# For the Record

## A DOCUMENTARY HISTORY

## OF AMERICA

# For the Record

## A DOCUMENTARY HISTORY
## OF AMERICA

### FIFTH EDITION

VOLUME 1

From First Contact through Reconstruction

DAVID E. SHI AND HOLLY A. MAYER

W · W · NORTON & COMPANY     NEW YORK · LONDON

*W. W. Norton & Company has been independent since its founding in 1923, when William Warder Norton and Mary D. Herter Norton first published lectures delivered at the People's Institute, the adult education division of New York City's Cooper Union. The firm soon expanded its program beyond the Institute, publishing books by celebrated academics from America and abroad. By mid-century, the two major pillars of Norton's publishing program—trade books and college texts—were firmly established. In the 1950s, the Norton family transferred control of the company to its employees, and today—with a staff of four hundred and a comparable number of trade, college, and professional titles published each year—W. W. Norton & Company stands as the largest and oldest publishing house owned wholly by its employees.*

Editor: Jon Durbin
Project Editor: Caitlin Moran
Media Editor: Steve Hoge
Associate Media Editor: Lorraine Klimowich
Assistant Editor: Justin Cahill
Editorial Assistant: Stefani Wallace
Production Manager: Ashley Horna
Photo Editor: Stephanie Romeo
Text Permissions: Bethany Salminen

Composition: Jouve North America
Manufacturing: Maple-Vail Book Group

Library of Congress Cataloging-in-Publication Data.

Shi, David E.
    For the record : a documentary history of America / David E. Shi and Holly A. Mayer. — Fifth edition.
        pages cm
    Includes bibliographical references.
    ISBN 978-0-393-91940-0 (Volume 1 : paperback) — ISBN 978-0-393-91941-7 (volume 2 : paperback)
    1. United States — History — Sources.   I. Mayer, Holly A. (Holly Ann), 1956–   II. Title.
    E173.S487 2013
    973—dc23

                                                                                    2012040081

W. W. Norton & Company, Inc., 500 Fifth Avenue, New York, N.Y. 10110-0017
wwnorton.com

W. W. Norton & Company Ltd., Castle House, 75/76 Wells Street, London W1T 3QT

3  4  5  6  7  8  9  0

DAVID E. SHI is a professor of history and president emeritus of Furman University. He is the author of several books on American cultural history, including *The Simple Life: Plain Living and High Thinking in American Culture* and *Facing Facts: Realism in American Thought and Culture (1850–1920)*.

HOLLY A. MAYER is an historian at Duquesne University in Pittsburgh, Pennsylvania, who has published a book and articles on women and war in late eighteenth-century America. A recent publication is "Bearing Arms, Bearing Burdens: Women Warriors, Camp Followers, and Home-front Heroines of the American Revolution," in *Gender, War, and Politics: Transatlantic Perspectives, 1775–1820* (2010).

For George Tindall

---

For our students

# CONTENTS

## CHAPTER 3 ◌ COLONIAL WAYS OF LIFE    42

## CHAPTER 4 ◌ FROM COLONIES TO STATES    82

## CHAPTER 5 ◌ THE AMERICAN REVOLUTION    124

## CHAPTER 6 ✑ SHAPING A FEDERAL UNION    155

## CHAPTER 7 ✑ THE FEDERALIST ERA    184

## CHAPTER 8 ✑ THE EARLY REPUBLIC    207

# CHAPTER 9 ᧡ THE DYNAMICS OF GROWTH   232

# CHAPTER 10 ᧡ NATIONALISM AND SECTIONALISM   254

# CHAPTER 11 ᧡ THE JACKSONIAN ERA   287

# INTERPRETING VISUAL SOURCES: PICTURING DEVELOPMENT VERSUS NATURE    311

# CHAPTER 12 ✑ THE OLD SOUTH    320

# CHAPTER 13 ✑ RELIGION, ROMANTICISM, AND REFORM    343

# INTERPRETING VISUAL SOURCES:
# PICTURING THE CIVIL WAR    457

# CHAPTER 17 ∼ RECONSTRUCTION:
# NORTH AND SOUTH    467

# PREFACE FOR INSTRUCTORS

We know from our experiences in the classroom that students can benefit greatly from studying the original sources that historians have used to craft their interpretations of the past. And students can use such sources to develop their own historical perspectives. The exchange that occurs between students and instructors when working with primary sources is an exciting and invaluable part of the learning process. This passion has motivated our work and helped guide our selection process across all five editions of *For The Record*.

This new edition of the reader features 250 primary source documents, both textual and visual, drawn from a vast range of media, including government documents, newspapers, speeches, letters, novels, and images. Twenty-four new selections offer strengthened coverage of African American history, and the table of contents has been revised to reflect the latest structure of *America: A Narrative History*, Ninth Edition. If you haven't looked seriously at *For the Record* in awhile or ever before, now is a great time to do so, as you think about putting together the lowest-price main text and companion reader package by far in the marketplace!

In selecting these documents, we have sought to represent the wide spectrum of historical developments by striking a balance among political, diplomatic, economic, social, and cultural perspectives. In general, we have tried to provide entire documents or substantial portions rather than brief snippets, which so often are pedagogically unsound and intellectually unsatisfying. We have edited several of these documents to eliminate extraneous material and to make them more accessible to the reader. Ellipses and asterisks indicate where passages or portions have been omitted. In a few cases, we have also modernized spelling and punctuation, taking care not to change the meaning of the original selection.

Chapter introductions set the stage for the accompanying selections by describing each historical period and highlighting key issues and actors. Each document in turn is introduced by a headnote that places it in the context of the period and suggests its historical significance. And each document is followed by a list of review questions to stimulate reflections about the material.

One of the unique features of *For the Record* is its recognition that visual artifacts are also important primary sources for the historian. Each volume contains two special sections intended to help students learn how to analyze and interpret visual sources. The four visual features include the following:

- *Picturing Development versus Nature* presents examples of the relationship between words and images that, in turn, describe the relationship between the man-made and natural America.
- *Picturing the Civil War* explores the Civil War as the first "total war" represented through the camera lens of Mathew Brady and his associates.
- *Photography and Progressive Reform* explores the Progressive era through the famous and controversial photos of the immigrant reformer Jacob Riis.
- *Photographs of the Civil Rights Movement* explores the courageous and controversial efforts to gain racial equality and justice during the twentieth century.

*For the Record: A Documentary History of America* is primarily a companion reader for *America: A Narrative History*. With a rich collection of 250 primary-source documents, it can also be readily used on its own or in conjunction with other survey texts.

New Selections in the Fifth Edition

- Thomas Gage, FROM *The English-American: A New Survey of the West Indies* (1648)
- William Moraley, FROM *Memoirs of an Indentured Servant* (1743)
- Phillis Wheatley, On the Death of General Wooster (1778)
- Reflections on the Cession of Louisiana to the United States (1803)
- David Walker, *Appeal to the Coloured Citizens of the World* (1829)
- Samuel Ennals and Philip Bell, An Address to the Citizens of New-York (1831)
- George Skipwith, Letters from "Your Servant" (1847)
- Interesting from Minnesota (1849)
- Jourdon Anderson, Letter to My Old Master (1865)
- Sojourner Truth, Address to the First Annual Meeting of the American Equal Rights Association (1867)
- Kelly Miller, The Risk of Woman Suffrage (1915)
- W. E. B. Du Bois, Woman Suffrage (1915)

- W. E. B. Du Bois, Returning Soldiers (1919)
- LIFE Magazine, Busy Wife's Achievements (1956)
- LIFE Magazine, Their Sheltered Honeymoon (1959)
- Gloria Steinem, Equal Rights for Women—Yes and No (1970)
- Phyllis Schlafly, What's Wrong with "Equal Rights" for Women? (1972)
- Richard M. Nixon and John Dean, The President and John Dean in the Oval Office (1973)
- Philip Caputo, FROM A Rumor of War (1977)
- Jesse Jackson, FROM Democratic Nominating Convention Speech (1984)
- Alan Wolfe, The Politics of Privacy, Right and Left (1993)
- Patrick Buchanan, The Culture War for the Soul of America (1992)
- *The Economist*, FROM One World? (1997)
- Barack Obama, A New Beginning (2009)

Taken as a whole, *For the Record* reveals the diversity of sources that contribute to our understanding of American history. In the process, it introduces students to important public documents and powerful personal accounts of events and experiences. The result is a more textured and comprehensive understanding of the ways in which we recreate and understand the past.

In compiling *For the Record*, we have benefited from the insights and talents of the editorial and marketing staff at W. W. Norton & Company. Jon Durbin has been our guide and our goad for this edition. He has provided wonderful advice in the first role and has been properly, thankfully amicably, persistent in the second. Kudos also go to Justin Cahill, Caitlin Moran, and Kate Feighery, who did truly fine work in shaping the final product.

# WHERE TO BEGIN

This checklist contains a series of questions that can be used to analyze most of the documents in this reader.

---

✔ What type of document is it?

✔ Why does the document exist? What motives prompted the author to write the material in this form?

✔ Who wrote this document?

✔ Who or what is left out of the document—women, children, other minorities, members of the majority?

✔ In addition to the main subject, what other kinds of information can be obtained from the document?

✔ How do the subjects of the document relate to what we know about broader society?

✔ What was the meaning of the document in its own time? What is its meaning for the reader today?

✔ What does the document tell us about change in society?

---

# For the Record

## A DOCUMENTARY HISTORY

## OF AMERICA

# 1 ⊱ THE COLLISION OF CULTURES

When Christopher Columbus sailed into view of the island he named San Salvador in October 1492, he was greeted by inhabitants he erroneously called Indians because of his preconceived notions of the world. He was not the only one to operate under cultural concepts that undermined first and subsequent contact. Preconceptions operated on both sides as eastern and western Atlantic peoples tried to make sense of each other from within their own frames of reference.

During the initial years of mutual discovery, some seventy-five million people inhabited the continents later known as the Americas. The ancestors of these aborigines had themselves migrated from Asia thousands of years earlier. Over the centuries, these peoples had created richly diverse civilizations. Some of these "Indian" societies had formed highly complex cultural, political, and economic organizations. They had conceptualized intricate cosmologies, built magnificent cities, and established mighty dominions based on agriculture and trade. The most powerful native empire at the time of Spanish exploration was that of the Aztecs. Far to the northeast, the French, Dutch, and English confronted a number of mighty tribes, in particular the Iroquois Federation. Other cultures, practicing different beliefs, operated as nomadic tribes, relying on hunting, fishing, and gathering for their subsistence. Yet as strong as they all were in their own sense of self, community, and the world, none of them was prepared to deal with the impact of the European invasion.

The Europeans who crossed the Atlantic came from different empires or kingdoms and spoke various languages, but their home cultures were not dissimilar. Thus there were similarities as well as differences in how they viewed and treated the natives. These Europeans may have had mixed motives for exploring and exploiting the New World, but they all carried with them powerful biological, cultural, and technological weapons. They sowed germs, wielded the cross, and fired guns. Many did so while seeking gold, spices, and other precious commodities. Others, both Catholics and Protestants, saw the Native Americans as potential

*converts to the Christian faith. In the New World, Spanish authorities were re-*
*quired to read a statement (the* requirimiento) *to the Indians, inviting them to*
*embrace Christianity. If they did not, the Spanish could then subjugate them by*
*force. Variations on this precedent were practiced in other areas of the New World*
*by the expansionistic and evangelistic Europeans.*

 *The people on each side of the cultural divides viewed others through the*
*prisms of their own ethnocentrism. This caused each to over- and underestimate*
*the capabilities of the other as they clashed over such ideological concerns as gov-*
*ernmental and religious doctrines and fought over such material matters as min-*
*eral resources and territory. Yet despite the ethnocentrism of everyone involved, not*
*all thought contact should be a synonym for conflict. There were individuals*
*among the Europeans and aborigines who sought to understand, if not appreciate,*
*other peoples. Humanity as well as inhumanity was inherent to cultural contact.*

# BARTOLOMÉ DE LAS CASAS

# In Defense of the Indians (c. 1550)

*Hernando Cortés and subsequent* conquistadores *of the Americas acted on the belief that conquest of the New World's native peoples as a means to increase Spanish wealth and sovereignty was justified by the expansion of civilization and Christianity. Some Catholic missionaries, however, protested against the plundering of Indian property, the enslavement of Indians, and other atrocities. Pope Paul III responded in 1537 by issuing a papal bull calling for the Indians to be treated humanely. Then Charles, king of Spain, called for an assembly in 1542 to determine what was going on in the New World and what should be done. Those infuriated by the resulting proposed reforms recruited their own apologists, and foremost among such defenders was the theologian and royal historian Ginés Sepúlveda. One of Sepúlveda's ablest foes was the Dominican priest Bartolomé de Las Casas (1474–1566). Las Casas spent most of his ninety-two years in the New World intent upon converting and defending the natives. According to Las Casas, Sepúlveda proclaimed that because the Indians were barbaric, ignorant, incapable of higher learning or reasoning, and prone to vice and cruelty, there was just cause for their subordination and, should they resist that, subjugation by the forces of those wiser and more virtuous. After summarizing Sepúlveda's position, Las Casas refuted it point by point as he argued against Sepúlveda and other "Persecutors and Slanderers of the Peoples of the New World Discovered Across the Seas."*

From Chapter 4, *In Defense of the Indians,* translated and edited by Stafford Poole, C. M. Used with permission of Northern Illinois University Press.

\*      \*      \*

From the fact that the Indians are barbarians it does not necessarily follow that they are incapable of government and have to be ruled by others, except to be taught about the Catholic faith and to be admitted to the holy sacraments. They are not ignorant, inhuman, or bestial. Rather, long before they had heard the word Spaniard they had properly organized states, wisely ordered by excellent laws, religion, and custom. They cultivated friendship and, bound together in common fellowship, lived in populous cities in which they wisely administered the affairs of both peace and war justly and equitably, truly governed by laws that at very many points surpass ours, and could have won the admiration of the sages of Athens. . . .

Now if they are to be subjugated by war because they are ignorant of polished literature, let Sepúlveda hear Trogus Pompey:

> Nor could the Spaniards submit to the yoke of a conquered province until Caesar Augustus, after he had conquered the world, turned his victorious armies against them and organized that barbaric and wild people as a province, once he had led them by law to a more civilized way of life.

Now see how he called the Spanish people barbaric and wild. I would like to hear Sepúlveda, in his cleverness, answer this question: Does he think that the war of the Romans against the Spanish was justified in order to free them from barbarism? And this question also: Did the Spanish wage an unjust war when they vigorously defended themselves against them?

Next, I call the Spaniards who plunder that unhappy people torturers. Do you think that the Romans, once they had subjugated the wild and barbaric peoples of Spain, could with secure right divide all of you among themselves, handing over so many head of both males and females as allotments to individuals? And do you then conclude that the Romans could have stripped your rulers of their authority and consigned all of you, after you had been deprived of your liberty, to wretched labors, especially in searching for gold and silver lodes and mining and refining the metals? And if the Romans finally did that, as is evident from Diodorus, [would you not judge] that you also have the right to defend your freedom, indeed your very life, by war? Sepúlveda, would you have permitted Saint James to evangelize your own people of Córdoba in that way? For God's sake and man's faith in him, is this the way to impose the yoke of Christ on Christian men? Is this the way to remove wild barbarism from the minds of barbarians? Is it not, rather, to act like thieves, cut-throats, and cruel plunderers and to drive the gentlest of people headlong into despair? The Indian race is not that barbaric, nor are they dull witted or stupid, but they are easy to teach and very talented in learning all the liberal arts, and very ready to accept, honor, and observe the Christian religion and correct their sins (as experience has taught) once priests have introduced them to the sacred mysteries and taught them the word of God. They have been endowed with excellent conduct, and before the coming of the Spaniards, as we have said, they had political states that were well founded on beneficial laws.

Furthermore, they are so skilled in every mechanical art that with every right they should be set ahead of all the nations of the known world on this score, so very beautiful in their skill and artistry are the things this people produces in the grace of its architecture, its painting, and its needlework. But Sepúlveda despises these mechanical arts, as if these things do not reflect inventiveness, ingenuity, industry, and right reason. For a mechanical art is an operative habit of the intellect that is usually defined as "the right way to make things, directing the acts of the reason, through which the artisan proceeds in orderly fashion, easily, and unerringly in the very act of reason." So these men are not stupid, Reverend Doctor. Their skillfully fashioned works of superior refinement awaken the admiration of all nations. . . .

In the liberal arts that they have been taught up to now, such as grammar and logic, they are remarkably adept. With every kind of music they charm the ears of their audience with wonderful sweetness. They write skillfully and quite elegantly, so that most often we are at a loss to know whether the characters are handwritten or printed. . . .

Now if Sepúlveda had wanted, as a serious man should, to know the full truth before he sat down to write with his mind corrupted by the lies of tyrants, he should have consulted the honest religious who have lived among those peoples for many years and know their endowments of character and industry, as well as the progress they have made in religion and morality. Indeed, Rome is far from Spain, yet in that city the talent of these people and their aptitude and capacity for grasping the liberal arts have been recognized. Here is Paolo Giovio, Bishop of Nocera, in praise of those peoples whom you call dull witted and stupid. In his *History of His Times* he has left this testimony for later generations to read:

> Hernán Cortés, hurrying overland to the kingdoms of Mexico after defeating the Indians, occupied the city of Tenochtitlân, after he had conquered in many battles, using boats which he had built, that city set upon a salt lagoon—wonderful like the city of Venice in its buildings and the size of its population.

As you see, he declares that the Indian city is worthy of admiration because of its buildings, which are like those of Venice.

As to the terrible crime of human sacrifice, which you exaggerate, see what Giovio adds in the same place. "The rulers of the Mexicans have a right to sacrifice living men to their gods, provided they have been condemned for a crime." Concerning the natural gifts of that people, what does he assert? "Thus it was not altogether difficult for Cortés to lead a gifted and teachable people, once they had abandoned their superstitious idolatry, to the worship of Christ. For they learn our writing with pleasure and with admiration, now that they have given up the hieroglyphics by which they used to record their annals, enshrining for posterity in various symbols the memory of their kings."

This is what you, a man of such great scholarship, should have done in ascertaining the truth, instead of writing, with the sharp edge of your pen poised for the whispers of irresponsible men, your little book that slanders the Indian inhabitants of such a large part of the earth. . . .

From this it is clear that the basis for Sepúlveda's teaching that these people are uncivilized and ignorant is worse than false. Yet even if we were to grant that this race has no keenness of mind or artistic ability, certainly they are not, in consequence, obliged to submit themselves to those who are more intelligent and to adopt their ways, so that, if they refuse, they may be subdued by having war waged against them and be enslaved, as happens today. For men are obliged by the natural law to do many things they cannot be forced to do against their will. We are bound by the natural law to embrace virtue and imitate the uprightness of good men. No one, however, is punished for being bad unless he is guilty of rebellion. Where the Catholic faith has been preached in a Christian manner and as it ought to be, all men are bound by the natural law to accept it, yet no one is forced to accept the faith of Christ. No one is punished because he is sunk in vice, unless he is rebellious or harms the property and persons of others.

No one is forced to embrace virtue and show himself as a good man. One who receives a favor is bound by the natural law to return the favor by what we call antidotal obligation. Yet no one is forced to this, nor is he punished if he omits it, according to the common interpretation of the jurists.

To relieve the need of a brother is a work of mercy to which nature inclines and obliges men, yet no one is forced to give alms. . . . Therefore, not even a truly wise man may force an ignorant barbarian to submit to him, especially by yielding his liberty, without doing him an injustice. This the poor Indians suffer, with extreme injustice, against all the laws of God and of men and against the law of nature itself. For evil must not be done that good may come of it. . . .

\*      \*      \*

# REVIEW QUESTIONS

1. Las Casas argues that although the Indians are barbarians according to certain definitions, it does not follow that others must rule them. Why not?
2. How does Las Casas use historical and religious examples to turn the argument against those who would subjugate the Indians by force? How does he make ethics a part of his argument?
3. What does Las Casas offer as evidence that the Indians were not as barbaric as their enemies proclaimed?

## Juan de Oñate

### FROM Letter from New Mexico (1599)

*Juan de Oñate (b. 1552) was a* criollo, *someone born in New Spain to Spanish parents. He married Isabel de Tolosa Cortés de Montezuma, the granddaughter of the Spanish conqueror and great-granddaughter of the Aztec emperor. Although his status as a colonial may have hurt him, his family's wealth helped as Oñate pushed for permission to lead an expedition into the North. In 1595 King Philip II of Spain finally gave him the authority to proceed—and to spread Catholicism, collect tribute from Indians, grant lands to followers, and establish mines as well as assorted other powers— in return for a percentage of the anticipated riches. Oñate quickly assembled an expedition of hundreds of men, women, and children of European, Indian, and African origins, but then had to wait for over two years because of delays engendered by the new viceroy of New Spain, Don Gaspar de Zúñiga y Acovedo, Count of Monterrey. He finally got under way in early 1598. After an arduous trek through northern Mexico, his expedition eventually made it to the fording place that became known as El Paso. On 30 April 1598, the soldiers, settlers, slaves, and missionaries held a thanksgiving celebration during which Oñate proclaimed possession of El Nuevo Mexico for his king. The expedition shortly thereafter crossed the Rio Bravo del Norte (Rio Grande) into New Mexico and made its way through the pueblos and rancherias of the native peoples. Oñate was a stern, even ruthless, governor as he dealt with mutiny in his own party and "treason" ( for he had proclaimed them subjects of the king) by Native Americans. This colonial conquistador was ultimately recalled to Mexico City, where he was convicted on charges of cruelty in 1608. He cleared his name on appeal and ended his days in Spain.*

From Herbert Eugene Bolton, ed., *Spanish Exploration in the Southwest, 1542–1706* (New York: Charles Scribner's Sons, 1916), pp. 216–21. [Editorial insertions appear in square brackets—*Ed.*]

\*   \*   \*

There must be in this province[1] and in the others above-mentioned,[2] to make a conservative estimate, seventy thousand Indians, settled after our custom, house adjoining house, with square plazas.

They have no streets, and in the pueblos, which contain many plazas or wards, one goes from one plaza to the other through alleys. They are of two and three stories, of an *estado*[3] and a half or an *estado* and a third each, which latter is not so common; and some houses are of four, five, six, and seven stories. Even whole pueblos dress in very highly colored cotton *mantas*, white or black, and some of thread—very good clothes. Others wear

---

[1] The region, in what is now New Mexico and Texas, populated by the Tegua people (now more commonly known as the Tiwa).

[2] Native American communities ranging from El Paso northward.

[3] A unit of measurement equal to a man's height.

buffalo hides, of which there is a great abundance. They have most excellent wool, of whose value I am sending a small example.

It is a land abounding in flesh of buffalo, goats with hideous horns, and turkeys; and in Mohoce there is game of all kinds. There are many wild and ferocious beasts, lions, bears, wolves, tigers, *penicas*, ferrets, porcupines, and other animals, whose hides they tan and use. Towards the west there are bees and very white honey, of which I am sending a sample. Besides, there are vegetables, a great abundance of the best and greatest salines in the world, and a very great many kinds of very rich ores. . . . There are very fine grape vines, rivers, forests of many oaks, and some cork trees, fruits, melons, grapes, watermelons, Castilian plums, *capuli*, pinenuts, acorns, ground-nuts, and *coralejo*, which is a delicious fruit, and other wild fruits. There are many and very good fish in this Rio del Norte, and in others. From the ores here are made all the colors which we use, and they are very fine.

The people are in general very comely; their color is like those of that land, and they are much like them in manner and dress, in their grinding, in their food, dancing, singing, and many other things, except in their languages, which are many, and different from those there. Their religion consists in worshipping idols, of which they have many; and in their temples, after their own manner, they worship them with fire, painted reeds, feathers, and universal offering of almost everything they get, such as small animals, birds, vegetables, etc. In their government they are free, for although they have some petty captains, they obey them badly and in very few things.

We have seen other nations such as the Querechos,[4] or herdsmen, who live in tents of tanned hides, among the buffalo. The Apaches, of whom we have also seen some, are innumerable. . . . They are a people whom I have compelled to render obedience to His Majesty, although not by means of legal instruments like the rest of the provinces. This has caused me much labor, diligence, and care, long journeys, with arms on the shoulders, and not a little watching and circumspection; indeed, because my *maese de campo* was not as cautious as he should have been, they killed him with twelve companions in a great pueblo and fortress called Acóma, which must contain about three thousand Indians. As punishment for its crime and its treason against his Majesty, to whom it had already rendered submission by a public instrument, and as a warning to the rest, I razed and burned it completely. . . . All these provinces, pueblos, and peoples, I have seen with my own eyes.

There is another nation, that of the Cocóyes,[5] an innumerable people with huts and agriculture. Of this nation and of the large settlements at the source of the Rio del Norte and of those to the northwest and west and towards the South Sea, I have numberless reports, and pearls of remarkable size from the said sea, and assurance that there is an infinite number of them on the coast of this country. And as to the east [there is a pueblo of herdsmen] . . . situated in the midst of the multitude of buffalo, which are so numerous that my *sargento mayor*, who hunted them and brought back their hides, meat, tallow, and suet, asserts that in one herd alone he saw more than there are of our cattle in the combined three ranches of Rodrigo del Rio, Salvago, and Jeronimo Lopez, which are famed in those regions.

I should never cease were I to recount individually all of the many things which occur to me. I can only say that with God's help I shall see them all, and give new worlds, new, peaceful, and grand, to his Majesty, greater than the good Marquis[6] gave to him, although he did so much, if you, Illustrious Sir,[7] will give to me the aid, the protection, and the help which I expect from such a hand. And although I confess that I am crushed at having been so out of favor when I left that country . . . it is nevertheless true that I never have and never shall lose hope of receiving many and very great favors at the hand of

---

[4]The Pueblo name for the buffalo-hunting Apache to the east.

[5]More commonly known as the Pecos.
[6]That is, Cortés.
[7]That is, New Spain's viceroy.

your Lordship, especially in matters of such importance to his Majesty. And in order that you, Illustrious Sir, may be inclined to render them to me, I beg that you take note of the great increase which the royal crown and the rents of his Majesty have and will have in this land, with so many and such a variety of things, each one of which promises very great treasures. I shall only note these four, omitting the rest as being well known and common:

First, the great wealth which the mines have begun to reveal and the great number of them in this land, whence proceed the royal fifths and profits. Second, the certainty of the proximity of the South Sea, whose trade with Pirú, New Spain, and China is not to be depreciated, for it will give birth in time to advantageous and continuous duties, because of its close proximity, particularly to China and to that land. And what I emphasize in this matter as worthy of esteem is the traffic in pearls, reports of which are so certain, as I have stated, and of which we have had ocular experience from the shells. Third, the increase of vassals and tributes, which will increase not only the rents, but his renown and dominion as well, if it be possible that for our king these can increase. Fourth, the wealth of the abundant salines, and of the mountains of brimstone, of which there is a greater quantity than in any other province. Salt is the universal article of traffic of all these barbarians and their regular food, for they even eat or suck it alone as we do sugar. These four things appear as if dedicated solely to his Majesty. I will not mention the founding of so many republics, the many offices, their quittances, vacancies, provisions, etc., the wealth of the wool and hides of buffalo, and many other things, clearly and well known, or, judging from the general nature of the land, the certainty of wines and oils.

In view, then, Illustrious Sir, of things of such honor, profit, and value, and of the great prudence, magnanimity, and nobility of your Lordship, who in all matters is bound to prosper me and overcome the ill fortune of my disgrace, I humbly beg and supplicate, since it is of such importance to the service of God and of his Majesty, that the greatest aid possible be sent to me, both for settling and pacifying, your Lordship giving your favor, mind, zeal, and life for the conservation, progress, and increase of this land, through the preaching of the holy gospel and the founding of this republic, giving liberty and favor to all, opening wide the door to them, and, if it should be necessary, even ordering them to come to serve their king in so honorable and profitable a matter, in a land so abundant and of such great beginnings of riches. I call them beginnings, for although we have seen much, we have not yet made a beginning in comparison with what there is to see and enjoy. And if the number should exceed five hundred men, they all would be needed, especially married men, who are the solid rock on which new republics are permanently founded; and noble people, of whom there is such a surplus there. . . .

\*    \*    \*

# REVIEW QUESTIONS

1. How do Oñate's descriptions of the land and its people reflect his cultural notions of what is common and uncommon, right and wrong?
2. What was Oñate's argument to the Count of Monterrey, viceroy of New Spain, for increased support of his expedition? What of his supporting evidence appears to be based in fact and what in fancy?
3. How did Oñate propose to give "liberty and favor to all" in the new territory?

# THOMAS HARRIOT AND JOHN WHITE

## FROM *A Briefe and true report of the new found land of Virginia* (1590)

*In April 1585 an expedition organized by Sir Walter Raleigh, but commanded by Sir Richard Grenville, left England to sail across the Atlantic and establish a colony in the New World. By July the explorer-colonists had secured a foothold on Roanoke Island in the newly named Virginia territory. With the expedition were two professional observers: Thomas Harriot and John White. While Harriot identified and described the new discoveries—whether flora, fauna, or human—in words, White recorded them in detailed drawings and paintings. After this first attempt at colonization failed in 1586, White, under Raleigh's aegis, would lead another group to attempt settlement again in 1587. In the meantime the printer-publisher Theodor de Bry set to work typesetting Harriot's words and engraving White's drawings for the book A Briefe and true report of the new found land of Virginia. Published in 1590, it served to publicize the wonders of the New World—with particular attention paid to the Indian village of Secoton, which lay across the sound from Roanoke.*

From Paul Hulton, *America, 1585: The Complete Drawings of John White* (Chapel Hill: University of North Carolina Press, 1984), p. 126.

THE TOWN OF SECOTA
Library of Congress

## The Towne of Secota

Their townes that are not inclosed with poles aire commonlye fayrer. Then suche as are inclosed, as appereth in this figure which liuelye expresseth the towne of Secotam. For the howses are Scattered heer and ther, and they haue gardein expressed by the letter E. wherin groweth Tobacco which the inhabitants call Vppowoc. They haue also groaues wherin thei take deer, and fields vherin they sowe their corne. In their corne fields they builde as yt weare a scaffolde wher on they sett a cottage like to a rownde chaire, signiffied by F. wherin they place one to watche. For there are suche number of fowles, and beasts, that vnless they keepe the better watche, they would soone deuoure all their corne. For which cause the watcheman maketh continual cryes and noyse. The Sowe their corne with a certaine distance noted by H. other wise one stalke would choke the growthe of another and the corne would not come vnto his rypeurs G. For the leaves therof are large, like vnto the leaues of great reedes. They haue also aseuerall broade plotte C. whear they meete with their neighbours, to celebrate their cheefe solemne feastes as the 18. picture doth declare: and a place D. whear after they haue ended their feaste they make merrie togither. Ouer against this place they haue a rownd plott B. wher they assemble themselves to make their solemne prayers. Not far from which place ther is a lardge buildinge A. wherin are the tombes of their kings and princes, as will appere by the 22. figure likewise they haue garden notted bey the letter I. wherin

they vse to sowe pompions. Also a place marked with K. wherin the make a fyre att their solemne feasts, and hard without the towne a riuer L. from whence they fetche their water. This people therfore voyde of all coutousnes lyue cherfullye and att their harts ease. Butt they solemnise their feasts in the nigt, and therfore they keepe verye great fyres to auodye darkenes, ant to testifie their loye.

## REVIEW QUESTIONS

1. The description was reproduced in the original language and spelling (except that the Old English β was converted to the modern *s*). What does this example of sixteenth-century English tell you about the language and the culture that used it?

2. What does the engraving reveal about the artist's talent and the engraver's skill and tools?

3. How may people's imaginations and perceptions of the New World have been shaped by such publicists?

4. What kinds of crops did the Indians cultivate?

5. What were some of the activities described and illustrated by Harriot and White?

6. Why did these two observers particularly mark these activities? How were such products or activities significant to an understanding of Native American life or to European plans?

7. Did Harriot and White provide idealistic or realistic portrayals of Indian culture? Why or why not?

# PAUL LE JEUNE AND JEROME LALEMANT

# FROM *The Jesuit Relations* (1640)

*The Jesuit priests Paul Le Jeune and Jerome Lalemant were missionaries to the native peoples in the territories claimed by France. In the* Relation of 1640, *Father Le Jeune reported from Quebec while Father Lalemant corresponded from the mission among the Hurons. These highly educated and dedicated men, along with other missionaries, learned the languages and gained an understanding of the cultures of the native peoples as they lived among them and worked to convert them to Christianity. They wrote extensively of their experiences among the Algonquin and Iroquoian peoples. While the missionaries expressed some appreciation of certain aspects of native cultures, such as a lack of avariciousness, they did not see the cultures as civilized. Their observations thus reveal not only native ways but also how Europeans thought of Indians in comparison to themselves. In 1639 and 1640, a smallpox epidemic spread through the St. Lawrence Valley and into the interior of Canada. Reports on the contagion show not only its fatal course but also how women in religious orders were integral to the mission. On the other hand, the reports also show how the spreading sickness increased the animosity of many natives toward the priests in their midst. Some Native Americans saw the "Black Robes" as evil sorcerers while the missionaries, in turn, often denigrated the natives' spirits and spiritual leaders as demons.*

---

From Reuben Gold Thwaites, ed., *The Jesuit Relations and Allied Documents: Travels and Explorations of the Jesuit Missionaries in New France, 1610–1791.* Volume XVII: *Huron and Quebec: 1640* (New York: Pageant Book Co., 1959), pp. 9–13, 21–25, 87–97, 115–17. [Editorial insertions appear in brackets—*Ed.*]

## Of the Hospital.

The hospital Nuns arrived at Kébec on the first day of the month of August of last year. Scarcely had they disembarked before they found themselves overwhelmed with patients. The hall of the Hospital being too small, it was necessary to erect some cabins, fashioned like those of the Savages, in their garden. Not having enough furniture for so many people, they had to cut in two or three pieces part of the blankets and sheets they had brought for these poor sick people. In a word, instead of taking a little rest, and refreshing themselves after the great discomforts they had suffered upon the sea, they found themselves so burdened and occupied that we had fear of losing them and their hospital at its very birth. The sick came from all directions in such numbers, their stench was so insupportable, the heat so great, the fresh food so scarce and so poor, in a country so new and strange, that I do not know how these good sisters, who almost had not even leisure in which to take a little sleep, endured all these hardships. . . . All the French born

in the country were attacked by this contagion, as well as the Savages. . . .

In brief, from the month of August until the month of May, more than one hundred patients entered the hospital, and more than two hundred poor Savages found relief there, either in temporary treatment or in sleeping there one or two nights, or more. There have been seen as many as ten, twelve, twenty, or thirty of them at a time. Twenty poor sick people have received holy Baptism there; and about twenty-four, quitting this house of mercy, have entered the regions of glory. . . .

. . . Father Claude Pijard, who has had charge of the instruction of the poor of this house, during the entire winter, has given me a little relation, couched in these terms: "In the morning, we had the Savages say prayers, and, some time after, the holy Mass was celebrated, at which those who had been baptized were present; after dinner, we had them recite the catechism, and then gave them a little explanation of it, usually adding some pious story that one of the Savages repeated. In the evening, they made their examination of conscience; they confessed and received communion every two weeks, and would have done so oftener if we had permitted them. They showed their devotion by often visiting the most holy Sacrament, by saying their rosary several times a day, by singing spiritual canticles, which have succeeded their barbarous songs,—in short, by fasting throughout the sacred forty days, for those who could do so. . . ."

\*    \*    \*

"I have often wondered," says the Mother [Superior], "how these persons, so different in country, age, and sex, can agree so well. In France, a Nun has to be on her guard every day in our houses, to prevent disputes among our poor, or to quell them; and all winter we have not observed the least discord among our sick Savages,—not even a slight quarrel has arisen.

"The remedies that we brought from Europe are very good for the Savages, who have no difficulty in taking our medicines, nor in having themselves bled. The love of the mothers toward their children is very great, for they take in their own mouths the medicine intended for their children, and then pass it into the mouths of their little ones." Thus the good Mother wrote to me.

\*    \*    \*

The Savages who leave the hospital, and who come to see us again at St. Joseph, or at the three Rivers, say a thousand pleasant things about these good Nuns. They call them "the good," "the liberal," "the charitable." The Mother Superior having fallen sick, these poor Savages were very sorry, the sick blaming themselves for it. "It is we who have made her sick," they said; "she loves us too much; why does she do so much for us?" When this good Mother, having recovered, entered the hall of the poor, they knew not how to welcome her enough. They have good reason to love these good Mothers: for I do not know that parents have so sweet, so strong, and so constant an affection for their children as these good women have for their patients. I have often seen them so

overwhelmed that they were utterly exhausted; yet I have never heard them complain, either of the too great number of their patients, or of the infection, or of the trouble they gave them. They have hearts so loving and so tender towards these poor people that, if occasionally some little present were given them, one could be very certain that they would not taste it, however greatly they might need it, everything being dedicated and consecrated to their sick. This charity had to be moderated, and an order was given them to eat at least a part of the little gifts that were made to them, especially when they were not strong. I am not surprised if the Savages, who recognize very clearly this great charity, love, cherish, and honor them.

Father Buteux wrote, some days ago, to the Reverend Father Superior that a woman who had remained a long time at the hospital did a great deal of good among the Savages of her nation, instructing them with much fervor. This is the common practice of those who have passed the winter in this holy house; they afterwards preach to their compatriots with great zeal.

\*    \*    \*

## [Of the Condition of the Country.]

Let us come to the disease which, having put everything in desolation, gave us much exercise, but was also an occasion of much consolation to us,—God having given us hardly any other harvest than from that quarter.

It was upon the return from the journey which the Hurons had made to Kébec, that it started in the country,—our Hurons, while again on their way up here, having thoughtlessly mingled with the Algonquins, whom they met on the route, most of whom were infected with smallpox. The first Huron who introduced it came ashore at the foot of our house, newly built on the bank of a lake,— whence being carried to his own village, about a league distant from us, he died straightway after. Without being a great prophet, one could assure one's self that the evil would soon be spread abroad through all these regions: for the Hurons—no matter what plague or contagion they may have—live in the midst of their sick, in the same indifference, and community of all things, as if they were in perfect health. In fact, in a few days, almost all those in the cabin of the deceased found themselves infected; then the evil spread from house to house, from village to village, and finally became scattered throughout the country.

## Of the Persecutions Excited Against Us.

The villages nearer to our new house having been the first ones attacked, and most afflicted, the devil did not fail to seize his opportunity for reawakening all the old imaginations, and causing the former complaints of us, and of our sojourn in these quarters, to be renewed; as if it were the sole cause of all their misfortunes, and especially of the sick. They no longer speak of aught else, they cry aloud that the French must be massacred. These barbarians animate one another to that effect; the death of their nearest relatives takes away their reason, and increases their rage against us so strongly in each village that the best informed can hardly believe that we can survive so horrible a storm. They observed, with some sort of reason, that, since our arrival in these lands, those who had been the nearest to us, had happened to be the most ruined by the diseases, and that the whole villages of those who had received us now appeared utterly exterminated; and certainly, they said, the same would be the fate of all the others if the course of this misfortune were not stopped by the massacre of those who were the cause of it. This was a common opinion, not only in private conversation but in the general councils held on this account, where the plurality of the votes went for our death,—there being only a few elders who thought they greatly obliged us by resolving upon banishment.

What powerfully confirmed this false imagination was that, at the same time, they saw us dispersed throughout the country,—seeking all sorts of ways to enter the cabins, instructing and baptizing those most ill with a care which they had never seen. No doubt, they said, it must needs be that we had a secret understanding with the disease (for they believe that it is a demon), since we alone were all full of life and health, although we constantly breathed nothing but a totally infected air,—staying whole days close by the side of the most foul-smelling patients, for whom every one felt horror; no doubt we carried the trouble with us, since, wherever we set foot, either death or disease followed us.

In consequence of all these sayings, many had us in abomination; they expelled us from their cabins, and did not allow us to approach their sick, and especially children: not even to lay eyes on them,—in a word, we were dreaded as the greatest sorcerers on earth.

Wherein truly it must be acknowledged that these poor people are in some sense excusable. For it has happened very often, and has been remarked more than a hundred times, that where we were most welcome, where we baptized most people, there it was in fact where they died the most; and, on the contrary, in the cabins to which we were denied entrance, although they were sometimes sick to extremity, at the end of a few days one saw every person prosperously cured. We shall see in heaven the secret, but ever adorable, judgments of God therein. . . .

The reasons which we have thus far adduced, on account of which the barbarians suspect us of being the cause of their diseases, seem to have some foundation; but the devil did not stop there,—it would be a miracle if he did not build the worst of his calumnies on sheer lies.

Robert le Coq, one of our domestics, had returned from Kébec in a state of sickness which caused as much horror as compassion to all those who had courage enough to examine the ulcers with which all his limbs were covered. Never would a Huron have believed that a body so filled with miseries could have returned to health; regarding him then as good as dead, there were found slanderers so assured in their falsehood that they publicly maintained that this young Frenchman had told them in confidence that the Jesuits alone were the authors and the cause of the diseases which from year to year kept depopulating the country. . . .

*    *    *

But let us return to our Savages, excited against us on account of the disease, and to those impostors who had maintained that Robert le Coq had so confidentially informed them of the black magic arts and the execrable spells with which we were causing them all to die. It was not very difficult to refute these calumnies, since he who was said to have been the sole source of all these rumors—not being dead, as they had supposed, but having recovered perfect health—could belie all those who previously maintained they had heard the thing from his lips. But what? falsehood gets the better of the truth; the slanderers find more credit than the one who justifies us. . . . but the demons are like thunders, which make more noise than they do harm,—for all these threats have had but little effect. We are alive, thank God, all full of life and health. It is indeed true that the crosses have been stricken down from above our houses; that people have entered our cabins, hatchet in hand, in order to deal some evil blow there; they have, it is said, awaited some of ours on the roads, with the intention of killing them; the hatchet has been lifted above others, and the blow brought within a finger-length of their bare heads; the Crucifixes which were carried to the sick have been violently snatched from us; blows with a club have been mightily inflicted upon one of our missionaries, to prevent him from conferring some baptism. *Sed nondum usque ad sanguinem restitimus*; our blood and our lives have not yet been poured out for him to whom we owe all our hearts. Our soul is in our hands, and this is the greatest favor that we hope to receive from the great Master who employs us,—namely, to die for his holy name, after having suffered much.

Not that I do not forever praise this great God of goodness, for having thus far protected us with so much love: for it is truly an unspeakable happiness for us, in the midst of this barbarism, to hear the roarings of the demons, and to see all hell and almost all men animated and filled with fury against a little handful of people who would not defend themselves; to see ourselves shut up in a place fifteen hundred leagues from our native land, where all the powers of the earth could not warrant us against the anger of the weakest man who might have designs on our lives, and where we have not even a bag of corn which has not been furnished us by those who incessantly parley about killing us; and to feel at the same time so special a confidence in the goodness of God, so firm an assurance in the midst of dangers, a zeal so active, and a courage so resolute to do all and to suffer all for the glory of our Master, so indefatigable a constancy in the labors which increase from day to day. So that it is easy to conceive that God is the one who espouses our cause; that it is he alone who protects us, and that his providence takes pleasure in manifesting itself where we see least of the human.

## REVIEW QUESTIONS

1. Was saving the sick or saving souls the first priority for the missionaries? How did the former affect the latter?
2. How did Le Jeune describe the Indians, nuns, and priests? What did those descriptions reveal of his beliefs about the three groups?
3. How does Lalemant believe the disease spread? What did the Hurons believe caused and spread the disease? What do those sentiments reveal about how these people explained catastrophe?
4. How did Lalemant react to the increasing animosity and aggressiveness of the Hurons? What does that say about the influence of religious beliefs in European expansion?

# THOMAS GAGE

## FROM *The English-American: A New Survey of the West Indies* (1648)

*Thomas Gage was born in England (c. 1600) to a family that had remained defiantly Catholic in the face of the English Reformation and that sent its sons to study abroad so as to serve the Catholic Church and perhaps eventually restore England to its fold. Gage had originally studied with the Jesuits at Valladolid, but he resisted the Spanish priests' discipline and attempts to Hispanicize their students. Gage instead joined the Dominicans and volunteered to serve in the Philippines. As the Spanish Crown barred Englishmen from its colonies, Gage had himself smuggled aboard a ship bound for Mexico in 1625. His plan was to travel across that country to the Pacific and then sail on, but instead he ended up serving in Spanish America, primarily Guatemala, for twelve years. While there Gage came to question Catholic doctrine and practices: he claimed the Catholic Church practiced idolatry even as it persecuted Indians for the offense, and he condemned how priests and friars enriched themselves at the expense of the native peoples even as he did the same as a means to fund his escape. Furthermore, as he noted in his book, he was an Englishman who became "American" but never Spanish-American. It may also be, as an historian has posited, that Gage had been acting as a spy for England. While that is unproven, he did change his vestments once he settled again in England. By 1640 he had joined the Anglican Church. He also informed against some priests in England, which resulted in their execution. Finally, Gage proselytized for England to expand its empire overseas and urged that it take Spain's territories. To that end, his book was not just a condemnation of Spanish conversion and colonization practices but also a briefing on "the state, condition, strength, and commodities of those countries which lie southward from Mexico" (109). Ultimately Oliver Cromwell consulted with Gage and appointed him chaplain to an expedition against Hispaniola in 1654. The attack there failed but the expedition did take Jamaica, making it England's first Caribbean colony. Gage died there in 1656. Although Gage offers numerous fascinating descriptions of nature and peoples in his book, of note here is his account of some privateers in 1637. Privateers, who had government commissions to attack the shipping of enemy countries, and pirates, who had no commission but their own, helped define the transatlantic world in the diversity of their targets and their crews. Indeed, some might argue that Gage was a form of pirate in both words (he may have borrowed passages of his book from others) and deeds (in how he harassed his enemies).*

From *The English-American: A New Survey of the West Indies, 1648*, edited by A. P. Newton (1928; special ed.: Guatemala City: El Patio, 1946), pp. 348–52. [Editorial insertions appear in square brackets—*Ed.*]

The master of the frigate [at the River Suere—today Pacuare—in Costa Rica] was exceeding glad of our company, and offered to carry me for nothing, but for my prayers to God for him, and for a safe passage; which he hoped would not be above three or four days' sailing. What he carried was nothing but some honey, hides, bacon, meal, and fowls. The greatest danger he told us of, was the setting out from the river (which runs in some places with a very strong stream, is shallow and full of rocks in other places) till we come forth to the main sea [Caribbean Sea]. Whither we got out safely and had not sailed on above twenty leagues when we discovered two ships making towards us; our hearts began to quake, and the master himself of the frigate we perceived was not without fear, who suspected that they were English, or Holland ships; we had no guns nor weapons to fight with, save only four or five muskets and half a dozen swords; we thought the wings of our nimble frigate might be our best comfort, and flying away our chiefest safety. But this comfort soon began to fail us, and our best safety was turned into near approaching danger; for before we could fly on five leagues towards Portobello, we could from our top mast easily perceive the two ships to be Hollanders, and too nimble for our little vessel, which presently one of them (which being a man-of-war was too much and too strong for our weakness) fetched up, and with a thundering message made us strike sail. Without any fighting we durst not but yield, hoping for better mercy. But O, what sad thoughts did here run to and fro my dejected heart, which was struck down lower than our sail! How did I sometimes look upon death's frighting visage! But if again I would comfort and encourage myself against this fear of death; how then did I begin to see an end of all my hopes of ever more returning to my wished and desired country! How did I see that my treasure of pearls, precious stones, and pieces of eight, and golden pistoles, which by singing [clerical duties] I had got in twelve years' space, now within one half hour ready to be lost with weeping, and become a sure prey to those who with as much ease as I got them, and with laughing, were ready to spoil me of all that with the sound of flutes, waits, and organs I had so long been hoarding up! Now I saw I must

forcedly and feignedly offer up to a Hollander what superstitious, yea also forced and feigned, offerings of Indians to their saints of Mixco, Pinola, Amatitlan, and Petapa had for a while enriched me. My further thoughts were soon interrupted by the Hollanders who came aboard our frigate with more speed than we desired. Though their swords, muskets and pistols did not a little terrify, yet we were somewhat comforted when we understood who was their chief captain and commander, and hoped for more mercy from him, who had been born and brought up amongst Spaniards, than from the Hollanders, who as they were little bound unto the Spanish nation for mercy, so did we expect little from them. The captain of this Holland ship which took us was a mulatto born and bred in Havana, whose mother I saw and spoke with afterwards that same year, when the galleons struck into that port to expect there the rest that were to come from Vera Cruz. This mulatto, for some wrongs which had been offered unto him from some commanding Spaniards in Havana, ventured himself desperately in a boat out to the sea, where were some Holland ships waiting for a prize, and with God's help getting unto them, yielded himself to their mercy, which he esteemed far better than that of his own countrymen, promising to serve them faithfully against his own nation, which had most injuriously and wrongfully abused, yea and (as I was afterwards informed) whipped him in Havana.

This mulatto proved so true and faithful in his good services unto the Hollanders, that they esteemed much of him, married him to one of their nation, and made him captain of a ship under that brave and gallant Hollander whom the Spaniards then so much feared, and named *Pie de Palo*, or Wooden Leg. This famous mulatto it was that with his sea soldiers boarded our frigate, in the which he had found little worth his labour had it not been for the Indians' offering which I carried with me, of which I lost that day the worth of four thousand pataciones or pieces of eight in pearls and precious stones, and near three thousand more in money. The other Spaniards lost some hundreds apiece, which was so rich a prize that it made the Hollanders' stomach loath the rest of our gross provision of bacon, meal and fowls, and our money tasted sweeter unto them than the honey which our frigate also afforded them. Other things I had (as a quilt to lie on, some books, and *laminas,* which are pictures in brass, and clothes) which I begged of that noble captain the mulatto, who considering my orders and calling, gave me them freely, and wished me to be patient, saying that he could do no otherwise than he did with my money and pearls, and using that common proverb at sea,—*oy por mi, mañana por ti,* today fortune hath been for me, tomorrow it may be for thee.

I had some comfort left in a few pistoles, some single, some double, which I had sewed up in my quilt (which the captain restored unto me, saying it was the bed I lay in) and in the doublet which I had at that present, which mounted to almost a thousand crowns, and in their searching was not found out. After the captain and soldiers had well viewed their prize, they thought of refreshing their stomachs with some of our provision; the good captain made a stately dinner in our frigate, and invited me unto it, and knowing that I was going towards Havana, besides many other *brindis* or healths, he drank one unto his mother, desiring me to see her, and to remember him unto her, and how that for her sake he had used me well and courteously in what he could; and further at table he said that for my sake he would give us our frigate that we might return again to land, and that I might find out from thence some safer way and means to get to Portobello, and to continue on my journey unto Spain. After dinner I conferred with the captain alone, and told him that I was no Spaniard, but an Englishman born, shewing him the licence which I had from Rome to go to England, and that therefore I hoped, not being of an enemy nation to the Hollanders, he would restore unto me what goods were mine. But all this was of little consequence with him, who had already taken possession of mine, and all other goods in the ship: he told me I must suffer with those amongst whom I was found, and that I might as well claim all the goods in the ship for mine. I desired him then to carry me along with him to Holland, that from thence I might get to England, which also he refused to do, telling me that he went about from one place to another, and knew not when he should go to Holland, and that he was

daily ready to fight with any Spanish ship, and if he should fight with the Spaniards whilst I was in his ship, his soldiers in their hot blood might be ready to do me a mischief, thinking I would do them harm if in fight they should be taken by the Spaniards. With these his answers I saw there was no hope of getting again what now was lost, therefore (as before) I commended myself again to God's providence and protection.

The soldiers and mariners of the Holland ship made haste that afternoon to unlade the goods of our frigate into their man-of-war, which took them up that, and part of the next day, whilst we as prisoners were wafting up and down the sea with them. And whereas we thought our money had satisfied them enough, and to the full, we found the next day that they had also a stomach to our fowls and bacon, and wanted our meal to make them bread, and our honey to sweeten their mouths, and our hides for shoes and boots, all which they took away, leaving me my quilt, books, and brass pictures, and to the master of the frigate some small provision, as much as might carry us to land, which was not far off, and thus they took their leaves of us, thanking us for their good entertainment.

\*    \*    \*

# REVIEW QUESTIONS

1. What were a single merchant ship's defenses against a privateer's (or pirate's) offensive actions?
2. What does the merchant ship's cargo and the personal property of its passengers disclose about the material culture and economy of Spanish America?
3. How does this engagement illuminate the give and take of transatlantic competition for America's wealth?
4. What does Gage's account reveal about early seventeenth-century Caribbean societies on land and sea (including pirate ships)?
5. What do Gage's thoughts and actions reveal about him?

Gage was shrewd trying to pull the English card.

# 2 &infin; BRITAIN AND ITS COLONIES

As the Old World pushed some peoples out, the New World pulled them over
the Atlantic. Over the course of the seventeenth century, English colonists
shipped out for a number of reasons, including those of economics, politics, and
religion. Their motives were reflected in where they settled and how they sowed,
nurtured, and defended their cuttings from that hardy oak called English civilization. In the course of transplantation, the colonists took with them certain
shared attitudes and behaviors, but they also carried with them localized variations depending on where in England they came from and why they decided to
emigrate. Further modification or deviation occurred as the offshoots took root
in new soils, were nurtured by new fertilizers, and not only survived but thrived
due to grafts from aborigine, African, and other European cultures. Thus,
although the colonies had much in common as they developed, they also differed
in their religious, political, and social establishments.

The English colonists compared themselves to and defined themselves against
native peoples, including the Powhatans, Pequots, and Mohawks, and immigrant
groups, such as the Dutch and African. Coming in contact with those cultures
made many colonists more aware and more defensive of their own. While
adopting what they deemed useful from the other cultures, they simultaneously
established their own identity—or identities—through their interactions with
these groups and with English settlers in other colonies. Thus these colonists
proclaimed their English identity, while developing regional—as New Englanders
or Virginians, for instance—and ethnic or racial ones. Cultural interchange
differed in kind and amount because colonists in some areas had more contact
with diverse groups than did the colonists in others. Intent on implementing their
own version of civilization, however, the English colonists—as well as other
European colonists—attempted to control this cultural interchange wherever,
whenever, and however it happened by imposing their own legal and social
principles.

*Controlling intercultural exchanges was but one of the complex tasks inherent to colonization; commanding the colonists themselves was another. Military, political, social, and religious leaders found it difficult to impose order in the colonies. From the first, the often dreadful demands of survival challenged the colonists' plans and attempts to create properly regulated and cohesive societies; although the need to survive caused some people to work together, it led others to strive for their own ends at the expense of others. Although the vastness of the land and the different peoples that inhabited it frightened some settlers into huddling their houses close together and accepting strict regulation for protection, others embraced the wilderness for the implied freedom it promised from nosy neighbors and government's rules. Then, as settlement proceeded, other factors, such as the growing diversity of religions and immigrants, complicated social transplantation. Whereas many colonists had hoped to reconstruct traditional social structures and mores, they found that circumstances sometimes demanded new constructions or adaptations. Each colony addressed such problems in different ways: some rooted out those who did not conform to their religious and social prescripts, whereas others attempted limited toleration and even inclusion. Such reactions, and the results they produced, illuminate both the initial challenges inherent to colonization as well as the developing nature of the different colonial societies.*

# CAPTAIN JOHN SMITH

## FROM *The Generall Historie* (1624)

*The Virginia Company, after receiving its charter from King James I in 1606, moved quickly to plant a colony within the territory granted to it. Within a year approximately a hundred men—called adventurers—encompassing artisans, soldiers, gentlemen, and a few farmers, sailed across the Atlantic Ocean and in May 1607 established a* plantation—*a term that meant "settlement" to them—and fort on a river off the Chesapeake Bay. They named both the river and their small settlement after their monarch.*

*The adventurers had hoped to find readily exploitable natural resources and native peoples to serve as laborers, but such expectations did not, literally, bear fruit. As they struggled with the reality of the land and its indigenous people, the colonists discovered just how ill-prepared they actually were. Captain John Smith, who was admitted to the governing council in June 1607 and then elected its president in the fall of 1608, strove to correct the settlers' deficiencies, subordinate the Native Americans, and make the colony a profitable operation. His actions ensured the survival of the colony, but his authoritarian leadership alienated many of its people. Due to his enemies' efforts, company reorganization, and a wound he suffered when some gunpowder exploded, Smith quit the colony in the fall of 1609.*

From John Lankford, ed., *Captain John Smith's America: Selections from His Writings* (New York: Harper Torchbooks, 1967), pp. 81–83. [Editorial insertions appear in brackets—*Ed.*]

[In the fall of 1608 Captain Christopher Newport took some of the men on an expedition up and down the peninsula to find mineral resources and to open trade relations with native inhabitants.]

\*     \*     \*

Trade they would not, and find their corn we could not; for they had hid[den] it in the woods: and being thus deluded, we arrived at Jamestown, half sick, all complaining, and tired with toil, famine, and discontent, to have only but discovered our gilded hopes, and such fruitless certainties, as Captain Smith foretold us. . . .

No sooner were we landed, but the President dispersed so many as were able, some for glass, others for tar, pitch, and soap ashes, leaving them with the fort to the Council's oversight.

But 30 of us he conducted down the river some 5 miles from Jamestown, to learn to make clapboard, cut down trees, and [to make] lye in [the] woods. Amongst the rest he had chosen Gabriel Beadle, and John Russell, the only two gallants of this last supply, and both proper gentlemen. Strange were these pleasures to their conditions; yet lodging, eating, and drinking, working or playing, they but doing as the President did himself. All these things were carried so pleasantly as within a week they became masters: making it their delight to hear the trees thunder as they fell; but the axes so oft blistered their tender fingers, that many times every third blow had a loud oath to drown the echo; for remedy of which sin, the President devised how to have every man's oaths numbered, and at night for every oath to have a can of water poured down his sleeve, with which every offender was so washed (himself and all) that a man should scarce hear an oath in a week. . . .

By this, let no man think that the President and these gentlemen spent their times as common wood haggers [cutters] at felling of trees, or such other like labors; or that they were pressed to it as hirelings, or common slaves; for what they did, after they were but once a little inured, it seemed and some conceited it, only as a pleasure and recreation: yet 30 or 40 of such voluntary gentlemen would do more in a day than 100 of the rest that must be pressed to it by compulsion; but twenty good workmen had been better than them all.

Master Scrivener, Captain Waldo, and Captain Winne at the fort, every one in like manner carefully regarded their charge. The President returning from amongst the woods, seeing the time consumed and no provision gotten, (and the ship lay idle at a great charge and did nothing) presently embarked himself in the discovery barge, giving order to the Council to send Lieutenant Percy after him with the next barge that arrived at the fort; two barges he had himself and 18 men, but arriving at *Chickahominy*, that dogged nation was too well acquainted with our wants, refusing to trade, with as much scorn and insolency as they could express. The President perceiving it was Powhatan's policy to starve us, told them he came not so much for their corn, as to revenge his imprisonment [December 1607], and the death of his men murdered by them; and so landing his men and ready to charge them, they immediately fled: and presently after sent their ambassadors with corn, fish, fowl, and what they had to make their peace; (their corn being that year but bad) they complained extremely of their own wants, yet fraughted our boats with a hundred bushels of corn, and in like manner Lieutenant Percy's that not long after arrived, and having done the best they could to content us, we parted good friends, and returned to Jamestown.

Though this much contented the company (that feared nothing more than starving), yet some so envied his good success, that they rather desired to hazard a starving, than his pains should prove so much more effectual than theirs. Some projects there were

invented by Newport and Ratcliffe [the former president], not only to have deposed him, but to have kept him out of the fort . . . but their horns were so much too short to effect it, as they themselves more narrowly escaped a greater mischief.

All this time our old tavern made as much of all them that had either money or ware as could be desired: by this time they were become so perfect on all sides (I mean the soldiers, sailors, and savages) as there was ten times more care to maintain their damnable and private trade, than to provide for the colony things that were necessary. Neither was it a small policy in Newport and the mariners to report in England we had such plenty, and bring us so many men without victuals, when they had so many private factors [business agents] in the fort, that within six or seven weeks, of two or three hundred axes, chisels, hoes, and pick-axes, scarce[ly] twenty could be found: and for pike-heads, shot, powder, or anything they could steal from their fellows, [which] was vendible; they knew as well (and as secretly) how to convey them to trade with the savages for furs, baskets, *mussaneeks*, young beasts, or such like commodities, as exchange them with the sailors for butter, cheese, beef, pork, aqua vitae, beer, biscuit, oatmeal, and oil: and then feign all was sent them from their friends. And though Virginia afforded no furs for the store, yet one master in one voyage hath got so many by this indirect means, as he confessed to have sold in England for £30.

Those are the saint-seeming worthies of Virginia (that have notwithstanding all this, meat, drink, and wages); but now they begin to grow weary, their trade being both perceived and prevented.

None hath been in Virginia, that hath observed anything, [who] knows not this to be true: and yet the loss, the scorn, the misery, and shame, was the poor officers', gentlemen's, and careless governors', who were all thus bought and sold; the adventurers cozened, and the action overthrown by their false excuses, informations, and directions. By this let all men judge, how this business could prosper, being thus abused by such pilfering occasions. And had not Captain Newport cried *peccavi* [admitted his mistake], the President would have discharged the ship, and caused him to have stayed one year in Virginia, to learn to speak of his own experience.

Master Scrivener was sent with the barges and pinnace to *Werowocómoco*, where he found the savages more ready to fight than trade: but his vigilancy was such as prevented their projects, and by the means of Namontack, [he] got three or four hogsheads of corn; and as much *puccoon*, which is a red root, which then was esteemed an excellent dye.

Captain Newport being dispatched [December 1608], with the trials [samples] of pitch, tar, glass, frankincense, soap ashes; with that clapboard and wainscot that could be provided met with Master Scrivener at Point Comfort, and so

returned [to] England. We remaining were about two hundred.

\*    \*    \*

## REVIEW QUESTIONS

1. How did each group, native and newcomer, act toward the other? What impact did that have on the colonists' settlement?
2. What kind of work did Smith have the men do? Were they productive?
3. What undermined Smith's efforts to secure and stabilize the colony?

# RICHARD FRETHORNE

## FROM An Indentured Servant's Letter Home (1623)

*Despite deteriorating relations with the Native Americans, often miserable environmental conditions, and a high mortality rate, Englishmen—along with some Englishwomen and, after 1619, some Africans—continued to colonize Virginia by planting more settlements. Although the later colonists were still fundamentally adventurers, more and more of them came prepared to seek their fortune through agriculture, specifically the cultivation of tobacco. Tobacco was a labor-intensive crop; thus success and profit depended on the acquisition and utilization of enough workers. Although Virginia planters would eventually come to rely on slaves, for most of the seventeenth century they turned to indentured laborers: colonists who contracted to work for a master for a specified number of years in return for passage to America along with room and board and other benefits as noted in the contract. Thousands of men and women accepted that challenge of hard work in the hope of future reward, only to realize once they were in America that they were not willing or able to work quite so hard in such conditions. Richard Frethorne was one of them. He was an indentured servant working at Martin's Hundred, a plantation a few miles away from Jamestown, a year after the 1622 Indian attack that left hundreds dead there and in the surrounding area. This was also a year before the royal government took over the struggling colony.*

From "An Indentured Servant's Letter Home," in Major Problems in the History of American Workers, Eileen Boris and Nelson Lichtenstein (Lexington, MA: D.C.Heath, 1991), pp. 34–36. Copyright © 1991 by Houghton Mifflin Company. [The spelling in the selection has been modernized. Editorial insertions that appear in square brackets are from Boris and Lichtenstein.—*Ed.*]

oving and kind father and mother:

My most humble duty remembered to you, hoping in God of your good health, as I myself am at the making hereof. This is to let you understand that I your child am in a most heavy case by reason of the nature of the country, [which] is such that it causeth much sickness, [such] as the scurvy and the bloody flux and diverse other diseases, which maketh the body very poor and weak. And when we are sick there is nothing to comfort for us; for since I came out of the ship I never ate anything but peas, and loblollie (that is, water gruel). As for deer or venison I never saw any since I came into this land. There is indeed some fowl, but we are not allowed to go and get it, but must work hard both early and late for a mess of water gruel and a mouthful of bread and beef. A mouthful of bread for a penny loaf must serve for four men which is most pitiful. [You would be grieved] if you did know as much as [I do], when people cry out day and night— Oh! that they were in England without their limbs—and would not care to lose any limb to be in England again, yea, though they beg from door to door. For we live in fear of the enemy [Powhatan Indians] every hour, yet we have had a combat with them on the Sunday before Shrovetide [Monday before Ash Wednesday], and we took two alive and made slaves of them. But it was by policy, for we are in great danger; for our plantation is very weak by reason of the death and sickness of our company. For we came but twenty for the merchants, and they are half dead just; and we look very hour when two more should go. Yet there came some four other men yet to live with us, of which there is but one alive; and our Lieutenant is dead, and [also] his father and his brother. And there was some five or six of the last year's twenty, of which there is but three left, so that we are fain to get other men to plant with us; and yet we are but 32 to fight against 3000 if they should come. And the nighest help that we have is ten miles of us, and when the rogues overcame this place [the] last [time] they slew 80 persons. How then shall we do, for we lie even in their teeth? . . .

And I have nothing to comfort me, nor there is nothing to be gotten here but sickness and death, except [in the event] that one had money to lay out in some things for profit. But I have nothing at all—no, not a shirt to my back but two rags (2), nor no clothes but one poor suit, nor but one pair of shoes, but one pair of stockings, but one cap, [and] but two bands. My cloak is stolen by one of my own fellows, and to his dying hour [he] would not tell me what he did with it; but some of my fellows saw him have butter and beef out of a ship, which my cloak, I doubt [not], paid for. So that I have not a penny, nor a penny worth, to help me to either spice or sugar or strong waters, without the which one cannot live here. For as strong beer in England doth fatten and strengthen them, so water here doth wash and weaken these here [and] only keeps [their] life and soul together. But I am not half a quarter so strong as I was in England, and all is for want of victuals; for I do protest unto you that I have eaten more in [one] day at home than I have allowed me here for a week. You have given more than my day's allowance to a beggar at the door; and if Mr. Jackson had not relieved me, I should be in a poor case. But he like a father and she like a loving mother doth still help me.

For when we go up to Jamestown (that is 10 miles of us) there lie all the ships that come to land, and there they must deliver their goods. And when we went up to town, as it may be, on Monday at noon, and come there by night, [and] then load the next day by noon, and go home in the afternoon, and unload, and then away again in the night, and [we would] be up about midnight. Then if it rained or blowed never so hard, we must lie in the boat on the water and have nothing but a little bread. . . . But that Goodman Jackson pitied me and made me a cabin to lie in always when I [would] come up, and he would give me some poor jacks [fish] [to take] home with me, which comforted me more than peas or water gruel. Oh, they be very godly folks, and love me very well, and will do anything for me. And he much marvelled that you would send me a servant to the Company; he saith I had been better knocked on the head.

And indeed so I find it now, to my great grief and misery; and [I] saith that if you love me you will redeem me suddenly, for which I do entreat and beg. And if you cannot get the merchants to redeem me for some little money, then for God's sake get a gathering or entreat some good folks to lay out some little sum of money in meal and cheese and butter and beef. . . . But for God's sake send beef and cheese and butter, or the more of one sort and none of another. But if you send cheese, it must be very old cheese; and . . . you must have a care how you pack it in barrels; and you must put cooper's chips between every cheese, or else the heat of the hold will rot them. And look whatsoever you send me—be it never so much—look, what[ever] I make of it, I will deal truly with you. I will send it over and beg the profit to redeem me; and if I die before it come, I have entreated Goodman Jackson to send you the worth of it, who hath promised he will. If you send, you must direct your letters to Goodman Jackson, at Jamestown, a gunsmith. (You must set down his freight, because there be more of his name there.) Good father, do not forget me, but have mercy and pity. . . . I pray you to remember my love to all my friends and kindred. I hope all my brothers and sisters are in good health, and as for my part I have set down my resolution that certainly will be; that is, that the answer of this letter will be life or death to me. Therefore, good father, send as soon as you can; and if you send me anything let this be the mark.

ROT

Richard Frethorne,
Martin's Hundred

## REVIEW QUESTIONS

1. What sense of community did Frethorne note in this early settlement?
2. Although Frethorne worked primarily at the Martin's Hundred plantation, what other task did this company servant commonly have to perform?
3. What were Frethorne's major complaints?
4. What did Frethorne want of his parents?

# NATHANIEL BACON

## FROM Bacon's Manifesto (1676)

*Later colonists in Virginia echoed Frethorne's complaints as they struggled with the hardships of settlement. They also started to grumble about how some colonists who had managed to establish themselves earlier were limiting the opportunities of others by amassing the best lands and controlling the government. By the 1670s most new immigrants and servants just freed from their indentures found that they could not afford lands in the settled areas, so they had to push on to the frontier. As they pushed out, the Native Americans pushed back. These issues led to a split between the colonists: those who supported Governor William Berkeley's Indian policies and defended his administration against those who favored Nathaniel Bacon's ideas. Bacon's Rebellion (1676), which was ultimately a battle over who was to rule the settlement, showed that Indian actions could pose not only external threats but also internal ones. In the latter case, their actions produced violent schisms within settler communities. Bacon was a recent immigrant to Virginia and a young man still in his twenties*

*when he challenged Governor Berkeley's authority. Representing the small farmers of
the frontier who had been battling native peoples, Bacon called for the extermination
of the Indians so as to secure the territory. When Berkeley appeared to be more interested in subduing the frontiersmen, Bacon and his supporters marched against the
government in Jamestown to force the issue. Having been declared a rebel, pardoned,
and then condemned again, Bacon rebutted the charges against him and other rebels
in a public declaration that outlined their motivation and purpose.*

. . . [I]f there bee as sure there is, a just God to appeal too, if Religion and Justice be a sanctuary here,
If to plead the cause of the oppressed, If sincerely
to aime at his Majesties Honour and the Publick
good without any reservation or by Interest, If to
stand in the Gap after soe much blood of our dear
Brethren bought and sold, If after the losse of a
great part of his Majesties Colony deserted and dis-
peopled, freely with our lives and estates to in-
deavor to save the remaynders bee Treason God
Almighty Judge and lett guilty dye, But since wee
cannot in our hearts find one single spott of Rebellion or Treason or that wee have in any manner
aimed at subverting the setled Government or attempting of the Person of any either magistrate or
private man not with standing the severall Reproaches and Threats of some who for sinister
ends were disaffected to us and censured our
ino[cent][1] and honest designes, and since all people in all places where wee have yet bin can attest
our civill quiet peaseable behaviour farre different
from that of Rebellion and tumultuous persons let
Trueth be bold and all the world know the real
Foundations of pretended giult, Wee appeale to
the Country itselfe what and of what nature their
Oppressions have bin or by what Caball and mis-
tery the designes of many of those whom wee call
great men have bin transacted and caryed on, but

let us trace these men in Authority and Favour to
whose hands the dispensation of the Countries
wealth has been commited; let us observe the
sudden Rise of their Estates composed with the
Quality in which they first entered this Country Or
the Reputation they have held here amongst wise
and discerning men, And lett us see wither their
extractions and Education have not bin vile, And
by what pretence of learning and vertue they
could soe soon into Imployments of so great Trust
and consequence, let us consider their sudden advancement and let us also consider wither any
Publick work for our safety and defence or for the
Advancement and propogation of Trade, liberall
Arts or sciences is here Extant in any [way]
adaquate to our vast chardg, now let us compare
these things togit[her] and see what spounges have
suckt up the Publique Treasure and wither it hath
not bin privately contrived away by unworthy
Favourites and juggling Parasites whose tottering
Fortunes have bin repaired and supported at the
Publique chardg, now if it be so Judg what greater
giult can bee then to offer to pry into these and to
unriddle the misterious wiles of a powerfull Cabal let
all people Judge what can be of more dangerous Import then to suspect the soe long Safe proceedings of
Some of our Grandees and wither People may with
safety open their Eyes in soe nice a Concerne.

Another main article of our Giult is our open
and manifest aversion of all, not onely the Foreign
but the protected and Darling Indians, this wee

---

[1] Further editorial insertions that appear in square
brackets are from Billings.

are informed is Rebellion of a deep dye For that both the Governour and Councell are by Colonell Coales Assertion bound to defend the Queen and Appamatocks with their blood Now whereas we doe declare and can prove that they have bin for these Many years enemies to the King and Country, Robbers and Theeves and Invaders of his Majesties' Right and our Interest and Estates, but yet have by persons in Authority bin defended and protected even against His Majesties loyall Subjects and that in soe high a nature that even the Complaints and oaths of his Majesties Most loyall Subjects in a lawfull Manner proffered by them against those barborous Outlawes have bin by the right honourable Governour rejected and the Delinquents from his presence dismissed not only with pardon and indemnitye but with all incouragement and favour. . . .

Another main article of our Giult is our Design not only to ruine and extirpate all Indians in Generall but all Manner of Trade and Commerce with them, Judge who can be innocent that strike at this tender Eye of Interest; Since the Right honourable the Governour hath bin pleased by his Commission to warrant this trade who dare oppose it, or opposing it can be innocent, Although Plantations be deserted, the blood of our dear Brethren Split. . . .

Another Article of our Giult is To Assert all those neighbour Indians as well as others to be outlawed, wholly unqualifyed for the benefitt and Protection of the law, For that the law does reciprocally protect and punish, and that all people offending must either in person or Estate make equivalent satisfaction or Restitution according to the manner and merit of the Offences Debts or Trespasses; Now since the Indians cannot according to the tenure and forme of any law to us known be prosecuted, Seised or Complained against, Their Persons being difficulty distinguished or known, Their many nations languages, and their subterfuges such as makes them incapeable to make us Restitution or satisfaction would it not be very giulty to say They have bin unjustly defended and protected these many years.

If it should be said that the very foundation of all these disasters the Grant of the Beaver trade to the Right Honourable Governour was illegall and not granteable by any power here present as being a monopoly, were not this to deserve the name of Rebell and Traytor.

Judge therefore all wise and unprejudiced men who may or can faithfully or truely with an honest heart attempt the country's good, their vindication and libertie without the aspersion of Traitor and Rebell, since as soe doing they must of necessity gall such tender and dear concernes, But to manifest Sincerity and loyalty to the World, and how much wee abhorre those bitter names, may all the world know that we doe unanimously desire to represent our sad and heavy grievances to his most sacred Majesty as our Refuge and Sanctuary, where wee doe well know that all our Causes will be impartially heard and Equall Justice administred to all men.

# REVIEW QUESTIONS

1. Whom did Bacon think should judge whether he and his followers had engaged in rebellion and treason?
2. Whom did he believe should bear the guilt for the colony's problems? Why?
3. How did he argue that the protection of the Indians under the law is unjust? Was it a valid argument? Why or why not?

# JOHN WINTHROP

# FROM General Observations AND Model of Christian Charity (1629–30)

*The Puritans, like the Pilgrims, felt impelled to emigrate to escape religious persecution. Puritans were dissenters who strove to "purify" the Anglican Church of vestiges of Catholicism and reform it through a stronger application of Calvinism. Condemned and harassed by crown and church officials, some decided to move to the New World. There they planned to establish, as their governor John Winthrop phrased it, a "city upon a hill" that was to set a shining example of piety and community for the rest of the world. Instead of pursuing property and profit, the Puritans were on a mission—though they certainly prayed that peace and prosperity would attend their piety. In 1629, as Winthrop, the forty-one-year-old Suffolk county squire, prepared to lead the first contingent of Puritans to the Massachusetts Bay colony, he listed some of the reasons why he was emigrating and why others should too. Then in 1630, while aboard the* Arbella, *as the colonists struggled with homesickness, seasickness, and fear of the unknown, he both chastised and encouraged them by reminding them that they were engaged in a labor of love and that their endeavors would be judged.*

Reprinted courtesy of the Massachusetts Historical Society. John Winthrop, "A Modell of Christian Charity," in *Winthrop Papers*, ed. Stewart Mitchell (Boston: Massachusetts Historical Society, 1931), 2:282, 292–295.
Reprinted courtesy of the Massachusetts Historical Society. John Winthrop, "General Observations," in *Winthrop Papers*, ed. Stewart Mitchell (Boston: Massachusetts Historical Society, 1931), 2:114–115.

## General Observations, 1629

1. It wilbe a service to the Churche of great Consequence to carrye the Gospell into those partes of the world, and to rayse a bullwarke against the kingdom of Antichrist which the Jesuites labour to reare vp in all places of the worlde.

2. All other Churches of Europe are brought to desolation, and it cannot be, but the like Judgment is comminge vpon vs: and who knows, but that God hathe provided this place, to be a refuge for manye, whom he meanes to save out of the general destruction?

3. This land growes wearye of her Inhabitantes, so as man which is the most pretious of all Creatures, is heere more vile and base, then the earthe they treade vpon: so as children neighbours and freindes (especi[ally] if they be poore) are rated the greatest burdens, which if things were right, would be the cheifest earthly bless[ings].

4. We are growne to that height of Intemperance in all excesse of Ryot, as no mans estate all most will suffice to keepe sayle with his equalls: and he that fayles in it, must liue in scorn and contempt: hence it comes, that all artes and trades are carried in that deceiptful and vnrighteous course, as it is allmost imposs[ible] for a good and vpright man to maintaine his charge and liue comfortably in any of them.

5. The fountains of learninge and Relig[ion] are so corrupted, as (besides the vnsupport[able] chardge of their educat[ion]) most Children, even

the best wittes and of fayrest hopes, are perverted corrupted and vttrly overthrowne by the multitude of evill examples and the licentious government of those seminaryes.

6. The whole earthe is the Lordes garden: and he hathe given it to the sons of men to be tilld and improved by them: why then should we stand striving heere for places of habitation etc. (many men spending as muche labor and cost to recover or keepe sometyme an Acre or 2 of lande, as would procure him many C [hundred] acres as good or better in another place) and in the mene tyme suffere whole countrys as fruitfull and convenient for the vse of man, to lye waste without any improvement?

7. What can be a better worke and more honorable and worthy [a Christian then to helpe] rayse and supporte a partic[ular] Churche while it is in the infancye, and to ioine our forces with suche a Companye of faithfull people, as by a tymely assistance maye growe stronge and prosper, and for want of it may be putt to great hazard, if not wholly ruined?

8. If suche as are knowne to be godly and liue in wealthe and prosperitye heere, shall forsake all this to ioine themselves to this Churche, and to runne the hazard with them of a harde and meane condition, it wilbe an example of great vse, bothe for removinge the schandale of worldly and sinister respectes to give more life to the Faithe of Godes people in their prayers for the plantation, and allso to incourage others to ioyne the more willingly in it.

\*   \*   \*

# Christian Charitie. A Modell Hereof [1630]

God Almightie in his most holy and wise providence hath soe disposed of the Condicion of mankinde, as in all times some must be rich some poore, some highe and eminent in power and dignitie; others meane and in subieccion.

\*   \*   \*

It rests now to make some applicacion of this discourse by the present designe which gaue the occasion of writeing of it. Herein are 4 things to be propounded: first the persons, 2ly, the worke, 3ly, the end, 4ly the meanes.

I. For the persons, wee are a Company professiong our selues fellow members of Christ, In which respect only though wee were absent from eache other many miles, and had our imploymentes as farre distant, yet wee ought to account our selues knitt together by this bond of loue, and liue in the exercise of it. . . .

2ly. For the worke wee haue in hand, it is by a mutuall consent through a speciall overruleing providence, and a more then an ordinary approbation of the Churches of Christ to seeke out a place of Cohabitation and Consorteshipp vnder a due forme of Government both ciuill and ecclesiasticall. In such cases as this the care of the publique must oversway all private respects, by which not onely conscience, but meare Ciuill pollicy doth binde vs; for it is a true rule that perticular estates cannott subsist in the ruine of the publique.

3ly. The end is to improue our liues to doe more seruice to the Lord the comforte and encrease of the body of christe whereof wee are members that our selues and posterity may be the better preserued from the Common corrupcions of this euill world to serue the Lord and worke out our Salvacion vnder the power and purity of his holy Ordinances.

4ly. For the meanes whereby this must bee effected, they are 2fold, a Conformity with the worke and end wee aime at, these wee see are extraordinary, therefore wee must not content our selues with vsuall ordinary meanes whatsoever wee did or ought to haue done when wee liued in England, the same must wee doe and more allsoe where we goe: That which the most in theire Churches maineteine as a truthe in profession onely, wee must bring into familiar and constant practise. . . . neither must wee think that the lord will beare with such faileings at our hands as hee dothe from those among whome wee haue liued, and that for 3 Reasons.

I. In regard of the more neare bond of mariage, betweene him and vs, wherein he hath taken vs to be his after a most strickt and peculiar manner which will make him the more Jealous of our loue and obedience soe he tells the people of Israell, you onely haue I knowne of all the families of the Earthe therefore will I punishe you for your Transgressions.

2ly, because the lord will be sanctified in them that come neare him. Wee know that there were many that corrupted the seruice of the Lord some setting vpp Alters before his owne, others offering both strange fire and strange Sacrifices allsoe; yet there came noe fire from heaven, or other sudden Judgement vpon them as did vpon Nadab and Abihu whoe yet wee may thinke did not sinne presumptuously.

3ly When God giues a speciall Commission he lookes to haue it stricktly obserued in every Article, when hee gaue Saule a Commission to destroy Amaleck hee indented with him vpon certaine Articles and because hee failed in one of the least, and that vpon a faire pretence, it lost him the kingdome, which should haue beene his reward, if hee had obserued his Commission: Thus stands the cause between God and vs, wee are entered into Covenant with him for this worke, wee haue taken out a Commission, the Lord hath giuen vs leaue to drawe our owne Articles . . . wee haue herevpon besought him of favour and blessing: Now if the Lord shall please to heare vs, and bring vs in peace to the place wee desire, then hath hee ratified this Covenant and sealed our Commission, [and] will expect a strickt performance of the Articles contained in it, but if we shall neglect the observacion of these Articles which are the ends wee haue propounded, and dissembling with our God, shall fall to embrace this present world and prosecute our carnall intencions, seekeing greate things for our selues and our posterity, the Lord will surely breake out in wrathe against vs be revenged of such a periured people and make vs knowe the price of the breache of such a Covenant.

Now the onely way to avoyde this shipwracke and to provide for our posterity is to followe the Counsell of Micah, to doe Justly, to loue mercy, to walke humbly with our God, for this end, wee must be knitt together in this worke as one man, wee must entertaine each other in brotherly Affeccion, wee must be willing to abridge our selues of our superfluities, for the supply of others necessities, we must vphold a familiar Commerce together in all meekenes, gentlenes, patience and liberal-lity, wee must delight in eache other, make others Condicions our owne reioyce together, mourne together, labour, and suffer together, allwayes haueing before our eyes our Commission and Community in the worke, our Community as members of the same body, soe shall wee keepe the vnitie of the spirit in the bond of peace, the Lord will be our God and delight to dwell among vs, as his owne people and will commaund a blessing vpon vs in all our wayes, soe that wee shall see much more of his wisdome power goodnes and truthe then formerly wee haue beene acquainted with, wee shall finde that the God of Israell is among vs, when tenn of vs shall be able to resist a thousand of our enemies, when hee shall make vs a prayse and glory, that men shall say of succeeding plantacions: the lord make it like that of New England: for wee must Consider that wee shall be as a Citty vpon a Hill, the eies of all people are vppon vs; soe that if wee shall deale falsely with our god in this worke wee haue vndertaken and soe cause him to withdrawe his present help from vs, wee shall be made a story and a by-word through the world, wee shall open the mouthes of enemies to speake euill of the wayes of god and all professours for Gods sake; wee shall shame the faces of many of gods worthy seruants, and cause theire prayers to be turned into Cursses vpon vs til wee be consumed out of the good land whether wee are goeing: And to shutt vpp this discourse with that exhortacion of Moses that faithfull seruant of the Lord in his last farewell to Israell Deut. 30. Beloued there is now sett before vs life, and good, deathe and euill in that wee are Commaunded this day to loue the Lord our God, and to loue one another to walke in his wayes and to keepe his Commaundements and his Ordinance, and his lawes, and the Articles of our Covenant with him that wee may liue and be multiplyed, and that the Lord our God may blesse vs in the land whether wee goe to possesse it: But if our heartes shall turne away soe that wee will not obey, but shall be seduced and worshipp other Gods our pleasures, and proffitts, and serue them; it is propounded vnto vs this day, wee shall surely perishe out of the good Land whether wee passe over this vast Sea to possesse it;

> Therefore lett vs choose life,
> that wee, and our Seede,
> may liue; by obeying his
> voyce, and cleaueing to him,
> for hee is our life, and
> our prosperity.

## REVIEW QUESTIONS

1. Did Winthrop focus on what pushed the Puritans out of England or what was pulling them to the New World when promoting emigration in 1629? How does this selection compare with his 1630 address?
2. How did dissent from the English establishment and consensus among themselves affect the movement of Puritans to the New World and the establishment of their city upon a hill?
3. Why did Winthrop think that the Puritans were a special people? And why did he believe that they had to be especially careful in their new endeavor?
4. How might the Puritans' creation and interpretation of a covenant have affected the relationships between church and state and people?

# The Massachusetts Bay Colony Case against Anne Hutchinson (1637)

*The Puritans' struggle to practice their own religion freely did not extend to toleration for those who questioned church policies, as Anne Hutchinson, the intelligent, well-read, forty-six-year-old wife of a prosperous merchant, discovered. In 1637 Hutchinson faced prosecution for practices and beliefs deemed threatening to the stability of church and commonwealth. The ministers and magistrates did not think her weekly meetings unseemly when she began them in 1635, but revised their opinions as her audience, interpretation, and instruction of scripture changed. Hutchinson attacked some doctrinal premises, such as blaming Eve—and, correspondingly, women—for Original Sin, while denouncing some ministers for not properly teaching Puritan dogma. She also revealed that she had an inclination to mysticism. For her antinomianism (beliefs against the law) the magistrates exiled Hutchinson. She then moved with her family into what became Rhode Island, helping found Portsmouth there, and then on to Long Island, where she and most of her children were later slain by Indians.*

Reprinted by permission of the publisher from *The History of the Colony and Province of Massachusetts Bay: Volume II* by Thomas Hutchinson, edited by Lawrence Shaw Mayo, pp. 366–84, Cambridge, Mass.: Harvard University Press, Copyright © 1936 by President and Fellows of Harvard College.

*Mr. Winthrop, governor.* Mrs. Hutchinson, you are called here as one of those that have troubled the peace of the commonwealth and the churches here; you are known to be a woman that hath had a great share in the promoting and divulging of those opinions that are causes of this trouble, and to be nearly joined not only in affinity and affection with some of those the court had taken notice of and passed censure upon. But you have spoken divers things as we have been informed very prejudicial to the honour of the churches and ministers thereof, and you have maintained a meeting and an assembly in your house that hath been condemned by the general assembly as a thing not tolerable nor comely in the sight of God nor fitting for your sex; and notwithstanding that was cried down, you have continued the same. Therefore we have thought good to send for you to understand how things are. . . .

\*     \*     \*

*Mrs. Hutchinson.* What have I said or done?

*Gov.* Why for your doings, this you did harbour and countenance those that are parties in this faction that you have heard of.

*Mrs. H.* That's matter of conscience, Sir.

*Gov.* Your conscience you must keep, or it must be kept for you. . . .

\*     \*     \*

*Gov.* Why do you keep such a meeting at your house as you do every week upon a set day?

*Mrs. H.* It is lawful for me so to do, as it is all your practices; and can you find a warrant for yourself and condemn me for the same thing? . . .

*Gov.* For this, that you appeal to our practice you need no confutation. If your meeting had answered to the former it had not been offensive, but I will say that there was no meeting of women alone. But your meeting is of another sort, for there are sometimes men among you.

*Mrs. H.* There was never any man with us.

*Gov.* Well, admit there was no man at your meeting and that you was sorry for it, there is no warrant for your doings; and by what warrant do you continue such a course?

*Mrs. H.* I conceive there is a clear rule in Titus, that the elder women should instruct the younger; and then I must have a time wherein I must do it.

*Gov.* All this I grant you, I grant you a time for it; but what is this to the purpose that you, Mrs. Hutchinson, must call a company together from their callings to come to be taught of you?

*Mrs. H.* Will it please you to answer me this and to give me a rule, for then I will willingly submit to any truth? If any come to my house to be instructed in the ways of God, what rule have I to put them away?

*Gov.* But suppose that a hundred men come unto you to be instructed, will you forbear to instruct them?

*Mrs. H.* As far as I conceive I cross a rule in it.

*Gov.* Very well and do you not so here?

*Mrs. H.* No Sir, for my ground is they are men.

*Gov.* Men and women all is one for that, but suppose that a man should come and say, "Mrs. Hutchinson, I hear that you are a woman that God hath given his grace unto and you have knowledge in the word of God. I pray instruct me a little." Ought you not to instruct this man?

*Mrs. H.* I think I may.—Do you think it not lawful for me to teach women, and why do you call me to teach the court?

*Gov.* We do not call you to teach the court but to lay open yourself.

*Mr. Dudley, dep. gov.* Here hath been much spoken concerning Mrs. Hutchinson's meetings and among other answers she saith that men come not there. I would ask you this one question then, whether never any man was at your meeting?

*Gov.* There are two meetings kept at their house.

*Dep. Gov.* How; is there two meetings?

*Mrs. H.* Ey Sir, I shall not equivocate, there is a meeting of men and women, and there is a meeting only for women.

*Dep. Gov.* Are they both constant?

*Mrs. H.* No, but upon occasions they are deferred.

*Mr. Endicot.* Who teaches in the men's meetings, none but men? Do not women sometimes?

*Mrs. H.* Never as I heard, not one. . . .

*Dep. Gov.* Now it appears by this woman's meeting that Mrs. Hutchinson hath so forestalled the minds of many by their resort to her meeting that now she hath a potent party in the country. Now if all these things have endangered us as from that foundation, and if she in particular hath disparaged all our ministers in the land that they have preached a covenant of works, . . . why this is not to be suffered. And therefore being driven to the foundation, and it being found that Mrs. Hutchinson is she that hath depraved all the ministers and hath been the cause of what is fallen out, why we must take away the foundation and the building will fall.

*Mrs. H.* I pray, Sir, prove it that I said they preached nothing but a covenant of works.

*Dep. Gov.* Nothing but a covenant of works? Why, a Jesuit may preach truth sometimes.

*Mrs. H.* Did I ever say they preached a covenant of works, then?

*Dep. Gov.* If they do not preach a covenant of grace clearly, then they preach a covenant of works.

*Mrs. H.* No Sir, one may preach a covenant of grace more clearly than another, so I said.

*Dep. Gov.* We are not upon that now, but upon position.

*Mrs. H.* Prove this then, Sir, that you say I said.

*Dep. Gov.* When they do preach a covenant of works, do they preach truth?

*Mrs. H.* Yes Sir, but when they preach a covenant of works for salvation, that is not truth.

*Dep. Gov.* I do but ask you this: when the ministers do preach a covenant of works, do they preach a way of salvation?

*Mrs. H.* I did not come hither to answer to questions of that sort.

*Dep. Gov.* Because you will deny the thing.

*Mrs. H.* Ey, but that is to be proved first.

*Dep. Gov.* I will make it plain that you did say that the ministers did preach a covenant of works.

*Mrs. H.* I deny that.

*Dep. Gov.* And that you said they were not able ministers of the new testament. . . .

*Mrs. H.* If ever I spake that, I proved it by God's word.

*Court.* Very well, very well. . . .

*Mrs. H.* If you please to give me leave, I shall give you the ground of what I know to be true. Be-

ing much troubled to see the falseness of the constitution of the church of England, I had like to have turned separatist; whereupon I kept a day of solemn humiliation and pondering of the thing; this scripture was brought unto me—he that denies Jesus Christ to be come in the flesh is antichrist—This I considered of, and in considering found that the papists did not deny him to be come in the flesh, nor we did not deny him—who then was antichrist? Was the Turk antichrist only? The Lord knows that I could not open scripture; he must by his prophetical office open it unto me. So after that, being unsatisfied in the thing, the Lord was pleased to bring this scripture out of the Hebrews. He that denies the testament denies the testator, and in this did open unto me and give me to see that those which did not teach the new covenant had the spirit of antichrist, and upon this he did discover the ministry unto me and ever since. I bless the Lord, he hath let me see which was the clear ministry and which the wrong. Since that time I confess I have been more choice, and he hath let me to distinguish between the voice of my beloved and the voice of Moses, the voice of John Baptist and the voice of antichrist, for all those voices are spoken of in scripture. Now if you do condemn me for speaking what in my conscience I know to be truth, I must commit myself unto the Lord.

*Mr. Nowell.* How do you know that that was the spirit?

*Mrs. H.* How did Abraham know that it was God that bid him offer his son, being a breach of the sixth commandment?

*Dep. Gov.* By an immediate voice.

*Mrs. H.* So to me by an immediate revelation.

*Dep. Gov.* How! an immediate revelation.

*Mrs. H.* By the voice of his own spirit to my soul. I will give you another scripture, Jer. 46. 27, 28—out of which the Lord shewed me what he would do for me and the rest of his servants.—But after he was pleased to reveal himself to me, I did presently like Abraham run to Hagar. And after that, he did let me see the atheism of my own heart, for which I begged of the Lord that it might not remain in my heart; and being thus, he did shew me this (a twelvemonth after) which I told you of before. Ever since that time I have been confident of what he hath revealed unto me. . . . You see this scripture fulfilled this day, and therefore I desire you that as you tender the Lord and the church and commonwealth to consider and look what you do. You have power over my body, but the Lord Jesus hath power over my body and soul; and assure yourselves thus much, you do as much as in you lies to put the Lord Jesus Christ from you; and if you go on in this course you begin, you will bring a curse upon you and your posterity, and the mouth of the Lord hath spoken it.

*Dep. Gov.* What is the scripture she brings?

*Mr. Stoughton.* Behold I turn away from you.

*Mrs. H.* But now having seen him which is invisible, I fear not what man can do unto me.

*Gov.* Daniel was delivered by miracle. Do you think to be deliver'd so too?

*Mrs. H.* I do here speak it before the court. I look that the Lord should deliver me by his providence.

*Mr. Harlakenden.* I may read scripture and the most glorious hypocrite may read them and yet go down to hell.

*Mrs. H.* It may be so. . . .

*Mr. Endicot.* I would have a word or two with leave of that which hath thus far been revealed to the court. I have heard of many revelations of Mr. Hutchinson's, but they were reports, but Mrs. Hutchinson I see doth maintain some by this discourse; and I think it is a special providence of God to hear what she hath said. Now there is a revelation you see which she doth expect as a miracle. She saith she now suffers, and let us do what we will she shall be delivered by a miracle. I hope the court takes notice of the vanity of it and heat of her spirit.

## REVIEW QUESTIONS

1. What were the charges brought against Anne Hutchinson?
2. What do you suppose were the most serious: those having to do with faith or with practices? Why?
3. How did Hutchinson respond to the various accusations? What did she say gave her the authority to interpret scripture?
4. What was the court's response to her answer?
5. Which side had the stronger case? Why?

# WILLIAM PENN

## FROM The Frame of Government and Laws Agreed upon in England (1682)

*William Penn the junior (1644–1718) was the son of Admiral Sir William Penn, a man knighted by Charles II as a reward for services rendered to the Stuarts during the English Civil War and the restoration of the monarchy. The younger Penn, however, was imprisoned for appearing to subvert the authority of the crown and security of the country by promoting the Quaker religion. As religious persecution continued in England and Europe, the younger Penn looked to America as the only place where he could establish a refuge for his religious compatriots and create a model of Christian liberty. Therefore, after his father's death, he asked the king to give him a grant of land in lieu of the payment still owed on the crown's debt to his father. Charles II, after considering the advantages of the exchange, granted Penn the charter to Pennsylvania in 1681. Penn then vigorously planned and promoted his colony, which included writing (with many revisions based on advisors' comments) a constitution. In this constitution, Penn incorporated treasured elements from the English legal system while altering or adding others that reflected both his personal experiences with persecution and contemporary political thought about the allocation of political powers or sovereignty and the guarantee of individual rights.*

From Richard S. Dunn and Mary Maples Dunn, eds., *The Papers of William Penn. Volume II: 1680–1684* (Philadelphia: University of Pennsylvania Press, 1982), pp. 211–26. [Editorial insertions appear in square brackets—*Ed.*]

# The FRAME of the GOVERNMENT of the Province of Pennsilvania in AMERICA: Together with certain LAWS Agreed upon in England by the GOVERNOUR and Divers FREE-MEN of the aforesaid PROVINCE. The PREFACE.

When the *Great* and *Wise God* had made the World, of all his Creatures it pleased him to chuse *Man* his *Deputy* to Rule it: And to fit him for so great a Charge and Trust, he did not only qualifie him with *Skill* and *Power*, but with *Integrity* to use them justly. This *Native Goodness* was equally his Honour and his Happiness; and whilst he stood here, all went well: There was no need of *Coercive* or *Compulsive means*; the Precept of *Divine Love* and *Truth*, in his own Bosom was the *Guide* and *Keeper* of his Innocency. But *Lust* prevailing against *Duty*, made a lamentable Breach upon it; and the *Law*, that before had no Power over him, took place upon him and his Disobedient Posterity, that such as would not live conformable to the *holy Law within*, should fall under the Reproof and Correction of the *just Law without* in a Judicial Administration.

This the Apostle teaches in divers of his Epistles: *The Law* (says he) *was added because of Transgression:* In another place; *Knowing that the Law was not made for the Righteous Man, but for the Disobedient and Ungodly, for Sinners, for Unholy and Prophane, for Murderers, for Whore-mongers, for them that Defile themselves with Mankind, and for Man-stealers, for Lyars, for Perjured Persons, &c.* But this is not all, he opens and carries the matter of *Government* a little farther; *Let every Soul be subject to the higher Powers; for there is no Power but of God. The Powers that be, are ordained of God: Whosoever therefore resisteth the Power, resisteth the Ordinance of God. For Rulers are not a Terror to good Works, but to Evil: Wilt thou then not be afraid of the Power, Do that which is good, and thou shalt have Praise of the same—He is the Minister of God to thee for good—Wherefore, ye must needs be subject, not only for Wrath, but for Conscience sake.* This settles the *Divine Right* of *Government* beyond Exception, and that for two ends: First, *To Terrifie Evil-Doers:* Secondly, *To Cherish those that do Well;* which gives *Government* a Life beyond Corruption, and makes it as *durable* in the World, as *Good Men* shall be. So that *Government* seems to me a part of *Religion* it self, a thing *Sacred* in its *Institution* and *End:* for if it does not directly remove the *Cause*, it crushes the *Effects* of *Evil*, and is as such (though a lower, yet) an Emanation of the same *Divine Power*, that is both *Author* and *Object* of *Pure Religion;* the Difference lying here, that the One is more *Free* and *Mental*, the Other, more *Corporal* and *Compulsive* in its Operations: But that is only to *Evil-doers;* *Government* in it self being otherwise as capable of *Kindness, Goodness* and *Charity* as a more private Society. They weakly Err, that think there is no other use for *Government*, than *Correction*, which is the coursest part of it: Daily experience tells us, that the Care and Regulation of many other Affairs, more soft and daily necessary, make up much the greatest part of *Government;* and which must have followed the *Peopling* of the *World*, had *Adam* never fell, and will continue among Men on Earth under the highest Attainments they may arrive at, by the Coming of the blessed *Second Adam,* the *Lord from Heaven.*—Thus much of *Government* in *General*, as to its Rise and End.

For *particular Frames* and *Models*, . . . [m]y Reasons are, *First*, That the *Age* is too *nice*[1] and *difficult* for it, there being nothing the *Wits* of *Men* are more *busie* and *divided* upon. 'Tis true, they seem to agree in the *end*, to wit, *Happiness;* but in the *means* they differ, as to Divine, so to this Humane *Felicity;* and the cause is much the same, not alwayes want of *Light* and *Knowledge*, but want of using them rightly. Men side with their *Passions* against their *Reason;* and their *sinister Interests* have so strong a Byass upon their minds, that they lean to them against the good of the things they know.

*Secondly*, I do not find a Model in the World, that *Time, Place* and some singular *Emergencies* have not necessarily alter'd; nor is it easie to frame a *Civil Government*, that shall serve all places alike.

*Thirdly*, I know what is said by the several Admirers of *Monarchy, Aristocracy* and *Democracy*, which are the Rule of *One*, a *Few* and *Many*, and are the *Three Common Idea's* of *Government*, when men discourse of that Subject. But I chuse to solve the Controversie with this small Distinction, and it belongs to all *three:* Any *Government* is **Free** to the People under it (what-ever be the Frame) **where the Laws Rule, and the People are a Party to those Laws,** and more then this is *Tyranny, Oligarchy* or *Confusion.*

But *Lastly*, when all is said, there is hardly one *Frame* of *Government* in the World so ill design'd by its first Founders, that in *good hands* would not do well enough; and Story[2] tells us, The *Best* in *Ill Ones* can do nothing that is *great* or *good;* witness the *Jewish* and *Roman* States. *Governments*, like Clocks, go from the motion Men give them; and as *Governments* are made and mov'd by *Men*, so by *Them* are Ruin'd too: wherefore *Governments* rather depend upon *Men*, then *Men* upon *Governments.* Let *Men* be *good*, and the *Government* can't be *bad;* if it be *ill*, they will cure it: but if *Men* be *bad*, let the *Government* be never so *good*, they will endeavour to warp and spoil it to their Turn.

\* \* \*

These Considerations of the Weight of *Government*, and the nice and various Opinions about It, made it uneasie to Me to think of publishing the ensuing *Frame* and *Conditional Laws*, foreseeing, both the Censures they will meet with from Men of differing Humors and engagements, and the occasion they may give of discourse beyond my design.

But next to the Power of *Necessity*, (which is a Solicitor that will take no denial) this induc'd me to a Compliance, that we have (with *Reverence* to God and *good Conscience* to Men) to the best of our Skill contrived and composed the **Frame** and **Laws** of this **Government** to the great *End* of all *Government*, viz. **To support Power in Reverence with the People, And to secure the People from the abuse of Power;** that they may be *Free* by their *just Obedience*, and the Magistrates *Honourable* for their *just Administration:* For *Liberty* without *Obedience* is Confusion, and *Obedience* without *Liberty* is Slavery. To carry this Evenness is partly owing to the *Constitution*, and partly to the *Magistracy;* where either of these fail, *Government* will be subject to

---

[1]That is, critical.

[2]That is, history.

*Convulsions*: but where *both* are wanting, it must be totally subverted: Then where *both* meet, the *Government* is like to endure: Which I humbly pray and hope, God will please to make the *Lot of This* of **Pennsilvania**: *Amen.*

William Penn.

# The FRAME of the Government of Pennsylvania in AMERICA, &c.

\*    \*    \*

**Now Know Ye,** That for the *Well-being* and *Government* of the said *Province*, and for the *Encouragement* of all the **Free-men** and **Planters** that may be therein concerned, . . . I the said **William Penn** . . . by these Presents for **Me,** my **Heirs** and **Assigns** do *Declare, Grant* and *Confirm* unto all the **Free-men, Planters** and **Adventurers** of, in and to the said Province These **Liberties, Franchises** and **Properties** to be held, enjoyed and kept by the **Free-men, Planters** and **Inhabitants** of and in the said *Province* of **Pennsilvania** forever.

*Imprimis*, That the *Government* of this *Province* shall, according to the *Powers* of the *Patent*, consist of the **Governour** and **Free-men** of the said *Province*, in the Form of a **Provincial Council** and **General Assembly,** by whom all *Laws* shall be made, Officers chosen and publick Affairs Transacted, as is hereafter respectively declared. . . .

\*    \*    \*

V. That the **Provincial Council** in all Cases and Matters of Moment, as their *Arguing upon Bills to be past into Laws, Erecting Courts of Justice, giving Judgment upon Criminals Impeached, and Choice of Officers in such manner as is herein after mentioned,* Not less than *Two Thirds* of the whole **Provincial Council** shall make a *Quorum*; and that the Consent and Approbation of *Two Thirds* of such *Quo-*

*rum* shall be had in all such Cases or Matters of Moment. And moreover, that in all Cases and Matters of lesser Moment, Twenty Four Members of the said **Provincial Council** shall make a *Quorum,* the *Majority* of which twenty four shall and may always Determine in such Cases & Causes of lesser Moment.

VI. That in this **Provincial Council** the **Governour** or his *Deputy* shall or may always *preside* and have a *Treble Voice.* . . .

VII. That the **Governour** and **Provincial Council** shall prepare and propose to the **General Assembly,** hereafter mentioned, all **Bills,** which they shall at any time think fit to be past into Laws within the said *Province*; which **Bills** shall be Publisht and Affixed to the most noted Places in the Inhabited Parts thereof **Thirty** Dayes before the Meeting of the **General Assembly,** in order to the passing of them into Laws, or rejecting of them, as the **General Assembly** shall see meet.

VIII. That the **Governour** and **Provincial Council** shall take Care, that all *Laws, Statutes* and *Ordinances,* which shall at any time be made within the said *Province*, be duely and diligently Executed.

IX. That the **Governour** and **Provincial Council** shall at all times have the Care of the *Peace* and *Safety* of the *Province.* . . .

X. That the **Governour** and **Provincial Council** shall at all times settle and order the Scituation of all *Cities, Ports* and *Market-Towns* in every *County*, modelling therein all publick *Buildings, Streets* and *Market-Places*; and shall appoint all necessary *Roads* and *Highwayes* in the *Province.*

XI. That the *Governour* and *Provincial Council* shall at all times have Power to inspect the Management of the publick *Treasury*, and punish those who shall Convert any part thereof to any other use, than what hath been agreed upon by the **Governour, Provincial Council** and **General Assembly.**

XII. That the **Governour** and **Provincial Council** shall erect and order all *publick Schools*, and encourage and reward the Authors of *useful Sciences* and *laudable Inventions* in the said Province.

*    *    *

XIV. And to the end that all Laws prepared by the **Governour** and **Provincial Council** aforesaid, may yet have the more full Concurrence of the **Free-men** of the *Province*, It is Declared, Granted and Confirmed, that at the time and Place or Places, for the Choice of a **Provincial Council,** as aforesaid, the said **Free-men** shall Yearly chuse *Members* to serve in a **General Assembly,** as their *Representatives*, not exceeding Two Hundred Persons, who shall Yearly meet on the Twentieth Day of the second Moneth,[3] which shall be in the Year 1683, following, in the *Capital Town* or *City* of the said *Province*, where during Eight Dayes the several *Members* may freely Confer with one another; and if any of them see meet, with a *Committee* of the **Provincial Council** . . . which shall be at that time purposely Appointed to receive from any of them Proposals for the Alteration or Amendment of any of the said proposed and promulgated *Bills;* and on the Ninth Day from their so meeting, the said **General Assembly,** after the reading over of the proposed *Bills* by the Clark of the **Provincial Council,** and the Occasions and Motives for them being opened by the **Governour** or his **Deputy,** shall give their **Affirmative** or **Negative,** which to them seemeth best, in such manner as hereafter is exprest: But not less than *two Thirds* shall make a *Quorum* in the Passing of Laws and Choice of such Officers as are by them to be Chosen.

XV. That the Laws so prepared and proposed as aforesaid, that are Assented to by the **General Assembly,** shall be Enrolled, as Laws of the *Province*, with this Stile, **By the Governour, with the Assent and Approbation of the Free-men in Provincial Council and General Assembly.**

XVI. That for the better Establishment of the *Government* and *Laws* of this *Province*, and to the end there may be an Universal Satisfaction in the laying of the *Fundamentals* thereof, the **General Assembly** shall or may for the first Year consist of all the **Free-men** of and in the said Province; and ever after it shall be yearly Chosen, as aforesaid: which Number of **Two Hundred** shall be Enlarged as the Country shall Encrease in People, so as it do not Exceed **Five Hundred** at any time. . . .

XVII. That the **Governour** and the **Provincial Council** shall Erect from time to time *standing Courts of Justice* in such Places and Number, as they shall judge Convenient for the good Government of the said *Province*. And that the **Provincial Council** shall on the *Thirteenth Day* of the First Moneth[4] Yearly Elect and Present to the **Governour** or his *Deputy* a double Number of Persons to serve for *Judges, Treasurers, Masters* of *Rolls* within the said *Province* for the Year next ensuing. And the **Free-men** of the said *Province* in their *County-Courts*, when they shall be erected, and till then, in the **General Assembly** shall on the *Three and Twentieth* Day of the Second Moneth[5] yearly Elect and Present to the **Governour** or his *Deputy a Double Number* of Persons to serve for *Sheriffs, Justices* of *Peace* and *Coroners* for the Year next ensuing; Out of which Respective *Elections* and *Presentments* the **Governour** or his *Deputy* shall Nominate and Commissionate the proper Number for each Office the *Third day* after the said respective Presentments, or else the First named in such Presentment for each Office shall stand and serve for that Office the Year ensuing.

*    *    *

XXII. That as often as any day of the Moneth, mentioned in any Article of this Charter, shall fall upon the *First Day* of the Week, commonly called the *Lords Day*, the Business appointed for that day shall be deferred till the next day, unless in case of Emergency.

---

[3]According to their calendar, 20 April.

[4]13 March.
[5]23 April.

XXIII. That no *Act, Law* or *Ordinance* whatsoever, shall at any time hereafter be made or done by the **Governour** of this *Province,* his **Heirs** or **Assigns,** or by the **Free-men** in the **Provincial Council,** or the **General Assembly,** to *Alter, Change* or *Diminish* the *Form* or *Effect* of this **Charter,** or any *Part* or *Clause* thereof, or contrary to the true Intent and Meaning thereof, *without the Consent of the* **Governour,** *his* **Heirs** *or* **Assigns,** *and Six Parts of Seven of the said* **Free-men** *in* **Provincial Council** and **General Assembly.**

XXIV. And *Lastly,* That I, the said **William Penn,** for **My Self,** my **Heirs** and **Assigns** have *Solemnly Declared, Granted* and *Confirmed,* and do hereby *Solemnly Declare, Grant* and *Confirm,* That neither **I,** My **Heirs** nor **Assigns** *shall procure or do any thing or things, whereby the* Liberties *in this* Charter *contained and expressed, shall be infringed or broken.* . . .

*William Penn.*

**Laws agreed upon in England.** . . .

I. THAT the **Charter** of **Liberties** Declared, Granted and Confirmed the Five and Twentieth day of the Second Moneth called *April,* 1682, before divers Witnesses by **William Penn, Governour** and *Chief Proprietor* of *Pennsylvania,* to all the **Free-Men** and **Planters** of the said *Province,* is hereby declared and approved, and shall be forever held for a *Fundamental* in the *Government* thereof, according to the Limitations mentioned in the said *Charter.*

II. That every Inhabitant in the said *Province* that is or shall be a Purchaser of One Hundred Acres of Land or upwards, his Heirs and Assigns; and every Person who shall have paid his Passage, and taken up One Hundred Acres of Land at *One Penny* an Acre,[6] and have cultivated *Ten Acres* thereof; and every Person that hath been a *Ser-vant* or *Bonds-man,* and is *Free* by his *Service,* that shall have taken up his Fifty Acres of Land, and culti-

vated *Twenty* thereof; and every *Inhabitant, Artificer* or other, resident in the said *Province,* that payes **Scot** and **Lot** to the *Government,* **shall** be deemed and accounted a **Freeman** of the said *Province*; and every such Person shall and may be capable of Electing or being elected **Representatives** of the People in **Provincial Council** or **General Assembly** in the said *Province.*

III. That all **Elections** of Members or **Representatives** of the People and Free-men of the *Province* of *Pennsilvania,* to serve in **Provincial Council** or **General Assembly,** to be held within the said *Province,* shall be Free and Voluntary: And that the **Elector,** that shall receive any **Reward** or **Gift** in Meat, Drink, Moneys, or otherwise, shall forfeit his Right to Elect: And such Person as shall directly or indirectly give, promise or bestow any such *Reward* as aforesaid, to be *Elected,* shall forfeit his **Election,** and be thereby incapable to serve, as aforesaid. And the **Provincial Council** and **General Assembly** shall be the *sole Judges* of the Regularity or Irregularity of the **Elections** of their own respective Members.

IV. That no **Money** or *Goods* shall be raised upon, or paid by any of the People of this *Province, by way of a publick* **Tax,** Custom or Contribution, but by a *Law* for that purpose made: And whosoever shall Leavy, Collect or Pay any **Money** or *Goods* contrary thereunto, shall be held a *publick Enemy* to the Province, and a *Betrayer* of the *Liberty* of the People thereof.

V. That all **Courts** shall be open, and *Justice* shall neither be sold, denyed nor delayed.

VI. That in **Courts** all Persons of **all Perswasions** may freely appear in *their own Way,* and according to *their own Manner,* and there Personally *Plead* their own Cause themselves, or if unable, by their Friends. . . .

VII. That all **Pleadings,** Processes and Records in Courts shall be short, and in *English,* and in an ordinary and plain Character, that they may be understood, and Justice speedily administered.

---

[6]That is, in rent.

VIII. That all **Tryals** shall be by **Twelve Men,** and as near as may be, *Peers* or *Equals,* and of the *Neighbourhood,* and men without just Exception. . . .

\*    \*    \*

X. That all **Prisons** shall be *Work-houses* for *Felons, Vagrants* and Loose and Idle Persons, whereof one shall be in every County.

XI. That all *Prisoners* shall be Baylable by sufficient Sureties, unless for *Capital Offenses,* where the Proof is evident, or the Presumption great.

XII. That all Persons *Wrongfully Imprisoned,* or prosecuted at Law, shall have *Double Damages* against the *Informer* or *Prosecutor.*

XIII. That all *Prisons* shall be Free, as to *Fees, Food* and *Lodging.*

XIV. That all *Lands* and *Goods* shall be liable to pay **Debts,** except where there be *Legal Issue,* and then all the *Goods,* and *One Third* of the *Land* only.

\*    \*    \*

XIX. That all **Marriages** (not forbidden by the Law of God, as to nearness of Blood and Affinity by Marriage) shall be encouraged; but the *Parents* or *Guardians* shall be first consulted, and the *Marriage* shall be published before it be solemnized, & it shall be solemnized by *taking one another as Husband and Wife* before Credible Witnesses: And a *Certificate* of the whole, under the hands of Parties and Witnesses shall be brought to the proper Register of that County, and shall be Registered in his Office.

XX. And to prevent Frauds and Vexatious Suits within the said Province, That all **Charters,** Gifts, Grants and Conveyances of Land (except Leases for a Year, or under) and all **Bills,** Bonds and Specialties above Five Pound, and not under three Moneths, made in the said Province, shall be Enrolled or Registered in the publick Enrollment-Office of the said Province. . . .

\*    \*    \*

XXII. That there shall be a **Register** for Births, Marriages, Burials, Wills and Letters of Administration distinct from the other Registry.

XXIII. That there shall be a Registry for all **Servants,** where their Names, Time, Wages, and Dayes of Payment shall be Registred.

XXIV. That all Lands and Goods of **Fellons** shall be liable to make satisfaction to the Party wronged Twice the Value; and for want of Lands or Goods, the Fellon shall be Bonds-man, to work in the Common-Prison or Work-house, or otherwise, till the Party injured be satisfied.

XXV. That the Estates of Capital Offenders, as **Traitors** and **Murderers,** shall go one third to the next of Kin to the Sufferer, and the remainder to the next of Kin to the Criminal.

XXVI. That all **Witnesses** coming or called to testifie their Knowledge in or to any Matter or Thing in any Court, or before any lawful Authority within the said Province, shall there give or deliver in their Evidence or Testimony by solemnly Promising *To speak the Truth, the Whole Truth, and nothing but the Truth* to the Matter or Thing in question. And in case any Person so called to Evidence, shall afterwards be convicted of Wilfull Falsehood, such Person shall suffer and undergo such Damage or Penalty as the Person or Persons, against whom he or she bore false Witness, did or should undergo, and shall also make Satisfaction to the Party wronged, and be publickly exposed as a *False Witness,* never to be credited in any Court or before any Magistrate in the said Province.

XXVII. And to the end that all **Officers** chosen to serve within this Province, may with more care and diligence answer the Trust reposed in them, It is agreed, that no such Person shall enjoy more than one publick Office at one time.

XXVIII. That all **Children** within this Province of the Age of Twelve Years shall be taught some useful **Trade** or Skill, to the end none may be *Idle,* but the Poor may Work to live, and the Rich, if they become Poor, may not want.

XXIX. That **Servants** be not kept longer than their time; and such as are Careful be both justly and kindly used in their Service, and put in fitting Equipage at the expiration thereof, according to Custom.

XXX. That all Scandalous and Malicious *Reporters*, Backbiters, Defamers and Spreaders of false News, whether against Magistrates or private Persons, shall be accordingly severely punished, as *Enemies* to the *Peace* and *Concord* of this *Province*.

\* \* \*

XXXIV. That all **Treasurers,** Judges, Masters of the Rolls, Sheriffs, Justices of the Peace, and other Officers or Persons whatsoever, relating to Courts or Tryals of Causes, or any other Service in the Government, and all Members elected to serve in **Provincial Council** and **General Assembly;** and all that have Right to elect such Members, shall be such as profess **Faith** in **Jesus Christ,** and that are not convicted of Ill Fame, or unsober and dishonest Conversation, and that are of One and Twenty Years of Age at least: and that all such so qualified, shall be capable of the said several Employments and Priviledges, as aforesaid.

XXXV. That all Persons living in this Province, who confess and acknowledge the One Almighty and Eternal God, to be the Creator, Upholder and Ruler of the World, and that hold themselves obliged in Conscience to live peaceably and justly in *Civil Society*, shall in no wayes be molested or prejudiced for their Religious Perswasion or Practice in matters of *Faith* and *Worship*, nor shall they be compelled at any time to frequent or maintain any Religious **Worship,** Place or **Ministry** whatever.

XXXVI. That according to the good Example of the Primitive Christians, and for the ease of the Creation, every *First Day* of the Week called the

*Lords Day*, People shall abstain from their common daily Labour, that they may the better dispose themselves to Worship God according to their Understandings.

XXXVII. That as a Careless and Corrupt Administration of Justice draws the Wrath of God upon Magistrates, so the Wildness and Looseness of the People provoke the Indignation of God against a Country; Therefore,——

**That All** such Offences against God, as Swearing, Cursing, Lying, Prophane Talking, Drunkenness, Drinking of Healths, Obscene words, Incest, Sodomy, Rapes, Whoredom, Fornication and other uncleanness (not to be repeated:) **All** Treasons, Misprisons, Murders, Duels, Fellonies, Sedition, Mayhems, Forcible Entries and other Violencies to the Persons and Estates of the Inhabitants within this Province: **All** Prizes, Stage-Plays, Cards, Dice, May-Games, Gamesters, Masques, Revels, Bull-baitings, Cock-fightings, Bear-baitings and the like, which excite the People to Rudeness, Cruelty, Looseness and Irreligion, shall be respectively discouraged and severely punished, according to the appointment of the **Governour** and **Free-men** in **Provincial Council** and **General Assembly,** as also all Proceedings contrary to these Laws, that are not here made expressly penal.

\* \* \*

XXXIX. That there shall be at no time any Alteration of any of these Laws without the Consent of the **Governour,** his Heirs or Assigns, and Six parts of Seven of the **Free-men** met in **Provincial Council** and **General Assembly.**

XL. That **All** other Matters and Things not herein provided for, which shall and may concern the publick Justice, Peace or Safety of the said Province, and the raising and imposing Taxes, Customs, Duties, or other Charges whatsoever, shall be and are hereby referred to the Order, Prudence and Determination of the **Governour** and **Free-men** in **Provincial Council** and **General Assembly,** to be held from time to time in the said Province.

## REVIEW QUESTIONS

1. How did Penn integrate faith and reason in preparing his constitution?
2. What are some of the respective powers of the governor, Provincial Council, and General Assembly?
3. What are the requirements for political power listed in the constitution?
4. How are justice and other legal issues to be administered, according to Penn's constitution?
5. How does religion pertain to rights and rights to religion in Penn's constitution?

# 3  &#x2767;  COLONIAL WAYS OF LIFE

*Colonization was both a destructive and constructive act. While immigrants and Native Americans often sought to purge themselves of undesirable elements, whether of the Old World or New, they also experimented with and embraced new ideas and methods of doing things. Cultural transference—processes and products transmitted from one group of people to another—was thus neither complete nor unilateral. This was especially true for the colonists. In the process of adapting to novel conditions and establishing their versions of European civilization in the new settlements, the colonists laid the foundations for an American civilization.*

*A variety of factors influenced the formation of colonial society and culture, including the beliefs and social ranks of the immigrants, the people who came as leaders and those who became ones, the need for laborers (both free and unfree), the impact of the land and its peoples on newcomers, and their impact on the same. The colonists did not always recognize changes as they occurred, but when they did, reactions ranged from satisfied acceptance to dismay to determined rejection. Yet, whether fully conscious of it, the colonists felt a freedom to experiment with ideas, both imported and domestic. This experimentation occurred in the public domain of government, in the public and private spheres of social relations, and in the spiritual realm of religion.*

*Colonization meant hard work and hard times for everyone, but the tasks and rewards differed according to one's rank, religion, region, and race. Most colonists of the seventeenth and early eighteenth centuries, in accord with their contemporaries across the ocean, believed that social hierarchy, strict legal codes, and uniform religious beliefs and practices were essential to public order. This appeared to be especially true in early New England, where civil and religious authorities collaborated to impose order in the wilderness. Religious equality among the saints was not supposed to translate into social equality. People were expected to act according to their place, and that place was proscribed by birth, worth, gender, and age.*

*The colonists faced both internal and external threats to their societies. Non-conformists represented the former, whereas Indians represented the latter kind of menace. Native Americans attacked the immigrant groups that threatened their persons, property, and cultures. Some of the settlers taken prisoner through raids died in captivity, others decided that they preferred the Indian way of life and stayed (a rejection that rebutted the vaunted European superiority), while still others were eventually released or managed to escape. A few of those who returned, as they embraced even more fervently their society's beliefs and lifestyles, narrated accounts that served not only as cautionary tales to prove that the native peoples were enemies but as allegories to describe the struggle between good and evil, civilization and barbarism on the cultural frontier.*

*The struggle to survive and prosper did affect traditional gender relations to some degree and to a lesser extent gender perceptions, but it did not radically change them. Indeed, there are indications that as the colonists became more secure in the American provinces the more likely they were to insist on maintaining separate roles or spheres for men and women. Some women chafed at these strictures, but they generally did not (or could not) rebel against them. For most people, the issue of greatest importance to gender relations was marriage to a good wife or provident husband.*

*In the eighteenth century, colonial culture—the developing Anglo- or Euro-American civilization—was affected by two major cultural movements: the Enlightenment and the Great Awakening. Although there were some European Enlightenment philosophers who advocated radical social change, most provincials adopted more moderate interpretations; but they not only professed these new ideas, they acted upon them. The emphasis on reason during the Enlightenment caused some people to question religious doctrines, but it also gave ministers, and others, new ways to answer those questions as well as counter the challenges raised by life in an increasingly complex and consumerist society. Ultimately, however, the Great Awakening focused not on the human ability to reason—an ability that varied from person to person—as the way to understand and command the natural order but on revelation—a most democratic gift embraced by many Americans—as the route by which to comprehend God's design.*

*Many colonists credited God's design for the creation and expansion of Euro-American culture (without acknowledging the African element), but some also recognized that it was due to human design, and human accident. With some divinely inspired and others not, the colonists created new, amalgam cultures within the British Empire.*

# MARY ROWLANDSON

## FROM A Captivity Narrative (1676)

*During Metacomet's or, using the colonists' name for that leader of the Wampanoags, King Philip's War (1675–78), bands of Indians attacked numerous frontier settlements. After the February 10, 1676, attack on Lancaster, Massachusetts, the warriors led away a group of captives, among whom was Mary Rowlandson. She was the wife of the minister Joseph Rowlandson and the mother of four children. Rowlandson remained a captive until ransomed in May for the £20 raised by the women of Boston. Her account, published a few years after her ordeal, stands as one of the premier examples of a distinctive form of colonial literature: the captivity narrative.*

From *The Narrative of the Captivity and Restoration of Mrs. Mary Rowlandson* (Cambridge, Mass.: Samuel Greer, 1682; Lancaster, Mass.: John Wilson & Son, 1903), pp. 1–11, 15–17, 19, 22–24, 30–31, 43–44, 46, 48–50, 53–55, 59, 64, 72. [Spelling and punctuation modernized—*Ed.*]

On the tenth of *February* 167[6]. Came the *Indians* with great numbers upon *Lancaster*: Their first coming was about Sun-rising; bearing the noise of some Guns, we looked out; several Houses were burning, and the Smoke ascending to Heaven. There were five persons taken in one house, the Father, and the Mother and a sucking Child they knockt on the head; the other two they took and carried away alive. Their were two others, who being out of their Garison upon some occasion were set upon; one was knockt on the head, the other escaped: Another their was who running aroug was shot and wounded, and fell down; he begged of them his life, promising them Money (as they told me) but they would not hearken to him but knockt him in head, and stript him naked, and split open his Bowels. . . .

At length they came and beset our own house, and quickly it was the dolefullest day that ever mine eyes saw. The House stood upon the edg of a hill; some of the *Indians* got behind the hill, others into the Barn, and others behind any thing that could shelter them; from all which places they shot against the House, so that the Bullets seemed to f[l]y like hail; and quickly they wounded one man among us, then another, and then a third, About two hours (according to my observation, in that amazing time) they had been about the house before they prevailed to fire it (which they did with Flax and Hemp, which they brought out of the Barn . . . they fired it once and one ventured out and quenched it, but they quickly fired it again, and that took. . . . Then I took my Children (and one of my sisters, hers) to go forth and leave the house: but as soon as we came to the dore and appeared, the *Indians* shot so thick that the bulletts rattled against the House, as if one had taken an handfull of stones and threw them, so that we were fain to give back. . . . But out we must go, the fire increasing, and coming along behiad us, roaring, and the *Indians* gaping before us with their Guns, Spears and Hatchets to devour us. No sooner were we out of the House, but my Brother in Law (being before wounded, in defending the house, in or near the throat) fell down dead, whereat the *Indians* scornfully shouted, and hallowed, and were presently upon him, stripping off his cloaths, the bulletts flying thick, one went through my side, and the same (as would seem) through the bowels and hand of my dear Child in my arms. One of my elder Sisters Children, named *William*, had then his Leg broken, which the *Indians* perceiving, they knockt him on head. Thus were we butchered by those merciless Heathen, standing amazed, with the blood running down to our heels. . . .

*      *      *

## The first Remove

Now away we must go with those Barbarous Creatures, with our bodies wounded and bleeding, and our hearts no less than our bodies. About a mile we went that night, up upon a hill within sight of the Town where they intended to lodge, . . . To add to the dolefulness of the former day, and the dismalness of the present night: my thoughts ran up on my losses and sad bereaved condition. . . .

*      *      *

## The second Remove

*But now, the next morning, I must turn my back upon the Town, and travel with them into the vast and desolate Wilderness, I knew not whither.* It is not my tongue, or pen can express the sorrows of my heart, and bitterness of my spirit, that I had at this departure: but God was with me, in a wonderfull manner, carrying me along, and bearing up my spirit, that it did not quite fail. One of the Indians carried my poor wounded Babe upon a horse, it went moaning all along, I shall dy, I shall dy. I went on foot after it, with sorrow that cannot be express. At length I took it off the horse, and carried it in my armes till my strength failed, and I fell down with it: Then they set me upon a horse with my wounded Child in my lap, and there being no furniture upon the horse back; as we were going down a steep hill, we both fell over the horses head, at which they like inhumane creatures laught, and rejoyced to see it, though I thought we should there have ended our dayes, as overcome with so many difficulties. But the Lord renewed my strength still,

and carried me along, that I might see more of his Power; yea, so much that I could never have thought of, had I not experienced it.

*      *      *

## The third Remove

*The morning being come, they prepared to go on their way. One of the Indians got up upon a horse, and they set me up behind him, with my poor sick Babe in my lap.* A very wearisome and tedious day I had of it; what with my own wound, and my Childs being so exceeding sick, and in a lamentable condition with her wound. It may be easily judged what a poor feeble condition we were in, there being not the least crumb of refreshing that came within either of our mouths, from *Wednesday* night to *Saturday* night, except only a little cold water. This day in the afternoon, about an hour by Sun, we came to the place where they intended, *viz.* an *Indian* Town, called *Wenimesset*, Norward of *Quabaug*. When we were come, Oh the number of Pagans (now merciless enemies) that there came about me, . . . The next day was the Sabbath: I then remembered how careless I had been of Gods holy time how many Sabbaths I had lost and mispent, and how evily I had walked in Gods sight: which lay so closs unto my spirit, that it was easie for me to see how righteous it was with God to cut off the threed of my life, and cast me out of his presence for ever. . . . I sat much alone with a poor wounded Child in my lap, which moaned night and day, having nothing to revive the body, or cheer the spirits of her, but instead of that, sometimes one *Indian* would come and tell me one hour, that your Master will knock your Child in the head, and then a second, and then a third, your Master will quickly knock your Child in the head.

*This was the comfort I had from them,* . . . Thus nine dayes I sat upon my knees, with my Babe in my lap, till my flesh was raw again; my Child being even ready to depart this sorrowfull world, they bade me carry it out to another Wigwam (I suppose because they would not be troubled with such spectacles) Whither I went with a very heavy heart, and down I sat with the picture of death on my lap. About two houres in the night, my sweet Babe, like a Lambe departed this life, on *Feb. 18, 167[6]*. It being about *six yeares*, and *five months* old. . . . I have thought since of the wonderfull goodness of God to me, in preserving me in the use of my reason and senses, in that distressed time, that I did not use wicked and violent means to end my own miserable life. . . .

*Now the lad, began to talk of removing from this place, some one way, and some another.* There were now besides my self nine, *English* Captives in this place (all of them Children, except one Woman) I got an opportunity to go and take my leave of them; they being to go one way, and I another, I *asked them whether they were earnest with God for deliverance*, they told me, they did as they were able, and it was some comfort to me, that the Lord stirred up *Children to look to him*. . . .

## The fourth Remove

*And now I must part with that little Company I had.* Here I parted from my Daughter *Mary*, (whom I never saw again till I saw her in *Doroester* [Dorchester], returned from Captivity, and from four little Cousins and Neighbours, some of which I never saw afterward: the Lord only knows the end of them. Amongst them also was that poor Woman before mentioned, who came to a sad end, as some of the company told me in my travel: She having much grief upon her Spirit, about her miserable condition, being so near her time, she would be often asking the *Indians* to let her go home; they not being willing to that, and yet vexed with her importunity, gathered a great company together about her, and stript her naked, and set her in the midst of them; and when they had sung and danced about her (in their hellish manner) as long as they pleased, they knockt her on head, and the child in her arms with her: when they had done that, they made a fire and put them both into it, and told the other Children that were with them, that if they attempted to go home, they would serve them in like manner: The Children said, she did not shed one tear, but prayed all the while. . . .

\*    \*    \*

## The fifth Remove

*The occasion (as I thought) of their moving at this time, was, the* English *Army it being near and following them*: For they went, as if they had gone for their lives, for some considerable way, and then they made a stop, and chose some of their stoutest men, and sent them back to hold the *English* Army in play whilst the rest escaped: . . .

*The first week of my being among them, I hardly ate any thing; the second week, I found my stomach grow very faint for want of something; and yet it was very hard to get down their filthy trash: but the third week, though I could think how formerly my stomach would turn against this or that, and I could starve and dy before I could eat such things, yet they were sweet and savoury to my taste*. . . .

\*    \*    \*

## The eighth Remove

On the morrow morning we must go over the River, *i.e. Connecticot*, to meet with King *Philip*, two *Cannoos* full, they had carried over, the next turn i my self was to go; but as my foot was upon the *Cannoo* to step in, there was a sudden out-cry among them, and i must step back; and instead of going over the River, i must go four or five miles up the River farther Northward. Some of the *Indians* ran one way, and some another. The cause of this rout was, as i thought, their espying some *English Scouts*, who were thereabout. In this travel up the River; about noon the Company made a stop, and sate down; some to eat, and others to rest them. As I sate amongst them, musing of things past, my Son *Joseph* unexpectedly came to me: we asked of each others welfare, bemoaning our dolefull condition, and the change that had come upon uss. . . . We travelled on till night; and in the morning, we must go over the River to *Philip*'s Crew. When I was in the Cannoo, I could not but be amazed at the numerous crew of Pagans that were on the Bank on the other side. When I came ashore, they gathered all about me, I sitting alone in the midst: I observed they asked one another questions, and laughed, and rejoyced over their Gains and Victories. Then my heart began to fail: and I fell a weeping which was the first time to my remembrance, that I wept before them. . . . There one of them asked me, why I wept, I could hardly tell what to say: yet I answered, they would kill me: No, said he, none will hurt you. Then came one of them and gave me two spoonfulls of Meal to comfort me, and another gave me half a pint of Pease; which was more worth than many Bushels at another time. Then I went to see King *Philip*, he bade me come in and sit down, and asked me whether I would smoke it (a usual Complement now adayes amongst Saints and Sinners) but this no way suited me. For though I had formerly used Tobacco, yet I had left it ever since I was first taken. It *seems to be a Bait, the Devil layes to make men loose their precious time*: I remember with shame, how formerly, when I had taken two or three pipes, I was presently ready for another, such a bewitching thing it is: But I thank God, he has now given me power over it; surely there are many who may be better imployed than to ly sucking a stinking Tobacco-pipe.

*       *       *

## The twelfth Remove

. . . This morning i asked my master whither he would sell me to my Husband; he answered me *Nux*, which did much rejoyce my spirit. My mistriss, before we went, was gone to the burial of a *Papoos*, and returning, she found me sitting and reading in my Bible; she snatched it hastily out of my hand, and threw it out of doors; I ran out and catcht it up, and put it into my pocket, and never let her see it afterward. Then they pack'd up their things to be gone, and gave me my load: I complained it was too heavy whereupon she gave me a slap in the face, and bade me go; I lif[t]ed up my heart to God, hoping the Redemption was not far off: and the rather because their insolency grew worse and worse.

*But the thoughts of my going homeward* for *so we bent our courses much cheared my Spirit, and made my burden seem light, and almost nothing at all.* . . .

*       *       *

## The sixteenth Remove

*We began this Remove with wading over* Baquag *River: the water was up to the knees, and the stream very swift, and so cold that I thought it would have cut me in sunder.* i was so weak and feeble, that I reeled as I went along, and thought there I must end my dayes at last, after my bearing and getting thorough so many difficulties; the *Indians* stood laughing to see me staggering along: but in my distress the Lord gave me experience of the truth, and goodness of that promise, Isai. 43.2. *When thou passest thorough the Waters, I will be with thee, and through the Rivers, they shall not overflow thee.* Then I sat down to put on my stockins and shoos, with the teares running down mine eyes, and many sorrowfull thoughts in my heart, but I gat up to go along with them. Quickly there came up to us an *Indian*, who informed them, that I must go to *Wachusit* to my master, for there was a Letter come from the Council to the *Saggamores*, about redeeming the Captives, and that there would be another in fourteen dayes, and that I must be there ready. My heart was so heavy before that I could scarce speak or go in the path; and yet now so light, that I could run. My strength seemed to come again, and recruit my feeble knees, and aking heart: . . .

*       *       *

## The nineteenth Remove

*They said, when we went out, that we must travel to* Wachusit *this day.* But a bitter weary day I had of it, travelling now three dayes together, without resting any day between. . . .

*       *       *

*Then came* Tom *and* Peter, *with the second Letter from the Council, about the Captives.* Though they were *Indians,* i gat them by the hand, and burst out into tears; my heart was so full that I could not speak to them; but recovering my self, I asked them how my husband did, & all my friends and acquain[t]ances they said, *They are all very well but melancohly.* They brought me two Biskets, and a pound of Tobacco. . . . When the Letter was come, the *Saggamores* met to consult about the Captives, and called me to them to enquire how much my husband would give to redeem me, when I came I sate down among them, as I was wont to do, as their manner is: *Then they bade me stand up, and said, they were the General Court. They bid me speak what I thought he would give,* Now knowing that all we had was destroyed by the *Indians.* I was in a great strait: I thought if I should speak of but a little, it would be slighted, and hinder the matter; if of a great sum, I knew not where it would be procured: yet at a venture, I said *Twenty pounds,* yet desired them to take less; but they would not hear of that, but sent that message to *Boston,* that for *Twenty pounds* I should be redeemed. . . .

\*      \*      \*

## The twentieth Remove

*It was their usual manner to remove, when they had done any mischief, lest they should be found out: and so they did at this time.* We went about three or four miles, and there they built a great *Wigwam,* big enough to hold an hundred *Indians,* which they did in preparation to a great day of Dancing. . . . The *Indians* now began to come from all quarters, against their merry dancing day. Among some of them came one *Goodwife Kettle:* I told her my heart was so heavy that it was ready to break: so is mine too said she, but yet said, I hope we shall hear some good news shortly. I could hear how earnestly my Sister desired to see me, & I as earnestly desired to see her: and yet neither of us could get an opportunity. My Daughter was also now about a mile off, and I had not seen her in nine or ten weeks, as I had not seen my Sister since

our first taking. I earnestly desired them to let me go and see them: yea, I intreated, begged, and perswaded them, but to let me see my Daughter; and yet so hard hearted were they, that they would not suffer it. They made use of their tyrannical power whilst they had it; but through the Lords wonderfull mercy, their time was now but short.

\*      \*      \*

On *Tuesday morning* they called their *General* Court (as they call it) to consult and determine, whether I should go home or no: And they all as one man did seemingly consent to it, that I should go home; except *Philip,* who would not come among them.

\*      \*      \*

. . . I may well say as his Psal. 107.12. *Oh give thanks unto the Lord for he is good, for his mercy endureth for ever.* Let the Redeemed of the Lord say so, whom he hath redeemed from the hand of the Enemy, especially that I should come away in the midst of so many hundreds of Enemies quietly and peacably, and not a Dog moving his tongue. So I took my leave of them, and in coming along my heart melted into tears, more then all the while I was with them, and I was almost swallowed up with the thoughts that ever I should go home again. . . .

\*      \*      \*

*Before I knew what affliction meant, I was ready sometimes to wish for it.* When I lived in prosperity; having the comforts of the World about me, my relations by me, my Heart chearfull: and taking little care for any thing; and yet seeing many, whom I preferred before my self, under many tryals and afflictions, in sickness, weakness, poverty, losses, crosses, and cares of the World, I should be sometimes jealous least I should have my portion in this life, and that Scripture would come to my mind, *Heb.* 12.6. *For whom the Lord loveth he chasteneth, and scourgeth every Son whom he receivith.* But now I see the Lord had his time to scourge and chasten me. The portion of some is to have their afflictions by drops, now one drop and then another; but the dregs of the Cup, the Wine of astonishment: like a sweeping rain that leaveth no food, did the Lord prepare to be my portion Affliction I wanted, and affliction I had, full measure (I thought) pressed down and running over; yet I see, when God calls a Person to any shing, and through never so many difficulties, yet he is fully able to carry them through and make them see, and say they have been gainers thereby. And I hope I can say in some measure, As *David* did, *It is good for me that I have been afflicted*: The Lord hath shewed me the vanity of these outward things. That they are the *Vanity of vanities, and vexation of spirit*; that they are but a shadow, a blast, a bubble, and things of no continuance. That we must rely on God himself, and our whole dependance must be upon him. If trouble from smaller matters begin to arise in me, I have something at hand to check myself with, and say, why am I troubled? It was but the other day that if I had had the world, I would have given it for my freedom, or to have been a Servant to a Christian. I have learned to look beyond present and smaller troubles, and to be quieted under them, as *Moses* said, *Exod.* 14.13. *Stand still and see the salvation of the Lord.*

## REVIEW QUESTIONS

1. How did the Native Americans treat their captives? Was what they expected of their captives very different from what they expected of themselves?
2. What did Rowlandson's observations—especially those that surprised her—reveal about native lifestyles and the colonists' lives and prejudices?
3. Rowlandson was most vulnerable at the very beginning of her captivity when she was suffering from shock. How did she start to recover? What did she say supported her through all her afflictions?
4. How did she explain this episode in her life to herself and others?
5. What does this story reveal when analyzed as a Puritan sermon? What does it reveal when interpreted as a frontier epic?

# COTTON MATHER

# FROM Accounts of the Salem Witchcraft Trials (1693)

*Cotton Mather (1639–1728), a respected minister in Boston, straddled both the seventeenth and eighteenth centuries. By birth—as the son and grandson of Puritan divines—education, and profession, he was primarily a man of the earlier century, but as a profoundly curious intellectual, he proved himself ready to consider and adopt some new ideas. Mather's belief in witchcraft and fear of the devil's work in New England reveal his seventeenth-century mental map, but his embrace of a new and controversial medical procedure, smallpox inoculation, in 1723, shows how he later adapted—both consciously and unconsciously—that map to a new age.*

*A communal hysteria over witchcraft engulfed Salem and Andover, Massachusetts, in 1692 and 1693. Historians able to focus a more objective, wide-angle lens on the phenomenon have shown how the accusations and trials reveal that these were communities experiencing various crises: problems of growth, gender, generations, and antagonistic groups. As a contemporary observer, however, Mather interpreted the personal and community antagonisms and actions as evidence of Satan's work and New England's fall from grace.*

From *Cotton Mather on Witchcraft: Being the Wonders of the Invisible World First Published at Boston in Octr. 1692 and now Reprinted, with Additional Matter. . . .* (1693; New York: Dorset Press, 1991), pp. 113–20, 170–71.

## The Tryal of Susanna Martin at the Court of Oyer and Terminer, Held by Adjournment at Salem, June 29, 1692

SUSANNA MARTIN, pleading *Not Guilty* to the Indictment of *Witchcraft*, brought in against her, there were produced the Evidences of many Persons very sensibly and grievously Bewitched; who all complained of the Prisoner at the Bar, as the Person whom they believed the cause of their Miseries. And now, as well as in the other Trials, there was an extraordinary Endeavour by *Witchcrafts*, with Cruel and frequent Fits, to hinder the poor Sufferers from giving in their Complaints, which the Court was forced with much Patience to obtain, by much waiting and watching for it.

2. There was now also an account given of what passed at her first Examination before the Magistrates. The Cast of her *Eye*, then striking the afflicted People to the Ground, whether they saw that Cast or no; there were these among other Passages between the Magistrates and the Examinate.

*Magistrate.* Pray, what ails these People?

*Martin.* I don't know.

*Magistrate.* But what do you think ails them?

*Martin.* I don't desire to spend my Judgment upon it.

*Magistrate.* Don't you think they are bewitch'd?

*Martin.* No, I do not think they are.

*Magistrate.* Tell us your Thoughts about them then.

*Martin.* No, my thoughts are my own, when they are in, but when they are out they are anothers. Their Master——

*Magistrate.* Their Master? who do you think is their Master?

*Martin.* If they be dealing in the Black Art, you may know as well as I.

*Magistrate.* Well, what have you done towards this?

*Martin.* Nothing at all.

*Magistrate.* Why, 'tis you or your Appearance.

*Martin.* I cannot help it.

*Magistrate.* Is it not *your* Master? How comes your Appearance to hurt these?

*Martin.* How do I know? He that appeared in the Shape of *Samuel*, a glorified Saint, may appear in any ones Shape.

It was then also noted in her, as in others like her, that if the Afflicted went to approach her, they were flung down to the Ground. And, when she was asked the reason of it, she said, *I cannot tell; it may be, the Devil bears me more Malice than another.*

\*       \*       \*

4. *John Atkinson* testifi'd, That he exchanged a Cow with a Son of *Susanna Martin's*, whereat she muttered, and was unwilling he should have it. Going to receive this Cow, tho he Hamstring'd her, and Halter'd her, she, of a Tame Creature, grew so mad, that they could scarce get her along. She broke all the Ropes that were fastned unto her, and though she were ty'd fast unto a Tree, yet she made her escape, and gave them such further trouble, as they could ascribe to no cause but Witchcraft.

\*       \*       \*

6. *Robert Downer* testified, That this Prisoner being some Years ago prosecuted at Court for a Witch, he then said unto her, *He believed she was a Witch.*

Whereat she being dissatisfied, said, *That some She-Devil would shortly fetch him away!*

Which words were heard by others, as well as himself. The Night following, as he lay in his Bed, there came in at the Window, the likeness of a *Cat*, which flew upon him, took fast hold of his Throat, lay on him a considerable while, and almost killed him. At length he remembered what *Susanna Martin* had threatned the Day before; and with much striving he cried out, *Avoid, thou She-Devil! In the Name of God the Father, the Son, and the Holy Ghost, Avoid!* Whereupon it left him, leap'd on the Floor, and flew out at the Window.

And there also came in several Testimonies, that before ever *Downer* spoke a word of this Accident, *Susanna Martin* and her Family had related, *How this* Downer *had been handled!*

7. *John Kembal* testified, that *Susanna Martin*, upon a Causeless Disgust, had threatned him, about a certain Cow of his, *That she should never do him any more Good:* and it came to pass accordingly. For soon after the Cow was found stark dead on the dry Ground, without any Distemper to be discerned upon her. Upon which he was followed with a strange Death upon more of his Cattle, whereof he lost in one Spring to the value of Thirty Pounds.

\*       \*       \*

12. But besides all of these Evidences, there was a most wonderful Account of one *Joseph Ring*, produced on this occasion. This Man has been strangely carried about by *Dæmons*, from one *Witch-meeting* to another, for near two years together; and for one quarter of this time, they have made him, and keep him Dumb, tho' he is now again able to speak. . . .

. . . this poor Man would be visited with unknown shapes . . . which would force him away with them, unto unknown Places, where he saw Meetings, Feastings, Dancings; . . . When he was brought until these hellish Meetings, one of the first Things they still did unto him, was to give him a knock on the Back, whereupon he was ever as if bound with Chains, uncapable of stirring out of the place, till they should release him. He related,

that there often came to him a Man, who presented him a *Book*, whereto he would have him set his Hand; promising to him, that he should then have even what he would; and presenting him with all the delectable Things, Persons, and Places, that he could imagin. But he refusing to subscribe, the business would end with dreadful Shapes, Noises and Screeches, which almost scared him out of his Wits. Once with the Book, there was a Pen offered him, and an Ink-horn with Liquor in it, that seemed like Blood: But he never toucht it.

This Man did now affirm, That he saw the Prisoner at several of those hellish Randezvouzes. Note, this Woman was one of the most impudent, scurrilous, wicked Creatures in the World; and she did now throughout her whole Tryal, discover her self to be such an one. Yet when she was asked, what she had to say for her self? Her chief Plea was, *That she had lead a most virtuous and holy Life.*

\*       \*       \*

Here were in *Salem*, *June* 10, 1692, about 40 persons that were afflicted with horrible torments by *Evil Spirits*, and the afflicted have accused 60 or 70 as Witches, for that they have *Spectral appearances* of them, tho the Persons are absent when they are tormented. When these Witches were Tryed, several of them confessed a contract with the Devil, by signing his Book, and did express much sorrow for the same, declaring also their *Confederate Witches*, and said the Tempters of them desired 'em to sign the *Devils Book*, who tormented them till they did it. There were at the time of *Examinations*, before many hundreds of Witnesses, strange Pranks play'd; such as the taking Pins out of the Clothes of the afflicted, and thrusting them into their flesh, many of which were taken out again by the *Judges* own hands. Thorns also in like kind were thrust into their flesh; the accusers were sometimes *struck dumb, deaf, blind*, and sometimes lay as if they were dead for a while, and all foreseen and declared by the afflicted just before 't was done. Of the afflicted there were two Girls, about 12 *or* 13 years of age, who saw all that was done, and were therefore called the *Visionary Girls*; they would say, *Now he, or she, or they, are going to bite* or *pinch the Indian*;

and all there present in Court saw the visible marks on the *Indians* arms; they would also cry out, *Now look, look, they are going to bind such an ones Legs*, and all present saw the same person spoken of, fall with her Legs twisted in an extraordinary manner; Now say they, we shall all fall, and immediately 7 or 8 of the afflicted fell down, with *terrible shrieks and Out-crys*: at the time when one of the Witches was *sentenc'd, and pinnion'd* with a Cord, at the same time was the afflicted *Indian* Servant going home, (being about 2 or 3 miles out of town,) and had both his Wrists at the same instant bound about with a like Cord, in the same manner as she was when she was sentenc'd, but with that violence, that the Cord entred into his flesh, not to be untied, nor hardly cut—Many *Murders* are suppos'd to be in this way committed; for these Girls, and others of the afflicted, say, *they see Coffins, and bodies in Shrouds*, rising up, and looking on the accused, crying, *Vengeance, Vengeance on the Murderers*—Many other strange things were transacted before the Court in the time of their Examination; and especially one thing which I had like to have forgot, which is this, One of the accus'd, whilst the rest were under Examination, was drawn up by a Rope to the Roof of the house where he was, and would have been choak'd in all probability, had not the Rope been presently cut; the Rope hung at the Roof by some *invisible tye*, for there was no hole where it went up; but after it was cut the *remainder* of it was found in the Chamber just above, lying by the very place where it hung down.

In *December* 1692, the Court sate again at *Salem* in *New-England*, and cleared about 40 persons suspected for Witches, and Condemned three. The Evidence against these three was the same as formerly, so the Warrant for their Execution was sent, and the *Graves digged* for the said three, and for about five more that had been Condemned at *Salem* formerly, but were Reprieved by the Governour.

\*    \*    \*

## REVIEW QUESTIONS

1. Why was Susanna Martin accused of witchcraft? What was the evidence presented against her?
2. How did she defend herself?
3. Who were the chief accusers in many of the cases brought before the Salem court? What kind of proof did they proffer?
4. Did most accusations result in convictions?

## BENJAMIN FRANKLIN

# *Articles of Belief* (1728)

*Benjamin Franklin (1706–1790) was born in Boston to a large artisan family with strong Calvinist roots. He departed from both in his teens. Franklin's father apprenticed him at the age of twelve to his brother James, a printer. At the age of seventeen, Franklin ran away from his brother in Boston and sailed to Philadelphia, where he first worked for another printer and then set up his own print shop. Industrious and shrewd, Franklin prospered. As he worked, Franklin also studied, and those studies led him to rebel against the religious orthodoxy of his parents and embrace deistic concepts of God, man, and nature. Deism reflected the Enlightenment idea that reality operated by natural laws that people could figure out and use to perfect human knowledge, virtue, and society. Although many people tried to marry natural reasoning and divine revelation, it was not easy, and thus some rejected religion in favor of reason as the way to understand and improve human existence, whereas others chose to have faith in revealed truth as recorded in scripture. The latter focused on piety and soul-searching as necessary conditions, though not guarantees of salvation. The former, Franklin among them, acknowledged God as the creator of the universe and its natural laws but defined virtue as something other than devotion to religious precepts or duties. Deists emphasized ethics, which they tended to define as the moral practices and judgments by which one may achieve individual and social welfare and happiness. Franklin's* Articles of Belief and Acts of Religion, *which he wrote as a personal catechism for private contemplation, reflects this focus.*

From Leonard W. Labaree, ed., *The Papers of Benjamin Franklin*, vol. 1 (New Haven, Conn.: Yale University Press, 1959), pp. 102–05.

## First Principles

I believe there is one Supreme most perfect Being, Author and Father of the Gods themselves.

For I believe that Man is not the most perfect Being but One, rather that as there are many Degrees of Beings his Inferiors, so there are many Degrees of Beings superior to him.

Also, when I stretch my Imagination thro' and beyond our System of Planets, beyond the visible fix'd Stars themselves, into that Space that is every Way infinite, and conceive it fill'd with Suns like ours, each with a Chorus of Worlds for ever moving round him, then this little Ball on which we move, seems, even in my narrow Imagination, to be almost Nothing, and my self less than nothing, and of no sort of Consequence.

When I think thus, I imagine it great Vanity in me to suppose, that the *Supremely Perfect*, does in the least regard such an inconsiderable Nothing as Man. More especially, since it is impossible for me to have any positive clear Idea of that which is infinite and incomprehensible, I cannot conceive otherwise, than that He, *the Infinite Father*, expects or requires no Worship or Praise from us, but that he is even INFINITELY ABOVE IT.

But since there is in all Men something like a natural Principle which enclines them to DEVOTION or the Worship of some unseen Power;

And since Men are endued with Reason superior to all other Animals that we are in our World acquainted with;

Therefore I think it seems required of me, and my Duty, as a Man, to pay Divine Regards to SOMETHING.

\*    \*    \*

It is that particular wise and good God, who is the Author and Owner of our System, that I propose for the Object of my Praise and Adoration.

For I conceive that he has in himself some of those Passions he has planted in us, and that, since he has given us Reason whereby we are capable of observing his Wisdom in the Creation, he is not above caring for us, being pleas'd with our Praise, and offended when we slight Him, or neglect his Glory.

I conceive for many Reasons that he is a *good Being*, and as I should be happy to have so wise, good and powerful a Being my Friend, let me consider in what Manner I shall make myself most acceptable to him.

Next to the Praise due, to his Wisdom, I believe he is pleased and delights in the Happiness of those he has created; and since without Virtue Man can have no Happiness in this World, I firmly believe he delights to see me Virtuous, because he is pleas'd when he sees me Happy.

And since he has created many Things which seem purely design'd for the Delight of Man, I believe he is not offended when he sees his Children solace themselves in any manner of pleasant Exercises and innocent Delights, and I think no Pleasure innocent that is to Man hurtful.

I *love* him therefore for his Goodness and I *adore* him for his Wisdom.

Let me then not fail to praise my God continually, for it is his Due, and it is all I can retrn for his many Favours and great Goodness to me; and let me resolve to be virtuous, that I may be happy, that I may please Him, who is delighted to see me happy. Amen.

*    *    *

### (1)

Powerful Goodness, &c.

O Creator, O Father, I believe that thou art Good, and that thou art *pleas'd with the Pleasure* of thy Children.

Praised be thy Name for Ever.

### (2)

By thy Power has thou made the glorious Sun, with his attending Worlds; from the Energy of thy mighty Will they first received [their prodigious] Motion, and by thy Wisdom hast thou prescribed the wondrous Laws by which they move.

Praised be thy Name for ever.

### (3)

By thy Wisdom hast thou formed all Things, Thou hast created Man, bestowing Life and Reason, and plac'd him in Dignity superior to thy other earthly Creatures.

Praised be thy Name for ever.

### (4)

Thy Wisdom, thy Power, and thy GOODNESS are every where clearly seen; in the Air and in the Water, in the Heavens and on the Earth; Thou providest for the various winged Fowl, and the innumerable Inhabitants of the Water; Thou givest Cold and Heat, Rain and Sunshine in their Season, and to the Fruits of the Earth Increase.

Praised be thy Name for ever.

### (5)

I believe thou hast given Life to thy Creatures that they might Live, and art not delighted with violent Death and bloody Sacrifices.

Praised be thy Name for Ever.

### (6)

Thou abhorrest in thy Creatures Treachery and Deceit, Malice, Revenge, [*Intemperance*] and every other hurtful Vice; but Thou art a Lover of Justice and Sincerity, of Friendship, Benevolence and every Virtue, Thou art my Friend, my Father, and my Benefactor.

Praised be thy Name, O God, for Ever.
Amen.

*    *    *

## REVIEW QUESTIONS

1. What is Franklin's perception of the supreme deity? Is his a kind or stern "father"? Why might that be significant?
2. What does Franklin's deity want from humankind?
3. How does the natural world or universe, rather than religious dogma, figure prominently in Franklin's personal creed?

# JONATHAN EDWARDS

## Some Thoughts Concerning the Present Revival of Religion (1743)

*Jonathan Edwards (1703–1758), a Congregationalist minister in New England, was a vigorous intellectual who studied Enlightenment philosophy but preferred the rich, challenging Calvinist theology of the earlier Puritan church. Edwards believed that people had fallen away from the demanding faith, with its emphasis on God's grace, that was so essential to their salvation. With that in mind, the great theologian began a revival in his Northampton, Massachusetts, church in the 1730s that became part of the general revival movement called the Great Awakening. As critics supporting order and orthodoxy increased their attacks against the movement, Edwards emerged as one of its strongest champions.*

From *Some Thoughts Concerning the Present Revival of Religion in New England* in *The Works of President Edwards*, vol. 6 (1817; New York: Burt Franklin, 1968), pp. 31–36, 44–49, 54–57.

## Part I, Sect. IV.

### The Nature of the Work in General.

Whatever imprudences there have been, and whatever sinful irregularities; whatever vehemence of the passions, and heats of the imagination, transports, and ecstasies: whatever error in judgment, and indiscreet zeal; and whatever outcries, faintings, and agitations of body; yet, it is manifest and notorious, that there has been of late a very uncommon influence upon the minds of a very great part of the inhabitants of *New England*, attended with the best effects. There has been a great increase of seriousness, and sober consideration of eternal things; a disposition to hearken to what is said of such things, with attention and affection; a disposition to treat matters of religion with solemnity, and as of great impor-

tance; to make these things the subject of conversation; to hear the word of God preached, and to take all opportunities in order to it; to attend on the public worship of God, and all external duties of religion, in a more solemn and decent manner; so that there is a remarkable and general alteration in the face of *New England* in these respects. Multitudes in all parts of the land, of vain, thoughtless, regardless persons, are quite changed, and become serious and considerate. There is a vast increase of concern for the salvation of the precious soul, and of that inquiry, *What shall I do to be saved?* The hearts of multitudes have been greatly taken off from the things of the world, its profits, pleasures, and honours. Multitudes in all parts have had their consciences awakened, and have been made sensible of the pernicious nature and consequences of sin, and what a dreadful thing it is to be under guilt and the displeasure of God, and to live without peace and reconciliation with him. They have also been awakened to a sense of the shortness and uncertainty of life, and the reality of another world and future judgment, and of the necessity of an interest in Christ. They are more afraid of sin, more careful and inquisitive that they may know what is contrary to the mind and will of God, that they may avoid it, and what he requires of them, that they may do it, more careful to guard against temptations, more watchful over their own hearts, earnestly desirous of knowing, and of being diligent in the use of the means that God has appointed in his word, in order to salvation. Many very stupid, senseless sinners, and persons of a vain mind, have been greatly awakened.

There is a strange alteration almost all over *New England* amongst young people: by a powerful invisible influence on their minds, they have been brought to forsake, in a general way, as it were at once, those things of which they were extremely fond, and in which they seemed to place the happiness of their lives, and which nothing before could induce them to forsake; as their frolicking, vain company-keeping, night-walking, their mirth and jollity, their impure language, and lewd songs. In vain did ministers preach against those things before, in vain were laws made to restrain them, and in vain was all the vigilance of magistrates and civil officers; but now they have almost every where dropt them as it were of themselves. And there is great alteration amongst old and young as to drinking, tavern-haunting, prophane speaking, and extravagance in apparel. Many notoriously vicious persons have been reformed, and become externally quite new creatures. Some that are wealthy, and of a fashionable, gay education; some great beaux and fine ladies, that seemed to have their minds swallowed up with nothing but the vain shews and pleasures of the world, have been wonderfully altered, have relinquished these vanities, and are become serious, mortified, and humble in their conversation. It is astonishing to see the alteration there is in some towns, where before there was but little appearance of religion, or any thing but vice and vanity. And now they are transformed into another sort of people; their former vain, worldly, and vicious conversation and dispositions seem to be forsaken, and they are, as it were,

gone over to a new world. Their thoughts, their talk, and their concern, affections and inquiries, are now about the favour of God, an interest in Christ, a renewed sanctified heart, and a spiritual blessedness, acceptance, and happiness in a future world.

Now, through the greater part of *New England*, the holy Bible is in much greater esteem and use than before. The great things contained in it are much more regarded, as things of the greatest consequence, and are much more the subjects of meditation and conversation; and other books of piety that have long been of established reputation, as the most excellent, and most tending to promote true godliness, have been abundantly more in use. The Lord's day is more religiously and strictly observed. And much has been lately done at making up differences, confessing faults one to another, and making restitution: probably more within two years, than was done in thirty years before.... And many have been deeply affected with a sense of their own ignorance and blindness, and exceeding helplessness, and so of their extreme need of the divine pity and help.

Multitudes in *New England* have lately been brought to a new and great conviction of the truth and certainty of the things of the gospel; to a firm persuasion that Christ Jesus is the son of God, and the great and only Saviour of the world; and that the great doctrines of the gospel touching reconciliation by his blood, and acceptance in his righteousness, and eternal life and salvation through him, are matters of undoubted truth.... And not only do these effects appear in new converts, but great numbers of those who were formerly esteemed the most sober and pious people, have, under the influence of this work, been greatly quickened, and their hearts renewed with greater degrees of light, renewed repentance and humiliation, and more lively exercises of faith, love and joy in the Lord.... And now, instead of meetings at taverns and drinking-houses, and of young people in frolics and vain company, the country is full of meetings of all sorts and ages of persons—young and old, men, women and little children—to read and pray, and sing praises, and to converse of the things of God and another world. In very many places the main of the conversation in all companies turns on religion, and things of a spiritual nature. . . . And there has been this alteration abiding on multitudes all over the land, for a year and a half, without any appearance of a disposition to return to former vice and vanity.

And, under the influences of this work, there have been many of the remains of those wretched people and dregs of mankind, the poor *Indians*, that seemed to be next to a state of brutality, and with whom, till now, it seemed to be to little more purpose to use endeavours for their instruction and awakening, than with the beasts. Their minds have now been strangely opened to receive instruction, and been deeply affected with the concerns of their precious souls; they have reformed their lives, and forsaken their former stupid, barbarous and brutish way of living; . . . And many of the poor *Negroes* also have been in like manner wrought upon and changed. Very many little children have been remarkably enlightened, and their hearts wonderfully affected and enlarged, and their mouths opened, expressing themselves in a manner far beyond their years, and to the just astonishment of those who have heard them. . . .

The divine power of this work has marvellously appeared in some instances I have been acquainted with; in supporting and fortifying the heart under great trials, such as the death of children, and extreme pain of body; and in wonderfully maintaining the serenity, calmness and joy of the soul, in an immoveable rest in God, and sweet resignation to him. And some under the blessed influences of this work have, in a calm, bright and joyful frame of mind, been carried through the valley of the shadow of death.

And now let us consider;——Is it not strange that in a Christian country, and such a land of light as this is, there are many at a loss to conclude whose work this is, whether the work of God or the work of the devil? Is it not a shame to *New England* that such a work should be much doubted of here? . . . We have a rule near at hand, a sacred book that God himself has put into our hands, with clear and infallible marks, sufficient to resolve us in things of this nature; which book I think we must reject, not only in some particular passages, but in the substance of it, if we reject such a work as has now been described, as not being the work of God. The whole tenor of the gospel proves it; all the notion of religion that the scripture gives us confirms it.

I suppose there is scarcely a minister in this land, but from sabbath to sabbath is used to pray that God would pour out his Spirit, and work a reformation and revival of religion in the country, and turn us from our intemperance, profaneness, uncleanness, worldliness and other sins; and we have kept from year to year, days of public fasting and prayer to God, to acknowledge our backslidings, and humble ourselves for our sins, and to seek of God forgiveness and reformation: And now when so great and extensive a reformation is so suddenly and wonderfully accomplished, in those very things that we have sought to God for, shall we not acknowledge it? or, do it with great coldness, caution and reserve, and scarcely take any notice of it in our public prayers and praises, or mention it but slightly and cursorily, and in such a manner as carries an appearance as though we would contrive to say as little of it as ever we could, and were glad to pass from it? And that because the work is attended with a mixture of error, imprudences, darkness and sin; because some persons are carried away with impressions, and are indiscreet, and too censorious with their zeal; and because there are high transports of religious affections; and some effects on their bodies of which we do not understand the reason.

*    *    *

# Sect. VI.

## *This Work is very Glorious.*

Now if such things are enthusiasm, and the fruits of a distempered brain, let my brain be evermore possessed of that happy distemper! If this be distraction, I pray God that the world of mankind

may be all seized with this benign, meek, beneficent, beatifical, glorious distraction! . . . The great
affections and high transports, that others have
lately been under, are in general of the same kind
with those in the instance that has been given,
though not to so high a degree, and many of them
not so pure and unmixed, and so well regulated. I
have had opportunity to observe many instances
here and elsewhere; and though there are some
instances of great affections in which there has
been a great mixture of nature with grace, and in
some, a sad degenerating of religious affections; yet
there is that uniformity observable, which makes it
easy to be seen, that in general it is the same spirit
from whence the work in all parts of the land has
originated. And what notions have they of religion,
that reject what has been described, as not true
religion! . . .

Those who are waiting for the fruits, in order to
determine whether this be the work of God or no,
would do well to consider, what they are waiting
for: Whether it be not to have this wonderful religious influence, and then to see how they will behave themselves? That is, to have grace subside, and
the actings of it in a great measure to cease, and to
have persons grow cold and dead; and then to see
whether, after that, they will behave themselves with
that exactness and brightness of conversation, that
is to be expected of lively Christians, or those that
are in the vigorous exercises of grace. There are
many that will not be satisfied with any exactness
or laboriousness in religion now, while persons
have their minds much moved, and their affections
are high; for they lay it to their flash of affection,
and heat of zeal, as they call it; they are waiting to
see whether they will carry themselves as well when
these affections are over; that is, they are waiting to
have persons sicken and lose their strength, that
they may see whether they will then behave themselves like healthy strong men. I would desire that
they would also consider, whether they be not waiting for more than is reasonably to be expected, supposing this to be really a great work of God, and
much more than has been found in former great
out-pourings of the Spirit of God, that have been
universally acknowledged in the Christian church?

Do not they expect fewer instances of apostacy and
evidences of hypocrisy in professors, than were after that great out-pouring of the Spirit in the apos-
tles' days, or that which was in the time of the
reformation? And do not they stand prepared to
make a mighty argument of it against this work, if
there should be *half* so many? And, they would do
well to consider how *long* they will wait to see the
good fruit of this work, before they will determine
in favour of it. Is not their waiting unlimited? The
visible fruit that is to be expected of a pouring out
of the Spirit of God on a country, is a visible reformation in that country. What reformation has lately
been brought to pass in *New England*, by this work,
has been before observed. And has it not continued
long enough already, to give reasonable satisfaction?
If God cannot work on the hearts of a people after
such a manner, as reasonably to expect it should be
acknowledged in a year and a half, or two years'
time; yet surely it is unreasonable that our expectations and demands should be unlimited, and our
waiting without any bounds.

As there is the clearest evidence, from what has
been observed, that this is the work of God; so it is
evident that it is a very great and wonderful, and exceeding glorious work.—This is certain, that it is a
great and wonderful event, a strange revolution, an
unexpected, surprising overturning of things, suddenly brought to pass; such as never has been seen
in *New England*, and scarce ever has been heard of
in any land. Who that saw the state of things in *New
England* a few years ago, would have thought that in
so short a time there would be such a change? . . .

Such a work is, in its nature and kind, the most
glorious of any work of God whatsoever, and is always so spoken of in scripture. It is the work of redemption (the great end of all the other works of
God, and of which the work of creation was but a
shadow) in the event, success, and end of it: It is
the work of new creation, which is infinitely more
glorious than the old. . . .

This work is very glorious both in its *nature*,
and in its *degree* and *circumstances*. It will appear
very glorious, if we consider the unworthiness of
the people who are the subjects of it; what obligations God has laid us under by the special privi-

leges we have enjoyed for our souls' good, and the great things God did for us at our first settlement in the land; how he has followed us with his goodness to this day, and how we have abused his goodness; how long we have been revolting more and more, (as all confess,) and how very corrupt we were become at last; in how great a degree we had forsaken the fountain of living waters; how obstinate we have been under all manner of means that God has used to reclaim us; how often we have mocked God with hypocritical pretences of humiliation, as in our annual days of public fasting, and other things, while, instead of reforming, we only grew worse and worse; and how dead a time it was every where before this work began. If we consider these things, we shall be most stupidly ungrateful, if we do not acknowledge God's visiting us as he has done, as an instance of the glorious triumph of free and sovereign grace.

The work is very glorious, if we consider the *extent* of it; being in this respect vastly beyond any that ever was known in *New England*. There has formerly sometimes been a remarkable awakening and success of the means of grace, in some particular congregations; and this used to be much noticed, and acknowledged to be glorious, though the towns and congregations round about continued dead: But now God has brought to pass a new thing, he has wrought a great work, which has extended from one end of the land to the other, besides what has been wrought in other *British* colonies in *America*.

The work is very glorious in the great *numbers* that have, to appearance, been turned from sin to God, and so, delivered from a wretched captivity to sin and Satan, saved from everlasting burnings, and made heirs of eternal glory. . . .

The work has been very glorious and wonderful in many *circumstances* and events of it, wherein God has in an uncommon manner made his hand visible and his power conspicuous; as in the extraordinary degrees of awakening, and the suddenness of conversions in innumerable instances. How common a thing has it been for a great part of a congregation to be at once moved by a mighty invisible power? and for six, eight, or ten souls to be converted to God (to all appearance) in an exercise, in whom the visible change still continues? How great an alteration has been made in some towns, yea, some populous towns, the change still abiding? And how many very vicious persons have been wrought upon, so as to become visibly new creatures? God has also made his hand very visible, and his work glorious, in the multitudes of little children that have been wrought upon. I suppose there have been some hundreds of instances of this nature of late, any one of which formerly would have been looked upon so remarkable, as to be worthy to be recorded, and published through the land. The work is very glorious in its influences and effects on many who have been very ignorant and barbarous, as I before observed of the *Indians* and *Negroes*.

The work is also exceeding glorious in the high attainments of Christians, in the extraordinary degrees of light, love and spiritual joy, that God has bestowed upon great multitudes. In this respect also, the land in all parts has abounded with such instances, any one of which, if they had happened formerly, would have been thought worthy to be noticed by God's people throughout the *British* dominions. The *New-Jerusalem* in this respect has begun to come down from heaven, and perhaps never were more of the prelibations of heaven's glory given upon earth.

\*    \*    \*

# Part II, Sect. II.

## *The Latter-Day Glory, is probably to begin in America.*

It is not unlikely that this work of God's Spirit, so extraordinary and wonderful, is the dawning, or at least, a prelude of that glorious work of God, so often foretold in scripture, which, in the progress and issue of it, shall renew the world of mankind. If we consider how long since the things foretold as what should precede this great event, have been accomplished; and how long this event has been expected by the church of God, and thought to be nigh by the most eminent men of God, in the church; and withal consider what the state of things now is, and has for a considerable time been, in the church of God, and the world of mankind; we cannot reasonably think otherwise, than that the beginning of this great work of God must be near. And there are many things that make it probable that this work will begin in *America*.—It is signified that it shall begin in some very remote part of the world, with which other parts have no communication but by navigation, in Isa. lx. 9. *Surely the isles shall wait for me, and the ships of* Tarshish *first, to bring my sons from far.* It is exceeding manifest that this chapter is a prophecy of the prosperity of the church, in its most glorious state on earth, in the latter days; and I cannot think that any thing else can be here intended but *America* by the isles that are far off, from whence the first-born sons of that glorious day shall be brought. . . .

God has made as it were two worlds here below, two great habitable continents, far separated one from the other: The latter is as it were now but newly created; it has been, till of late, wholly the possession of *Satan*, the church of God having never been in it, as it has been in the other continent, from the beginning of the world. This new world is probably now discovered, that the new and most glorious state of God's church on earth might commence there; that God might in it begin a new world in a spiritual respect, when he creates the *new heavens* and *new earth.*

God has already put that honour upon the other continent, that Christ was born there literally, and there made the *purchase of redemption.* So, as Providence observes a kind of equal distribution of things, it is not unlikely that the great spiritual birth of Christ, and the most glorious *application of redemption*, is to begin in this. . . .

*    *    *

The old continent has been the source and original of mankind, in several respects. The first parents of mankind dwelt there; and there dwelt *Noah* and his sons; there the second *Adam* was born, and crucified and raised again: And it is probable that, in some measure to balance these things, the most glorious renovation of the world shall originate from the new continent, and the church of God in that respect be from hence. And so it is probable that will come to pass in spirituals, which has taken place in temporals, with respect to *America*; that whereas, till of late, the world was supplied with its silver, and gold, and earthly treasures from the old continent, now it is supplied chiefly from the new; so the course of things in spiritual respects will be in like manner turned.— And it is worthy to be noted, that *America* was discovered about the time of the reformation, or but little before: Which reformation was the first thing that God did towards the glorious renovation of the world, after it had sunk into the depths of darkness and ruin, under the great antichristian apostacy. So that, as soon as this new world stands forth in view, God presently goes about doing some great thing in order to make way for the introduction of the church's latter-day glory—which is to have its first seat in, and is to take its rise from that new world.

*    *    *

## REVIEW QUESTIONS

1. According to Edwards, what was New England like before the Great Awakening? After? What do his descriptions reveal about colonial society? What do they reveal about him?
2. While he noted that all sorts of people were affected by the Awakening, whom did he indicate were most affected by it? Why do you suppose this concerned both proponents and opponents of the movement?
3. How did Edwards answer critics who believed that the dissension and disorder of the Awakening might be a manifestation of the devil's, rather than God's, work?
4. Did Edwards champion the Awakening as a democratic as well as a providential process?
5. How did Edwards interpret the Awakening as a sign of the possible destiny of America? Did his argument reflect earlier ideas about America or foreshadow later ones? Explain.

# ELIZA LUCAS PINCKNEY

# Letters from South Carolina
# (1740–42, 1760–61)

*Eliza Lucas Pinckney (1722–1793) not only represented the southern planting elite but was in some ways a self-made woman. She built on the wealth, position, and education she received as a child and became a powerful figure in South Carolina. She was born in Antigua in the West Indies to a British military officer who later became lieutenant governor there. Her father moved his two daughters and their sickly mother to the family's Wappoo plantation near Charlestown, South Carolina, in 1738. When he returned to the West Indies in 1739, he left Eliza in charge of that and two other plantations. The young Eliza Lucas was more than a caretaker: she was an innovator and shrewd businesswoman. She worked herself and her slaves hard as she developed the cultivation and processing of indigo in the colony (and thus helped British mercantilism, for then England did not have to buy the blue dye from other countries). She also experimented with other crops, continued her intellectual pursuits, maintained an active social life, and kept up an extensive correspondence with her father, brothers, friends, and, later, her children. She married the widower Charles Pinckney in 1745. She had four children, one of whom died young. After her husband died in 1758, she continued to manage the family's estates and took especial care in the education of her children, including that of her daughter Harriott. Her two sons, Thomas and Charles Cotesworth Pinckney, became notable revolutionaries.*

From *The Letterbook of Eliza Lucas Pinckney, 1739–1762*, edited by Elise Pinckney, with an introduction by Walter Muir Whitehill (Chapel Hill: University of North Carolina Press, 1972), pp. 6–8, 29–35, 39–40, 154–55, 164–65. [Editorial insertions appear in brackets—*Ed.*]

To my good friend Mrs. Boddicott

Dear Madam,                    May the 2nd [1740]

I flatter myself it will be a satisfaction to you to hear I like this part of the world, as my lott has fallen here—which I really do. I prefer England to it, 'tis true, but think Carolina greatly preferable to the West Indias, and was my Papa here I should be very happy.

We have a very good acquaintance from whom we have received much friendship and Civility. Charles Town, the principal one in this province, is a polite, agreeable place. The people live very Gentile and very much in the English taste. The Country is in General fertile and abounds with Venison and wild fowl; the Venison is much higher flavoured than in England but 'tis seldom fatt.

My Papa and Mama's great indulgence to me leaves it to me to chose our place of residence either in town or Country, but I think it more prudent as well as most agreeable to my Mama and self to be in the Country during my Father's absence. We are

17 mile by land and 6 by water from Charles Town—where we have about 6 agreeable families around us with whom we live in great harmony.

I have a little library well furnished (for my papa has left me most of his books) in which I spend part of my time. My Musick and the Garden, which I am very fond of, take up the rest of my time that is not imployed in business, of which my father has left me a pretty good share—and indeed, 'twas inavoidable as my Mama's bad state of health prevents her going through any fatigue.

I have the business of 3 plantations to transact, which requires much writing and more business and fatigue of other sorts than you can imagine. But least you should imagine it too burthensom to a girl at my early time of life, give me leave to answer you: I assure you I think myself happy that I can be useful to so good a father, and by rising very early I find I can go through much business. But least you should think I shall be quite moaped with this way of life I am to inform you there is two worthy Ladies in Charles Town, Mrs. Pinckney [Elizabeth Lamb Pinckney, d. January 1744, first wife of Charles Pinckney] and Mrs. Cleland, who are partial enough to me to be always pleased to have me with them, and insist upon my making their houses my home when in town and press me to relax a little much oftener than 'tis in my honor to accept of their obliging intreaties. But I some times am with one or the other for 3 weeks or a month at a time, and then enjoy all the pleasures Charles Town affords, . . .

*     *     *

[To Miss Bartlett]
Dr. Miss B                                [March 1742]

I am willing you should participate of the pleasure we enjoyed yesterday by hearing Mr. B[ryan] is come to his sences and acknowledges with extream concern he was guided by a spirit of delusion. . . . Poor man! with what anguish must he reflect on making the spirit of God the author of his weakneses, and of disturbing the whole community, who tho' they knew him to be no prophet dreaded the consiquence of his prophecys coming to the ears of the African Hosts, as he calls them. I hope he will be a warning to all pious minds not to reject reason and revelation and set up in their stead their own wild notions. He fancied indeed he was soported in his oppinions by the sacred Oracles, and (as a father of our church observes) so did all the broachers of herisey in the primitive church. But why should we not expect to be deluded when we refuse that assistance which the bountiful Author of our being has naturally revealed to us and set up in every mans mind, without which 'tis impossible to understand his will supernaturally revealed. For tho' their may be things in the Xtian sistem above reason such as the incarnation of our Saviour, etc., yet surely they highly dishonour our religion who affirm there is any thing in it contrary to reason.

Dont you by this time wish my preachment at an End and repent telling me you think my letters too short? But I cant conclude yet till I have told you I see the Comett Sir I. Newton foretold should appear in 1741 and which in his opinion is that that will destroy the world. How long it may be traveling down to us he does not say; but I think it does not concern us much as our time of action is over at our death, the exact time of which is uncertain; tho' we may reasonably expect it within the utmost limits mentioned by the psalmist. . . .

*     *     *

Memdam. March 11th, 1741. [/2]. Wrote a long letter to my father about the Indigo and all the plantation affairs, and that Mr. H. B. [Hugh Bryan] had been very much deluded by his own fancys and imagined he was assisted by the divine spirrit to prophesey: Charles Town and the Country as farr as Ponpon Bridge should be destroyed by fire and sword, to be executed by the Negroes before the first day of next month. . . . People in general were very uneasey tho' convinced he was no prophet, but they dreaded the consiquence of such a thing being put in to the head of the slaves and the advantage they might take of us. . . .

*     *     *

[To Miss Bartlett]
Dr. Miss B                    [c. March–April, 1742]

By your enquiry after the Comett I find your curiosity has not been strong enough to raise you out of your bed so much before your usual time as mine has been. But to answer your querie: The Comett had the appearance of a very large starr with a tail and to my sight about 5 or 6 foot long— its real magnitude must then be prodigious. The tale was much paler than the Commet it self and not unlike the milkey way. 'Twas about a fortnight ago that I see it.

The brightness of the Committ was too dazleing for me to give you the information you require. I could not see whether it had petticoats on or not, but I am inclined to think by its modest appearance so early in the morning it wont permitt every Idle gazer to behold its splendour, a favour it will only grant to such as take pains for it—from hence I conclude if I could have discovered any clothing it would have been the female garb. Besides if it is any mortal transformed to this glorious luminary, why not a woman.

The light of the Comitt to my unphilosophical Eyes seems to be natural and all its own. How much it may really borrow from the sun I am not astronomer enough to tell. . . .

*       *       *

[To Miss Bartlett]
Dr. Miss B                    [c. March–April, 1742]

I admire your resolution of conquering the Lazey deity Somnus you talk off. I assure you the sight of a commit is not the only pleasure you lose if you lie late a bed in a morning; for this, like every other pernisious custome, gains upon us the more we indulge it. I cant help calling it pernicious, and I devide it into heads like a Sermon: 1st, because by loseing so much of our time we lose so much of life; 2dy because 'tis unhealthy; 3dly and lastly, because we lose by farr the pleasanest part of the day. From all which I could draw some useful inferences, but whether it will be so agreeable to you to hear preaching any where but in a pulpitt I am in doubt.

An old lady in our Neighbourhood is often querrelin with me for riseing so early as 5 o'Clock in the morning, and is in great pain for me least it should spoil my marriage, for she says it will make me look old long before I am so; in this, however, I believe she is mistaking for what ever contributes to health and pleasure of mind must also contribute to good looks. But admiting what she says, I reason with her thus: If I should look older by this practice I really am so; for the longer time we are awake the longer we live. Sleep is so much the Emblem of death that I think it may be rather called breathing than living. Thus then I have the advantage of the sleepers in point of long life, so I beg you will not be frighted by such sort of apprehensions as those suggested above and for fear of your pretty face give up your late pious resolution of early rising.

My Mama joyns with me in Compliments to Mr. and Mrs. Pinckney. I send herewith Colo. Pinckneys books and shall be much obliged to him for Virgils works; notwithstanding this same old Gentlewoman (who I think too has a great friendship for me) has a great spite at my books and had like to have thrown a volume of my Plutarchs lives into the fire the other day. She is sadly afraid, she says, I shall read my self mad. . . .

*       *       *

[To Miss Bartlett]
Dr. Miss B

. . . Why, my dear Miss B, will you so often repeat your desire to know how I triffle away my time in our retirement in my fathers absence. . . . to show you my readiness in obeying your commands, here it is.

In general then I rise at five o'Clock in the morning, read till Seven, then take a walk in the garden or field, see that the Servants are at their respective business, then to breakfast. The first hour after breakfast is spent at my musick, the next is constantly employed in recolecting something I have learned least for want of practise it should be quite lost, such as French and short hand. After that I devote the rest of the time till I dress for dinner to our little Polly and two black girls who I teach to read, and if I have my paps's approbation (my Mamas I have got) I intend [them] for school mistres's for the rest of the Negroe children—another scheme you see. [She was not the only person to think about educating African Americans so that they could then teach others, but it was a radical and rare notion.] But to proceed, the first hour after dinner as the first after breakfast at musick, the rest of the afternoon in Needle work till candle light, and from that time to bed time read or write. 'Tis the fashion here to carry our work abroad with us so that having company, without they are great strangers, is no interruption to that affair; but I have particular matters for particular days, which is an interruption to mine. Mondays my musick Master is here. Tuesdays my friend Mrs. Chardon (about 3 mile distant) and I are constantly engaged to each other, she at our house one Tuesday—I at hers the next and this is one of the happiest days I spend at Woppoe. Thursday the whole day except what the necessary affairs of the family take up is spent in writing, either on the business of the plantations, or letters to my friends. Every other Fryday, if no company, we go a vizeting so that I go abroad once a week and no oftener.

. . . I have planted a large figg orchard with design to dry and export them. I have reckoned my expence and the prophets to arise from these figgs, but was I to tell you how great an Estate I am to make this way, and how 'tis to be laid out you would think me far gone in romance. Your good Uncle I know has long thought I have a fertile brain at schemeing. I only confirm him in his opinion; but I own I love the vegitable world extremly. I think it an innocent and useful amusement. . . .

\*      \*      \*

[To Thomas Lucas]
May 22nd, 1742

I am now set down, my Dear Brother, to obey your commands and give you a short discription of the part of the world I now inhabit. South Carolina then is a large and Extensive Country Near the Sea. Most of the settled parts of it is upon a flatt—the soil near Charles Town sandy, but further distant clay and swamplands. It abounds with fine navigable rivers, and great quantities of fine timber. The Country at a great distance, that is to say about a hundred or a hundred and fifty mile from Charles Town, [is] very hilly.

The Soil in general [is] very fertile, and there is very few European or American fruits or grain but what grow here. The Country abounds with wild fowl, Venison and fish. Beef, veal and motton are here in much greater perfection than in the Islands [West Indies], tho' not equal to that in England; but their pork exceeds any I ever tasted any where. The Turkeys [are] extreamly fine, especially the wild, and indeed all their poultry is exceeding good; and peaches, Nectrons and mellons of all sorts extreamly fine and in profusion, and their Oranges exceed any I ever tasted in the West Indies or from Spain or Portugal.

The people in general [are] hospitable and honest, and the better sort add to these a polite gentile behaviour. The poorer sort are the most indolent people in the world or they could never be wretched in so plentiful a country as this. The winters here are very fine and pleasant, but 4 months in the year is extreamly disagreeable, excessive hott, much thunder and lightening, and muskatoes and sand flies in abundance.

Charles Town, the Metropolis, is a neat pretty place. The inhabitants [are] polite and live in a very gentile manner; the streets and houses regularly built; the ladies and gentlemen gay in their dress. Upon the whole you will find as many agreeable people of both sexes for the size of the place as almost any where. St. Phillips church in Charles Town is a very Eligant one, and much frequented. There are several more places of publick worship in this town and the generallity of people [are] of a religious turn of mind.

I began in haste and have observed no method or I should have told you before I came to Summer that we have a most charming spring in this country, especially for those who travel through the Country for the scent of the young mirtle and Yellow Jesamin with which the woods abound is delightful.

The staple comodity here is rice and the only thing they export to Europe. Beef, pork and lumber they send to the West Indias. . . .

*     *     *

Crs. Town, So. Carolina, March 12th, 1760 [To Vigorous Edwards]

. . . May the Almighty long continue that health to you [which you] inform me you have injoyed since we left England, and be assured I account it among the first of temporal blessings to know that the much valued friends of my beloved Mr. Pinckney are well and happy; I mean as much so as this uncertain state will admit— . . . We are not to fix our happiness on any thing beneath the supream Good nor Idolize the best man on Earth, or pay dearly for it. Nor must we express real and lasting comfort to the torn heart till it returns to its duty by patience and submission to The Infinitely good as well as Wise disposer of all Events. To Him I desire to be resigned in all things, and To Him I recommend my dear children and trust he will preserve them from all evil, natural and moral. I know 'tis only in His protection they can be safe whether they are with me or from me—and in that they are, be they where they will. Yet so weak am I, that my heart bleeds at our separation and I long more than I can express to be with them. [Yet she left her sons in England to advance their education.]

Accept Good Sir, my grateful acknowledgments for your friendship and notice of them and for mentioning them so particularly to me in your letter. . . .

The Cheerokee Indians have been very insolent the last year and commited many murders on our back Settlements; and in all probability we should by this time have been engaged in an Indian War, the most dreadful of all war, had our Gov. acted with less judgment and resolution. He marched an army up into their Country and demanded satisfaction at the head of it for the Murders they had commited or would then take it. They were much alarmed, pretended it was only some of their hot headed young men, and not aproved by the whole; would have excused giving the Criminals up by saying they could not be found, but after some time brought some of them in and gave Hostages

for the rest. A treaty of peace and friendship was concluded upon it, and I hope and we have great reason to think, we are upon a better footing with those people than we have been many years. [But not for long, for hostilities soon resumed.] . . .

[To Mr. Morly]

Dear Sir                                   March 14th, 1760

. . . The beginning of this Year there was such a fine prospect on our plantations of a great Crop that I was hopeful of clearing all the mony that was due upon the Estate, but the great drought in most parts of the Country, such as I never remember here, disapointed those expectations so much that all that we make from the planting interest will hardly defray the charges of the plantations. And upon our arrival here we found they wanted but every thing and [were] every way in bad order, with ignorant or dishonest Over Seers.

My Nephew had no management of the planting interest, and my brother who had, by a stroak of the palsey, had been long incapable of all business. I thank God there is now a good prospect of things being deferently conducted. I have prevailed upon a conscientious good man . . . to undertake the dircction and inspection of the overseers. He is an excellent planter, a Dutchman, originally Servant and Overseer to Mr. Golightly, who has been much solicited to undertake for many Gentlemen; but as he has no family but a wife and is comfortable enough in his circumstances, refuses to do it for any but women and children that are not able to do it for themselves. . . .

I find it requires great care, attention and activity to attend properly to a Carolina Estate, tho' but a moderate one, to do ones duty and make it turn to account, that I find I have as much business as I can go through of one sort or other. Perhaps 'tis better for me, and I believe it is. Had there not been a necessity for it, I might have sunk to the grave by this time in that Lethargy of stupidity which had seized me after my mind had been violently agitated by the greatest shock it ever felt. But a variety of imployment gives my thoughts a relief from melloncholy subjects, . . .

*     *     *

[To Mrs. Evance]
March 15th, [17]60

. . . A great cloud seems at present to hang over this province. We are continually insulted by the Indians on our back settlements, and a violent kind of small pox rages in Charles Town that almost puts a stop to all business. [The *South Carolina Gazette* reported in April that thousands "took the Disease" either naturally or by inoculation since February and that hundreds died of it.] Several of those I have to transact business with are fled into the Country, but by the Divine blessing I hope a month or two will change the prospect. We expect shortly troops from Gen. Amherst [Jeffery Amherst, Commander in Chief of American operations], which I trust will be able to manage these savage Enemies. And the small pox, as it does not spread in the Country, must be soon over for want of subjects.

I am now at Belmont to keep my people out of the way of the violent distemper for the poor blacks have died very fast even by inocculation. But the people in Charles Town were inocculation mad, I think I may call it, and rushed into it with such presipitation that I think it impossible they could have had either a proper preparation or attendance had there been 10 Doctors in town to one. The Doctors could not help it—the people would not be said nay. . . .

\*    \*    \*

[To Mr. George Morly]
Dear Sir                    Belmont. July 19th, 1760

Having been some time in the Country I but just heard of these ships sailing to-morrow to London, so that I shall not now be able to write to my dear children or any of my friends but your self and to Mrs. King to acknowledge the receipt of the very gentile present she sent to Harriott by Capt. Muir. . . .

Our Indian affairs are in a poor way. Col. Mongomerie at the head of 16 hundred men including rangers marched into the middle Cherokee Towns and destroyed 5 towns, which raised the spirits of people much. But while we imag-

ined he was proceeding to Fort Loudon he began his march towards Charles Town in order to return to Genl. Amherst, in consiquence of whose orders 'tis said he returns. [Archibald Montgomery's combined force of regular and provincial troops destroyed the lower towns but were unsuccessful against middle ones. When he pulled out his troops, he doomed Fort Loudoun.] The Gov. by the desire of the assembly has sent to desire his continuing in the nation. We impatiently wait his answer, as we also do one to an express sent from hence to Genl. Amherst. We have no doubt but the Creeks will soon joyn the Cherookees. . . .

[To Mrs. King]
Dr. Madm.                    Belmont. July 19th, 1760

I had the honour of yours of the 16th Febr. last with yours and the young ladies very gentile present to Harriott. Indeed, Madam, you are too good to us. Either of the three would have showed us the honour you do us in remembering us, expecially as there is such a risk of things being taken at this time. 'Tis a most compleat suit and universally admired. The fann I think a curiosity and the pompon the prettiest we ever saw. The little girl is quite happy, and the more so as they are the first that have reached this part of the world, so she has an opportunity of seting the fashion. I doubt whether she would part with them to purchase a peace with the Cherokees who are become extreamly troublesome to us. Nor have the highland troops under Col. Mongomery, sent by Genl. Amherst, done much more than exasperated the Indians to more cruel revenge. And they are now about to leave us to the mercy of these Barbarians.

I hope the good people of England wont give all their superfluous mony away to French prisoners and to build foreign churches, but reserve some for their poor fellow subjects in America. For if they go on to make new conquests in America and neglect the protection of their old Colonys, you may soon have importations of distressed people from the southwardmost part of North America to exercise their charity upon.

\*    \*    \*

To the Honble. Mrs. King

Dr. Madm.                                    April 13th, 1761

I cant resist the temptation of paying you my respects when a fleet sails though I did my self the honor To write you by the Man of War in Feb.— which letter with the Seeds for Mr. King I hope are safe arrived by this time.

Our hopes and Expectations are a good deal raised by the great fleet we are told that is bound from England for America this spring. We flatter our selves they will take The Mississippi in their way, which if they succeed inn must put an end to all our Indian Warrs, as they could never molest us if the French from thence did not supply them with arms and Ammunition. Our army has marched for the Cheerokee nation. They consist of regular troops and provincials. 'Tis a disagreeable Service but they have this to comfort them, that whether they are successful or other ways they may be pretty sure of gathering Laurels from the bounty of the English news writers; for after the incomiums opon the last Cheerokee expedition, there surely can nothing be done there that dont merrit praise.

If the 50 Mohocks arrive safe that we expect from Genl. Amherst, I hope we shall be able to quel those Barbarians; for the Mohocks are very fine men—five of them are now here—and they are looked upon by the rest of the Indians with both dread and respect for they think them the greatest warriors in the world. [Lieutenant Colonel James Grant commanded a force of over 2,800 men and was aided by Mohawk and Stockbridge Indian scouts. His troops destroyed the Cherokee Middle Towns.]

Many thanks to good Mr. King for my beer, which came in very good order and is extreamly good, though it had a long voyage and went first to Lisbon.

My most respectful Compliments wait on My Lady and Lord King and the young Ladies. Harriott is out of Town with Lady Mary Drayton and dont know when the fleet sails or would do her self the honour to write to Miss Whilhelmine by it.

I am with great gratitude and affection.

Dr. Madm.

Your most obliged and most obedt.

Servant

E. Pinckney

# REVIEW QUESTIONS

1. What did it take to run a plantation? What did Eliza Lucas Pinckney believe made her successful?
2. What is the evidence that Pinckney cared for at least some of her slaves and yet worried about the possibility of slave revolts?
3. How did religious beliefs and other cultural issues affect Pinckney's conceptions of her world and society? Was there evidence that she might have been affected by Enlightenment philosophy or the religious Great Awakening?
4. How did she think of herself as a woman and about the proper roles and interests of a woman? Did her thoughts and actions appear to be a reflection of general social norms or more an indication of her elite status?
5. What were some of her major concerns in terms of the security and stability of her family, society, and colony? How did she handle such concerns?

## BENJAMIN FRANKLIN

# The Way to Wealth (1757)

*Benjamin Franklin became the editor and publisher of the* Pennsylvania Gazette *in 1729 and started publishing* Poor Richard's Almanack, *an annual best-seller, in 1732. Franklin did so well that he was able to retire from the greater part of his printing business—namely as editor and publisher of the* Pennsylvania Gazette*— while still in his forties (1748). He then had ample time to devote to other interests, which included science and politics. He continued, however, to publish* Poor Richard's Almanack *until 1757. In its final edition, Franklin, in his persona of "Richard Saunders" (that is, "Poor Richard"), made up a story about an old man who advised some people on work and financial matters at a vendue (public sale). Delighted by the old man's use of Poor Richard's principles (which Franklin admitted reflected sayings in general use at the time), Franklin, as Saunders, ended the piece by saying he intended to follow his own advice and recommended that his readers do the same.*

From *Benjamin Franklin: The Autobiography and Other Writings*, edited by Kenneth Silverman (New York: Penguin Books, 1986), pp. 215–25.

\*     \*     \*

. . . I stopt my Horse lately where a great Number of People were collected at a Vendue of Merchant Goods. The Hour of Sale not being come, they were conversing on the Badness of the Times, and one of the Company call'd to a plain clean old Man, with white Locks, *Pray, Father Abraham, what think you of the Times? Won't these heavy Taxes quite ruin the Country? How shall we be ever able to pay them? What would you advise us to?*—Father Abraham stood up, and reply'd, If you'd have my Advice, I'll give it you in short, for a *Word to the Wise is enough,* and *many Words won't fill a Bushel,* as *Poor Richard says.* They join'd in desiring him to speak his Mind, and gathering round him, he proceeded as follows;

Friends, says he, and Neighbours, the Taxes are indeed very heavy, and if those laid on by the Government were the only Ones we had to pay, we might more easily discharge them; but we have many others, and much more grievous to some of us. We are taxed twice as much by our *Idleness,* three times as much by our *Pride,* and four times as much by our *Folly,* and from these Taxes the Commissioners cannot ease or deliver us by allowing an Abatement. However let us hearken to good Advice, and something may be done for us; *God helps them that help themselves,* as *Poor Richard* says, in his Almanack of 1733.

It would be thought a hard Government that should tax its People one tenth Part of their *Time,* to be employed in its Service. But *Idleness* taxes many of us much more, if we reckon all that is spent in absolute *Sloth,* or doing of nothing, with that which is spent in idle Employments or Amusements, that amount to nothing. . . . If Time be of all Things the most precious, *wasting Time* must be, as *Poor Richard* says, *the greatest Prodigality,* since, as he elsewhere tells us, *Lost Time is never found again;* and what we call *Time-enough, always proves little enough:* Let us then be up and be doing, and doing to the Purpose; so by Diligence shall we do more with less Perplexity. *Sloth makes all Things difficult, but Industry all easy,* as *Poor Richard* says; and *He that riseth late, must trot all Day, and shall scarce overtake his Business at Night.* While *Laziness travels so slowly, that Poverty soon overtakes him,* as we read in *Poor Richard,* who adds, *Drive thy Business, let not that drive thee;* and *Early to Bed, and early to rise, makes a Man healthy, wealthy and wise.*

So what signifies *wishing* and *hoping* for better Times. We may make these Times better if we bestir ourselves. *Industry need not wish,* as *Poor Richard* says, and *He that lives upon Hope will die fasting. There are no Gains, without Pains;* then *Help Hands, for I have no Lands,* or if I have, they are smartly taxed. And, as *Poor Richard* likewise observes, *He that hath a Trade hath an Estate,* and *He that hath a Calling hath an Office of Profit and Honour;* but then the *Trade* must be worked at, and the *Calling* well followed, or neither the *Estate,* nor the *Office,* will enable us to pay our Taxes.—If we are industrious we shall never starve; for, as *Poor Richard* says, *At the working Man's House* Hunger *looks in, but dares not enter.* Nor will the Bailiff nor the Constable enter, for *Industry pays Debts, while Despair encreaseth them,* says *Poor Richard. . . .* If you were a Servant, would you not be ashamed that a good Master should catch you idle? Are you then your own Master, *be ashamed to catch yourself idle,* as *Poor Dick* says. When there is so much to be done for yourself, your Family, your Country, and your gracious King, be up by Peep of Day; *Let not the Sun look down and say, Inglorious here he lies. . . .*

Methinks I hear some of you say, *Must a Man afford himself no Leisure?*— I will tell thee, my Friend, what *Poor Richard* says, *Employ thy Time well if thou meanest to gain Leisure;* and, *since thou art not sure of a Minute, throw not away an Hour.* Leisure, is Time for doing something useful; this Leisure the diligent Man will obtain, but the lazy Man never; so that, as *Poor Richard* says, a *Life of Leisure and a Life of Laziness are two Things. . . .*

But with our Industry, we must likewise be *steady, settled* and *careful,* and oversee our own Affairs *with our own Eyes,* and not trust too much to others; for, as *Poor Richard* says, . . . *Keep thy Shop, and thy Shop will keep thee;* and again, *If you would have your Business done, go; If not, send. . . .*

And again, *The Eye of a Master will do more Work than both his Hands;* and again, *Want of Care does us more Damage than Want of Knowledge;* and again, *Not to oversee Workmen, is to leave them your Purse open.* Trusting too much to others Care is the Ruin of many; for, as the *Almanack* says, *In the Affairs of this World, Men are saved, not by Faith, but by the Want of it;* but a Man's own Care is profitable; for, saith *Poor Dick, Learning is to the Studious,* and *Riches to the Careful,* as well as *Power to the Bold,* and *Heaven to the Virtuous.* And farther, *If you would have a faithful Servant, and one that you like, serve yourself.* And again, he adviseth to Circumspection and Care, even in the smallest Matters, because sometimes *a little Neglect may breed great Mischief;* adding, *For want of a Nail the Shoe was lost; for want of a Shoe the Horse was lost; and for want of a Horse the Rider was lost,* being overtaken and slain by the Enemy, all for want of Care about a Horse-shoe Nail.

So much for Industry, my Friends, and Attention to one's own Business; but to these we must add *Frugality,* if we would make our *Industry* more certainly successful. A Man may, if he knows not how to save as he gets, *keep his Nose all his Life to the Grindstone,* and die not worth a *Groat* at last. . . .

*If you would be wealthy,* says he, in another Almanack, *think of Saving as well as of Getting: The Indies have not made Spain rich, because her* Outgoes *are greater than her* Incomes. Away then with your expensive Follies, and you will not have so much Cause to complain of hard Times, heavy Taxes, and chargeable Families; for, as *Poor Dick* says,

> *Women and Wine, Game and Deceit,*
> *Make the Wealth small, and the Wants great.*

And farther, *What maintains one Vice, would bring up two Children.* You may think perhaps, That a *little* Tea, or a *little* Punch now and then, Diet a *little* more costly, Clothes a *little* finer, and a *little* Entertainment now and then, can be no *great* Matter; but remember what *Poor Richard* says, . . . *Beware of* little *Expences; a small Leak will sink a great Ship*; and again, *Who Dainties love, shall Beggars prove*; and moreover, *Fools make Feasts, and wise Men eat them.*

Here you are all got together at this Vendue of *Fineries* and *Knicknacks*. You call them *Goods*, but if you do not take Care, they will prove *Evils* to some of you. You expect they will be sold *cheap*, and perhaps they may for less than they cost; but if you have no Occasion for them, they must be *dear* to you. Remember what *Poor Richard* says, *Buy what thou hast no Need of, and ere long thou shalt sell thy Necessaries.* And again, *At a great Pennyworth pause a while:* He means, that perhaps the Cheapness is *apparent* only, and not *real*; or the Bargain, by straitning thee in thy Business, may do thee more Harm than Good. . . . Many a one, for the Sake of Finery on the Back, have gone with a hungry Belly, and half starved their Families; *Silks and Sattins, Scarlet and Velvets*, as *Poor Richard* says, *put out the Kitchen Fire.* These are not the *Necessaries* of Life; they can scarcely be called the *Conveniencies*, and yet only because they look pretty, how many *want* to *have* them. The *artificial* Wants of Mankind thus become more numerous than the *natural*; and, as *Poor Dick* says, *For one* poor *Person, there are an hundred* indigent. By these, and other Extravagancies, the Genteel are reduced to Poverty, and forced to borrow of those whom they formerly despised, but who through *Industry* and *Frugality* have maintained their Standing; in which Case it appears plainly, that a *Ploughman on his Legs is higher than a Gentleman on his Knees*, as *Poor Richard* says. . . . *If you would know the Value of Money, go and try to borrow some*; for, *he that goes a borrowing goes a sorrowing*; and indeed so does he that lends to such People, when he goes *to get it in again* . . .

\*      \*      \*

But what Madness must it be to *run in Debt* for these Superfluities! We are offered, by the Terms of this Vendue, *Six Months Credit*; and that perhaps has induced some of us to attend it, because we cannot spare the ready Money, and hope now to be fine without it. But, ah, think what you do when you run

in Debt; *You give to another Power over your Liberty.* If you cannot pay at the Time, you will be ashamed to see your Creditor; you will be in Fear when you speak to him; you will make poor pitiful sneaking Excuses, and by Degrees come to lose your Veracity, and sink into base downright lying; for, as *Poor Richard* says, *The second Vice is Lying, the first is running in Debt.* And again, to the same Purpose, *Lying rides upon Debt's Back.* Whereas a freeborn Englishman ought not to be ashamed or afraid to see or speak to any Man living. But Poverty often deprives a Man of all Spirit and Virtue: *'Tis hard for an empty Bag to stand upright*, as *Poor Richard* truly says. What would you think of that Prince, or that Government, who should issue an Edict forbidding you to dress like a Gentleman or a Gentlewoman, on Pain of Imprisonment or Servitude? Would you not say, that you are free, have a Right to dress as you please, and that such an Edict would be a Breach of your Privileges, and such a Government tyrannical? And yet you are about to put yourself under that Tyranny when you run in Debt for such Dress! Your Creditor has Authority at his Pleasure to deprive you of your Liberty, by confining you in Goal for Life, or to sell you for a Servant, if you should not be able to pay him! When you have got your Bargain, you may, perhaps, think little of Payment; but *Creditors, Poor Richard* tells us, *have better Memories than Debtors*; and in another Place says, *Creditors are a superstitious Sect, great Observers of set Days and Times.* The Day comes round before you are aware, and the Demand is made before you are prepared to satisfy it. Or if you bear your Debt in Mind, the Term which at first seemed so long, will, as it lessens, appear extreamly short. *Time* will seem to have added Wings to his Heels as well as Shoulders. *Those have a short Lent*, saith *Poor Richard*, *who owe Money to be paid at Easter.* Then since, as he says, *The Borrower is a Slave to the Lender, and the Debtor to the Creditor*, disdain the Chain, preserve your Freedom; and maintain your Independency: Be *industrious* and *free*; be *frugal* and *free*. . . .

This Doctrine, my Friends, is *Reason* and *Wisdom*; but after all, do not depend too much upon your own *Industry*, and *Frugality*, and *Prudence*, though excellent Things, for they may all be blasted without the

Blessing of Heaven; and therefore ask that Blessing humbly, and be not uncharitable to those that at present seem to want it, but comfort and help them. Remember *Job* suffered, and was afterwards prosperous.

And now to conclude, *Experience keeps a dear School, but Fools will learn in no other, and scarce in that*; for it is true, *we may give Advice, but we cannot give Conduct*, as *Poor Richard* says: However, remember this, *They that won't be counselled, can't be helped*, as *Poor Richard* says: And farther, That *if you will not hear Reason, she'll surely rap your Knuckles.*

Thus the old Gentleman ended his Harangue. The People heard it, and approved the Doctrine, and immediately practised the contrary, just as if it had been a common Sermon; for the Vendue opened, and they began to buy extravagantly, notwithstanding all his Cautions, and their own Fear of Taxes. . . .

## REVIEW QUESTIONS

1. What did Franklin believe was the key to making money? He provided plenty of aphorisms to make that point. Of those, which do you believe provided the best advice? Why?
2. What did Franklin say about holding on to money? What do you believe was the most pertinent piece of that advice? Why?
3. What does this story, and the advice in it, reveal about colonial society? About Franklin?

# WILLIAM MORALEY

# FROM Memoirs of an Indentured Servant (1743)

*As more people, especially in the South, bought the bodies and labors of African slaves, others continued to buy the time and labor of European servants. Anyone traveling through the middle colonies in the early to mid-eighteenth century would have seen a mixture of free, indentured, and slave laborers working in shops and fields. These laborers were essential to the growing colonial economies, but their treatment and opportunities reflected growing social stratification and legal limitations. William Moraley (1699–1762), after squandering an opportunity to study law, trained as a clock and watchmaker under his father. Then in 1729 "oppress'd by Dame Fortune"—after his father left him little in his will, the spendthrift son traveled to London where he found no work, only debtors' prison—Moraley signed an indenture binding himself to five years of labor in the colonies. The new servant chafed at the conditions of his indenture as he compared and contrasted his restrictions with those of slaves. Moraley also complained about the handicaps he faced when trying to establish himself afterward. He wandered a while as an itinerant watchmaker, tinsmith, and blacksmith but ultimately left the land of opportunity to return to England in 1734. Moraley's story shows that not every immigrant to America stayed nor was every immigrant a success.*

From Susan E. Klepp and Billy G. Smith, eds., *The Infortunate: The Voyages and Adventures of William Moraley, an Indentured Servant* (University Park: Penn State University Press, 1992), pp. 77, 82–83, 87–89, 93–97. [Editorial insertions appear in square brackets—*Ed.*]

I left *Philadelphia*, to go to *Burlington* to my Master [Isaac Pearson, clockmaker], I went in a Boat, where I got my self Drunk for the first time after my Arrival, and then first experienced the Strength of Rum. About Twelve we landed there, and I was conveyed to my Master, where I dined upon Dumplings, boil'd Beef, and Udder; when I became enamour'd with Mrs *Sarah* ["Mrs" indicates Sarah Pearson's superior social status as the master's daughter, not her marital status.], the Daughter. I was stripp'd of my Rags, and received in lieu of them a torn Shirt, and an old Coat. They tell me, it was only for the present, for I might expect better.

\* \* \*

My Master employed me in his Business: I continued satisfied with him for sometime; but being desirous to settle at *Philadelphia*, during the rest of my Servitude, I declared to him, I would stay no longer, and desired him to dispose of me to some other Master, and insisted upon it, agreeably to the Tenour of my Indenture. This Demand made him cross to me, and I attempted an Escape, but was taken, and put into Prison; but was soon released, with a promise to satisfy my Demand. About a Fortnight after, we went to the Mayor of *Philadelphia*, his Name was *Griffith* [Thomas Griffitts], a Man of exact Justice, tho' an *Irishman*, who reconciled us; so I returned back to *Burlington*, and continued with him three Years, he forgiving me the other Two: I was ever after perfectly pleased with my Master's Behaviour to me, which was generous.

\* \* \*

Our Family consisted of a Wife and two Daughters, with a Nephew, a Negro Slave, a bought Servant [Aaron Middleton], and myself, with the aforesaid Gentlewoman. We had a next Door Neighbour, called *William Cullum*, a *Lincolnshire* Man, and a Baker: He came to us one Day, as my master and myself were making Nails for a Bellows for a Forge; and laying down upon the Bellows Board Three-pence and Sugar, writ the following Words in Chalk, and left the Place, we not knowing from whence the money came.

*Here's Money, Sugar, fetch some Rum,*
*And when the Liquors made, I come.*

My Master perceiving it, said, Well, this is *William Cullum's*, in order to shew his Wit, and order'd me to answer it Extempore. I first fetched the Rum, then made the Liquor, which was *Bombo*, and writ under the foregoing Lines.

*The Liquor's made, besure to come,*
*Or send more Sugar, and more Rum.*

Which my Friend perceived, laughed, and gave me a Shilling, with which I merrily quaffed.

One Night as I was in Bed with my Fellow Servant, being awake, the Chamber Door opened without any Noise, and I perceiv'd something coming cross the Floor, like a Ghost, in White, with a black Face. The Sight was so terrifying, that I shrunk under the Bed Cloaths, and sweated heartily, and endeavoured to wake my Friend, but to no Purpose. It came to the Bedside, and stooping, grined, and stared me in the Face, and beckened with its Hand: At which I shiver'd so much, and my Chops chatter'd, as if beating a March; but recollecting myself, I demanded of it what it wanted. Then it beckoned again, and left the Room; but soon after came again, looked earnestly at me. When I said, *Lord! why do you come here?* It answer'd, *Nothing with you*, as I well remember, and then went away, the Door shooting after it, without any Noise. I was very positive it was a Spirit, and told the Family the next Morning; who said, it was a Negro killed some Years since by her Master, and that they had often seen it.

\* \* \*

Before I observed, that I continued with my Master at *Burlington*, in perfect Concord. I acting as a Watchmaker, he often detached me into the Country to clean Clocks and Watches: It was in these Journeys I had an Opportunity of discovering what I have observed relating to the several Descriptions contained in this Book.

Almost every inhabitant, in the Country, have a Plantation, some two or more; there being no

Land lett as in *England* [an exaggeration], where Gentlemen live on the Labour of the Farmer, to whom he grants a short Lease, which expiring, he is either raised in his Rent, or discharged his Farm. Here they improve their Lands themselves, with the Assistance both of bought Servants and Negroes. They raise *Indian* Corn, for the Subsistence of their Families, after this Method: The Ears of Corn of the last Years growth is sown in the Beginning of *April;* they dig a Trench in the Ground, about five Inches deep, into which they strew the Grains, a few at a Time, for fear they should Sprout out too thick, and cover them lightly with Earth. After six Weeks it shoots out, then the Planters rake with a Hough the Ground, round the Stalk, to strengthen it: This is done every six Weeks, till the Corn is confirmed, which is brought to perfection the Beginning of *September,* when they strip the Corn from the Stalks, which they convey to their Granaries, leaving the Stalks to rot, which fertilizes their Land. With this Corn they make a kind of hasty Pudding, boiling it in Salt and Water, till it is thick; then pour it into a Dish, and serve it up with Milk, sometimes with Butter, but most commonly with Treacle [a sugar syrup]. It is a hungry Food, and is called *Mush,* being not unlike a Dish called *Cous Cous,* used in the Kingdoms of *Fez* and *Morocco.* They make use of it for Puddings, both boiled and baked, which with Eggs, is as good as a Rice Pudding. Raisins and Currants are seldom used, by reason of their Dearness, being Twelve-pence a Pound.

This Country produces not only almost every Fruit, Herb, and Root, as grows in *Great Britain,* but divers Sorts unknown to us. Bread Corn is superior to ours for Whiteness, and Cheaper. Barley is not so good, tho' they make Beer of it: Our Ten Shilling Small Beer is infinitely preferrable to any brewed there. Butter is very good, but Eight-pence a Pound; so Fish is generally eaten with the Butter it is fried in, with a little Vinegar to make it sharp. Butchers Meat, particularly Pork, is cheaper and better than with us; being fed with *Indian* Corn and Acrons. I have seen the Planters shake the Peach Trees to the Hogs.

The Country is every where diversify'd with Woods, and well manured Farms: And the hospitable Inhabitants dispence their Favours to the Traveller, the Poor and Needy. I have travelled some Hundreds of Miles at no Expense, Meat and Drink being bestowed upon all the subjects of *Great Britain;* for they strive to out-do one another in Works of good Nature and Charity. In short, it is the best poor Man's Country in the World; and, I believe, if this was sufficiently known by the miserable Objects we have in our Streets, Multitudes would be induced to go thither. Journeymens Wages are Five Shillings a Day, and is paid to Joiners, Carpenters, Bricklayers, and Barbers, &c.

The Rivers are well stored with Fish, as Roaches, Pearch, Trout, Cat Fish, which makes excellent Broth. Sturgeon I have bought one eight Foot long for Ten-pence; Flounders, Eels, Sun-Fish, Rock-Fish, better than our Cod; Oysters larger than *English* ones, and much better, the Shells are one Foot long. Here are Swans, Peacocks, Geese, Turkies, Ducks, Pidgeons, both Wild and Tame; Cocks and Hens are cheap, a fat Hen is sold for Two-pence Half-penny in the Markets; Pheasants, Partridges, Woodcocks, Quails, Plover, Snipes, besides small Birds unknown to us.

Here are Rabbits, but they are rather Hares, smaller than ours, they are seldom larger than *English* Rabbits, and the Flesh tasting like the Flesh of *English* Hares. Squirrels are of different Kinds, the smallest having Wings like a Bat, which helps them to fly from Tree to Tree. Panthers, Wolves, and Bears, are common; besides Horses, the hardiest in the World, for after a Riding of many Miles, being hot, they leave them standing in the Streets all Night, without catching Cold.

Otters, Badgers, Wild Cats, and a Beast called Scunck, who if you approach near them, will piss on their Tails, and switch them in your Face, and the Stink will continue above a Week. The Possum, which will retire to a tree when pursued, where hanging by its Tail, which it twists round the Branches, will defend itself against its Enemies, with the young in its Belly, which is a false one, for that use.

Here are Foxes, both Red, Grey, and White; besides Racoons, of the same Nature and Qualities, of whose Furs, worked up with Beaver, are made the best of Hats. Frogs are numerous, and of different Colours; their Legs are much longer than those of *Europe;* some are coloured like a 'Leopard, others streak'd like a Tyger with black and yellow Spots, which makes them of a frightful appearance. Here are no Toads; Lizards are of various Sorts and Colours, but not Poisonous; and are looked upon as Forerunners of Snakes, which are of many Sorts; as First,

The Rattle Snake, about six or seven Feet in Length, and so Poisonous, that if the Party bitten, does not cut off the Part bit, Death immediately ensues. . . .

*       *       *

Before I left *America* there was such a prodigious Flight of Pidgeons seen that almost darkened the Air, and infested the Fields and Villages, and so tame, that they became the Food of the Inhabitants for a Month together. They alighted in whole Flocks, and rested upon the Tops of Houses and Barns in a starving Condition, being by Necessity drove from some other Country. In 1732, in *July* and *September* an Insect called a Locust appeared, which was looked upon as a bad Omen, and it accordingly happened, for presently after, they came in such Swarms, that the Trees were covered with them, and devour'd the Leaves and Fruit: . . .

Here are Many Sorts of Butterflies, larger than those in *England,* so finely coloured, as causes in the Beholder both Wonder and Delight: . . . So admirable are the Effects of the Divine Providence in supporting the most minute of his Productions, that makes me break out in the Words of *David, How manifold, 0 Lord! are all thy Works; in Wisdom hast thou created them.*

At the first Peopling [of] these Colonies, there was a Necessity of employing a great Number of Hands, for the clearing the Land, being over-grown with Wood for some Hundred of Miles; to which Intent, the first Settlers not being sufficient of themselves to improve those Lands, were not only obliged to purchase a great Number of *English* Servants to assist them, to whom they granted great Immunities, and at the Expiration of their Servitude, Land was given to encourage them to continue there; but were likewise obliged to purchase Multitudes of Negro Slaves from *Africa,* by which Means they are become the richest Farmers in the World, paying no Rent, nor giving Wages either to purchased Servants or Negro Slaves; so that instead of finding the Planter Rack-rented, as the *English* Farmer, you will taste of their Liberality, they living in Affluence and Plenty.

The Condition of the Negroes is very bad, by reason of the Severity of the Laws, there being no Laws made in Favour of these unhap[p]y Wretches: For the least Trespass, they undergo the severest Punishment; but their Masters make them some amends, by suffering them to marry, which makes them easier, and often prevents their running away. The Consequence of their marrying is this, all their Posterity are Slaves without Redemption; and it is in vain to attempt an Escape, tho' they often endeavour it; for the Laws against them are so severe, that being caught after running away, they are unmercifully whipped; and if they die under the Discipline, their Masters suffer no Punishment, there being no Law against murdering them. So if one Man kills another's Slave, he is only obliged to pay his Value to the Master, besides Damages that may accrue for the Loss of him in his Business.

The Masters generally allow them a Piece of Ground, with Materials for improving it. The Time of working for themselves, is *Sundays,* when they raise on their own Account divers Sorts of Corn and Grain, and sell it in the Markets. They buy with the Money Cloaths for themselves and Wives; as for the Children, they belong to the Wives Master, who bring them up; so the Negro need fear no Expense, his Business being to get them for his Master's use, who is as tender of them as his own Children. On *Sundays* in the evening they converse with their Wives, and drink Rum, or Bumbo, and smoak Tobacco, and the next Morning return to their Master's Labour.

They are seldom made free, for fear of being burthensome to the Provinces, there being a Law, that no Master shall manumise them, unless he gives Security they shall not be thrown upon the

Province, by settling Land [life interest, not full ownership] on them for their Support.

∗    ∗    ∗

. . . I have often heard them say, they did not think God made them Slaves, any more than other Men, and wondered that Christians, especially *Englishmen,* should use them so barbarously. But there is a Necessity of using them hardly, being of an obdurate, stubborn Disposition; and when they have it in their Power to rebel, are extremely cruel.

The Condition of bought Servants is very hard, notwithstanding their indentures are made in *England,* wherein it is expressly stipulated, that they shall have, at their Arrival, all the Necessaries specified in those Indentures, to be given 'em by their future Masters, such as Clothes, Meat, and Drink; yet upon Complaint made to a Magistrate against the Master for Nonperformance, the Master is generally heard before the Servant, and it is ten to one if he does not get his Licks for his Pains, as I have experienced upon the like Occassion, to my Cost.

If they endeavor to escape, which is next to impossible, there being a Reward for taking up any Person who travels without a Pass, which is extended all over the *British* Colonies, their Masters immediately issue out a Reward for the apprehending them, from Thirty Shillings to Five Pound, as they think proper, and this generally brings them back again. Printed and Written Advertisements are also set up against the Trees and publick Places in the Town, besides those in the News-papers. Notwithstanding these Difficulties, they are perpetually running away, but seldom escape; for a hot Pursuit being made, brings them back, when a Justice settles the Expences, and the Servant is oblig'd to serve a longer time.

## REVIEW QUESTIONS

1. What was Moraley's relationship to his master?
2. What does Moraley reveal about living and working in an artisan household?
3. How did Moraley compare America to Great Britain? What did he see as positive points and what were some negative ones?
4. Discuss Moraley's analysis of slave and indentured servitude. How were they similar and how different? Did he believe the conditions of labor were changing? Consider what he revealed about himself as well as about the labor systems he saw and experienced.

NEWSPAPERS

# Ads for Runaway Servants and Slaves (1733–72)

*Both slavery and freedom thrived in colonial America. Desire for the latter meant that people constantly sought opportunities to escape the former. As the number of indentured servants and slaves rose, so too did the number of runaways. Many such runaways, or fugitives, were soon caught, or they voluntarily returned to their masters. If they did not do so, and if the owners believed the expense and effort (and indeed the servants or slaves) worthwhile, then they published advertisements in the provincial newspapers. These ads often provided physical descriptions of the runaways, accounts of what kind of work these laborers performed, and why their masters believed they ran away. Such observations can reveal much about the society and individuals, specifically about masters and servants, and about the differences in such working relationships over time and place.*

From Lathan A. Windley, comp., *Runaway Slave Advertisements: A Documentary History from the 1730s to 1790*. Volume 2: *Maryland* (Westport, Conn.: Greenwood Press, 1983), pp. 22–23, 26–27, 41–42, 93–94; and Volume 3: *South Carolina*, pp. 6–7, 81, 158–59, 220. Billy G. Smith and Richard Wojtowicz, eds., *Blacks Who Stole Themselves: Advertisements for Runaways in the Pennsylvania Gazette, 1728–1790* (Philadelphia: University of Pennsylvania Press, 1989), pp. 54–55. [Editorial insertions appear in brackets—*Ed.*]

## South-Carolina Gazette (Whitemarsh), April 28 to May 5, 1733.

Run away three Weeks ago, a Negro Man named Hampshire, belonging to Mrs. Elizabeth Bampfield. Whoever will bring the said Negro to his Mistress, shall have 40 s. Reward, and if taken out of the Town, any reasonable Charge as the Law allows. The aforesaid Negro is to be sold, as is another young Fellow named Stafford, who has been bred a Butcher, and a Negro Woman that is a very good Cook, Washer, and understanding any Sort of Houshold [*sic*] Work. Enquire of

Elizabeth Bampfield.

## South-Carolina Gazette (Whitemarsh), May 26 to June 2, 1733.

Run away the 14th of last month, a Mustee Wench, that may be taken for an Indian, about 20 Years of Age, speaks good English, and can do anything about House, as spinning, carding, needle-work &c. [S]he is a short, well sett, fat Wench, and may be taken to be a Free Wench, and has her Tongue at Pleasure, and her Back will shew the Marks of her former Misdeeds. Whoever will bring the said Wench to James Mackewn, at Stono, shall have 5 l. Reward.

## South-Carolina Gazette (Timothy), February 22 to February 29, 1748.

Run-away on the 20th Inst. from Silas Parvin, at Cobausey in New-Jersey, a very lusty Negro Man named Sampson, aged about 58 Years, and has some mixture of Indian Blood in him, he is Hip shot and goes very Lame. He has taken with him a Boy about 12 or 14 Years of Age named Sam, who was born of an Indian Woman, and looks much like an Indian only his Hair. They were both well Cloathed, only the Boy is barefoot, they have taken with them a gun and Ammunition, and two Ruggs. They both talk Indian very well, and it is likely have dress'd themselves in an Indian Dress, and gone towards Carolina. Whoever secures the said Slaves so that their Master may have them again, or delivers them to Thomas Shute in Charles-Town, shall have THIRTY POUNDS Reward, from the said Shute or Silas Parvin.

## Annapolis *Maryland Gazette*, March 20, 1755.

### Ten Pistoles Reward.

Kent County, Maryland, March 19, 1755.

WHEREAS there were several Advertisements, (some of which were printed, and others of the same Signification written), dispers'd through this

Province, describing, and offering a Reward of Two Pistoles, &c. for taking up a Servant Man, named James Francis, and a Mulatto Man Slave call'd Toby, both belonging to the Subscriber, and ran away on the 11th Instant: And whereas it has been discover'd since the Publishing of the said Advertisements, that they carried with them many more Things than is therein described, I do hereby again and farther give Notice, that the white Man, James Francis, is aged about 21 Years, his Stature near five Feet and an half, slender bodied, with a smooth Face, almost beardless, born in England, and bred a Farmer. The Mulatto is a lusty, well-set Country born Slave, with a great Nose, wide Nostrils, full mouth'd, many Pimples in his Face, very slow in Speech, he is a tolerable good Cooper and House-Carpenter, and no doubt will endeavour to pass for a Free-Man: Each hath a Felt Hat, Country Cloth Vest and Breeches, and Yarn Stockings; one of them has a light colour'd loose Coat of Whitney or Duffel: the white Man a dark close bodied Coat, a striped short Vest of Everlasting, another of blue Fearnothing, with other Cloaths. The Slave has also many other more valuable Garments; they took with them likewise a Gun, Powder and Shot, and are suppos'd either to cross, or go down the Bay in a Pettiauger.

Whoever brings the said Servant and Slave to the Subscriber on the Mouth of Chester River, or to Thomas Ringgold at Chester-Town, shall have for a Reward Ten Pistoles, and all reasonable Charges in taking and securing the said Servant and Slave, paid by

James Ringgold.

THAT this Slave shou'd ran away and attempt getting his Liberty, is very alarming, as he has been always too kindly used, if any Thing, by his Master, and one in whom his Master has put great Confidence, and depended on him to overlook the rest of his Slaves, and he had no kind of Provocation to go off. It seems to be the Interest, at least of every Gentleman that has Slaves, to be active in the beginning of these Attempts, for whilst we have the French such near Neighbours, we shall not have the least Security in that kind of Property. I should be greatly obliged to any Gentleman that shall hear of these Fellows, to endeavour to get certain Intelligence which Way they have taken, and to inform me of it by Express, and also to employ some active Person or Persons immediately to take their Track and pursue them and secure them, and I will thankfully acknowledge the Favour, and immediately answer the Expence attending it.

Thomas Ringgold.

## Annapolis *Maryland Gazette*, November 11, 1756.

RAN away on the 10th of October last, from the Subscriber, living near George-Town on Rock-Creek, in Frederick County, a Mulatto Woman Slave, named Kate, who formerly belonged to Mr. Benjamin Lane in Anne-Arundel County, and bought of him last June; she is a pert pallavering Wench, of a middle Size, about 30 Years old. She took with her a small Black Horse, branded on the near Buttock with a large S: And as she is pretty well dressed may sometimes pass for a free Woman where she is not known to be otherwise. It is supposed she is secreted by a Mulatto Slave called Jemmy (a Carpenter by Trade), belonging to Mr. Thomas Sprigg, on West-River, with the Assistance and Contrivance of some other Slaves in the neighbourhood where she was bought, who (it seems she has bragg'd) had promised to conceal her whenever she would run away from me. I understand she has been a great Rambler, and is well known in Calvert and Anne-Arundel Counties, besides other Parts of the Country. She may indulge herself a little in visiting her old Acquaintance; but it is most probable she will spend the greater Part of her Time with or near wherever the aforesaid Mulatto Slave of Mr. Sprigg's may be at Work.

Whoever brings the said Wench to the Subscriber, shall have Two Pistoles for their Trouble, besides a good Reward if they discover the Persons that harbour her, so that they may be brought to Justice.

HENRY THRELKELD.

## South-Carolina Gazette (Timothy), October 13, 1757.

RUN AWAY from the Subscriber, at Wando, a negro woman named KATE, about 32 years old, of a yellowish complexion, hollow jaw'd, a pouting look, all her upper fore-teeth gone, and speaks good English, formerly belong'd to Mrs. L'Escott, and afterwards to Paul Villepontoux, of whom she was purchased. She is well known in Charles-Town, and it's supposed has changed her name and is harboured there (as she formerly was for 23 months together); and 'tis probable she will get into some of the negro washing-houses or kitchens, to be employ'd in them, and say she belongs to Mr. Villepontoux aforesaid. She is 7 months gone with child; and carried with her, her son Billy (a squat well-set boy about 13 years of age, who is apt to stutter when spoke smartly to), and her daughter Alce [*sic?*] (a girl about 5 years old, with a mark in her forehead and another somewhere about her breast, occasioned by accidental burns, and silver drops in her ears. She will no doubt change her dress, but had on when she went away, a blue jacket (the sleeves scolloped) and petticoat. As this inhuman creature, when she went away, left myself extreme ill in one bed, her mistress in another, and two of my children, not one able to help the other, she must be conscious of some very atrocious crime: I therefore humbly request every friend and acquaintance I have, in town and country, to use their utmost endeavours, in taking and delivering the said wench and children to me, or to the warden of the work-house; hereby promising a reward of 10 l. for so doing, and 20 l. to whoever will prove where she is harboured or employed.

STEPHEN HARTLEY

## Annapolis *Maryland Gazette,* August 20, 1761.

### *Fairfax County (Virginia) August 11, 1761.*

RAN away from a Plantation of the Subscriber's, on Dogue-Run in Fairfax, on Sunday the 9th Instant, the following Negroes, viz.

Peres, 35 or 40 Years of Age, a well-set Fellow, of about 5 Feet 8 Inches high, yellowish Complexion, with a very full round Face, and full black Beard, his Speech is something slow and broken, but not in so great a Degree as to render him remarkable. He had on when he went away, a dark colour'd Cloth Coat, a white Linen Waist-coat, white Breeches and white Stockings.

Jack, 30 Years (or thereabouts) old, a slim, black, well made Fellow, of near 6 Feet high, a small Face, with Cuts down each Cheek, being his Country Marks, his Feet are large (or long) for he requires a great Shoe. The Clothing he went off in cannot be well ascertained, but it is thought in his common working Dress, such as Cotton Waistcoat (of which he had a new One) and Breeches, and Osnabrig Shirt.

Neptune, aged 25 or 30, well-set, and of about 5 Feet 8 or 9 Inches high, thin jaw'd, his Teeth stragling and fil'd sharp, his Back, if rightly remember'd, has many small Marks or Dots running from both Shoulders down to his Waistband, and his Head was close shaved: Had on a Cotton Waistcoat, black or dark colour'd Breeches, and an Osnabrig Shirt.

Cupid, 23 or 25 Years old, a black well made Fellow, 5 Feet 8 or 9 Inches high, round and full faced, with broad Teeth before, the Skin of his Face is coarse, and inclined to be pimpley, he has no other distinguishable Mark that can be recollected; he carried with him his common working Cloaths, and an old Osnabrigs Coat made Frockwise.

The two last of these Negroes were bought from an African Ship in August 1759, and talk very broken and unintelligible English; the second one, Jack, is Countryman to those, and speaks pretty good English, having been several Years in the Country. The other, Peres, speaks much better than either, indeed has little of his Country Dialect left, and is esteemed a sensible judicious Negro.

As they went off without the least Suspicion, Provocation, or Difference with any Body, or the least angry Word or Abuse from their Overseers, 'tis supposed they will hardly lurk about in the Neighbourhood, but steer some direct Course (which cannot even be guessed at) in Hopes of an

Escape: Or, perhaps, as the Negro Peres has lived many Years about Williamsburg, and King-William County, and Jack in Middlesex, they may possibly bend their Course to one of those Places.

Whoever apprehends the said Negroes, so that the Subscriber may readily get them, shall have, if taken up in this County, Forty Shillings Reward, beside what the Law allows; and if at any greater Distance, or out of the Colony, a proportionable Recompence paid them, by

GEORGE WASHINGTON.

## Pennsylvania Gazette, April 29, 1762

### New-York, Printing-Office, in Beaver-Street, April 17, 1762.

Run away, on Monday the 12th Instant, from the Subscriber, a Mulattoe Servant Man, named CHARLES, and known by the Name of CHARLES ROBERTS, or GERMAN. He is a likely well set Fellow, 28 or 30 Years of Age, about 5 Feet 6 Inches high, and has had the Small-Pox. He has a Variety of Clothes, some of them very good, affects to dress very neat and genteel, and generally wears a Wig. He took with him two or three Coats or Suits, viz. A dark brown, or Chocolate coloured Cloth Coat, pretty much worn; a dun, or Dove coloured Cloth, or fine Frize, but little worn; and a light blue grey Summer coat, of Grogram, Camblet, or some such Stuff; a Straw coloured Waistcoat, edged with a Silver Cord, almost new; and several other Waistcoats, Breeches, and Pairs of Stockings; a blue Great coat, and a Fiddle. His Behaviour is excessively complaisant, obsequious and insinuating; he speaks good English, smoothly and plausibly, and generally with a Cringe and a Smile; he is extremely artful, and ready at inventing specious Pretences to conceal villainous Actions or Designs. He plays on the Fiddle, can read and write tolerably well, and understands a little of Arithmetick and Accounts. I have Reason to believe some evil minded Persons in town have encouraged, and been Accomplices with him in villain-

ous Designs; and it is probable he will contrive the most specious Forgeries to give him the Appearance of being a Free Man: I have already been informed of a Writing he has shewn for that Purpose, by which he has imposed upon many People; who may all be easily satisfied that he has no legal Claim to Freedom, even from Slavery, nor any Pretence to it but by the very Law by which he is my Servant for 40 Years, as the Records of the Superior Court at New Haven will Witness. At that Place, where the former Owner of the said Slave lived, he was guilty of a Variety of Crimes and Felonies, for which he was several Times publickly whipped, and only escaped the Gallows by want of Prosecution. When he became my Servant, I intended to have shipped him to the West Indies, and sold him there; and kept him in Prison till I should get an Opportunity; but on his earnest Request, solemn Promises of his good Behaviour, and seeming Penitence, I took him into my Family upon Trial, where for some Time he behaved well, and was very serviceable to me. Deceived by his seeming Reformation, I placed some Confidence in him, which he has villainously abused; having embezzled Money sent by him to pay for Goods, borrowed Money, and taken up Goods in my Name unknown to me, and also on his own Account, pretending to be a Freeman. By this villainous Proceeding I suppose he has collected a considerable Sum of Money, and am also apprehensive that he has been an Accomplice in some of the late Robberies committed in and near this City. Whoever will take up the said Servant, and bring him to me, or secure him in some of His Majesty's Goals, so that I may get him again, if taken up in the City of New-York, shall have Five Pounds Reward, and a greater, if taken up at a greater Distance. Any Persons who take him up, are desired to be careful to carry him before the next Magistrate, and have him well searched, leaving all the Money and Goods found upon him, except the necessary Clothes he has on, in the Hands of the said Magistrate; and to be very watchful against an Escape, or being deceived by him, for he is one of the most artful of Villains.

JOHN HOLT.

## South-Carolina Gazette (Timothy), August 7 to August 14, 1762.

### Five Pounds Reward.

RUN away about 12 days ago, a negro girl named MARY, about 20 years old, well known in Charles-Town, and has been entertained in several houses at needle-work, &c. to whom she has past herself for free. Whoever will apprehend the said negro girl, and deliver her to the warden of the work-house, or to the subscriber, shall receive five pounds currency reward, besides all reasonable charges, and thirty pounds reward to any person who will inform me of her being harboured by a white person, on conviction of the offender, or five pounds to a negro: She has on a blue negro cloth habit, and a strip'd jacket under, with a coat of the same; she is artful and speaks good English, but fast, and stutters a little; by pretending to be free may endeavor to get on board some vessel, as she has a mother that lives at Winyah; or may make for John's or James-Island where she has a father and brother: She is said to have changed her name, and says she belongs to Mrs. Matthews. All persons are hereby forbid to carry off or har-bour the said slave, as they may depend on being prosecuted by

JOHN-PAUL GRIMKE.

N.B. If the said negro wench will return home, she shall be forgiven.

## Annapolis *Maryland Gazette*, July 16, 1772.

### Ten Pounds Reward.

July 6, 1772.

RAN away from the Subscribers, living near Soldiers Delight, in Baltimore County, Maryland, a dark Mulatto Slave, who goes by the Name of CHARLES HARDING, but formerly by the Name of DICK; about 30 Years of Age, 5 Feet 7 Inches high, large Nose, hollow eyed, low Forehead, has upwards of Forty Scars on his Head of different Sizes, well made, has a small Scar on the upper Part of his Nose on the left Side, a small Scar on the right Side his under Lip, close knee'd, his Shins bend forwards, some Scars on the small of his legs occasioned by wearing of irons, a large Scar on the Outside of his left Leg occasioned by a Burn, a Scar on one of his Thumbs, he has been unmercifully whipped from his Neck to his Knees, which he says was by his former Master, is a Carpenter and Joiner by Trade, and can paint, which he learned of Lewis Allmorn, of Nanceman County in Virginia, who sold him to Edward Voss, a Bricklayer by Trade, and worked in sundry Parts of Virginia, and when the said Slave ran away from him, lived in King and Queen County near Rapahannah, got by Water to Philadelphia, and from thence travelled through Lancaster and York Counties to Hanover-Town, and worked there about a Year, and from thence into Baltimore County near Baltimore-Town, where he continued, from about the Year 1765 to the Year 1772, as a free Man, and since he left his former Masters in Virginia, has learnt to read and write, and to play on the Violin; it is possible he may forge a Pass and change his Name, as he has done before: Took with him a Castor Hat, a Suit of white Russia Drab Cloaths, a blue Cloth Coat, red striped Jacket, a new redish brown Broad-Cloth Jacket much too large for him, new dark-ish coloured Cotton Velvet Breeches with large old fashioned Pocket Flaps, Shirts, Stockings and Shoes of different Sorts, and large plated Buckles. Whoever secures the above Slave in any jail, so that his Masters get him again, shall receive Five Pounds, and if 50 Miles from Home Seven Pounds Ten Shillings, and if 100 Miles the above Reward, and reasonable Charges if brought Home, paid by

SAMUEL OWINGS, jun.
ALEXANDER WELLS.

## REVIEW QUESTIONS

1. What kind of physical characteristics were mentioned in the ads? Why may these have been deemed significant enough to mention? What do they reveal about the composition of slave society?

2. What kind of work did the slaves noted in these ads perform? What does this indicate about the slave labor force?

3. Do these advertisements state or suggest why the slaves may have run away? What may have been some of these reasons?

4. What do the notices reveal about the masters who submitted them?

5. What do these pieces suggest about colonial-American slavery in general?

# 4 ❧ FROM COLONIES TO STATES

*English subjects at home and abroad gloried in the growth of the first British Empire. As succeeding monarchs, ministers, and members of Parliament tried to tighten imperial control, however, they faced challenges from colonists who began to hold different views on the form and function of the empire. These subjects, many who by the end of the seventeenth century were born in America, accepted that they were provincials within the empire, but they refused to accept that they had little power over legislation that directly affected their survival and prosperity. These provincials insisted vehemently, and at times violently, that the privileges they believed to have been granted them by English birth, charter, or previous colonial practices be recognized. They did not see themselves as revolutionaries in their recalcitrance: they were merely insisting that the power and liberties acquired by the people over time—from the Magna Carta through the English Revolution of 1649 to the Glorious Revolution of 1688—be applied to them as well.*

*Although diversions at home, such as civil war, regicide, and revolution, sometimes led the British ministry to neglect colonial affairs, the government did want the colonies bound to the empire by law as well as by culture. It established trade regulations, issued orders, and sent over officials and sometimes troops to secure its territories. Colonial wars, however, strained the sinews of empire as conflicts against native peoples and other European powers sometimes led to hostilities between different interest groups within the colonies as well as between colonists and mother country. The desires of an empire that wished to encourage trade with the Indians and minimize the expenses of security in the New World occasionally clashed with the expansionist wishes of the settlers.*

*Native tribes, England, France, and Spain all jockeyed for power and position in North America in a series of armed conflicts that culminated in what the colonists called the French and Indian War. Actions with the British army and having to acquiesce to the results of British diplomacy over the course of these wars began to make some colonists question the notion that colonial needs and British desires could always be met concurrently. Those questions increased after 1763. Then the questions led to protests and the protests to declarations.*

*James Otis, who was labeled an incendiary by Lieutenant Governor Thomas Hutchinson in 1766, was still praising the British government in 1764. He wrote, "I believe there is not one man in an hundred (except in Canada) who does not think himself under the best national civil constitution in the world. . . . Their affection and reverence for their mother country is unquestionable. They yield the most cheerful and ready obedience to her laws, particularly to the power of that august body the parliament of Great Britain, the supreme legislative of the kingdom and in dominions." The events of 1765 changed his mind. Insanity soon felled this early champion of colonists' rights, but others carried on the fight. And a fight it was, for not all of the colonists rejected the mother country.*

*Colonists resisted British policies for both materialistic and idealistic reasons. Initially their protests seemed to be grounded in economics, but in time constitutional issues (which were instrumental in the move to revolution) assumed greater importance. The colonists presented their grievances by way of petitions, boycotts, speeches, and ultimately spectacles, such as the Boston Tea Party in December 1773. By that time, and certainly after Parliament's punishing response, most colonists were taking a stand: some actively promoted rebellion, some advocated self-interested or disinterested neutrality, while others profusely professed loyalty to the king and his government.*

*By 1774 the initiative had clearly shifted from the imperial government to the colonies. Members of Parliament, responding to the growing dissent across the Atlantic, began to concentrate on coercive tactics to bring the colonists in line, while colonists debated the possibility of creating a new system of government within—or perhaps outside of—the British Empire. The radicals sent delegates to a continental congress, which in turn considered a plan of union, endorsed the Suffolk Resolves, and adopted a Declaration of American Rights along with the Continental Association. That declaration served as an ideological defense, while the association became an economic offense. The conflict continued to escalate. As the Pilgrims had removed themselves from the Church of England to escape the corruption they had perceived there, so by 1776 did some Americans propose to remove themselves from the perceived corruption of the British government. By that time, when provincials had to choose between rebellion or supporting the sovereignty of king and Parliament, many conservative colonists chose the latter course and then found themselves condemned as Tories while their opponents retained the name Whig, and later Patriot, for themselves.*

# JOHN LOCKE

## FROM *The Second Treatise on Civil Government* (1689)

*James II ascended the throne of England in 1685. His Catholicism, among other things, made him unpopular from the start, but his harsh actions against the first rebels who tried to unseat him and his moves against Protestantism, in addition to his filling Parliament with loyal Tories and his scheming with the French monarch, led to outright revolt. In the Glorious Revolution of 1688, Parliament deposed the hated king and invited William of Orange, the husband of James's daughter Mary, to lead forces against him. James fled England, and Parliament then declared William and Mary to be king and queen. This established Parliamentary supremacy within a constitutional monarchy. Colonists added to the Glorious Revolution by challenging royal and proprietary control in New England, New York, and Maryland.*

*The English philosopher John Locke (1632–1704), a supporter of the Glorious Revolution, had probably been at work on his two treatises of government well before the revolution, and the ideas he expresses in them had certainly been debated before he so clearly articulated his arguments. In his first treatise on civil government, Locke attacked the divine right of kings. In his second treatise, the one excerpted here, he promulgated the idea that government rests in the will of the people; thus, those people have the right to challenge and change their rulers and government. The colonists readily accepted this notion, but it was a later generation of provincials who applied this concept in another great revolution.*

From *The Second Treatise of Civil Government*, edited by John W. Gough (Oxford: Basil Blackwell, 1946), pp. 4, 15, 48–50, 66–72, 107–09, 118–19.

## Of the State of Nature

To understand political power aright, and derive it from its original, we must consider what estate all men are naturally in, and that is, a state of perfect freedom to order their actions, and dispose of their possessions and persons as they think fit, within the bounds of the law of Nature, without asking leave or depending upon the will of any other man.

A state also of equality, wherein all the power and jurisdiction, is reciprocal, no one having more than another, there being nothing more evident than that creatures of the same species and rank, promiscuously born to all the same advantages of Nature, and the use of the same faculties, should also be equal one amongst another, without subordination or subjection, unless the lord and master of them all should, by any manifest declaration of his will, set one above another, and confer on him, by an evident and clear appointment, an undoubted right to dominion and sovereignty. . . .

## Of Property

\*   \*   \*

God, who hath given the world to men in common, hath also given them reason to make use of it to the best advantage of life and convenience. The earth and all that is therein is given to men for the support and comfort of their being. And though all the fruits it naturally produces, and beasts it feeds, belong to mankind in common, as they are produced by the spontaneous hand of Nature, and nobody has originally a private dominion exclusive of the rest of mankind in any of them, as they are thus in their natural state, yet being given for the use of men, there must of necessity be a means to appropriate them some way or other before they can be of any use, or at all beneficial, to any particular men. The fruit or venison which nourishes the wild Indian, who knows no enclosure, and is still a tenant in common, must be his, and so his—i.e., a part of him, that another can no longer have any right to it before it can do him any good for the support of his life.

Though the earth and all inferior creatures be common to all men, yet every man has a "property" in his own "person." This nobody has any right to but himself. The "labor" of his body and the "work" of his hands, we may say, are properly his. Whatsoever, then, he removes out of the state that Nature hath provided and left it in, he hath mixed his labor with it, and joined to it something that is his own, and thereby makes it his property. It being by him removed from the common state Nature placed it in, it hath by this labor something annexed to it that excludes the common right of other men. For this "labor" being the unquestionable property of the laborer, no man but he can have a right to what that is once joined to, at least where there is enough, and as good left in common for others. . . .

# Of the Beginning of Political Societies

Men being, as has been said, by nature all free, equal, and independent, no one can be put out of this estate and subjected to the political power of another without his own consent, which is done by agreeing with other men, to join and unite a community for their comfortable, safe, and peaceable living, one amongst another, in a secure enjoyment of their properties, and a greater security against any that are not of it. This any number of men may

do, because it injures not the freedom of the rest; they are left, as they were, in the liberty of the state of Nature. When any number of men have so consented to make one community or government, they are thereby presently incorporated, and make one body politic, wherein the majority have a right to act and conclude the rest.

For, when any number of men have, by the consent of every individual, made a community, they have thereby made that community one body, with a power to act as one body, which is only by the will and determination of the majority. . . .

And thus every man, by consenting with others to make one body politic under one government, puts himself under an obligation to everyone of that society to submit to the determination of the majority, and to be concluded by it; or else this original compact, whereby he with others incorporates into one society, would signify nothing, and be no compact if he be left free and under no other ties than he was in before in the state of Nature. . . .

Whosoever, therefore, out of a state of Nature unite into a community, must be understood to give up all the power necessary to the ends for which they unite into society to the majority of the community, unless they expressly agreed in any number greater than the majority. And this is done by barely agreeing to unite into one political society, which is all the compact that is, or needs be, between the individuals that enter into or make up a commonwealth. And thus, that which begins and actually constitutes any political society is nothing but the consent of any number of freemen capable of majority, to unite and incorporate into such a society. And this is that, and that only, which did or could give beginning to any lawful government in the world. . . .

# Of the Extent of the Legislative Power

The great end of men's entering into society being the enjoyment of their properties in peace and safety, and the great instrument and means of that being the laws established in that society, the first and fundamental positive law of all common-wealths is the establishing of the legislative power, as the first and fundamental natural law which is to govern even the legislative. Itself is the preservation of the society and (as far as will consist with the public good) of every person in it. This legislative is not only the supreme power of the commonwealth, but sacred and unalterable in the hands where the community have once placed it. Nor can any edict of anybody else, in what form soever conceived, or by what power soever backed, have the force and obligation of a law which has not its sanction from that legislative which the public has chosen and appointed; for without this the law could not have that which is absolutely necessary to its being a law, the consent of the society, over whom nobody can have a power to make laws but by their own consent and by authority received from them; and therefore all the obedience, which by the most solemn ties anyone can be obliged to pay, ultimately terminates in this supreme power, and is directed by those laws which it enacts. Nor can any oaths to any foreign power whatsoever, or any domestic subordinate power, discharge any member of the society from his obedience to the legislative, acting pursuant to their trust, nor oblige him to any obedience contrary to the laws so enacted or farther than they do allow, it being ridiculous to imagine one can be tied ultimately to obey any power in the society which is not the supreme.

Though the legislative, whether placed in one or more, whether it be always in being or only by intervals, though it be the supreme power in every commonwealth, yet, first, it is not, nor can possibly be, absolutely arbitrary over the lives and fortunes of the people. For it being but the joint power of every member of the society given up to that person or assembly which is legislator, it can be no more than those persons had in a state of Nature before they entered into society, and gave it up to the community. For nobody can transfer to another more power than he has in himself, and nobody has an absolute arbitrary power over himself, or over any other, to destroy his own life, or take away the life or property of another. A man, as has

been proved, cannot subject himself to the arbitrary power of another; and having, in the state of Nature, no arbitrary power over the life, liberty, or possession of another, but only so much as the law of Nature gave him for the preservation of himself and the rest of mankind, this is all he does, or can give up to the commonwealth, and by it to the legislative power, so that the legislative can have no more than this. Their power in the utmost bounds of it is limited to the public good of the society. It is a power that has no other end but preservation, and therefore can never have a right to destroy, enslave, or designedly to impoverish the subjects; the obligations of the law of Nature cease not in society, but only in many cases are drawn closer, and have, by human laws, known penalties annexed to them to enforce their observation. Thus the law of Nature stands as an eternal rule to all men, legislators as well as others. The rules that they make for other mens' actions must, as well as their own and other men's actions, be comfortable to the law of Nature—i.e., to the will of God, of which that is a declaration, and the fundamental law of Nature being the preservation of mankind, no human sanction can be good or valid against it.

Secondly, the legislative or supreme authority cannot assume to itself a power to rule by extemporary arbitrary decrees, but is bound to dispense justice and decide the rights of the subject by promulgated standing laws, and known authorized judges. For the law of Nature being unwritten, and so nowhere to be found but in the minds of men, they who, through passion or interest, shall miscite or misapply it, cannot so easily be convinced of their mistake where there is no established judge; and so it serves not as it ought, to determine the rights and fence the properties of those that live under it, especially where everyone is judge, interpreter, and executioner of it too, and that in his own case; and he that has right on his side, having ordinarily but his own single strength, hath not force enough to defend himself from injuries or punish delinquents. To avoid these inconveniences which disorder men's properties in the state of Nature, men unite into societies that they may have the united strength of the whole society to secure and defend their properties, and may have standing rules to bound it by which everyone may know what is his. To this end it is that men give up all their natural power to the society they enter into, and the community put the legislative power into such hands as they think fit, with this trust, that they shall be governed by declared laws, or else their peace, quiet, and property will still be at the same uncertainty as it was in the state of Nature.

Absolute arbitrary power, or governing without settled standing laws, can neither of them consist with the ends of society and government, which men would not quit the freedom of the state of Nature for, and tie themselves up under, were it not to preserve their lives, liberties, and fortunes, and by stated rules of right and property to secure their peace and quiet. It cannot be supposed that they should intend, had they a power so to do, to give anyone or more an absolute arbitrary power over their persons and estates, and put a force into the magistrate's hand to execute his unlimited will arbitrarily upon them; this were to put themselves into a worse condition than the state of Nature, wherein they had a liberty to defend their right against the injuries of others, and were upon equal terms of force to maintain it, whether invaded by a single man or many in combination. . . . And, therefore, whatever form the commonwealth is under, the ruling power ought to govern by declared and received laws, and not by extemporary dictates and undetermined resolutions, for then mankind will be in a far worse condition than in the state of Nature if they shall have armed one or a few men with the joint power of a multitude, to force them to obey at pleasure the exorbitant and unlimited decrees of their sudden thoughts, or unrestrained, and till that moment, unknown wills, without having any measures set down which may guide and justify their actions. For all the power the government has, being only for the good of the society, as it ought not to be arbitrary and at pleasure, so it ought to be exercised by established and promulgated laws, that both the people may know their duty, and be safe and secure within the limits of the law, and the rulers, too, kept within their due

bounds, and not be tempted by the power they have in their hands to employ it to purposes, and by such measures as they would not have known, and own not willingly.

Thirdly, the supreme power cannot take from any man any part of his property without his own consent. For the preservation of property being the end of government, and that for which men enter into society, it necessarily supposes and requires that the people should have property, without which they must be supposed to lose that by entering into society which was the end for which they entered into it; too gross an absurdity for any man to own. Men, therefore, in society having property, they have such a right to the goods, which by the law of the community are theirs, that nobody has a right to take them, or any part of them, from them without their own consent; without this they have no property at all. . . . Hence it is a mistake to think that the supreme or legislative power of any commonwealth can do what it will, and dispose of the estates of the subject arbitrarily, or take any part of them at pleasure. This is not much to be feared in governments where the legislative consists wholly or in part in assemblies which are variable, whose members upon the dissolution of the assembly are subjects under the common laws of their country, equally with the rest. But in governments where the legislative is in one lasting assembly, always in being, or in one man as in absolute monarchies, there is danger still, that they will think themselves to have a distinct interest from the rest of the community, and so will be apt to increase their own riches and power by taking what they think fit from the people. For a man's property is not at all secure, though there be good and equitable laws to set the bounds of it between him and his fellow-subjects, if he who commands those subjects have power to take from any private man what part he pleases of his property, and use and dispose of it as he thinks good.

*    *    *

It is true governments cannot be supported without great charge, and it is fit everyone who enjoys his share of the protection should pay out of his estate his proportion for the maintenance of it. But still it must be with his own consent—i.e., the consent of the majority, giving it either by themselves or their representatives chosen by them; for if anyone shall claim a power to lay and levy taxes on the people by his own authority, and without such consent of the people, he thereby invades the fundamental law of property, and subverts the end of government. For what property have I in that which another may by right take when he pleases to himself?

Fourthly, the legislative cannot transfer the power of making laws to any other hands, for it being but a delegated power from the people, they who have it cannot pass it over to others. The people alone can appoint the form of the commonwealth, which is by constituting the legislative, and appointing in whose hands that shall be. And when the people have said, "We will submit, and be governed by laws made by such men, and in such forms," nobody else can say other men shall make laws for them; nor can they be bound by any laws but such as are enacted by those whom they have chosen and authorized to make laws for them.

These are the bounds which the trust that is put in them by the society and the law of God and Nature have set to the legislative power of every commonwealth, in all forms of government. First, they are to govern by promulgated established laws, not to be varied in particular cases, but to have one rule for rich and poor, for the favorite at Court, and the countryman at plow. Secondly, these laws also ought to be designed for no other end ultimately but the good of the people. Thirdly, they must not raise taxes on the property of the people without the consent of the people given by themselves or their deputies. And this properly concerns only such governments where the legislative is always in being, or at least where the people have not reserved any part of the legislative to deputies, to be from time to time chosen by themselves. Fourthly, legislative neither must nor can transfer the power of making laws to anybody else, or place it anywhere but where the people have.

# Of the Dissolution of Government

\*     \*     \*

The reason why men enter into society is the preservation of their property; and the end while they choose and authorize a legislative is that there may be laws made, and rules set, as guards and fences to the properties of all the society, to limit the power and moderate the dominion of every part and member of the society. For since it can never be supposed to be the will of the society that the legislative should have a power to destroy that which everyone designs to secure by entering into society, and for which the people submitted themselves to legislators of their own making: whenever the legislators endeavor to take away and destroy the property of the people, or to reduce them to slavery under arbitrary power, they put themselves into a state of war with the people, who are thereupon absolved from any farther obedience, and are left to the common refuge which God hath provided for all men against force and violence. Whensoever, therefore, the legislative shall transgress this fundamental rule of society, and either by ambition, fear, folly, or corruption, endeavor to grasp themselves, or put into the hands of any other, an absolute power over the lives, liberties, and estates of the people, by this breach of trust they forfeit the power the people had put into their hands for quite contrary ends, and it devolves to the people, who have a right to resume their original liberty, and by the establishment of a new legislative (such as they shall think fit), provide for their own safety and security, which is the end for which they are in society.

What I have said here concerning the legislative in general holds true also concerning the supreme executor, who having a double trust put in him, both to have a part in the legislative and the supreme execution of the law, acts against both, when he goes about to set up his own arbitrary will as the law of the society. He acts also contrary to his trust when he employs the force, treasure, and offices of the society to corrupt the representatives and gain them to his purposes, when he openly pre-engages the electors, and prescribes, to their choice, such whom he has, by solicitation, threats, promises, or otherwise, won to his designs, and employs them to bring in such who have promised beforehand what to vote and what to enact. Thus to regulate candidates and electors, and new model the ways of election, what is it but to cut up the government by the roots, and poison the very fountain of public security? For the people having reserved to themselves the choice of their representatives as the fence to their properties, could do it for no other end but that they might always be freely chosen, and so chosen, freely act and advise as the necessity of the commonwealth and the public good should, upon examination and mature debate, be judged to require. This, those who give their votes before they hear the debate, and have weighed the reasons on all sides, are not capable of doing. To prepare such an assembly as this, and endeavor to set up the declared abettors of his own will, for the true representatives of the people, and the law-makers of the society, is certainly as great a breach of trust, and as perfect a declaration of a design to subvert the government, as is possible to be met with. To which, if one shall add rewards and punishments visibly employed to the same end, and all the arts of perverted law made use of to take off and destroy all that stand in the way of such a design, and will not comply and consent to betray the liberties of their country, it will be past doubt what is doing. . . .

Here it is like the common question will be made: Who shall be judge whether the prince or legislative act contrary to their trust? This, perhaps, ill-affected and factious men may spread amongst the people, when the prince only makes use of his due prerogative. To this I reply, The people shall be judge; for who shall be judge whether his trustee or deputy acts well and according to the trust reposed in him, but he who deputes him and must, by having deputed him, have still a power to discard him when he fails in his trust? If this be reasonable in particular cases of private men, why should it be otherwise in that of the greatest moment, where the welfare of millions is concerned and also where the evil, if not prevented, is greater, and the redress very difficult, dear, and dangerous?

But, farther, this question, Who shall be judge? cannot mean that there is no judge at all. For where there is no judicature on earth to decide controversies amongst men, God in heaven is judge. He alone, it is true, is judge of the right. But every man is judge for himself, as in all other cases so in this, . . .

If a controversy arise betwixt a prince and some of the people in a matter where the law is silent or doubtful, and the thing be of great consequence, I should think the proper umpire in such a case should be the body of the people. For in such cases where the prince hath a trust reposed in him, and is dispensed from the common, ordinary rules of the law, there, if any men find themselves aggrieved, and think the prince acts contrary to, or beyond that trust, who so proper to judge as the body of the people (who at first lodged that trust in him) how far they meant it should extend? But if the prince, or whoever they be in the administration, decline that way of determination, the appeal then lies nowhere but to Heaven. Force between either persons who have no known superior on earth, or which permits no appeal to a judge on earth, being properly a state of war, wherein the appeal lies only to Heaven; and in that state the injured party must judge for himself when he will think fit to make use of that appeal and put himself upon it.

To conclude. The power that every individual gave the society when he entered into it can never revert to the individuals again, as long as the society lasts, but will always remain in the community; because without this there can be no community—no commonwealth, which is contrary to the original agreement; so also when the society hath placed the legislative in any assembly of men, to continue in them and their successors, with direction and authority for providing such successors, the legislative can never revert to the people whilst that government lasts; because, having provided a legislative with power to continue forever, they have given up their political power to the legislative, and cannot resume it. But if they have set limits to the duration of their legislative, and made this supreme power in any person or assembly only temporary; or else when, by the miscarriages of those in authority, it is forfeited; upon the forfeiture of their rulers, or at the determination of the time set, it reverts to the society, and the people have a right to act as supreme, and continue the legislative in themselves or place it in a new form, or new hands, as they think good.

## REVIEW QUESTIONS

1. According to Locke, what is accorded all humans in a state of nature?

2. Why or how is property a basis for political society?

3. When people in a state of nature unite to form a political society, is creation an act of consensus or conflict?

4. If such a society rests on majority rule, then what kind of government is established? What are the limits of this government?

5. What are legitimate reasons for dissolving a government?

6. How do some of Locke's ideas compare to what Penn established in his *Frame of Government* (see Chapter 2)?

# WILLIAM BYRD II

# Representation of Mr. Byrd Concerning Proprietary Governments (1699)

*William Byrd II (1674–1744) was born in Virginia and educated in England. A prominent plantation owner, he served in the colony's government, both in its House of Burgesses and then in its council. He also represented his colony's interests as an agent in London between 1697 and 1704. During that time he corresponded with his father, William Byrd, and brother-in-law, Robert Beverley, both of whom were concerned about the powers of governors and proprietors, intercolonial relations, Indian affairs, the preservation of property, and the pursuit of prosperity. William Byrd the younger presented the concerns they shared with other planters to the Board of Trade. The following document is a draft of a memorial that was, or was to be, presented to the board to get it to make some reforms in the colonial system.*

"Representation of Mr. Byrd Concerning Propriety Governments," from Louis B. Wright, ed., *An Essay Upon the Government of the English Plantations on the Continent of America,* pp. 58–63. Reprinted with the permission of the Henry E. Huntington Library. [Editorial insertions appear in squared brackets—*Ed.*]

Every one I believe is convinc'd of the great Importance that some of the American Plantations are to the Kingdom of England; how much they improve our Trade, advance our Manufactures, multiply our Seamen, promote our Navigation, employ our Poor, and help to ballance our

Trade with other Countrys, which wou'd otherwise Draw away our mony and by that means prey upon our Vitals By these means they abundantly Compensate for the multitude of People they have drain'd from hence, which England cou'd ill part with but upon the Termes of their being more usefull abroad, than they would be at home.

Now it is demonstrable that in Virginia, Maryland, Jamaica, Barbados, and the Leward Ilands, every Single Hand finds employment for two People in England, by the Effects they send over. And it is much to be lamented that the other English Colonys in America are not made more beneficial than they have hitherto proved. New England indeed affords some fine masts for the Kings Navy, but I believe if right measures were taken, all sorts of navel Stores might be produc'd there. New York subsists principally by the Plantation Trade, haveing no staple Commodity of its own, whereas Pitch, Tar, Rosin, Hemp, and Flax, might be there easily propagated. The People of East and West Jerzey have very little Trade, unless it be to the West India Islands, but live for the most part upon the product of their own Country. Pensilvania has little Trade with England but pretty much with the West Indies, and are not precize in Consulting what Trade is lawfull, and what is not. In the lower parts of this Country they make one year with another about Fifteen hundred hogsheads of Tobacco, which they seldome send over hither. And then for Carolina so much Celebrated by the Flying Post, it is pretty notorious, that neither Gospell, acts of Parliament nor the Interest of England are ever Consulted there, and the Chief of their Traffique is with Surinam, Curassow [Dutch colonies; the first was in South America and the latter, Curaçao was in the West Indies] and their old friends the Pyrates. And the truth of it is, none of the Propriety governments are at all scrupulous in these matters. The Acts of Navigation are of no force in those Countrys and the Governors want either honesty or power to put them in execution. For which reason tis high time these Governments were reduc'd under a better administration.

I would not be understood to be of opinion, that any Particular Persons should be wrong'd in their Propriety, as long as they keep to the Conditions upon which they are granted, but if they will keep to no Terms, nor observe any laws, but run counter to the Interest of the Crown under which they claime, there is all the reason in the world, that His Majesty should appoint such Governors as may have authority to put the Laws in execution, and to take care of promoteing the advantages of England. And I am humbly of opinion, that all the Propriety Governments shou'd be put under the Kings Direction and that for these severall Reasons.

1. Because they have made an ill use of His Majestys grant, by their frequent harbouring of Pyrates, by their recieveing and furnishing them with Provisions and other necessarys, by which they have supported 'em in the Carrying on of their Villany. By all the Laws in the world those People that recieve, assist, and encourage Rogues, make themselves Accessary to the Crimes they Committ, for without such Recievers and Abettors, it were impossible for those Free booters to subsist. Every one knows what Enimys to Mankind Pyrates are, how much they interrupt and discourage Trade how many outrages of all kind they are guilty of, how they corrupt and intice away our Seamen, and Draw them off from the service of the Nation to be the most Dangerous Enimys it has; how often their hands reak with innocent bloud, and how many other barbaritys Concur to make them the most profligate Wretches under Heaven. And since this is their just Character, tis easy to Concieve, how Criminal it is to entertain and encourage them.

Now when Governments connive at these crimes, and maintain and abet those that commit them, may they not be justly accounted the cause that those outlaws are so much encreas'd, and is not this then an offence heinous enough to forfeit the Priviledge of appointing Governors, and to devolve that Right to the King who woud appoint such Governors as might restrain this growing Evil. When his Majesty grants a Charter to any of his Subjects there is always this Condition imply'd, that neither the Grantee nor his Assigns shall by means of such grant, commit any thing against his Crown and Dignity, or to the Prejudice of his other good subjects; and nobody can deny but that Pyracy and all sorts of aiding and assisting of it is the highest breach of that Condition: and that all Governments now in Proprietors hands, have often offended in these respects, every body must acknowledge that knows any thing of those Countrys, And Consequently there is all the Reason in the world that his Majesty shou'd take all those Governments into his own hands, to put some stop to a Mischief, that will otherwise prove the ruine of the west India-Trade.

2. They have abus'd his Majestys grant by permitting and maintaining of illegal Trade, to the great prejudice of England, and in Contempt of all the Acts of Parliament made against it. It is to the disadvantage of England because they supply themselves with a great many goods from Suranam and Curassow for which otherwise they must be beholden to England and in return for these goods, they send to those Dutch Colonys, several of their Productions, for which they coud find no Market any where else, and for that reason were it not for this unlawfull Trade, they woud be forc't to apply themselves to something or other, that might be for the Interest of their Mother-Country.

All the Acts of Navigation, and other Statutes against these lawless Practices, are of no Effect in these Proprietys and the Governors and naval offices are either brib'd or forct into a Connivance. Now in this particular the People of Carolina have been the most enormous, where if by Chance any of their Governors have had the courage to examine into this matter with more Curiosity than their Predecessors, they have been either clappt up into the Logg-house, or else forc't to run for their lives, and save themselves in some of the Roiall-Governments. A Governor has very little authority amongst 'em, as being onely the Deputy of their fellow Subjects, and therefore they think themselves under no hazard in disobeying either Him or the laws of their mother country. By this means People do what seems good in their eys, and are in a fair way of shakeing off their Dependance upon England. Nay to break all the laws made to kirb them by the authority of King and Parliament, is a

virtual throwing of their Dependance, for that Country can't be said to depend upon another, that refuses to pay obedience to its laws: Now nothing is more Notorious than that all the Proprietys more or less have been Criminal in this particular, as appears amongst a great many other Proofes, by the multitude of Dutch Wares that are seen in all those Countrys; And therefore tis high time to reduce those Governments into the Kings hands and by that means to purge their foul Trade and bring 'em back to their obedience.

3. These governments, as they are now order'd, do greatly encourage offences of every kind in the more usefull Plantations. They entice Servants to run away from their Masters, in the neighbour Colonys, by refuseing to give them up to their right owners, by which they both deprive the master of the Servants that run away, and spoil those that stay behind to the great Discouragement of Industry. They receive with open arms all such Malefactors as fly to them, and so, cover them from Justice. For the business of Proprietors is to get People, and they are not over Scrupulous in the manner of procureing them. This encourages men to commit several Crimes, which they woud not Dare to do, unless they could rely upon this Sanctuary. If such Malefactors can but escape from Virginia to Carolina; to Pensilvania from Maryland (which tho a Propriety is now brought under the Kings Government) to the Jerseys from New York, or New England they are sure of protection, tho their offences have been never so great. This if duely consider'd is a Mischief of fatal Consequence for it drains away People from those Colonys, where their Labour is profitable to England, and removes them to such Countrys, as by their wrong management are rather a Detriment to England than an advantage, which is another argument why these governments ought to be brought under the Kings Direction.

4. These colonys as they stand now in the hands of Proprietors, are several ways hurtfull to England for all the People that flock thither from hence, and all those that are tempted from the other Plantations, are truly, a dead loss to this Nation. And as a

great many People have removd Considerable Estates to those Countrys, so what ever they carryd away has been another article of loss to England, because that mony has not been employd upon the produceing any Commodity to be sent home but upon Provisions for their own Subsistance, and to supply some foreign Plantations. And all this proves no benefit to us but rather an Injury, by supplying those Countrys with such necessarys as otherwise they might be obligd to have from hence. So that what they've hitherto betaken themselves to, dos not make amends for our loss of People, that have remov'd themselves to those Parts. Whereas if the King had those governments in his own hands, and shoud send over Governors able and zealous for the good of their Country, there is no doubt but they might first Correct all the abuses of Trade, and then lead the People into such Manufactures as might be improvd to the benefit of England.

5. Another reason for vesting the Propriety governments in the King, and which imports the Interest of England very nearly, is, for that the French Power has been sufferd to encrease very much upon that Continent, and to extend it self a great way along the back of our Plantations, And we have lately reciev'd the unwelcome news, that the French are in a fair way of drawing the five nations, the most powerfull of all the Indians into their Interest. This it must be Confesst, has been brought about, either by very great artifice on the French side, or by great negligence on ours. But be it how it will, it is certain, that this puts it in the Power of the French to annoy us extreamly in case of a war. They omit no opportunity of enlargeing their Power, and no care or encouragement is wanting to make them grow stronger, while we use no precautions to traverse their designs, or to put our Colonys in Condition to oppose them. This Diligence on their Side, and Security on ours, may in a Little time grow very Dangerous to our Interest there. Which Consideration ought to alarm and make us Carefull to put those Plantations into the best Condition of Defence we can, which I am sure is quite impracticable in the Propriety-governments. For there is too little Discipline, and too great a Contempt of Governors ever to have the best measures taken for their defence.

In Pensilvania the Quakers under the management of mr. Pen can't find in their Conscience to gird on the Carnal Sword, so that they are very Liable to become a Prey to any Invader, and New Jerzey by reason of the multitude of Quakers is pretty near in the same Condition. Carolina is as Defenceless as either of the Countrys before mentiond, tho not from the same tenderness of Conscience, but from the Confusion of their Government. Their Governors have no Command, as being without the Roiall authority, and therefore all is anarchy and Confusion. So that under these wretched Circumstances, there is no Likelihood to make those Countrys Capable of repulsing any Enimy, that shall please to attaque them. For this Reason tis highly necessary that His Majesty should take back these Governments into his own Hands, and Constitute such Governors over them, as may be best able to put them in a good posture of defence, that so they may no longer lye at the mercy of our Enimys.

These Reasons are I hope sufficient to Convince any Person that is impartial, how necessary it now is that these Proprietys should no longer have the Priviledge of appointing their own Governors. And tho it shoud be objected, (which seems very improbable) that all the unlawfull Practices mentioned before, are not sufficient to occasion a forfeiture of the whole Grants, yet at least it might be allow'd that the Proprietors ought to be forejudgd of that part, that relates to the Goverment. Neither will that be any great Prejudice to the Proprietors, for notwithstanding the Government be adjudgd to the King yet that dos not hinder, but they may have the Quit Rents, as the Lord Baltimore has now from Maryland. And tho there was no cause of forfeiture at all, yet the safety of those Countrys dos at this juncture absolutely require, that his Majesty shoud Constitute Governors over them, who may have authority to execute his Laws and take care of the defence of his People.

## REVIEW QUESTIONS

1. How do the American colonies contribute to the English empire?
2. In what ways does Byrd think colonial production could be increased and the economic connection between mother country and colonies strengthened?
3. What are his complaints about the proprietary governments? Why does he believe the settlements should be made royal colonies and brought more directly under the king's control?
4. Do you suppose his being a Virginian played a part in his complaints and suggestions?
5. What does this document reveal about the intercolonial relations?
6. How does Byrd interpret the respective powers and duties of colonial governments versus those of the English government? How does his interpretation compare to the thoughts of the Massachusetts men who opposed Andros and the Maryland Associators who protested their proprietorship?

# THE ALBANY CONGRESS

## FROM *The Albany Plan of Union* (1754)

*Throughout the colonial period British settlers, French colonists, and Native Americans were constantly in conflict with each other as they tried to expand and/or secure their territories. Advances spurred attacks that sometimes led to war. In many cases this border warfare was limited by the time, territory, and people involved. In 1754, however, a border skirmish near the Forks of the Ohio escalated into what the British colonists called the French and Indian War. Lieutenant Colonel George Washington's Virginia troops and Indian allies attacked a French detachment on 28 May. French forces then issued out from Fort Duquesne to return the favor—defeating Washington at Fort Necessity on 4 July. While Virginia conducted that military venture, delegates from seven northern colonies met at Albany, New York, to consult on defense matters and reestablish friendly relations with the Iroquois. They managed the latter to a limited degree by 9 July. The former became more complicated when the delegates decided to create a plan of union for all the colonies to ensure better common defenses and to secure the frontier as they expanded. Benjamin Franklin had advocated such a union, and it was primarily from his plan that the delegates chose to work (though they did incorporate ideas from other plans submitted). The final product was ultimately ignored or rejected by the imperial and colonial governments, but it served as an example and basis for later plans of union.*

From "The Albany Plan of the Union," *Roots of the Republic: American Founding Documents Interpreted*, Stephen L. Schechter, ed. (Madison, WI: Madison House Publishers, 1990) pp. 114–17. Used by permission. [Editorial insertions that appear in brackets are from Schechter—*Ed.*]

Plan of a proposed Union of the Several Colonies of Massachusetts Bay, New Hamphire, Connecticut, Rhode Island, New York, New Jersey, Pensil-vania, Maryland, North Carolina, and South Carolina, for their mutual defence & Security & for the Extending the British Settlements in North America.

That humble application be made for an act of the Parliament of Great Britain by virtue of which one General Government may be formed in America including all the said Colonies within & under which Government each Colony may retain it present constitution except in the Perticulars wherein a Change may be directed by the said act as Hereafter follows.—

That the said General Government be administered by a President General to be appointed & supported by the Crown, & a Grand Council to be chosen by the Representatives of the People of the several Colonies met in their respective Assemblies.

That within ——— Months after the passing of such act, the House of Representatives in the several Assemblies that happens to be sitting within that time or that shall be exspecially for that purpose convened may & Shall chuse Members for the Grand Council in the following proportions that is to say.

| Massachusetts Bay | 7 |
|---|---|
| New Hampshire | 2 |
| Connecticut | 5 |
| Rhode Island | 2 |
| New York | 4 |
| New Jersey | 3 |
| Pensilvania | 6 |
| Maryland | 4 |
| Virginia | 7 |
| North Carolina | 4 |
| South Carolina | 4 |
| | 48 |

Who shall meet for the first time at the City of Philadelphia in Pensilvania being called by the President General as soon as conveniently may be after his Appointment.

That there shall be a new Election of members for the Grand Council every three Years, & on the Death or resignation of any Member, his place shall be Supplyed by a new choice at the next sitting of the Assembly of the Colony he represented.

That after the first three years when the proportion of Money arising out of each Colony, to the General Treasury can be known, the Number of Members to be chosen for each Colony shall from time to time in all Ensuing Elections be regulated by that proportion yet so as that the Number to be chosen by any one Province be not more than Seven nor less than two.

That the Grand Council shall meet once in every year and oftener if occasion require at such time & place as they shall adjourn to at the last preceding meeting or as they shall be called to meet at by the President General on any Emergency he having first obtained in Writing the consent of Seven of the Members to such Call, & sent due & timely notice to the whole.

That the Grand Council have power to chuse their Speaker & shall neither be dissolved, prorogued, nor continue Sitting longer than Six Weeks at one time, without the[ir] own consent or the Special Command of the Crown.

That the Members of the Grand Council shall be allowed for their Service ten Shillings Sterling per diem during their Sessions and Journey to & from the place of meeting; twenty Miles to be reckoned a Days Journey.

That the assent of the President General be requisite to all Acts of the Grand Council, & that it be his Office & duty to cause them to be Carried into Execution.

That the President General with the advice of the Grand Council hold or direct all Indian Treaties in which the General Interest or Welfare of the Colonies may be concerned, & to make Peace or declare War with Indian Nations. That they make such Laws as they judge necessary for regulating all Indian Trade. That they make all purchases from Indians for the Crown, of Lands now not within the bounds of particular Colonies or that Shall not be within their Bounds when some of them are reduced to more Convenient Dimensions. That they make New Settlements on such Purchases by Granting Lands in the Kings name reserving a Quit Rent to the Crown for the use of the General Treasury. That they make Laws for Regulating & Governing such new Settlements till the Crown shall think fit to form them into particular Governments. That they may raise & pay Soldiers, and build Forts for the Defence of any of the Colonies, & equip Vessels of force to guard the Coast and protect the Trade on the Ocean Lakes or great Rivers, but they shall not impress men in any Colony without the consent of its Legislature— That for these Purposes they have power to make Laws, & lay, & levy such General Dutys Imposts or Taxes as to themselves appear most equal & just considering the ability & other Circumstances of the Inhabitants in the Several Colonies, & such as may be collected with the least Inconvenience to the People, rather discorageing Luxury, than loading Industry with unnecessary Burthens—that they may appoint a general Treasurer, and a perticular Treasurer in each Government when necessary and from time to time may order the Sums in the Treasuries of each Government into the General Treasury, or draw on them for special Payments as they find most convenient, Yet no money to Issue but by joint orders of the President General and Grand Council except where Sums have been appropriated to perticular purposes, and the President General is previously impowered by an Act to draw for Such Sums—That the General Accounts shall be yearly settled & reported to the Several Assemblies.—that a Quorum of the Grand Counsil, impowered to Act with the President General do consist of Twenty Five Members among who there shall be one or more from a Majority of the Colonies.—That the Laws made by them for the purposes aforesaid shall not be repugnant but as near as may be agreeable to the Laws of England and shall be transmitted to the King in Council for approbation as soon as may be after their passing and if not disapproved within three years after presentation to remain in force.—That in case of

the Death of the President General the Speaker of the Grand Council for the time being shall Succeed and be vested with the same power and authorities & continue till the Kings pleasure be known.

That all Military Commission Officers whether for Land or Sea Service to act under this General Constitution Shall be nominated by the President General, but the approbation of the Grand Council is to be obtained before they receive their Commissions And all civil Officers are to be nominated by the Grand Council, and to receive the President Generals approbation before they officiate But in case of Vacancy by Death or removal of any Officer civil or Military under this Constitution, the Governor of the Provinces in which such Vacancy happens may appoint till the Pleasure of the President General and Grand Council be known.—That the perticular Military as well as civil Establishments in each Colony remain in their present State, this General Constitution notwithstanding; and that on Sudden Emergenceys any Colony may defend itself, and lay the Accounts of Expence Thence arisen before the President General and Grand Council, who may allow and order payment of the same as far as they judge such Accounts just and reasonable.

## REVIEW QUESTIONS

1. What was to be the imperial government's relationship with the newly formed General Government? What would define the relationship between this government and those of the individual colonies?
2. How did the delegates propose to organize this government?
3. What were to be the main duties of the General Government?
4. What power would enable this government to carry out these duties?

# Letters about War and Trade (1760)

*When the French and Indian War, the American theater of the Seven Years' War, began, the British government tried to subordinate colonial troops and legislatures to the commanders in chief, such as Lord Loudoun, that it assigned there. Colonists delayed complying with, and sometimes outright declined to follow, requests and orders. When William Pitt (Britain's secretary of state in 1757 and later prime minister) took greater control of Britain's war strategy and policy in 1758, he decided to treat the colonists more as allies than as subjects. He asked them to raise money, supplies, and troops to support the empire's campaigns in America, and in return he promised to reimburse them. The colonists accepted that deal, and the combined forces of the British and provincial armies started to turn the war around in 1758. They took Quebec in September 1759 and Montreal a year later. By 1760 some colonial legislatures, depending perhaps on how secure their colonists felt, started to resist requests for continued support. But, although battles with the French in Canada ceased in 1760, there remained problems with the Native Americans, and Pitt still had to fight the war elsewhere to secure the expanded empire. Thus colonists who refused to assist Britain and colonists who continued to trade with the enemy, especially in the Louisiana country and West Indies, undermined imperial aims. Pitt issued strong orders to the governors to stop the trade. The governors, as revealed in these letters, tried to make their colonies better serve the empire both economically and militarily, but despite some successes—or perhaps wishful thinking—they found that they could not compel obedience.*

Gertrude Selwyn Kimball, ed., *Correspondence of William Pitt*, vol. II (New York: Macmillan, 1906; New York: Kraus Reprint Co., 1969), pp. 274–76, 320–21, 343–44, 362–63. [Editorial insertions appear in brackets—*Ed.*]

## Governor [Horatio] Sharpe to Pitt

ANNAPOLIS the 14th of April 1760.

*Sir,*

I now do myself the honour to inform you that having convened the Assembly of this Province immediately on the Receit of your Letter dated the 7th of Jan[y] I communicated to them the Contents of it, pressing them at the same time to embrace the Opportunity which it offered them of effacing the Remembrance of their past Failures & of manifesting their Duty Affection & Gratitude to our most gracious Sovereign & to the mother Country by raising & supporting such a Number of Troops to assist in the Operations of the ensuing Campaign as His Majesty was pleased to expect from this Province & as the Inhabitants can well afford to furnish, but Sir tis with concern I must also inform you that an Address which the members of the Lower House sent me the second Day after they met gave me great reason to apprehend, & some Resolves which the House made soon afterwards left me no room to doubt but that they were determined at all Events to avoid complying with His Majesty's Requisition, for altho I laid before them together with Your Letter the Opinion of His Majesty's Attorney General M[r] Pratt on the Supply Bill which they had at several times within these three years offered to the Upper House, in which Opinion he had Remarked on several Parts of the Bill & declared it to be such a one as the other Branches of our Legislature could not consistent with Honour or their Duty agree to, yet the Gentlemen of the Lower House Resolved that they would again offer the same Bill, & that as they could not agree in opinion with M$^r$ Pratt that it was either unreasonable or unconstitutional they would still adhere to it; Accordingly they sent their Bill a few Days afterwards to the Gentlemen of the Upper House not expecting their Concurrence, but conceiving that it would have a better Appearance for them to Vote Supplies & then propose to raise them by a Bill which they knew would be rejected, than at once to declare themselves entirely averse to granting any Money for His Majesty's Service. Such being the Resolutions of the Lower House, & the Gentlemen of the Upper House being confirmed by M$^r$ Pratt's Remarks & Observations in the opinion which they always entertained of the Bill that was now for the sixth time offered them, it is I imagine almost unnecessary for me to add that they have again broke up without enabling me to send General Amherst or the Officer that is appointed to Command His Majesty's Forces in this Part of America the least Assistance; nor can I since the opinion of His Majesty's Attorney General hath had so little weight with them flatter myself that they will be ever prevailed on to raise & support any more Troops during the Continuance of this War, especially as I am convinced that a Majority of their Constituents (now they think themselves secure from Danger) are really averse to being burthened with any more Taxes—Hoping that the Almighty will continue to bless the Arms of our most gracious Sovereign during this Campaign with as great & signal Successes as were obtained by His Majestys Fleets & armies during the Course of the last year, on which I presume most heartily to congratulate You, I remain with the utmost Respect &c

## Governor [James] Hamilton to Pitt

PENNSYLVANIA. 15 April 1760.

Sir,

I do myself the honour to acquaint you, that, in obedience to his Majesty's Command signified by your Excellency's letter of the 7° of January, relative to the raising of a Body of Men by this province for the Service of the ensuing Campaign; An Act of Assembly was passed here on the 12° instant, for raising Cloathing and paying Twenty seven hundred Men, till the 25° of November next.—That these troops are to act in Conjunction with His Majesty's British forces, and to be under the supreme command of the officer appointed by the General to command in these parts, agreable to his Majesty's directions.—and that I am preparing, with all possible diligence to raise the Men; so that they, or a good part of them, may be in readiness at the time and place of rendezvous appointed by General Stanwix, which is on the 12° of May.

I further do myself the honour to acquaint You, that in the passing of this Bill, I have been obliged to do violence to my own Judgment, and to make a Sacrifice both of the property, and just powers of Government of the Proprietary's of this Province to the Assembly, who would take no step towards forwarding the Service recommended, but at the price of obtaining the most unjust advantages over their Proprietaries, with whom they are contending. And to which nothing could have induced me to submit, but my Zeal for the General Service, and my fears of depriving the King of so considerable an Aid at this most critical juncture; of which, so far as regards the Proprietaries, I humbly hope, his Majesty will be graciously pleas'd to take a favourable notice.

I have the honour to be with the greatest respect Sir

Your Excellency's most obedient and most humble Servant

JAMES HAMILTON.

## Pitt to Governors in North America and the West Indies

WHITEHALL. August 23$^d$ 1760.

Sir,

The Commanders of His Majesty's Forces, and Fleets, in North America, and the West Indies, having transmitted repeated and certain Intelligence of an illegal and most pernicious Trade, carried on by the King's Subjects, in North America, and the West Indies, as well to the French Islands, as to the French Settlements on the Continent of America, and particularly to the Rivers Mobile, and Mississippi, by which the Enemy is, to the greatest Reproach, & Detriment, of Government, supplyed with Provisions, and other Necessaries, whereby they are, principally, if not alone, enabled to sustain, and protract, this long and expensive War; And It farther appearing, that large Sums, in Bullion, are also sent, by the King's Subjects, to the above Places, in return whereof, Commodities are taken, which interfere with the Produce of the British Colonies themselves, in open Contempt of the Authority of the Mother Country, as well as to the most manifest Prejudice of the Manufactures and Trade of Great Britain: In order, therefore, to put the most speedy and effectual Stop to such flagitious Practises, so utterly subversive of all Law, and so highly repugnant to the Honor, and well-being, of this Kingdom, It is His Majesty's express will and Pleasure, that you do forthwith make the strictest and most diligent Enquiry into the State of this dangerous and ignominious Trade, that you do use every Means in your Power, to detect and discover persons concerned, either as Principals, or Accessories, therein, and that you do take every Step, authorized by Law, to bring all such heinous Offenders to the most exemplary and condign Punishment; And you will, as soon as may be, and from time to time, transmit to me, for the King's Information, full and particular Accounts of the Progress, you shall have made, in the Execution of these His Majesty's Commands, to which the King expects that you do pay the most exact Obedience. And you are farther to use your utmost Endeavours to trace out, and investigate the various Artifices, and Evasions, by which the Dealers in this iniquitous Intercourse find means to cover their criminal Proceedings, and to elude the Law, in order that, from such Lights, due and timely Consideration may be had, what further Provisions shall be necessary to restrain an Evil of such extensive and pernicious Consequences.

I am &c.[a]

W. PITT.

# Governor [Benning] Wentworth to Pitt

PORTSMOUTH October 19th 1760.

*May it please your Honor*

By His Majesty's ship the Winchester I have the Honor to congratulate you on the Glorious Success of His Majesty's Arms, under the conduct of General Amherst, against Montreal[1] and the whole Country of Canada, A Conquest not only worthy the Author & promoter of it, but must be of inestimable Value to Great Brittain, as the peopling of this Continent, cannot fail of Creating a full Employ for the Manufacturers of our Mother Country more especially for such as are Employed in making the Courser woolens, & every Species of Iron Ware; with an Innumerable Number of other Articles, which the Inhabitants must be supplyed with from Great Brittain, for cloathing themselves & familys, for cultivating, & Improving the Wilderness lands.

Wealth will arise to the Inhabitants of these Colonys by slow degrees, the tedious winter will call for all the Industry of the farmer in Summer, to defend himself & Cattle against the Inclemency of the Winter, notwithstanding this Continent when more fully peopled may be as advantageous to England as thô it abounded in Riches. I have the Honor to be with the greatest Respect Sir

Your most faithfull Serv![t]

B. WENTWORTH.

# Governor Wentworth to Pitt

PORTSMOUTH December 9th 1760.

*May it Please your Honor*

I have the Honor to make answer to your letter of the 23rd of August, relative to an Illegal, and a most pernicious trade carried on by His Majesty's Subjects in North America, both to the West Indies, & French Settlements on the Continent, whereby the Enemy has received great Supplys of Provisions & Mony, and the French Kings Subjects

---

[1]Montreal surrendered on 8 September 1760.

on the Missisippy, have been enabled to assist the Indians contiguous to that River, & other Nations in Friendship with them, to carry on the war with greater vigor, than otherwise they possibly could have done, and by the last Accounts from South Carolina, that Province feels the fatall Effects of these Iniquitous Proceedings.

You may justly Sir, & with the greatest propriety on an affair of so much Importance to the Nation, expect from the Governors of the respective Provinces, where it can be suspected, this destructive Intercourse has been carried on, a Justification of their particular Conduct, respecting granting Commissions to Masters of Merchantmen for Flaggs of Truce, under pretence of redeeming Seamen in Captivity in the French Colonys.

This practise I am informed gave birth to the dangerous, & Infamous Commerce so Justly complained of, by the Commanders of His Majesty's Armys & Fleets, but of late years by the Vigilance of the Commanders of His Majesty's Ships of War these Adventurers have been very unsuccessful, notwithstanding I am informed the Traders of the Southern Governments, are making new Attempts, to open a Trade, with some of the small French Settlements on Hispaniola, at present I cannot get Information of the Names of the Ports or Bays, but I am useing my utmost diligence to obtain it, and shall be punctual in transmitting every material Circumstance agreable to your Commands.

With respect to the Government under my Command, I am certain the Trade has been carried on with great Exactness, and confined to His Majesty's Sugar Colonys only.

With respect to myself, although in the last, and beginning of the present war, Applications were made to me for Commissions for Flaggs of Truce, for Issueing of which, I might have received Considerable Sums of Mony, yet I ever treated the Applications with the greatest Contempt and disdain, which when known, freed me from future trouble, and was the means of keeping the port pure.

It has been my constant practise, and I hope never to depart from it, not to do anything, but what I could justifie to the King, His Ministers & my own Conscience, and neither directly, or Indirectly to be Instrumental in Strengthning the hands of His Majesty's enemies, and so long as I continue to act on these principles I shall hope for a continuance of His Majesty's favours and your kind protection. I am with the greatest Respect Sir
Your Honors most faithfull Servant
B. WENTWORTH.

# REVIEW QUESTIONS

1. According to Governor Sharpe, how did the Lower House in the Maryland Assembly manage to avoid financing the king's forces while appearing to support imperial requests for aid? Yet the Lower House passed its supply bill while the Upper House did not, so which house was the problem? How does this reveal power struggles within the colony's political structure as well as between colonists and their mother country?

2. How did the Pennsylvania Assembly respond to Pitt's and the colonial governor's requests for the same support? Why was Governor Hamilton more successful than Governor Sharpe?

3. Even as the governors wrestled with legislatures about financing and supplying military forces, Pitt demanded that they take action against "an illegal and most pernicious Trade." What was that trade and why was it so pernicious? How did Pitt expect the governors to correct it?

4. Governor Wentworth of New Hampshire was well aware that Britain's aim in winning the war was to ensure not only that the colonies were secure but also that they could then enrich the empire. How were they to do so? Given that, what did Wentworth think and do about the "pernicious trade"? What does his response reveal about how he saw himself and others?

5. Compare these letters to William Byrd's 1699 essay about problems with proprietary governments. What does the comparison suggest about the difficulties in regulating and ruling colonies?

# STAMP ACT CONGRESS

# FROM Declaration of Rights and Grievances of the Colonies (1765)

*The king's chief minister in 1765, George Grenville, was determined to have the colonies help defray the costs of the vast empire of which they were a part. Among the various solutions he proposed that were enacted by Parliament was a stamp duty. Starting in November of that year, the colonists were to buy and affix stamps to all sorts of printed matter. These stamps did not represent postage fees, nor were they to help regulate trade; they were to be used simply as a way to raise money for the government from within the colonies. Although the Stamp Act was easily passed in Parliament, its implementation in the colonies was another matter altogether. In the midst of riots and other mob actions, the representative bodies of various colonial governments, such as the House of Burgesses in Virginia, met and drew up resolutions that not only denounced the act but established the constitutional argument for denying Parliament's right to tax the colonies. To send a stronger message across the Atlantic, nine of the colonies also acted in concert: their representatives met that October in New York City in what became known as the Stamp Act Congress. These delegates issued resolutions and petitions to both the king and the two houses of Parliament establishing the colonial position. The combination of both economic and ideological interests can be seen in the resolutions passed by the Stamp Act Congress in October 1765.*

From *Journal of the First Congress of the American Colonies in Opposition to the Tyrannical Acts of the British Parliament, 1775* (New York, 1845), pp. 27–29.

The members of this Congress, sincerely devoted with the warmest sentiments of affection and duty to His Majesty's person and Government, inviolably attached to the present happy establishment of the Protestant succession, and with minds deeply impressed by a sense of the present and impending misfortunes of the British colonies on this continent; having considered as maturely as time will permit the circumstances of the said colonies, esteem it our indispensable duty to make the following declarations of our humble opinion respecting the most essential rights and liberties of the colonists, and of the grievances under which they labour, by reason of several late Acts of Parliament.

I. That His Majesty's subjects in these colonies owe the same allegiance to the Crown of Great Britain that is owing from his subjects born within the realm, and all due subordination to that august body the Parliament of Great Britain.

II. That His Majesty's liege subjects in these colonies are intitled to all the inherent rights and liberties of his natural born subjects within the kingdom of Great Britain.

III. That it is inseparably essential to the freedom of a people, and the undoubted right of

Englishmen, that no taxes be imposed on them but with their own consent, given personally or by their representatives.

IV. That the people of these colonies are not, and from their local circumstances cannot be, represented in the House of Commons in Great Britain.

V. That the only representatives of the people of these colonies are persons chosen therein by themselves, and that no taxes ever have been, or can be constitutionally imposed on them, but by their respective legislatures.

VI. That all supplies to the Crown being free gifts of the people, it is unreasonable and inconsistent with the principles and spirit of the British Constitution, for the people of Great Britain to grant to His Majesty the property of the colonists.

VII. That trial by jury is the inherent and invaluable right of every British subject in these colonies.

VIII. That the late Act of Parliament, entitled *An Act for granting and applying certain stamp duties, and other duties, in the British colonies and plantations in America, etc.*, by imposing taxes on the inhabitants of these colonies; and the said Act, and several other Acts, by extending the jurisdiction of the courts of Admiralty beyond its ancient limits, have a manifest tendency to subvert the rights and liberties of the colonists.

IX. That the duties imposed by several late Acts of Parliament, from the peculiar circumstances of these colonies, will be extremely burthensome and grievous; and from the scarcity of specie, the payment of them absolutely impracticable.

X. That as the profits of the trade of these colonies ultimately center in Great Britain, to pay for the manufactures which they are obliged to take from thence, they eventually contribute very largely to all supplies granted there to the Crown.

XI. That the restrictions imposed by several late Acts of Parliament on the trade of these colonies will render them unable to purchase the manufactures of Great Britain.

XII. That the increase, prosperity, and happiness of these colonies depend on the full and free enjoyments of their rights and liberties, and an intercourse with Great Britain mutually affectionate and advantageous.

XIII. That it is the right of the British subjects in these colonies to petition the King or either House of Parliament.

Lastly, That it is the indispensable duty of these colonies to the best of sovereigns, to the mother country, and to themselves, to endeavour by a loyal and dutiful address to His Majesty, and humble applications to both Houses of Parliament, to procure the repeal of the Act for granting and applying certain stamp duties, of all clauses of any other Acts of Parliament, whereby the jurisdiction of the Admiralty is extended as aforesaid, and of the other late Acts for the restriction of American commerce.

## REVIEW QUESTIONS

1. Did the members of the congress deny the authority of Parliament over the colonies?
2. What did they deem to be at issue here: their duties to the government or their rights as English subjects?
3. What were their grievances?
4. Did they appear more concerned about the constitutional issues raised by this act or the possible economic repercussions? Why?

# JOHN DICKINSON

## FROM *Letters from a Farmer in Pennsylvania* (1767–68)

*In 1767 John Dickinson, a well-educated and wealthy lawyer in his thirties, began writing the popular essays that in the following year were collected and published together as* Letters from a Farmer in Pennsylvania. *Dickinson was no radical (as a member of the Second Continental Congress he abstained in the vote for independence), but he was determined to protect his fellow colonists' rights to life, liberty, and property. In a moderate, reasonable tone, Dickinson articulated the American position against the Townshend Acts. Before he died, Charles Townshend, chancellor of the Exchequer, had pushed the acts through in his determination to raise money in America that could be used not only to help defray the costs of the troops in the colonies but also to pay the royal officials there so that they would be independent of popular control. Dickinson outlined a reasonable program of protest but, unfortunately for the moderates in the colonies, it was doomed when expectations on both sides of the Atlantic were not met.*

From *Empire and Nation: Letters from a Farmer in Pennsylvania, John Dickinson, Letters from the Federal Farmer, Richard Henry Lee*, introduction by Forrest McDonald (Englewood Cliffs, N.J.: Prentice-Hall, 1962), pp. 7–20. [Editorial insertions appear in brackets—*Ed.*]

## Letter II

*My dear Countrymen,*

There is another late act of parliament, which appears to me to be unconstitutional, and as destructive to the liberty of these colonies, as that mentioned in my last letter; that is, the act for granting the duties on paper, glass, etc.

The parliament unquestionably possesses a legal authority to *regulate* the trade of *Great Britain*, and all her colonies. Such an authority is essential to the relation between a mother country and her colonies; and necessary for the common good of all. He who considers these provinces as states distinct from the *British Empire*, has very slender notions of *justice*, or of their *interests*. We are but parts of a *whole*; and therefore there must exist a power somewhere, to preside, and preserve the connection in due order. This power is lodged in the parliament; and we are as much dependent on *Great Britain*, as a perfectly free people can be on another.

I have looked over *every statute* relating to these colonies, from their first settlement to this time; and I find every one of them founded on this principle, till the *Stamp Act* administration. *All before*, are calculated to regulate trade, and preserve or promote a mutually beneficial intercourse between the several constituent parts of the empire; and though many of them imposed duties on trade, yet those duties were always imposed *with design* to restrain the commerce of one part, that was injurious to another, and thus to promote the general welfare. . . . Never did the *British* parliament, till the period above mentioned, think of imposing duties in *America* FOR THE PURPOSE OF RAISING A REVENUE. . . .

\* \* \*

This I call an innovation: and a most dangerous innovation. It may perhaps be objected, that *Great Britain* has a right to lay what duties she pleases upon her exports, and it makes no difference to us, whether they are paid here or there.

To this I answer. These colonies require many things for their use, which the laws of *Great Britain* prohibit them from getting any where but from her. Such are paper and glass.

That we may legally be bound to pay any *general* duties on these commodities, relative to the regulation of trade, is granted; but we being *obliged by her laws* to take them from *Great Britain*, any *special* duties imposed on their exportation *to us only, with intention to raise a revenue from us only*, are as much *taxes* upon us, as those imposed by the *Stamp Act*.

What is the difference in *substance* and *right*, whether the same sum is raised upon us by the rates mentioned in the *Stamp Act*, on the *use* of paper, or by these duties, on the *importation* of it. It is only the edition of a former book, shifting a sentence from the end to the *beginning*.

\*     \*     \*

. . . [T]he *Stamp Act* was said to be a law THAT WOULD EXECUTE ITSELF. For the very same reason, the last act of parliament, if it is granted to have any force here, WILL EXECUTE ITSELF, and will be attended with the very same consequences to *American* liberty.

Some persons perhaps may say that this act lays us under no necessity to pay the duties imposed because we may ourselves manufacture the articles on which they are laid; . . .

\*     \*     \*

. . . But can any man, acquainted with *America*, believe this possible? I am told there are but two or three *Glass-Houses* on this continent, and but very few *Paper-Mills*; . . . This continent is a country of planters, farmers, and fishermen; not of manufacturers. . . .

Inexpressible therefore must be our distresses in evading the late acts, by the disuse of *British* paper and glass. Nor will this be the extent of our misfortune, if we admit the legality of that act.

Great Britain has prohibited the manufacturing *iron* and *steel* in these colonies, without any objection being made to her *right* of doing it. The *like* right she must have to prohibit any other manu-facture among us. Thus she is possessed of an undisputed *precedent* on that point. This authority, she will say, is founded on the *original intention* of settling these colonies; that is, that she should manufacture for them, and that they should supply her with materials. . . .

\*     \*     \*

Here then, my dear countrymen, ROUSE yourselves, and behold the ruin hanging over your heads. If you ONCE admit, that *Great Britain* may lay duties upon her exportations to us, *for the purpose of levying money on us only*, she then will have nothing to do, but to lay those duties on the articles which she prohibits us to manufacture—and the tragedy of *American* liberty is finished. . . . if *Great Britain* can order us to come to her for necessaries we want, and can order us to pay what taxes she pleases before we take them away, or when we land them here, we are as abject slaves as *France* and *Poland* can show in wooden shoes and with uncombed hair.[1]

\*     \*     \*

. . . [T]he single question is, whether the parliament can legally impose duties to be paid *by the people of these colonies only*, FOR THE SOLE PURPOSE OF RAISING A REVENUE, *on commodities which she obliges us to take from her alone*, or, in other words, whether the parliament can legally take money out of our pockets, without our consent. If they can, our boasted liberty is but

> *Vox et praeterea nihil.*
> A sound and nothing else.

# Letter III

*My dear Countrymen,*

\*     \*     \*

. . . [T]he meaning of [these letters] is, to convince the people of these colonies that they are at this

---

[1] Dickinson remarked in a footnote that French peasants wore wooden shoes and that Polish vassals had uncombable matted hair.

moment exposed to the most imminent dangers; and to persuade them immediately, vigorously, and unanimously, to exert themselves in the most firm, but most peaceable manner, for obtaining relief.

The cause of *liberty* is a cause of too much dignity to be sullied by turbulence and tumult. It ought to be maintained in a manner suitable to her nature. Those who engage in it, should breathe a sedate, yet fervent spirit, animating them to actions of prudence, justice, modesty, bravery, humanity and magnanimity.

\*      \*      \*

I hope, my dear countrymen, that you will, in every colony, be upon your guard against those who may at any time endeavor to stir you up, under pretenses of patriotism, to any measures disrespectful to our Sovereign, and our mother country. Hot, rash, disorderly proceedings, injure the reputation of the people as to wisdom, valor, and virtue, without procuring them the least benefit. . . .

Every government at some time or other falls into wrong measures. These may proceed from mistake or passion. But every such measure does not dissolve the obligation between the governors and the governed. The mistake may be corrected; the passion may subside. It is the duty of the governed to endeavor to rectify the mistake, and to appease the passion. They have not at first any other right, than to represent their grievances, and to pray for redress, unless an emergency is so pressing as not to allow time for receiving an answer to their applications, which rarely happens. If their applications are disregarded, then that kind of *opposition* becomes justifiable which can be made without breaking the laws or disturbing the public peace. . . .

If at length it becomes UNDOUBTED that an inveterate resolution is formed to annihilate the liberties of the governed, the *English* history affords frequent examples of resistance by force. What particular circumstances will in any future case justify such resistance can never be ascertained till they happen. Perhaps it may be allowable to say generally, that it never can be justifiable until the people

are FULLY CONVINCED that any further submission will be destructive to their happiness.

When the appeal is made to the sword, highly probable is it, that the punishment will exceed the offense; and the calamities attending on war outweigh those proceeding it. . . .

To these reflections on this subject, it remains to be added, and ought for ever to be remembered, that resistance, in the case of colonies against their mother country, is extremely different from the resistance of a people against their prince. A nation may change their king, or race of kings, and, retaining their ancient form of government, be gainers by changing. Thus *Great Britain*, under the illustrious house of *Brunswick* [Hanover], a house that seems to flourish for the happiness of mankind, has found a felicity unknown in the reigns of the *Stuarts*. But if once we are separated from our mother country, what new form of government shall we adopt, or where shall we find another *Britain* to supply our loss? Torn from the body, to which we are united by religion, liberty, laws, affections, relation, language and commerce, we must bleed at every vein.

In truth—the prosperity of these provinces is founded in their dependence on *Great Britain*; and when she returns to her "old good humor, and her old good nature," as Lord *Clarendon* expresses it, I hope they will always think it their duty and interest, as it most certainly will be, to promote her welfare by all the means in their power.

We cannot act with too much caution in our disputes. Anger produces anger; and differences, that might be accommodated by kind and respectful behavior, may, by imprudence, be enlarged to an incurable rage. . . .

The constitutional modes of obtaining relief are those which I wish to see pursued on the present occasion; that is, by petitions of our assemblies, or where they are not permitted to meet, of the people, to the powers that can afford us relief.

We have an excellent prince, in whose good dispositions toward us we may confide. We have a generous, sensible and humane nation, to whom we may apply. They may be deceived. They may, by artful men, be provoked to anger against us. I cannot believe they will be cruel and unjust; or that their anger will be implacable. Let us behave like dutiful children who have received unmerited blows from a beloved parent. Let us complain to our parent; but let our complaints speak at the same time the language of affliction and veneration.

If, however, it shall happen, by an unfortunate course of affairs, that our applications . . . prove ineffectual, let us then take *another step*, by withholding from *Great Britain* all the advantages she has been used to receive from us. . . . Let us all be united with one spirit, in one cause. . . .

## REVIEW QUESTIONS

1. Why did Dickinson believe the Townshend duties to be unconstitutional?
2. How does he argue that the taxes on certain enumerated goods such as glass and paper were particularly pernicious? In forming his argument, does he condemn the actor (Parliament) as well as the act?
3. Why did he, an author who was trying to persuade people to exert themselves vigorously against encroachments on their liberty, condemn those who more violently stirred up the populace?
4. Why did he want protest to be reasonable and limited? Was that a reasonable desire?

## THOMAS PAINE

## FROM *Common Sense* (1776)

*As the instruments of protest became sticks, stones, and muskets in addition to words, American reformers and radicals had to decide if they were indeed rebels (as King George had declared them) and, even more important, revolutionaries. Thomas Paine (1737–1809) played a major role in effecting their transformation. Paine arrived in Philadelphia in November 1774 with a history of misfortune both in work and marriage. The New World, however, offered him a fresh start, and he soon established himself as a political revolutionary. In January 1776, he published* Common Sense, *which immediately became, using today's term, a best-seller. Hundreds of thousands of copies were sold. Americans read and debated the pamphlet: some denounced the sentiments it expressed while others embraced and acted on them. In Common Sense, Paine not only provided clear, material arguments for separation but articulated the revolutionaries' sense of mission: to be free at home and to serve as an example to the world.*

From Merrill Jensen, ed., *Tracts of the American Revolution, 1763–1776* (New York: Bobbs-Merrill, 1967), pp. 418–27, 431–38, 441–46.

## Thoughts, on the Present State of American Affairs

\*   \*   \*

Volumes have been written on the subject of the struggle between England and America. Men of all ranks have embarked in the controversy, from different motives, and with various designs; but all have been ineffectual, and the period of debate is closed. Arms as the last resource decide the contest; the appeal was the choice of the King, and the Continent has accepted the challenge.

\*   \*   \*

The Sun never shined on a cause of greater worth. 'Tis not the affair of a City, a County, a Province or a Kingdom; but of a Continent—of at least one eighth part of the habitable Globe. 'Tis not the concern of a day, a year, or an age; posterity are virtually involved in the contest, and will be more or less affected even to the end of time by the proceedings now. Now is the seed time of Continental union, faith, and honour. The least fracture now, will be like a name engraved with the point of a pin on the tender rind of a young oak; the wound will enlarge with the tree, and posterity read it in full grown characters.

By referring the matter from argument to arms, a new era for politics is struck—a new method of thinking hath arisen. All plans, proposals, &c. prior to the 19th of April, i.e. to the commencement of hostilities, are like the almanacks of the last year; which tho' proper then, are superceded and useless now. Whatever was advanced by the advocates on either side of the question then, terminated in one and the same point, viz. a union with Great-Britain; the only difference between the parties, was the method of effecting it; the one proposing force, the other friendship; but it hath so far happened that the first hath failed, and the second hath withdrawn her influence.

As much hath been said of the advantages of reconciliation, which like an agreeable dream, hath passed away and left us as we were, it is but right, that we should examine the contrary side of the argument, and enquire into some of the many material injuries which these Colonies sustain, and always will sustain, by being connected with and dependant on Great-Britain. To examine that connection and dependance on the principles of nature and common sense, to see what we have to trust to if separated, and what we are to expect if dependant.

I have heard it asserted by some, that as America hath flourished under her former connection with Great-Britain, that the same connection is necessary towards her future happiness and will always have the same effect—Nothing can be more fallacious than this kind of argument: . . . America would have flourished as much, and probably much more had no European power taken any notice of her. The commerce by which she hath enriched herself are the necessaries of life, and will always have a market while eating is the custom of Europe.

But she has protected us say some. That she hath engrossed us is true, and defended the Continent at our expence as well as her own is admitted; and she would have defended Turkey from the same motive viz. the sake of trade and dominion.

Alas! we have been long led away by ancient prejudices and made large sacrifices to superstition. We have boasted the protection of Great Britain, without considering, that her motive was *interest* not *attachment;* that she did not protect us from *our enemies* on *our account,* but from *her enemies* on *her own account,* from those who had no quarrel with us on any *other account,* and who will always be our enemies on the *same account.* Let Britain wave her pretensions to the Continent, or the Continent throw off the dependance, and we should be at peace with France and Spain were they at war with Britain. The miseries of Hanover last war ought to warn us against connections.

It hath lately been asserted in parliament, that the Colonies have no relation to each other but through the Parent Country, *i.e.* that Pennsylvania and the Jerseys and so on for the rest, are sister Colonies by the way of England; this is certainly a very roundabout way of proving relationship, but it is the nearest and only true way of proving enmity (or enemyship, if I may so call it.) France and Spain never were, nor perhaps ever will be our enemies as *Americans* but as our being the *subjects of Great Britain.*

But Britain is the parent country say some. Then the more shame upon her conduct. Even brutes do not devour their young, nor savages make war upon their families; wherefore the assertion if true, turns to her reproach; but it happens not to be true, or only partly so, and the phrase, *parent* or *mother country*, hath been jesuitically adopted by the King and his parasites, with a low papistical design of gaining an unfair bias on the credulous weakness of our minds. Europe and not England is the parent country of America. This new World hath been the asylum for the persecuted lovers of civil and religious liberty from *every part* of Europe. Hither have they fled, not from the tender embraces of the mother, but from the cruelty of the monster; and it is so far true of England, that the same tyranny which drove the first emigrants from home, pursues their descendants still.

*If freed from Britain, then free from animosity w/ the rest of Europe.*

Much hath been said of the united strength of Britain and the Colonies, that in conjunction they might bid defiance to the world: But this is mere presumption, the fate of war is uncertain, neither do the expressions mean any thing, for this Continent would never suffer itself to be drained of inhabitants, to support the British Arms in either Asia, Africa, or Europe.

Besides, what have we to do with setting the world at defiance? Our plan is commerce, and that well attended to, will secure us the peace and friendship of all Europe, because it is the interest of all Europe to have America a free port. Her trade will always be a protection, and her barrenness of gold and silver will secure her from invaders.

I challenge the warmest advocate for reconciliation, to shew, a single advantage that this Continent can reap, by being connected with Great Britain. I repeat the challenge, not a single advantage is derived. Our corn will fetch its price in any market in Europe and our imported goods must be paid for buy them where we will.

But the injuries and disadvantages we sustain by that connection, are without number, and our duty to mankind at large, as well as to ourselves, instruct us to renounce the alliance: because any submission to, or dependance on Great Britain, tends directly to involve this Continent in European wars and quarrels. As Europe is our market for trade, we ought to form no political connection with any part of it. 'Tis the true interest of America, to steer clear of European contentions, which she never can do, while by her dependance on Britain, she is made the make-weight in the scale of British politics.

Europe is too thickly planted with Kingdoms, to be long at peace, and whenever a war breaks out between England and any foreign power, the trade of America goes to ruin, *because of her connection with Britain.* The next war may not turn out like the last, and should it not, the advocates for reconciliation now, will be wishing for separation then, because neutrality in that case, would be a safer convoy than a man of war. Every thing that is right or reasonable pleads for separation. The blood of the slain, the weeping voice of nature cries. 'TIS TIME TO PART. Even the distance at which the Almighty hath placed England and America, is a strong and natural proof, that the authority of the one over the other, was never the design of Heaven. The time likewise at which the Continent was discovered, adds weight to the argument, and the manner in which it was peopled encreases the force of it. The Reformation was preceded by the discovery of America as if the Almighty graciously meant to open a sanctuary to the persecuted in future years, when home should afford neither friendship nor safety.

The authority of Great Britain over this Continent is a form of Government which sooner or later must have an end: . . .

Though I would carefully avoid giving unnecessary offence, yet I am inclined to believe, that all those who espouse the doctrine of reconciliation, may be included within the following descriptions. Interested men who are not to be trusted, weak

*America = Religious freedoms*

men who cannot see, prejudiced men who will not see, and a certain set of moderate men who think better of the European world than it deserves; and this last class, by an ill-judged deliberation, will be the cause of more calamities to this Continent, than all the other three.

It is the good fortune of many to live distant from the scene of present sorrow; the evil is not sufficiently brought to their doors to make them feel the precariousness with which all American property is possessed. But let our imaginations transport us for a few moments to Boston; that seat of wretchedness will teach us wisdom, and instruct us for ever to renounce a power in whom we can have no trust. The inhabitants of that unfortunate city who but a few months ago were in ease and affluence, have now no other alternative than to stay and starve, or turn out to beg. Endangered by the fire of their friends if they continue within the city, and plundered by government if they leave it. In their present condition they are prisoners without the hope of redemption, and in a general attack for their relief, they would be exposed to the fury of both armies.

Men of passive tempers look somewhat lightly over the offences of Britain, and still hoping for the best, are apt to call out: *Come, come, we shall be friends again for all this.* But examine the passions and feelings of mankind: bring the doctrine of reconciliation to the touchstone of nature, and then tell me, whether you can hereafter love, honour, and faithfully serve the power that hath carried fire and sword into your land? . . .

. . . 'Tis not in the power of England or of Europe to conquer America, if she doth not conquer herself by delay and timidity. The present winter is worth an age if rightly employed, but if lost or neglected, the whole Continent will partake of the misfortune; and there is no punishment which that man doth not deserve, be he who, or what, or where he will, that may be the means of sacrificing a season so precious and useful.

\*    \*    \*

Every quiet method for peace hath been ineffectual. Our prayers have been rejected with disdain; and hath tended to convince us that nothing flat-

ters vanity or confirms obstinacy in Kings more than repeated petitioning—and nothing hath contributed more, than that very measure, to make the Kings of Europe absolute. Witness Denmark and Sweden. Wherfore, since nothing but blows will do, for God's sake let us come to a final separation, and not leave the next generation to be cutting throats under the violated unmeaning names of parent and child.

To say they will never attempt it again is idle and visionary, we thought so at the repeal of the stamp-act, yet a year or two undeceived us; as well may we suppose that nations which have been once defeated will never renew the quarrel.

As to government matters 'tis not in the power of Britain to do this Continent justice: the business of it will soon be too weighty and intricate to be managed with any tolerable degree of convenience, by a power so distant from us, and so very ignorant of us; for if they cannot conquer us, they cannot govern us. To be always running three or four thousand miles with a tale or a petition, waiting four or five months for an answer, which when obtained requires five or six more to explain it in, will in a few years be looked upon as folly and childishness—There was a time when it was proper, and there is a proper time for it to cease.

Small islands not capable of protecting themselves are the proper objects for government to take under their care: but there is something very absurd, in supposing a Continent to be perpetually governed by an island. In no instance hath nature made the satellite larger than its primary planet, and as England and America with respect to each other reverse the common order of nature, it is evident they belong to different systems. England to Europe: America to itself.

\*    \*    \*

If there is any true cause of fear respecting independance, it is because no plan is yet laid down. . . .

. . . Let a Continental Conference be held in the following manner, and for the following purpose.

A Committee of twenty six members of Congress, viz. Two for each Colony. Two Members from each House of Assembly, or Provincial Convention; and five Representatives of the people at large, to be chosen in the capital city or town of each Province, for, and in behalf of the whole Province, by as many qualified voters as shall think proper to attend from all parts of the Province for that purpose: or if more convenient, the Representatives may be chosen in two or three of the most populous parts thereof. In this conference thus assembled, will be united the two grand principles of business, *knowledge* and *power*. The Members of Congress, Assemblies, or Conventions, by having had experience in national concerns, will be able and useful counsellors, and the whole, by being impowered by the people, will have a truly legal authority.

The conferring members being met, let their business be to frame a Continental Charter, or Charter of the United Colonies; (answering, to what is called the Magna Charta of England) fixing the number and manner of choosing Members of Congress, Members of Assembly, with their date of sitting, and drawing the line of business and jurisdiction between them: Always remembering, that our strength is Continental not Provincial. Securing freedom and property to all men, and above all things, the free exercise of religion, according to the dictates of conscience; with such other matters as is necessary for a charter to contain. Immediately after which, the said conference to dissolve, and the bodies which shall be chosen conformable to the said charter, to be the Legislators and Governors of this Continent, for the time being: Whose peace and happiness, may GOD preserve. AMEN.

*     *     *

But where say some is the King of America? I'll tell you friend, he reigns above; and doth not make havoc of mankind like the Royal Brute of Great Britain. Yet that we may not appear to be defective even in earthly honours, let a day be solemnly set a part for proclaiming the Charter; let it be brought forth placed on the Divine Law, the Word of God; let a crown be placed thereon, by which the world may know, that so far as we approve of monarchy, that in America THE LAW IS KING. For as

in absolute governments the King is law, so in free countries the law ought to be king; and there ought to be no other. But lest any ill use should afterwards arise, let the Crown at the conclusion of the ceremony be demolished, and scattered among the people whose right it is.

A government of our own is our natural right: and when a man seriously reflects on the precariousness of human affairs, he will become convinced, that it is infinitely wiser and safer, to form a constitution of our own, in a cool deliberate manner, while we have it in our power, than to trust such an interesting event to time and chance. . . .

*     *     *

O ye that love mankind! Ye that dare oppose not only the tyranny but the tyrant, stand forth! Every spot of the old world is over-run with oppression. Freedom hath been hunted round the Globe. Asia and Africa have long expelled her. Europe regards her like a stranger, and England hath given her warning to depart. O! receive the fugitive, and prepare in time an asylum for mankind.

## Of the Present Ability of America, With Some Miscellaneous Reflections.

*     *     *

'Tis not in numbers but in unity that our great strength lies: yet our present numbers are sufficient to repel the force of all the world. The Continent hath at this time the largest disciplined army of any power under Heaven: and is just arrived at that pitch of strength, in which no single Colony is able to support itself, and the whole, when united, is able to do any thing. . . .

*     *     *

The debt we may contract doth not deserve our regard if the work be but accomplished. No nation ought to be without a debt. A national debt is a national bond: and when it bears no interest is in no case a grievance. Britain is oppressed with a debt of upwards of one hundred and forty millions sterling, for which she pays upwards of four millions interest. And as a compensation for her debt, she has a large navy; America is without debt, and without a navy; but for the twentieth part of the English national debt, could have a navy as large again. . . .

No country on the globe is so happily situated, or so internally capable of raising a fleet as America. Tar, timber, iron, and cordage are her natural produce. We need go abroad for nothing. Whereas the Dutch, who make large profits by hiring out their ships of war to the Spaniards and Portuguese, are obliged to import most of the materials they use. We ought to view the building a fleet as an article of commerce, it being the natural manufactory of this country. 'Tis the best money we can lay out. A navy when finished is worth more than it cost: And is that nice point in national policy, in which commerce and protection are united. Let us build; if we want them not, we can sell; and by that means replace our paper currency with ready gold and silver.

\*     \*     \*

In point of safety, ought we to be without a fleet? We are not the little people now, which we were sixty years ago, at that time we might have trusted our property in the streets, or fields rather, and slept securely without locks or bolts to our doors and windows. The case now is altered, and our methods of defence, ought to improve with our encrease of property. . . .

Another reason why the present time is preferable to all others is, that the fewer our numbers are, the more land there is yet unoccupied, which instead of being lavished by the king on his worthless dependants, may be hereafter applied, not only to the discharge of the present debt, but to the constant support of government. No nation under Heaven hath such an advantage as this.

The infant state of the Colonies, as it is called, so far from being against, is an argument in favour of independance. We are sufficiently numerous, and were we more so, we might be less united. 'Tis a matter worthy of observation, that the more a country is peopled, the smaller their armies are. In

military numbers the ancients far exceeded the moderns: and the reason is evident, for trade being the consequence of population, men become too much absorbed thereby to attend to any thing else. Commerce diminishes the spirit both of Patriotism and military defence. And history sufficiently informs us that the bravest achievements were always accomplished in the non-age of a nation. With the encrease in commerce, England hath lost its spirit. . . .

Youth is the seed time of good habits as well in nations as in individuals. It might be difficult, if not impossible to form the Continent into one Government half a century hence. The vast variety of interests occasioned by an increase of trade and population would create confusion. Colony would be against Colony. Each being able would scorn each others assistance: and while the proud and foolish gloried in their little distinctions, the wise would lament that the union had not been formed before. Wherefore, the present time is the true time for establishing it. The intimacy which is contracted in infancy, and the friendship which is formed in misfortune, are of all others, the most lasting and unalterable. Our present union is marked with both these characters: we are young and we have been distressed; but our concord hath withstood our troubles, and fixes a memorable Æra for posterity to glory in.

The present time likewise, is that peculiar time, which never happens to a nation but once, viz. the time of forming itself into a government. Most nations have let slip the opportunity, and by that means have been compelled to receive laws from their conquerors, instead of making laws for themselves. . . .

\*     \*     \*

TO CONCLUDE, however strange it may appear to some, or however unwilling they may be to think so, matters not, but many strong and striking reasons may be given to shew, that nothing can settle our affairs so expeditiously as an open and determined declaration for independence. Some of which are,

*First*—It is the custom of Nations when any two are at war, for some other powers not engaged in the quarrel, to step in as mediators and bring about the preliminaries of a peace: But while America calls herself the subject of Great Britain, no power however well disposed she may be, can offer her mediation. Wherefore in our present state we may quarrel on for ever.

*Secondly*—It is unreasonable to suppose, that France or Spain will give us any kind of assistance, if we mean only to make use of that assistance, for the purpose of repairing the breach, and strengthening the connection between Britain and America; because, those powers would be sufferers by the consequences.

*Thirdly*—While we profess ourselves the subjects of Britain, we must in the eye of foreign nations be considered as Rebels. The precedent is some-what dangerous to their peace, for men to be in arms under the name of subjects: we on the spot can solve the paradox; but to unite resistance and subjection, requires an idea much too refined for common understanding.

*Fourthly*—Were a manifesto to be published and dispatched to foreign Courts, setting forth the miseries we have endured, and the peaceable methods we have ineffectually used for redress, declaring at the same time, that not being able any longer to live happily or safely, under the cruel disposition of the British Court, we had been driven to the necessity of breaking off all connections with her; at the same time, assuring all such Courts, of our peaceable disposition towards them, and of our desire of entering into trade with them: such a memorial would produce more good effects to this Continent, than if a ship were freighted with petitions to Britain.

Under our present denomination of British Subjects, we can neither be received nor heard abroad: the custom of all Courts is against us, and will be so, until by an independance we take rank with other nations.

These proceedings may at first appear strange and difficult, but like all other steps which we have already passed over, will in a little time become familiar and agreeable: and until an independance is declared, the Continent will feel itself like a man who continues putting off some unpleasant business from day to day, yet knows it must be done, hates to set about it, wishes it over, and is continually haunted with the thoughts of its necessity.

FINIS

# REVIEW QUESTIONS

1. What does Paine say are some of the "material injuries" the colonies had sustained due to their dependence on Great Britain? What are the strengths and weaknesses in his argument?
2. Was Paine right to say that "Europe and not England is the parent country of America"? Why should that concept be considered a factor for separation?
3. What interests could America better pursue if independent?
4. What does Paine say would guarantee American success? Why?
5. Why did he argue for a declaration of independence and for immediate action?

# JAMES CHALMERS

## FROM *Plain Truth* (1776)

*Common Sense? Nonsense! James Chalmers, an immigrant from Scotland by way of the West Indies who had established himself as a major planter in Maryland, was incensed by Thomas Paine's "Insidious Tenets" and exasperated by the exuberant popular response. He believed that "intemperate zeal" damaged liberty while "a manly discussion of facts" preserved it. Chalmers, under the pen name Candidus, responded to Paine with* Plain Truth; Addressed to the Inhabitants of America, Containing, Remarks On a Late Pamphlet, entitled Common Sense. *He published the first edition of* Plain Truth *in Philadelphia in March 1776 and followed it in April with* Additions to Plain Truth. *Later that year a London publisher took Chalmers's and Paine's pamphlets and released them together in multiple editions.* Common Sense, *or even the* Declaration of Independence, *therefore, did not end the verbal battle for people's hearts and minds. Chalmers parried Paine's emotional rhetoric with appeals to reason. He asked his readers to consider the benefits of the British constitution and mercantile system and to give further thought to military readiness and foreign affairs. Chalmers said he adored his country, but he, like others labeled Tories, found that one could not be both a loyal Briton and an American patriot. After serving as an officer in the first Battalion of Maryland Loyalists during the war, Chalmers lived out the rest of his life in England.*

From Merrill Jensen, ed., *Tracts of the American Revolution, 1763–1776* (New York: Bobbs-Merrill, 1967), pp. 459–62, 465–67, 474–77, 480–81, 483–88. [Editorial insertions appear in square brackets—*Ed.*]

\*     \*     \*

I shall humbly endeavour to shew, that our author[1] shamefully misrepresents facts, is ignorant of the true state of Great Britain and her Colonies, utterly unqualified for the arduous task, he has presumptuously assumed; and ardently intent on seducing us to that precipice on which himself stands trembling. . . . the judicious reader will remember, that true knowledge of our situation, is as essential to our safety, as ignorance thereof may endanger it. In the English provinces, exclusive of negroe and other slaves, we have one hundred and sixty thousand, or one hundred and seventy thousand men capable of bearing arms. If we deduct

the people called Quakers, Anabaptists, and other religionists averse to arms; a considerable part of the emigrants, and those having a grateful predilection for the ancient constitution and parent state, we shall certainly reduce the first number to sixty or seventy thousand men. Now admitting those equal to the Roman legions, can we suppose them capable of defending against the power of Britain, a country nearly twelve hundred miles extending on the ocean. Suppose our troops assembled in New England, if the Britons see not fit to assail them, they haste to and desolate our other provinces, which eventually would reduce New England. If by dividing our forces, we pretend to defend our provinces, we also are infallibly undone. Our most fertile provinces, filled with unnumbered

---

[1] That is, Paine.

domestic enemies, slaves, intersected by navigable rivers, every where accessible to the fleets and armies of Britain, can make no defence. If without the medium of passion and prejudice, we view our other provinces, half armed, destitute of money and a navy: We must confess, that no power ever engaged such POTENT ANTAGONISTS, under such peculiar circumstances of infelicity. In the better days of Rome, she permitted no regular troops to defend her. Men destitute of property she admitted not into her militia, (her only army.) I have been extremely concerned at the separation of the Connecticut men from our army. It augur'd not an ardent enthusiasm for liberty and glory. We still have an army before Boston, and I should be extremely happy to hear substantial proofs of their glory. I am still hopeful of great things from our army before Boston, when joined by the regiments now forming, which WANT OF BREAD will probably soon fill. Notwithstanding the predilection I have for my countrymen, I remark with grief, that hitherto our troops have displayed but few marks of Spartan or Roman enthusiasm. . . . I am under no doubt, however, that we shall become as famed for martial courage, as any nation ever the sun beheld. Sanguine as I am, respecting the virtue and courage of my countrymen, depending on the history of mankind, since the Christian Æra, I cannot however imagine, that zeal for liberty will animate to such glorious efforts of heroism, as religious enthusiasm hath often impelled its votaries to perform. . . .

With the utmost deference to the honorable Congress, I do not view the most distant gleam of aid from foreign powers. The princes alone, capable of succouring us, are the Sovereigns of France and Spain. If according to our Author, we possess an eighth part of the habitable globe, and actually have a check on the West India commerce of England, the French indigo and other valuable West India commodities, and the Spanish galeons, are in great jeopardy from our power. The French and Spaniards are therefore wretched politicians, if they do not assist England, in reducing her colonies to obedience.——Pleasantry apart! Can we be so deluded, to expect aid from those princes, which inspiring their subjects with a relish for liberty, might eventually shake their arbitrary thrones. Natural avowed enemies to our sacred cause: Will they cherish, will they support the flame of liberty in America? Ardently intent on extinguishing its latent dying sparks in their respective dominions. Can we believe that those princes will offer an example so dangerous to their subjects and colonies, by aiding those provinces to independence? If independent, aggrandized by infinite numbers from every part of Europe, this Continent would rapidly attain power astonishing to imagination. Soon, very soon would we be conditioned to conquer Mexico, and all their West India settlements, which to annoy, or possess, we indeed are most happily situated. Simple and obvious as these truths are, can they be unknown to the people and princes of Europe? . . . I say, be it admitted, that those princes regardless of future consequences, and the ineptitude of the times, are really disposed to succour us. Say, ye friends of liberty and mankind, would no danger accrue from an army of French and Spaniards in the bosom of America? Would ye not dread their junction with the Canadians and Savages, and with the numerous Roman catholics, dispersed throughout the Colonies? . . .

*     *     *

"Much" says our author, "has been said of the strength of Britain and the Colonies, that in conjunction they might bid defiance to the world; but this is mere presumption, the fate of war is uncertain."

Excellent reasoning, and truly consistent with our author. We of ourselves are a match for Europe, nay for the world; but in junction with the most formidable power on earth; why then, the matter is mere presumption. The fate of war is uncertain. It is indeed humiliating to consider, that this author should vamp up a form of government, for a considerable part of mankind; and in case of its succeeding, that he probably would be one of our tyrants, until we prayed some more illustrious tyrant of the army, to spurn him to his primeval obscurity, from all his ill-got honours flung, turned to that dirt from whence he sprung. "A government of our own, is our natural right," says our author.

> "Had right decided, and not fate the cause,
> Rome had preserv'd her Cato and her laws."

Unfortunately for mankind, those are fine sounding words, which seldom or ever influence human affairs. If they did, instead of appropriating the vacant lands to schemes of ambition, we must instantly deputise envoys to the Indians, praying them to re-enter their former possessions, and permit us quietly to depart to the country of our ancestors, where we would be welcome guests. But continues our author,

> What have we to do with setting the world at defiance? our plan is commerce, and that well attended to, will secure us the peace and friendship of all Europe; because it is the interest of all Europe to have America a free port, her trade will always be her protection, and her barrenness of gold and silver, will secure her from invaders.

I am perfectly satisfied, that we are in no condition to set the world at defiance, that commerce and the protection of Great Britain will secure us peace, and the friendship of all Europe; but I deny that it is the interest of all Europe to have America a free-port, unless they are desirous of depopulating their dominions. His assertions, that barrenness of gold and silver will secure us from invaders, is indeed highly pleasant. Have we not a much better security from invasions, viz. the most numerous and best disciplined army under heaven. . . .

\*    \*    \*

. . . "The infant state of the Colonies as it is called, so far from being against, is an argument in favor of Independence." This assertion is as absurd, as if he had maintained, that twenty is inferior in number to two. "But the injuries and disadvantages we sustain by that connection, are without number, and our duty to mankind at large, as well as to ourselves, instruct us to renounce the alliance; because any submission to, or dependence upon Great Britain, tends directly to involve this Continent in European wars and quarrels. As Europe is our market for trade, we ought to form no political connection with any part of it." Innumerable are the advantages of our connection with Britain; and a just dependence on her, is a sure way to avoid the horrors and calamities of war. Wars in Europe, will probably than heretofore become less frequent; religious rancour, which formerly animated princes to arms, is succeeded by a spirit of philosophy extremely friendly to peace. The princes of Europe are or ought to be convinced by sad experience, that the objects of conquest, are vastly inadequate to the immense charge of their armaments. Prudential motives, therefore, in future, will often dictate negociation, instead of war. Be it however admitted, that our speculations are nugatory, and that as usual, we are involved in war. In this case we really do not participate a twentieth part of the misery and hardships of war, experienced by the other subjects of the empire. . . .

Our author surely forgets, that when independent, we cannot trade with Europe, without political connections, and that all treaties made by England or other commercial states are, or ought to be, ultimately subservient to their commerce. "But" (says our author,) "admitting that matters were now made up, what would be the event? I answer the ruin of the Continent, and that for several reasons." Reconciliation would conduct us to our former happy state. The happiness of the governed is without doubt the true interest of the governors, and if we aim not at independence, there cannot be a doubt, of receiving every advantage relative to laws and commerce that we can desire. Montesquieu speaking of the people of England, says, "They know better than any people on earth, how to value at the same time these three great advantages, religion, liberty, and commerce." "It is a matter worthy of observation, that the more a country is peopled, the smaller their armies are." This indeed would be worthy of observation, did not daily experience contravert it. The armies of Russia, France, Austria, England, and Prussia, are certainly more numerous than those of Spain, Sweden, Denmark, Portugal, and Sardinia. . . . "In military numbers, the ancients far exceeded the moderns, and the reason is evident, for trade being the consequences of population, men become too much absorbed thereby, to attend to any thing else, commerce diminishes the spirit both of patriotism, and military defence."

Every man of sense, now rejects the fabulous numbers of the army of Xerxes, and other fabled armies of antiquity. The ancient armies, did not exceed in numbers the armies of the moderns. If so, their states had been desolated by the horrid carnage of their battles, arising from the military spirit of defence, from the nature of their arms, and the arrangement of their armies, which permitted the combatants to buckle together, who seldom gave quarter. . . . Notwithstanding my ardour for liberty, I do most fervently pray, that we may never exchange the spirit of commerce, for that of military defence, even at the price of augmenting our armies. Let us hear the testimony of Montesquieu in favor of commerce: "Commerce," says he,

> is a cure for the most destructive prejudices, for it is almost a general rule, that wherever we find agreeable manners, their commerce flourishes. Let us not be astonished then, if our manners are now less savage than formerly. Commerce has every where diffused a knowledge of all nations, these are compared one with another, and from this comparison arise the greatest advantages. Peace is the natural effect of trade, &c.

. . . In short, could we enumerate the infinite train of misfortunes inflicted on mankind, in every clime and age by this self-same spirit of military defence; our readers will surely join us in opinion, that commerce has most happily humanized mankind. I am not unaware, that there are many declamations against commerce, these I have ever regarded as trials of wit, rather than serious productions. Our author's antipathy, and extreme aversion to commerce, is easily accounted for. If his independence takes place, I do aver, that commerce will be as useless, as our searching for the philosopher's stone. "And history (says he,) sufficiently informs us, that the bravest achievements were always accomplished in the non-age of a nation." The Greeks in their early state were pirates, and the Romans robbers, and both warred in character.

Their glorious actions were performed, (if I may so express myself) in the manhood of their empire. Carthage, Greece, Asia, Spain, Gaul, and Britain, were not indeed conquered during the non-age of the republic. Agincourt, Cressey, Oudenard, Ramillies, Blenheim, Dettingen, and Minden, surely were not fought in the infancy of the English Empire. "With the encrease of commerce, England has lost her spirit." This is really a curious discovery; who is unacquainted, that the English are the lords and factors of the universe, and that Britain joins to the commerce of Tyre, Carthage and Venice, the discipline of Greece, and the fire of old Rome. . . .

\*    \*    \*

. . . "It is the custom of nations," (says our author) "when any two are at war, for some other powers not engaged in the quarrel, to step in as mediators, and bring about the preliminaries of a peace. But while America calls herself the subject of Britain, no power, however well disposed she may be, can offer her mediation. Wherefore in our present state we may quarrel on forever."

Nations, like individuals, in the hour of passion attend to no mediation. But when heartily drubbed, and tired of war, are very readily reconciled, without the intervention of mediators; by whom, belligerents were never reconciled, until their interests or passions dictated the pacification. If we may use our author's elegant language, mediation is "farsical." I grant however, that the idea of our forcing England by arms to treat with us is brilliant. "It is unreasonable" (continues our author) "to suppose that France and Spain will give us any kind of assistance, if we mean only to make use of that assistance for the purpose of repairing the breach, and strengthening the connection between Britain and America; because those powers would be sufferers by the consequences."

Considering "we have the most numerous, and best disciplined army under Heaven; and a fleet fit to contend with the navy of Britain," we must suppose our Author's brain affected by dwelling constantly on his beloved independency, else he would not have the imbecility to require the assistance of France and Spain. The manner of his prevailing on

France and Spain to assist us, is also a strong proof of his insanity. Did those powers hesitate to succour the Scotch rebels in 1745, because they did not declare themselves independent. It then was their interest to create a diversion, alas! too serious in the sequel for the deluded rebels in that kingdom; and were they now interested in aiding us, they undoubtedly would do it in spite of quibbles. . . . "Were a manifesto (says our author) dispatched to foreign courts, &c." This also is a conclusive proof of our author's maniacum delirium. Our author "challenges the warmest advocate for reconciliation to shew a single advantage this Continent can reap by being connected with Great Britain. I repeat the challenge, not a single advantage is derived: Our corn will fetch its price in any market in Europe." Were the author's assertions respecting our power, as real as delusive, a reconciliation on liberal principles with Great Britain, would be most excellent policy. I wave similarity of manners, laws, and customs, most friendly indeed to perpetual alliance. The greatest part of our plank, staves, shingles, hoops, corn, beef, pork, herrings, and many other articles, could find no vent, but in the English Islands. The demand for our flour would also be considerably lessened. The Spaniards have no demand for these articles and the French little or none. Britain would be a principal mart for our lumber, part of our grain, naval stores, tobacco, and many other articles, which perhaps are not generally wanted in any kingdom in Europe. . . .

\*     \*     \*

. . . It now behoves us well to consider, whether it were better to enter the harbour of peace with Great Britain, or plunge the ship into all the horrors of war.—Of civil war. As peace and a happy extension of commerce, are objects infinitely better for Great Britain, than war and a diminution of her commerce. It therefore is her interest to grant us every species of indulgence, consistent with our constitutional dependence, should war continue, there can be no doubt of the annihilation of our ships, ports and commerce, by Great Britain. The King's ships now in New England, unhappily are more than sufficient to ruin the ports and commerce of these provinces. New York is already secured; and I should be extremely grieved to hear that a small armament were destined against Philadelphia. In the opinion of the best officers of the navy, Philadelphia is accessible to a few forty and fifty gunships, in despite of our temporary expedients to fortify the river Delaware. If such opinion is groundless, the ministry by their imbecillity have befriended us; since by guarding the River Delaware with a few frigates only, they had precluded us from arming our vessels and strengthening the river Delaware. I would remind our author of the constant language, and apparent purport of all ranks in opposition to Great Britain: "We have" (say they) "been the happiest people on earth, and would continue to be so, should Great Britain renounce her claim of taxation. We have no sinister views, we claim not independence; No! Perish the thought." Such I believe also was the tenor of the petitions from the Congress to his Majesty. Now I would ask every man of sentiment, what opinion our friends in Great Britain, nay the whole world will entertain of us, if ingratefully, and madly adopting our author's frantic schemes, we reject reasonable terms of reconciliation? Will they not most assuredly believe, that our popular leaders, have by infinite art, deluded the unwary people into their pre-concerted schemes; on supposition, *that the time had found us?* Those acquainted with Britain must confess, that the minority in parliament, hitherto have been our main prop. Now independency for ever annihilates this our best resource. . . .—If my remarks are founded on truth, it results, *that the time hath not found us;* that independency is inexpedient, ruinous, and impracticable, and that reconciliation with Great Britain on good terms, is our sole resource. 'Tis this alone, will render us respectable; it is this alone, will render us numerous; it is this only, will make us happy.

I shall no longer detain my reader, but conclude with a few remarks on our Author's scheme. The people of those Colonies would do well to consider the character, fortune, and designs of our Author, and his independents; and compare them with those of the most amiable and venerable personages in, and out of the Congress, who abominate such nefarious measures. I would humbly observe, that the specious science of politics, is of all others, the most delusive. . . . It is perhaps possible to form a specious system of government on paper which may seem practicable, and to have the consent of the people; yet it will not answer in practice, nor retain their approbation upon trial. "All plans of government (says Hume) which suppose great reformation in the manners of mankind, are merely imaginary."

The fabricators of Independency have too much influence to be entrusted in such ardous and important concerns. This reason alone, were sufficient at present, to deter us from altering the Constitution.[2] It would be as inconsistent in our leaders in this hour of danger to form a government, as it were for a Colonel forming his battalion in the face of an enemy, to stop to write an essay on war.

This author's[3] Quixotic system, is really an insult to our understanding; it is infinitely inferior to Hume's idea of a perfect Common Wealth, which notwithstanding his acknowledged greatness of genius, is still reprehensible. It is not our business to examine, in what manner this author's associates, acquired their knowledge in national affairs; but we may predict, that his scheme of independency would soon, very soon give way to a government imposed on us, by some Cromwell of our armies. . . . Let us however admit that our [hypothetical] General and troops, contradicting the experience of ages, do not assume the sovereignty. Released from foreign war, we would probably be plunged into all the misery of anarchy and intestine war. Can we suppose that the people of the south, would submit to have the seat of Empire at Philadelphia, or in New England; or that the people oppressed by a change of government, contrasting their misery

with their former happy state, would not invite Britain to reassume the sovereignty.

A failure of commerce precludes the numerous tribe of planters, farmers and others, from paying their debts contracted on the faith of peace and commerce. They cannot, nor perhaps ought not to pay their debts. A war will ensue between the creditors and their debtors, which will eventually end in a general spunge or abolition of debts, which has more than once happened in other States on occasions similar.

\*    \*    \*

Volumes were insufficient to describe the horror, misery and desolation, awaiting the people at large in the Syren form of American independence. In short, I affirm that it would be most excellent policy in those who wish for TRUE LIBERTY to submit by an advantageous reconciliation to the authority of Great Britain; "to accomplish in the long run, what they cannot do by hypocrisy, fraud and force in the short one."

INDEPENDENCE AND SLAVERY
ARE SYNONYMOUS TERMS.

FINIS

# REVIEW QUESTIONS

1. What weaknesses did Chalmers argue would undermine the rebels' ability to wage war?
2. How does Chalmers contradict Paine's assertions that foreign powers would aid America?
3. What were some of the benefits to staying connected to Great Britain?
4. Why, do you suppose, didn't Chalmer's *Plain Truth* trump Paine's *Common Sense* in 1776?

---

[2]That is, the British Constitution.
[3]That is, Paine's.

# Thomas Jefferson

# Draft of the *Declaration of Independence* (1776)

*Thomas Jefferson (1743–1826), a Virginia planter and lawyer who emerged from the Revolution renowned as an American statesman and philosopher, levied his first major charge against the British government when he wrote* A Summary View of the Rights of British America *in 1774. While arguing against Parliament's power, however, he still promoted allegiance to the king. Two years later he advocated the severance of that tie. After Richard Henry Lee, a delegate from Virginia to the Continental Congress, made the resolution that the colonies were and had the right to be independent states, the congress created a committee to draft a declaration to that effect. The committee, in turn, handed over the task to the person they believed most suited to it: Jefferson. A product of his period and place, Jefferson wrote later in 1825 that in the* Declaration of Independence *he had attempted to produce "an expression of the American Mind." Other congressional delegates had their own interpretations and agendas, however, and insisted on alterations. Jefferson recorded the changes that were made to the draft he submitted by underlining and sometimes bracketing what the delegates omitted and showing what they added in the margins.*

"The Declaration of Independence," Boyd, Julian P.; *The Papers of Thomas Jefferson, Vol. 1: 1760–1776.* © 1950 Princeton University Press, 1978 renewed Princeton University Press. Reprinted by permission of Princeton University Press.

A Declaration by the representatives of the United states of America, in General Congress assembled.

When in the course of human events it becomes necessary for one people to dissolve the political bands which have connected them with another, and to assume among the powers of the earth the separate & equal station to which the laws of nature and of nature's god entitle them, a decent respect to the opinions of mankind requires that they should declare the causes which impel them to the separation.

We hold these truths to be self evident: that all men are created equal; that they are endowed by their creator with ∧ inherent and inalienable rights; that among    ∧ certain these are life, liberty & the pursuit of happiness: that to secure these rights, governments are instituted among men, deriving their just powers from the conesent of the governed; that whenever any form of government becomes destructive of these ends, it is the right of the people to alter or to abolish it, & to institute new government, laying it's foundation on such principles, & organising it's powers in such form, as to them shall seem most likely to effect their safety & happiness. prudence indeed will dictate that governments long established should not be changed for light & transient causes; and accordingly all experience hath shewn that mankind are more disposed to suffer while evils are sufferable than to right themselves by abolishing the forms to which they are accustomed. but when a long train of abuses & usurpations [begun at a distinguished period and] pursuing invariably the same object, evinces a design to reduce them under absolute despotism it is their right, it is their duty to throw off such government, & to provide new guards for their future security. such has been the patient sufferance of these colonies; & such is now the necessity which constrains them to ∧ [expunge] their ∧ alter former systems of government. the history of the present king of Great Britain is a history of ∧ [unremitting] injuries & usurpations, [among which appears no ∧ repeated solitary fact to contradict the uniform tenor of the rest but all have] ∧ in direct ∧ all having object the establishment of an absolute tyranny over these states. to prove this let facts be submitted to a candid world [for the truth of which we pledge a faith yet unsullied by falsehood.]

he has refused his assent to laws the most wholsome & necessary for the public good.

he has forbidden his governors to pass laws of immediate & pressing importance, unless suspended in their operation till his assent should be obtained; & when so suspended, he has utterly neglected to attend to them.

he has refused to pass other laws for the accomodation of large districts of people, unless those people would relinquish the right of representation in the legislature, a right inestimable to them, & formidable to tyrants only.

he has called together legislative bodies at places unusual, uncomfortable, and distant from the depository of their public records, for the sole purpose of fatiguing them into compliance with his measures.

he has dissolved representative houses repeatedly [& continually] for opposing with manly firmness his invasions on the rights of the people.

he has refused for a long time after such dissolutions to cause others to be elected, whereby the legislative powers, incapable of annihilation, have returned to the people at large for their exercise, the state remaining in the mean time exposed to all the dangers of invasion from without & convulsions within.

he has endeavored to prevent the population of these states; for that purpose obstructing the laws for naturalization of foreigners, refusing to pass others to encourage their migrations hither, & raising the conditions of new appropriations of lands.

he has ∧ [suffered] the administration of justice [totally to cease in some of ∧ obstructed these states] ∧ refusing his assent to laws for establishing judiciary powers. ∧ by

he has made [our] judges dependant on his will alone, for the tenure of their offices, & the amount & paiment of their salaries.

he has erected a multitude of new offices [by a self assumed power] and sent hither swarms of new officers to harrass our people and eat out their substance.

he has kept among us in times of peace standing armies [and ships of war] without the consent of our legislatures.

he has affected to render the military independant of, & superior to the civil power.

he has combined with others to subject us to a jurisdiction foreign to our constitutions & unacknoleged by our laws, giving his assent to their acts of pretended legislation for quartering large bodies of armed troops among us; for protecting them by a mock-trial from punishment for any murders which they should commit on the inhabitants of these states; for cutting off our trade with all parts of the world; for imposing taxes on us without our consent; for depriving us ∧ [∧ in many cases] of the benefits of trial by jury; for transporting us beyond seas to be tried for pretended offences; for abolishing the free system of English laws in a neighboring province, establishing therein an arbitrary government, and enlarging it's boundaries, so as to render it at once an example and fit instrument for introducing the same absolute rule into these ∧ [∧ colonies] [states]; for taking away our charters, abolishing our most valuable laws, and altering fundamentally the forms of our governments; for suspending our own legislatures, & declaring themselves invested with power to legislate for us in all cases whatsoever.

he has abdicated government here ∧ [∧ by declaring us out of his protection & waging war against us.] [withdrawing his governors, and declaring us out of his allegiance & protection]

he has plundered our seas, ravaged our coasts, burnt our towns, & destroyed the lives of our people.

he is at this time transporting large armies of foreign mercenaries to compleat the works of death, desolation & tyranny already begun with circumstances of cruelty and perfidy ∧ [∧ scarcely paralleled in the most barbarous ages, & totally] unworthy the head of a civilized nation.

he has constrained our fellow citizens taken captive on the high seas to bear arms against their country, to become the executioners of their friends & brethren, or to fall themselves by their hands.

he has ∧ [∧ excited domestic insurrections amongst us, & has] endeavored to bring on the inhabitants of our frontiers the merciless Indian savages, whose known rule of warfare is an undistinguished destruction of all ages, sexes, & conditions [of existence.]

[he has incited treasonable insurrections of our fellow-citizens, with the allurements of forfeiture & confiscation of our property.

he has waged cruel war against human nature itself, violating it's most sacred rights of life and liberty in the persons of a distant people who never offended him, captivating & carrying them into slavery in another hemisphere or to incur miserable death in their transportation thither. this piratical warfare, the opprobrium of *infidel* powers, is the warfare of the *Christian* king of Great Britain. determined to keep open a market where *Men* should be bought & sold, he has prostituted his negative for suppressing every legislative attempt to prohibit or to restrain this execrable commerce. and that this assemblage of horrors might want no fact of distinguished die, he is now exciting those very people to rise in arms among us, and to purchase that liberty of which he has deprived them, by murdering the people on whom he also obtruded them: thus paving off former crimes committed against the *Liberties* of one people, with crimes which he urges them to commit against the *lives* of another.]

In every stage of these oppressions we have petitioned for redress in the most humble terms: our repeated petitions have been answered only by repeated injuries. a prince whose character is thus marked by every act which may define a tyrant is unfit to be the ruler of a ∧ [∧ free] people [who mean to be free. future ages will scarcely believe that the hardiness of one man adventured, within the short compass of twelve years only, to lay a foundation so broad & so undisguised for tyranny over a people fostered & fixed in principles of freedom.]

Nor have we been wanting in attentions to our British brethren. we have warned them from time to time of attempts by their legislature to extend ∧ [a] jurisdiction over ∧ [these our states.] we have reminded them of the circumstances of our emigration & settlement here, [no one of which could warrant so strange a pretension: that these were effected at the expence of our own blood & treasure, unassisted by the wealth or the strength of Great Britain: that in constituting indeed our several forms of government, we had adopted one common king, thereby laying a foundation for perpetual league & amity with them: but that submission to their parliament was no part of our constitution, nor ever in idea, if history may be credited: and,] we ∧ appealed to their native justice and magnanimity ∧ [as well as to] the ties of our common kindred to disavow these usurpations which ∧ [were likely to] interrupt our connection and correspondence. they too have been deaf to the voice of justice & of consanguinity, [and when occasions have been given them, by the regular course of their laws, of removing from their councils the disturbers of our harmony, they have, by their free election, re-established them in power. at this very time too they are permitting their chief magistrate to send over not only souldiers of our common blood, but Scotch & foreign mercenaries to invade & destroy us. these facts have given the last stab to agonizing affection, and manly spirit bids us to renounce for ever these unfeeling brethren. we must endeavor to forget our former love for them, and to hold them as we hold the rest of mankind enemies in war, in peace friends. we might have been a free and a great people together; but a communication of grandeur & of freedom it seems is below their dignity. be it so, since they will have it. the road to happiness & to glory is open to us too. we will tread it apart from them, and] ∧ acquiesce in the necessity which denounces our [eternal] separation ∧ !

∧ an unwarrantable

∧ us

∧ have
∧ and we have conjured them by
∧ would inevitably

∧ we must therefore
∧ and hold them as we hold the rest of mankind, enemies in war, in peace friends.

We therefore the representatives of the United states of America in General Congress assembled do in the name, & by the authority of the good people of these [states reject & renounce all allegiance & subjection to the kings of Great Britain & all others who may hereafter claim by, through or under them: we utterly dissolve all political connection which may heretofore have subsisted between us & the people or parliament of Great Britain: & finally we do assert & declare these colonies to be free & independant states,] & that as free & independant states, they have full power to levy war, conclude peace, contract alliances, establish commerce, & to do all other acts &

We therefore the representatives of the United states of America in General Congress assembled, appealing to the supreme judge of the world for the rectitude of our intentions, do in the name, & by the authority of the good people of these colonies, solemnly publish & declare that these United colonies are & of right ought to be free & independant states; that they are absolved from all allegiance to the British crown, and that all political connection between them & the state of Great Britain is, & ought to be, totally dissolved; & that as free & independant states they have full power to levy war, conclude peace, contract alliances, establish commerce & to do all other acts & things

things which independant states may of right do. and for the support of this declaration we mutually pledge to each other our lives, our fortunes & our sacred honour.

which independant states may of right do. and for the support of this declaration, with a firm reliance on the protection of divine providence we mutually pledge to each other our lives, our fortunes & our sacred honour.

# REVIEW QUESTIONS

1. What were the charges against the king? Why were most of the condemnations addressed against him?
2. How did Jefferson's interpretation of the American mind differ from that presented by the Continental Congress via its alterations? Which version appears to be the harsher condemnation of the British government and people? Why?
3. What does this difference suggest about American perceptions and feelings toward the mother country?
4. What is distinctive about the approved concluding paragraph versus the one proposed by Jefferson? What does this difference reveal about the original author and those who altered his document?
5. How did the declaration justify independence?
6. Is this a document of construction as well as destruction? How so?
7. Does it reveal one unified nation and people or a group of states and peoples working together?

# 5 ∽ THE AMERICAN REVOLUTION

*The American Revolution began when colonists protested English acts that infringed on the privileges granted them as British subjects. These protests became rebellion as the issue of privileges became one of rights. As James Thacher, a young physician, wrote one January day in 1775, "In no country . . . is the love of liberty more deeply rooted, or the knowledge of the rights inherent to freemen more generally diffused, or better understood, than among the British American Colonies." Although loyal British subjects in both mother country and colonies could point out the benefits of living under the British constitution, once the discontented colonists determined that a corrupt imperial government threatened their natural rights, as well as their privileges as citizens, the resistance movement exploded into both a revolution and a war for independence.*

*In the course of destroying the fetters of empire and forging new national bonds, the revolutionaries grappled with novel ideas and institutions. They did not act on or implement everything that was proposed, nor was everything that was initiated successful, but there were revolutionaries of all sorts active in all facets of change—political, military, and social.*

*Political revolutionaries lambasted loyalists and lauded separatists in their struggle for the allegiance of Americans. They also bickered, dickered, and philosophized their way through the establishment of new state and national governments. Militaristic revolutionaries focused their minds and might on winning the War for American Independence. Whether serving in the Continental Army or the state regiments and militia, they battled against foreign and domestic enemies. These two groups of revolutionaries, after many setbacks, met with success, but success brought with it both questions and challenges. Many of those challenges were delivered by those who also wanted to see a societal revolution. Social revolutionaries, from those who had only begun to question established hierarchies and conventions to those who wanted to overthrow them, presented some of the most troublesome issues of the era. While they helped initiate some changes—as seen in wider suffrage, an increase in private manumissions, the abolition of slavery in some states, and a greater separation between church and state—they did not meet with the same success as the other revolutionaries.*

*A major issue confronting the revolutionaries was how to act on the words that initiated and described the new world they wanted to create. They voted in new state constitutions and governments, and they took up arms to ensure independence, but many stopped short—some in humorous disbelief and others in horror—when some of their associates grabbed hold of the words and applied them literally and liberally. To many revolutionaries the formation of a republic based on the notion that all free, white, adult males were legally and politically equal was quite radical enough. Indeed, they were right—it was a radical change from what was practiced in most of the world. But others argued for a new order in that new world: for all men to be equal, neither creed nor color must matter. If "men" meant humankind, then gender must be irrelevant. But in this case, at that time, such a definition was too demanding: most revolutionaries were unable or unwilling to free themselves of the social and cultural constraints by which they defined their world. Even so, the words remained, and were—and are— dynamic elements of revolution in American history.*

# JAMES THACHER

## FROM *Military Journal of the American Revolution* (1775–77)

*James Thacher (1754–1844) had just completed his medical studies and apprentice-ship under a doctor in Barnstable, Massachusetts, when his country erupted into full-fledged rebellion. He started to keep a journal in which he recorded not just the events but the sentiments—feelings and opinions—of the war years. His entries show an immediacy reflective of living through the events noted, but as Thacher first published his journal in 1823, some also hint at later contemplation and possible revision. His journal may thus present the strong nationalism of the mature veteran as well as the burning patriotism of the young man who initially wrote the journal's entries. In June 1775 as the colonies were abuzz with news of the battle at Bunker (Breed's) Hill, Thacher became determined to combine his profession and patriotism. He said that friends tried to discourage him from taking sides in a civil war that might end with him on the gallows, while Tories warned him of the dire consequences for fighting the king and his powerful army. Nonetheless he sought a position with the medical department then being organized. After passing a medical board's examination that July, he became a surgeon's mate in the provincial hospital at Cambridge. He served there until February 1776, at which time, due to the reorganization of the medical department and reduction of surgeon's mates at the hospital, he was reassigned as mate to the surgeon attached to Colonel Asa Whitcomb's Massachusetts regiment (later 6th Continental Infantry). Over time, and as circumstances dictated, his assignments changed. Thacher generally preferred to record political and military events in his journal, but on occasion he mentioned his duties and thus revealed some of the hardships and horrors of this war.*

From *Military Journal of the American Revolution, From the Commencement to the Disbanding of the American Army* (1862; reprint, New York: Arno Press, 1969), pp. 29–30, 33–34, 44–46, 51–52, 78, 82–83, 85–86, 96–97, 99–03, 112–13. [Editorial insertions appear in brackets—*Ed.*]

[July 1775] . . . Having received my appointment by the [Massachusetts] Provincial Congress, I commenced my duty in the hospital, July 15th. Several private, but commodious, houses in Cambridge are occupied for hospitals, and a considerable number of soldiers who were wounded at Breed's hill, and a greater number of sick of various diseases, require all our attention. . . .

I am informed that General George Washington arrived at our provincial camp, in this town, on the 2d July; having been appointed, by the unanimous voice of the Continental Congress at Philadelphia, general and commander-in-chief of all the troops raised, and to be raised, for the defence of the United Colonies, as they are now termed. . . . General Washington is a native of

Virginia; he was in General Braddock's defeat in 1755, and having had considerable experience in the wars with the French and Indians on the frontiers of that colony, in former years, he is supposed to possess ample qualifications for the command of our army, and the appointment gives universal satisfaction. . . . General Washington has established his head-quarters in a convenient house, about half a mile from Harvard College, and in the vicinity of our hospital. The provincial army is encamped in various parts of this town and Roxbury, and some works have been erected on Prospect hill, and on an eminence near Roxbury church, within cannon-shot of Boston. The amount of our forces I have not ascertained; but we are daily increasing in numbers, both of militia and enlisted soldiers. The operations of the war have interrupted the progress of education at college; the students have returned to their homes, and the college buildings are occupied by our soldiery.

*July 20th.*—This day is devoted to a Public Fast throughout the United Colonies, by the recommendation of Congress, to implore the Divine benediction on our country; that any further shedding of blood may be averted; and that the calamities with which we are afflicted may be removed. This is the first general or Continental Fast ever observed since the settlement of the colonies. I have been much gratified this day with a view of General Washington. His excellency was on horseback, in company with several military gentlemen. It was not difficult to distinguish him from all others; his personal appearance is truly noble and majestic; being tall and well proportioned. His dress is a blue coat with buff-colored facings, a rich epaulette on each shoulder, buff under dress, and an elegant small sword; a black cockade in his hat.

\*        \*        \*

[October 1775] . . . The term for which the continental soldiers enlisted will expire in a few weeks, and it is understood that the recruits for a future army will be enlisted to serve to the 1st of December next, unless sooner discharged, as hopes are yet entertained that a settlement of our difficulties with Great Britain may be effected. Reports are in circulation that an attack on the town of Boston is contemplated. . . . The public appear to be impatient to have our inveterate enemies expelled from our territories.

*November.*—Our hospitals are considerably crowded with sick soldiers from camp; the prevailing diseases are autumnal fevers and dysenteric complaints, which have proved fatal in a considerable number of instances. It is highly gratifying to observe, that these brave men, while in the service of their country, receive in sickness all the kind attention from physicians and nurses, which their circumstances require; they have the prayers and consolations of pious clergymen, and are destitute of nothing but the presence of their dearest friends to alleviate their sufferings. . . . Several other store vessels have been taken by our privateers, with cargoes of provision and various kinds of stores, to a very considerable amount, which greatly augments the distresses of the troops and people in Boston, and affords us a very opportune and essential supply. It is now represented that the distresses of the inhabitants and troops in Boston exceed the possibility of description. They are almost in a state of starvation, for the want of food and fuel. The inhabitants, totally destitute of vegetables, flour and fresh provisions, have actually been obliged to feed on horse flesh; and the troops confined to salt provisions; by means of which they have become very sickly. They have taken down a number of houses, removed the pews from the church, and are digging up the timber at the wharves for fuel.

. . . [December] *4th.*—A considerable number of Connecticut troops have left our service and returned home; no persuasion could induce them to continue in service after their time of enlistment had expired. Enlisting officers are distributed in various parts of New England; but it is reported that voluntary enlistments go on slowly. The people seem to be unwilling to engage in the public service, and require higher wages. The spirit of patriotism appears in some degree to have subsided, and the militia are to be employed.

\*        \*        \*

*May* [1776]—As the small-pox is in many parts of the town among both the inhabitants and soldiers, I was advised by my friends to have recourse to inoculation for my own safety, though contrary to general orders. I was accordingly inoculated by my friend Dr. John Homans, and have passed through the disease in the most favorable manner, not suffering one day's confinement. . . .

*July 3d.*—Orders are given to inoculate for the small-pox, all the soldiers and inhabitants in town, as a general infection of this terrible disease is apprehended. Dr. Townsend and myself are now constantly engaged in this business.

*12th.* . . . The very important intelligence from Philadelphia is now proclaimed, that on the 4th instant, the American Congress declared the thirteen United Colonies, "*Free, Sovereign, Independent States.*" The subject has for some time agitated the public mind, and various opinions have been entertained relative to this momentous transaction. Opinions of much weight and authority have been and still are in collision, and it has been considered very doubtful whether the grand object would be accomplished at the present time. Objections, however, have yielded to imperious necessity, and a new epoch for United America has now commenced. We are now, in the 16th year of the reign of his Majesty King George the Third, absolved from all allegiance to the British crown; and all political connexion between us, as subjects, and his government is totally and for ever dissolved, unless indeed Providence shall so order, that we shall be again reduced to a state of dependence and vassalage.

\*     \*     \*

*August 1st.*—The continental army, under the immediate command of General Washington, is stationed at New York; and it is expected that the British army, under command of General Howe, will endeavor to take possession of that city the present season.

*5th.*—Colonel Whitcomb's regiment, consisting of five hundred men, has now gone through the small-pox in this town by inoculation, and all, except one negro, have recovered.

*7th.*—This regiment, with Colonel Sargeant's, are preparing to march to Ticonderoga. A number of teams are procured to transport the baggage and stores, and this morning, at seven o'clock, they marched out of town with colors displayed and drums beating. Being myself indisposed, I am permitted to tarry in town till my health is restored, and in the mean time I am directed to take charge of the sick soldiers that remain here.

*20th.*—Having recovered my health, and being prepared to follow our regiment, I am this day to bid adieu to the town of Boston, where I have resided very pleasantly for the last five months. I am destined to a distant part of our country, and know not what suffering and hazards I shall be called to encounter, while in the discharge of my military duty. . . .

*September.*—We took our route through Worcester, Springfield, Charlestown, in New Hampshire, and over the Green Mountains to Skeensboro'; which is the place of rendezvous for the continental troops and militia destined to Ticonderoga. Here boats are provided at the entrance of Lake Champlain, which are continually passing to and from this place. We embarked on the 6th instant, and with good oarsmen and sails we arrived the same day, and joined our regiment here, a distance of thirty miles. While on our march, we received alarming reports respecting some military operations between our army, commanded by General Washington, and the British, under command of General Howe, on Long Island, near New York. The report states that our army has suffered a complete defeat with great loss, and that two of our general officers are taken prisoners. The inhabitants through the country are in great alarm; but have not obtained the particulars; as the account at present is vague, and somewhat contradictory, we hope and trust that a particular detail will prove the event to be more favorable to our cause.

\*     \*     \*

*April 1st.* [1777]—The term of service of Colonel Whitcomb's regiment having expired, they have now left the service, and returned to New England. Having received an invitation from

Dr. Jonathan Potts, the surgeon-general in this department, to accept the office of surgeon's-mate in the general hospital, I have received the said appointment, and commenced my official duties accordingly at this place [Ticonderoga]; Dr. D. Townsend being at the same time appointed senior surgeon. We find here about eighty soldiers laboring under various diseases, and eight or ten that have been cruelly wounded by the savages who have been skulking in the woods in the vicinity. In our retired situation here, we are unacquainted with any military transactions in other quarters till they transpire in the public papers.

\*    \*    \*

*July 2d.*—The British army is now approaching; some of their savage allies have been seen in the vicinity of our out works, which, with the block-house beyond the old French lines, has this day been abandoned. On the 3d and 4th, the enemy are making their approaches and gaining as is supposed some advantages. They have taken possession of Mount Hope, our batteries are now opened, and a cannonading has commenced. General St. Clair endeavors to animate the troops, and orders every man to repair to the alarm-posts at morning and evening roll call, and to be particularly alert and vigilant. There seems to be a diversity of opinion whether General Burgoyne intends to besiege our garrison, or to attempt to possess himself of it by an assault on our lines.

*5th.*—It is with astonishment that we find the enemy have taken possession of an eminence called *Sugar-loaf Hill*, or *Mount Defiance*, which, from its height and proximity, completely overlooks and commands all our works at Ticonderoga and Mount Independence. . . . The situation of our garrison is viewed as critical and alarming. . . .

*14th.*—By reason of an extraordinary and unexpected event, the course of my Journal has been interrupted for several days. At about twelve o'clock, in the night of the 5th instant, I was urgently called from sleep, and informed that our army was in motion, and was instantly to abandon Ticonderoga and Mount Independence. I could scarcely believe that my informant was in earnest,

but the confusion and bustle soon convinced me that it was really true, and that the short time allowed demanded my utmost industry. It was enjoined on me immediately to collect the sick and wounded, and as much of the hospital stores as possible, and assist in embarking them on board the batteaux and boats at the shore. Having with all possible despatch completed our embarkation, at three o'clock in the morning of the 6th, we commenced our voyage up the South bay to Skeensboro', about thirty miles. Our fleet consisted of five armed gallies and two hundred batteaux and boats deeply laden with cannon, tents, provisions, invalids and women. We were accompanied by a guard of six hundred men, commanded by Colonel Long, of New Hampshire. . . . [They reached Skenesboro only to find themselves still pursued by Burgoyne's forces. They then marched for Fort Anne, but within a few days had to abandon that to find refuge at Fort Edward.]

The abandonment of Ticonderoga and Mount Independence has occasioned the greatest surprise and alarm. No event could be more unexpected nor more severely felt throughout our army and country. This disaster has given to our cause a dark and gloomy aspect, but our affairs are not desperate, and our exertions ought to be in proportion to our misfortunes and our exigencies. The conduct of General St. Clair on this occasion has rendered him very unpopular, and subjected him to general censure and reproach; there are some, indeed, who even accuse him of treachery; but time and calm investigation must decide whether he can vindicate himself as a judicious and prudent commander. There is much reason to suppose that neither the strength of Burgoyne's army, nor the weakness of our garrison were properly considered or generally understood. It must be universally conceded, that when the enemy had effected their great object by hoisting cannon from tree to tree, till they reached the summit of *Sugar-loaf Hill*, the situation of our garrison had become perilous in the extreme. General Schuyler is not altogether free from public reprehension, alleging that he ought in duty to have been present at Ticonderoga during the critical period. It is predicted by some of our well-informed and respectable characters, that this event, apparently so calamitous, will ultimately prove advantageous, by drawing the British army into the heart of our country, and thereby place them more immediately within our power. . . .

25*th*.—The sick soldiers under my care at this place have been accommodated in barracks and tents. I have now received orders to accompany them to the hospital at Albany, about fifty-five miles; boats being provided, we embarked about forty sick and invalids, and proceeded down the North river, and arrived on the third day at the place of our destination.

\*    \*    \*

13*th*. [September]—There is a constant intercourse kept up between this city and our army near Stillwater, by which we are regularly apprised of daily occurrences. It is now ascertained that Burgoyne has crossed the Hudson, and encamped at Saratoga, about thirty-six miles above Albany.

17*th*.—General Gates, reposing full confidence in the courage and strength of his army, seems to have determined to march and confront his formidable enemy, and endeavor to force him and his troops back to Canada, . . .

18*th and* 19*th*.—Our army is advancing towards the enemy in three columns, under Generals Lincoln and Arnold, General Gates in the centre. A terrible conflict is daily expected; both parties appear to be determined to commence the work of destruction.

20*th*.—By express arrived in this city last night, it is announced that the two armies fought in the field, yesterday, a very sanguinary battle, the particulars of which are not fully understood; but it is reported that from the closeness and obstinacy of the combat, the carnage on both sides was prodigious. It is with inexpressible satisfaction that we learn our troops behaved with that undaunted bravery which has secured to them the victory, and were it not for the darkness of the evening when the battle closed, it would have been more complete.

21*st and* 22*d*.—A considerable number of officers and soldiers who were wounded in the late battle, have been brought here to be accommodated in our hospital, or in private houses in this city. Several of these unfortunate but brave men have received wounds of a very formidable and dangerous nature, and many of them must be subjected to capital operations.

\*    \*    \*

*October* 1*st*.—The situation of the royal army under Burgoyne, is now considered extremely precarious; his march to Albany is deemed absolutely impracticable, and a retreat to Canada must be attended with insurmountable difficulties and dangers. It is well understood, that he calculates on the coöperation of Sir Henry Clinton, by sending from New York a force up the North river to endeavor to effect a passage to Albany, or at least to occasion such alarm, as to draw off a part of General Gates' army from before him. Messengers or persons in the character of spies, are frequently suspected of passing from one British commander to the other. A man, by name Nathan Palmer, was, a few days since, seized in General Putnam's camp, at Peekskill, under suspicious circumstances, and on trial was found to be a lieutenant in the tory new levies, and he was executed as a spy.

4*th*.—By intelligence from camp, it appears that Burgoyne has thrown up a line of intrenchments in front of his camp, and is making every possible effort to strengthen his position and prepare for another conflict. The Canadians and his savage allies being greatly dissatisfied and discouraged, have deserted his standard since the last battle. The advantages obtained over the enemy on this occasion, excites the greatest exultation and rejoicing throughout our army and country. It is indeed a remarkable fact, which must animate the heart of every friend to the cause of America, that our troops, so little accustomed to encounter the prowess of European veterans, and the peculiar warfare of the savages, should face these enemies with such undaunted courage and intrepidity. Sanguine hopes are now entertained that we shall, by the help of Providence, be finally enabled to destroy or capture the whole British army. Our troops are panting for another opportunity of displaying their valor, and another dreadful conflict is daily expected; alternate hopes and fears continually agitate our minds, and create the greatest anxiety and solicitude. What can excite ideas more noble and sublime, than impending military events, on which depend the destiny of a nation?

\*    \*    \*

8*th.*—The anticipated important intelligence has just reached us, that a most severe engagement took place yesterday, between the two armies, at a place between Stillwater and Saratoga, called Bemis' Heights. It is supposed to be the hardest fought battle, and the most honorable to our army, of any since the commencement of hostilities. The enemy was completely repulsed in every quarter, and his defeat was attended with irreparable loss of officers, men, artillery, tents and baggage. Our officers and men acquired the highest honor; they fought like heroes, and their loss is very inconsiderable. General Arnold has received a wound in his leg. I am impatient to receive the particular details of this capital event.

\*    \*    \*

11*th.*—The night after the battle, Burgoyne silently moved from his position, and on the 8th there was considerable skirmishing through the day, with some loss on both sides. We have to lament the misfortune of Major-General Lincoln, who, while reconnoitring the enemy, advanced so near, that a whole volley of musketry was discharged at him, and he received a dangerous wound in his leg. It is reported that, the day after the battle, upwards of one hundred of the enemy's dead were found unburied in the field. General Gates having detached a body of troops to get into the rear of the British army, Burgoyne took the alarm, and resolved to retreat immediately to Saratoga; accordingly in the night of the 9th instant, he silently moved off, leaving in our possession his hospital, containing three hundred sick and wounded, with medicinal stores, and two hundred barrels of flour, &c. It is a fact, both unaccountable and disgraceful, that on their retreat they committed the most wanton devastations, burning

and destroying almost every house within their reach; the elegant and valuable country seat of General Schuyler, near Saratoga, did not escape their fury. The situation of the royal army is now extremely deplorable, and there is scarcely a possibility of their final escape. General Gates has so arranged his forces as to cut off their retreat, and is endeavoring to surround them on every quarter. May the Almighty Ruler grant that our efforts may be crowned with still more glorious success!

12*th.*—The wounded officers and soldiers of our army, and those of the enemy who have fallen into our hands, are crowding into our hospital, and require our constant attention. The last night I watched with the celebrated General Arnold, whose leg was badly fractured by a musket-ball while in the engagement with the enemy on the 7th instant. He is very peevish, and impatient under his misfortunes, and required all my attention during the night, but I devoted an hour in writing a letter to a friend in Boston, detailing the particulars of the late battle.

\*    \*    \*

21*st.*—The captive Generals Burgoyne, Phillips, Reidesel, &c. with a number of ladies of high rank, arrived last evening at the hospitable mansion of General Schuyler in this city. . . .

22*d.*—The magnanimous General Schuyler, with his lady and daughters, have given their unfortunate guests a friendly and polite reception, characteristic of this noble spirited family. Notwithstanding General Burgoyne destroyed their beautiful villa at Saratoga, they appear disposed to console them in their misfortune by all the civilities and attention in their power.

23*d.*—General Burgoyne gratefully acknowledged the generous treatment received from General Schuyler, and observed to him, "You show me great kindness, sir, though I have done you much injury." To which he magnanimously replied, "*That was the fate of war!* let us say no more about it."

24*th.*—This hospital is now crowded with officers and soldiers from the field of battle; those belonging to the British and Hessian troops, are accommodated in the same hospital with our own men, and receive equal care and attention. The foreigners are under the care and management of their own surgeons. I have been present at some of their capital operations, and remarked that the English surgeons perform with skill and dexterity, but the Germans, with a few exceptions, do no credit to their profession; some of them are the most uncouth and clumsy operators I ever witnessed, and appear to be destitute of all sympathy and tenderness towards the suffering patient. Not less than one thousand wounded and sick are now in this city; the Dutch church, and several private houses are occupied as hospitals. We have about thirty surgeons, and mates; and all are constantly employed. I am obliged to devote the whole of my time, from eight o'clock in the morning to a late hour in the evening, to the care of our patients. Here is a fine field for professional improvement. Amputating limbs, trepanning fractured skulls, and dressing the most formidable wounds, have familiarized my mind to scenes of woe. A military hospital is peculiarly calculated to afford examples for profitable contemplation, and to interest our sympathy and commiseration. If I turn from beholding mutilated bodies, mangled limbs and bleeding, incurable wounds, a spectacle no less revolting is presented, of miserable objects, languishing under afflicting diseases of every description—here, are those in a mournful state of despair, exhibiting the awful harbingers of approaching dissolution—there, are those with emaciated bodies and ghastly visage, who begin to triumph over grim disease and just lift their feeble heads from the pillow of sorrow. No parent, wife or sister, to wipe the tear of anguish from their eyes, or to soothe the pillow of death, they look up to the physician as their only earthly friend and comforter, and trust the hands of a stranger to perform the last mournful duties. Frequently have I re-marked their confidence in my friendship, as though I was endeared to them by brotherly ties. Viewing these unfortunate men as the faithful defenders of the liberties of our country, far separated from their dearest friends, who would be so lost to the duties of humanity, patriotism, and benevolence, as not to minister to their comfort, and pour into their wounds the healing balm of consolation? It is my lot to have twenty wounded men committed to my care, by Dr. Potts, our surgeon-general; one of whom, a young man, received a musket-ball through his cheeks, cutting its way through the teeth on each side, and the substance of the tongue; his sufferings have been great, but he now begins to articulate tolerably well. Another had the whole side of his face torn off by a cannon-ball, laying his mouth and throat open to view. A brave soldier received a musket-ball in his forehead, observing that it did not penetrate deep, it was imagined that the ball rebounded and fell out; but after several days, on examination, I detected the ball laying flat on the bone, and spread under the skin, which I removed. No one can doubt but he received his wound while facing the enemy, and it is fortunate for the brave fellow that his skull proved too thick for the ball to penetrate. . . .

## REVIEW QUESTIONS

1. What images does Thacher present of the Continental officers and forces? Of the British? Consider why he thought them noteworthy enough to record.
2. What were Thacher's duties as a surgeon's mate?
3. Describe the conditions of war as Thacher saw them.
4. How does he account for the soldiers withstanding such conditions?

## A CHAPLAIN

# An Address to General St. Clair's Brigade (1776)

*James Thacher may well have been in the audience when a minister addressed the troops at Fort Ticonderoga on 20 October 1776. The Continental Congress and its army's commander in chief both supported the recruitment of chaplains. As Washington noted in 1776: divine providence is always necessary but especially in dangerous times. In recognition of the troops' religious pluralism, Washington also advocated that each regiment choose its own chaplain to best fit the particular religious sentiments of its soldiers. Not all regiments had a chaplain all the time, but it appears that in the fall of 1776 there may have been up to eight chaplains with the state and continental units at Fort Ticonderoga and Mount Independence, the fortifications guarding a narrow channel on Lake Champlain. In their sermons, chaplains generally expounded on a biblical passage that they believed addressed a particular concern (such as immorality) or situation (an imminent battle). Like some civilian ministers, many added Enlightenment philosophy and revolutionary political ideas to religious doctrine. The author of the following address, which is not fully a sermon, shows the connection between sacred and secular duties. Finding the authors of works published anonymously is often difficult, but researchers have suggested that the following people may have written the address: John Hurt, chaplain of the Sixth Virginia Regiment; William Tennent, of a Connecticut state regiment; and, perhaps most likely, David Jones, of the Third Pennsylvania.*

*An Address to General St. Clair's Brigade, at Ticonderoga, when the Enemy were hourly expected*, October 20, 1776 (Philadelphia: Steiner & Cist, 1777). Historical Society of Pennsylvania document at the Library Company of Philadelphia.

*My Countrymen, Fellow-soldiers and Friends,*

I am sorry that during this campaign I have been favoured with so few opportunities of addressing you on subjects of the greatest importance both with respect to this life and that which is to come, but what is past cannot be recalled, and NOW time will not admit an enlargement, as we have the greatest reason to expect the advancement of our enemies as speedily as Heaven will permit:[1] Therefore, at present, let it suffice to bring to your remembrance some *necessary truths.*

It is our *common faith*, and a very just one too, that all events on earth are under the notice of that GOD in whom we live, move and have our being; therefore we must believe, that in this important struggle with the worst of enemies, he has assigned us our post here at Ticonderoga.

Our situation is such, that if properly defended, we shall give our enemies a fatal blow, and in great measure prove the *means* of the *salvation* of North America.

Such is our present case, that we are fighting for all that is near and *dear* to us, whilst our enemies are engaged in the worst of causes, their design being to subjugate, plunder and enslave a free

---

[1]Depending on the wind, which blew strongly to the north.

people that have done them no harm. Their tyrannical views are so glaring, their cause so horridly bad, that there still remain too much goodness and humanity in Great-Britain to engage unanimously against us, therefore they have been obliged (and at a most amazing expence too) to hire the assistance of a barbarous, mercenary people, that would cut your throats for the small reward of sixpence. No doubt these have hopes of being our taskmasters, and would rejoice at our calamities.

Look, oh! look therefore at your respective States, and anticipate the consequences if these vassals are suffered to enter! It would fail the most fruitful imagination to represent in a proper light what anguish, what horror, what distress would spread over the whole! See, oh! see the dear wives of your bosoms forced from their peaceful habitations, and perhaps used with such indecency that modesty would forbid the discription. Behold the fair virgins of your land, whose benevolent souls are now filled with a thousand good wishes and hopes of seeing their *admirers* return home crowned with victory, would not only meet with a doleful disappointment, but also with such insults and abuses that would induce their tender hearts to pray for the shades of death. See your children exposed as vagabonds to all the calamities of this life! Then, oh! then adieu to all felicity this side of the grave!

Now all these calamities may be prevented, if our GOD be for us, and who can doubt of this who observes the point in which the wind blows,[2] if you will only acquit yourselves like men, and with firmness of mind go forth against your enemies, resolving either to return with victory, or to die gloriously. Every one that may fall in this dispute, will be justly esteemed a *Martyr* to liberty, and his name will be had in precious *memory* while the love of freedom remains in the breasts of men. All whom GOD will favour to see a glorious victory, will return to their respective States with every mark of honour, and be received with joy and gladness of heart by all friends to liberty and lovers of mankind.

As our present case is singular, I hope therefore that the candid will excuse me, if I now conclude with an uncommon address in substance principally extracted from the writings of the servants of GOD in the old testament; though at the same time it is freely acknowledged that I am not possessed of any similar power either of blessing or cursing.

1. Blessed be that man who is possessed of true love to liberty; and let all the people say, *Amen*.
2. Blessed be that man who is a friend to the common rights of mankind; and let all the people say, *Amen*.
3. Blessed be that man who is a friend to the United States of America; and let all the people say, *Amen*.
4. Blessed be that man who will use his utmost endeavour to oppose the tyranny of Great-Britain, and to vanquish all her forces invading North-America; and let all the people say, *Amen*.
5. Blessed be that man who is resolved never to submit to Great-Britain; and let all the people say, *Amen*.
6. Blessed be that man who in the present dispute esteems not his life too good to fall a sacrifice in defence of his country;—let his posterity, if any he has, be blessed with riches, honour, virtue and true religion; and let all the people say, *Amen*.

Now on the other hand, as far as is consistent with the holy scriptures, let all these blessings be turned into curses to him who deserts the noble cause in which we are engaged; and turns his back to the enemy before he receives proper orders to retreat; and let all the people say, *Amen*.

Let him be abhorred by all the United States of America.

Let faintness of heart and fear never forsake him on earth.

Let him be a magor missabib, a terror to himself and all around him.

Let him be accursed in his outgoing, and cursed in his incoming; cursed in lying down, and

---

[2]The wind blew north, preventing vessels from reaching Crown Point.

cursed in uprising; cursed in basket, and cursed in store.

Let him be cursed in his *connexions*, 'till his *wretched* head with dishonour is laid low in the dust; and let all the soldiers say, *Amen.*

And may the GOD of all grace, in whom we live, enable us, in defence of our country, to acquit ourselves like men, to his honour and praise. *Amen and Amen.*

## REVIEW QUESTIONS

1. What are the author's "necessary truths" and how do they compare to Thomas Paine's "common sense" and James Chalmers's "plain truth"?
2. How does the author intermingle spiritual and temporal means and ends?
3. What does the author want his listeners (and, by extension, his readers) to do?

# PHILLIS WHEATLEY

# On the Death of General Wooster (1778)

*Poetry sang the sentiments of both the Patriots and Loyalists, and women as well as men contributed to the Revolution's verses as they did to its events. One notable woman scribe was Mercy Otis Warren (1728–1814), a well-born, well-connected writer who published her work anonymously until the 1790s. Another was Phillis Wheatley (c. 1753–1784), who was born in Africa, enslaved, educated by the family that bought her, and then, with her master's help, published a book of poetry in 1773 in London. In both cases, Warren as a woman of privilege and Wheatley as a privileged female slave, these exceptional women faced challenges to being heard, but certainly Wheatley faced greater ones, which may be a reason that Warren was more forthright in her thoughts and Wheatley more subtle. Wheatley was ultimately freed upon the deaths of her mistress and then master, Boston merchant John Wheatley. She married, but when her husband was jailed for debt, she had to work as a maid. She continued to write poetry, but the loss of patrons and the upheavals of revolution meant she was not able to publish another volume as she did in 1773; instead some pieces were published individually in newspapers. Although slavery rarely figured in her poems, Wheatley did slip in references as she wrote about religious and revolutionary matters. The latter was the case when she wrote an elegy marking the death of General David Wooster. Years earlier Wheatley had written Wooster, then a Connecticut merchant, about her trip to England in 1773 to promote her book. Wooster, who had served in the invasion of Canada in 1775, was in command of Connecticut's militia forces when he was mortally wounded at the Battle of Ridgefield on 27 April 1777 (he died on 2 May).*

From *The Collected Works of Phillis Wheatley*, edited by John Shields (New York: Oxford University Press, 1988), pp. 149–50.

From this the Muse rich consolation draws
He nobly perish'd in his Country's cause
His Country's Cause that ever fir'd his mind
Where martial flames, and Christian virtues join'd.
How shall my pen his warlike deeds proclaim                    5
Or paint them fairer on the list of Fame—
Enough, great Chief-now wrapt in Shades around,
Thy grateful Country shall thy praise resound—
Tho not with mortals' empty praise elate
That vainest vapour to th' immortal State                     10
Inly serene the expiring hero lies
And thus (while heav'nward roll his swimming eyes):

   "Permit, great power, while yet my fleeting breath
And Spirits wander to the verge of Death—
Permit me yet to point fair freedom's charms                 15
For her the Continent shines bright in arms,
By thy high will, celestial prize she came—
For her we combat on the field of fame
Without her presence vice maintains full sway
And social love and virtue wing their way                    20
O still propitious be thy guardian care
And lead Columbia thro' the toils of war.
With thine own hand conduct them and defend
And bring the dreadful contest to an end—
For ever grateful let them live to thee                      25
And keep them ever Virtuous, brave, and free—
But how, presumptuous shall we hope to find
Divine acceptance with th' Almighty mind—
While yet (O deed Ungenerous!) they disgrace
And hold in bondage Afric's blameless race?                  30
Let Virtue reign—And thou accord our prayers
Be victory our's, and generous freedom theirs."
The hero pray'd—the wond'ring spirits fled
And sought the unknown regions of the dead—
Tis thine, fair partner of his life, to find                35
His virtuous path and follow close behind—
A little moment steals him from thy sight
He waits thy coming to the realms of light
Freed from his labours in the ethereal Skies
Where in succession endless pleasures rise!                  40

# REVIEW QUESTIONS

1. Phillis Wheatley sent this poem to Mary Wooster, the general's widow. What consolation did the poet offer the widow?

2. What does Wheatley have to say about "fair freedom's charms" and champions?

3. How are the Revolution's champions ungenerous? What may they do to increase their virtue?

# Petition to the Assembly of Pennsylvania against the Slave Trade (March 1780)

*African Americans, both free and enslaved, fought in the armies of both sides of the American Revolution and desired, in turn, to benefit from such service. Others had not joined in the military fight, but they also hoped that the rhetoric of the Revolution would translate into freedom and rights for blacks. "A Black Whig" wrote a sermon in 1782 glorifying American independence. As he focused on America's righteousness, he slipped in a request that Americans remember the slaves: "And now my virtuous fellow citizens, let me intreat you, that, after you have rid yourselves of the British yoke, that you will also emancipate those who have been all their life time subject to bondage."*

*As Americans created new state constitutions and legislation, they grappled with the issue. Although not all acted immediately, nor provided for immediate emancipation, states from the Middle Atlantic region to New England did move to abolish slavery. Pennsylvania, for instance, passed an act for gradual emancipation in 1780 that allowed owners to retain the slaves they already had, but stipulated that children born to a slave mother after the act's passage would be servants until the age of twenty-eight and then be freed. To retain the slaves they already had, owners had to register them by November 1780; if they did not, they could lose their slaves (and a number of unregistered slaves did gain immediate freedom). Furthermore, slaves brought into the state could not be held in servitude longer than seven years unless they came in under the age of twenty-one; then they could be kept until they were twenty-eight. Finally, the act nullified laws that discriminated against blacks, stating that blacks were to be judged and punished just like other inhabitants. States south of Pennsylvania, however, did not accept general emancipation, though most did relax manumission laws that allowed owners to liberate slaves individually.*

---

"Petition to the Assembly of Pennsylvania against the Slave Trade, March 1780," Historical Society of Pennsylvania. *Sermon, On the Present Situation of the Affairs of America and Great-Britain.* Written by a Black, and printed at the Request of several Persons of distinguished Characters (Philadelphia: T. Bradford & P. Hall, 1782, Library Company of Philadelphia).

---

To the Representatives of the Freemen of the Commonwealth of Pennsylvania, in General Assembly met,

The Representation and Petition of the Subscribers, Citizens of Pennsylvania.

Your Petitioners have observed, with great satisfaction, the salutary effects of the Law of this State, passed on the first day of March, 1780, for the "gradual abolition of slavery."—They have also seen, with equal satisfaction, the progress which the humane and just principles of that Law have made in other States.

They, however, find themselves called upon, by the interesting nature of those principles, to suggest to the General Assembly, that vessels have been publicly equipt in this Port for the Slave Trade, and that several other practices have taken place which they conceive to be inconsistent with the spirit of the Law abovementioned; and that these, and other circumstances relating to the afflicted Africans, do, in the opinion of your Petitioners, require the further interposition of the Legislature.

Your Petitioners, therefore, earnestly request that you will again take this subject into your serious consideration, and that you will make such additions to the said Law, as shall effectually put a stop to the Slave Trade being carried on directly or indirectly in this Commonwealth, and to answer other purposes of benevolence and justice to an oppressed part of the human species.

1688 signatures

## REVIEW QUESTIONS

1. Why, given that the state had just passed an act providing for gradual emancipation, did Pennsylvania citizens again petition their assembly about slavery in March 1780?
2. What was their argument?
3. Pennsylvania did not pass legislation complying with their request until 1788. Why do you think it took so long?

# FROM *Massachusetts Bill of Rights* (1780)

*As the armies clashed on fields of battle, and as soldiers fought for reasons both patriotic and personal, American politicians and statesmen gathered in conventions, congresses, and legislatures to formulate, fight over, and finally install new governments based on principles espoused in new constitutions. The* Massachusetts Bill of Rights *leads off that state's constitution of 1780. The* Declaration of Rights *and* Frame of Government *that together formed the constitution were the result of much thought on the nature of the Revolution and the proper relationship between a people and their government. In 1778, when Massachusetts's provisional legislature presented its draft of a constitution to the people for ratification, the people rejected it. They did not like some of its provisions, its lack of a bill of rights, and, very important, the government writing its own "compact." They believed that the people should create the contract that in turn begets the government. The legislature's response in 1780 was to allow a constitutional convention to meet and decide on the issue, one that resulted in a constitution that embodied such Enlightenment principles as social contract, popular sovereignty, and separation of powers.*

From Francis N. Thorpe, ed., *The Federal and State Constitutions*, vol. 3 (Washington, D.C., 1909), pp. 1888–95.

The end of the institution, maintenance, and administration of government, is to secure the existence of the body-politic, to protect it, and to furnish the individuals who compose it with the power of enjoying in safety and tranquillity their natural rights, and the blessings of life: and whenever these great objects are not obtained, the people have a right to alter the government, and to take measures necessary for their safety, prosperity, and happiness.

The body-politic is formed by a voluntary association of individuals; it is a social compact by which the whole people covenants with each citizen and each citizen with the whole people that all shall be governed by certain laws for the common good. It is the duty of the people, therefore, in framing a constitution of government, to provide for an equitable mode of making laws, as well as for an impartial interpretation and a faithful execution of them; that every man may, at all times, find his security in them.

We, therefore, the people of Massachusetts, acknowledging, with grateful hearts the goodness of the great Legislator of the universe, in affording us, in the course of His Providence, an opportunity, deliberately and peaceably, without fraud, violence, or surprise, of entering into an original, explicit, and solemn compact with each other; and of forming a new constitution of civil government, for ourselves and posterity; and devoutly imploring His direction in so interesting a design, do agree upon, ordain, and establish the following Declaration of Rights, and Frame of Government, as the Constitution of the Commonwealth of Massachusetts.

# A Declaration of the Rights of the Inhabitants of the Commonwealth of Massachusetts

Article I. All men are born free and equal, and have certain natural, essential and unalienable rights; among which may be reckoned the right of enjoying and defending their lives and liberties; that of acquiring, possessing, and protecting property; in fine, that of seeking and obtaining their safety and happiness.

II. It is the right as well as the duty of all men in society, publicly, and at stated seasons, to worship the Supreme Being, the great Creator and Preserver of the universe. And no subject shall be hurt, molested, or restrained, in his person, liberty, or estate, for worshipping God in the manner and season most agreeable to the dictates of his own conscience; or for his religious profession of sentiments; provided he doth not disturb the public peace, or obstruct others in their religious worship. . . .

As the happiness of a people and the good order and preservation of civil government essentially depend upon piety, religion, and morality, and as these cannot be generally diffused through a community but by the institution of the public worship of God and of public instructions, in piety, religion, and morality. Therefore to promote their happiness and secure the good order and preservation of their government, the people of this commonwealth have a right to invest their legislature with power to authorize and require, and the legislature shall from time to time authorize and require, the several towns. . . . and other bodies—politic or religious societies, to make suitable provision, at their own expense, for the institution of the public worship of God and the support and maintenance of public Protestant teachers of piety, religion, and morality. . . .

And the people of this commonwealth. . . . do invest their legislature with authority to enjoin upon all the subjects an attendance upon the instructions of the public teachers aforesaid. . . .

And every denomination of Christians, demeaning themselves peaceably and as good subjects of the commonwealth, shall be equally under the protection of the law; and no subordination of any one sect or denomination to another shall ever be established by law.

IV. The people of this commonwealth have the sole and exclusive right of governing themselves, as a free, sovereign, and independent State, and do, and forever hereafter shall, exercise and enjoy every power, jurisdiction, and right, which is not, or may not hereafter be, by them expressly delegated to the United States of America, in Congress assembled.

V. All power residing originally in the people, and being derived from them, the several magistrates and officers of government, vested with authority, whether legislative, executive, or judicial, are their substitutes and agents, and are at all times accountable to them.

VI. No man, nor corporation, or association of men, have any other title to obtain advantages, or particular and exclusive privileges, distinct from those of the community, than what arises from the consideration of services rendered to the public; and this title being in nature neither hereditary, nor transmissible to children, or descendants, or relations by blood; the idea of a man born a magistrate, lawgiver, or judge, is absurd and unnatural.

VII. Government is instituted for the common good, for the protection, safety, prosperity, and happiness of the people and not for the profit, honor or private interest of any one man, family, or class of men; therefore the people alone have an incontestible unalienable, and indefeasible right to institute government; and to reform, alter, or totally change the same, when their protection, safety, prosperity, and happiness require it.

VIII. In order to prevent those who are vested with authority from becoming oppressors, the people have a right, at such periods and in such manner as they shall establish by their frame of government, to cause their public officers to return to private life; and to fill up vacant places by certain and regular elections and appointments.

IX. All elections ought to be free; and all the inhabitants of this commonwealth, having such qualifications as they shall establish by their frame of government, have an equal right to elect officers, and to be elected, for public employments.

X. Each individual of the society has a right to be protected by it in the enjoyment of his life, liberty, and property. . . . No part of the property of any individual can, with justice, be taken from him, or applied to public uses, without his own consent, or that of the representative body of the people. . . . And whenever the public exigencies require that the property of any individual should be appropriated to public uses, he shall receive a reasonable compensation therefor.

XI. Every subject of the commonwealth ought to find a certain remedy, by having recourse to the laws, for all injuries or wrongs which he may receive in his person, property, or character. He ought to obtain right and justice freely, and without being obliged to purchase it; completely, and without any denial; promptly, and without delay, conformably to the laws.

XII. No subject shall be held to answer for any crimes or offence, until the same is fully and plainly . . . described to him; or be compelled to accuse, or furnish evidence against himself. And every subject shall have a right to produce all proofs that may be favorable to him; to meet the witnesses against him face to face, and to be fully heard in his defence by himself, or his counsel, at his election. And no subject shall be arrested . . . or deprived of his life, liberty, or estate, but by the judgement of his peers, or the law of the land.

And the legislature shall not make any law that shall subject any person to a capital or infamous punishment, excepting for the government of the army and navy, without trial by jury. . . .

XIV. Every subject has a right to be secure from all unreasonable searches, and seizures, of his person, his houses, his papers, and all his possessions. . . . And no warrant ought to be issued but in cases, and with the formalities prescribed by the laws.

XV. In all controversies concerning property, and in all suits between two or more persons . . . the parties have a right to a trial by jury; and this method of procedure shall be held sacred. . . .

XVI. The liberty of the press is essential to the security of freedom in a state it ought not, therefore, to be restricted in this commonwealth.

XVII. The people have a right to keep and to bear arms for the common defence. And as, in time of peace, armies are dangerous to liberty, they ought not to be maintained without the consent of the legislature; and the military power shall always be held in an exact subordination to the civil authority, and be governed by it.

XVIII. A frequent recurrence to the fundamental principles of the constitution, and a constant adherence to those of piety, justice, moderation, temperance, industry and frugality, are absolutely necessary to preserve the advantages of liberty, and to maintain a free government. The people ought, consequently, to have a particular attention to all those principles, in the choice of their officers and representatives: and they have a right to require of their lawgivers and magistrates an exact and constant observance of them, in the formation and execution of the laws necessary for the good administration of the commonwealth.

XIX. The people have a right, in an orderly and peaceable manner to assemble to consult upon the common good; give instructions to their representatives, and to request of the legislative body, by the way of addresses, petitions, or remonstrances, redress of the wrongs done them, and of the grievances they suffer.

XX. The power of suspending the laws, or the execution of the laws, ought never to be exercised but by the legislature, or by authority derived from it, to be exercised in such particular cases only as the legislature shall expressly provide for.

XXI. The freedom of deliberation, speech, and debate, in either house of the legislature, is so essential to the rights of the people, that it cannot be the foundation of any accusation or prosecution, action or complaint, in any other court or place whatsoever.

XXII. The legislature ought frequently to assemble for the redress of grievances, for correcting, strengthening, and confirming the laws, and for making new laws, as the common good may require.

XXIII. No subsidy, charge, tax, impost, or duties ought to be established, fixed, laid or levied, under any pretext whatsoever, without the consent of the people or their representatives in the legislature.

XXIV. Laws made to punish for actions done before the existence of such laws, and which have not been declared crimes by preceding laws, are unjust, oppressive, and inconsistent with the fundamental principles of a free government.

XXV. No subject ought, in any case, or in any time, to be declared guilty of treason or felony by the legislature.

XXVI. No magistrate or court of law shall demand excessive bail or sureties, impose excessive fines, or inflict cruel or unusual punishments.

XXVII. In time of peace, no soldier ought to be quartered in any house without the consent of the owner; and in time of war, such quarters ought not to be made but by the civil magistrate, in a manner ordained by the legislature.

XXVIII. No person can in any case be subject to law-martial, or to any penalties or pains, by virtue of that law, except those employed in the army or navy, and except the militia in actual service, but by authority of the legislature.

XXIX. It is essential to the preservation of the rights of every individual, his life, liberty, property, and character, that there be an impartial interpretation of the laws, and administration of justice. It is the right of every citizen to be tried by judges as free, impartial, and independent as the lot of humanity will admit. It is, therefore, not only the best policy, but for the security of the rights of the people, and of every citizen, that the judges of the supreme judicial court should hold their offices as long as they behave themselves well; and that they should have honorable salaries ascertained and established by standing laws.

XXX. In the government of this commonwealth, the legislative department shall never exercise the executive and judicial powers, or either of them: the executive shall never exercise the legislative and judicial powers, or either of them: the judicial shall never exercise the legislative and executive powers, or either of them: to the end it may be a government of laws and not of men.

## REVIEW QUESTIONS

1. What human rights are listed in this document? Of those, which appear to have been the most important to the people of Massachusetts? Why?

2. How did the framers balance the rights of the one—the individual—against the rights of the many—the community?

3. How did the framers ensure that political power would remain with the people; in other words, by what means was the government made answerable to the will of the people?

4. How revolutionary were the thoughts expressed in this *Bill of Rights*?

# FROM *Virginia Statute of Religious Liberty* (1786)

*Shortly after Virginia established a new government under its constitution of 1776, Thomas Jefferson, along with other like-minded representatives in the House of Delegates, started to propose numerous bills to reform even more fully both government and society. The Virginia Assembly quickly accepted a few of the bills, which dealt with such matters as inheritance of property, slavery, crime, education, and religion, rejected some others that seemed to require too radical a change, and then slowly worked its way through the rest, approving many of them after the war was over, when Jefferson was away representing the country in France. Jefferson's* Bill for Establishing Religious Freedom *was one of the latter proposals and was in response to the colony of Virginia's having sanctioned and supported the Church of England by way of law and taxes. Jefferson proposed that the state of Virginia support religious freedom instead of any one church. The Assembly passed the bill in January 1786.*

From William W. Hering, ed., *The Statutes at Large of Virginia*, 13 vols. (New York, 1819–23), 12:86.

January 16, 1786

## An Act for establishing Religious Freedom

I. WHEREAS Almighty God hath created the mind free; that all attempts to influence it by temporal punishments or burthens, or by civil incapacitations, tend only to beget habits of hypocrisy and meanness, and are a departure from the plan of the Holy author of our religion, who being Lord both of body and mind, yet chose not to propagate it by coercions on either, as was in his Almighty power to do; that the impious presumption of legislators and rulers, civil as well as ecclesiastical, who being themselves but fallible and uninspired men, have assumed dominion over the faith of others, setting up their own opinions and modes of thinking as the only true and infallible, and as such endeavouring to impose them on others, hath established and maintained false religions over the greatest part of the world, and through all time; that to compel a man to furnish contributions of money for the propagation of opinions which he disbelieves, is sinful and tyrannical; that even the forcing him to support this or that teacher of his own religious persuasion, is depriving him of the comfortable liberty of giving his contributions to the particular pastor whose morals he would make his pattern, and whose powers he feels most persuasive to righteousness, and is withdrawing from the ministry those temporary rewards, which proceeding from an approbation of their personal conduct, are an additional incitement to earnest and unremitting labours for the instruction of mankind; that our civil rights have no dependence on our religious opinions, any more than our opinions in physics or geometry; that therefore the proscribing any citizen as unworthy the public confidence by laying upon him an incapacity of being called to offices of trust and emolument, unless he profess or renounce this or that religious opinion, is depriving him injuriously of those privileges and advantages to which in common with his fellow-citizens he has a natural right, that it tends only to corrupt the principles of that religion it is meant to encourage, by bribing with a monopoly of worldly honours and emoluments, those who will externally profess and conform to it; that though indeed these are criminal who do not withstand such temptation, yet neither are those innocent who lay the bait in their way; that to suffer the civil magistrate to intrude his powers into the field of opinion, and to restrain the profession or propagation of principles on supposition of their ill tendency, is a dangerous fallacy, which at once destroys all religious liberty, because he being of course judge of that tendency will make his opinions the rule of judgment, and approve or condemn the sentiments of others only as they shall square with or differ from his own; that it is time enough for the rightful purposes of civil government, for its officers to interfere when principles break out into overt acts against peace and good order; and finally, that truth is great and will prevail if left to herself, that she is the proper and sufficient antagonist to error, and has nothing to fear from the conflict, unless by human interposition disarmed of her natural weapons, free argument and debate, errors ceasing to be dangerous when it is permitted freely to contradict them.

II. Be it enacted by the General Assembly, that no man shall be compelled to frequent or support any religious worship, place or ministry whatsoever, nor shall be enforced, restrained, molested, or burthened in his body or goods, nor shall otherwise suffer on account of his religious opinions or belief; but that all men shall be free to profess, and by argument to maintain, their opinion in matters of religion, and that the same shall in no wise diminish, enlarge or affect their civil capacities.

III. And though we well know that this assembly, elected by the people for the ordinary purposes of legislation only, have no power to restrain the acts of succeeding assemblies, constituted with powers equal to our own, and that therefore to declare this act to be irrevocable would be of no effect in law; yet as we are free to declare, and do declare, that the rights hereby asserted are of the natural rights of mankind and that if any act shall hereafter be passed to repeal the present, or to narrow its operation, such act will be an infringement of natural right.

## REVIEW QUESTIONS

1. What was the purpose of section one?
2. Did Jefferson effectively prove his case for religious freedom? How did he answer those people with religious reservations?
3. How was freedom of religion defined in this statute?
4. Why was it deemed a natural right? And why must it be a civil liberty?

# FROM The Articles of Confederation (Ratified 1781)

*On 12 June 1776, just five days after Richard Henry Lee had moved that a resolution be adopted declaring the colonies to be free and independent states, the Second Continental Congress appointed a committee to draft a constitution for the new nation's government. Independence was declared before the committee was ready to report back, but soon thereafter, on 12 July, the committee submitted its proposal to Congress. The committee's draft, a revision of one written by John Dickinson, made Congress—as a body of national government—stronger than the states. The delegates did not approve. Reflecting Americans' fears of too strong a central government, the representatives made major changes that switched the seat of power back to the states. Writing and deciding on these revisions was a lengthy and interrupted process because Congress had a war to run as well, but on 17 November 1777 Congress approved the Articles of Confederation and submitted them to the states for ratification. Although a few states signified their approval by July 1778, full ratification came neither quickly nor easily, for many thought the powers granted Congress were still too great. The major issue, however, became that of control over the western lands. Maryland refused to ratify until Virginia ceded her western land claims to the United States. When Virginia made that concession in January 1781, Maryland ratified in February, and the Articles officially went into effect on 1 March.*

From James D. Richardson, comp., *A Compilation of the Messages and Papers of the Presidents, 1789–1902*, vol. 1 (Washington, D.C., Bureau of National Literature and Art, 1904), pp. 9–18.

## Agreed to by Congress November 15, 1777; Ratified and in Force, March 1, 1781

TO ALL TO WHOM these Presents shall come, we the undersigned Delegates of the States affixed to our Names send greeting. Whereas the Delegates of the United States of America in Congress assembled did on the fifteenth day of November in the Year of our Lord One Thousand Seven Hundred and Seventy seven, and the Second Year of the Independence of America agree to certain articles of Confederation and perpetual Union . . . in the Words following, viz. "Articles of Confederation and perpetual Union between the states. . . .

Art. I. The Stile of this confederacy shall be "The United States of America."

Art. II. Each state retains its sovereignty, freedom and independence, and every Power, Jurisdiction and right, which is not by this confederation expressly delegated to the United States, in Congress assembled.

Art. III. The said states hereby severally enter into a firm league of friendship with each other, for their common defence, the security of their Liberties, and their mutual and general welfare, binding themselves to assist each other, against all force offered to, or attacks made upon them, or any of them, on account of religion, sovereignty, trade, or any other pretence whatever.

Art. IV. The better to secure and perpetuate mutual friendship and intercourse among the people of the different states in this union, the free inhabitants of each of these states, paupers, vagabonds and fugitives from Justice excepted, shall be entitled to all privileges and immunities of free citizens in the several states; and the people of each state shall have free ingress and regress to and from any other state, and shall enjoy therein all the privileges of trade and commerce, subject to the same duties, impositions and restrictions as the inhabitants thereof respectively, provided that such restriction shall not extend so far as to prevent the removal of property imported into any state, to any other state of which the Owner is an inhabitant; provided also that no imposition, duties or restriction shall be laid by any state, on the property of the united states, or either of them.

If any Person guilty of, or charged with treason, felony, or other high misdemeanor in any state, shall flee from Justice, and be found in any of the united states, he shall upon demand of the Governor or executive power, of the state from which he fled, be delivered up and removed to the state having jurisdiction of his offence.

Full faith and credit shall be given in each of these states to the records, acts and judicial proceedings of the courts and magistrates of every other state.

Art. V. For the more convenient management of the general interests of the united states, delegates shall be annually appointed in such manner as the legislature of each state shall direct, to meet in Congress on the first Monday in November, in every year, with a power reserved to each state, to recall its delegates, or any of them, at any time within the year, and to send others in their stead, for the remainder of the Year.

No state shall be represented in Congress by less than two, nor by more than seven Members; and no person shall be capable of being a delegate for more than three years in any term of six years; nor shall any person, being a delegate, be capable of holding any office under the united states, for which he, or another for his benefit receives any salary, fees or emolument of any kind.

Each state shall maintain its own delegates in a meeting of the states, and while they act as members of the committee of the states.

In determining questions in the united states, in Congress assembled, each state shall have one vote.

Freedom of speech and debate in Congress shall not be impeached or questioned in any Court, or place out of Congress, and the members of congress shall be protected in their persons from arrests and imprisonments, during the time of their going to and from, and attendance on congress, except for treason, felony, or breach of the peace.

Art. VI. No state without the Consent of the united states in congress assembled, shall send any embassy to, or receive any embassy from, or enter into any conference, agreement, or alliance or treaty with any King, prince or state; nor shall any person holding any office of profit or trust under the united states, or any of them, accept of any present, emolument, office or title of any kind

whatever from any king, prince or foreign state; nor shall the united states in congress assembled, or any of them, grant any title of nobility.

No two or more states shall enter into any treaty, confederation or alliance whatever between them, without the consent of the united states in congress assembled, specifying accurately the purposes for which the same is to be entered into, and how long it shall continue.

No state shall lay any imposts or duties, which may interfere with any stipulations in treaties, entered into by the united states in congress assembled, with any king, prince or state, in pursuance of any treaties already proposed by congress, to the courts of France and Spain.

No vessels of war shall be kept up in time of peace by any state, except such number only, as shall be deemed necessary by the united states in congress assembled, for the defence of such state, or its trade; nor shall any body of forces be kept up by any state, in time of peace, except such number only as in the judgment of the united states, in congress assembled, shall be deemed requisite to garrison the forts necessary for the defence of such state; but every state shall always keep up a well regulated and disciplined militia, sufficiently armed and accoutred, and shall provide and constantly have ready for use, in public stores, a due number of field pieces and tents, and a proper quantity of arms, ammunition and camp equipage.

No state shall engage in any war without the consent of the united states in congress assembled, unless such state be actually invaded by enemies, or shall have received certain advice of a resolution being formed by some nation of Indians to invade such state, and the danger is so imminent as not to admit of a delay, till the united states in congress assembled can be consulted: nor shall any state grant commissions to any ships or vessels of war, nor letters of marque or reprisal, except it be after a declaration of war by the united states in congress assembled, and then only against the kingdom or state and the subjects thereof, against which war has been so declared, and under such regulations as shall be established by the united states in congress assembled, unless such state be infested by pirates, in which case vessels of war may be fitted out for that occasion, and kept so long as the danger shall continue, or until the united states in congress assembled shall determine otherwise. . . .

Art. VIII. All charges of war, and all other expences that shall be incurred for the common defence or general welfare, and allowed by the united states in congress assembled, shall be defrayed out of a common treasury, which shall be supplied by the several states, . . .

Art. IX. The united states in congress assembled, shall have the sole and exclusive right and power of determining on peace and war, except in the cases mentioned in the sixth article—of sending and receiving ambassadors—entering into treaties and alliances, provided that no treaty of commerce shall be made whereby the legislative power of the respective states shall be restrained from imposing such imposts and duties on foreigners, as their own people are subjected to, or from prohibiting the exportation or importation of any species of goods or commodities whatsoever—of establishing rules for deciding in all cases, what captures on land or water shall be legal, and in what manner prizes taken by land or naval forces in the service of the united states shall be divided or appropriated.—of granting letters of marque and reprisal in times of peace—appointing courts for the trial of piracies and felonies committed on the high seas and establishing courts for receiving and determining finally appeals in all cases of captures, provided that no member of congress shall be appointed a judge of any of the said courts.

The united states in congress assembled shall also be the last resort on appeal in all disputes and differences now subsisting or that hereafter may arise between two or more states concerning boundary, jurisdiction or any other cause whatever; which authority shall always be exercised in the manner following. . . .

The united states in congress assembled shall also have the sole and exclusive right and power of regulating the alloy and value of coin struck by their own authority, or by that of the respective

states—fixing the standard of weights and measures throughout the united states.—regulating the trade and managing all affairs with the Indians, not members of any of the states, provided that the legislative right of any state within its own limits be not infringed or violated—establishing and regulating post-offices from one state to another, throughout all the united states, and exacting such postage on the papers passing thro' the same as may be requisite to defray the expences of the said office—appointing all officers of the land forces, in the service of the united states, excepting regimental officers.—appointing all the officers of the naval forces, and commissioning all officers whatever in the service of the united states—making rules for the government and regulation of the said land and naval forces, and directing their operations.

The united states in congress assembled shall have authority to appoint a committee, to sit in the recess of congress, to be denominated "A Committee of the States," and to consist of one delegate from each state; and to appoint such other committees and civil officers as may be necessary for managing the general affairs of the united states under their direction—to appoint one of their number to preside, provided that no person be allowed to serve in the office of president more than one year in any term of three years; to ascertain the necessary sums of Money to be raised for the service of the united states, and to appropriate and apply the same for defraying the public expences—to borrow money, or emit bills on the credit of the united states, transmitting every half year to the respective states an account of the sums of money so borrowed or emitted,—to build and equip a navy—to agree upon the number of land forces, and to make requisitions from each state for its quota, in proportion to the number of white inhabitants in such state; which requisition shall be binding, and thereupon the legislature of each state shall appoint the regimental officers, raise the men and cloath, arm and equip them in a soldier like manner, at the expence of the united states, and the officers and men so cloathed, armed and equipped shall march to the place appointed, and within the time agreed on by the united states in congress assembled: . . .

The united states in congress assembled shall never engage in a war, nor grant letters of marque and reprisal in time of peace, nor enter into any treaties or alliances, nor coin money, nor regulate the value thereof, nor ascertain the sums and expences necessary for the defence and welfare of the united states, or any of them, nor emit bills, nor borrow money on the credit of the united states, nor appropriate money, nor agree upon the number of vessels of war, to be built or purchased, or the number of land or sea forces to be raised, nor appoint a commander in chief of the army or navy, unless nine states assent to the same: nor shall a question on any other point, except for adjourning from day to day be determined, unless by the votes of a majority of the united states in congress assembled. . . .

Art. X. The committee of the states, or any nine of them, shall be authorised to execute, in the recess of congress, such of the powers of congress as the united states in congress assembled, by the consent of nine states, shall from time to time think expedient to vest them with; provided that no power be delegated to the said committee, for the exercise of which, by the articles of confederation, the voice of nine states in the congress of the united states assembled is requisite.

Art. XI. Canada acceding to this confederation, and joining in the measures of the united states, shall be admitted into, and entitled to all the advantages of this union: but no other colony shall be admitted into the same, unless such admission be agreed to by nine states.

Art. XII. All bills of credit emitted, monies borrowed and debts contracted by, or under the authority of congress, before the assembling of the united states, in pursuance of the present confederation, shall be deemed and considered as a charge against the united states, for payment and satisfaction whereof the said united states, and the public faith are hereby solemnly pledged.

Art. XIII. Every state shall abide by the determinations of the united states in congress assembled, on all questions which by this confederation are submitted to them. And the Articles of this confederation shall be inviolably observed by every state, and the union shall be perpetual; nor shall any alteration at any time hereafter be made in any of them; unless such alteration be agreed to in a congress of the united states, and be afterwards confirmed by the legislatures of every state.

AND WHEREAS it hath pleased the Great Governor of the World to incline the hearts of the legislatures we respectively represent in congress, to approve of, and to authorize us to ratify the said articles of confederation and perpetual union. . . . In Witness whereof we have hereunto set our hands in Congress. Done at Philadelphia in the state of Pennsylvania the ninth Day of July in the Year of our Lord one Thousand seven Hundred and Seventy-eight, and in the third year of the independence of America.

# REVIEW QUESTIONS

1. Was this a radical or conservative document?
2. What do you think are its strengths and weaknesses?
3. What powers are assigned to Congress?
4. How do the Articles safeguard the states against encroachment from the central government?
5. What are the controls placed on and the privileges granted to the representatives?

# ABIGAIL AND JOHN ADAMS

## FROM Family Letters on Revolutionary Matters (1776–83)

*Abigail Adams recognized that the constituting of a new government was a chance to rectify gender inequities inherent in law, politics, and society. A problem for historians, however, is determining whether she was exceptional or representative of her female contemporaries. While it may be impossible to discover how many thought as she did, it is probable that those who did advocate such change tried to influence their friends and family—especially the men who participated in politics—to effect reform. Adams spent much of the war separated from her husband John, but the loving couple kept postriders busy with their constant letters on family, local, and national affairs. They also maintained a voluminous correspondence with many other people, such as their good friend Mercy Otis Warren (the learned wife of politician Joseph Warren, she would later write a history of the Revolution), and John Thaxter Sr., the husband of Abigail Adams's aunt. While John Adams was off in Philadelphia creating a new nation or overseas in Europe representing the United States, his wife—in this act representative of so many other women—took command on the homefront. Adams and other female patriots did without their usual comforts, boycotted British goods, and took on additional burdens to maintain family farms and businesses.*

Excerpts from select letters reprinted by permission of the publisher from *The Adams Papers: Adams Family Correspondence, Volume I: December 1761–May 1776* and *The Adams Papers: Adams Family Correspondence, Volume II: June 1776–March 1778*, edited by L. H. Butterfield Cambridge, Mass.: The Belknap Press of Harvard University Press. Copyright © 1963 by the Massachusetts Historical Society; *The Adams Papers: Adams Family Correspondence, Volume V: October 1782–November 1784*, edited by Richard Alan Ryerson, Joanna Revelas, Celeste Walker, Gregg Lint and Humphrey Costello Cambridge, Mass.: The Belknap Press of Harvard University Press. Copyright © 1993 by the Massachusetts Historical Society. [Editorial insertions appear in brackets—*Ed.*]

## John Adams to Abigail Adams

March 19, 1776

\*    \*    \*

You ask, what is thought of Common sense [Paine's pamphlet]. Sensible Men think there are some Whims, some Sophisms, some artfull Addresses to superstitious Notions, some keen attempts upon the Passions, in this Pamphlet. But all agree there is a great deal of good sense, delivered in a clear, simple, concise and nervous Style.

His Sentiments of the Abilities of America, and of the Difficulty of a Reconciliation with G.B. are generally approved. But his Notions, and Plans of Continental Government are not much applauded. Indeed this Writer has a better Hand at pulling down than building.

. . . This Writer seems to have very inadequate Ideas of what is proper and necessary to be done, in order to form Constitutions for single Colonies, as well as a great Model of Union for the whole.

\*    \*    \*

## Abigail Adams to John Adams

Braintree March 31 1776

I wish you would ever write me a Letter half as long as I write you; and tell me if you may where your Fleet are gone? What sort of Defence Virginia can make against our common Enemy? Whether it is so situated as to make an able Defence? Are not the Gentery Lords and the common people vassals, are they not like the uncivilized Natives Brittain represents us to be? I hope their Riffel Men who have shewen themselves very savage and even Blood thirsty; are not a specimen of the Generality of the people.

I am willing to allow the Colony great merrit for having produced a Washington but they have been shamefully duped by a Dunmore.

I have sometimes been ready to think that the passion for Liberty cannot be Eaquelly Strong in the Breasts of those who have been accustomed to deprive their fellow Creatures of theirs. Of this I am certain that it is not founded upon that generous and christian principal of doing to others as we would that others should do unto us.

\*      \*      \*

I feel very differently at the approach of spring to what I did a month ago. We knew not then whether we could plant or sow with safety, whether when we had toild we could reap the fruits of our own industery, whether we could rest in our own Cottages, or whether we should not be driven from the sea coasts to seek shelter in the wilderness, but now we feel as if we might sit under our own vine and eat the good of the land.

\*      \*      \*

Tho we felicitate ourselves, we sympathize with those who are trembling least the Lot of Boston should be theirs. But they cannot be in similar circumstances unless pusilanimity and cowardise should take possession of them. They have time and warning given them to see the Evil and shun it.—I long to hear that you have declared an independancy—and by the way in the new Code of Laws which I suppose it will be necessary for you to make I desire you would Remember the Ladies, and be more generous and favourable to them than your ancestors. Do not put such unlimited power into the hands of the Husbands. Remember all Men would be tyrants if they could. If perticuliar care and attention is not paid to the Laidies we are determined to foment a Rebelion, and will not hold ourselves bound by any Laws in which we have no voice, or Representation.

That your Sex are Naturally Tyrannical is a Truth so thoroughly established as to admit of no dispute, but such of you as wish to be happy willingly give up the harsh title of Master for the more tender and endearing one of Friend. Why then, not put it out of the power of the vicious and the Lawless to use us with cruelty and indignity with impunity. Men of Sense in all Ages abhor those customs which treat us only as the vassals of your Sex. Regard us then as Beings placed by providence under your protection and in immitation of the Supreem Being make use of that power only for our happiness.

## John Adams to Abigail Adams

Ap. 14 1776

You justly complain of my short Letters, but the critical State of Things and the Multiplicity of Avocations must plead my Excuse.—You ask where the Fleet is. The inclosed Papers will inform you. You ask what Sort of Defence Virginia can make. I believe they will make an able Defence. Their Militia and minute Men have been some time employed in training them selves, and they have Nine Battallions of regulars as they call them, maintained among them, under good Officers, at the Continental Expence. They have set up a Number of Manufactories of Fire Arms, which are busily employed. They are tolerably supplied with Powder, and are successfull and assiduous, in making Salt Petre. Their neighbouring Sister or rather Daughter Colony of North Carolina, which is a warlike Colony, and has several Battallions at the Continental Expence, as well as a pretty good Militia, are ready to assist them, and they are in very good Spirits, and seem determined to make a brave Resistance.—The Gentry are very rich, and the common People very poor.

This Inequality of Property, gives an Aristocratical Turn to all their Proceedings, and occasions a strong Aversion in their Patricians, to Common Sense. But the Spirit of these Barons, is coming down, and it must submit.

It is very true, as you observe they have been duped by Dunmore. But this is a Common Case. All the Colonies are duped, more or less, at one Time and another. . . .

*     *     *

As to Declarations of Independency, be patient. Read our Privateering Laws, and our Commercial Laws. What signifies a Word.

As to your extraordinary Code of Laws, I cannot but laugh. We have been told that our Struggle has loosened the bands of Government every where. That Children and Apprentices were disobedient—that schools and Colledges were grown turbulent—that Indians slighted their Guardians and Negroes grew insolent to their Masters. But your Letter was the first Intimation that another Tribe more numerous and powerfull than all the rest were grown discontented.—This is rather too coarse a Compliment but you are so saucy, I wont blot it out.

Depend upon it, We know better than to repeal our Masculine systems. Altho they are in full Force, you know they are little more than Theory. We dare not exert our Power in its full Latitude. We are obliged to go fair, and softly, and in Practice you know We are the subjects. We have only the Name of Masters, and rather than give up this, which would compleatly subject Us to the Despotism of the Peticoat, I hope General Washington, and all our brave Heroes would fight. I am sure every good Politician would plot, as long as he would against Despotism, Empire, Monarchy, Aristocracy, Oligarchy, or Ochlocracy.—A fine Story indeed. I begin to think the Ministry as deep as they are wicked. After stirring up Tories, Landjobbers, Trimmers, Bigots, Canadians, Indians, Negroes, Hanoverians, Hessians, Russians, Irish Roman Catholicks, Scotch Renegadoes, at last they have stimulated the [————] to demand new Priviledges and threaten to rebell.

# Abigail Adams to Mercy Otis Warren

Braintree April 27 1776

*     *     *

I dare say [John Adams] writes to no one unless to Portia[1] oftner than to your Friend [Warren's husband], because I know there is no one besides in whom he has an eaquel confidence. His Letters to me have been generally short, but he pleads in Excuse the critical state of affairs and the Multiplicity of avocations and says further that he has been very Busy, . . .

He is very sausy to me in return for a List of Female Grievances which I transmitted to him. I think I will get you to join me in a petition to Congress. I thought it was very probable our wise Statesmen would erect a New Government and form a new code of Laws. I ventured to speak a word in behalf of our Sex, who are rather hardly dealt with by the Laws of England which gives such unlimitted power to the Husband to use his wife Ill.

I requested that our Legislators would consider our case and as all Men of Delicacy and Sentiment are averse to Excercising the power they possess, yet as there is a natural propensity in Humane Nature to domination, I thought the most generous plan was to put it out of the power of the Arbitary and tyranick to injure us with impunity by Establishing some Laws in our favour upon just and Liberal principals.

I believe I even threatned fomenting a Rebellion in case we were not considerd, and assured him we would not hold ourselves bound by any Laws in which we had neither a voice, nor representation.

In return he tells me he cannot but Laugh at My Extrodonary Code of Laws. That he had heard their Struggle had loosned the bands of Goverment, that children and apprentices were dissabedient, that Schools and Colledges were grown turbulent, that Indians slighted their Guardians, and Negroes grew insolent to their Masters. But my

---

[1] Adams and Warren gave each other classical nicknames: Portia for Adams, Marcia for Warren.

Letter was the first intimation that another Tribe more numerous and powerfull than all the rest were grown discontented. This is rather too coarse a complement, he adds, but that I am so sausy he wont blot it out.

So I have help'd the Sex abundantly, but I will tell him I have only been making trial of the Disintresstedness of his Virtue, and when weigh'd in the balance have found it wanting.

It would be bad policy to grant us greater power say they since under all the disadvantages we Labour we have the assendancy over their Hearts

And charm by accepting, by submitting sway.

I wonder Apollo and the Muses could not have indulged me with a poetical Genious. I have always been a votary to her charms but never could assend Parnassus myself.

\*       \*       \*

## Abigail Adams to John Adams

B[raintre]e May 7 1776

\*       \*       \*

A Goverment of more Stability is much wanted in this colony, and they are ready to receive it from the Hands of the Congress, and since I have begun with Maxims of State I will add an other viz. that a people may let a king fall, yet still remain a people, but if a king let his people slip from him, he is no longer a king. And as this is most certainly our case, why not proclaim to the World in decisive terms your own importance?

Shall we not be dispiced by foreign powers for hesitateing so long at a word?

I can not say that I think you very generous to the Ladies, for whilst you are proclaiming peace and good will to Men, Emancipating all Nations, you insist upon retaining an absolute power over Wives. But you must remember that Arbitary power is like most other things which are very hard, very liable to be broken—and notwithstanding all your wise Laws and Maxims we have it in our power not only to free ourselves but to subdue

our Masters, and without voilence throw both your natural and legal authority at our feet[.]

\*       \*       \*

## John Adams to Abigail Adams

Philadelphia July 3 1776

\*       \*       \*

Yesterday the greatest Question was decided, which ever was debated in America, and a greater perhaps, never was or will be decided among Men. A Resolution was passed without one dissenting Colony "that these united Colonies, are, and of right ought to be free and independent States, and as such, they have, and of Right ought to have full Power to make War, conclude Peace, establish Commerce, and to do all the other Acts and Things, which other States may rightfully do." You will see in a few days a Declaration setting forth the Causes, which have impell'd Us to this mighty Revolution, and the Reasons which will justify it, in the Sight of God and Man. A Plan of Confederation will be taken up in a few days.

When I look back to the Year 1761, and recollect the Argument concerning Writs of Assistance, in the Superiour Court, which I have hitherto considered as the Commencement of the Controversy, between Great Britain and America, and run through the whole Period from that Time to this, and recollect the series of political Events, the Chain of Causes and Effects, I am surprized at the Suddenness, as well as Greatness of this Revolution. Britain has been fill'd with Folly, and America with Wisdom, at least this is my Judgment.—Time must determine. It is the Will of Heaven, that the two Countries should be sundered forever. It may be the Will of Heaven that America shall suffer Calamities still more wasting and Distresses yet more dreadfull. If this is to be the Case, it will have this good Effect, at least: it will inspire Us with many Virtues, which We have not, and correct many Errors, Follies, and Vices, which threaten to disturb, dishonour, and destroy Us.—The Furnace of Affliction produces Refinement, in States as well as Individuals. And the new Governments we are assuming, in every Part, will require a Purification from our Vices, and an Augmentation of our Virtues or they will be no Blessings. The People will have unbounded Power. And the People are extreamly addicted to Corruption and Venality, as well as the Great.—I am not without Apprehensions from this Quarter. But I must submit all my Hopes and Fears, to an overruling Providence, in which, unfashionable as the Faith may be, I firmly believe.

## Abigail Adams to John Adams

August 14 1776

\*    \*    \*

You remark upon the deficiency of Education in your Countrymen. It never I believe was in a worse state, at least for many years. The Colledge is not in the state one could wish, the Schollars complain that their professer in Philosophy is taken of by publick Buisness to their great detriment. In this Town I never saw so great a neglect of Education. The poorer sort of children are wholly neglected, and left to range the Streets without Schools, without Buisness, given up to all Evil. The Town is not as formerly divided into Wards. There is either too much Buisness left upon the hands of a few, or too little care to do it. We daily see the Necessity of a regular Goverment. . . .

If you complain of neglect of Education in sons, What shall I say with regard to daughters, who every day experience the want of it. With regard to the Education of my own children, I find myself soon out of my debth, and destitute and deficient in every part of Education.

I most sincerely wish that some more liberal plan might be laid and executed for the Benefit of the rising Generation, and that our new constitution may be distinguished for Learning and Virtue. If we mean to have Heroes, Statesmen and Philosophers, we should have learned women. The world perhaps would laugh at me, and accuse me of vanity, But you I know have a mind too enlarged and liberal to disregard the Sentiment. If much depends as is allowed upon the early Education of

youth and the first principals which are instilld take the deepest root, great benifit must arise from litirary accomplishments in women.

\*    \*    \*

## Abigail Adams to Mercy Otis Warren

August 14. 1777. Braintree
This is the memorable fourteenth of August. This day 12 years the Stamp office was distroyd. Since that time what have we endured? What have we suffer'd? Many very many memorable Events which ought to be handed down to posterity will be buried in oblivion merely for want of a proper Hand to record them, whilst upon the opposite side many venal pens will be imployd to misrepresent facts and to render all our actions odious in the Eyes of future Generations. I have always been sorry that a certain person who once put their Hand to the pen, should be discouraged, and give up so important a service. Many things would have been recorded by the penetrateing Genious of that person which thro the multiplicity of Events and the avocations of the times will wholly escape the notice of any future Historian.

The History and the Events of the present day must fill every Humane Breast with Horrour. Every week produces some Horrid Scene perpetrated by our Barbarous foes, not content with a uniform Series of cruelties practised by their own Hands, but they must let loose the infernal Savages "those dogs of War" and cry Havock to them. Cruelty, impiety and an utter oblivion of the natural Sentiments of probity and Honour with the voilation of all Laws Humane and Divine rise at one veiw and characterise a George, a How and a Burgoine.

O my dear Friend when I bring Home to my own Dwelling these tragical Scenes which are every week presented in the publick papers to us, and only in Idea realize them, my whole Soul is distress'd. Were I a man I must be in the Feild. I could not live to endure the Thought of my Habitation desolated, my children Butcherd, and I an inactive Spectator.

\*    \*    \*

## Abigail Adams to John Thaxter

Dear Sir                    Braintree Febry 15 1778

\*    \*    \*

It gives me pleasure to see so distinguished a Genious as Mrs. Macauly[2] Honourd with a Statue, yet she wanted it not to render her Name immortal. The Gentleman who erected it has sullied the glory of his deed by the narrow contracted Spirit which he discovers in the inscription, . . . Even the most Excellent monody which he wrote upon the Death of his Lady will not atone for a mind contracted enough to wish that but one woman in an age might excell, and she only for the sake of a prodigy. What must be that Genious which cannot do justice to one Lady, but at the expence of the whole Sex?

It is really mortifying Sir, when a woman possessd of a common share of understanding considers the difference of Education between the male and female Sex, even in those families where Education is attended too. Every assistance and advantage which can be procured is afforded to the sons, whilst the daughters are totally neglected in point of Literature. Writing and Arithmetick comprise all their Learning. Why should children of the same parents be thus distinguished? Why should the Females who have a part to act upon the great Theater, and a part not less important to Society, (as the care of a family and the first instruction of Children falls to their share, and if as we are told that first impressions are most durable), is it not of great importance that those who are to instill the first principals should be suiteably qualified for the Trust, Especially when we consider that families compose communities, and individuals make up the sum total. Nay why should your sex wish for such a disparity in those whom they one day intend for companions and associates. Pardon me Sir if I cannot help sometimes suspecting that this Neglect arises in some measure from an ungenerous

jealosy of rivals near the Throne—but I quit the Subject or it will run away with my pen.

\*    \*    \*

## John Thaxter to Abigail Adams

Dear Madam           York Town March 6th. 1778

Your much esteemed favor came to hand this day, in which you inform me of the departure of your "dearest Friend."[3] I sincerely wish for your sake it had been convenient and safe for you to have accompanied him: But the danger you mention must, I think, have made the voyage disagreeable and had the event taken place, doubly aggravating on his part. . . . The principle, on which you assented to his departure, was noble, and marks that zeal and attachment to the cause of our country, which has so eminently distinguished you. Honor or profit weighed not with either of you, I am certain. . . .

\*    \*    \*

I cannot pass over that part of your agreeable favor which contain some strictures on the statue of [Mrs.] McCaulay, and the difference in point of Education between [male] and female, without an acknowledgment of the justice of the observations. They are so ingenious, and at the same time so just, that if complaisance did not suggest silence, Reason would tell me that the subterfuges of sophistication would be defyed in breaking silence and attempting to explain them away. After mentioning that our sex wish a disparity, you subjoin a suspicion that Jealousy of rivalship is the foundation of the neglect of your sex. Madam, I am positive it is too often the case. It is an "ungenerous Jealousy" as you justly term it.

\*    \*    \*

---

[2] Catherine Macaulay, British philosopher and author.

[3] John Adams left with his son, John Quincy Adams, on a diplomatic mission to Europe.

## John Adams to Abigail Adams 2d

My Dear Daughter                    Paris, August 13th
                                         [i.e. 14th], 1783

I have received your affectionate letter of the 10th of May, with great pleasure, and another from your mother of the 28th and 29th of April, which by mistake I omitted to mention in my letter to her to-day. Your education and your welfare, my dear child, are very near my heart; and nothing in this life would contribute so much to my happiness, next to the company of your mother, as yours. I have reason to say this by the experience I have had of the society of your brother, whom I brought with me from the Hague. He is grown to be a man, and the world says they should take him for my younger brother, if they did not know him to be my son. I have great satisfaction in his behaviour, as well as in the improvements he has made in his travels, and the reputation he has left behind him wherever he has been. He is very studious and delights in nothing but books, which alarms me for his health; because, like me, he is naturally inclined to be fat. His knowledge and his judgment are so far beyond his years, as to be admired by all who have conversed with him. I lament, however, that he could not have his education at Harvard College, where his brothers shall have theirs, if Providence shall afford me the means of supporting the expense of it. . . .

You have reason to wish for a taste for history, which is as entertaining and instructive to the female as to the male sex. My advice to you would be to read the history of your own country, which although it may not afford so splendid objects as some others, before the commencement of the late war, yet since that period, it is the most interesting chapter in the history of the world, and before that period is intensely affecting to every native American. You will find among your own ancestors, by your mother's side at least, characters which deserve your attention. It is by the female world, that the greatest and best characters among men are formed. I have long been of this opinion to such a degree, that when I hear of an extraordinary man, good or bad, I naturally, or habitually inquire who was his mother? There can be nothing in life more honourable for a woman, than to contribute by her virtues, her advice, her example, or her address, to the formation of an husband, a brother, or a son, to be useful to the world.

Heaven has blessed you, my daughter, with an understanding and a consideration, that is not found every day among young women, and with a mother who is an ornament to her sex. You will take care that you preserve your own character, and that you persevere in a course of conduct, worthy of the example that is every day before you. With the most fervent wishes for your happiness, I am your affectionate father,

                                              John Adams

## REVIEW QUESTIONS

1. How conversant was Abigail Adams with the public ideas and issues of the day? Did she simply echo her husband's ideas or did she have her own opinions?

2. What did Adams think about men's attitudes and actions toward women? What did she want her husband to do about these issues? How did John Adams respond?

3. Why did Abigail Adams take up the cause of educational reform? Was that revolutionary?

4. Was her husband in agreement with her on this issue? Was her uncle John Thaxter?

5. How did the Adams family correspondents display a regional bias even as they labored to establish a united American nation? What would have been the significance of such an attitude if held by many revolutionaries?

# 6   SHAPING A FEDERAL UNION

*To borrow a phrase from a twentieth-century cartoon character, "We have met the enemy and he is us."[1] In the early years of the American Revolution, and on through the War for Independence, revolutionaries distanced themselves from local opponents both in word and action. Calling themselves patriots and Americans while cursing the loyalists as Tories, they tried, and often succeeded, in driving out these enemies. They also focused on and fought fiercely against the external threat: Great Britain and its armies. The necessity of dealing with these threats, as well as a shared idealistic desire to initiate a new civil millennium, tended to steer the revolutionaries through myriad political conflicts into consensus on what they wanted to achieve: republican states and nation. Consensus, however, although firmly founded on certain key ideas about rights and government, was in fact a rather fragile construct. Fissures and weak spots soon appeared in the philosophical and governmental systems that the revolutionaries had engineered, and the persons who discovered and exposed these were not outsiders, they were Americans. The Revolution, therefore, did not end with the ratification of the Articles of Confederation and state constitutions; nor did it end with victory in the war. It continued through the 1780s as Americans struggled with themselves over the interpretation and implementation through law and government of such ideas as life, liberty, property, and the pursuit of happiness.*

 *At times it may seem that governing in peace is more difficult than governing in war, and so it appeared in the immediate postwar years. That transition from war to peace, from fighting for independence to living with it, proved quite difficult for Americans in the 1780s. There was much to which they had to adjust, both in personal and political affairs. Issues that had been repressed, ignored, or temporarily compromised on during the greater emergency now*

---

[1] *Pogo* by Walt Kelly, 1970 cartoon.

*demanded resolution along with the new problems that cropped up. People and events, both foreign and domestic, constantly challenged the plans and programs, including The Articles of Confederation, that leaders had drawn up during the war. While they certainly reflected revolutionary political philosophy, these schemes had also been the result of expediency and speculation as to what the nation and its people would face and want in the future. Once the future became the present, and that present became marked by problems, many, but not all, Americans clamored for amendments.*

*For people who tended to define "pursuit of happiness" in economic terms, the financial fiascoes of the postwar era proved especially disconcerting. Americans did not simply want to muddle through the adjustments that had to be made; they wanted solutions—with many demanding that they be democratic ones— that would allow them to prosper. The nation and states struggled to meet those desires as they also strove to ensure the security of the United States.*

*In the course of trying to cure the nation's ills, some American leaders fostered another one. They prescribed changing the federal compact and government, which raised a fever among Americans. At issue was the degree of change acceptable to the majority at that time. Some Americans wanted to slow down the changes and create a stability in which they could find the time to think things through before taking the next step. Some thought there had already been too much change. There was a fear that their dearly bought win would lead to loss. The heated debates that ensued ranged over the need for radical change versus more moderate reforms, who would lead during and after the change, and how the change would define the nation and people.*

# DANIEL GRAY

# FROM A Proclamation of Shaysite Grievances (1786)

*In the mid-1780s western Massachusetts farmers, many of whom had supported the Revolution through military service, found their pursuit of happiness challenged by the fiscal policies of the state. Anxiety and anger boiled into direct action in the summer of 1786 after the state legislature voted for more taxes but did not reform the state's monetary policy. The legislature's lack of responsiveness to the westerners' problems and requests reflected the political power of the eastern mercantile and creditor interests, but it may also have been due to an earlier lack of strong, direct participation in government by the westerners. The farmers set out to rectify that. Farmers who had already suffered through foreclosure on their lands due to their inability to pay taxes were joined by those who faced ruin because of the new taxes. Under such leaders as Daniel Shays, who had been a captain in the Continental Army, the farmers formed their own political committees (chaired by such compatriots as Daniel Gray) and armed forces. They closed courts while opening their own conventions in the counties, for they wanted to make sure that their grievances were not only heard but acted on. Governor James Bowdoin certainly did react, but not in the way they wanted: he first suspended habeas corpus and then called out an army.*

From George R. Minot, *The History of the Insurrection in Massachusetts in 1786 and of the Rebellion Consequent Thereon* (1788; New York: Da Capo Press, 1971), pp. 82–83.

## Shays's Rebellion 1786

1. An ADDRESS to the People of the several towns in the county of Hampshire, now at arms.

GENTLEMEN,

We have thought proper to inform you of some of the principal causes of the late risings of the people, and also of their present movement, viz.

1st. The present expensive mode of collecting debts, which by reason of the great scarcity of cash, will of necessity fill our gaols with unhappy debtors, and thereby a reputable body of people rendered incapable of being serviceable either to themselves or the community.

2d. The monies raised by impost and excise being appropriated to discharge the interest of governmental securities, and not the foreign debt, when these securities are not subject to taxation.

3d. A suspension of the writ of Habeas Corpus, by which those persons who have stepped forth to assert and maintain the rights of the people, are liable to be taken and conveyed even to the most distant part of the Commonwealth, and thereby subjected to an unjust punishment.

4th. The unlimited power granted to Justices of the Peace and Sheriffs, Deputy Sheriffs, and Constables, by the Riot Act, indemnifying them to the prosecution thereof; when perhaps, wholly actuated from a principle of revenge, hatred, and envy.

*Furthermore*, Be assured, that this body, now at arms, despise the idea of being instigated by British emissaries, which is so strenuously propagated by the enemies of our liberties: And also wish the most proper and speedy measures may be taken, to discharge both our foreign and domestick debt.

Per Order,

DANIEL GRAY,

Chairman of the Committee.

## REVIEW QUESTIONS

1. How did this address serve as an assurance that the rebels were not enemies of the people or the Revolution?
2. Did the rebels perceive their cause to be a matter of rights or economics?
3. Did the reasons the rebels presented justify rebellion?
4. How did the rebels' grievances indicate a breakdown in the newly constituted political processes? How did they indicate an erosion in social and political deference?

## GEORGE WASHINGTON

# Letters about Shays's Rebellion (1786)

*The rebellion in Massachusetts ignited public and private outbursts within and well beyond the state. Newspaper publishers filled column upon column with reports of the insurgents' as well as the government's actions, while correspondents penned their opinions of the legality, morality, and repercussions of the rebellion. Some Americans supported the rebellion, but many others feared, deplored, and condemned it. The strong reactions showed how sensitive many Americans, including George Washington, were to both the image and the implementation of their republican experiment. Washington, who had resigned his commission and returned to private life as a planter after the war, was still vitally concerned about the security and interests of the new nation. To that end he encouraged attendance at the Annapolis Convention in September 1786, and when that failed to draw enough delegates, he supported the call for a convention to take place the following year in Philadelphia. In almost constant communication with other leading revolutionaries, he continued to influence events as he offered his opinions and advice.*

From John C. Fitzpatrick, ed., *The Writings of George Washington*, vol. 29 (Washington, D.C., U.S. Government Printing Office, 1939), pp. 50–52, 121–24.

## To James Madison

Mount Vernon, November 5, 1786

My dear Sir: . . . Fain would I hope, that the great, and most important of all objects, the fœderal governmt., may be considered with that calm and deliberate attention which the magnitude of it so loudly calls for at this critical moment. Let prejudices, unreasonable jealousies, and local interest yield to reason and liberality. Let us look to our National character, and to things beyond the present period. No morn ever dawned more favourably than ours did; and no day was ever more clouded than the present! Wisdom, and good examples are necessary at this time to rescue the political machine from the impending storm. Virginia has now an opportunity to set the latter, and has enough of the former, I hope, to take the lead in promoting this great and arduous work. Without some alteration in our political creed, the superstructure we have been seven years raising at the expence of so much blood and treasure, must fall. We are fast verging to anarchy and confusion!

A letter which I have just received from Genl Knox, who had just returned from Massachusetts (whither he had been sent by Congress consequent of the commotion in that State) is replete with melancholy information of the temper, and designs of a considerable part of that people. Among other things he says,

> there creed is, that the property of the United States, has been protected from confiscation of Britain by the joint exertions of *all*, and therefore ought to be the *common property* of all. And he that attempts opposition to this creed is an enemy to equity and justice, and ought to be swept from off the face of the Earth.

again

> They are determined to anihillate all debts public and private, and have Agrarian Laws, which are easily effected by the means of unfunded paper money which shall be a tender in all cases whatever.

He adds

> The numbers of these people amount in Massachusetts to about one fifth part of several populous Counties, and to them may be collected, people of similar sentiments from the States of Rhode Island, Connecticut, and New Hampshire, so as to constitute a body of twelve or fifteen thousand desperate, and unprincipled men. They are chiefly of the young and active part of the Community.

How melancholy is the reflection, that in so short a space, we should have made such large strides towards fulfilling the prediction of our transatlantic foe! "leave them to themselves, and their government will soon dissolve." Will not the wise and good strive hard to avert this evil? Or will their supineness suffer ignorance, and the arts of self-interested designing disaffected and desperate characters, to involve this rising empire in wretchedness and contempt? What stronger evi-

dence can be given of the want of energy in our governments than these disorders? If there exists not a power to check them, what security has a man for life, liberty, or property? To you, I am sure I need not add aught on this subject, the consequences of a lax, or inefficient government, are too obvious to be dwelt on. Thirteen Sovereignties pulling against each other, and all tugging at the f;oederal head will soon bring ruin on the whole; whereas a liberal, and energetic Constitution, well guarded and closely watched, to prevent incroachments, might restore us to that degree of respectability and consequence, to which we had a fair claim, and the brightest prospect of attaining. With sentiments of the sincerest esteem etc.

## To Henry Knox

Mount Vernon, December 26, 1786

My dear Sir. . . .

Lamentable as the conduct of the Insurgents of Massachusetts is, I am exceedingly obliged to you for the advices respecting them; and pray you, most ardently, to continue the acct. of their proceedings; because I can depend upon them from you without having my mind bewildered with those vague and contradictory reports which are handed to us in Newspapers, and which please one hour, only to make the moments of the next more bitter. I feel, my dear Genl. Knox, infinitely more than I can express to you, for the disorders which have arisen in these States. Good God! who besides a tory could have foreseen, or a Briton predicted them! were these people wiser than others, or did they judge of us from the corruption, and depravity of their own hearts? The latter I am persuaded was the case, and that notwithstanding the boasted virtue of America, we are far gone in every thing ignoble and bad.

I do assure you, that even at this moment, when I reflect on the present posture of our affairs, it seems to me to be like the vision of a dream. My mind does not know how to realize it, as a thing in actual existence, so strange, so wonderful does it appear to me! In this, as in most other matter, we are too slow. When this spirit first dawned, probably it might easily have been checked; but it is scarcely within the reach of human ken, at this moment, to say when, where, or how it will end. There are combustibles in every State, which a spark might set fire to. In this State, a perfect calm prevails at present, and a prompt disposition to support, and give energy to the federal System is discovered, if the unlucky stirring of the dispute respecting the navigation of the Mississippi does not become a leaven that will ferment, and sour the mind of it.

The resolutions of the prest. Session respecting a paper emission, military certificates, &ca., have stamped justice and liberality on the proceedings of the Assembly, and By a late act, *it* seems very desirous of a General Convention to revise and amend the fœderal Constitution. Apropos, what prevented the Eastern States from attending the September meeting at Annapolis? Of all the States in the Union it should have seemed to me, that a measure of this sort (distracted as they were with internal commotions, and experiencing the want of energy in the government) would have been most pleasing to them. What are the prevailing sentiments of the one now proposed to be held at Philadelphia, in May next? and how will it be attended? . . .

*   *   *

In both your letters you intimate, that the men of reflection, principle and property in New England, feeling the inefficacy of their present government, are contemplating a change; but you are not explicit with respect to the nature of it. It has been supposed, that, the Constitution of the State of Massachusetts was amongst the most energetic in the Union; May not these disorders then be ascribed to an endulgent exercise of the powers of Administration? If your laws authorized, and your powers were adequate to the suppression of these tumults, in the first appearances of them, delay and temporizing expedients were, in my opinion improper; these are rarely well applied, and the same causes would produce similar effects in any form of government, if the powers of it are not enforced. I

ask this question for information, I know nothing of the facts.

That G. B. will be an unconcerned Spectator of the present insurrections (if they continue) is not to be expected. That she is at this moment sowing the Seeds of jealousy and discontent among the various tribes of Indians on our frontier admits of no doubt, in my mind. And that she will improve every opportunity to foment the spirit of turbulence within the bowels of the United States, with a view of distracting our governments, and promoting divisions, is, with me, not less certain. Her first Manœuvres will, no doubt, be covert, and may remain so till the period shall arrive when a decided line of conduct may avail her. . . . We ought not therefore to sleep nor to slumber. Vigilance in watching, and vigour in acting, is, in my opinion, become indispensably necessary. If the powers are inadequate amend or alter them, but do not let us sink into the lowest state of humiliation and contempt, and become a by-word in all the earth. I think with you that the Spring will unfold important and distressing Scenes, unless much wisdom and good management is displayed in the interim. . . .

## REVIEW QUESTIONS

1. Compare Washington's summary of Henry Knox's account of the rebels' grievances to the proclamation on p. 157. Do the two support one another?
2. Does the Knox account as accepted and echoed by Washington show any interpretative biases? If so, what does it reveal about their shared attitude to the rebellion?
3. Did Washington believe the insurgents to be a small faction found only in Massachusetts? Did he believe their attitude and actions to be a threat not only to their state but to others? Why or why not?
4. What does Washington say caused the problem? What did he believe to be the solution?
5. How did Washington use the rebellion to support his argument for governmental reform?

# CONSTITUTIONAL CONVENTION

# Debates on Slavery (1787)

*Delegates from twelve states (Rhode Island did not appoint a representative), tasked with reforming the Articles of Confederation, met in a Grand Convention in Philadelphia from May to September 1787. Their mission, as announced and accepted by Congress, the state governments, and the public was reform, not revolution. Yet once the delegates settled down to work, key members such as James Madison and Alexander Hamilton immediately began to push for radical change. In the debates that ensued, members argued over revolutionary social and political issues. One such issue was slavery. Many of the nation's founders desired the abolition of that institution. Just a year before, in September 1786, George Washington had written, "I never mean (unless some particular circumstance should compel me to it) to possess another slave by purchase; it being among my first wishes to see some plan adopted, by which slavery in this country may be abolished by slow, sure, and imperceptible degrees." Washington and others like him did not propose immediate emancipation, for they did not wish to upset or undermine state societies and economies, but they did want to deal with the moral and ideological dilemma that slavery posed. Their sentiments, however, did not match the resolve of the slaveholding interests.*

From *Notes of Debates in the Federal Convention of 1787 Reported by James Madison*, intro. Adrienne Koch (Athens: Ohio University Press. Intro. Copyright 1966; new indexed ed. 1984), pp. 502–08, 530–32. [Editorial insertions that appear in brackets are from the 1984 edition—*Ed.*]

## [Tuesday, August 21]

M[r] L. MARTIN, proposed to vary the Sect: 4. art VII. so as to allow a prohibition or tax on the importation of slaves. 1. as five slaves are to be counted as 3 free men in the apportionment of Representatives; such a clause wd. leave an encouragement to this trafic. 2. slaves weakened one part of the Union which the other parts were bound to protect: the privilege of importing them was therefore unreasonable. 3. it was inconsistent with the principles of the revolution and dishonorable to the American character to have such a feature in the Constitution.

M[r] RUTLIDGE did not see how the importation of slaves could be encouraged by this Section. He was not apprehensive of insurrections and would readily exempt the other States from the obligation to protect the Southern against them.—Religion & humanity had nothing to do with this question. Interest alone is the governing principle with nations. The true question at present is whether the South[n] States shall or shall not be parties to the Union. If the Northern States consult their interest, they will not oppose the increase of Slaves which will increase the commodities of which they will become the carriers.

M[r] ELSEWORTH was for leaving the clause as it stands. let every State import what it pleases. The morality or wisdom of slavery are considerations belonging to the States themselves. What enriches a part enriches the whole, and the States are the best judges of their particular interest. The old confederation had not meddled with this point, and he did not see any greater necessity for bringing it within the policy of the new one:

Mr PINKNEY. South Carolina can never receive the plan if it prohibits the slave trade. In every proposed extension of the powers of the Congress, that State has expressly & watchfully excepted that of meddling with the importation of negroes. If the States be all left at liberty on this subject, S. Carolina may perhaps by degrees do of herself what is wished, as Virginia & Maryland have already done.

Adjourned

# Wednesday August 22. in Convention

Art VII sect 4. resumed. Mr SHERMAN was for leaving the clause as it stands. He disapproved of the slave trade; yet as the States were now possessed of the right to import slaves, as the public good did not require it to be taken from them, & as it was expedient to have as few objections as possible to the proposed scheme of Government, he thought it best to leave the matter as we find it. He observed that the abolition of Slavery seemed to be going on in the U. S. & that the good sense of the several States would probably by degrees compleat it. He urged on the Convention the necessity of despatching its business.

Col. MASON. This infernal trafic originated in the avarice of British Merchants. The British Govt constantly checked the attempts of Virginia to put a stop to it. The present question concerns not the importing States alone but the whole Union. The evil of having slaves was experienced during the late war. Had slaves been treated as they might have been by the Enemy, they would have proved dangerous instruments in their hands. But their folly dealt by the slaves, as it did by the Tories. . . . Maryland & Virginia he said had already prohibited the importation of slaves expressly. N. Carolina had done the same in substance. All this would be in vain if S. Carolina & Georgia be at liberty to import. The Western people are already calling out for slaves for their new lands, and will fill that Country with slaves if they can be got thro' S. Carolina & Georgia. Slavery discourages arts & manufactures. The poor despise labor when performed by slaves. They prevent the immigration of Whites, who really enrich & strengthen a Country. They produce the most pernicious effect on manners. Every master of slaves is born a petty tyrant. They bring the judgment of heaven on a Country. As nations can not be rewarded or punished in the next world they must be in this. By an inevitable chain of causes & effects providence punishes national sins, by national calamities. He lamented that some of our Eastern brethren had from a lust of gain embarked in this nefarious traffic. As to the States being in possession of the Right to import, this was the case with many other rights, now to be properly given up. He held it essential in every point of view that the Genl Govt should have power to prevent the increase of slavery.

Mr ELSWORTH. As he had never owned a slave could not judge of the effects of slavery on character: He said however that if it was to be considered in a moral light we ought to go farther and free those already in the Country.—As slaves also multiply so fast in Virginia & Maryland that it is cheaper to raise than import them, whilst in the sickly rice swamps foreign supplies are necessary, if we go no farther than is urged, we shall be unjust towards S. Carolina & Georgia. Let us not intermeddle. As population increases poor laborers will be so plenty as to render slaves useless. Slavery in time will not be a speck in our Country. Provision is already made in Connecticut for abolishing it. And the abolition has already taken place in Massachusetts. As to the danger of insurrections from foreign influence, that will become a motive to kind treatment of the slaves.

Mr PINKNEY. If slavery be wrong, it is justified by the example of all the world. He cited the case of Greece Rome & other antient States; the sanction given by France England, Holland & other modern States. In all ages one half of mankind have been slaves. If the S. States were let alone they will probably of themselves stop importations. He wd himself as a Citizen of S. Carolina vote for it. An attempt to take away the right as proposed will produce serious objections to the Constitution which he wished to see adopted.

General PINKNEY declared it to be his firm opinion that if himself & all his colleagues were to sign the Constitution & use their personal influence, it would be of no avail towards obtaining the assent of their Constituents. S. Carolina & Georgia cannot do without slaves. As to Virginia she will gain by stopping the importations. Her slaves will rise in value, & she has more than she wants. It would be unequal to require S. C. & Georgia to confederate on such unequal terms. He said the Royal assent before the Revolution had never been refused to S. Carolina as to Virginia. He contended that the importation of slaves would be for the interest of the whole Union. The more slaves, the more produce to employ the carrying trade; The more consumption also, and the more of this, the more of revenue for the common treasury. He admitted it to be reasonable that slaves should be dutied like other imports, but should consider a rejection of the clause as an exclusion of S. Carolª from the Union.

Mr BALDWIN had conceived national objects alone to be before the Convention, not such as like the present were of a local nature. Georgia was decided on this point. . . .

Mr GERRY thought we had nothing to do with the conduct of the States as to Slaves, but ought to be careful not to give any sanction to it.

Mr DICKENSON considered it as inadmissible on every principle of honor & safety that the importation of slaves should be authorised to the States by the Constitution. The true question was whether the national happiness would be promoted or impeded by the importation, and this question ought to be left to the National Govt not to the States particularly interested. If Engd & France permit slavery, slaves are at the same time excluded from both those Kingdoms. Greece and Rome were made unhappy by their slaves. He could not believe that the Southn States would refuse to confederate on the account apprehended; especially as the power was not likely to be immediately exercised by the Genl Government.

Mr WILLIAMSON stated the law of N. Carolina on the subject, to wit that it did not directly prohibit the importation of slaves. It imposed a duty of £5. on each slave imported from Africa. £10 on each from elsewhere, & £50 on each from a State licensing manumission. He thought the S. States could not be members of the Union if the clause shd. be rejected, and that it was wrong to force any thing down, not absolutely necessary, and which any State must disagree to.

Mr KING thought the subject should be considered in a political light only. If two States will not agree to the Constitution as stated on one side, he could affirm with equal belief on the other, that great & equal opposition would be experienced from the other States. He remarked on the exemption of slaves from duty whilst every other import was subjected to it, as an inequality that could not fail to strike the commercial sagacity of the Northn. & middle States.

Mr LANGDON was strenuous for giving the power to the Genl Govt. He cd not with a good conscience leave it with the States who could then go on with the traffic, without being restrained by the opinions here given that they will themselves cease to import slaves.

Genl PINKNEY thought himself bound to declare candidly that he did not think S. Carolina would stop her importations of slaves in any short time, but only stop them occasionally as she now does. He moved to commit the clause that slaves might be made liable to an equal tax with other imports which he he thought right & wch wd remove one difficulty that had been started.

Mr RUTLIDGE. If the Convention thinks that N. C. S. C. & Georgia will ever agree to the plan, unless their right to import slaves be untouched, the expectation is vain. The people of those States will never be such fools as to give up so important an interest. He was strenuous agst striking out the Section, and seconded the motion of Genl Pinkney for a commitment.

\*        \*        \*

Mr SHERMAN said it was better to let the S. States import slaves than to part with them, if they made that a sine qua non. He was opposed to a tax on slaves imported as making the matter worse, because it implied they were *property*. He acknowledged that if the power of prohibiting the importation should be given to the Gen.l Government that it would be exercised. He thought it would be its duty to exercise the power.

\*    \*    \*

M.r RANDOLPH was for committing in order that some middle ground might, if possible, be found. He could never agree to the clause as it stands. He w.d sooner risk the constitution. He dwelt on the dilemma to which the Convention was exposed. By agreeing to the clause, it would revolt the Quakers, the Methodists, and many others in the States having no slaves. On the other hand, two States might be lost to the Union. Let us then, he said, try the chance of a commitment.

On the question for committing the remaining part of Sect. 4 & 5. of art: 7. N. H. no. Mas. abs.t Con.t ay N. J. ay P.a no. Del. no Mary.d ay. V.a ay. N. C. ay S. C. ay. Geo. ay.

\*    \*    \*

## [From Saturday August 25, 1787. In Convention.]

The Report of the Committee of eleven [see friday the 24.th instant] being taken up.

Gen.l PINKNEY moved to strike out the words "the year eighteen hundred" as the year limiting the importation of slaves, and to insert the words "the year eighteen hundred and eight"

M.r GHORUM 2.ded the motion

M.r MADISON. Twenty years will produce all the mischief that can be apprehended from the liberty to import slaves. So long a term will be more dishonorable to the National character than to say nothing about it in the Constitution.

On the motion; which passed in the affirmative. N. H. ay. Mas. ay. C.t ay. N. J. no. P.a no. Del. no. M.d ay. V.a no. N. C. ay. S. C. ay. Geo. ay.

M.r Gov.r MORRIS was for making the clause read at once, "importation of slaves into N. Carolina, S. Carolina & Georgia shall not be prohibited &c." This he said would be most fair and would avoid the ambiguity by which, under the power

with regard to naturalization, the liberty reserved to the States might be defeated. He wished it to be known also that this part of the Constitution was a compliance with those States. If the change of language however should be objected to by the members from those States, he should not urge it.

Col: MASON was not against using the term "slaves" but ag.nt naming N. C. S. C. & Georgia, lest it should give offence to the people of those States.

M.r SHERMAN liked a description better than the terms proposed, which had been declined by the old Cong.r & were not pleasing to some people. M.r CLYMER concurred with M.r Sherman

M.r WILLIAMSON said that both in opinion & practice he was, against slavery; but thought it more in favor of humanity, from a view of all circumstances, to let in S. C. & Georgia on those terms, than to exclude them from the Union.

M.r Gov.r MORRIS withdrew his motion.

M.r DICKENSON wished the clause to be confined to the States which had not themselves prohibited the importation of slaves, and for that purpose moved to amend the clause so as to read "The importation of slaves into such of the States as shall permit the same shall not be prohibited by the Legislature of the U- S- until the year 1808"—which was disagreed to nem: cont:

The first part of the report was then agreed to, amended as follows.

"The migration or importation of such persons as the several States now existing shall think proper to admit, shall not be prohibited by the Legislature prior to the year 1808."

N. H. Mas. Con. M.d N. C. S. C. Geo: ay

N. J. P.a Del. Virg.a . . . . . . . . . . . . . . . no

M.r BALDWIN in order to restrain & more explicitly define "the average duty" moved to strike out of the 2.d part the words "average of the duties laid on imports" and insert "common impost on articles not enumerated" which was agreed to nem: cont:

M.r SHERMAN was ag.st this 2.d part, as acknowledging men to be property, by taxing them as such under the character of slaves.

M.r KING & M.r LANGDON considered this as the price of the I.st part.

Gen.l PINKNEY admitted that it was so.

Col: M<small>ASON</small>. Not to tax, will be equivalent to a bounty on the importation of slaves.

M<sup>r</sup> G<small>HORUM</small> thought that M<sup>r</sup> Sherman should consider the duty, not as implying that slaves are property, but as a discouragement to the importation of them.

M<sup>r</sup> Gov<sup>r</sup> M<small>ORRIS</small> remarked that as the clause now stands it implies that the Legislature may tax freemen imported.

M<sup>r</sup> S<small>HERMAN</small> in answer to M<sup>r</sup> Ghorum observed that the smallness of the duty shewed revenue to be the object, not the discouragement of the importation.

M<sup>r</sup> M<small>ADISON</small> thought it wrong to admit in the Constitution the idea that there could be property in men. The reason of duties did not hold, as slaves are not like merchandize, consumed, &c

Col. M<small>ASON</small> (in answ<sup>r</sup> to Gov<sup>r</sup> Morris) the provision as it stands was necessary for the case of Convicts in order to prevent the introduction of them.

It was finally agreed nem: contrad: to make the clause read "but a tax or duty may be imposed on such importation not exceeding ten dollars for each person," and then the 2d. part as amended was agreed to.

*    *    *

## REVIEW QUESTIONS

1. During the debates, what were the arguments for and against the importation of slaves—and by extension, for and against the entire institution of slavery?
2. How and why did the delegates finally arrive at a compromise if not a consensus on this issue?
3. How did these debates affect the representation and regulation of slavery (in particular, see Art. I, Sections 2 & 9; Art. IV, Section 2) in the Constitution?
4. Given that the Constitution did not abolish slavery, do the arguments presented here indicate that the Revolution initiated change with respect to that institution both in attitude and practice?

# Constitution of the United States (1787)

*Hot as it was outside the Pennsylvania State House (now called Independence Hall), it was even hotter within as the delegates to the Constitutional Convention debated behind closed doors and windows. While some representatives hoped that reforms would include moral and ideological imperatives, most saw the creation of a federal government that would work more effectively and protect the nation's interests as the first priority. After many debates, committee meetings, and compromises over the proper form and function of their national government, the twelve state delegations (minus some delegates who had left earlier and three who refused to sign) approved the final draft of the Constitution on September 17. They then sent it on to Congress.*

From James D. Richardson, comp., *A Compilation of the Messages and Papers of the Presidents, 1789–1902*, vol. I (Washington, DC, Bureau of National Literature and Art, 1904), pp. 21–38.

We the people of the United States, in order to form a more perfect Union, establish Justice, insure domestic Tranquility, provide for the common defence, promote the general Welfare, and secure the Blessings of Liberty to ourselves and our Posterity, do ordain and establish this Constitution for the United States of America.

# Article. I

*Section. 1.* All legislative Powers herein granted shall be vested in a Congress of the United States, which shall consist of a Senate and House of Representatives.

*Section. 2.* The House of Representatives shall be composed of Members chosen every second Year by the People of the several States, and the Electors in each State shall have the Qualifications requisite for Electors of the most numerous Branch of the State Legislature.

No Person shall be a Representative who shall not have attained to the Age of twenty five Years, and been seven Years a Citizen of the United States, and who shall not, when elected, be an Inhabitant of that State in which he shall be chosen.

Representatives and direct Taxes shall be apportioned among the several States which may be included within this Union, according to their respective Numbers, which shall be determined by adding to the whole Number of free Persons, including those bound to Service for a Term of Years, and excluding Indians not taxed, three fifths of all other Persons. The actual Enumeration shall be made within three Years after the first Meeting of the Congress of the United States, and within every subsequent Term of ten Years, in such Manner as they shall by Law direct. The Number of Representatives shall not exceed one for every thirty Thousand, but each State shall have at Least one Representative; and until such enumeration shall be made, the State of New Hampshire shall be entitled to chuse three, Massachusetts eight, Rhode-Island and Providence Plantations one, Connecticut five, New-York six, New Jersey four,

Pennsylvania eight, Delaware one, Maryland six, Virginia ten, North Carolina five, South Carolina five, and Georgia three.

When vacancies happen in the Representation from any state, the Executive Authority thereof shall issue Writs of Election to fill such Vacancies.

The House of Representatives shall chuse their Speaker and other Officers; and shall have the sole Power of Impeachment.

*Section. 3.* The Senate of the United States shall be composed of two Senators from each State, chosen by the legislature thereof, for six Years; and each Senator shall have one Vote.

Immediately after they shall be assembled in Consequence of the first Election, they shall be divided as equally as may be into three Classes. The Seats of the Senators of the first Class shall be vacated at the Expiration of the second Year, of the second Class at the Expiration of the fourth Year, and of the third Class at the Expiration of the sixth Year, so that one third maybe chosen every second Year; and if Vacancies happen by Resignation, or otherwise, during the Recess of the Legislature of any State, the Executive thereof may make temporary Appointments until the next Meeting of the Legislature, which shall then fill such Vacancies.

No Person shall be a Senator who shall not have attained to the Age of thirty Years, and been nine Years a Citizen of the United States, and who shall not, when elected, be an Inhabitant of that State for which he shall be chosen.

The Vice President of the United States shall be President of the Senate, but shall have no Vote, unless they be equally divided.

The Senate shall chuse their other Officers, and also a President pro tempore, in the Absence of the Vice President, or when he shall exercise the Office of President of the United States.

The Senate shall have the sole Power to try all Impeachments. When sitting for that Purpose, they shall be on Oath or Affirmation. When the President of the United States is tried, the Chief Justice shall preside: And no Person shall be convicted without the Concurrence of two thirds of the Members present.

Judgment in Cases of Impeachment shall not extend further than to removal from Office, and disqualification to hold and enjoy any Office of honor, Trust or Profit under the United States: but the Party convicted shall nevertheless be liable and subject to Indictment, Trial, Judgment and Punishment, according to Law.

*Section. 4.* The Times, Places and Manner of holding Elections for Senators and Representatives, shall be prescribed in each State by the Legislature thereof, but the Congress may at any time by Law make or alter such Regulations, except as to the Places of chusing Senators.

The Congress shall assemble at least once in every Year, and such Meeting shall be on the first Monday in December, unless they shall by Law appoint a different Day.

*Section. 5.* Each House shall be the Judge of the Elections, Returns and Qualifications of its own Members, and a Majority of each shall constitute a Quorum to do Business; but a smaller Number may adjourn from day to day, and may be authorized to compel the Attendance of absent Members, in such Manner, and under such Penalties as each House may provide.

Each House may determine the Rules of its Proceedings, punish its Members for disorderly Behaviour, and, with the Concurrence of two thirds, expel a Member.

Each House shall keep a Journal of its Proceedings, and from time to time publish the same, excepting such Parts as may in their Judgment require Secrecy; and the Yeas and Nays of the Members of either House on any question shall, at the Desire of one fifth of those Present, be entered on the Journal.

Neither House, during the Session of Congress, shall, without the Consent of the other, adjourn for more than three days, nor to any other Place than that in which the two Houses shall be sitting.

*Section. 6.* The Senators and Representatives shall receive a Compensation for their Services, to be ascertained by Law, and paid out of the Treasury of the United States. They shall in all Cases, except Treason, Felony and Breach of the Peace, be privileged from Arrest during their Attendance at the Session of their respective Houses, and in going to and returning from the same; and for any Speech or Debate in either House, they shall not be questioned in any other Place.

No Senator or Representative shall, during the Time for which he was elected, be appointed to any civil Office under the Authority of the United States, which shall have been created, or the Emoluments whereof shall have been encreased during such time; and no Person holding any Office under the United States, shall be a Member of either House during his Continuance in Office.

*Section. 7.* All Bills for raising Revenue shall originate in the House of Representatives; but the Senate may propose or concur with Amendments as on other Bills.

Every Bill which shall have passed the House of Representatives and the Senate, shall, before it become a Law, be presented to the President of the United States; If he approve he shall sign it, but if not he shall return it, with his Objections to that House in which it shall have originated, who shall enter the Objections at large on their Journal, and proceed to reconsider it. If after such Reconsideration two thirds of that House shall agree to pass the Bill, it shall be sent, together with the Objections, to the other House, by which it shall likewise be reconsidered, and if approved by two thirds of that House, it shall become a Law. But in all such Cases the Votes of both Houses shall be determined by yeas and Nays, and the Names of the Persons voting for and against the Bill shall be entered on the Journal of each House respectively. If any Bill shall not be returned by the President within ten Days (Sundays excepted) after it shall have been presented to him, the Same shall be a Law, in like Manner as if he had signed it, unless the Congress by their Adjournment prevent its Return, in which Case it shall not be a Law.

Every Order, Resolution, or Vote to which the Concurrence of the Senate and House of

Representatives may be necessary (except on a question of Adjournment) shall be presented to the President of the United States; and before the Same shall take Effect, shall be approved by him, or being disapproved by him, shall be repassed by two thirds of the Senate and House of Representatives, according to the Rules and Limitations prescribed in the Case of a Bill.

*Section. 8.* The congress shall have Power To lay and collect Taxes, Duties, Imposts and Excises, to pay the Debts and provide for the common Defence and general Welfare of the United States; but all Duties, Imposts and Excises shall be uniform throughout the United States.

To borrow Money on the credit of the United States;

To regulate Commerce with foreign Nations, and among the several States, and with the Indian Tribes;

To establish an uniform Rule of Naturalization, and uniform Laws on the subject of Bankruptcies throughout the United States;

To coin Money, regulate the Value thereof, and of foreign Coin, and fix the Standard of Weights and Measures;

To provide for the Punishment of counterfeiting the Securities and current Coin of the United States;

To establish Post Offices and Post Roads;

To promote the Progress of Science and useful Arts, by securing for limited Times to Authors and Inventors the exclusive Right to their respective Writings and Discoveries;

To constitute Tribunals inferior to the supreme Court;

To define and punish Piracies and Felonies committed on the high Seas, and Offences against the Law of Nations;

To declare War, grant Letters of Marque and Reprisal, and make Rules concerning Captures on land and Water;

To raise and support Armies, but no Appropriation of Money to that Use shall be for a longer Term than two Years;

To provide and maintain a Navy;

To make Rules for the Government and Regulation of the land and naval Forces;

To provide for calling forth the Militia to execute the Laws of the Union, suppress Insurrections and repel Invasions;

To provide for organizing, arming, and disciplining, the Militia, and for governing such Part of them as may be employed in the Service of the United States, reserving to the States respectively, the Appointment of the Officers, and the Authority of training the Militia according to the discipline prescribed by Congress;

To exercise exclusive Legislation in all Cases whatsoever, over such District (not exceeding ten Miles square) as may, by Cession of particular States, and the Acceptance of Congress, become the Seat of the Government of the United States, and to exercise like Authority over all Places purchased by the Consent of the Legislature of the State in which the Same shall be, for the Erection of Forts, Magazines, Arsenals, dock-Yards, and other needful Buildings;—And

To make all Laws which shall be necessary and proper for carrying into Execution the foregoing Powers, and all other Powers vested by this Constitution in the Government of the United States, or in any Department or Officer thereof.

*Section. 9.* The Migration or Importation of such Persons as any of the States now existing shall think proper to admit, shall not be prohibited by the Congress prior to the Year one thousand eight hundred and eight, but a Tax or duty may be imposed on such Importation, not exceeding ten dollars for each Person.

The Privilege of the Writ of Habeas Corpus shall not be suspended, unless when in Cases of Rebellion or Invasion the public Safety may require it.

No Bill of Attainder or ex post facto Law shall be passed.

No Capitation, or other direct, Tax shall be laid, unless in Proportion to the Census or Enumeration herein before directed to be taken.

No Tax or Duty shall be laid on Articles exported from any State.

No Preference shall be given by any Regulation of Commerce or Revenue to the Ports of one State over those of another: nor shall Vessels bound to, or from, one State, be obliged to enter, clear, or pay Duties in another.

No Money shall be drawn from the Treasury, but in Consequence of Appropriations made by Law; and a regular Statement and Account of the Receipts and Expenditures of all public Money shall be published from time to time.

No Title of Nobility shall be granted by the United States: And no Person holding any Office of Profit or trust under them, shall, without the Consent of the Congress, accept of any present, Emolument, Office, or Title, of any kind whatever, from any King, prince, or foreign State.

*Section. 10.* No State shall enter into any Treaty, Alliance, or Confederation; grant Letters of Marque and Reprisal; coin Money; emit Bills of Credit; make any Thing but gold and silver Coin a Tender in Payment of Debts; pass any Bill of Attainder, ex post facto Law, or Law impairing the Obligation of Contracts, or grant any Title of Nobility.

No State shall, without the Consent of the Congress, lay any Imposts or Duties on Imports or Exports, except what may be absolutely necessary for executing it's inspection Laws: and the net Produce of all Duties and Imposts, laid by any State on Imports or Exports, shall be for the Use of the Treasury of the United States; and all such Laws shall be subject to the Revision and Controul of the Congress.

No State shall, without the Consent of Congress, lay any Duty of Tonnage, keep Troops, or Ships of War in time of Peace, enter into any Agreement or Compact with another State, or with a foreign Power, or engage in War, unless actually invaded, or in such imminent Danger as will not admit of delay.

# Article. II

*Section. 1.* The executive Power shall be vested in a President of the United States of America. He shall hold his Office during the term of four Years, and,

together with the Vice President, chosen for the same Term, be elected, as follows.

Each State shall appoint, in such Manner as the Legislature thereof may direct, a Number of Electors, equal to the whole Number of Senators and Representatives to which the State may be entitled in the Congress: but no Senator or Representative, or Person holding an Office of Trust or Profit under the United States, shall be appointed an Elector.

The Electors shall meet in their respective States, and vote by Ballot for two Persons, of whom one at least shall not be an Inhabitant of the same State with themselves. And they shall make a List of all the Persons voted for, and of the Number of Votes for each; which List they shall sign and certify, and transmit sealed to the Seat of the Government of the United States, directed to the President of the Senate. The President of the Senate shall, in the Presence of the Senate and House of Representatives, open all the Certificates, and the Votes shall then be counted. The Person having the greatest Number of Votes shall be the President, if such Number be a Majority of the whole Number of Electors appointed; and if there be more than one who have such Majority, and have an equal Number of Votes, then the House of Representatives shall immediately chuse by Ballot one of them for President; and if no Person have a Majority, then from the five highest on the List the said House shall in like Manner chuse the President. But in chusing the President, the Votes shall be taken by States, the Representation from each State having one Vote; A quorum for this Purpose shall consist of a Member or Members from two thirds of the States, and a Majority of all the States shall be necessary to a Choice. In every Case, after the Choice of the President, the Person having the greatest Number of Votes of the Electors shall be the Vice President. But if there should remain two or more who have equal Votes, the Senate shall chuse from them by Ballot the Vice President.

The Congress may determine the Time of chusing the Electors, and the Day on which they shall give their Votes; which Day shall be the same throughout the United States.

No Person except a natural born Citizen, or a Citizen of the United States, at the time of the Adoption of this Constitution, shall be eligible to the Office of President, neither shall any Person be eligible to that Office who shall not have attained to the Age of thirty five Years, and been fourteen Years a Resident within the United States.

In Case of the Removal of the President from office, or of his Death, Resignation, or Inability to discharge the Powers and Duties of the said Office, the Same shall devolve on the Vice President, and the Congress may by Law provide for the Case of Removal, Death, Resignation or Inability, both of the President and Vice President, declaring what Officer shall then act as President, and such Officer shall act accordingly, until the Disability be removed, or a President shall be elected.

The President shall, at stated Times, receive for his Services, a Compensation, which shall neither be encreased or diminished during the Period for which he shall have been elected, and he shall not receive within that Period any other Emolument from the United States, or any of them.

Before he enters on the Execution of his Office, he shall take the following Oath or Affirmation:—"I do solemnly swear (or affirm) that I will faithfully execute the Office of President of the United States, and will to the best of my Ability, preserve, protect and defend the Constitution of the United States."

*Section. 2.* The President shall be Commander in Chief of the Army and Navy of the United States, and of the Militia of the several States, when called into the actual Service of the United States; he may require the Opinion, in writing, of the principal Officer in each of the executive Departments, upon any Subject relating to the Duties of their respective Offices, and he shall have Power to grant Reprieves and Pardons for Offences against the United States, except in Cases of Impeachment.

He shall have Power, by and with the Advice and Consent of the Senate, to make Treaties, provided two thirds of the Senators present concur; and he shall nominate, and by and with the Advice and Consent of the Senate, shall appoint Ambassadors, other public Ministers and Consuls, Judges

of the supreme Court, and all other Officers of the United States, whose Appointments are not herein otherwise provided for, and which shall be established by Law; but the Congress may by Law vest the Appointment of such inferior Officers, as they think proper, in the President alone, in the Courts of Law, or in the Heads of Departments.

The President shall have Power to fill up all Vacancies that may happen during the Recess of the Senate, by granting Commissions which shall expire at the End of their next Session.

*Section. 3.* He shall from time to time give to the Congress Information of the State of the Union, and recommend to their Consideration such Measures as he shall judge necessary and expedient; he may, on extraordinary Occasions, convene both Houses, or either of them, and in Case of Disagreement between them, with Respect to the Time of Adjournment, he may adjourn them to such Time as he shall think proper; he shall receive Ambassadors and other public Ministers; he shall take Care that the Laws be faithfully executed, and shall Commission all the Officers of the United States.

*Section. 4.* The President, Vice President and all civil Officers of the United States, shall be removed from Office on Impeachment for, and Conviction of, Treason, Bribery, or other high Crimes and Misdemeanors.

# Article. III

*Section. 1.* The judicial Power of the United States, shall be vested in one supreme Court, and in such inferior Courts as the Congress may from time to time ordain and establish. The Judges, both of the supreme and inferior Courts, shall hold their Offices during good Behavior, and shall, at stated Times, receive for their Services, a Compensation, which shall not be diminished during their Continuance in Office.

*Section. 2.* The judicial Power shall extend to all Cases, in Law and Equity, arising under this Constitution, the Laws of the United States, and Treaties made, or which shall be made, under their Authority;—to all Cases affecting Ambassadors, other public Ministers and Consuls;—to all Cases of admiralty and maritime Jurisdiction;—to Controversies to which the United States shall be a Party;—to Controversies between two or more States;—between a State and Citizens of another State;—between Citizens of different States;—between Citizens of the same State claiming Lands under Grants of different States, and between a State, or the Citizens thereof, and foreign States, Citizens or Subjects.

In all cases affecting Ambassadors, other public Ministers and Consuls, and those in which a State shall be Party, the supreme Court shall have original Jurisdiction. In all the other Cases before mentioned, the supreme Court shall have appellate Jurisdiction, both as to Law and Fact, with such Exceptions, and under such Regulations as the Congress shall make.

The Trial of all Crimes, except in Cases of Impeachment, shall be by Jury; and such Trial shall be held in the State where the said Crimes shall have been committed; but when not committed within any State, the Trial shall be at such Place or Places as the Congress may by Law have directed.

*Section. 3.* Treason against the United States, shall consist only in levying War against them, or in adhering to their Enemies, giving them Aid and Comfort. No Person shall be convicted of Treason unless on the Testimony of two Witnesses to the same overt Act, or on Confession in open Court.

The Congress shall have Power to declare the Punishment of Treason, but no Attainder of Treason shall work Corruption of Blood, or Forfeiture except during the Life of the Person attainted.

# Article. IV

*Section. 1.* Full Faith and Credit shall be given in each State to the public Acts, Records, and judicial Proceedings of every other State. And the Congress may by general Laws prescribe the Manner in which such Acts, Records and Proceedings shall be proved, and the Effect thereof.

*Section. 2.* The Citizens of each State shall be entitled to all Privileges and Immunities of Citizens in the several States.

A Person charged in any State with Treason, Felony, or other Crime, who shall flee from Justice, and be found in another State, shall on Demand of the executive Authority of the State from which he fled, be delivered up, to be removed to the State having Jurisdiction of the Crime.

No Person held to Service or Labour in one State, under the Laws thereof, escaping into another, shall, in Consequence of any Law or Regulation therein, be discharged from such Service or Labour, but shall be delivered up on Claim of the Party to whom such Service or Labour may be due.

*Section. 3.* New States may be admitted by the Congress into this Union; but no new State shall be formed or erected within the Jurisdiction of any other State; nor any State be formed by the Junction of two or more States, or Parts of States, without the consent of the Legislatures of the States concerned as well as of the Congress.

The Congress shall have Power to dispose of and make all needful Rules and Regulations respecting the Territory or other Property belonging to the United States; and nothing in this Constitution shall be so construed as to Prejudice any Claims of the United States, or of any particular States.

*Section. 4.* The United States shall guarantee to every State in this Union a Republican Form of Government, and shall protect each of them against Invasion; and on Application of the Legislature, or of the Executive (when the Legislature cannot be convened) against domestic Violence.

# Article. V

The Congress, whenever two thirds of both Houses shall deem it necessary, shall propose Amendments to this Constitution, or, on the

Application of the Legislatures of two thirds of the several States shall call a Convention for proposing Amendments, which, in either Case, shall be valid to all Intents and Purposes, as Part of this Constitution, when ratified by the Legislatures of three fourths of the several States, or by Conventions in three fourths thereof, as the one or the other Mode of Ratification may be proposed by the Congress; Provided that no Amendment which may be made prior to the Year One thousand eight hundred and eight shall in any Manner affect the first and fourth Clauses in the Ninth Section of the first Article; and that no State, without its Consent, shall be deprived of its equal Suffrage in the Senate.

## Article. VI

All Debts contracted and Engagements entered into, before the Adoption of this Constitution, shall be as valid against the United States under this Constitution, as under the Confederation.

This Constitution, and the Laws of the United States which shall be made in Pursuance thereof; and all Treaties made, or which shall be made, under the Authority of the United States, shall be the supreme Law of the Land; and the Judges in every State shall be bound thereby, any Thing in the Constitution or Laws of any State to the Contrary notwithstanding.

The Senators and Representatives before mentioned, and the Members of the several State Legislatures, and all executive and judicial Officers, both of the United States and of the several States, shall be bound by Oath or Affirmation, to support this Constitution; but no religious Test shall ever be required as a Qualification to any Office or public Trust under the United States.

## Article. VII

The Ratification of the Conventions of nine States, shall be sufficient for the Establishment of this Constitution between the States so ratifying the Same.

Done in Convention by the Unanimous Consent of the States present the Seventeenth Day of September in the Year of our Lord one thousand seven hundred and Eighty seven and of the Independence of the United States of America the Twelfth. In witness thereof We have hereunto subscribed our Names,

Gº: WASHINGTON—Presidᵗ
and deputy from Virginia

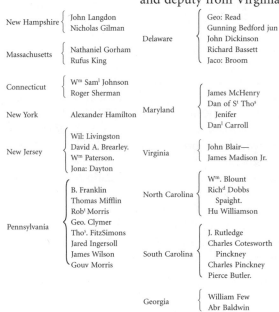

New Hampshire { John Langdon / Nicholas Gilman

Massachusetts { Nathaniel Gorham / Rufus King

Connecticut { Wᵐ Samˡ Johnson / Roger Sherman

New York    Alexander Hamilton

New Jersey { Wil: Livingston / David A. Brearley. / Wᵐ Paterson. / Jona: Dayton

Pennsylvania { B. Franklin / Thomas Mifflin / Robᵗ Morris / Geo. Clymer / Thoˢ. FitzSimons / Jared Ingersoll / James Wilson / Gouv Morris

Delaware { Geo: Read / Gunning Bedford jun / John Dickinson / Richard Bassett / Jaco: Broom

Maryland { James McHenry / Dan of Sᵗ Thoˢ / Jenifer / Danˡ Carroll

Virginia { John Blair— / James Madison Jr.

North Carolina { Wᵐ. Blount / Richᵈ Dobbs / Spaight. / Hu Williamson

South Carolina { J. Rutledge / Charles Cotesworth / Pinckney / Charles Pinckney / Pierce Butler.

Georgia { William Few / Abr Baldwin

## REVIEW QUESTIONS

1. What major political principles are not only articulated but also activated by the Constitution?
2. How does the Constitution reveal not only the intellectual background of the Founders but also their practical experiences as well?
3. Can you tell which provisions are the result of consensus and which are due to compromise? What does such a comparison reveal about the founders and the foundation of the government?
4. What provisions appear to be most open to differing interpretations? Why are the different possibilities for interpretation significant?

# PATRICK HENRY AND GEORGE MASON

## FROM Arguments against Ratification at the Virginia Convention (1788)

*As the Constitution—and the government it would create—could be ratified only by the people, the Confederation Congress submitted the document to the states where the issue would be decided by special ratifying conventions. That was a noble nod to government by the people, but the convention delegates also bowed to political necessity in Article VII of the Constitution: only nine of the state conventions had to vote aye for the Constitution to be ratified. But to found the new government on the acceptance of only nine states would not have boded well for the strength and unity of the new nation, so the Constitution's supporters set out to make ratification a unanimous mandate for change. It was not quite the mandate they sought, for while all of the states did eventually ratify the Constitution, North Carolina and Rhode Island waiting until after the new government had commenced operations, unanimity came only after vigorous debate with and concessionary promises to those against the proposed change.*

*When the delegates to the Virginia convention debated the Constitution in June 1788, they did so under the assumption that an aye vote there would provide the vital, deciding ninth affirmative needed for ratification. As it turned out, New Hampshire provided that necessary vote, but acting without that knowledge and aware that other states deemed Virginia's acceptance critical to the success of a new government, these delegates were especially primed to do battle. Adding to the dynamism of this particular convention was the caliber of the participants: there were exceptional men among both the proponents of and opponents to the Constitution. Among its champions were Edmund Pendleton, James Madison, George Nicholas, and John Marshall. Opposing them was a formidable team that included, to name just a few, George Mason, Richard Henry Lee, James Monroe, and its leader Patrick Henry. Henry had served as a wartime governor of the state but had made his reputation through his inflammatory rhetoric as a young revolutionary. In the following selection he once again uses his oratory talents as well as his legal skills to try to guide public affairs as he presents impassioned, imaginative, and negative arguments.*

From Jonathan Elliot, ed., *The Debates in the Several State Conventions on the Adoption of the Federal Constitution*, vol. 3 (1836; New York: Burt Franklin Reprints, 1974), pp. 6, 21–23, 29–34, 44–59, 445–48, 589–91.

Wednesday, 4 June 1788

The Convention, according to the order of the day, resolved itself into a committee of the whole Convention, to take into consideration the proposed plan of government, Mr. Wythe in the chair.

Mr. HENRY moved,—

That the act of Assembly appointing deputies to meet at Annapolis to consult with those from some other states, on the situation of the commerce of the United States—the act of Assembly appointing deputies to meet at Philadelphia, to revise the Articles of Confederation—and other public papers relative thereto—should be read.

Mr. PENDLETON then spoke to the following effect: Mr. Chairman, we are not to consider whether the federal Convention exceeded their powers. It strikes my mind that this ought not to influence our deliberations. This Constitution was transmitted to Congress by that Convention; by the Congress transmitted to our legislature; by them recommended to the people; the people have sent us hither to determine whether this government be a proper one or not. I did not expect these papers would have been brought forth. Although those gentlemen were only directed to consider the defects of the old system, and not devise a new one, if they found it so thoroughly defective as not to admit a revising, and submitted a new system to our consideration, which the people have deputed us to investigate, I cannot find any degree of propriety in reading those papers.

Mr. HENRY then withdrew his motion.

The clerk proceeded to read the preamble, and the two first sections of the first article.

\*    \*    \*

Mr. HENRY. Mr. Chairman, the public mind, as well as my own, is extremely uneasy at the proposed change of government. Give me leave to form one of the number of those who wish to be thoroughly acquainted with the reasons of this perilous and uneasy situation, and why we are brought hither to decide on this great national question. I consider myself as the servant of the people of this commonwealth, as a sentinel over their rights, liberty, and happiness. I represent their feelings when I say that they are exceedingly uneasy at being brought from that state of full security, which they enjoyed, to the present delusive appearance of things. A year ago, the minds of our citizens were at perfect repose. Before the meeting of the late federal Convention at Philadelphia, a general peace and a universal tranquillity prevailed in this country; but, since that period, they are exceedingly uneasy and disquieted. When I wished for an appointment to this Convention, my mind was extremely agitated for the situation of public affairs. I conceived the republic to be in extreme danger. If our situation be thus uneasy, whence has arisen this fearful jeopardy? It arises from this fatal system; it arises from a proposal to change our government—a proposal that goes to the utter annihilation of the most solemn engagements of the states—a proposal of establishing nine states into a confederacy, to the eventual exclusion of four states. It goes to the annihilation of those solemn treaties we have formed with foreign nations.

The present circumstances of France—the good offices rendered us by that kingdom—require our most faithful and most punctual adherence to our treaty with her. We are in alliance with the Spaniards, the Dutch, the Prussians; those treaties bound us as thirteen states confederated together. Yet here is a proposal to sever that confederacy. Is it possible that we shall abandon all our treaties and national engagements?—and for what? I expected to hear the reasons for an event so unexpected to my mind and many others. Was our civil polity, or public justice, endangered or sapped? Was the real existence of the country threatened, or was this preceded by a mournful progression of events? This proposal of altering our federal government is of a most alarming nature! Make the best of this new government—say it is composed by any thing but inspiration—you ought to be extremely cautious, watchful, jealous of your liberty; for, instead of securing your rights, you may lose them forever. . . . It will be necessary for this Convention to have a faithful historical detail of the facts that preceded the session of the federal Convention, and the reasons that actuated its members in proposing an entire alteration of government, and to demonstrate the dangers that awaited us. If they were of such awful magnitude as to warrant a proposal so extremely perilous as this, I must assert, that this Convention has an absolute right to a thorough discovery of every circumstance relative to this great event. And here I would make this inquiry of those worthy characters who composed a part of the late federal Convention. I am sure they were fully impressed with the necessity of forming a great consolidated government, instead of a confederation. That this is a consolidated government is demonstrably clear; and the danger of such a government is, to my mind, very striking. I have the highest veneration for those gentlemen; but, sir, give me leave to demand, What right had they to say, *We, the people*? My political curiosity, exclusive of my anxious solicitude for the public welfare, leads me to ask, Who authorized them to speak the language of, *We, the people*, instead of, *We, the states*? States are the characteristics and the soul of a confederation. If the states be not the agents of this compact, it must be one great, consolidated, national government, of the people of all the states. . . . It is not mere curiosity that actuates me: I wish to hear the real, actual, existing danger, which should lead us to take those steps, so dangerous in my conception, Disorders have arisen in other parts of America; but here, sir, no dangers, no insurrection or tumult have happened; every thing has been calm and tranquil. But, notwithstanding this, we are wandering on the great ocean of human affairs. . . . The federal Convention ought to have amended the old system; for this purpose they were solely delegated; the object of their mission extended to no other consideration. You must, therefore, forgive the solicitation of one unworthy member to know what danger could have arisen under the present Confederation, and what are the causes of this proposal to change our government.

*          *          *

Mr. GEORGE MASON. Mr. Chairman, whether the Constitution be good or bad, the present clause clearly discovers that it is a national government, and no longer a Confederation. I mean that clause which gives the first hint of the general government laying direct taxes. The assumption of this power of laying direct taxes does, of itself, entirely change the confederation of the states into one consolidated government. This power, being at discretion, unconfined, and without any kind of control, must carry every thing before it. The very idea of converting what was formerly a confederation to a consolidated government, is totally subversive of every principle which has hitherto governed us. This power is calculated to annihilate totally the state governments. Will the people of this great community submit to be individually taxed by two different and distinct powers? Will they suffer themselves to be doubly harassed? These two concurrent powers cannot exist long together; the one will destroy the other: the general government being paramount to, and in every respect more powerful than the state governments, the latter must give way to the former. Is it to be supposed that one national government will suit so extensive a country, embracing so many climates, and containing inhabitants so very different in manners, habits, and customs? It is ascertained, by history, that there never was a government over a very extensive country without destroying the liberties of the people: history also, supported by the opinions of the best writers, shows us that monarchy may suit a large territory, and despotic governments ever so extensive a country, but that popular governments can only exist in small territories. . . . It would be impossible to have a full and adequate representation in the general government; it would be too expensive and too unwieldy. We are, then, under the necessity of having this a very inadequate representation. Is this general representation to be compared with the real, actual, substantial representation of the state legislatures? It cannot bear a comparison. To make representation real and actual, the number of representatives ought to be adequate; they ought to mix with the people, think as they think, feel as they feel,—ought to be perfectly amenable to them, and thoroughly acquainted with their interest and condition. Now, these great ingredients are either not at all, or in a small degree, to be found in our federal representatives; so that we have no real, actual, substantial representation: but I acknowledge it results from the nature of the government. The necessity of this inconvenience may appear a sufficient reason not to argue against it; but, sir, it clearly shows that we ought to give power with a sparing hand to a government thus imperfectly constructed. To a government which, in the nature of things, cannot but be defective, no powers ought to be given but such as are absolutely necessary. There is one thing in it which I conceive to be extremely dangerous. Gentlemen may talk of public virtue and confidence; we shall be told that the House of Representatives will consist of the most virtuous men on the continent, and that in their hands we may trust our dearest rights. This, like all other assemblies, will be composed of some bad and some good men; and, considering the natural lust of power so inherent in man, I fear the thirst of power will prevail to oppress the people. . . . But my principal objection is, that the Confederation is converted to one general consolidated government, which, from my best judgment of it, (and which perhaps will be shown, in the course of this discussion, to be really well founded,) is one of the worst curses that can possibly befall a nation. Does any man suppose that one general national government can exist in so extensive a country as this? I hope that a government may be framed which may suit us, by drawing a line between the general and state governments, and prevent that dangerous clashing of interest and power, which must, as it now stands, terminate in the destruction of one or the other. When we come to the judiciary, we shall be more convinced that this government will terminate in the annihilation of the state governments: the question then will be, whether a consolidated government can preserve the freedom and secure the rights of the people.

If such amendments be introduced as shall exclude danger, I shall most gladly put my hand to it. When such amendments as shall, from the best information, secure the great essential rights of the people, shall be agreed to by gentlemen, I shall most heartily make the greatest concessions, and concur in any reasonable measure to obtain the desirable end of conciliation and unanimity. . . .

\* \* \*

Thursday, 5 June 1788

Mr. HENRY. . . .

I rose yesterday to ask a question which arose in my own mind. When I asked that question, I thought the meaning of my interrogation was obvious. The fate of this question and of America may depend on this. Have they said, We, the states? Have they made a proposal of a compact between states? If they had, this would be a confederation. It is otherwise most clearly a consolidated government. The question turns, sir, on that poor little thing—the expression, We, the *people*, instead of the *states*, of America. I need not take much pains to show that the principles of this system are extremely pernicious, impolitic, and dangerous. Is this a monarchy, like England—a compact between prince and people, with checks on the former to secure the liberty of the latter? Is this a confederacy, like Holland—an association of a number of independent states, each of which retains its individual sovereignty? It is not a democracy, wherein the people retain all their rights securely. Had these principles been adhered to, we should not have been brought to this alarming transition, from a confederacy to a consolidated government. . . . Here is a resolution as radical as that which separated us from Great Britain. It is radical in this transition; our rights and privileges are endangered, and the sovereignty of the states will be relinquished: and cannot we plainly see that this is actually the case? The rights of conscience, trial by jury, liberty of the press, all your immunities and franchises, all pretensions to human rights and privileges, are rendered insecure, if not lost, by this change, so loudly talked of by some, and inconsiderately by others. Is this tame relinquishment of rights worthy of freemen? Is it worthy of that manly fortitude that ought to characterize republicans? . . . You are not to inquire how your trade may be increased, nor how you are to become a great and powerful people, but how your liberties can be secured; for liberty ought to be the direct end of your government.

\*     \*     \*

What, sir, is the genius of democracy? Let me read that clause of the bill of rights of Virginia which relates to this: 3d clause:—that government is, or ought to be, instituted for the common benefit, protection, and security of the people, nation, or community. Of all the various modes and forms of government, that is best, which is capable of producing the greatest degree of happiness and safety, and is most effectually secured against the danger of mal-administration; and that whenever any government shall be found inadequate, or contrary to those purposes, a majority of the community hath an indubitable, unalienable, and indefeasible right to reform, alter, or abolish it, in such manner as shall be judged most conducive to the public weal.

This, sir, is the language of democracy—that a majority of the community have a right to alter government when found to be oppressive. But how different is the genius of your new Constitution from this! How different from the sentiments of freemen, that a contemptible minority can prevent the good of the majority! If, then, gentlemen, standing on this ground, are come to that point, that they are willing to bind themselves and their posterity to be oppressed, I am amazed and inexpressibly astonished. . . .

A standing army we shall have, also, to execute the execrable commands of tyranny; and how are you to punish them? Will you order them to be punished? Who shall obey these orders? Will your mace-bearer be a match for a disciplined regiment? In what situation are we to be? The clause before you gives a power of direct taxation, unbounded and unlimited, exclusive power of legislation, in all cases whatsoever, for ten miles square, and over all places purchased for the erection of forts, magazines, arsenals, dockyards, &c. What resistance could be made? The attempt would be madness. You will find all the strength of this country in the hands of your enemies; their garrisons will naturally be the strongest places in the country. Your militia is given up to Congress,

also, in another part of this plan: they will therefore act as they think proper: all power will be in their own possession. . . .

\*     \*     \*

. . . An opinion has gone forth, we find, that we are contemptible people: the time has been when we were thought otherwise. Under the same despised government, we commanded the respect of all Europe: wherefore are we now reckoned otherwise? The American spirit has fled from hence: it has gone to regions where it has never been expected; it has gone to the people of France, in search of a splendid government—a strong, energetic government. Shall we imitate the example of those nations who have gone from a simple to a splendid government? Are those nations more worthy of our imitation? What can make an adequate satisfaction to them for the loss they have suffered in attaining such a government—for the loss of their liberty? If we admit this consolidated government, it will be because we like a great, splendid one. Some way or other we must be a great and mighty empire; we must have an army, and a navy, and a number of things. When the American spirit was in its youth, the language of America was different: liberty, sir, was then the primary object. We are descended from a people whose government was founded on liberty: our glorious forefathers of Great Britain made liberty the foundation of every thing. That country is become a great, mighty, and splendid nation; not because their government is strong and energetic, but, sir, because liberty is its direct end and foundation. We drew the spirit of liberty from our British ancestors: by that spirit we have triumphed over every difficulty. But now, sir, the American spirit, assisted by the ropes and chains of consolidation, is about to convert this country into a powerful and mighty empire. If you make the citizens of this country agree to become the subjects of one great consolidated empire of America, your government will not have sufficient energy to keep them together. Such a government is incompatible with the genius of republicanism. There will be no checks, no real balances, in this government. What can avail your specious, imaginary balances, your rope-dancing, chain-rattling, ridiculous ideal checks and contrivances? But, sir, we are not feared by foreigners; we do not make nations tremble. Would this constitute happiness, or secure liberty? I trust, sir, our political hemisphere will ever direct their operations to the security of those objects.

Consider our situation, sir: go to the poor man, and ask him what he does. He will inform you that he enjoys the fruits of his labor, under his own fig-tree, with his wife and children around him, in peace and security. Go to every other member of society,—you will find the same tranquil ease and content; you will find no alarms or disturbances. Why, then, tell us of danger, to terrify us into an adoption of this new form of government? And yet who knows the dangers that this new system may produce? They are out of the sight of the common people: they cannot foresee latent consequences. I dread the operation of it on the middling and lower classes of people: it is for them I fear the adoption of this system. . . .

\*   \*   \*

Monday, 14 June 1788

Mr. HENRY. Mr. Chairman, the necessity of a bill of rights appears to me to be greater in this government than ever it was in any government before. I have observed already, that the sense of the European nations, and particularly Great Britain, is against the construction of rights being retained which are not expressly relinquished. I repeat, that all nations have adopted this construction—that all rights not expressly and unequivocally reserved to the people are impliedly and incidentally relinquished to rulers, as necessarily inseparable from the delegated powers. It is so in Great Britain; for every possible right, which is not reserved to the people by some express provision or compact, is within the king's prerogative. It is so in that country which is said to be in such full possession of freedom. . . .

\*   \*   \*

If you intend to reserve your unalienable rights, you must have the most express stipulation; for, if implication be allowed, you are ousted of those rights. If the people do not think it necessary to reserve them, they will be supposed to be given up. How were the congressional rights defined when the people of America united by a confederacy to defend their liberties and rights against the tyrannical attempts of Great Britain? The states were not then contented with implied reservation. No, Mr. Chairman. It was expressly declared in our Confederation that every right was retained by the states, respectively, which was not given up to the government of the United States. But there is no such thing here. You, therefore, by a natural and unavoidable implication, give up your rights to the general government.

\*   \*   \*

. . . A bill of rights is a favorite thing with the Virginians and the people of the other states likewise. It may be their prejudice, but the government ought to suit their geniuses; otherwise, its operation will be unhappy. A bill of rights, even if its necessity be doubtful, will exclude the possibility of dispute; and, with great submission, I think the best way is to have no dispute. In the present Constitution, they are restrained from issuing general warrants to search suspected places, or seize persons not named, without evidence of the commission of a fact, &c. There was certainly some celestial influence governing those who deliberated on that Constitution; for they have, with the most cautious and enlightened circumspection, guarded those indefeasible rights which ought ever to be held sacred! . . .

\*   \*   \*

Tuesday, 24 June 1788 [Mr. Henry]

\*   \*   \*

With respect to that part of the proposal which says that every power not granted remains with the people, it must be previous to adoption, or it will involve this country in inevitable destruction. To talk of it as a thing subsequent, not as one of your unalienable rights, is leaving it to the casual opinion of the Congress who shall take up the consideration of that matter. They will not reason with you about the effect of this Constitution. They will not take the opinion of this committee concerning its operation. They will construe it as they please. If you place it subsequently, let me ask the consequences. Among ten thousand *implied powers* which they may assume, they may, if we be engaged in war, liberate every one of your slaves if they please. And this must and will be done by men, a majority of whom have not a common interest with you. They will, therefore, have no feeling of your interests. It has been repeatedly said here, that the great object of a national government was national defence. That power which is said to be intended for security and safety may be rendered detestable and oppressive. If they give power to the general government to provide for the *general defence*, the means must be commensurate to the end. All the means in the possession of the people must be given to the government which is intrusted with the public defence. In this state there are two hundred and thirty-six thousand blacks, and there are many in several other states. But there are few or none in the Northern States; and yet, if the Northern States shall be of opinion that our slaves are numberless, they may call forth every national resource. May Congress not say, *that every black man must fight*? Did we not see a little of this last war? We were not so hard pushed as to make emancipation general; but acts of Assembly passed that every slave who would go to the army should be free. Another thing will contribute to bring this event about. Slavery is detested. We feel its fatal effects—we deplore it with all the pity of humanity. Let all these considerations, at some future period, press with full force on the minds of Congress. Let that urbanity, which I trust will distinguish America, and the necessity of national defence,—let all these things operate on their minds; they will search that paper, and see if they have power of manumission. And have they not, sir? Have they not power to provide for the general defence and welfare? May they not think that these call for the abolition of slavery? May they not pronounce all slaves free, and will they not be warranted by that power? This is no ambiguous implication or logical deduction. The paper speaks to the point: they have the power in clear, unequivocal terms, and will clearly and certainly exercise it. As much as I deplore slavery, I see

that prudence forbids its abolition. I deny that the general government ought to set them free, because a decided majority of the states have not the ties of sympathy and fellow-feeling for those whose interest would be affected by their emancipation. The majority of Congress is to the north, and the slaves are to the south.

In this situation, I see a great deal of the property of the people of Virginia in jeopardy, and their peace and tranquillity gone. I repeat it again, that it would rejoice my very soul that every one of my fellow-beings was emancipated. As we ought with gratitude to admire that decree of Heaven which has numbered us among the free, we ought to lament and deplore the necessity of holding our fellowmen in bondage. But is it practicable, by any human means, to liberate them without producing the most dreadful and ruinous consequences? We ought to possess them in the manner we inherited them from our ancestors, as their manumission is incompatible with the felicity of our country. But we ought to soften, as much as possible, the rigor of their unhappy fate. I know that, in a variety of particular instances, the legislature, listening to complaints, have admitted their emancipation. Let me not dwell on this subject. I will only add that this, as well as every other property of the people of Virginia, is in jeopardy, and put in the hands of those who have no similarity of situation with us. This is a local matter, and I can see no propriety in subjecting it to Congress.

With respect to subsequent amendments, proposed by the worthy member, I am distressed when I hear the expression. It is a new one altogether, and such a one as stands against every idea of fortitude and manliness in the states, or any one else. Evils admitted in order to be removed subsequently, and tyranny submitted to in order to be excluded by a subsequent alteration, are things totally new to me. . . . I ask, does experience warrant such a thing from the beginning of the world to this day? Do you enter into a compact first, and afterwards settle the terms of the government? . . .

\*    \*    \*

## REVIEW QUESTIONS

1. How did Patrick Henry define the difference between a confederation and a consolidated, national government? Why did he see the latter as so dangerous?
2. How did Henry address local, material concerns? How did he present ideological, political ones?
3. Did he appear to be more worried about states' rights or people's rights?
4. What were George Mason's particular worries? How did his argument supplement Henry's?
5. Were Patrick Henry and George Mason reactionaries in their distrust of constitutional innovation or were they still revolutionaries?

# JAMES MADISON

# *The Federalist Papers,* No. 45 (1788)

*James Madison, a principal framer of the Constitution at the Federal (later called Constitutional) Convention, defended this conception of a new, stronger, central government at the Virginia ratifying convention. His powerful rebuttals and counter-arguments were the products of his extensive study of governments, his participation in the Constitutional Convention's debates, and his writing a great many of the essays published under the title of* The Federalist.

*Alexander Hamilton devised* The Federalist Papers *to overwhelm the strong opposition to the Constitution's ratification in New York. He planned the series of letters to illuminate both the pros of a new government under the Constitution and the cons of a government under The Articles of Confederation. To help him in the intensive writing campaign (which resulted in eighty-five essays between October 1787 and May 1788), he recruited Madison and John Jay. All three wrote under the pseudonym "Publius." The letters originally appeared in New York newspapers and were then collected into a two-volume book, which Hamilton hoped would influence the delegates at the New York ratification convention; Madison wished for the same in Virginia. In each case, the essays were not as persuasive as their authors had desired, but* The Federalist Papers *did help people interpret the Constitution once it was adopted.*

From Alexander Hamilton, James Madison, and John Jay, *The Federalist Papers*, edited by Garry Wills (New York: Bantam Books, 1982), pp. 232–37.

# The Federalist No. 45

January 26, 1788

*To the People of the State of New York.*

Having shewn that no one of the powers transferred to the federal Government is unnecessary or improper, the next question to be considered is whether the whole mass of them will be dangerous to the portion of authority left in the several States.

The adversaries to the plan of the Convention instead of considering in the first place what degree of power was absolutely necessary for the purposes of the federal Government, have exhausted themselves in a secondary enquiry into the possible consequences of the proposed degree of power, to the Governments of the particular States. But if the Union, as has been shewn, be essential, to the security of the people of America against foreign danger; if it be essential to their security against contentions and wars among the different States; if it be essential to guard them against those violent and oppressive factions which embitter the blessings of liberty, and against those military establishments which must gradually poison its very fountain; if, in a word the Union be essential to the happiness of the people of America, is it not preposterous, to urge as an objection to a government without which the objects of the Union cannot be attained, that such a Government may derogate from the importance of the Governments of the individual States? Was then the American revolution effected, was the American confederacy formed, was the precious blood of thousands spilt, and the hard earned substance of millions lavished, not that the people of America should enjoy peace, liberty and safety; but that the Governments of the individual States, that particular municipal establishments, might enjoy a certain extent of power, and be arrayed with certain dignities and attributes of sovereignty? We have heard of the impious doctrine in the old world that the people were made for kings, not kings for the people. Is the same doctrine to be revived in the new, in another shape,

that the solid happiness of the people is to be sacrificed to the views of political institutions of a different form? It is too early for politicians to presume on our forgetting that the public good, the real welfare of the great body of the people is the supreme object to be pursued; and that no form of Government whatever, has any other value, than as it may be fitted for the attainment of this object. Were the plan of the Convention adverse to the public happiness, my voice would be, reject the plan. Were the Union itself inconsistent with the public happiness, it would be, abolish the Union. In like manner as far as the sovereignty of the States cannot be reconciled to the happiness of the people, the voice of every good citizen must be, let the former be sacrificed to the latter. How far the sacrifice is necessary, has been shewn. How far the unsacrificed residue will be endangered, is the question before us.

Several important considerations have been touched in the course of these papers, which discountenance the supposition that the operation of the federal Government will by degrees prove fatal to the State Governments. The more I revolve the subject the more fully I am persuaded that the balance is much more likely to be disturbed by the preponderancy of the last than of the first scale.

We have seen in all the examples of ancient and modern confederacies, the strongest tendency continually betraying itself in the members to despoil the general Government of its authorities, with a very ineffectual capacity in the latter to defend itself against the encroachments. Although in most of these examples, the system has been so dissimilar from that under consideration, as greatly to weaken any inference concerning the latter from the fate of the former; yet as the States will retain under the proposed Constitution a very extensive portion of active sovereignty, the inference ought not to be wholly disregarded. In the Achæan league, it is probable that the federal head had a degree and species of power, which gave it a considerable likeness to the government framed by the Convention. The Lycian confederacy, as far as its principles and form are transmitted, must have borne a still greater analogy to it. Yet history does not inform us that either of them ever degenerated or tended to degenerate into one consolidated government. On the contrary, we know that the ruin of one of them proceeded from the incapacity of the federal authority to prevent the dissentions, and finally the disunion of the subordinate authorities. These cases are the more worthy of our attention, as the external causes by which the component parts were pressed together, were much more numerous and powerful than in our case; and consequently, less powerful ligaments within, would be sufficient to bind the members to the head, and to each other.

*    *    *

The State Governments will have the advantage of the federal Government, whether we compare them in respect to the immediate dependence of the one or the other; to the weight of personal influence which each side will possess; to the powers respectively vested in them; to the predilection and probable support of the people; to the disposition and faculty of resisting and frustrating the measures of each other.

The State Governments may be regarded as constituent and essential parts of the federal Government; whilst the latter is nowise essential to the operation or organisation of the former. Without the intervention of the State Legislatures, the President of the United States cannot be elected at all. They must in all cases have a great share in his appointment, and will perhaps in most cases of themselves determine it. The Senate will be elected absolutely and exclusively by the State Legislatures. Even the House of Representatives, though drawn immediately from the people, will be chosen very much under the influence of that class of men, whose influence over the people obtains for themselves an election into the State Legislatures. Thus each of the principal branches of the federal Government will owe its existence more or less to the favor of the State Governments, and must consequently feel a dependence, which is much more likely to beget a disposition too obsequious, than too overbearing towards them. On the other side, the component parts of the State Governments will

in no instance be indebted for their appointment to the direct agency of the federal government, and very little if at all, to the local influence of its members.

The number of individuals employed under the Constitution of the United States, will be much smaller, than the number employed under the particular States. There will consequently be less of personal influence on the side of the former, than of the latter. The members of the legislative, executive and judiciary departments of thirteen and more States; the justices of peace, officers of militia, ministerial officers of justice, with all the county corporation and town-officers, for three millions and more of people, intermixed and having particular acquaintance with every class and circle of people, must exceed beyond all proportion, both in number and influence, those of every description who will be employed in the administration of the federal system. Compare the members of the three great departments, of the thirteen States, excluding from the judiciary department the justices of peace, with the members of the corresponding departments of the single Government of the Union; compare the militia officers of three millions of people, with the military and marine officers of any establishment which is within the compass of probability, or I may add, of possibility, and in this view alone, we may pronounce the advantage of the States to be decisive. If the federal Government is to have collectors of revenue, the State Governments will have theirs also. And as those of the former will be principally on the sea-coast, and not very numerous; whilst those of the latter will be spread over the face of the country, and will be very numerous, the advantage in this view also lies on the same side. It is true that the confederacy is to possess, and may exercise, the power of collecting internal as well as external taxes throughout the States: But it is probable that this power will not be resorted to, except for supplemental purposes of revenue; that an option will then be given to the States to supply their quotas by previous collections of their own; and that the eventual collection under the immediate authority of the Union, will generally be made by the officers, and according to the rules, appointed by the several States. Indeed it is extremely probable that in other instances, particularly in the organisation of the judicial power, the officers of the States will be cloathed with the correspondent authority of the Union. Should it happen however that separate collectors of internal revenue should be appointed under the federal Government, the influence of the whole number would not be a comparison with that of the multitude of State officers in the opposite scale. . . .

The powers delegated by the proposed Constitution to the Federal Government, are few and defined. Those which are to remain in the State Governments are numerous and indefinite. The former will be exercised principally on external objects, as war, peace, negociation, and foreign commerce; with which last the power of taxation will for the most part be connected. The powers reserved to the several States will extend to all the objects, which, in the ordinary course of affairs, concern the lives, liberties and properties of the people; and the internal order, improvement, and prosperity of the State.

The operations of the Federal Government will be most extensive and important in times of war and danger; those of the State Governments, in times of peace and security. As the former periods will probably bear a small proportion to the latter, the State Governments will here enjoy another advantage over the Federal Government. The more adequate indeed the federal powers may be rendered to the national defence, the less frequent will be those scenes of danger which might favour their ascendency over the governments of the particular States.

If the new Constitution be examined with accuracy and candour, it will be found that the change which it proposes, consists much less in the addition of NEW POWERS to the Union, than in the invigoration of its ORIGINAL POWERS. The regulation of commerce, it is true, is a new power; but that seems to be an addition which few oppose, and from which no apprehensions are entertained. The powers relating to war and peace, armies and fleets, treaties and finance, with the other more considerable powers, are all vested in the existing Congress by the articles of Confederation. The proposed change does not enlarge these powers; it only substitutes a more effectual mode of administering them. The change relating to taxation, may be regarded as the most important. And yet the present Congress have as compleat authority to REQUIRE of the States indefinite supplies of money for the common defence and general welfare, as the future Congress will have to require them of individual citizens; and the latter will be no more bound than the States themselves have been, to pay the quotas respectively taxed on them. Had the States complied punctually with the articles of confederation, or could their compliance have been enforced by as peaceable means as may be used with success towards single persons, our past experience is very far from countenancing an opinion that the State Governments would have lost their constitutional powers, and have gradually undergone an entire consolidation. To maintain that such an event would have ensued, would be to say at once, that the existence of the State Governments is incompatible with any system whatever that accomplishes the essential purposes of the Union.

PUBLIUS.

# REVIEW QUESTIONS

1. What anti-federalist arguments does Madison counter in this essay?
2. Why does Madison begin his essay with questions about the ends or goals of a federal government? What does he say is the ultimate goal of government?
3. How does Madison try to neutralize fears of stronger federal authority? Does he provide speculations or certainties?
4. How does he compare federal and state powers? Why does he say the latter would generally still have the advantage?

# 7 ✍ THE FEDERALIST ERA

*The citizens of the new nation may have ratified their Constitution, but they still had to translate the words into actions. They proceeded by inaugurating a new government in 1789. Yet again, that was not enough, for they had to figure out what that government truly could and could not do. With that in mind, the American people debated the initiation, amendment, and interpretation of the rules by which they wanted to live. The revolutionaries had taken historical and transatlantic intellectual and political concepts, translated them into a language and form—an idiom—readily understood by Americans, and applied them to the American situation. The Founders then had to make those words serve the new government—which involved some reinterpretation. As they labored to create a government and govern at the same time, the Founders debated fiercely over whether they were undermining some of their revolutionary and constitutional concepts in the process. In the midst of these debates, having already established the Constitution as the organic law of the United States, the founders proceeded to build on it with both administrative and statutory constructions. In doing so, they set precedents by which later generations governed and judged themselves.*

*Federalists gained power first and set out to create not only a government in their image but also a nation to fit their vision. In many ways they succeeded, but not without encountering opposition, a resistance that had first been mounted against the ratification of the Constitution. In what was both a concession to the merit of their opponents' arguments and an expediency to gain ratification, the Federalists compromised over incorporating a Bill of Rights into the Constitution. Their subsequent policies and programs, whether on domestic or foreign issues, were also challenged—and sometimes changed—by the opponents who came to be known as the Democratic Republicans.*

*Although most Americans said they deplored the rise of factionalism that undermined consensus, they continued to fight over how the Constitution was to be interpreted and implemented, thus contributing to the rise of a new institution—*

*the political party—during the administrations of George Washington and John Adams. Both parties wanted to make the United States a viable nation. Both Federalists and Republicans were concerned about national honor, interests, and security. These issues were top priorities in the 1790s as the nation tried to counter foreign intrigues directed against it at home as well as the foreign conflicts that encroached on its endeavors abroad. The Federalists and Republicans wanted a stable government that was respected nationally and internationally, and both wanted to ensure citizen rights. But they could not always agree on how to define or ensure these ends. For instance, the Federalists and Republicans differed on what was economically (a manufacturing or agricultural orientation) and diplomatically (fostering British or French connections) important. Therefore debates over programs that addressed immediate material concerns often became battles over differing visions for America's future and over constitutional interpretation.*

*These conflicts revealed that consensus was an ideal that was often surrendered to more pragmatic compromise. Union, at times, seemed more important than unity. While some may have deplored compromise as the lesser sibling to consensus, others accepted it as another check within the new system they had created. The factions or parties checked one another as they dealt with sectionalism, economic interests, and competing images of America's future.*

# DAVID RAMSAY

## A Dissertation on the Manner of Acquiring the Character and Privileges of a Citizen of the United States (1789)

*David Ramsay (1749–1815) graduated from the College of New Jersey (later renamed Princeton University) when he was sixteen. He then taught school for a while until he entered the medical school of the College of Philadelphia (later the University of Pennsylvania). He practiced medicine for a year in Maryland before settling in Charleston, South Carolina, in 1774. He married well (more than once) and pursued a political career, serving in the South Carolina legislature and, for short periods, in the Continental and Confederation Congresses. He also managed to find the time to write political tracts and volumes on American history, including one of the first full accounts of the American Revolution, so as to promote and help shape an emerging nationalism. In this piece he addresses the transformation of civic identity: who and what are we, and how did we become so?*

A Dissertation on the Manner of Acquiring the Character and Privileges of a Citizen of the United States (Charleston, 1789), Historical Society of Pennsylvania document at the Library Company of Philadelphia.

The *United States* are a new nation, or political society, formed at first by the declaration of independence, out of those *British subjects* in *America*, who were thrown out of royal protection by act of parliament, passed in *December,* 1775.

A citizen of the *United States,* means a member of this new nation. The principle of government being radically changed by the revolution, the political character of the people was also changed from subjects to citizens.

The difference is immense. Subject is derived from the latin words, *sub* and *jacio,* and means one who *is under* the power of another; but a citizen is an *unit* of a mass of free people, who, collectively, possess sovereignty.

Subjects look up to a master, but citizens are so far equal, that none have hereditary rights superior to others. Each citizen of a free state contains, within himself, by nature and the constitution, as much of the common sovereignty as another. In the eye of reason and philosophy, the political condition of citizens is more exalted than that of noblemen. Dukes and earls are creatures of kings, and may be made by them at pleasure: but citizens possess in their own right original sovereignty.

There is also a great difference between citizens, and inhabitants or residents.

Any person living within a country or state, is an inhabitant of it, or resident in it.

Negroes are inhabitants, but not citizens. Citizenship confers a right of voting at elections, and many other privileges not enjoyed by those who are no more than inhabitants.

The precise difference may be thus stated: The citizen of a free state is so united to it as to possess an individual's proportion of the common sovereignty; but he who is no more than an inhabitant, or resident, has no farther connection with the state in which he resides, than such as gives him security for his person and property, agreeably to fixed laws, without any participation in its government.

Republics, both ancient and modern, have been jealous of the rights of citizenship. The new constitution carries this matter so far, as to require not only present citizenship in federal representatives and senators, but antecedent citizenship for the term of seven and nine years. The time and manner of acquiring the high character of a citizen of the *United States*, is therefore well worthy of public discussion.

The following appear to be the only modes of acquiring this distinguishing privilege.

1st. By being parties to the original compact, the declaration of independence.

2d. By taking an oath of fidelity to some one of the *United States*, agreeably to law.

3d. By tacit consent and acquiescence.

4th. By birth or inheritance.

5th. By adoption. Of each of these in their order.

1st. By the declaration of independence congress proclaimed to the world, that their constituents, "the people of the united colonies, were absolved from all allegiance to the crown of *England*," and that the late colonies were "free and independent states." For the support of this bold measure, they confederated together, by pledging to each other "their lives, fortunes, and sacred honour." By this eventful declaration, "a nation was born in a day." Nearly three millions of people who had been subjects, became citizens. Their former political connection with *George* the third was done away, and a new one was formed, not with another king, but among themselves, by which they became coequal citizens, and, collectively, assumed all the rights of sovereignty. As this was done by the representatives of the people of this country, and in their name, and on their behalf, all who had concurred in investing congress with power, acquired citizenship, by being parties to this solemn act. These original citizens were the founders of the *United States*. Citizenship could not be acquired in this way by absentees from *America*, for two reasons; 1st. Such were not thrown out of *British protection* by the restraining act of parliament, and therefore continued *British subjects*, under the obligations, and in quiet possession of their *British allegiance*: And, secondly, Such could not be parties to the constitution of congress. The members of that body were not their deputies, or agents, and therefore could not bind them, or act for them.

2d. To cement the people of *America* more firmly together, oaths of fidelity to the states were respectively administered soon after the declaration of independence, to all above a certain age. By these oaths, a compact was established between the state and the individuals; and those who took them acquired or confirmed their citizenship by their own personal act. By swearing to do the duty of citizens, they, by law, acquired a right to the privileges and protection of citizens. Those who refused, were ordered to depart, as being persons unfriendly to the revolution.

3d. As the war drew near a close, the administration of oaths being less necessary, was less frequent. Citizenship was then, and now is, daily acquired by tacit consent or acquiescence. Minors who were not old enough to be parties to the declaration of independence, or to take the oaths of fidelity to the states at the time they were imposed, became citizens in consequence of their continuing to reside in the *United States* after they had arrived to mature age, especially if at the same time they claimed the protection, and performed the duties of citizens.

At twenty-one years of age, every freeman is at liberty to chuse his country, his religion, and his allegiance. Those who continue after that age in the allegiance under which they have been educated, become, by tacit consent, either subjects or citizens, as the case may be. In this manner, young men are now daily acquiring citizenship, without the intervention of an oath.

It is to be observed, that in order that such persons may acquire citizenship in this way, their residence subsequent to the revolution is indispensably necessary, previous to the commencement of their citizenship: for no man can be said so far to acquiesce in, or consent to a government, before he has lived under it, as to become a citizen thereof by tacit consent.

Citizenship, when acquired in this way by an absentee at the time of the declaration of independence, can therefore only be dated from the time in which the claimant of that high privilege became a resident under the independent government of the state of which he claims to be a citizen.

4th. None can claim citizenship as a birth-right, but such as have been born since the declaration of independence, for this obvious reason: no man can be born a citizen of a state or government, which did not exist at the time of his birth. Citizenship is the inheritance of the children of those who have taken a part in the late revolution: but this is confined exclusively to the children of those who were themselves citizens. Those who died before the revolution, could leave no political character to their children, but that of subjects, which they themselves possessed. If they had lived, no one could be certain whether they would have adhered to the king or to congress. Their children, therefore, may claim by inheritance the rights of *British subjects*, but not of *American citizens*.

5th. Persons born in any country may have acquired citizenship by adoption, or naturalization, agreeably to law.

The citizenship of such must be dated from the time of their adoption.

From these observations, the following inferences result.

Citizenship is an adventitious[1] character to every adult in the *United States*: and there was a certain period in the lives of such persons, when they ceased to be subjects, and began to be citizens.

The citizenship of no man could be previous to the declaration of independence, and, as a natural right, belongs to none but those who have been born of citizens since the 4th of *July*, 1776.

This accounts for the use of the word *resident* in that paragraph of the new constitution, which describes the qualification of the president of the *United States*. The senators must be *citizens* nine years, and the representatives seven years; but it is not said, that the president must be a citizen for fourteen years. The thing was impossible, for independence was then not quite twelve years declared; therefore the word *resident* was introduced in order to comprehend time before the declaration of independence.

By the same paragraph, the distinction between a citizen and a resident is constitutionally recognized; for tho' it is necessary, that the president must have been "fourteen years a *resident*," it is sufficient for him to have become a *citizen* "at the time of the adoption of the constitution." By this it is acknowledged, that one may be much longer a resident within the *United States*, than a citizen of the same. The precision of this paragraph, in respect to language, is worthy of observation. It is not said, that the president must have been a resident *in*, or an inhabitant *of* the *United States*, for fourteen years. The word used is *within*, which as explained by Doctor *Johnson*, means, "in the compass of,"— "the inclosure of." The sentence, therefore, when analysed, means nothing more than that the president must have been a resident within the *limits* of the *United States* for fourteen years.

Though the states have not existed as states for fourteen years; yet, their geographical boundaries, or limits, have existed from the first settlement of *America*. But to proceed with inferences. From the premises already established, it may be farther inferred, that citizenship, by inheritance, belongs to none but the children of those *Americans*, who, having survived the declaration of independence, acquired that adventitious character in their own right, and transmitted it to their offspring. The children of those who died before the revolution, who are now citizens, must have acquired that privilege in their own right, and by their own personal act; that is, by joining their country at or since the revolution.

Citizenship, acquired by tacit consent, is exclusively confined to the cases of persons who have resided within the *United States* since the declaration of independence, and could not have

---

[1] Not necessarily inherent, but rather added.

commenced prior to their actual residence under their new and independent governments.

From the whole it is plain, that no private individual, tho' a native, who was absent from this country at the time independence was declared, could have acquired citizenship with the *United States*, prior to his returning and actually joining his countrymen subsequent to the revolution.

Dangerous consequences would follow from admitting that birth and residence, before the declaration of independence in the country now called the *United States*, were sufficient to confer the rights of citizenship on persons who were absent during the late war, before they returned to their native country.

If this should be established, many persons, hostile to our liberties and independence, might put in their claim to be citizens. All the children born in the interval between the peace of *Paris*, 1763, and the declaration of independence in 1776, within the *British* posts on our north-western frontier, now wrongfully held from us, would be citizens. Our *East-India* trade would be laid open to many adventures, who have contributed nothing towards the establishment of our liberties: for the natives of this country, born before the revolution, who are now dispersed over the world, might, on that principle, fit out ships, make voyages to *India*, come here and sell their goods, under the character of citizens, from the circumstance of their having been born among us thirty or forty years ago,

and return with the net proceeds of their cargoes, to their present residence in foreign countries. These, and many other consequences, injurious to the liberties and commerce of these states, would result from admitting the dangerous position, that birth and residence in this country, before the revolution, conferred citizenship on absentees, antecedent to their return after that event had taken place. FINIS.

## REVIEW QUESTIONS

1. Which came first: American citizens or the United States?
2. How and why are citizens, residents, and inhabitants different?
3. What makes a citizen? Were some people denied citizenship?
4. How did a person actively become a citizen? How did a person passively become one?
5. Why did Ramsay think that living in the country was so important to acquiring citizenship? And given that, why did Ramsay argue that being American-born did not automatically make some people citizens of the United States? Consider the context of Ramsay's argument and why that may have prompted him to focus on time and timing.

# THOMAS JEFFERSON

## FROM *Notes on the State of Virginia* (1785)

*As the first secretary of the United States Treasury, Alexander Hamilton wanted not only to manage the country's finances but also to promote a diversified economy that emphasized trade and manufacturing. He believed that the United States should have an economic system that was as exceptional as its political one. Secretary of State Thomas Jefferson, like most other Americans, agreed with that idea in principle but disagreed on the particulars. Jefferson articulated the prevailing agrarian vision when he described his dream for America in his Notes on the State of Virginia. Besides extolling the virtues of an agriculture-based economy, Jefferson also commented on American flora and fauna, Native American issues, the problem of slavery, the promise of education, and the organization of government. Jefferson began the work as a series of essay answers to a questionnaire sent out by an official, François Barbé-Marbois, with the French legation at Philadelphia in 1780, sending him his original answers in December 1781. Jefferson revised and added new material to the work until it was published as a book, first in Paris in 1785 and then in London. He continued to espouse these ideas years later.*

From *Notes on the State of Virginia*, introduction by Thomas Perkins Abernathy (New York: Harper Torch Books, 1964), pp. 156–58.

# Query XIX

*The present state of manufactures, commerce, interior and exterior trade?*

We never had an interior trade of any importance. Our exterior commerce has suffered very much from the beginning of the present contest. During this time we have manufactured within our families the most necessary articles of clothing. Those of cotton will bear some comparison with the same kinds of manufacture in Europe; but those of wool, flax and hemp are very coarse, unsightly, and unpleasant; and such is our attachment to agriculture, and such our preference for foreign manufactures, that be it wise or unwise, our people will certainly return as soon as they can, to the raising raw materials, and exchanging them for finer manufactures than they are able to execute themselves.

The political economists of Europe have established it as a principle, that every State should endeavor to manufacture for itself; and this principle, like many others, we transfer to America, without calculating the difference of circumstance which should often produce a difference of result. In Europe the lands are either cultivated, or locked up against the cultivator. Manufacture must therefore be resorted to of necessity not of choice, to support the surplus of their people. But we have an immensity of land courting the industry of the husbandman. Is it best then that all our citizens should be employed in its improvement, or that one half should be called off from that to exercise manufactures and handicraft arts for the other? Those who labor in the earth are the chosen people of God, if ever He had a chosen people, whose breasts He has made His peculiar deposit for substantial and genuine virtue. It is the focus in which he keeps alive that sacred fire, which otherwise might escape from the face of the earth. Corruption of morals in the mass of cultivators is a phenomenon of which no age nor nation has furnished an example. It is the mark set on those, who, not looking up to heaven, to their own soil and industry, as does the husbandman, for their subsistence, depend for it on casualties and caprice of customers. Dependence begets subservience and venality, suffocates the germ of virtue, and prepares fit tools for the designs of ambition. This, the natural progress and consequence of the arts, has sometimes perhaps been retarded by accidental circumstances; but, generally speaking, the proportion which the aggregate of the other classes of citizens bears in any State to that of its husbandmen, is the proportion of its unsound to its healthy parts, and is a good enough barometer whereby to measure its degree of corruption. While we have land to labor then, let us never wish to see our citizens occupied at a workbench, or twirling a distaff. Carpenters, masons, smiths, are wanting in husbandry; but, for the general operations of manufacture, let our workshops remain in Europe. It is better to carry provisions and materials to workmen there, than bring them to the provisions and materials, and with them their manners and principles. The loss by the transportation of commodities across the Atlantic will be made up in happiness and permanence of government. The mobs of great cities add just so much to the support of pure government, as sores do to the strength of the human body. It is the manners and spirit of a people which preserve a republic in vigor. A degeneracy in these is a canker which soon eats to the heart of its laws and constitution.

## REVIEW QUESTIONS

1. Why does Jefferson dismiss European political-economic theory as irrelevant to or improper for the American situation?
2. What does Jefferson say differentiated America from Europe?
3. Why did he believe an agrarian economy begat a better society?
4. Are Jefferson's comments those of an economist or a revolutionary?

# GEORGE WASHINGTON

# FROM Farewell Address (1796)

*The Founders wanted to make the United States independent in an economic as well as political sense, and yet, in their promotion of a diversified economy, they also advocated the expansion of foreign trade. They wanted to create more markets abroad to offset the use of this country as a market for other nations. Such a plan generally meant establishing ties to other nations, but American leaders tried to avoid such connections by supporting a concept of free trade. Most Americans wanted to be free of entangling alliances as they pursued their interests abroad as well as at home. Unfortunately for them, European nations, especially Britain and France, were not willing to grant the Americans such autonomy in international relations. Struggling to maintain their power and contain adversaries in an era of revolution and war, these countries challenged and intervened in the domestic and foreign affairs of the United States. President Washington strove to counter these attacks on the nation's honor and interests as he labored to ensure the nation's security. He addressed these issues in the valedictory statement that he published in the* American Daily Advertiser *on 19 September 1796. After informing the American people that he was retiring from office, he offered them some advice. His recommendations as they pertained to foreign relations influenced the creation and implementation of American foreign policy into the twentieth century.*

From *The Writings of George Washington from the Original Manuscript Sources, 1745–1799*, vol. 35, edited by John C. Fitzpatrick (Washington, D.C.: U.S. Government Printing Office, 1940), pp. 214–36. [Editorial insertions appear in brackets—*Ed.*]

United States, September 19, 1796

\*         \*         \*

. . . [A] solicitude for your welfare, which cannot end but with my life, and the apprehension of danger, natural to that solicitude, urge me on an occasion like the present, to offer to your solemn contemplation, and to recommend to your frequent review, some sentiments; which are the result of much reflection, of no inconsiderable observation, and which appear to me all important to the permanency of your felicity as a People. . . .

\*         \*         \*

The Unity of Government which constitutes you one people is also now dear to you. It is justly so; for it is a main Pillar in the Edifice of your real independence, the support of your tranquility at home; your peace abroad; of your safety; of your prosperity; of that very Liberty which you so highly prize. But as it is easy to foresee, that from different causes and from different quarters, much pains will be taken, many artifices employed, to weaken in your minds the conviction of this truth; as this is the point in your political fortress against which the batteries of internal and external enemies will be most constantly and actively (though often covertly and insidiously) directed, it is of infinite moment, that you should properly estimate the immense value of your national Union to your collective and individual happiness; that you should cherish a cordial, habitual and immoveable attachment to it; accustoming yourselves to think and speak of it as of the Palladium of your political safety and prosperity; watching for its preservation with jealous anxiety; discountenancing whatever may suggest even a suspicion that it can in any event be abandoned, and indignantly frowning upon the first dawning of every attempt to alienate any portion of our Country from the rest, or to enfeeble the sacred ties which now link together the various parts.

For this you have every inducement of sympathy and interest. Citizens by birth or choice, of a common country, that country has a right to concentrate your affections. The name of AMERICAN, which belongs to you, in your national capacity, must always exalt the just pride of Patriotism, more than any appellation derived from local discriminations. With slight shades of difference, you have the same Religeon, Manners, Habits and political Principles. You have in a common cause fought and triumphed together. The independence and liberty you possess are the work of joint councils, and joint efforts; of common dangers, sufferings and successes.

But these considerations, however powerfully they address themselves to your sensibility are greatly outweighed by those which apply more immediately to your Interest. Here every portion of our country finds the most commanding motives for carefully guarding and preserving the Union of the whole.

The *North*, in an unrestrained intercourse with the *South*, protected by the equal Laws of a common government, finds in the productions of the latter, great additional resources of Maratime and commercial enterprise and precious materials of manufacturing industry. The *South* in the same Intercourse, benefitting by the Agency of the *North*, sees its agriculture grow and its commerce expand. Turning partly into its own channels the seamen of the *North*, it finds its particular navigation envigorated; and while it contributes, in different ways, to nourish and increase the general mass of the National navigation, it looks forward to the protection of a Maratime strength, to which itself is unequally adapted. The *East*, in a like intercourse with the *West*, already finds, and in the progressive improvement of interior communications, by land and water, will more and more find a valuable vent for the commodities which it brings from abroad, or manufactures at home. The *West* derives from the *East* supplies requisite to its growth and comfort, and what is perhaps of still greater consequence, it must of necessity owe the *secure* enjoyment of indispensable *outlets* for its own productions to the weight, influence, and the future Maritime strength of the Atlantic side of the Union, directed by an indissoluble community of Interest as *one Nation*. Any other tenure by which the *West* can hold this essential advantage, whether derived from its own seperate strength, or from an apostate and unnatural connection with any foreign Power, must be intrinsically precarious.

While then every part of our country thus feels an immediate and particular Interest in Union, all the parts combined cannot fail to find in the united mass of means and efforts greater strength, greater resource, proportionably greater security from external danger, a less frequent interruption of their Peace by foreign Nations; and, what is of inestimable value! they must derive from Union an exemption from those broils and Wars between themselves, which so frequently afflict neighbouring countries, not tied together by the same government; . . . Hence likewise they will avoid the necessity of those overgrown Military establishments, which under any form of Government are inauspicious to liberty, and which are to be regarded as particularly hostile to Republican Liberty: In this sense it is, that your Union ought to be considered as a main prop of your liberty, and that the love of the one ought to endear to you the preservation of the other.

\*      \*      \*

In contemplating the causes wch. may disturb our Union, it occurs as matter of serious concern, that any ground should have been furnished for characterizing parties by *Geographical* discriminations: *Northern* and *Southern*; *Atlantic* and *Western*; whence designing men may endeavour to excite a belief that there is a real difference of local interests and views. One of the expedients of Party to acquire influence, within particular districts, is to misrepresent the opinions and aims of other Districts. You cannot shield yourselves too much against the jealousies and heart burnings which spring from these misrepresentations. They tend to render Alien to each other those who ought to be bound together by fraternal affection. . . .

To the efficacy and permanency of Your Union, a Government for the whole is indispensable. No Alliances however strict between the parts can be an adequate substitute. They must inevitably experience the infractions and interruptions which all Alliances in all times have experienced. Sensible of this momentous truth, you have improved upon your first essay, by the adoption of a Constitution of Government, better calculated than your former for an intimate Union, and for the efficacious management of your common concerns. This government, . . . has a just claim to your confidence and your support. Respect for its authority, compliance with its Laws, acquiescence in its measures, are duties enjoined by the fundamental maxims of true Liberty. The basis of our political systems is the right of the people to make and to alter their Constitutions of Government. But the Constitution which at any time exists, 'till changed by an explicit and authentic act of the whole People, is sacredly obligatory upon all. The very idea of the power and the right of the People to establish Government presupposes the duty of every Individual to obey the established Government.

All obstructions to the execution of the Laws, all combinations and Associations, under whatever plausible character, with the real design to direct, controul counteract, or awe the regular deliberation and action of the Constituted authorities are distructive of this fundamental principle and of fatal tendency. They serve to organize faction, to give it an artificial and extraordinary force; to put in the place of the delegated will of the Nation, the will of a party; often a small but artful and enterprizing minority of the Community; and, according to the alternate triumphs of different parties, to make the public administration the Mirror of the ill concerted and incongruous projects of faction, rather than the organ of consistent and wholesome plans digested by common councils and modefied by mutual interests. . . .

\*      \*      \*

[The Spirit of Party] serves always to distract the Public Councils and enfeeble the Public administration. It agitates the Community with ill founded jealousies and false alarms, kindles the animosity of one part against another, foments occasionally riot and insurrection. It opens the door to foreign influence and corruption, which find a facilitated access to the government itself through the channels of party passions. Thus the policy and and [*sic*][1] the will of one country, are subjected to the policy and will of another.

There is an opinion that parties in free countries are useful checks upon the Administration of the Government and serve to keep alive the spirit of Liberty. This within certain limits is probably true, and in Governments of a Monarchical cast Patriotism may look with endulgence, if not with favour, upon the spirit of party. But in those of the popular character, in Governments purely elective, it is a spirit not to be encouraged. From their natural tendency, it is certain there will always be enough of that spirit for every salutary purpose. And there being constant danger of excess, the effort ought to be, by force of public opinion, to mitigate and assuage it. . . .

It is important, likewise, that the habits of thinking in a free Country should inspire caution in those entrusted with its administration, to confine themselves within their respective Constitutional spheres; avoiding in the exercise of the Powers of one department to encroach upon another. The spirit of encroachment tends to consolidate the powers of all the departments in one, and thus to create whatever the form of government, a real despotism. . . .

\*   \*   \*

'Tis substantially true, that virtue or morality is a necessary spring of popular government. The rule indeed extends with more or less force to every species of free Government. Who that is a sincere friend to it, can look with indifference upon attempts to shake the foundation of the fabric

Promote then as an object of primary importance, Institutions for the general diffusion of knowledge. In proportion as the structure of a government gives force to public opinion, it is essential that public opinion should be enlightened

As a very important source of strength and security, cherish public credit. One method of preserving it is to use it as sparingly as possible: avoiding occasions of expence by cultivating peace,

but remembering also that timely disbursements to prepare for danger frequently prevent much greater disbursements to repel it; avoiding likewise the accumulation of debt, not only by shunning occasions of expence, but by vigorous exertions in time of Peace to discharge the Debts which unavoidable wars may have occasioned, not ungenerously throwing upon posterity the burthen which we ourselves ought to bear. The execution of these maxims belongs to your Representatives, but it is necessary that public opinion should cooperate. To facilitate to them the performance of their duty, it is essential that you should practically bear in mind, that towards the payment of debts there must be Revenue; that to have Revenue there must be taxes; that no taxes can be devised which are not more or less inconvenient and unpleasant; . . .

Observe good faith and justice towds. all Nations. Cultivate peace and harmony with all. Religion and morality enjoin this conduct; and can it be that good policy does not equally enjoin it? It will be worthy of a free, enlightened, and, at no distant period, a great Nation, to give to mankind the magnanimous and too novel example of a People always guided by an exalted justice and benevolence. . . .

In the execution of such a plan nothing is more essential than that permanent, inveterate antipathies against particular Nations and passionate attachments for others should be excluded; and that in place of them just and amicable feelings towards all should be cultivated. The Nation, which indulges towards another an habitual hatred, or an habitual fondness, is in some degree a slave. It is a slave to its animosity or to its affection, either of which is sufficient to lead it astray from its duty and its interest. . . .

\*   \*   \*

Against the insidious wiles of foreign influence, (I conjure you to believe me fellow citizens) the jealousy of a free people ought to be *constantly* awake; since history and experience prove that foreign influence is one of the most baneful foes of Republican Government. But that jealousy to be useful must be impartial; else it becomes the instrument

---

[1] Editorial insertion from Fitzpatrick's edition.

of the very influence to be avoided, instead of a defence against it. . . .

The Great rule of conduct for us, in regard to foreign Nations is in extending our commercial relations to have with them as little *political* connection as possible. So far as we have already formed engagements let them be fulfilled, with perfect good faith. Here let us stop.

Europe has a set of primary interests, which to us have none, or a very remote relation. Hence she must be engaged in frequent controversies, the causes of which are essentially foreign to our concerns. Hence therefore it must be unwise in us to implicate ourselves, by artificial ties, in the ordinary vicissitudes of her politics, or the ordinary combinations and collisions of her friendships, or enmities:

Our detached and distant situation invites and enables us to pursue a different course. If we remain one People, under an efficient government, the period is not far off, when we may defy material injury from external annoyance; when we may take such an attitude as will cause the neutrality we may at any time resolve upon to be scrupulously respected; when belligerent nations, under the impossibility of making acquisitions upon us, will not lightly hazard the giving us provocation; when we may choose peace or war, as our interest guided by our justice shall Counsel.

Why forego the advantages of so peculiar a situation? Why quit our own to stand upon foreign ground? Why, by interweaving our destiny with that of any part of Europe, entangle our peace and prosperity in the toils of European Ambition, Rivalship, Interest, Humour or Caprice?

'Tis our true policy to steer clear of permanent Alliances, with any portion of the foreign world. So far, I mean, as we are now at liberty to do it, for let me not be understood as capable of patronising infidelity to existing engagements (I hold the maxim no less applicable to public than to private affairs, that honesty is always the best policy). I repeat it therefore, let those engagements be observed in their genuine sense. But in my opinion, it is unnecessary and would be unwise to extend them.

Taking care always to keep ourselves, by suitable establishments, on a respectably defensive posture, we may safely trust to temporary alliances for extraordinary emergencies.

Harmony, liberal intercourse with all Nations, are recommended by policy, humanity and interest. But even our Commercial policy should hold an equal and impartial hand: neither seeking nor granting exclusive favours or preferences; consulting the natural course of things; diffusing and deversifying by gentle means the streams of Commerce, but forcing nothing; establishing with Powers so disposed; in order to give to trade a stable course, to define the rights of our Merchants, and to enable the Government to support them; conventional rules of intercourse, the best that present circumstances and mutual opinion will permit, but temporary, and liable to be from time to time abandoned or varied, as experience and circumstances shall dictate; constantly keeping in view, that 'tis folly in one Nation to look for disinterested favors from another; that it must pay with a portion of its Independence for whatever it may accept under that character; that by such acceptance, it may place itself in the condition of having given equivalents for nominal favours and yet of being reproached with ingratitude for not giving more. There can be no greater error than to expect, or calculate upon real favours from Nation to Nation. 'Tis an illusion which experience must cure, which a just pride ought to discard.

In offering to you, my Countrymen these counsels of an old and affectionate friend, I dare not hope they will make the strong and lasting impression, I could wish; that they will controul the usual current of the passions, or prevent our Nation from running the course which has hitherto marked the Destiny of Nations: But if I may even flatter myself, that they may be productive of some partial benefit, some occasional good; that they may now and then recur to moderate the fury of party spirit, to warn against the mischiefs of foreign Intriegue, to guard against the Impostures of pretended patriotism; this hope will be a full recompence for the solicitude for your welfare, by which they have been dictated.

\*       \*       \*

## REVIEW QUESTIONS

1. In voicing some concerns and offering advice, Washington revealed some of the problems and conflicts undermining the republic's stability and success. What were they?

2. What did he believe were the nation's particular strengths?

3. What did Washington recommend to preserve the nation's union and liberty?

4. Were his recommendations idealistic or practical? Why?

# FROM Alien and Sedition Acts (1798)

*Washington, his successor John Adams, and the Federalist Congress came under increasing attack by the public and in the press in the 1790s. It was difficult to determine whether the press was simply reporting public sentiment or feeding it, but the leaders being criticized tended to believe the latter. They deplored what was happening for personal reasons, but they also worried about the power of the press in fostering dissent and division.*

*Foreign affairs highlighted and contributed to domestic schisms. Washington had warned against hostile foreign influences in his Farewell Address, but the Federalist-dominated Congress, with President Adams's concurrence, moved beyond mere warnings to legislate for the containment of dissent—whether it was foreign or domestically generated. In 1798, a year already fraught with international problems, namely the growing conflict with France, Congress escalated the domestic political crisis by passing acts that could be interpreted as demanding deferential behavior and orderly, even unquestioning, compliance with national policies.*

From Richard Peters, ed., *The Public Statutes at Large of the United States of America from the Organization of the Government in 1789, to March, 1845*, vol. I (Boston: Little, Brown, 1853), pp. 566–69, 570–72, 577–78, 596–97.

## The Naturalization Act (18 June 1798; repealed 1802)

*CHAP. LIV.—An Act Supplementary to and to Amend the Act, Intituled "An Act to Establish an Uniform Rule of Naturalization; And to Repeal the Act Heretofore Passed on That Subject."*

———

SECTION 1. *Be it enacted by the Senate and House of Representatives of the United States of America in*

*Congress assembled,* That no alien shall be admitted to become a citizen of the United States, or of any state, unless in the manner prescribed by the act, intituled "An act to establish an uniform rule of naturalization; and to repeal the act heretofore passed on that subject," he shall have declared his intention to become a citizen of the United States, five years, at least, before his admission, and shall, at the time of his application to be admitted, declare and prove, to the satisfaction of the court having jurisdiction in the case, that he has resided within the United States fourteen years, at least, and within the state or territory where, or for which such court is at the time held, five years, at least, besides conforming to the other declarations, renunciations and proofs, by the said act required, any thing therein to the contrary hereof notwithstanding: *Provided*, that any alien, who was residing within the limits, and under the jurisdiction of the United States, before the twenty-ninth day of January, one thousand seven hundred and ninety-five, may, within one year after the passing of this act—and any alien who shall have made the declaration of his intention to become a citizen of the United States, in conformity to the provisions of the act, intituled "An act to establish an uniform rule of naturalization, and to repeal the act heretofore passed on that subject," may, within four years after having made the declaration aforesaid, be admitted to become a citizen, in the manner prescribed by the said act, upon his making proof that he has resided five years, at least, within the limits, and under the jurisdiction of the United States: *And provided also*, that no alien, who shall be a native, citizen, denizen or subject of any nation or state with whom the United States shall be at war, at the time of his application, shall be then admitted to become a citizen of the United States.

\*    \*    \*

SEC. 4. *And be it further enacted*, That all white persons, aliens, (accredited foreign ministers, consuls, or agents, their families and domestics, excepted) who, after the passing of this act, shall continue to reside, or who shall arrive, or come to reside in any port or place within the territory of the United States, shall be reported, if free, and of the age of twenty-one years, by themselves, or being under the age of twenty-one years, or holden in service, by their parent, guardian, master or mistress in whose care they shall be, to the clerk of the district court of the district, if living within ten miles of the port or place, in which their residence or arrival shall be, and otherwise, to the collector of such port or place, or some officer or other person there, or nearest thereto, who shall be authorized by the President of the United States, to register aliens: And report, as aforesaid, shall be made in all

cases of residence, within six months from and after the passing of this act, and in all after cases, within forty-eight hours after the first arrival or coming into the territory of the United States, and shall ascertain the sex, place of birth, age, nation, place of allegiance or citizenship, condition or occupation, and place of actual or intended residence within the United States, of the alien or aliens reported, and by whom the report is made. And it shall be the duty of the clerk, or other officer, or person authorized, who shall receive such report, to record the same in a book to be kept for that purpose, and to grant to the person making the report, and to each individual concerned therein, whenever required, a certificate of such report and registry; . . .

SEC. 5. *And be it further enacted*, That every alien who shall continue to reside, or who shall arrive, as aforesaid, of whom a report is required as aforesaid, who shall refuse or neglect to make such report, and to receive a certificate thereof, shall forfeit and pay the sum of two dollars; and any justice of the peace, or other civil magistrate, who has authority to require surety of the peace, shall and may, on complaint to him made thereof, cause such alien to be brought before him, there to give surety of the peace and good behaviour during his residence within the United States, or for such term as the justice or other magistrate shall deem reasonable, and until a report and registry of such alien shall be made, and a certificate thereof, received as aforesaid; and in failure of such surety, such alien shall and may be committed to the common gaol, and shall be there held, until the order which the justice or magistrate shall and may reasonably make, in the premises, shall be performed. And every person, whether alien, or other, having the care of any alien or aliens, under the age of twenty-one years, or of any white alien holden in service, who shall refuse and neglect to make report thereof, as aforesaid, shall forfeit the sum of two dollars, for each and every such minor or servant, monthly, and every month, until a report and registry, and a certificate thereof, shall be had, as aforesaid.

\*    \*    \*

# The Alien Act
# (25 June 1798; expired)

## CHAP. LVIII.—An Act concerning Aliens. (u)

SECTION 1. *Be it enacted by the Senate and House of Representatives of the United States of America in Congress assembled*, That it shall be lawful for the President of the United States at any time during the continuance of this act, to *order* all such *aliens* as he shall judge dangerous to the peace and safety of the United States, or shall have reasonable grounds to suspect are concerned in any reasonable or secret machinations against the government thereof, to depart out of the territory of the United States, within such time as shall be expressed in such order, which order shall be served on such alien by delivering him a copy thereof, or leaving the same at his usual abode, and returned to the office of the Secretary of State, by the marshal or other person to whom the same shall be directed. And in case any alien, so ordered to depart, shall be found at large within the United States after the time limited in such order for his departure, and not having obtained a *license* from the President to reside therein, or having obtained such *license* shall not have conformed thereto, every such alien shall, on conviction thereof, be imprisoned for a term not exceeding three years, and shall never after be admitted to become a citizen of the United States. *Provided always, and be it further enacted*, that if any alien so ordered to depart shall prove to the satisfaction of the President, by evidence to be taken before such person or persons as the President shall direct, who are for that purpose hereby authorized to administer oaths, that no injury or danger to the United States will arise from suffering such alien to reside therein, the President may grant a *license* to such alien to remain within the United States for such time as he shall judge proper, and at such place as he may designate. And the President may also require of such alien to enter into a bond to the United States, in such penal sum as he may direct, with one or more sufficient sureties to the satisfaction of the person authorized by the President to take the same, conditioned for the good behavior of such alien during his residence in the United States, and not violating his license, which license the President may revoke, whenever he shall think proper.

SEC. 2. *And be it further enacted*, That it shall be lawful for the President of the United States, whenever he may deem it necessary for the public safety, to order to be removed out of the territory thereof, any alien who may or shall be in prison in pursuance of this act; and to cause to be arrested and sent out of the United States such of those aliens as shall have been ordered to depart therefrom and shall not have obtained a license as aforesaid, in all cases where, in the opinion of the President, the public safety requires a speedy removal. And if any alien so removed or sent out of the United States by the President shall voluntarily return thereto, unless by permission of the President of the United States, such alien on conviction thereof, shall be imprisoned so long as, in the opinion of the President, the public safety may require.

\*    \*    \*

# The Alien Enemy Act
# (6 July 1798; expired)

## CHAP. LXVI.—An Act respecting Alien Enemies. (a)

SECTION 1. *Be it enacted by the Senate and House of Representatives of the United States of America in Congress assembled*, That whenever there shall be a declared war between the United States and any foreign nation or government, or any invasion or predatory incursion shall be perpetrated, attempted, or threatened against the territory of the United States, by any foreign nation or government, and the President of the United States shall make public proclamation of the event, all natives, citizens, denizens, or subjects of the hostile nation or government, being males of the age of fourteen years and upwards, who shall be within the United

States, and not actually naturalized, shall be liable to be apprehended, restrained, secured and removed as alien enemies. And the President of the United States . . . is hereby authorized, . . . to direct the conduct to be observed, on the part of the United States, towards the aliens who shall become liable, as aforesaid; the manner and degree of the restraint to which they shall be subject, and in what cases, and upon what security their residence shall be permitted, and to provide for the removal of those, who, not being permitted to reside within the United States, shall refuse or neglect to depart therefrom; and to establish any other regulations which shall be found necessary in the premises and for the public safety: Provided, that aliens resident within the United States, who shall become liable as enemies, in the manner aforesaid, and who shall not be chargeable with actual hostility, or other crime against the public safety, shall be allowed, for the recovery, disposal, and removal of their goods and effects, and for their departure, the full time which is, or shall be stipulated by any treaty, where any shall have been between the United States, and the hostile nation or government, of which they shall be natives, citizens, denizens or subjects: and where no such treaty shall have existed, the President of the United States may ascertain and declare such reasonable time as may be consistent with the public safety, and according to the dictates of humanity and national hospitality.

SEC. 2. *And be it further enacted,* That after any proclamation shall be made as aforesaid, it shall be the duty of the several courts of the United States, and of each state, having criminal jurisdiction, and of the several judges and justices of the courts of the United States, . . . upon complaint, against any alien or alien enemies, as aforesaid, . . . to cause such alien or aliens to be duly apprehended and convened before such court, judge or justice; and after a full examination and hearing on such complaint, and sufficient cause therefor appearing, shall and may order such alien or aliens to be removed out of the territory of the United States, or to give sureties of their good behaviour, or to be otherwise restrained, . . .

\*     \*     \*

# The Sedition Act
# (14 July 1798; expired)

## CHAP. LXXIV.—An Act in addition to the act, entitled "An act for the punishment of certain crimes against the United States."

SECTION 1. *Be it enacted by the Senate and House of Representatives of the United States of America, in Congress assembled,* That if any persons shall unlawfully combine or conspire together, with intent to oppose any measure or measures of the government of the United States, which are or shall be directed by proper authority, or to impede the operation of any law of the United States, or to intimidate or prevent any person holding a place or office in or under the government of the United States, from undertaking, performing or executing his trust or duty; and if any person or persons, with intent as aforesaid, shall counsel, advise or attempt to procure any insurrection, riot, unlawful assembly, or combination, whether such conspiracy, threatening, counsel, advice, or attempt shall have the proposed effect or not, he or they shall be deemed guilty of a high misdemeanor, and on conviction, before any court of the United States having jurisdiction thereof, shall be punished by a fine not exceeding five thousand dollars, and by imprisonment during a term not less than six months nor exceeding five years; and further, at the discretion of the court may be holden to find sureties for his good behaviour in such sum, and for such time, as the said court may direct.

SEC. 2. *And be it further enacted,* That if any person shall write, print, utter or publish, or shall cause or procure to be written, printed, uttered or published, or shall knowingly and willingly assist or aid in writing, printing, uttering or publishing any false, scandalous and malicious writing or writings against the government of the United States, or either house of the Congress of the United States, or the President of the United States, with intent to defame the said government, or either house of the said Congress, or the said President, or to

bring them, or either of them, into contempt or dis-
repute; or to excite against them, or either or any of
them, the hatred of the good people of the United
States, or to stir up sedition within the United
States, or to excite any unlawful combinations
therein, for opposing or resisting any law of the
United States, or any act of the President of the
United States, done in pursuance of any such law, or
of the powers in him vested by the constitution of
the United States, or to resist, oppose, or defeat any
such law or act, or to aid, encourage or abet any hostile designs of any foreign nation against the United
States, their people or government, then such person, being thereof convicted before any court of the
United States having jurisdiction thereof, shall be
punished by a fine not exceeding two thousand dollars, and by imprisonment not exceeding two years.

SEC. 3. *And be it further enacted and declared,*
That if any person shall be prosecuted under this
act, for the writing or publishing any libel aforesaid, it shall be lawful for the defendant, upon the
trial of the cause, to give in evidence in his defence,
the truth of the matter contained in the publication charged as a libel. And the jury who shall try
the cause, shall have a right to determine the law
and the fact, under the direction of the court, as in
other cases.

\*     \*     \*

# REVIEW QUESTIONS

1. By passing the Alien and Sedition Acts, were the
   Federalist legislators reacting to a national or a
   political threat?
2. What do these acts suggest about their conception of loyalty and citizenship?
3. How did the Alien Act pick up from and
   strengthen provisions in the Naturalization Act?
   Was the Alien Act anti-immigrant or pro-security?
4. Did the later two alien acts expand presidential
   power?
5. Was the Sedition Act a defense of order or an
   offense against citizens' rights? Did the act, in
   effect, define dissent as treachery?
6. How could a person charged under the provisions of this act defend herself or himself?

# FROM Kentucky and Virginia Resolutions
# (1798 and 1799)

*Federalists received neither the respect nor domestic peace they wanted with the Alien
and Sedition Acts; instead, the acts provoked more challenges by their opponents. Republicans denounced the legislation as unconstitutional. In their outrage and through
their endeavors to have the acts immediately repealed, some Republicans advanced
new or revised theories on how to check the powers of the national government. Their
ideas on state interposition and nullification of national legislation would be revised
by later theorists and used in even more divisive political wrangles. Thomas Jefferson
and James Madison presented these ideas in the Kentucky and Virginia Resolutions,
respectively (Jefferson drafted Kentucky's argument; John Breckinridge actually presented them to that state's legislature). Their proposals were controversial, so much so
that despite their attempts to persuade other states to pass supporting legislation,
many states passed statements—though none so short and scathing perhaps as*

*Delaware's—denouncing the resolutions. Despite such denunciations, however, many Americans agreed that the Federalists had overstepped their authority and infringed on the people's rights, and thus, although they lost this political battle, the Republicans won the "war" in the election of 1800.*

From Jonathan Elliot, ed., *The Debates in the Several State Conventions on the Adoption of the Federal Constitution*, vol. 4 (1836; New York: Burt Franklin Reprints, 1974), pp. 528–29, 532, 540–45.

# Kentucky Resolutions of 1798 and 1799.

[HOUSE OF REPRESENTATIVES, *November* 10, 1798]

1. *Resolved*, That the several states composing the United States of America are not united on the principle of unlimited submission to their general government; but that, by compact, under the style and title of a Constitution for the United States, and of amendments thereto, they constituted a general government for special purposes, delegated to that government certain definite powers, reserving, each state to itself, the residuary mass of right to their own self-government; and that whensoever the general government assumes undelegated powers, its acts are unauthoritative, void, and of no force; that to this compact each state acceded as a state, and is an integral party; that this government, created by this compact, was not made the exclusive or final judge of the extent of the powers delegated to itself, since that would have made its discretion, and not the Constitution, the measure of its powers; but that, as in all other cases of compact among parties having no common judge, *each party has an equal right to judge for itself, as well of infractions as of the mode and measure of redress.*

2. *Resolved*, That the Constitution of the United States having delegated to Congress a power to punish treason, counterfeiting the securities and current coin of the United States, piracies and felonies committed on the high seas, and offences against the laws of nations, and no other crimes whatever; and it being true, as a general principle, and one of the amendments to the Constitution having also declared "that the powers not delegated to the United States by the Constitution, nor prohibited by it to the states, are reserved to the states respectively, or to the people,"—therefore, also, the same act of Congress, passed on the 14th day of July, 1798, and entitled "An Act in Addition to the Act entitled 'An Act for the Punishment of certain Crimes against the United States;'" as also the act passed by them on the 27th day of June, 1798, entitled "An Act to punish Frauds committed on the Bank of the United States," (and all other their acts which assume to create, define, or punish crimes other than those enumerated in the Constitution,) are altogether void, and of no force; and that the power to create, define, and punish, such other crimes is reserved, and of right appertains, solely and exclusively, to the respective states, each within its own territory.

3. *Resolved*, That it is true, as a general principle, and is also expressly declared by one of the amendments to the Constitution, that "the powers not delegated to the United States by the Constitution, nor prohibited by it to the states, are reserved to the states respectively, or to the people;" and that, no power over the freedom of religion, freedom of speech, or freedom of the press, being delegated to the United States by the Constitution, nor prohibited by it to the states, all lawful powers respecting the same did of right remain, and were reserved to the states, or to the people; that thus was manifested their determination to retain to themselves the right of judging how far the licentiousness of speech, and of the press, may be abridged without lessening their useful freedom, and how far those abuses which cannot be separated from their use, should be tolerated rather than the use be destroyed; and thus also

they guarded against all abridgment, by the United States, of the freedom of religious principles and exercises, and retained to themselves the right of protecting the same, as this, stated by a law passed on the general demand of its citizens, had already protected them from all human restraint or interference; and that, in addition to this general principle and express declaration, another and more special provision has been made by one of the amendments to the Constitution, which expressly declares, that "Congress shall make no laws respecting an establishment of religion, or prohibiting the free exercise thereof, or abridging the freedom of speech, or of the press," thereby guarding, in the same sentence, and under the same words, the freedom of religion, of speech, and of the press, insomuch that whatever violates either throws down the sanctuary which covers the others,—and that libels, falsehood, and defamation, equally with heresy and false religion, are withheld from the cognizance of federal tribunals. That therefore the act of the Congress of the United States, passed on the 14th of July, 1798, entitled "An Act in Addition to the Act entitled 'An Act for the Punishment of certain Crimes against the United States,'" which does abridge the freedom of the press, is not law, but is altogether void, and of no force.

4. *Resolved*, That alien friends are under the jurisdiction and protection of the laws of the state wherein they are; that no power over them has been delegated to the United States, nor prohibited to the individual states, . . . [thus] the act of the Congress of the United States, passed the 22d day of June, 1798, entitled "An Act concerning Aliens," which assumes power over alien friends not delegated by the Constitution, is not law, but is altogether void and of no force.

5. *Resolved*, That, in addition to the general principle, as well as the express declaration, that powers not delegated are reserved, another and more special provision inserted in the Constitution from abundant caution, has declared, "that the migration or importation of such persons as any of the states now existing shall think proper to admit, shall not be prohibited by the Congress prior to the year 1808." That this commonwealth does admit the migration of alien friends described as the subject of the said act concerning aliens; . . .

6. *Resolved*, That the imprisonment of a person under the protection of the laws of this commonwealth, on his failure to obey the simple order of the President to depart out of the United States, as is undertaken by the said act, entitled, "An Act concerning Aliens," is contrary to the Constitution, one amendment in which has provided, that "no person shall be deprived of liberty without due process of law;" and that another having provided, "that, in all criminal prosecutions, the accused shall enjoy the right of a public trial by an impartial jury, to be informed as to the nature and cause of the accusation, to be confronted with the witnesses against him, to have compulsory process for obtaining witnesses in his favor, and to have assistance of counsel for his defence," the same act undertaking to authorize the President to remove a person out of the United States who is under the protection of the law, on his own suspicion, without jury, without public trial, without confrontation of the witnesses against him, without having witnesses in his favor, without defence, without counsel—contrary to these provisions also of the Constitution—is therefore not law, but utterly void, and of no force.

\*   \*   \*

7. *Resolved*, That the construction applied by the general government (as is evident by sundry of their proceedings) to those parts of the Constitution of the United States which delegate to Congress power to lay and collect taxes, duties, imposts, excises; to pay the debts, and provide for the common defence and general welfare, of the United States, and to make all laws which shall be necessary and proper for carrying into execution the powers vested by the Constitution in the government of the United States, or any department thereof, goes to the destruction of all the limits prescribed to their power by the Constitution; that words meant by that instrument to be subsidiary only to the execution of the limited powers, ought

not to be so construed as themselves to give un-limited powers, nor a part so to be taken as to de-stroy the whole residue of the instrument; that the proceedings of the general government, under color of those articles, will be a fit and necessary subject for revisal and correction at a time of greater tranquillity, while those specified in the preceding resolutions call for immediate redress.

\*       \*       \*

9. *Resolved*, lastly, That the governor of this com-monwealth be, and is, authorized and requested to communicate the preceding resolutions to the leg-islatures of the several states, to assure them that this commonwealth considers union for special na-tional purposes, and particularly for those speci-fied in their late federal compact, to be friendly to the peace, happiness, and prosperity, of all the states: that, faithful to that compact, according to the plain intent and meaning in which it was un-derstood and acceded to by the several parties, it is sincerely anxious for its preservation; that it does also believe, that, to take from the states all the powers of self-government, and transfer them to a general and consolidated government, without re-gard to the special government, and reservations solemnly agreed to in that compact, is not for the peace, happiness, or prosperity of these states; . . . that the friendless alien has been selected as the safest subject of a first experiment; but the citizen will soon follow, or rather has already followed; for already has a Sedition Act marked him as a prey: That these and successive acts of the same charac-ter, unless arrested on the threshold, may tend to drive these states into revolution and blood, and will furnish new calumnies against republican gov-ernments, and new pretexts for those who wish it to be believed that man cannot be governed but by a rod of iron; . . .

In questions of power, then, let no more be said of confidence in man, but bind him down from mis-chief by the chains of the Constitution. That this commonwealth does therefore call on its co-states for an expression of their sentiments on the acts concerning aliens, and for the punishment of cer-tain crimes herein before specified, plainly declaring whether these acts are or are not authorized by the federal compact. . . . That they will view this as seiz-ing the rights of the states, and consolidating them in the hands of the general government, with a power assumed to bind the states, not merely in cases made federal, but in all cases whatsoever, by laws made, not with their consent, but by others against their consent, that this would be to surren-der the form of government we have chosen, and live under one deriving its powers from its own will, and not from our authority; and that the co-states, recurring to their natural rights not made federal, will concur in declaring these void and of no force, and will each unite with this commonwealth in re-questing their repeal at the next session of Congress.

HOUSE OF REPRESENTATIVES,
*Thursday, Nov. 14, 1799.*

\*       \*       \*

The representatives of the good people of this commonwealth, in General Assembly convened, having maturely considered the answers of sundry states in the Union to their resolutions, passed the last session, respecting certain unconstitutional laws of Congress, commonly called the Alien and Sedition Laws, would be faithless, indeed, to them-selves, and to those they represent, were they silently to acquiesce in the principles and doctrines attempted to be maintained in all those answers, that of Virginia only excepted. To again enter the field of argument, and attempt more fully or forcibly to expose the unconstitutionality of those obnoxious laws, would, it is apprehended, be as un-necessary as unavailing. We cannot, however, but lament that, in the discussion of those interesting subjects by sundry of the legislatures of our sister states, unfounded suggestions and uncandid in-sinuations, derogatory to the true character and principles of this commonwealth, have been sub-stituted in place of fair reasoning and sound argument. . . . Lest, however, the silence of this commonwealth should be construed into an acquiescence in the doctrines and principles ad-vanced, and attempted to be maintained, by the said answers; or at least those of our fellow-citizens, throughout the Union, who so widely differ from us on those important subjects, should be deluded by the expectation that we shall be deterred from what we conceive our duty, or shrink from the principles contained in those resolutions,—therefore,

*Resolved*, That this commonwealth considers the federal Union, upon the terms and for the purposes specified in the late compact, conducive to the liberty and happiness of the several states: That it does now unequivocally declare its attachment to the Union, and to that compact, agreeably to its obvious and real intention, and will be among the last to seek its dissolution: That, if those who administer the general government be permitted to transgress the limits fixed by that compact, by a total disregard to the special delegations of power therein contained, an annihilation of the state governments, and the creation, upon their ruins, of a general consolidated government, will be the inevitable consequence: That the principle and construction, contended for by sundry of the state legislatures, that the general government is the exclusive judge of the extent of the powers delegated to it, stop not short of *despotism*—since the discretion of those who administer the government, and not the *Constitution*, would be the measure of their powers: That the several states who formed that instrument, being sovereign and independent, have the unquestionable right to judge of the infraction: and, *That a nullification, by those sovereignties, of all unauthorized acts done under color of that instrument, is the rightful remedy:* That this commonwealth does, under the most deliberate reconsideration, declare, that the said Alien and Sedition Laws are, in their opinion, palpable violations of the said Constitution; and, however cheerfully it may be disposed to surrender its opinion to a majority of its sister states, in matters of ordinary or doubtful policy, yet, in momentous regulations like the present, which so vitally wound the best rights of the citizen, it would consider a silent acquiescence as highly criminal: That, although this commonwealth, as a party to the federal compact, will bow to the laws of the Union, yet it does, at the same time, declare, that it will not now, or ever hereafter, cease to oppose, in a constitutional manner, every attempt, at what quarter soever offered, to violate that compact: And finally, in order that no pretext or arguments may be drawn from a supposed acquiescence, on the part of this commonwealth, in the constitutionality of those laws, and be thereby used as precedents for similar future violations of the federal compact, this commonwealth does now enter against them its solemn PROTEST.

\*   \*   \*

# Virginia Resolutions of 1798, Pronouncing the Alien and Sedition Laws to be Unconstitutional, and Defining the Rights of the States.

## *Drawn by Mr. Madison.*

IN THE VIRGINIA HOUSE OF DELEGATES, FRIDAY, *December* 21, 1798.

*Resolved*, That the General Assembly of Virginia doth unequivocally express a firm resolution to maintain and defend the Constitution of the United States, and the Constitution of this state, against every aggression, either foreign or domestic; and that they will support the government of the United States in all measures warranted by the former.

That this Assembly most solemnly declares a warm attachment to the union of the states, to maintain which it pledges its powers; and that, for this end, it is their duty to watch over and oppose every infraction of those principles which constitute the only basis of that union, because a faithful observance of them can alone secure its existence and the public happiness.

That this Assembly doth explicitly and peremptorily declare, that it views the powers of the federal government as resulting from the compact to which the states are parties, as limited by the plain sense and intention of the instrument constituting that compact, as no further valid than they are authorized by the grants enumerated in that compact; and that, in case of a deliberate, palpable, and dangerous exercise of other powers, not granted by the said compact, the states, who are parties thereto, have the right, and are in duty bound, to interpose, for arresting the progress of the evil, and for maintaining, within their respective limits, the authorities, rights, and liberties, appertaining to them.

That the General Assembly doth also express its deep regret, that a spirit has, in sundry instances, been manifested by the federal government to enlarge its powers by forced constructions of the constitutional charter which defines them; and that indications have appeared of a design to expound certain general phrases (which, having been copied from the very limited grant of powers in the former Articles of Confederation, were the less liable to be misconstrued) so as to destroy the meaning and effect of the particular enumeration which necessarily explains and limits the general phrases, and so as to consolidate the states, by degrees, into one sovereignty, the obvious tendency and inevitable result of which would be, to transform the present republican system of the United States into an absolute, or, at best, a mixed monarchy.

*That the General Assembly doth particularly PROTEST against the palpable and alarming infractions of the Constitution, in the two late cases of the "Alien and Sedition Acts," passed at the last session of Congress; the first of which exercises a power nowhere delegated to the federal government, and which, by uniting legislative and judicial powers to those of executive, subverts the general principles of free government, as well as the particular organization and positive provisions of the Federal Constitution; and the other of which acts exercises, in like manner, a power not delegated by the Constitution, but, on the contrary, expressly and positively forbidden by one of the amendments thereto—a power which, more than any other, ought to produce universal alarm, because it is levelled against the right of freely examining public characters and measures, and of free communication among the people thereon, which has ever been justly deemed the only effectual guardian of every other right.*

That this state having, by its Convention, which ratified the Federal Constitution, expressly declared that, among other essential rights, "the liberty of conscience and the press cannot be cancelled, abridged, restrained, or modified, by any authority of the United States," and from its extreme anxiety to guard these rights from every possible attack of sophistry and ambition, having, with other states, recommended an amendment for that purpose, which amendment was, in due time, annexed to the Constitution,—it would mark a reproachful inconsistency, and criminal degeneracy, if an indifference were now shown to the most palpable violation of one of the rights thus declared and secured, and to the establishment of a precedent which may be fatal to the other.

That the good people of this commonwealth, having ever felt, and continuing to feel, the most sincere affection for their brethren of the other states; the truest anxiety for establishing and perpetuating the union of all; and the most scrupulous fidelity to that Constitution, which is the pledge of mutual friendship, and the instrument of mutual happiness,—the General Assembly doth solemnly appeal to the like dispositions in the other states, in confidence that they will concur with this commonwealth in declaring, as it does hereby declare, that the acts aforesaid are unconstitutional; and that the necessary and proper measures will be taken *by each* for coöperating with this state, in maintaining unimpaired the authorities, rights, and liberties, reserved to the states respectively, or to the people.

\*      \*      \*

# State of Delaware.

IN THE HOUSE OF REPRESENTATIVES,
*February* 1, 1799.

*Resolved,* By the Senate and House of Representatives of the state of Delaware, in General Assembly met, that they consider the resolutions from the state of Virginia as a very unjustifiable interference with the general government and constituted authorities of the United States, and of dangerous tendency, and therefore not fit subject for the further consideration of the General Assembly.

*    *    *

# REVIEW QUESTIONS

1. What body, or bodies, did Jefferson argue had the right to determine the constitutionality of congressional acts? If an act was determined to be unconstitutional, could it be declared null and void?
2. Jefferson argued that not only the creation of such legislation by the national government but also its contents were unconstitutional. Is this second argument a defense of civil rights?
3. How does Jefferson's interpretation of the Constitution form the basis of his arguments? Was his a strict (literal) or broad (flexible) interpretation?
4. In the Virginia Resolutions, does Madison's assertion that the states were duty bound to interpose to arrest the progress of evil and maintain rights supplement or modify Jefferson's challenge? Does Madison's argument include an admonition against a broad or loose interpretation of the Constitution?
5. Why would Delaware's legislature have considered Virginia's (and, by inference, Kentucky's) resolutions to have been dangerous?

# 8   THE EARLY REPUBLIC

Americans inaugurated a new president and a new century in 1801. Revolutionary as it was for a nation's people to transfer power peacefully from a current head of state to a new one, and in the process from one interest group or political party to another, this was not another revolutionary era. While some citizens talked of radical change or embraced millennialist rhetoric, most sought assurance that the establishment created in the old century would continue in the new. As most of the nation's leaders had earned their original laurels in the Revolution, Americans could be assured that its principles and institutions would continue to be the foundation of government. But in moving into the future with a new president—one elected because he espoused a strict interpretation of the Constitution and a limited federal government—American citizens did indicate a desire for some course corrections on the nation's journey to security and prosperity.

 The new chief executive of the nation, Thomas Jefferson, and the new chief justice, John Marshall, jousted again and again over what should be the proper interpretation and implementation of the Constitution. The Federalists, voted out of the executive branch and relegated to minority status in the legislative branch, made the judiciary their bulwark. As the champions for each side battled in Congress, in courts, and finally in the Supreme Court itself, Marshall, Jefferson, and James Madison (first as Jefferson's secretary of state and then as president) further defined the powers of their own respective branches as well as the limits of the others. In the course of their political and legal contests, these leaders, like Washington and Hamilton before them, set precedents upon which later officials would base their decisions and actions.

 Jefferson presided over a growing nation—both in population and territory —which presented particular challenges to its government. Upon taking office, Jefferson faced a major foreign threat to the nation's interests and security: Napoleon Bonaparte. The general and first consul of France (emperor in 1804) wanted not only to extend France's domain in Europe but also to reestablish its *empire in North America. Jefferson learned of his plans and immediately took steps to counter them, engaging both explorers and diplomats to secure his country's claims to the Louisiana Territory.*

*While the United States thus resolved one impediment to its national interests, it was left with what many citizens deemed an even greater one: Native Americans holding prime lands and resisting physical and cultural encroachments. Jefferson was willing to protect Indian interests on what lands the tribes still held, but he and his successors not only bought Indian lands, they also promoted land exchanges in which Native Americans traded their lands east of the Mississippi for lands to the west of it. As most Indians were not willing to do this, successive presidential administrations continued to grapple with the problem of how to foster coexistence with and assimilation of Native Americans. Some citizens, in turn, wrestled with a similar, sometimes connected issue—that of assimilating other ethnic groups.*

*As the nation struggled with domestic challenges, it also tried to counter transatlantic threats to its interests. Problems had arisen because of European conflicts, primarily British-French warfare, and the continuing growth and strength of the British Empire. British dominance on the high seas led to disagreements over maritime rights. Americans, insecure because of the British presence in Canada, also accused the British of inciting Indians against them. As such American weaknesses were revealed, militants in both parties, but especially Republicans, called for a war to defend the nation's honor, rights, and institutions. The result was what some citizens called the "second war of American independence." The title was perhaps apt, for whereas the first had been a war for independence, this was a war coming out of American insistence that its independence and autonomy be not only acknowledged but respected. Yet, even with such a noble-sounding aim, the War of 1812 was not a popular one, or one well waged: it was a war that both united and divided Americans.*

# THOMAS JEFFERSON

## FROM First Inaugural Address (1801)

*The election of 1800 was not a polite political duel. There was much verbal mudslinging and intraparty and interparty blows and backstabbing. Alexander Hamilton's disputes with John Adams weakened the Federalist Party from within, while reactions to the administration's policies battered it from without. As a result of those conflicts and the Republican Party's attractive promises, Americans elected Thomas Jefferson to be the third president of the United States. The inauguration was conducted on 4 March in the new capital of the country, Washington, D.C., and—with the president figuratively honoring the people and states by whose power he served—at the new home of the Congress, the Capitol.*

From James D. Richardson, ed., *A Compilation of the Messages and Papers of the Presidents, 1789–1902*, vol. I (Washington, DC, Bureau of National Literature and Art, 1904), pp. 321–24. [Editorial insertions appear in square brackets—*Ed.*]

*Friends and Fellow-Citizens.*

Called upon to undertake the duties of the first executive office of our country, I avail myself of the presence of that portion of my fellow-citizens which is here assembled to express my grateful thanks for the favor with which they have been pleased to look toward me, to declare a sincere consciousness that the task is above my talents, and that I approach it with those anxious and awful presentiments which the greatness of the charge and the weakness of my powers so justly inspire. A rising nation, spread over a wide and fruitful land, traversing all the seas with the rich productions of their industry, engaged in commerce with nations who feel power and forget right, advancing rapidly to destinies beyond the reach of mortal eye—when I contemplate these transcendent objects, and see the honor, the happiness, and the hopes of this beloved country committed to the issue and the auspices of this day, I shrink from the contemplation, and humble myself before the magnitude of the undertaking. Utterly, indeed, should I despair did not the presence of many whom I here see remind me that in the other high authorities provided by our Constitution I shall find resources of wisdom, of virtue, and of zeal on which to rely under all difficulties. To you, then, gentlemen, who are charged with the sovereign functions of legislation, and to those associated with you, I look with encouragement for that guidance and support which may enable us to steer with safety the vessel in which we are all embarked amidst the conflicting elements of a troubled world.

During the contest of opinion through which we have passed the animation of discussions and of exertions has sometimes worn an aspect which might impose on strangers unused to think freely and to speak and to write what they think; but this being now decided by the voice of the nation, announced according to the rules of the Constitution, all will, of course, arrange themselves under the will of the law, and unite in common efforts for the common good. All, too, will bear in mind this sacred principle, that though the will of the majority is in all cases to prevail, that will to be rightful must be reasonable; that the minority possess their equal rights, which equal law must protect, and to violate would be oppression. Let us, then, fellow-citizens, unite with one heart and one mind. Let us restore to social intercourse that harmony and affection without which liberty and even life itself are but dreary things. And let us reflect that, having banished from our land that religious intolerance under which mankind so long bled and suffered, we have yet gained little if we countenance a political intolerance as despotic, as wicked, and capable of as bitter and bloody persecutions. . . . [E]very difference of opinion is not a difference of principle. We have called by different names brethren of the same principle. We are all Republicans, we are all Federalists. If there be any among us who would wish to dissolve this Union or to change its republican form, let them stand undisturbed as monuments of the safety with which error of opinion may be tolerated where reason is left free to combat it. I know, indeed, that some honest men fear that a republican government can not be strong, that this Government is not strong enough; but would the honest patriot, in the full tide of successful experiment, abandon a government which has so far kept us free and firm on the theoretic and visionary fear that this Government, the world's best hope, may by possibility want energy to preserve itself? I trust not. I believe this, on the contrary, the strongest Government on earth. I believe it the only one where every man, at the call of the law, would fly to the standard of the law, and would meet invasions of the public order as his own personal concern. Sometimes it is said that man can not be trusted with the government of himself. Can he, then, be trusted with the government of others? Or have we found angels in the forms of kings to govern him? Let history answer this question.

Let us, then, with courage and confidence pursue our own Federal and Republican principles, our attachment to union and representative government. Kindly separated by nature and a wide ocean from the exterminating havoc of one quarter of the globe; too high-minded to endure the degradations of the others; possessing a chosen country, with room enough for our descendants to the thousandth and thousandth generation; entertaining a due sense of our equal right to the use of our own faculties, to the acquisitions of our own

industry, to honor and confidence from our fellow-citizens, resulting not from birth, but from our actions and their sense of them; enlightened by a benign religion, professed, indeed, and practiced in various forms, yet all of them inculcating honesty, truth, temperance, gratitude, and the love of man; acknowledging and adoring an overruling Providence, which by all its dispensations proves that it delights in the happiness of man here and his greater happiness hereafter—with all these blessings, what more is necessary to make us a happy and a prosperous people? Still one thing more, fellow-citizens—a wise and frugal Government, which shall restrain men from injuring one another, shall leave them otherwise free to regulate their own pursuits of industry and improvement, and shall not take from the mouth of labor the bread it has earned. This is the sum of good government, and this is necessary to close the circle of our felicities.

About to enter, fellow-citizens, on the exercise of duties which comprehend everything dear and valuable to you, it is proper you should understand what I deem the essential principles of our Government, and consequently those which ought to shape its Administration. I will compress them within the narrowest compass they will bear, stating the general principle, but not all its limitations. Equal and exact justice to all men, of whatever state or persuasion, religious or political; peace, commerce, and honest friendship with all nations, entangling alliances with none; the support of the State governments in all their rights, as the most competent administrations for our domestic concerns and the surest bulwarks against antirepublican tendencies; the preservation of the General Government in its whole constitutional vigor, as the sheet anchor of our peace at home and safety abroad; a jealous care of the right of election by the people—a mild and safe corrective of abuses which are lopped by the sword of revolution where peaceable remedies are unprovided; absolute acquiescence in the decisions of the majority, the vital principle of republics, from which is no appeal but to force, the vital principle and immediate parent of despotism; a well-disciplined militia, our best reliance in peace and for the first moments of war, till regulars may relieve them; the supremacy of the civil over the military authority; economy in the public expense, that labor may be lightly burthened; the honest payment of our debts and sacred preservation of the public faith; encouragement of agriculture, and of commerce as its handmaid; the diffusion of information and arraignment of all abuses at the bar of the public reason; freedom of religion; freedom of the press, and freedom of person under the protection of the habeas corpus, and trial by juries impartially selected. These principles form the bright constellation which has gone before us and guided our steps through an age of revolution and reformation. The wisdom of our sages and blood of our heroes have been devoted to their attainment. They should be the creed of our political faith, the text of civic instruction, the touchstone by which to try the services of those we trust; and should we wander from them in moments of error or of alarm, let us hasten to retrace our steps and to regain the road which alone leads to peace, liberty, and safety.

. . . I have learnt to expect that it will rarely fall to the lot of imperfect man to retire from this station with the reputation and the favor which bring him into it. Without pretensions to that high confidence you reposed in our first and greatest revolutionary character, . . . I ask so much confidence only as may give firmness and effect to the legal administration of your affairs. I shall often go wrong through defect of judgment. When right, I shall often be thought wrong by those whose positions will not command a view of the whole ground. I ask your indulgence for my own errors, which will never be intentional, and your support against the errors of others, who may condemn what they would not if seen in all its parts. The approbation implied by your suffrage is a great consolation to me for the past, and my future solicitude will be to retain the good opinion of those who have bestowed it in advance, to conciliate that of others by doing them all the good in my power, and to be instrumental to the happiness and freedom of all.

\*    \*    \*

## REVIEW QUESTIONS

1. Does Jefferson speak of continuity or change?
2. How does he define the president's powers and relationship with the legislative branch?
3. How does he define the federal government's power and responsibilities?
4. Does he speak of or imply a belief in American exceptionalism?
5. Are the sentiments expressed in this address in agreement with his earlier opinions (see Chapters 4 and 7)?

# FROM *Marbury v. Madison* (1803)

*The Federalists lost Congress as well as the presidency in the elections of 1800, but before they handed over their seats and votes to the Jeffersonian Republicans, the Sixth Congress passed the Judiciary Act of 1801. Besides providing for a reduction in the number of Supreme Court justices, it also created sixteen circuit courts, with a judge for each, and increased the number of attorneys, clerks, and marshals associated with the judicial branch. Before leaving office, President Adams named John Marshall as chief justice and appointed a significant number of Federalists to the newly established positions. These last-minute commissions became known as the "midnight appointments." Unfortunately for some of those selected for the new offices, their commissions were not delivered before Jefferson took office. Jefferson, resisting the Federalist power play and trying to contain Federalist entrenchment in the judiciary, made a power play of his own by directing his secretary of state, James Madison, not to deliver the remaining commissions. When William Marbury did not receive his letter of appointment to a justice of the peace position in the District of Columbia, he sued for a writ of mandamus (an order issued by a higher court to a lower one or to other government agencies and officials) to force its delivery. When the Supreme Court, led by Marshall, ruled on the case in February 1803, it not only exercised its own power but expanded it.*

---

From William Cranch, ed., *Reports of Cases Argued and Adjudged in the Supreme Court of the United States, in August and December Terms, 1801, and February Term, 1803*, 3rd ed., vol. I (Philadelphia: Carey & Lea, 1830), pp. 49–72. [Editorial insertions appear in brackets—*Ed.*]

\*     \*     \*

Mr. Chief Justice MARSHALL delivered the opinion of the court.

At the last term, on the affidavits then read and filed with the clerk, a rule was granted in this case, requiring the secretary of state to show cause why a mandamus should not issue, directing him to deliver to William Marbury his commission as a justice of the peace for the county of Washington, in the district of Columbia.

No cause has been shown, and the present motion is for a mandamus. The peculiar delicacy of this case, the novelty of some of its circumstances, and the real difficulty attending the points which occur in it, require a complete exposition of the principles on which the opinion to be given by the court is founded.

\*     \*     \*

The first object of inquiry is,

1. Has the applicant a right to the commission he demands?

His right originates in an act of congress passed in February 1801, concerning the district of Columbia.

\*     \*     \*

It appears from the affidavits, that in compliance with this law, a commission for William Marbury as a justice of peace for the county of Washington was signed by John Adams, then president of the United States; after which the seal of the United States was affixed to it; but the commission has never reached the person for whom it was made out.

In order to determine whether he is entitled to this commission, it becomes necessary to inquire whether he has been appointed to the office. For if he has been appointed, the law continues him in office for five years, and he is entitled to the possession of those evidences of office, which, being completed, became his property.

The second section of the second article of the constitution declares, "the president shall nominate, and, by and with the advice and consent of the senate, shall appoint ambassadors, other public ministers and consuls, and all other officers of the United States, whose appointments are not otherwise provided for."

The third section declares, that "he shall commission all the officers of the United States."

An act of congress directs the secretary of state to keep the seal of the United States, "to make out and record, and affix the said seal to all civil commissions to officers of the United States to be appointed by the president, by and with the consent of the senate, or by the president alone; provided that the said seal shall not be affixed to any commission before the same shall have been signed by the president of the United States."

\*     \*     \*

The acts of appointing to office, and commissioning the person appointed, can scarcely be considered as one and the same; since the power to perform them is given in two separate and distinct sections of the constitution.

\* \* \*

It follows too, from the existence of this distinction, that, if an appointment was to be evidenced by any public act other than the commission, the performance of such public act would create the officer; and if he was not removable at the will of the president, would either give him a right to his commission, or enable him to perform the duties without it.

\* \* \*

This is an appointment made by the president, by and with the advice and consent of the senate, and is evidenced by no act but the commission itself. In such a case therefore the commission and the appointment seem inseparable; it being almost impossible to show an appointment otherwise than by proving the existence of a commission: still the commission is not necessarily the appointment; though conclusive evidence of it.

\* \* \*

The commission being signed, the subsequent duty of the secretary of state is prescribed by law, and not to be guided by the will of the president. He is to affix the seal of the United States to the commission, and is to record it.

This is not a proceeding which may be varied, if the judgment of the executive shall suggest one more eligible, but is a precise course accurately marked out by law, and is to be strictly pursued. It is the duty of the secretary of state to conform to the law, and in this he is an officer of the United States, bound to obey the laws. He acts, in this respect, as has been very properly stated at the bar, under the authority of law, and not by the instructions of the president. . . .

\* \* \*

It is therefore decidedly the opinion of the court, that when a commission has been signed by the president, the appointment is made; and that the commission is complete when the seal of the United States has been affixed to it by the secretary of state.

Where an officer is removable at the will of the executive, the circumstance which completes his appointment is of no concern; because the act is at any time revocable; and the commission may be arrested, if still in the office. But when the officer is not removable at the will of the executive, the appointment is not revocable and cannot be annulled. It has conferred legal rights which cannot be resumed.

The discretion of the executive is to be exercised until the appointment has been made. But having once made the appointment, his power over the office is terminated in all cases, where by law the officer is not removable by him. The right to the office is *then* in the person appointed, and he has the absolute, unconditional power of accepting or rejecting it.

Mr. Marbury, then, since his commission was signed by the president and sealed by the secretary of state, was appointed; and as the law creating the office gave the officer a right to hold for five years independent of the executive, the appointment was not revocable; but vested in the officer legal rights which are protected by the laws of his country.

To withhold the commission, therefore, is an act deemed by the court not warranted by law, but violative of a vested legal right.

This brings us to the second inquiry; which is,

2. If he has a right, and that right has been violated, do the laws of his country afford him a remedy?

The very essence of civil liberty certainly consists in the right of every individual to claim the protection of the laws, whenever he receives an injury. One of the first duties of government is to afford that protection. . . .

\* \* \*

The government of the United States has been emphatically termed a government of laws, and not of men. It will certainly cease to deserve this high appellation, if the laws furnish no remedy for the violation of a vested legal right.

If this obloquy is to be cast on the jurisprudence of our country, it must arise from the peculiar character of the case.

It behoves us then to inquire whether there be in its composition any ingredient which shall exempt from legal investigation, or exclude the injured party from legal redress. . . .

*      *      *

It follows then that the question, whether the legality of an act of the head of a department be examinable in a court of justice or not, must always depend on the nature of that act.

If some acts be examinable, and others not, there must be some rule of law to guide the court in the exercise of its jurisdiction.

In some instances there may be difficulty in applying the rule to particular cases; but there cannot, it is believed, be much difficulty in laying down the rule.

*      *      *

. . . [W]here the heads of departments are the political or confidential agents of the executive, merely to execute the will of the president, or rather to act in cases in which the executive possesses a constitutional or legal discretion, nothing can be more perfectly clear than that their acts are only politically examinable. But where a specific duty is assigned by law, and individual rights depend upon the performance of that duty, it seems equally clear that the individual who considers himself injured has a right to resort to the laws of his country for a remedy.

If this be the rule, let us inquire how it applies to the case under the consideration of the court.

The power of nominating to the senate, and the power of appointing the person nominated, are political powers, to be exercised by the president according to his own discretion. When he has made an appointment, he has exercised his whole power, and his discretion has been completely applied to the case. If, by law, the officer be removable at the will of the president, then a new appointment may be immediately made, and the rights of the officer are terminated. But . . . if the officer is by law not removable at the will of the president, the rights he has acquired are protected by the law, and are not resumable by the president. . . .

*      *      *

It is then the opinion of the court,

1. That by signing the commission of Mr. Marbury, the president of the United States appointed him a justice of peace for the county of Washington in the district of Columbia; and that the seal of the United States, affixed thereto by the secretary of state, is conclusive testimony of the verity of the signature, and of the completion of the appointment; and that the appointment conferred on him a legal right to the office for the space of five years.
2. That, having this legal title to the office, he has a consequent right to the commission; a refusal to deliver which is a plain violation of that right, for which the laws of his country afford him a remedy.

It remains to be inquired whether,

3. He is entitled to the remedy for which he applies. This depends on,
    1. The nature of the writ applied for. And,
    2. The power of this court.
    3. The nature of the writ.

*      *      *

This writ, if awarded, would be directed to an officer of government, and its mandate to him would be, to use the words of Blackstone,[1] "to do a particular thing therein specified, which appertains to his office and duty, and which the court has previously determined or at least supposes to be consonant to right and justice." Or, in the words of

---

[1] Sir William Blackstone (d. 1780), lawyer, historian, judge, and author of *Commentaries on the Laws of England—Ed.*

Lord Mansfield,[2] the applicant, in this case, has a right to execute an office of public concern, and is kept out of possession of that right.

These circumstances certainly concur in this case.

Still, to render the mandamus a proper remedy, the officer to whom it is to be directed, must be one to whom, on legal principles, such writ may be directed: and the person applying for it must be without any other specific and legal remedy.

1. With respect to the officer to whom it would be directed. The intimate political relation, subsisting between the president of the United States and the heads of departments, necessarily renders any legal investigation of the acts of one of those high officers peculiarly irksome, as well as delicate: . . . [I]t is not wonderful that in such a case as this, the assertion, by an individual, of his legal claims in a court of justice, to which claims it is the duty of that court to attend, should at first view be considered by some, as an attempt to intrude into the cabinet, and to intermeddle with the prerogatives of the executive.

It is scarcely necessary for the court to disclaim all pretensions to such a jurisdiction. . . . The province of the court is, solely, to decide on the rights of individuals, not to inquire how the executive, or executive officers, perform duties in which they have a discretion. Questions, in their nature political, or which are, by the constitution and laws, submitted to the executive, can never be made in this court.

But, if this be not such a question; if so far from being an intrusion into the secrets of the cabinet, it respects a paper, which, according to law, is upon record, . . . if it be no intermeddling with a subject, over which the executive can be considered as having exercised any control; what is there in the exalted station of the officer, which shall bar a citizen from asserting, in a court of justice, his legal rights, or shall forbid a court to listen to the claim; or to issue a mandamus, directing the performance of a duty, not depending on executive discretion, but on particular acts of congress and the general principles of law?

\*       \*       \*

This, then, is a plain case of a mandamus, either to deliver the commission, or a copy of it from the record; and it only remains to be inquired,

Whether it can issue from this court.

The act [Judiciary Act of 1789] to establish the judicial courts of the United States authorizes [via Section 13] the supreme court "to issue writs of mandamus, in cases warranted by the principles and usages of law, to any courts appointed, or persons holding office, under the authority of the United States."

The secretary of state, being a person, holding an office under the authority of the United States, is precisely within the letter of the description; and if this court is not authorized to issue a writ of mandamus to such an officer, it must be because the law is unconstitutional, and therefore absolutely incapable of conferring the authority, and assigning the duties which its words purport to confer and assign.

The constitution [Article III] vests the whole judicial power of the United States in one supreme court, and such inferior courts as congress shall, from time to time, ordain and establish. This power is expressly extended to all cases arising under the laws of the United States; and consequently, in some form, may be exercised over the present case because the right claimed is given by a law of the United States.

In the distribution of this power it is declared that "the supreme court shall have original jurisdiction in all cases affecting ambassadors, other public ministers and consuls, and those in which a state shall be a party. In all other cases, the supreme court shall have appellate jurisdiction."

It has been insisted at the bar, that as the original grant of jurisdiction to the supreme and inferior courts is general, and the clause [Section 2] assigning original jurisdiction to the supreme court, contains no negative or restrictive words; the power remains to the legislature to assign original

---

[2] William Murray, first Earl of Mansfield (d. 1793), Lord Chief Justice of the King's Bench, 1756–1788—*Ed.*

jurisdiction to that court in other cases than those specified in the article which has been recited; provided those cases belong to the judicial power of the United States.

If it had been intended to leave it in the discretion of the legislature to apportion the judicial power between the supreme and inferior courts according to the will of that body, it would certainly have been useless to have proceeded further than to have defined the judicial power, and the tribunals in which it should be vested. The subsequent part of the section is mere surplusage, is entirely without meaning, if such is to be the construction. If congress remains at liberty to give this court appellate jurisdiction, where the constitution has declared their jurisdiction shall be original; and original jurisdiction where the constitution has declared it shall be appellate; the distribution of jurisdiction made in the constitution, is form without substance.

Affirmative words are often, in their operation, negative of other objects than those affirmed; and in this case, a negative or exclusive sense must be given to them or they have no operation at all.

*    *    *

When an instrument organizing fundamentally a judicial system, divides it into one supreme, and so many inferior courts as the legislature may ordain and establish; then enumerates its powers, and proceeds so far to distribute them, as to define the jurisdiction of the supreme court by declaring the cases in which it shall take original jurisdiction, and that in others it shall take appellate jurisdiction, the plain import of the words seems to be, that in one class of cases its jurisdiction is original, and not appellate: in the other it is appellate, and not original. If any other construction would render the clause inoperative, that is an additional reason for rejecting such other construction, and for adhering to the obvious meaning.

To enable this court then to issue a mandamus, it must be shown to be an exercise of appellate jurisdiction, or to be necessary to enable them to exercise appellate jurisdiction.

It has been stated at the bar that the appellate jurisdiction may be exercised in a variety of forms, and that if it be the will of the legislature that a mandamus should be used for that purpose, that will must be obeyed. This is true; yet the jurisdiction must be appellate, not original.

It is the essential criterion of appellate jurisdiction, that it revises and corrects the proceedings in a cause already instituted, and does not create that case. Although, therefore, a mandamus may be directed to courts, yet to issue such a writ to an officer for the delivery of a paper, is in effect the same as to sustain an original action for that paper, and therefore seems not to belong to appellate, but to original jurisdiction. Neither is it necessary in such a case as this, to enable the court to exercise its appellate jurisdiction.

The authority, therefore, given to the supreme court, by the act establishing the judicial courts of the United States, to issue writs of mandamus to public officers, appears not to be warranted by the constitution; and it becomes necessary to inquire whether a jurisdiction, so conferred, can be exercised.

The question, whether an act, repugnant to the constitution, can become the law of the land, is a question deeply interesting to the United States; but, happily, not of an intricacy proportioned to its interest. . . .

That the people have an original right to establish, for their future government, such principles as, in their opinion, shall most conduce to their own happiness, is the basis on which the whole American fabric has been erected. The exercise of this original right is a very great exertion; nor can it nor ought it to be frequently repeated. The principles, therefore, so established are deemed fundamental. And as the authority, from which they proceed, is supreme, and can seldom act, they are designed to be permanent.

This original and supreme will organizes the government, and assigns to different departments their respective powers. It may either stop here; or establish certain limits not to be transcended by those departments.

The government of the United States is of the latter description. The powers of the legislature are defined and limited; and that those limits may not be mistaken or forgotten, the constitution is written. . . . The constitution is either a superior, paramount law, unchangeable by ordinary means, or it is on a level with ordinary legislative acts, and like other acts, is alterable when the legislature shall please to alter it.

If the former part of the alternative be true, then a legislative act contrary to the constitution is not law: if the latter part be true, then written constitutions are absurd attempts, on the part of the people, to limimit [*sic*] a power in its own nature illimitable.

Certainly all those who have framed written constitutions contemplate them as forming the fundamental and paramount law of the nation, and consequently the theory of every such government must be, that an act of the legislature repugnant to the constitution is void.

\* \* \*

If an act of the legislature, repugnant to the constitution, is void, does it, notwithstanding its invalidity, bind the courts and oblige them to give it effect? Or, in other words, though it be not law, does it constitute a rule as operative as if it was a law? This would be to overthrow in fact what was established in theory; and would seem, at first view, an absurdity too gross to be insisted on. It shall, however, receive a more attentive consideration.

It is emphatically the province and duty of the judicial department to say what the law is. Those who apply the rule to particular cases, must of necessity expound and interpret that rule. If two laws conflict with each other, the courts must decide on the operation of each.

So if a law be in opposition to the constitution: if both the law and the constitution apply to a particular case, so that the court must either decide that case conformably to the law, disregarding the constitution; or conformably to the constitution, disregarding the law: the court must determine which of these conflicting rules governs the case. This is of the very essence of judicial duty.

If then the courts are to regard the constitution; and the constitution is superior to any ordinary act of the legislature; the constitution, and not such ordinary act, must govern the case to which they both apply.

\* \* \*

The judicial power of the United States is extended to all cases arising under the constitution.

Could it be the intention of those who gave this power, to say that, in using it, the constitution should not be looked into? That a case arising under the constitution should be decided without examining the instrument under which it arises?

This is too extravagant to be maintained.

In some cases then, the constitution must be looked into by the judges. And if they can open it at all, what part of it are they forbidden to read, or to obey?

There are many other parts of the constitution which serve to illustrate this subject.

It is declared that "no tax or duty shall be laid on articles exported from any state." Suppose a duty on the export of cotton, of tobacco, or of flour; and a suit instituted to recover it. Ought judgment to be rendered in such a case? ought the judges to close their eyes on the constitution, and only see the law.

\* \* \*

"No person," says the constitution, "shall be convicted of treason unless on the testimony of two witnesses to the same overt act, or on confession in open court."

Here the language of the constitution is addressed especially to the courts. It prescribes, directly for them, a rule of evidence not to be departed from. If the legislature should change that rule, and declare *one* witness, or a confession *out* of court, sufficient for conviction, must the constitutional principle yield to the legislative act?

From these and many other selections which might be made, it is apparent, that the framers of the constitution contemplated that instrument as a rule for the government of *courts*, as well as of the legislature.

Why otherwise does it direct the judges to take an oath to support it? This oath certainly applies, in an especial manner, to their conduct in their official character. How immoral to impose it on them, if they were to be used as the instruments, and the knowing instruments, for violating what they swear to support!

\*    \*    \*

Why does a judge swear to discharge his duties agreeably to the constitution of the United States, if that constitution forms no rule for his government? if it is closed upon him and cannot be inspected by him.

\*    \*    \*

It is also not entirely unworthy of observation, that in declaring what shall be the supreme law of the land, the constitution itself is first mentioned; and not the laws of the United States generally, but those only which shall be made in pursuance of the constitution, have that rank.

Thus, the particular phraseology of the constitution of the United States confirms and strengthens the principle, supposed to be essential to all written constitutions, that a law repugnant to the constitution is void, and that courts, as well as other departments, are bound by that instrument.

The rule must be discharged.

## REVIEW QUESTIONS

1. What were the specific inquiries or issues brought before the court? How did Marshall justify or explain the opinion of the court on each of these issues?
2. Did the court illuminate an important duality in the duties of cabinet officers? How did it differentiate between political and legal responsibilities?
3. Why was there a question about the proper jurisdiction or procedure for this case? If the Judiciary Act of 1789 gave the Supreme Court the power to originate a writ of mandamus, why did the court dispute it?
4. Was the Supreme Court defining or checking the powers of the executive and judicial branches in this case? If so, how?

# Reflections on the Cession of Louisiana to the United States (1803)

*President Jefferson in his inaugural address spoke of Americans "possessing a chosen country, with room enough for our descendants to the thousandth and thousandth generation." Jefferson's hyperbole reflected the expansiveness of the land then claimed by the United States and echoed the thoughts both of Americans who believed that it would take generations to settle the territory out to the Mississippi and of those who already contemplated expansion to the Pacific Ocean. Given such an expansive mental map—as well as the threat to national interests and security should France occupy the interior of the continent—Jefferson's decision to acquire the Louisiana Territory was a reasonable one. While some people debated the constitutionality of the acquisition, many others preferred to discuss what to do with it. The expansion of territory fostered expansive dreams, which included not only reveries about individual opportunity but visions of social and political reforms.*

From "Extract from a pamphlet just published, entitled Reflections on the cession of Louisiana to the United States," *The National Intelligencer and Washington* [D.C.] *Advertiser*, Wednesday, 19 October 1803, Issue 467, col. A (available in the 19th Century US Newspapers database published by Gale). [Editorial insertions appear in square brackets—Ed.]

# Extract from a pamphlet just published, entitled Reflections on the cession of Louisiana to the United States.

"We now shall have it in our power to propose to the Indian nations now settled within the United States an exchange of lands beyond the Mississippi, for those which they now hold;[1] by this means we shall be able to dispose of all the lands on this side of the Mississippi to those who shall cultivate them, who are already civilized, who speak the same language with us, and who will be ready and willing to harmonise and become one people with us, if they be not so already. The lands which we may acquire in this manner will probably be amply sufficient to pay for ten times the purchase of Louisiana, and this remote treasure, so dangerous to be touched whilst it remains at a distance, may be brought with safety to our doors, and used as occasion shall require, without fear of the consequences.

Such an exchange, if it can be effected, of which I presume there can be little doubt, will strengthen and cement our union beyond any other event of which I am able to form an idea. Our whole country, except the ports on the Atlantic, and at the mouth of the Mississippi, will consist of an extensive and numerous agricultural people, detached from all the other civilized nations of the globe, forming one general and powerful confederacy of republican states, nursed in the lap of liberty, sprung from one common stock, cherishing the same fraternal sentiments towards each other, and the same devotion to their common country, liberty and happiness. The demon of discord is the only enemy from whose effects or malignity the United States could have just cause of apprehension; and he might be chained for centuries, beyond the Mississippi, if the policy which is here recommended be adopted.

Of the same nature, though of less practicable aspect, is another Utopean idea, which I presume to suggest to the genuine friends of freedom, yet, I confess, without any sanguine hope, that it will receive countenance. The southern parts of Louisiana bordering upon the gulph of Mexico lie under a climate more favorable for the African constitution than any part of the United States. Thither, if under the auspices of a divine Providence, the great work of the abolition of slavery should be accomplished in Virginia, or other southern states, we may colonise those unhappy people, whom our ancestors have brought in chains from their native country, and we continue to hold in bondage. Would to God, that I could flatter myself that this was not a mere visionary project!—Thither, at least, it may be adviseable to entice those to remove who have already, or may hereafter obtain their freedom, through the benevolence of their masters, and a relaxation of the rigid laws, which have heretofore existed to prevent emancipation. Thither, also, delinquents, whose lives may be forfeited to the considerations of self-preservation, may be banished for attempts to regain their native freedom. The distance of that part of Louisiana from the United States might recommend it as a place of exile, also for other criminals.—There they might form settlements, and perhaps repent, and become useful members of society among each other: but I am not more sanguine upon this subject, than the former. Time and experiment may enable us to judge better.

It formed no part of my plan in this essay to consider what temporary arrangements it might be necessary to adopt on this truly important occasion: many will no doubt be necessary—But if what I have offered against the settlement of Louisiana be worthy of attention, I would beg leave to hint, that a measure intimately connected with those already mentioned, would be to invite those, who are new settled in Louisiana, to remove into the United States, by proposing to them an advantageous exchange of lands. Thus should we make them a full recompence for whatever they might abandon on the other side of the Mississippi, and gain an accession of population in the United States, and at the same time relieve ourselves

---

[1] There are probably two hundred millions of acres of land in the United States to which the Indian title has not yet been extinguished.

from any expense necessary for the preservation of civil government among them. This, if it can be effected, will be happy counterpart of the proposed exchange with the Indian tribes.

The island of New Orleans will no doubt claim the immediate attention of Congress if we can obtain from Spain a cession of that part of West Florida which lies to the west of the Mobille, or even of the Pearl river, or of the river Amitie, it might be worthy of an amendment of the constitution to incorporate that territory, together with the territory of New Orleans, with the present United States government upon the Mississippi; and admit the whole into the Union as a new state, as soon as the population of it may entitle it to such admission. Such an arrangement would probably immediately conciliate the affections of the people of the ceded territory, and prove an additional motive to those beyond the Mississippi to remove to this side, where they might at once experience all the benefits of civil government, and the participation of the freest and happiest constitution upon the face of the globe.

Homer tells us that Ulysses on his return from Troy paid a visit to Eolus, the God of the winds; who, out of his great favor to that illustrious chief presented him with a bag, in which all the adverse winds and storms, which might retard or endanger his passage to his native kingdom, were tied up: his companions, fancying that this bag contained some precious treasure, took the first opportunity, whilst the Ithacan sage was asleep, to open it:—upon which, the winds and storms instantly making their escape, the ship with all his indiscreet companions was immediately swallowed up in the ocean.

May no imprudent use of our late successful negociation with France induce the application of this fable to the people of the United States!

## REVIEW QUESTIONS

1. How did the author propose to use the Louisiana Territory to solve Indian issues? What did he propose for the people already in the territory? How was this to be a matter of solving two problems in one stroke?
2. Why did the author think this acquisition would cement the union?
3. What was the author's utopian scheme in terms of using the new territory to foster abolitionist reform?
4. How was this new land of opportunity also to be a land of exile?
5. The author separated the disposition of West Florida and New Orleans from the rest of the Louisiana Territory. Why do you think he did that? What did he intend for that area?

# MERIWETHER LEWIS AND WILLIAM CLARK

## FROM Journals of Exploration (1804–05)

*Even before the Louisiana Purchase was complete, Jefferson authorized an expedition to explore the northwestern frontier. This was due to simple curiosity—a desire to know who and what was out there—as well as a need to know what the United States was acquiring. He appointed Meriwether Lewis, a captain in the regular army who had extensive frontier experience as well as an avid interest in nature, and William Clark, a former army officer, now recommissioned, who also was fascinated with nature, as commanders of the Corps of Discovery. Jefferson gave them a multi-faceted mission: they were to inform the native peoples of the government's acquisition, establish friendly relations with them, and record their languages and ways; they were to make topographical and horticultural studies; and, if possible, they were to find a viable trade route through the new territory. The expedition of forty to fifty men (of which only some were to go out to the Pacific) set out from the St. Louis area in May 1804. They traveled up the Missouri to Mandan territory in what is now North Dakota with the intention of wintering there before the permanent party continued west in the spring.*

---

From John Bakeless, ed., *The Journals of Lewis and Clark* (New York: Mentor Books, 1964), pp. 98–127. This is a heavily edited version of the Reuben G. Thwaites edition, with modern spelling and grammar. [Editorial insertions that appear in square brackets and footnotes are from Bakeless—*Ed.*]

\*   \*   \*

### 31st of October, 1804

A fine morning. The chief of the Mandans sent a second chief to invite us to his lodge to receive some corn and hear what he had to say. I walked down and, with great ceremony, was seated on a robe by the side of the chief. He threw a handsome robe over me, and after smoking the pipe with several old men around, the chief spoke:

Said he believed what we had told them, and that peace would be general, which not only gave him satisfaction but all his people: they could now hunt without fear, and their women could work in the fields without looking every moment for the enemy; and put off their moccasins at night. [Sign of peace: undress.] As to the Arikaras, we will show you that we wish peace with all, and do not make war on any without cause. That chief—pointing to the second—and some brave men will accompany the Arikara chief now with you to his village and nation, to smoke with that people. When you came up, the Indians in the neighboring villages, as well as those out hunting, when they heard of you, had great expectations of receiving presents. Those hunting, immediately on hearing, returned to the village; and all were disappointed, and some dissatisfied. As to himself, he was not much so; but his village was. He would go and see his Great Father, &c.

He had put before me two of the steel traps which were robbed from the French a short time ago, and about twelve bushels of corn, which were brought and put before me by the women of the village. After the chief finished and smoked in great ceremony, I answered the speech, which satisfied them very much, and returned to the boat. Met the principal chief of the third village, and the Little Crow, both of whom I invited into the cabin, and smoked and talked with for about one hour.

Soon after those chiefs left us, the grand chief of the Mandans came, dressed in the clothes we had given, with his two small sons, and requested to see the men dance, which they very readily gratified him in. . . .

### 1st of November, 1804

The wind hard from the N.W. Mr. McCracken, a trader, set out at 7 o'clock, to the fort on the Assiniboine. By him sent a letter (enclosing a copy of the British Minister's protection) to the principal agent of the Company.

At about 10 o'clock, the chiefs of the lower village came, and after a short time informed us they wished we would call at their village and take some corn; that they would make peace with the Arikaras; they never made war against them but after the Arikaras killed their chiefs. They killed them like birds, and were tired of killing them, and would send a chief and some brave men to the Arikaras to smoke with that people.

*     *     *

2nd November, 1804

This morning at daylight, I went down the river with my men, to look for a proper place to winter. Proceeded down the river three miles, and found a place well supplied with wood, and returned. Captain Lewis went to the village to hear what they had to say, and I fell down, and formed a camp, near where a small camp of Indians were hunting. Cut down the trees around our camp. In the evening, Captain Lewis returned with a present of 11 bushels of corn. Our Arikara chief set out, accompanied by one chief of Mandans and several brave men of Minnetarees and Mandans. He called for some small article which we had promised, but as I could not understand him, he could not get it. [Afterward he did get it.] The wind from the S.E. A fine day. Many Indians to view us today.

4th November, 1804

A fine morning. We continued to cut down trees and raise our houses. A Mr. Charbonneau[1] interpreter for the Gros Ventre nation, came to see us, and informed that he came down with several Indians from a hunting expedition up the river, to hear what we had told the Indians in council. This man wished to hire as an interpreter. The wind rose this evening from the east, and clouded up. Great numbers of Indians pass, hunting, and some on the return.

*     *     *

12th November, 1804

A very cold night. Early this morning, The Big White, principal chief of the lower village of the Mandans, came down. He packed about 100 pounds of fine meat on his squaw for us. We made some small presents to the squaw and child, gave a small ax with which she was much pleased.

Three men sick with the [blank in MS.]. Several. Wind changeable. Very cold evening. Freezing all day. Some ice on the edges of the river.

Swans passing to the south. The hunters we sent down the river to hunt have not returned.

The Mandans speak a language peculiar to themselves, very much [blank in MS.]. They can raise about 350 men; the Wetersoons or Mahas, 80; and the Big Bellies, or Minnetarees, about 600 or 650 men. The Mandans and Sioux have the same word for water. The Big Bellies or Minnetarees and Raven [Wetersoon, as also the Crow or Raven] Indians speak nearly the same language, and the presumption is they were originally the same nation. The Raven Indians have 400 lodges and about 1,200 men, and follow the buffalo, or hunt for their subsistence in the plains, and on the Côte Noire and Rocky Mountains, and are at war with the Sioux and Snake Indians.

The Big Bellies and Wetersoons are at war with the Snake Indians and Sioux, and were at war with the Arikaras until we made peace a few days past. The Mandans are at war with all who make war [on them—at present with the Sioux] only, and wish to be at peace with all nations. Seldom the aggressors.

*     *     *

22nd of November, 1804

A fine morning. Dispatched a pirogue and 5 men under the direction of Sergeant Pryor, to the second village, for 100 bushels of corn in ears, which Mr. Jussome let us have. [Did not get more than 30 bushels.] I was alarmed about 10 o'clock by the sentinel, who informed that an Indian was about to kill his wife, in the interpreter's fire [*i.e., lodge*] about 60 yards below the works. I went down and spoke to the fellow about the rash act he was likely to commit, and forbade any act of the kind near the Fort.

Some misunderstanding took place between this man and his wife, about 8 days ago, and she came to this place, and continued with the squaws of the interpreters. [He might lawfully have killed her for running away.] Two days ago, he returned to the village. In the evening of the same day, she

---

[1] "Mr. Charbonneau" was Toussaint Charbonneau, husband of Sacagawea, and of another Shoshone girl as well.

came to the interpreter's fire, apparently much beaten and stabbed in 3 places. We directed that no man of this party have any intercourse with this woman under the penalty of punishment. He, the husband, observed that one of our sergeants slept with his wife, and if he wanted her he would give her to him.

We directed the sergeant (Ordway) to give the man some articles, at which time I told the Indian that I believed not one man of the party had touched his wife except the one he had given the use of her for a night, in his own bed;[2] no man of the party should touch his squaw, or the wife of any Indian, nor did I believe they touched a woman if they knew her to be the wife of another man, and advised him to take his squaw home and live happily together in future. At this time the grand chief of the nation arrived, and lectured him, and they both went off, apparently dissatisfied.

\*       \*       \*

30th of November, 1804

This morning at 8 o'clock, an Indian called from the other side, and informed that he had something of consequence to communicate. We sent a pirogue for him, and he informed us as follows: "Five men of the Mandan nation, out hunting in a S.W. direction about eight leagues, were surprised by a large party of Sioux and Pawnees. One man was killed and two wounded with arrows, and 9 horses taken; 4 of the Wetersoon nation were missing, and they expected to be attacked by the Sioux, &c." We thought it well to show a disposition to aid and assist them against their enemies, particularly those who came in opposition to our councils. And I determined to go to the town with some men and, if the Sioux were coming to attack the nation, to collect the warriors from each village and meet them. Those ideas were also those of Captain Lewis.

---

[2] Among these Indians, a husband had the right to give (or sell) his wife's favors to anyone he pleased. Surreptitious adultery was an offense, which the husband might punish, practically as he pleased. But a woman who yielded to another at her husband's order was merely doing her duty as a wife.

I crossed the river in about an hour after the arrival of the Indian express with 23 men including the interpreters, and flanked the town and came up on the back part. The Indians, not expecting to receive such strong aid in so short a time, were much surprised, and a little alarmed at the formidable appearance of my party. The principal chiefs met me some distance from the town (say 200 yards) and invited me in to town. I ordered my party into different lodges, &c. I explained to the nation the cause of my coming in this formidable manner to their town was to assist and chastise the enemies of our dutiful children. I requested the grand chief to repeat the circumstances as they happened, which he did, as was mentioned by the express in the morning.

I then informed them that if they would assemble their warriors and those of the different towns, I would go to meet the army of Sioux, &c., and chastise them for taking the blood of our dutiful children, &c. After a conversation of a few minutes among themselves, one chief—The Big Man, a Cheyenne—said they now saw that what we had told them was the truth: that when we expected the enemies of their nation were coming to attack them, or had spilled their blood, we were ready to protect them, and kill those who would not listen to our good talk. His people had listened to what we had told them, and fearlessly went out to hunt in small parties believing themselves to be safe from the other nations, and were killed by the Pawnees and Sioux.

"I knew," said he, "that the Pawnees were liars, and told the old chief who came with you (to confirm a peace with us) that his people were liars and bad men, and that we killed them like the buffalo—when we pleased. We had made peace several times and your nation has always commenced the war. We do not want to kill you, and will not suffer you to kill us or steal our horses. We will make peace with you as our two fathers have directed, and they shall see that we will not be the aggressors. But we fear the Arikaras will not be at peace long. My father, those are the words I spoke to the Arikaras in your presence. You see they have not opened their ears to your good counsels, but have spilled our blood.

"Two Arikaras, whom we sent home this day, for fear of our people's killing them in their grief, informed us when they came here several days ago, that two towns of the Arikaras were making their moccasins, and that we had best take care of our horses, &c. Numbers of Sioux were in their towns and, they believed, not well disposed toward us. Four of the Wetersoons are now absent. They were to have been back in 16 days; they have been out 24. We fear they have fallen. My father, the snow is deep and it is cold. Our horses cannot travel through the plains. Those people who have spilt our blood have gone back. If you will go with us in the spring after the snow goes off, we will raise the warriors of all the towns and nations around about us, and go with you."

I told this nation that we should be always willing and ready to defend them from the insults of any nation who would dare to come to do them injury, during the time we remained in their neighborhood, and requested that they would inform us of any party who might at any time be discovered by their patrols or scouts. I was sorry that the snow in the plains had fallen so deep since the murder of the young chief by the Sioux as prevented their horses from traveling. I wished to meet those Sioux and all others who will not open their ears, but make war on our dutiful children, and let you see that the warriors of your Great Father will chastise the enemies of his dutiful children the Mandans, Wetersoons, and Minnetarees, who have opened their ears to his advice. You say that the Pawnees or Arikaras were with the Sioux. Some bad men may have been with the Sioux. You know there are bad men in all nations. Do not get mad with the Arikaras until we know if those bad men are countenanced by their nation, and we are convinced those people do not intend to follow our counsels. You know that the Sioux have great influence over the Arikaras, and perhaps have led some of them astray. You know that the Arikaras are dependent on the Sioux for their guns, powder, and ball; and it was policy in them to keep on as good terms as possible with the Sioux until they had some other means of getting those articles, &c. You know yourselves that you are compelled to put up with little insults from the Crees and Assiniboines (or Stone Indians) because if you go to war with those people, they will prevent the traders in the north from bringing you guns, powder, and ball, and by that means distress you very much. But when you will have certain supplies from your Great American Father of all those articles, you will not suffer any nation to insult you, &c.

After about two hours' conversation on various subjects, all of which tended toward their situation, &c., I informed them I should return to the Fort. The chief said they all thanked me very much for the fatherly protection which I showed toward them; that the village had been crying all the night and day for the death of the brave young man who fell, but now they would wipe away their tears and rejoice in their father's protection, and cry no more.

I then paraded and crossed the river on the ice, and came down on the north side. The snow so deep, it was very fatiguing. Arrived at the Fort after night, gave a little taffe[3] [dram] to my party. A cold night. The river rose to its former height. The chief frequently thanked me for coming to protect them; and the whole village appeared thankful for that measure.

1st of December, 1804

Wind from the N.W. All hands engaged in getting pickets, &c. At 10 o'clock, the half-brother of the man who was killed came and informed us that, after my departure last night, six Chiens [Cheyennes]—so called by the French—or Sharha Indians, had arrived with a pipe, and said that their nation was at one day's march and intended to come and trade, &c. Three Pawnees had also arrived from the nation. Their nation was then within 3 days' march, and were coming on to trade with us. Three Pawnees accompanied these Cheyennes. The Mandans call all Arikaras Pawnees; they don't use the name of Arikaras, but the Arikaras call themselves Arikaras. The Mandans apprehended danger from the Sharhas, as they were at peace with the Sioux; and wished to kill

---

[3] A local rum.

them and the Arikaras (or Pawnees), but the chiefs informed the nation it was our wish that they should not be hurt and forbid their being killed, &c. We gave a little tobacco, &c., and this man departed, well satisfied with our counsels and advice to him.

In the evening a Mr. G. Henderson arrived, in the employ of the Hudson's Bay Company, sent to trade with the Gros Ventres, or Big Bellies, so called by the French traders.

*    *    *

7th of December, 1804

A very cold day. Wind from the N.W. The Big White, grand chief of the first village, came and informed us that a large drove of buffalo was near, and his people were waiting for us to join them in a chase. Captain Lewis took 15 men and went out and joined the Indians who were, at the time he got up, killing the buffalo, on horseback with arrows, clothed. This man was not in the least injured. Customs, and the habits of those people, have inured them to bear more cold than I thought it possible for man to endure. Sent out 3 men to hunt elk, below, about 7 miles.

13th of January, 1805

A cold, clear day. Great numbers of Indians move down the river to hunt. Those people kill a number of buffalo near their villages and save a great proportion of the meat. Their custom of making [sharing] this article of life general leaves them more than half of their time without meat. Their corn and beans, &c., they keep for the summer, and as a reserve in case of an attack from the Sioux, of which they are always in dread, and seldom go far to hunt except in large parties. About ½ the Mandan nation passed today, to hunt on the river below. They will stay out some days. Mr. Charbonneau, our interpreter, and one man who accompanied him to some lodges of the Minnetarees near the Turtle Hill, returned, both frozen in their faces. Charbonneau informs me that the clerk of the Hudson's Bay Company, with the Minnetarees, has been speaking some few expressions unfavorable toward us, and that it is said the N.W.

Company intends building a fort at the Minnetarees. He saw the Grand Chief of the Big Bellies, who spoke slightingly of the Americans, saying if we would give our great flag to him he would come to see us.

*    *    *

Fort Mandan, April 7th, 1805

Having on this day at 4 P.M. completed every arrangement necessary for our departure, we dismissed the barge and crew, with orders to return without loss of time to St. Louis. A small canoe with two French hunters accompanied the barge. These men had ascended the Missouri with us the last year as *engagés*. The barge crew consisted of six soldiers and two [blank space in MS.] Frenchmen. Two Frenchmen and an Arikara Indian also take their passage in her as far as the Arikara villages, at which place we expect Mr. Tabeau to embark, with his peltry, who, in that case, will make an addition of two, perhaps four, men to the crew of the barge.

We gave Richard Warfington, a discharged corporal, the charge of the barge and crew, and confided to this care likewise our dispatches to the government, letters to our private friends, and a number of articles to the President of the United States. One of the Frenchmen, by the name of Joseph Gravelines, an honest, discreet man, and an excellent boatman, is employed to conduct the barge as a pilot. We have therefore every hope that the barge and, with her, our dispatches will arrive safe at St. Louis. Mr. Gravelines, who speaks the Arikara language extremely well, has been employed to conduct a few of the Arikara chiefs to the seat of government, who have promised us to descend in the barge to St. Louis with that view.

At the same moment that the barge departed from Fort Mandan, Captain Clark embarked with our party and proceeded up the river. As I had used no exercise for several weeks, I determined to walk on shore as far as our encampment of this evening. Accordingly I continued my walk on the north side of the river about six miles, to the upper village of the Mandans, and called on The Black Cat, or Posecopsehá, the Great Chief of the Mandans. He was not at home. I rested myself a few minutes and, finding that the party had not arrived, I returned about two miles and joined them at their encampment on the N. side of the river opposite the lower Mandan village.

\*      \*      \*

Our party now consisted of the following individuals:

| | |
|---|---|
| Sergeants: | John Ordway |
| | Nathaniel Pryor |
| | Patrick Gass |
| | |
| Privates: | William Bratton |
| | John Colter |
| | Reuben Fields |
| | Joseph Fields |
| | John Shields |
| | George Gibson |
| | George Shannon |
| | John Potts |
| | John Collins |
| | Joseph Whitehouse |
| | Richard Windsor |
| | Alexander Willard |
| | Hugh Hall |
| | Silas Goodrich |
| | Robert Frazer |
| | Peter Cruzat |
| | John Baptiste Lepage |
| | Francis Labiche |
| | Hugh McNeil |
| | William Warner |
| | Thomas P. Howard |
| | Peter Wiser |
| | John B. Thompson |

Interpreters: George Drouilliard and Toussaint Charbonneau; also a black man by the name of York, servant to Captain Clark; an Indian woman, wife to Charbonneau, with a young child; and a Mandan man who had promised us to accompany us as far as the Snake Indians, with a view to bring about a good understanding and friendly intercourse between that nation and his own, the Minnetarees and Amahamis.

Our vessels consisted of six small canoes and two large pirogues. This little fleet, although not quite so respectable as that of Columbus or Captain Cook, was still viewed by us with as much pleasure as those deservedly famed adventurers ever beheld theirs, and, I daresay, with quite as much anxiety for their safety and preservation. We were now about to penetrate a country at least two thousand miles in width, on which the foot of civilized man had never trod. The good or evil it had in store for us was for experiment yet to determine, and these little vessels contained every article by which we were to expect to subsist or defend ourselves. However, as the state of mind in which we are, generally gives the coloring to events, when the imagination is suffered to wander into futurity, the picture which now presented itself to me was a most pleasing one.

Entertaining as I do the most confident hope of succeeding on a voyage which had formed a darling project of mine for the last ten years, I could but esteem this moment of my departure as among the most happy of my life. The party are in excellent health and spirits, zealously attached to the enterprise, and anxious to proceed. Not a whisper or murmur of discontent to be heard among them, but all act in unison and with the most perfect harmony.

\*      \*      \*

## REVIEW QUESTIONS

1. Lewis and Clark wanted recognition, good relations, and assistance from the Mandan and the other local Native American tribes. What did these tribes want from the explorers in return?
2. What customs—social, political, and/or military—did the explorers find to be noteworthy?
3. What do these notes reveal about both the subjects and the writers?
4. What do the entries reveal about intertribal relations in the area?
5. Why do you think such relations and conflicts were important to the explorers and their government?

# MATHEW CAREY

# *The Olive Branch* (1818 edition)

*The full title of Mathew Carey's work is* The Olive Branch: or, Faults on Both Sides, Federal and Democratic. A Serious Appeal on the Necessity of Mutual Forgiveness and Harmony. *He published the first edition in 1814, two years after the War of 1812 began, and published the tenth edition in May 1818, three years after the United States and Great Britain ended the war with the ratification of the Treaty of Ghent. Carey's book shows, both in its contents and in the popularity that the many editions indicate, that while Americans were fighting outside foes, they were also battling each other over the necessity and conduct of the war. Furthermore, although peace ushered in a so-called "Era of Good Feelings," Americans continued the debate.*

*Carey (1760–1839), who settled in Philadelphia in 1784 after his political opinions made him unpopular with authorities in Ireland, switched from the Federalist to Democratic Republican Party in 1796. No matter which party he was in, however, Carey used his pen and printing press to push for national strength and unity. He advocated increasing the nation's military establishments, especially the navy, and he labored to expose and prevent what he believed was a conspiracy among disaffected New Englanders to dissolve the union. In his book he criticized the Democratic Republicans for leaving the nation ill prepared for war and condemned Federalists and other opponents of the war for not seeing its necessity. He branded as Jacobins (the name of radicals in the French Revolution) those who wanted to destroy the administration and the union, and he trumpeted the British actions, especially the impressment of American sailors, that he felt made war necessary for national security, prosperity, and honor.*

---

From *The Olive Branch: or, Faults on Both Sides, Federal and Democratic*, 10th ed. (Philadelphia: M. Carey and Son, 1818; reprint, Freeport, N.Y.: Books for Libraries Press, 1969), pp. 180–81, 207–17.

\*  \*  \*

An idea is very prevalent, that the impressment of our seamen by the British vessels of war is a grievance of little moment, to which the malice entertained by our administration against England, has attached an importance of which it is utterly undeserving. Hundreds of thousands of our citizens have been duped into the belief, that this item of grievance was created under Mr. Jefferson, or at least incalculably exaggerated by him and his successor. Never was there a more egregious error. Never was fraud more successful in propagating— never was fatuitous credulity more deceived in believing—a tale as foreign from the truth as Erebus is from Heaven.

Mr. Madison has been ten thousand times cursed for his folly and wickedness in involving this country in war for the purpose of securing a few seamen, said to be vagabond English, Irish, and Scotchmen, the scum of the earth, from the claims of their lawful prince. It has been asserted that few or none of the natives of this country are impressed—that when such *an accident takes place,* redress is easily had—and further, that England is, and has at all times been, ready to make any arrangement whereby our sailors may be guarded against impressment, provided she can be secured against the loss of hers.

These assertions are utterly false. From the commencement of the war of the French revolution, to the late declaration of hostilities, this has been a constant, unceasing subject of reclamation and complaint to the British government, as well under the administrations of General Washington and Mr. Adams, as under those of Mr. Jefferson and Mr. Madison. And disgraceful, dishonourable, and infamous, would it have been to any of the presidents, had they been deaf to the complaints, and callous to the sufferings, of the American slaves, stolen by force and fraud from their families, and freedom, and favoured country, to perish, fighting the battles of their enslavers.

"The practice has no parallel, either for atrocity or extent, in any thing of modern times, but the business of negro stealing on the coast of unfortunate Africa."

*       *       *

There is one strong and striking point of view in which the subject of impressment may be considered, and which really renders the tame acquiescence in it, which was lately contended for, pregnant with awful results. *England has impressed from our ships, Danes, Swedes, and Italians, as well as native Americans.* WE HAVE SUBMITTED TO IT. *And Mr. Pickering, Mr. King, governor Strong, H. G. Otis, &c. plead in favour of submission.* If this be just, what right, I demand, have we to prevent all belligerents whatever, and at all times, from copying the example? Suppose France, Spain, and Italy, at war. Are not the cruisers of each nation justified in searching our vessels for the subjects of the powers to which they respectively belong, and as fully entitled *to enslave the Danes, Portuguese, Swedes, and Englishmen on board, as the British cruizers are to enslave Frenchmen, Spaniards, Danes and Portuguese*? This is a horrible view of the subject, and must curdle the blood in the veins of every man possessed of American feeling. There is no calculating the extent or the enormity of the evil.

I must resume this topic. It is too important to be dismissed in a single paragraph. It deserves volumes. Would to heaven an abler pen were engaged in the discussion.

That British officers have been in the constant habit of impressing, without any scruple, and that they regard it as their right to impress, Danes, Portuguese, Frenchmen, Italians, and all other foreigners found on board our vessels, is true. . . .

If Great Britain have a right to impress Frenchmen, or Spaniards, or Dutchmen, on board our vessels, France, Spain, and Holland, have an equal right to impress Englishmen. Nothing can be more clear. Let us proceed.

The British captains assert that they find it difficult or impossible to discriminate between Englishmen and Americans. It must be far more difficult for French captains. And they will be still more excusable for any *mistakes*—and for enslaving Americans instead of Englishmen. What a frightful fate has faction prepared for our ill-starred sea-faring citizens!

I have stated that Messrs. Pickering, King, Strong, &c. "contended for submission to impressment." This requires explanation. They did not, it is true, *in words*, contend for impressment. But this was the inevitable result of their late course of proceeding; for, as I have already stated, and beg to repeat, they laboured most indefatigably to destroy the present administration, principally for the stand made to put an end to impressment; and the consequence of the violent opposition made to the government on the subject, has been to oblige it to postpone the discussion of that important question, which may probably lead to a future war.

A committee of the legislature of Massachusetts was appointed, at a late session, to enquire into the affair of impressment. The object of the appointment was to damn the character of the administration, by diminishing the enormity of this high-handed offence, against which the Levitical law pronounced the sentence of death:—

"*He that stealeth a man—and selleth him—or if he be found in his hand, he shall be put to death.*"

It is painful to state—but it is my duty to state to the world—that this committee by no means did justice to the subject. They acted with most palpable partiality. They reported—wonderful to tell—impossible to believe—that at the commencement of the war, the number of impressed Americans belonging to the great commercial state of Massachusetts, on board British vessels of war, was "*only eleven!!!*"—Yes—reader—it is really *eleven*—I have read it six times over, to convince myself that I was not mistaken. But it is absolutely true, that a committee of the legislature of Massachusetts did report to that body, that at the commencement of the war, THERE WERE BUT "ELEVEN" IMPRESSED MASSACHUSETTS' SAILORS on board the vessels of his Britannic majesty.

Now, reader, let me request you to consult the preceding documents carefully—and observe

1. That there were *ten Americans on board the Guerriere,* at the time of her engagement with the Constitution. This is established by the log book of one of her officers.[1]
2. That *there were thirteen Americans on board the Java,* when she was captured by Bainbridge.[2]
3. That there were on board the Moselle and Sappho, as appears by the muster-books of those vessels,[3] *at least thirty-five impressed Americans.*
4. That these plain facts stand on such ground as neither Timothy Pickering, Rufus King, governor Strong, George Cabot, Harrison Gray Otis, Daniel Webster, or A. C. Hanson will dare to dispute. I hereby publicly challenge them to a denial.
5. That I have thus clearly and indisputably established, that on board of four vessels there were 10, and 13, and 35 American slaves, being AN AVERAGE OF FOURTEEN TO EACH.
6. That there are about 500 British vessels constantly in commission.

7. That an average of fourteen amounts to 7000 on board the British fleet.
8. That this statement corresponds pretty nearly with the records of the secretary of state's office.

And then, reader, decide what judgment must be passed on the committee, when they gravely state, that there were on board the British vessels of war *only eleven natives of Massachusetts! ! !* It makes one sick to reflect on such obliquity of mind, and such monstrous perversion of fact.

It is, however, true, that this committee, though the world is grossly deceived by the form of expression in the report, have a salvo to prevent establishing against them the charge of falsehood. They state, that these are the results, "*as far as their enquiries went.*" But this saving clause escapes the mass of readers. They fasten on the strong allegation, that "the administration continued the war, on account of impressed seamen; and that there were only *eleven natives of Massachusetts impressed.*" All the rest escapes notice.

"*As far as their enquiries went*" is a very equivocal expression. They may have stopped at the threshold—or they may have gone half way—or they may have gone through the business completely. That their enquiries did not go very far, is, however, pretty certain.

The words "*American slaves,*" will startle some delicate ears. This strong expression is nevertheless correct. When an Algerine corsair attacks one of our vessels, and seizes it and the crew, *the latter are justly regarded as slaves. Yet their case is far better than that of the Americans impressed by British cruisers.* The Algerine slaves work for task-masters. So do the British slaves. The Algerine slaves are flogged if they refuse "to do their duty." So are the British. The Algerine slaves have wretched fare. So have the British. Thus far they are on a parallel. But here the parallel ceases. *The Algerine slave is never forced to jeopardize his life in battle—he is never forced to point a gun that may slaughter his countrymen.* But this the British slave must do, or "BE TIED TO THE MAST, AND SHOT AT LIKE A DOG! ! !" Is he not then the most miserable of slaves?

---

[1] The USS *Constitution* commanded by Captain Isaac Hull captured the HMS *Guerriere* on 19 August 1812.
[2] The USS *Constitution* under Bainbridge's command took HMS *Java* on 29 December 1812.
[3] The muster rolls of these brigs were found on a captured packet.

\*     \*     \*

The statement of commodore Rodgers, respecting the muster books of the Moselle and Sappho, is the most recent document on the subject, and is beyond the reach of suspicion.

To the reader I unhesitatingly submit the subject. Let him, whether Federalist or Democrat, honestly raise the scales of truth and justice—let him impartially weigh the evidence on both sides: and let him decide according to the credibility of these warring and irreconcilable documents.

In addition to the information contained in the preceding pages, I have now before me a most powerful document on the subject of impressment. It is

A statement of applications made to the British government on 1538 cases of impressed seamen, claiming to be citizens of the United States, from the eleventh of March, 1803, till the thirty-first of August, 1804; by George Erving, agent of the United States for the relief and protection of their seamen.

I subjoin an abstract:

| | |
|---|---:|
| Number of applications, - - - | 1538 |
| Of which are duplicates of former ones, - | 306 |
| Original applications, - - - - | 1232 |
| | 1538 |

| | |
|---|---:|
| Refused to be discharged, having no documents, | 383 |
| Ordered to be discharged, - - - | 437 |
| Said not to be on board the ships specified, | 105 |
| Refused to be discharged, said to have taken the bounty, and entered, - - - | 120 |
| Said to be married in England, - - | 17 |
| | 1062 |

| | |
|---|---:|
| Brought forward, - - - - | 1062 |
| Said to have deserted, - - - - | 13 |
| Said to have been drowned, or died, - - | 2 |
| Ships, on board of which stated not in commission, | 3 |
| Refused to be discharged, said to be British subjects, | 49 |
| Refused to be discharged, said to be prisoners of war, | 2 |
| Do not appear to have been impressed, - - | 6 |
| On board ships stated to be on a foreign station, | 22 |
| Ships lost, on board of which were stated to be - | 6 |

*Refused to be discharged, documents being insufficient, viz.*

| | |
|---|---:|
| 1. Protections from consuls and vice-consuls, - | 88 |
| 2. Notarial affidavits made in the United States, | 15 |
| 3. Notarial affidavits made in England, - - | 27 |
| 4. Collectors' protections, - - - | 41 |
| 5. Discharges granted from King's ships, they being American citizens, - - - - | 4 |
| 6. Of different descriptions, and which were kept by the impress officers, - - - | 35 |
| 7. Applications yet unanswered, - - | 163 |
| | 1538 |

This abstract deserves to be read and examined over and over. Every line of it claims the deepest and most serious consideration. It appears that in less than eighteen months, twelve hundred and thirty-two persons were impressed out of American vessels, exclusive of the very great number, who, we may reasonably conclude, had no means of conveying their applications for redress to the proper organ. An entire volume might be written as a commentary on this memorial of British outrage and injustice, and of American disgrace and dishonour.

The first item is hideous. Three hundred and eighty-three impressed Americans were doomed to remediless slavery, because they were not branded with the mark U. S. or provided with a badge, a pass, a license, or certificate! Suppose commodore Perry, or commodore Macdonough, or commodore Porter, had impressed three hundred and eighty-three men from on board of British vessels, under pretence of their being Americans—(and has the Almighty given any right to a British captain or commodore beyond what he has vested in an American captain or commodore?) and suppose Mr. Merry, Mr. Liston, Francis James Jackson, Mr. Rose, or Mr. Foster,[4] had demanded them— and that our secretary of state had peremptorily refused to surrender them, because they had not the regular brand of G. R. or a proper certificate or protection, would Great Britain have submitted to the slow process of further demanding and waiting for redress? Indubitably not.

---

[4]British envoys.

One hundred and five were doomed to slavery, by a removal from the vessels by which they were impressed, to others. An easy and summary process, by which the doors of redress are eternally barred with adamantine fastenings.

One hundred and twenty of these sufferers were withheld because they had taken the bounty, or voluntarily entered! In forming an estimate of the justice of this plea, we must not lose sight of the subsequent cruel tragedy acted by order of commodore Berkley, on board the Chesapeake, in order to seize men who had voluntarily entered on board that vessel. If this be not—*give no right—take no wrong*—I cannot divine what deserves the title.

I am tired of this vile, this odious, this detestable subject. It excites to loathing and abhorrence. I must draw to a close. But there is one more point that I must touch upon—and that is, that of the whole number of fifteen hundred and thirty-eight, there are only forty-nine asserted to be British subjects! The American, who, after these statements, can advocate the atrocious practice of impressment, must be utterly lost to a sense of justice for his countrymen, or regard to the national rights or national honour.

# REVIEW QUESTIONS

1. What was impressment? How long had that been an issue in U.S. foreign relations?
2. Carey was arguing on two levels: he argued against those who said that impressment was not a strong enough reason for war, and he argued that impressment was a great offense against the American people and their nation. How did he attack opponents of the war?
3. How and why did Carey equate impressment with slavery?
4. Did Carey primarily see impressment as undermining American material interests in shipping and trade or as an affront to national honor? Explain.
5. How well does Carey intertwine emotion, logic, and evidence to make his argument?

# 9 ❧ THE DYNAMICS OF GROWTH

*Opportunity plus improvements equaled growth, and growth, to most Americans, meant progress and prosperity. As the nation grew physically, it encompassed more people who ingeniously and energetically pursued individual and national improvements. Many of these people cultivated more and more land. Agriculture, however, blossomed not just because additional farmers worked on extensive homesteads; it flourished because other Americans, native born and immigrant, created better tools with which to work. Inventors devised mechanical aids, from the cotton gin that transformed the South to the mechanical seeders and reapers that, in the Old Northwest, helped turn sustenance farming into commercial agriculture.*

*The farmers then needed greater markets and ways to get their goods to them. Furthermore, those farmers became markets for other goods they could not easily or profitably produce. Well aware of the farmers' situation, Americans took a great interest in internal improvements—whether financed by the national or state governments.*

*While citizens wrangled over the type and sponsorship of improvements, their federal and local governments proceeded to build roadways and waterways. The National Road was the premier example of the former, and the latter included the numerous canals that gouged through the states, connecting rivers and lakes, cities and shipping terminals. Yet these did not represent the greatest innovations in transportation. People had long used the power supplied by air, earth, and water, but in harnessing the power created by a combination of those elements—steam power—they revolutionized the ways by which people traveled. Steamships began to ply the country's rivers, lakes, and shorelines, and heralded the beginning of the end for the great ocean sailing ships. Steam-powered locomotives, engines on wheels that moved on tracks, also energized the movement of people and products.*

*The most dynamic element in this transformation was the human one. People invented machines to benefit people. Laborers used the machines to make the tools and goods that the populace required. As demand for both workers and products grew, people streamed in from the countryside and from other countries to work in the factories. The resulting confluence of cultures, with all its attendant turbulence and debris, was a mixed blessing for American society. While some Americans liked to see customs challenged by the new realities of industrialization and urbanization, many others found the process, and certainly the consequences, profoundly disturbing.*

*The growth of manufacturing expanded the ranks of landless laborers and contributed to social and economic stratification as Americans started to define the value of such workers and their work. Many, planted deep in the yeoman farmer tradition, did not understand those who toiled in factories rather than fields. Although movement was an accepted part of the American experience when it included clearing new farms, the urban laborers' rootlessness was not. One result was that some Americans discriminated against industrial workers, especially when such laborers changed the face, figure, and speech of America's working class. When manufacturers readily hired women and children—they preferred them for some tasks—people worried about them working outside family control (working within it had always been acceptable). While factory work was a positive in that it gave some women and families greater economic options, it also led to exploitation. Natives and immigrants alike struggled with this and other dilemmas that were the by-products of industrialization.*

*Immigrants were vital to growth. The nation had natural resources in abundance, but while Americans were as energetic in populating the land as they were in planting crops, rail stakes, and factory foundations, they did not provide enough laborers. Fortunately for the nation—although some citizens believed that more misfortune than fortune attended their coming—immigrants flocked to these shores after 1820. Pushed from their motherlands by depression, famine, and political persecution, and pulled to America by images of prosperity, bountifulness, and tolerance, thousands upon thousands of peoples shipped off for the New World. Prominent among them were Germans and Irish, the two major European groups to migrate to the United States before 1860.*

*National power and prosperity benefited from the interplay of land, people, and technology. Yet what many hailed as progress was not welcomed by all. Some feared that manufacturing and cities spelled the doom not only of the yeoman farmer but also of the political system created for him. Others decried the influence of immigrants on American culture and thus espoused nativism. Yet as much as nativists wanted to preserve an idealized past in their culture, American civilization was just as dynamic an invention as the mechanical ones, and just as susceptible to those who wanted to improve it.*

## JOHN JAMES AUDUBON

# The Ohio (1830s)

*Birds fascinated John James Audubon (1785–1851), and he spent most of his life studying their habits as well as making detailed paintings of them. Born in Saint-Domingue (Haiti) and raised in France, he moved to America in 1803. In 1807 he and a partner established a general store in Louisville, Kentucky. A year later he married Lucy Bakewell. Throughout this period he developed the taxidermy and drawing skills that resulted in ever more lifelike drawings of birds and other animals. By 1811 he had moved his family to Henderson, Kentucky, and ended his earlier business partnership to enter a new one with his wife's brother. His business and other investment endeavors generally did not do well, but his combined artistic and scientific observations continued to develop, eventually resulting in the career for which he is known. He spent some time in the 1820s in England, where he gained the first subscribers for his work,* Birds of America. *He then returned to America and in 1831 published the first volume of his* Ornithological Biography *(others appeared in 1834, 1835, 1838, and 1839). Mixed in with those "bird biographies" were a number of essays, "Delineations of American Scenery and Manners," in which Audubon described his adopted country and people. In his early essays he tended to applaud their growth, but later he started to worry about development's cost to nature.*

From *Writings and Drawings* (New York: Library of America, 1999), pp. 520–24. [Editorial insertions appear in square brackets—*Ed.*]

. . . The natural features of that land are not less remarkable than the moral character of her inhabitants; and I cannot find a better subject with which to begin, than one of those magnificent rivers that roll the collected waters of her extensive territories to the ocean.

When my wife, my eldest son (then an infant), and myself were returning from Pennsylvania to Kentucky, we found it expedient, the waters being unusually low, to provide ourselves with a *skiff*, to enable us to proceed to our abode at Henderson. I purchased a large, commodious, and light boat of the denomination. We procured a mattress, and our friends furnished us with ready prepared viands. We had two stout Negro rowers, and in this trim we left the village of Shippingport, in expectation of reaching the place of our destination in a very few days.

It was in the month of October. [Poetic license? It appears that the family may have returned in July 1812.] The autumnal tints already decorated the shores of that queen of rivers, the Ohio. Every tree was hung with long and flowing festoons of different species of vines, many loaded with clustered fruits of varied brilliancy, their rich bronzed carmine mingling beautifully with the yellow foliage, which now predominated over the yet green leaves, reflecting more lively tints from the clear stream than ever landscape painter portrayed or poet imagined.

The days were yet warm. The sun had assumed the rich and glowing hue which at that season produces the singular phenomenon called there the "Indian Summer." The moon had rather passed the meridian of her grandeur. We glided down the river, meeting no other ripple of the water than that formed by the propulsion of our boat. Leisurely we moved along, gazing all day on the grandeur and beauty of the wild scenery around us.

Now and then a large catfish rose to the surface of the water, in pursuit of a shoal of fry, which, starting simultaneously from the liquid element, like so many silvery arrows, produced a shower of light, while the pursuer with open jaws seized the stragglers, and, with a splash of his tail, disappeared from our view. . . .

Nature, in her varied arrangements, seems to have felt a partiality towards this portion of our country. As the traveller ascends or descends the Ohio, he cannot help remarking that alternately, nearly the whole length of the river, the margin, on one side, is bounded by lofty hills and a rolling surface, while on the other, extensive plains of the richest alluvial land are seen as far as the eye can command the view. Islands of varied size and form rise here and there from the bosom of the water, and the winding course of the stream frequently brings you to places where the idea of being on a river of great length changes to that of floating on a lake of moderate extent. Some of these islands are of considerable size and value; while others, small and insignificant, seem as if intended for contrast, and as serving to enhance the general interest of the scenery. These little islands are frequently over-flowed during great *freshets* or floods, and receive at their heads prodigious heaps of drifted timber. We foresaw with great concern the alterations that cultivation would soon produce along those delightful banks.

As night came, . . . [t]he tinkling of bells told us that the cattle which bore them were gently roving from valley to valley in search of food, or returning to their distant homes. The hooting of the Great Owl, or the muffled noise of its wings as it sailed smoothly over the stream, were matters of interest to us; so was the sound of the boatman's horn, as it came winding more and more softly from afar. When daylight returned, many songsters burst forth with echoing notes, more and more mellow to the listening ear. Here and there the lonely cabin of a squatter struck the eye, giving note of commencing civilization. The crossing of the stream by a deer foretold how soon the hills would be covered with snow.

Many sluggish flat-boats we overtook and passed: some laden with produce from the different head-waters of the small rivers that pour their tributary streams into the Ohio; others, of less dimensions, crowded with emigrants from distant parts, in search of a new home. Purer pleasures I never felt; nor have you, reader, I ween, unless indeed you have felt the like, and in such company.

The margins of the shores and of the river were at this season amply supplied with game. A Wild Turkey, a Grouse, or a Blue-winged Teal, could be procured in a few moments; and we fared well, for, whenever we pleased, we landed, struck up a fire, and provided as we were with the necessary utensils, procured a good repast.

Several of these happy days passed, and we neared our home, when, one evening, not far from Pigeon Creek (a small stream which runs into the Ohio, from the State of Indiana), a loud and strange noise was heard, so like the yells of Indian warfare, that we pulled at our oars, and made for the opposite side as fast and as quietly as possible. The sounds increased, we imagined we heard cries of "murder;" and as we knew that some depredations had lately been committed in the country by dissatisfied parties of Aborigines, we felt for a while extremely uncomfortable. Ere long, however, our minds became more calmed, and we plainly discovered that the singular uproar was produced by an enthusiastic set of Methodists, who had wandered thus far out of the common way, for the purpose of holding one of their annual camp meetings, under the shade of a beech forest. Without meeting with any other interruption, we reached Henderson, distant from Shippingport by water about two hundred miles.

When I think of these times, and call back to my mind the grandeur and beauty of those almost uninhabited shores; when I picture to myself the dense and lofty summits of the forest, that everywhere spread along the hills, and overhung the margins of the stream, unmolested by the axe of the settler; when I know how dearly purchased the safe navigation of that river has been by the blood of many worthy Virginians; when I see that no longer any Aborigines are to be found there, and that the vast herds of elks, deer and buffaloes which once pastured on these hills and in these valleys, making for themselves great roads to the several salt-springs, have ceased to exist; when I reflect that all this grand portion of our Union, instead of being in a state of nature, is now more or less covered with villages, farms, and towns, where the din of hammers and machinery is constantly heard; that the woods are fast disappearing under the axe by day, and the fire by night, that hundreds of steam-boats are gliding to and fro, over the whole length of the majestic river, forcing commerce to take root and to prosper at every spot; when I see the surplus population of Europe coming to assist in the destruction of the forest, and transplanting civilization into its darkest recesses;—when I remember that these extraordinary changes have all taken place in the short period of twenty years, I pause, wonder, and, although I know all to be fact, can scarcely believe its reality.

Whether these changes are for the better or for the worse, I shall not pretend to say; but in whatever way my conclusions may incline, I feel with regret that there are on record no satisfactory accounts of the state of that portion of the country, from the time when our people first settled in it. This has not been because no one in America is able to accomplish such an undertaking. Our IRVINGS and our COOPERS [Washington Irving and James Fenimore Cooper] have proved themselves fully competent for the task. It has more probably been because the changes have succeeded each other with such rapidity, as almost to rival the movements of their pen. However, it is not too late yet; and I sincerely hope that either or both of them will ere long furnish the generations to come with those delightful descriptions which they are so well qualified to give, of the original state of a country that has been so rapidly forced to change her form and attire under the influence of increasing population. Yes; I hope to read, ere I close my earthly career, accounts from those delightful writers of the progress of civilization in our western country. They will speak of the CLARKS, the CROGHANS, the BOONS [including George Rogers Clark, his brother William Clark, William Croghan and his son George, and Daniel Boone, all of whom were important to Kentucky's history], and many other men of great and daring enterprise. They will analyze, as it were, into each component part, the country as it once existed, and will render the picture, as it ought to be, immortal.

## REVIEW QUESTIONS

1. How does Audubon juxtapose wilderness and civilization in this piece? Did he see equilibrium between them at that time?
2. What part did the Ohio River play in fostering both nature and development?
3. What does his comparison of the noise engendered by a Methodist camp meeting to the war yells of Native Americans reveal about his perceptions of the frontier's peoples?
4. Why does he think that the great authors of the age should describe the country as it was when the first settlers spread out through it? Why does he believe that "picture" ought to be immortal?

# JOSEPHINE L. BAKER

## FROM *The Lowell Offering* (1845)

*Lowell, Massachusetts, garnered much attention for the factory system that operated there. Of interest to everyone was not just the system of production but the social system that the manufacturers, the Boston Associates, engineered to support it. Along with the numerous cotton mills that they erected in Lowell starting in 1822, these industrialists built boardinghouses for their workers, most of whom were single young women. The Boston Associates deliberately set out to attract such laborers by offering higher wages than women could make at the other legal occupations open to them, and by guaranteeing respectable living conditions that included educational opportunities. When word got out, as it quickly did, young women who needed to support themselves as well as those who wanted to work for a few years to build dowries or help their families financially flocked to the mills. The investment in wages and living as well as working conditions paid off: the manufacturers paid a reliable and generally biddable workforce with wages that, though high for women, were still lower than those for men. Initially many people hailed this system as more humane than labor practices elsewhere and as an effective way of tapping underutilized human resources within the social order. As time went by, however, the physical plant of both factory and boardinghouse deteriorated. Supposedly benevolent paternalism turned into sometimes malevolent policing, especially when the mill workers protested, which they increasingly did. Their work and educational experiences so empowered some of the women that they were no longer as obedient or deferential as their managers wished. Josephine L. Baker revealed such sentiments when she described factory life in* The Lowell Offering, *a magazine edited by and for women after 1842.*

From Benita Eisler, ed., *The Lowell Offering: Writings by New England Mill Women (1840–1845)* (1977; New York: W. W. Norton, 1998), pp. 77–82.

\*　　\*　　\*

There is the "counting-room," a long, low, brick building, and opposite is the "store-house," built of the same material, after the same model. Between them, swings the ponderous gate that shuts the mills in from the world without. But, stop; we must get "a pass," ere we go through, or "the watchman will be after us." Having obtained this, we will stop on the slight elevation by the gate, and view the mills. The one to the left rears high its huge sides of brick and mortar, and the belfry, towering far above the rest, stands out in bold relief against the rosy sky. The almost innumerable windows glitter, like gems, in the morning sunlight. It is six and a half stories high, and, like the fabled monster of old, who guarded the sacred waters of Mars, it seems to guard its less aspiring sister to the right; that is five and a half stories high, and to it is attached the repair-shop. If you please, we will pass to the larger factory,—but be careful, or you will get lost in the mud, for this yard is not laid out in such beautiful order, as some of the factory yards are, nor can it be.

We will just look into the first room. It is used for cleaning cloth. You see the scrubbing and scouring machines are in full operation, and gigging and fulling are going on in full perfection. As it is very damp, and the labor is performed by the other half of creation, we will pass on, for fear of incurring their jealousy. But the very appearance might indicate that there are, occasionally, *fogs and clouds*; and not only fogs and clouds, but sometimes plentiful showers. In the second room the cloth is "*finished*," going through the various operations of burling, shearing, brushing, inking, fine-drawing, pressing, and packing for market. This is the pleasantest room on the corporation, and consequently they are never in want of help. The shearing, brushing, pressing and packing is done by males, while the burling, inking, marking and fine-drawing is performed by females. We will pass to the third room, called the "cassimere weaving-room," where all kinds of cloths are woven, from plain to the most exquisite fancy. There are between eighty and ninety looms, and part of the dressing is also done here. The fourth is the "broad weaving-room," and contains between thirty and forty looms; and broad sure enough they are. Just see how lazily the lathe drags backward and forward, and the shuttle—how spitefully it hops from one end of it to the other. But we must not stop longer, or perchance it will hop at us. You look weary; but, never mind! there was an end to Jacob's ladder, and *so* there is a termination to these stairs. Now if you please we will go up to the next room, where the spinning is done. Here we have spinning jacks or jennies that dance merrily along whizzing and singing, as they spin out their "long yarns," and it seems but pleasure to watch their movements; but it is hard work, and requires good health and much strength. Do not go too near, as we shall find that they do not understand the established rules of *etiquette*, and might unceremoniously knock us over. We must not stop here longer, for it is twelve o'clock, and we have the "carding-room" to visit before dinner. There are between twenty and thirty set of cards located closely together, and I beg of you to be careful as we go amongst them, or you will get caught in the machinery. You walk as

though you were afraid of getting blue. Please excuse me, if I ask you not to be afraid. 'Tis a wholesome color, and soap and water will wash it off. The girls, you see, are partially guarded against it, by over-skirts and sleeves; but as it is not *fashionable* to wear masks, they cannot keep it from their faces. You appear surprised at the hurry and bustle now going on in the room, but your attention has been so engaged that you have forgotten the hour. Just look at the clock, and you will find that it wants but five minutes to "bell time." We will go to the door, and be ready to start when the others do; and now, while we are waiting, just cast your eyes to the stair-way, and you will see another flight of stairs, leading to another spinning-room; a picker is located somewhere in that region, but I cannot give you a description of it, as I have never had the courage to ascend more than five flight of stairs at a time. And—but the bell rings.

Now look out—not for the engine—but for the rush to the stair-way. O mercy! what a crowd. I do not wonder you gasp for breath; but, keep up courage; we shall soon be on terra firma again. Now, safely landed, I hope to be excused for taking you into such a crowd. Really, it would not be fair to let you see the factory girls and machinery for nothing. I shall be obliged to hurry you, as it is some way to the boarding-house, and we have but thirty minutes from the time the bell begins to ring till it is done ringing again; and then all are required to be at their work. There is a group of girls yonder, going our way; let us overtake them, and hear what they are talking about. Something unpleasant I dare say, from their earnest gestures and clouded brows.

"Well, I do think it is too bad," exclaims one.

"So do I," says another. "This cutting down wages *is not* what they cry it up to be. I wonder how they'd like to work as hard as we do, digging and drudging day after day, from morning till night, and then, every two or three years, have their wages reduced. I rather guess it wouldn't set very well."

"And, besides this, who ever heard, of such a thing as their being raised again," says the first speaker. "I confess that I never did, so long as I've worked in the mill, and that's been these ten years."

"Well, it is real provoking any how," returned the other, "for my part I should think they had made a clean sweep this time. I wonder what they'll do next."

"Listeners never hear any good of themselves" is a trite saying, and, for fear it may prove true in our case, we will leave this busy group, and get some dinner. There is an open door inviting us to enter. We will do so. You can hang your bonnet and shawl on one of those hooks, that extend the length of the entry for that purpose, or you can lay them on the banisters, as some do. Please to walk into the dining-room. Here are two large square tables, covered with checked clothes and loaded down with smoking viands, the odor of which is very inviting. But we will not stop here; there is the long table in the front room, at which ten or fifteen can be comfortably seated. You may place yourself at the head. Now do not be bashful or wait to be helped, but comply with the oft-made request, "help yourself" to whatever you like best; for you have but a few minutes allotted you to spend at the table. The reason why, is because you are a rational, intelligent, thinking being, and ought to know enough to swallow your food whole; whereas a horse or an ox, or any other dumb beast knows no better than to spend an hour in the *useless* process of mastication. The bell rings again, and the girls are hurrying to the mills; you, I suppose, have seen enough of them for one day, so we will walk up stairs and have a *tete-a-tete.*

You ask, if there are so many things objectionable, why we work in the mill. Well, simply for this reason,—every situation in life, has its trials which must be borne, and factory life has no more than any other. There are many things we do not like; many occurrences that send the warm blood mantling to the cheek when they must be borne in silence, and many harsh words and acts that are not called for. There are objections also to the number of hours we work, to the length of time allotted to our meals, and to the low wages allowed for labor; objections that must and will be answered; for the time has come when something, besides the clothing and feeding of the body is to be thought of; when the mind is to be clothed and fed; and this cannot be as it should be, with the present system of labor. Who, let me ask, can find that pleasure in life which they should, when it is spent in this way. Without time for the laborer's own work, and the improvement of the mind, save the few evening hours; and even then if the mind is enriched and stored with useful knowledge, it must be at the expense of health. And the feeling too, that comes over us (there is no use in denying it) when we hear the bell calling us away from repose that tired nature loudly claims—the feeling, that we are *obliged to go.* And these few hours, of which we have spoken, are far too short, three at the most at the close of day. Surely, methinks, every heart that lays claim to humanity will feel 'tis not enough. But this, we hope will, ere long, be done away with, and labor made what it should be; pleasant and inviting to every son and daughter of the human family.

There is a brighter side to this picture, over which we would not willingly pass without notice, and an answer to the question, why we work here? The time we *do* have is our own. The money we earn comes promptly; more so than in any other situation; and our work, though laborious is the same from day to day; we know what it is, and when finished we feel perfectly free, till it is time to commence it again.

Besides this, there are many pleasant associations connected with factory life, that are not to be found elsewhere.

There are lectures, evening schools and libraries, to which all may have access. The one thing needful here, is the time to improve them as we ought.

There is a class, of whom I would speak, that work in the mills, and will while they continue in operation. Namely, the many who have no home, and who come here to seek, in this busy, bustling "City of Spindles," a competency that shall enable them in after life, to live without being a burden to society,—the many who toil on, without a murmur, for the support of an aged mother or orphaned brother and sister. For the sake of them, we earnestly hope labor may be reformed; that the miserable, selfish spirit of competition, now in our midst, may be thrust from us and consigned to eternal oblivion.

There is one other thing that must be mentioned ere we part, that is the practice of sending agents through the country to decoy girls away from their homes with the promise of high wages, when the market is already stocked to overflowing. This is certainly wrong, for it lessens the value of labor, which should be ever held in high estimation, as the path marked out by the right hand of GOD, in which man should walk with dignity.

*    *    *

## REVIEW QUESTIONS

1. Was there a moral to this story?
2. What criticisms did the author have about life and work in Lowell? What did she praise?
3. What were some of the different operations performed to manufacture cloth?
4. Which of the tasks was performed by the minority, in this workforce, the men?

## ANNA MARIA KLINGER

# Letters Home to Germany (1849–50s)

*Businessmen and families in need of laborers and servants often turned to immigrants. They could generally pay such workers less than they did native sons and expend less worry about "protecting" them than they did native daughters. Although most of the immigrants could offer only unskilled or semiskilled labor, there were artisans as well as professionals among them. Of the two major immigrant groups in the first half of the nineteenth century, the Germans, despite language problems, generally found greater acceptance than the Irish, mainly because there was already a strong German presence in America from the earlier colonial migrations and because they were often better educated and financially prepared. Germans were also religiously diverse; although there were some Catholics and Jews, the majority belonged to Protestant sects. Furthermore, while many Germans settled in the eastern cities, many more moved west to establish new farms and communities there. Poor harvests, too-small farms, and mechanized industry drove many Germans to America, where, once settled, they wrote home to entice friends and family to join them. Anna Maria Klinger came from a poor, winegrowing family in Württemberg. She arrived in America in 1849 and immediately found work with the family of a German-American pharmacist. She soon married another immigrant, Franz Schano, who had deserted from the Bavarian army. They, in turn, helped five other Klingers emigrate during the 1850s.*

From Walter D. Kamphoefner, Wolfgang Helbich, and Ulrike Sommer, eds., *News from the Land of Freedom: German Immigrants Write Home*, trans. by Susan Carter Vogel (Ithaca, Cornell University Press, 1991), pp. 534, 536–39. © Briefe aus Amerika. *Deutsche Auswanderer schreiben aus der Neuen Welt 1830–1930* by Walter Kamphoefner, Wolfgang Helbich, and Ulrike Sommer. München, Verlag C. H. Beck, 1988. Reprinted by permission of Verlag C. H. Beck. [Editorial insertions appear in square brackets—*Ed.*]

# Anna Maria Klinger

New Jork, March 18, 1849

Beloved parents and brothers and sisters,

Out of filial and sisterly love I feel obliged to inform you about my well-being in America. After a long and trying journey I arrived in New Jork safe and sound after all, and until now I have been quite well. . . . Now I want to tell you about my situation, that is that on the same day I arrived in New Jork, I went into service for a German family. I am content with my wages for now, compared to Germany, I make 4 dollars a month in our money [10] guilders, if you can speak English then it's considerably better, since the English pay a good wage, a servant gets 7 to 10 dollars a month, but if you can't speak or understand English you can't ask for so much pay. But I hope that things will get better, for it's always like that, no one really likes it at first, and especially if you are so lonely and forlorn in a foreign land like I am, no friends or relatives around. . . . The dear Lord is my shield and refuge. . . . I keep thinking you are fearful and worried about me because you have not received a letter for so long, first of all, we were at sea for one hundred and 5 days, 7 weeks we were docked at Blümuth [Plymouth] before our ship was done. You probably read in the letter I wrote to the mayor about the bad luck we had. From England to America things went well, we still had one big storm, but we suffered no more misfortune, there were 200 and 60 passengers on the ship. My journey from Stuttgart to Antwerben went well, I met up with those 3 girls who were also going from Stuttgart to America in Maintz, but they'd already met up with companions on the way, they started behaving so badly on the journey already, and at sea there were two tailor boys with those girls, I got annoyed because I couldn't stand such loose behavior, one of them went to Viladelfe [Philadelphia] and another in New Jork. . . .

The city of New Jork is the largest in America, it is so big you can't walk around it in one day, the religious institutions are like in Germany, there are 182 churches here, but belonging to different religions. Here you can find people from all corners of the world, there are about 4,000 German residents alone [actually, there were between fifty and sixty thousand]. I will be able to write more in the future when I have been here longer. But I do want to tell you this [that so many deserters] from the army have arrived here. . . . Gottlieb [her brother] should give my best to his cook where he was when I left, she only needs to come to America, it's very good for girls who have to work in service. I haven't regretted it yet. Write me, too, about what's happening in Stuttgart. Dear parents, my next letter will make you happier. . . .

# Anna Maria Schano, née Klinger

[New York, probably mid-1850]

[Beginning of letter missing] I've saved up to now in the time we've been married some 40 dollars in cash, not counting my clothes. Dear parents and brothers and sisters, I certainly don't want to tell you what to do, do what you want, for some like it here and some don't, but the only ones who don't like it here had it good in Germany, but I also think you would like it here since you never had anything good in Germany. I'm certainly glad not to be over there, and only those who don't want to work don't like it here, since in America you have to work if you want to amount to anything, you mustn't feel ashamed, that's just how you amount to something, and so I want to tell you again to do what you want, since it can seem too trying on the journey and in America as well, and then you heap the most bitter reproaches on those who talked you into coming, since it all depends on whether you have good luck, just like in Germany. Dear parents, you wrote me that Daniel wants to come to America and doesn't have any money, that is certainly a problem. Now I want to give you my opinion, I've often thought about what could be done, I thought 1st if he could borrow the money over there, then when he has saved enough over here then he could send it back over, like a lot of people do, and secondly, I thought we would like to pay for him to come over, but right now we can't since it costs 28 dollars a person and I also want to tell you since my husband wrote to you, the money we want to send you, whether you want to use it to have one or two come over here or if you want to spend it on yourselves, you just have to let us know so we have an idea how much you still need, and you'll have to see to it that you have some more money, too, since we can't pay it all. [ . . . ] Things in Daniel's *Profesion* are not the best, he shouldn't count on that, it would be better if he were a tailor or shoemaker, but it doesn't matter, a lot of people don't work in their *Profesion* and learn others or other businesses, since you don't have to pay to learn a trade in America. Dear parents and brothers and sisters, if one of you comes over here and comes to stay with us we will certainly take care of you, since we are now well known, and you needn't be so afraid of America, when you come to America, just imagine you were moving to Stuttgart, that's how many Germans you can see here.

And as far as the Americans are concerned, whites and blacks, they won't harm you, since the blacks are very happy when you don't do anything to them, the only thing is the problem with the language. It's not as easy to learn as you think, even now I don't know much, and there are many people here who don't even learn it in 6 to 8 years, but if you start off working for Americans then you can learn in one year as much as in 10 years living with Germans. Dear parents and brothers and sisters, I'd like to be with you, you will surely be pleased to get the picture of us, to see me again, and I would also be so happy to see you again. In my dreams I've often been with you and also in my old job in Germany, but when I woke up, it wasn't true, but still I am happy in any case that I am in America. . . . We would have liked to have sent a few dollars along with this letter but at the moment we don't have much money, since I can well imagine you could use it now, but things go slowly the first few years, you have to take care of yourself, since the motto in America is help yourself. . . .

## REVIEW QUESTIONS

1. What does Klinger reveal about the process of emigration/immigration?
2. How does she promote America to her relatives in Germany?
3. What does she believe to be the key(s) to doing well in America?

# JOHN FRANCIS MAGUIRE

## FROM *The Irish in America* (1867)

*The Irish were weighed down by many woes in the nineteenth century; prime among them were British dominion and the famine caused by the potato rot. The weight buried many at home and squeezed others out to find freedom and food abroad. These Irish immigrants, who by 1860 composed the largest foreign-born group in America, faced perhaps the greatest prejudice. John Francis Maguire, looking back on decades of Irish migration, tried to explain why to both Irish and American readers in his book,* The Irish in America.

From *The Irish in America*, 4th ed. (New York: D. & J. Sadlier, 1867), pp. 215–19, 240, 252, 281–84, 333–37.

\*   \*   \*

Irish emigrants of the peasant and labouring class were generally poor, and after defraying their first expenses on landing had little left to enable them to push their way into the country in search of such employment as was best suited to their knowledge and capacity: though had they known what was in store for too many of them and their children, they would have endured the severest privation and braved any hardship, in order to free themselves from the fatal spell in which the fascination of a city life has meshed the souls of so many of their race. Either they brought little money with them, and were therefore unable to go on; or that little was plundered from them by those whose trade it was to prey upon the inexperience or credulity of the new-comer. Therefore, to them, the poor or the plundered Irish emigrants, the first and pressing necessity was employment; and so splendid seemed the result of that employment, even the rudest and most laborious kind, as compared with what they were able to earn in the old country, that it at once predisposed them in favour of a city life. . . . Then there were old friends and former companions or acquaintances to be met with at every street-corner; and there was news to give, and news to receive—too often, perhaps, in the liquor-store or dram-shop kept by a countryman— probably 'a neighbour's child,' or 'a decent boy from the next ploughland.' Then 'the chapel was handy,' and 'a Christian wouldn't be overtaken for want of a priest;' then there was 'the schooling convenient for the children, poor things,'—so the glorious chance was lost; and the simple, innocent countryman, to whom the trees of the virgin forest were nodding their branches in friendly invitation, and the blooming prairie expanded its fruitful bosom in vain, became the denizen of a city, for which he was unqualified by training, by habit, and by association. Possibly it was the mother's courage that failed her as she glanced at the flock of little ones who clustered around her, or timidly clung to her skirts, and she thought of the new dangers and further perils that awaited them; and it was her maternal influence that was flung into the trembling balance against the country and in favour of the city. Or employment was readily found for one of the girls, or one or two of the boys, and things looked so hopeful in the fine place that all thoughts of the fresh, breezy, healthful plain or hill-side were shut out at that supreme moment of the emigrant's destiny; though many a time after did he and they long for one breath of pure air, as they languished in the stifling heat of a summer in a tenement house. Or the pioneer of the family—most likely a young girl—had found good employment, and, with the fruits of her honest toil, had gradually brought out brothers and sisters, father and mother, for whose companionship her heart ever yearned; and possibly her affection was stronger than her prudence, or she knew nothing of the West and its limitless resources. Or sickness, that had followed the emigrant's family across the ocean, fastened upon some member of the group as they touched the soil for which they had so ardently prayed, and though the fever or the cholera did not destroy a precious life, it did the almost as precious opportunity of a better future! the spring of that energy which was sufficient to break asunder the ties and habits of previous years—sufficient for flight from home and country—was broken, and those who faced America in high hope were thenceforth added to the teeming population of a city— to which class, it might be painful to speculate.

\*   \*   \*

This headlong rushing into the great cities has the necessary effect of unduly adding to their population, thereby overtaxing their resources, however large or even extraordinary these resources may be, and of rudely disturbing the balance of supply and demand. The hands—the men, women, and children—thus become too many for the work to be done, as the work becomes too little for the hands willing and able to do it. What is worse, there are too many mouths for the bread of independence; and thus the bread of charity has to supplement the bread which is purchased with the sweat of the brow. Happy would it be for the poor in the towns of America, as elsewhere, if the bread of charity were the *only* bread with which the bread of independence is supplemented. But there is also the bread of degradation, and the bread of crime. And when the moral principle is blunted by abject misery, or weakened by disappointments and privation, there is but a narrow barrier between poverty and crime; and this, too frequently, is soon passed. For such labour as is thus recklessly poured into the great towns there is constant peril. It is true, there are seasons when there is a glut of work, when the demand exceeds the supply—when some gigantic industry or some sudden necessity clamours for additional hands; but there are also, and more frequently, seasons when work is slack, seasons of little employment, seasons of utter paralysis and stagnation. Cities are liable to occasional depressions of trade, resulting from over production, or the successful rivalry of foreign nations, or even portions of the same country; or there are smashings of banks, and commercial panics, and periods of general mistrust. Or, owing to the intense severity of certain seasons, there is a total cessation of employments of particular kinds, by which vast numbers of people are flung idle on the streets. . . .

The evil of overcrowding is magnified to a prodigious extent in New York, which, being *the* port of arrival—the Gate of the New World—receives a certain addition to its population from almost every ship-load of emigrants that passes through Castle Garden. There is scarcely any city in the world possessing greater resources than New York, but these resources have long since been strained to the very uttermost to meet the yearly increasing demands created by this continuous accession to its inhabitants; . . .

As in all cities growing in wealth and in population, the dwelling accommodation of the poor is yearly sacrificed to the increasing necessities or luxury of the rich. While spacious streets and grand mansions are on the increase, the portions of the city in which the working classes once found an economical residence, are being steadily encroached upon—just as the artisan and labouring population of the City of London are driven from their homes by the inexorable march of city improvements, and streets and courts and alleys are

swallowed up by a great thoroughfare or a gigantic railway terminus. . . .

As stated on official authority, there are 16,000 tenement houses in New York, and in these there dwell more than half a million of people! This astounding fact is of itself so suggestive of misery and evil, that it scarcely requires to be enlarged upon; . . .

\*     \*     \*

It is not at all necessary that an Irish immigrant should go West, whatever and how great the inducements it offers to the enterprising. There is land to be had, under certain circumstances and conditions, in almost every State in the Union. And there is no State in which the Irish peasant who is living from hand to mouth in one of the great cities as a day-labourer, may not improve his condition by betaking himself to his natural and legitimate avocation—the cultivation of the soil. Nor is the vast region of the South unfavourable to the laborious and energetic Irishman. On the contrary, there is no portion of the American continent in which he would receive a more cordial welcome, or meet with more favourable terms. This would not have been so before the war, or the abolition of slavery, and the upset of the land system which was based upon the compulsory labour of the negro.

 . . . The policy of the South is to increase and strengthen the white population, so as not to be, as the South yet is, too much dependent on the negro; and the planter who, ten years ago, would not sever a single acre from his estate of 2,000, or 10,000, or 20,000 acres, will now readily divide, if not all, at least a considerable portion of it, into saleable quantities, to suit the convenience of purchasers. . . .

\*     \*     \*

Were I asked to say what I believed to be the most serious obstacle to the advancement of the Irish in America, I would unhesitatingly answer—*Drink*; meaning thereby the excessive use, or abuse, of that which, when taken in excess, intoxicates, deprives man of his reason, interferes with his industry, injures his health, damages his position, compromises his respectability, renders him unfit for the successful exercise of his trade, profession, or employment—which leads to quarrel, turbulence, violence, crime. I believe this fatal tendency to excessive indulgence to be the main cause of all the evils and miseries and disappointments that have strewed the great cities of America with those wrecks of Irish honour, Irish virtue, and Irish promise, which every lover of Ireland has had, one time or other, bitter cause to deplore. Differences of race and religion are but as a feather's weight in the balance; indeed these differences tend rather to add interest to the steady and self-respecting citizen. Were this belief, as to the tendency of the Irish to excess in the use of stimulants, based on the testimony of Americans, who might probably be somewhat prejudiced, and therefore inclined to judge unfavourably, or pronounce unsparingly, I should not venture to record it; but it was impressed upon me by Irishmen of every rank, class, and condition of life, wherever I went, North or South, East or West. It was openly deplored, or it was reluctantly admitted. I rarely heard an Irishman say that his country or his religion was an effectual barrier to his progress in the United States. . . .

The question here naturally arises,—do the Irish drink more than the people of any other nationality in America? The result of my observation and inquiries leads me to the conviction that *they do not.* How then comes it that the habit, if common to all is so pernicious to them? There are many and various reasons why this is so. In the first place, they are strangers, and, as such, more subject to observation and criticism than the natives of the country. They are, also, as a rule, of a faith different to that of the majority of the American people; and the fact that they are so does not render the observation less keen, nor does it render the criticism more gentle. Then, be it constitution, or temperament, or whatever else, excess seems to be more injurious to them than to others. They are genial, open-hearted, generous, and social in their tendencies; they love company, court excitement, and delight in affording pleasure or gratification to their friends. And not only are their very virtues leagued against them, but the prevailing custom of the country is a perpetual challenge to indulgence.

This prevailing custom or habit springs more from a spirit of kindness than from a craving for sensual gratification. Invitations to drink are universal, as to rank and station, time and place, hour and circumstance; they literally rain upon you. The Americans are perhaps about the most thoroughly wide-awake people in the world, yet they must have an 'eye-opener' in the morning. To prepare for meals, you are requested to fortify your stomach and stimulate your digestive powers with an 'appetizer.' To get along in the day, you are invited to accept the assistance of a 'pony.' If you are startled at the mention of 'a drink,' you find it difficult to refuse 'at least a nip.' And who but the most morose—and the Irishman is all geniality—can resist the influence of 'a smile?' Now a 'cocktail,' now a 'cobler'—here a 'julep,' there a 'smasher;' or if you shrink from the potency of the 'Bourbon,' you surely are not afraid of 'a single glass of lager beer!' To the generous, company loving Irishman there is something like treason to friendship and death to good-fellowship in refusing these kindly-meant invitations; but woe to the impulsive Irishman who becomes the victim of this custom of the country! The Americans drink, the Germans drink, the Scotch drink, the English drink—all drink with more or less injury to their health or circumstances, but whatever the injury to these, or any of these, it is far greater to the mercurial and light-hearted Irish than to races of hard head and lethargic temperament. . . .

It must be admitted that, in some cities of America—by no means in all, or anything like all—the Irish element figures unenviably in the police records, and before the inferior tribunals; and that in these cities the committals are more numerous than they should be in proportion to the numerical strength of the Irish population. . . . The deadly crimes—the secret poisonings, the deliberate murders, the deep-laid frauds, the cunningly-masked treachery, the dark villany, the spider-like preparation for the destruction of the unwary victim—these are not common to the Irish. Rows, riots, turbulence, acts of personal violence perpetrated in passion, are what are principally recorded of them in the newspapers; and in nine cases out of ten, these offences against the peace and order of the community, and which so deeply prejudice the public mind, not only against the perpetrators, but, what is far worse, against the ir-race and country, are attributable to one cause, and one cause alone—*drink. . . .*

*       *       *

. . . Whatever estimate Americans may form of their Irish fellow-citizens, be that estimate favourable or unfavourable, there is but one opinion as to the moral character of Irish women. Their reputation for purity does not rest on the boastful assertions of those who either regard all matters concerning their race or country from a favourable point of view, or who, to gratify a natural feeling, would wilfully exaggerate, or possibly misstate a fact: it is universally admitted. . . . Prejudices, strong prejudices, there are in the States, as in all countries in which diversity of race and religion exists; and where this diversity comprehends race and religion in the same individuals, these prejudices are certain to be the stronger and the more deeply rooted. The Irish Catholic has to contend against this double prejudice, which nevertheless is not powerful enough to interfere with the conviction, indeed admission, as to the moral character of the women of that country and that faith. The poor Irish emigrant girl may possibly be rude, undisciplined, awkward—just arrived in a strange land, with all the rugged simplicity of her peasant's training; but she is good and honest. Nor, as she rapidly acquires the refinement inseparable from an improved condition of life, and daily association with people of cultivated manners, does she catch the contagion of the vices of the great centres of wealth and luxury. Whatever her position,—and it is principally amongst the humble walks of life the mass of the Irish are still to be found,—she maintains this one noble characteristic: purity. In domestic service her merit is fully recognised. Once satisfied of the genuineness of her character, an American family will trust in her implicitly; and not only is there no locking up against her, but everything is left in her charge. Occasionally she may be hot tempered, difficult to be managed, per-

haps a little 'turbulent'—especially when her country is sneered at, or her faith is wantonly ridiculed; but she is cheerful and laborious, virtuous and faithful.

An instance of very legitimate 'turbulence' occurred not long since in one of the most rising of the great Western cities. There lived, as a 'help,' in the house of a Protestant family, an intelligent and high-spirited Irish girl, remarkable for her exemplary conduct, and the zeal with which she discharged the duties of her position. Kate acted as a mother to a young brother and sister, whom she was bringing up with the greatest care; and a happy girl was Kate when she received good tidings of their progress in knowledge and piety. Kate, like many other people in the world, had her special torment, and that special torment was a playful-minded preacher who visited at the house, and who looked upon 'Bridget'—he *would* call her Bridget—as a fair butt for the exercise of his pleasant wit, of which he was justly proud. It was Kate's duty to attend table; and no sooner did she make her appearance in the dining-room, than the playful preacher commenced his usual fun, which would be somewhat in this fashion: 'Well, Bridget, my girl! when did you pray last to the Virgin Mary? Tell me, Bridget, when were you with Father Pat? What did you give him, Bridget? What did the old fellow ask for the absolution this time? Now, I guess it was ten cents for the small sins, and $1 for the thumpers! Come now, Bridget, tell me what penance did that priest of yours give you?' Thus would the agreeable jester pelt the poor Irish girl with his generous pleasantries, to the amusement of the thoughtless, but to the serious annoyance of the fair-minded, who did not like to see her feelings so wantonly wounded. The mistress of the house mildly remonstrated with her servant's lively tormentor, though she did not herself admire 'Bridget's' form of prayer, and was willing to regard 'Father Pat's' absolution as a matter of bargain and sale. But the wit should have his way. 'Bridget' was a handsome girl, and the rogue liked to see the fire kindle in her grey eye, and the hot blood mantle over her fair round cheek; and then the laughter of his admirers was such delightful incense to his vanity, as peal after peal told how successfully the incorrigible wag 'roasted Bridget.' On one memorable day, however, his love of the humorous carried him just too far. A large company was assembled round the hospitable table of the mistress of the house. The preacher was present, and was brimming over with merriment. Kate entered the room, bearing a large tureen of steaming soup in her hands. 'Ho, ho, Bridget!—how are you, Bridget? Well, Bridget, what did you pay Father Pat for absolution this time? Come to me, Bridget, and I will give you as many dollars as will set you all straight with the old fellow for the next six months, and settle your account with purgatory too. Now, Bridget, tell us how many cents for each sin?' The girl had just reached the preacher as he finished his little joke; and if he wished to see the Irish eye flash out its light, and the Irish blood burn in the cheek, he had an excellent opportunity for enjoying that treat. It was Bridget's turn to be playful. Stopping next to his chair, and looking him steadily in his face, while she grasped the tureen of rich green-pea soup more firmly in her hands, she said: 'Now, sir, I often asked you to leave me alone, and not mind me, and not to insult me or my religion, what no real gentleman would do to a poor girl; and now, sir, as you want to know what I pay for absolution, here's my answer!' and, suiting the action to the word, she flung the hot steaming liquid over the face, neck, breast—entire person—of the playful preacher! . . . The sentiment—the generous American sentiment—was in Kate's favour, as she might have perceived in the manner of the guests. For the poor preacher, it may be said that the soup 'spoiled his dinner' for that day. He did not make his appearance again for some time; but when he did, it was as an altered and much-improved gentleman, who appeared to have lost all interest in the religious peculiarities of Kate, whom, strange to say, he never more called by the name of Bridget. The warm bath, so vigorously administered, had done him much service—Kate said, 'a power of good.'

\*    \*    \*

## REVIEW QUESTIONS

1. How was Maguire's book a commentary on American culture in general as well as on the Irish element within it in particular?
2. In combating prejudice against the Irish, did Maguire perpetuate or even promote other biases?
3. What does this piece reveal about gender and class as well as ethnic relations and attitudes in the mid–nineteenth century?
4. What did the author believe most injured Irish interests and advancement in America? Did he say this was a problem of perception or practice?
5. Could this piece be used as a source on reform ideas and movements as well as on immigration? Explain.

# SAMUEL F. B. MORSE

## FROM *Imminent Dangers to the Free Institutions of the United States* (1835)

*In another chapter of his book, John Maguire related the history of the Know-Nothing movement of the mid 1850s. He noted how adherents combined religious bigotry with nationalistic prejudice, all to the detriment of the Irish immigrant. He was quick to point out, however, that "there was nothing new in this Know-Nothingism. It was as old as the time of the Revolution, being Native Americanism under another name. Its animating spirit was hostility to the stranger—insane jealousy of the foreigner." While the elaborate organization and political power of the American (Know-Nothing) Party was a new development, Maguire had it right: this kind of intolerance was nothing new. Nativism grew as immigration increased. By the 1830s Americans fearful of possible immigrant power and cultural effects, including politicians and reformers, delivered impassioned arguments against unrestricted immigration. Prominent among them was Samuel F. B. Morse. Although he made a career of painting—an artist of some repute, he was chosen to paint a portrait of Lafayette for the city of New York in 1825—Morse achieved lasting renown for inventing the telegraph. He was not the only one working on the concept, but his invention was the first to show itself practicable. With congressional support, Morse was able to build a line from Washington to Baltimore, and on 24 May 1844 he sent a passage from the Bible, "What hath God wrought," over the wire. Raised in a deeply religious Protestant home, Morse developed a strong antagonism against Catholicism, which became marked during his European tour in the early 1830s—the same tour that gave him some of the foundational ideas for the telegraph. On his return to a changing America he went public with his concerns, and found a ready audience.*

---

From *Imminent Dangers to the Free Institutions of the United States through Foreign Immigration* . . . (1835; New York: Arno Press, 1969), pp. 6–15.

*    *    *

Our country, in the position it has given to foreigners who have made it their home, has pursued a course in relation to them, totally different from that of any other country in the world. This course, while it is liberal without example, subjects our institutions to peculiar dangers. In all other countries the foreigner, to whatever privileges he may be entitled by becoming a subject, can never be placed in a situation to be politically dangerous, for he has no share in the government of the country; . . .

. . . The writer believes, that since the time of the American Revolution, which gave the principles of Democratic liberty a home, those principles have never been in greater jeopardy than at the present moment. To his reasons for thus believing, he invites the unimpassioned investigation of every American citizen. If there is danger, let it arouse to defence. If it is a false alarm, let such explanations be given of most suspicious appearances as shall safely allay it. It is no *party* question, and the attempt to make it one, should be at once suspected. It concerns all of every party.

*There is danger of re-action from Europe*; and it is the part of common prudence to look for it, and to provide against it. The great political truth has recently been promulged at the capital of one of the principal courts of Europe, at Vienna, and by one of the profoundest scholars of Germany, (Frederick Schlegel, a devoted Roman Catholic, and one of the Austrian Cabinet,) the great truth, clearly and unanswerably proved, that the *political revolutions to which European governments have been so long subjected, from the popular desires for liberty, are the natural effects of the Protestant Reformation.* That *Protestantism* favours *Republicanism*, while *Popery* as naturally supports *Monarchical* power. In these lectures, . . . there is a *most important* allusion to this country; and as it demonstrates one of the principal connecting points between European and American politics, and is the key to many of the mysterious doings that are in operation against American institutions under our own eyes, let Americans treasure it well in their memories. This is the passage:—"THE GREAT NURSERY *of these destructive principles*, (the principles of Democracy,) *the* GREAT REVOLUTIONARY SCHOOL *for* FRANCE *and* THE REST OF EUROPE, *is* NORTH AMERICA!" Yes, (I address Democratic Americans,) the influence of this Republican government, of your democratic system, is vitally felt by Austria. She confesses it. It is proscribed by the Austrian Cabinet. This country is designated directly to all her people, and to her allied despots, as the great *plague spot* of the world, the poisoned fountain whence flow all the deadly evils which threaten their own existence. . . . Is it wonderful after such an avowal in regard to America, that she should do something to rid herself and the world of such a tremendous evil? . . . But how shall she attack us? She cannot send her armies, they would be useless. She has told us by the mouth of her Counsellor of Legation, that Popery, while it is the natural antagonist to Protestantism, is opposed in its whole character to Republican liberty, and is the promoter and supporter of arbitrary power. How fitted then is Popery for her purpose! This she can send without alarming our fears, or, at least, only the fears of those "*miserable*," "*intolerant fanatics*," and "*pious bigots*," who affect to see danger to the liberties of the country in the mere introduction of a *religious system* opposed to their own, and whose cry of danger, be it ever so loud, will only be regarded as the result of "*sectarian fear*," and the plot ridiculed as a "*quixotic dream*." But is there any thing so irrational in such a scheme? Is it not the most natural and obvious act for Austria to do, with her views of the influence of Popery upon the form of government, its influence to pull down Republicanism, and build up monarchy; I say, is it not her most obvious act *to send Popery to this country if it is not here, or give it a fresh and vigorous impulse if it is already here*? At any rate *she is doing it.* She has set herself to work with all her activity to disseminate throughout the country the *Popish religion*. Immediately after the delivery of Schlegel's lectures, which was in the year 1828, a great society was formed in the Austrian capital, in Vienna, in 1829. The late Emperor, and Prince Metternich, and the Crown Prince, (now Emperor,) and all the civil and ecclesiastical officers of the empire, with the princes of Savoy and Piedmont, uniting in it, and calling it after the name of a canonized King, *St. Leopold*. This society is formed for a great and express purpose. . . . "*of promoting the greater activity of Catholic missions in America;*" these are the words of their own reports. Yes; these Foreign despots are suddenly stirred up to combine and promote the greater activity of Popery in this country; and this, too, just after they had been convinced of the truth, or, more properly speaking, had their memories quickened with it, that *Popery is utterly opposed to Republican liberty*. These are the facts in the case. Americans, explain them in your own way. If any choose to stretch their charity so far as to believe that these crowned gentlemen have combined in this Society solely for *religious* purposes; that they have organized a Society to collect moneys to be spent in this country, and have sent Jesuits as their almoners, and shiploads of Roman Catholic emigrants, and for the sole purpose of converting us to the *religion* of Popery, and without any *political* design, credat Judæus Apella, non ego.

\*        \*        \*

Let us examine the operations of this Austrian Society, for it is hard at work all around us; yes, here in this country, from one end to the other, at our very doors, in this city. . . . Its emissaries are here. And who are these emissaries? They are JESUITS. This society of men, after exerting their tyranny for upwards of 200 years, at length became so formidable to the world, threatening the entire subversion of all social order, that even the Pope, whose *devoted subjects* they are, and must be, by the vow of their society, was compelled to dissolve them. They had not been suppressed, however, for 50 years, before the waning influence of Popery and Despotism required their useful labours, to resist the spreading light of Democratic liberty, and the Pope, (Pius VII,) simultaneously with the formation of the Holy Alliance, revived the order of the Jesuits in all their power. . . . And do Americans need to be told what *Jesuits* are? If any are ignorant, let them inform themselves of their history without delay; no time is to be lost: their workings are before you in every day's events: they are a *secret* society, a sort of Masonic order, with superadded features of most revolting odiousness, and a thousand times more dangerous. They are not confined to one class in society; they are not merely priests, or priests of one religious creed, they are merchants, and lawyers, and editors, and men of any profession, and no profession, having no outward badge, (in this country,) by which to be recognised; they are about in all your society. They can assume any character, that of angels of light, or ministers of darkness, to accomplish their one great end, the *service* upon which they are sent, whatever that service may be. "They are all educated men, prepared, and sworn to *start at any moment, in any direction,* and for any service, commanded by the general of their order, bound to no family, community, or country, by the ordinary ties which bind men; and *sold for life* to the cause of the Roman Pontiff."

*       *       *

Is there no danger to the Democracy of the country from such formidable foes arrayed against it? Is Metternich its friend? Is the *Pope* its friend? Are his official documents, now daily put forth, *Democratic* in their character?

O there is no danger to the Democracy; for those most devoted to the Pope, the Roman Catholics, especially the Irish Catholics, are all on the side of Democracy. Yes; to be sure they are on the side of Democracy. They are just where I should look for them. Judas Iscariot joined with the true disciples. Jesuits are not fools. They would not startle our slumbering fears, by bolting out their monarchical designs directly in our teeth, and by joining the opposing ranks, *except so far as to cover their designs.* This is a Democratic country, and the Democratic party is and ever must be the strongest party, unless ruined by traitors and Jesuits in the camp. Yes; it is in the ranks of Democracy I should expect to find them, and

for no good purpose be assured. Every measure of Democratic policy in the least exciting will be pushed to *ultraism,* so soon as it is introduced for discussion. Let every real Democrat guard against this common Jesuitical artifice of tyrants, an artifice which there is much evidence to believe is practising against them at this moment, an artifice *which if not heeded will surely be the ruin of Democracy*: it is founded on the well-known principle that "*extremes meet.*" The writer has seen it pass under his own eyes in Europe, in more than one instance. When in despotic governments popular discontent, arising from the intolerable oppressions of the tyrants of the people, has manifested itself by popular outbreakings, to such a degree as to endanger the throne, and the people seemed prepared to shove their masters from their horses, and are likely to mount, and seize the reins themselves; then, the popular movement, unmanageable any longer by resistance, is pushed to the extreme. The passions of the ignorant and vicious are excited to outrage by pretended friends of the people. Anarchy ensues; and then the mass of the people, who are always lovers of order and quiet, unite at once in support of the strong arm of force for protection; and despotism, perhaps, in another, but *preconcerted* shape, resumes its iron reign. Italy and Germany are furnishing examples every day. If an illustration is wanted on a larger scale, look at France in her late Republican revolution, and in her present relapse into despotism.

*       *       *

That Jesuits are at work upon the passions of the American community, managing in various ways to gain control, must be evident to all. They who have learned from history the general mode of proceeding of this crafty set of men, could easily infer that they were here, even were it not otherwise confirmed by unquestionable evidence in their correspondence with their foreign masters in Austria. There are some, perhaps, who are under the impression that the order of Jesuits is a purely religious Society for the dissemination of the Roman Catholic religion; and therefore comes within the protection of our laws, and must be tolerated. There cannot be a greater mistake. It was from the beginning a *political* organization, an absolute Monarchy masked by religion. It has been aptly styled "*tyranny by religion.*" . . .

\*      \*      \*

. . . It becomes important to inquire, then, what are the *principal materials* in our society with which Jesuits can accomplish the political designs of the Foreign Despots embodied in the Leopold Foundation. And here let me make the passing remark, that there has been a great deal of mawkish sensitiveness on the subject of introducing any thing concerning religion into political discussions. This sensitiveness, as it is not merely foolish, arising from ignorance of the true line which separates political and theological matters, but also exposes the political interests of the country to manifest danger, I am glad to see is giving way to a proper feeling on the subject. Church and State must be for ever separated, but it is the height of folly to suppose, that in political discussions, *Religion* especially, the *political* character *of any and every religious creed* may not be publicly discussed. The absurdity of such a position is too manifest to dwell a moment upon it. And in considering the materials in our society adapted to the purposes of hostile attack upon our Institutions, we must of necessity notice the Roman Catholic religion. *It is this form of religion* that is most implicated in the conspiracy against our liberties. It is in this sect that the Jesuits are organized. It is this sect that is proclaimed by one of its own most brilliant and profound literary men to be *hostile in its very nature to republican liberty*; and it is the active extension of this sect that Austria is endeavouring to promote throughout this Republic. And Americans will not be cowed into silence by the cries of *persecution, intolerance, bigotry, fanaticism,* and such puerile catchwords, perpetually uttered against those who speak or write ever so calmly against the dangers of Popery. I can say, once for all, that no such outcry weighs a feather with me, nor does it weigh a feather with the mass of the American people. They have good sense enough to discrimi-

nate, especially in a subject of such vital importance to their safety, between *words* and *things.* I am not tenacious of *words,* except for convenience sake, the better to be understood, but if detestation of Jesuitism and tyranny, whether in a civil or ecclesiastical shape, is in future to be called *intolerance,* be it so; only let it be generally understood, and I will then glory in *intolerance.* When that which is now esteemed *virtue,* is to be known by general consent only by the name *vice,* why I will not be singular, but glory in *vice,* since the word is used to embody the *essential qualities of virtue.* I will just add, that those who are so fond of employing these epithets, forget that by so constantly, loosely, and indiscriminately using them, they cease to convey any meaning, or to excite any emotions but those of disgust towards those who use them.

To return to the subject; it is in the Roman Catholic ranks that we are principally to look for the materials to be employed by the Jesuits, and in what condition do we find this sect at present in our country? We find it spreading itself into every nook and corner of the land; churches, chapels, colleges, nunneries and convents, are springing up as if by magic every where; an activity hitherto unknown among the Roman Catholics pervades all their ranks, and yet whence the means for all these efforts? Except here and there funds or favours collected from an inconsistent *Protestant,* (*so called* probably because born in a Protestant country, who is flattered or wheedled by some Jesuit artifice to give his aid to their cause,) the greatest part of the pecuniary means for all these works are from abroad. They are the contributions of his Majesty the Emperor of Austria, of Prince Metternich, of the late Charles X., and the other Despots combined in the Leopold Society. And who are the members of the Roman Catholic communion? What proportion are natives of this land, nurtured under our own institutions, and well versed in the nature of American liberty? Is it not notorious that the greater part are *Foreigners* from the various Catholic countries of Europe. Emigration has of late years been specially promoted among this class of Foreigners, and they have been in the proportion of three to one of all other emigrants arriving on our shores; they are from Ireland, Germany, Poland, and Belgium. From about the period of the formation of the Leopold Society, Catholic emigration increased in an amazing degree. Colonies of Emigrants, selected, perhaps, with a view to occupy particular places, (for, be it remembered, every portion of this country is as perfectly known at Vienna and Rome as in any part of our own country,) have been constantly arriving. The principal emigrants are from Ireland and Germany. We have lately been told by the captain of a lately arrived *Austrian vessel*, which, by the by, brought 70 emigrants from *Antwerp*! that a desire is suddenly manifested among the poorer class of the Belgian population, to emigrate to America. They are mostly, if not all, Roman Catholics, be it remarked, for Belgium is a Catholic country, and *Austrian vessels are bringing them here*. Whatever *the cause* of all this movement abroad to send to this country their poorer classes, the fact is certain, the class of emigrants is known, and the instrument, Austria, is seen in it—the same power that directs the Leopold Foundation.

\*       \*       \*

I have shown what are the *Foreign materials* imported into the country, with which the Jesuits can work to accomplish their designs. Let us examine this point a little more minutely. These materials are the *varieties of Foreigners* of the same Creed, the Roman Catholic, over all of whom the Bishops or Vicars General hold, as a matter of course, ecclesiastical rule; and we well know what is the nature of Roman Catholic ecclesiastical rule,—it is the double refined spirit of despotism, which, after arrogating to itself the prerogatives of Deity, and so claiming to bind or loose the *soul* eternally, makes it, in the comparison, but a mere trifle to exercise absolute sway in all that relates to the body. The notorious ignorance in which the great mass of these emigrants have been all their lives sunk, until their minds are dead, makes them but senseless machines; they obey orders mechanically, for it is the habit of their education, in the despotic countries

of their birth. And can it be for a moment supposed by any one that by the act of coming to this country, and being naturalized, their darkened intellects can suddenly be illuminated to discern the nice boundary where their *ecclesiastical obedience* to their priests *ends*, and their *civil independence* of them *begins*? The very supposition is absurd. They obey their priests as demigods, from the habit of their whole lives; they have been taught from infancy that their priests are infallible in the greatest matters, and can they, by mere importation to this country, be suddenly imbued with the knowledge that in civil matters their priests may err, and that they are not in these also their infallible guides? Who will teach them this? Will their priests? Let common sense answer this question. Must not the priests, as a matter almost of *certainty*, control the opinions of their ignorant flock in civil as well as religious matters? and do they not do it?

Mr. Jefferson, with that deep sagacity and foresight which distinguished him as a politician, foresaw, predicted, and issued his warning, on the great danger to the country of this introduction of foreigners. He doubted its policy, even when the advantages seemed to be greatest. He says, "The present desire of America, (in 1781,) is to produce rapid population by as great *importations of foreigners* as possible. *But is this founded in policy?*" \* \* \* "Are there no *inconveniences* to be thrown into the scale against the advantage expected from a multiplication of numbers by the importation of foreigners? It is for the happiness of those united in society to harmonize as much as possible in matters which they must of necessity transact together."

\*       \*       \*

What was dimly seen by the prophetic eye of Jefferson, is actually passing under our own eyes. Already have foreigners increased in the country to such a degree, that they justly give us alarm. They feel themselves so strong, as to organize themselves even as *foreigners* into *foreign bands*, and this for the purpose of influencing our elections. . . . That they are men who having *professed* to become Americans, by accepting our terms of naturalization, do yet, in direct contradiction to their professions, clan together as a separate interest, and retain their foreign appellation; that it is with such a separate foreign interest, organizing in the midst of us, that Jesuits in the pay of foreign powers are tampering; that it is this foreign corps of religionists that Americans of both parties have been for years in the habit of basely and traitorously encouraging to erect into an umpire of our political divisions, thus virtually surrendering the government into the hands of Despotic powers. In view of these facts, which every day's experience proves to be facts, is it not time, high time, that a true American spirit were roused to resist this alarming inroad of foreign influence upon our institutions, to avert dangers to which we have hitherto shut our eyes, and which if not remedied, and that immediately, will inevitably change the whole character of our government. I repeat what I first said, this is no party question, it concerns native Americans of all parties.

\*   \*   \*

## Review Questions

1. Why did Morse believe that the massive immigration from Europe was part of a vast conspiracy against the United States?
2. Did he see this conspiracy as primarily religious or political in its means and its ends?
3. Was his conspiracy theory logical and his evidence supportable? In other words, did he prove his case?
4. Did he acknowledge and argue against his opponents or did he simply disparage them as he believed they disparaged nativists?
5. Was he against all immigrants?

# 10 ∽ NATIONALISM AND SECTIONALISM

*As the revolutionary generation was dying off, transitional figures, such as James Monroe and John Quincy Adams, who had entered adulthood during the Revolution, applauded their predecessors even as they set about changing the setting, tempo, and temper of the republic. New generations of Americans reflected and acted on such issues as national history, honor, and improvement.*

*The developing nation had altered much, in form if not in substance. Americans had extended their country's borders, and within those borders they argued over and then implemented internal improvements, such as roads and the development of waterways, to foster prosperity and power. While most, if not all, Americans looked at these transportation networks primarily as commercial necessities, a few leaders also saw them as contributing to the nation's security—they could thus move the military more efficiently to meet threats posed by Indian tribes and foreign nations. As Native American resistance grew, so too did the response of the United States: the Seminoles and Andrew Jackson illustrated the dynamics of this aggression. The nation was also intent on containing British imperial possessions to the north in Canada and pushing Spain off the continent altogether.*

*Territorial and economic growth stimulated the growth of American nationalism. As the Federalist Party disappeared and Republicans adopted and adapted some of its ideas and projects—including a national bank—as their own, some Americans could hope that political partisanship was a thing of the past. That quickly proved to be wishful thinking, for one party could not accommodate all beliefs or all political players. Schisms developed within the party as its leaders jockeyed for power, and the intense rivalry and deal making that marked the election of Adams to the presidency in 1824 split the party. Andrew Jackson stormed out of its ranks and helped create the new Democratic Party, and then went on to win the election of 1828.*

Schisms also developed between sections of the country. There arose new North–South issues that were related to or exacerbated by the rise of the West. The question of Missouri statehood awakened people to the fact that the states had not surmounted all the domestic dangers to their union. The result was that even as citizens celebrated the nation's power, they started to worry about national dissolution.

Sectional sentiments challenged nationalism, but the latter remained strong among the American people. Nationalism also prevailed due to the ideologies and actions of the country's leaders in the executive and judicial branches. Adams and Monroe secured the United States as a continental power and endeavored to extend it as a hemispheric one. Although the United States was not a leading world power, Adams and Monroe were determined to maintain its national honor and autonomy. John Marshall, the Chief Justice of the Supreme Court, was just as determined to preserve the power of the national government from encroachments by the states.

## ANDREW JACKSON

# Report of Florida Expedition (1818)

*What became known as the First Seminole War began at the end of 1817 when American forces and Native Americans clashed as each tried to secure their interests in the area where Florida and the southwestern tip of Georgia meet. Each attacked the other. Then, after the Native Americans killed most of a group (which included some soldiers' wives) traveling up the Apalachicola River to get to Fort Scott across the Georgia border, Secretary of War John C. Calhoun ordered General Andrew Jackson to campaign against the Seminoles. Calhoun authorized Jackson to pursue the Seminoles into Spanish territory but did not give him orders to attack Spanish-held posts in the process. Jackson asked for President Monroe's permission to seize such posts to secure the area. Supposedly, according to Jackson, he received word—though cryptically and through unofficial channels—to do so. He seized St. Mark's on 7 April and then moved on to take Pensacola on 24 May.*

From John Spencer Bassett, ed., *Correspondence of Andrew Jackson*, vol. 2 (1927; reprint, New York: Kraus Reprint Co., 1969), pp. 365–68. [Editorial insertions appear in square brackets—*Ed.*]

## To Secretary Calhoun.

FORT GADSDEN [at the ruins of the "Negro Fort," which Jackson had ordered destroyed in 1816, on the Apalachicola River], May 5, 1818.

*Sir.* I returned to this post with my Army on the evening of the 2d instant, and embrace an early opportunity of furnishing you a detailed report of my operations to the east of the Apalachacola river. . . . This has been principally a war of movements; The Enemy cut off from their strong holds, or deceived in the promised foreign aid have uniformly avoided a general engagement. Their resistance has generally been feeble, and in the partial rencounters into which they seem to have been involuntarily forced; The Regulars, Volunteers, and militia under my command realised my expectations; Every privation, fatigue, and exposure was encountered with the spirit of soldiers, and danger was met with a degree of fortitude calculated to strengthen the confidence I had reposed in them.

On the commencement of my operations I was strongly impressed with a belief that this Indian War had been excited by some unprincipled Foreign, or private agents. The outlaws of the old red stick party [a group of Creek warriors who had fought to restore the traditional Creek way of life in 1813–1814 and who had fought American forces over land] had been too severely convinced, and the Seminoles were too weak in numbers to believe, that they could possibly alone maintain a war with even partial success against the United States. Firmly convinced therefore that succor had been promised from some quarter, or that they had been deluded into a belief that America dare not violate the neutrality of spain by penetrating to their Towns, I early determined to ascertain these facts, and so direct my movements as to undeceive the Indians. After the destruction of the Mekasukian [Mikasuki or Miccosukee] villages I marched direct for St Marks: The correspondence between myself and the Spanish Commandant in which I demanded the occupancy of that Fortress with an American Garrison, accompanies this. It had been reported to me direct from the Governor of Pensacola that the Indians and Negroes [those included runaway slaves and Black Seminoles] unfriendly to the United States, had demanded of the commandant of st Marks a supply of ammunition, munitions of war etc, threatning in the event of a non compliance to take possession of the Fort. The Spanish Commandant acknowledged the defenceless state of his fortress and his inability to defend it: and the Governor of Pensacola expressed similar apprehensions. The Spanish Agents throughout the Floridas had uniformly disavowed having any connection with the Indians, and acknowledged the obligations of his catholic Majesty under existing treaties to restrain their outrages against the citisens of the United States. Indeed they declared that the Seminole Indians were viewed as alike hostile to the spanish government, and that the will remained, though the power was wanting to inflict merited chastisement on this lawless Tribe. It was therefore to be supposed that the American Army impelled by the immutable laws of self defence to penetrate the territory of his Catholic Majesty, to fight his battles, and even to relieve from a cruel bondage some of his own subjects, would have been received as allies, hailed as deliverers, and every facility afforded to them to terminate speedily and successfully this savage war. Fort St Marks could not be maintained by the Spanish force garrisoning it. The Indians and Negroes viewed it as an asylum if driven from their Towns, and were preparing to occupy it in this event. It was necessary to anticipate their movements, independant of the position being deemed essential as a depot on which the success of my future operations measur[ab]ly depended. In the spirit of Friendship therefore I demanded its surrender to the Army of the u states untill the close of the seminole war. The Spanish Commandant required time to reflect, it was granted; a negotiation ensued, and an effort made to protract it to an unreasonable length. In the conversation between my Aid de camp Lt Gadsden and the Spanish Commandant circumstances transpired convicting him of a disposition to favour the Indians, and of having taken an active part in aiding and abetting them in this war. I hesitated therefore no longer, and as I could not be received in friendship, I entered the Fort by violence. Two light companies of the 7th Regt Infantry and one of the 4th under the command of Major Twigs was ordered to advance, lower the spanish colors, and hoist the star spangled banner on the ramparts of Fort St Marks. The order was executed promptly, no resistance attempted on the part of the Spanish garrison.

The duplicity of the Spanish Commandant of St Marks in professing friendship towards the United States while he was actually aiding and supplying her savage enemies; Throwing open the gates of his garrison to their free access, Appropriating the King's stores to their use, issuing amunition and munition of war to them, and knowingly purchasing of them property plundered from the Citisens of the U States is clearly evinced by the documents accompanying my correspondence.

In Fort St Marks as an inmate in the family of the Spanish Commandant an Englishman by the name of Abuthnot was found. Unable satisfactorily to explain the objects of his visiting this country, and their being a combination of circumstances to justify a suspicion that his views were not honest, he was ordered in close confinement. The capture of his Schooner near the mouth of Suwaney river by my aid de camp Mr Gadsden, and the papers found on board unvailed his corrupt transactions as well as those of a Capt Armbrister, late of the British Colonial marine Corps, taken as a prisoner near Bowlegs Town [town of King Bowlegs on Suwanee River]. These Individuals were tried under my orders by a special Court of select officers, legally convicted as exciters of this savage and negro War, legally condemned, and most justly punished for their iniquities. The proceedings of the Court martial in this case, with the volume of Testimony justifying their condemnation, presents scenes of wickedness, corruption, and barbarity at which the heart sickens and in which in this enlightened age it ought not scarcely to be believed that a christian nation would have participated, and yet the British government is involved in the agency. If Arbuthnot and Armbrister are not convicted as the Authorised Agents of Great Britain there is no room to doubt but that that Government had a knowledge of their assumed character, and was well advised of the measures which they had adopted to excite the negroes and Indians in East Florida to war against the U States. I hope the execution of these two unprincipled villains [Alexander Arbuthnot was hanged and Robert Ambrister shot on 29 April] will prove an awful example to the world, and convince the Government of Great Britain as well as her subjects that certain, if slow retribution awaits those uncristian wretches who by false promises delude and excite a Indian tribe to all the horrid deeds of savage war.

. . . It has been stated that the Indians at war with the U States have free access into Pensacola; That they are kept advised from that quarter of all our movements; that they are supplied from thence with amunition and munitions of war, and that they are now collecting in large bodies to the amount of 4 or 500 warriors in that city; That inroads from thence have lately been made on the alabama, in one of which 18 setlers fell by the tomahawk.

These statements compell me to make a movement to the West of the Apalachacola and should they prove correct Pensacola must be occupied with an American force, The Governor treated according to his deserts or as policy may dictate. I shall leave strong garrisons in Fort St Marks, Fort Gadsden, and Fort Scott, and in Pensacola should it become necessary to possess it. It becomes my duty to state it as my confirmed opinion, that so long as Spain has not the power, or will to enforce the treaties by which she is solemnly bound to preserve the Indians within her territory at peace with the U States, no security can be given to our Southern frontier without occupying a cordon of Posts along the Sea Shore. The moment the American Army retires from Florida, The War hatchet will be again raised, and the same scenes of indiscriminate murder with which our frontier setlers have been visited, will be repeated. So long as the Indians within the territory of spain are exposed to the delusions of false prophets, and the poison of foreign intrigue; so long as they can receive amunition, munitions of war etc from pretended Traders, or Spanish commandants it will be impossible to restrain their outrages. The burning of their Towns, the destroying of their stock and provisions will produce but temporary embarrassments, resupplied by spanish authorities they may concentrate, or disperse at will, and keep up a lasting predatory warfare against the Frontiers of the U States, as expensive as harrassing to her Troops. The Savages therefore must be made dependant on us, and cannot be kept at peace without [being] persuaded of the certainty of chastisement being inflicted on the commission of the first offence.

I trust therefore that the measures which have been persued will meet with the approbation of the President of the U States. They have been adopted in pursuance of your instructions, under a firm conviction that they alone were calculated to ensure "Peace and security to the southern frontier of Georgia." . . .

# REVIEW QUESTIONS

1. Why did Jackson believe he was justified in attacking Spanish fortifications?
2. Why did he believe that the responses of Spanish officials to his demands warranted his subsequent actions?
3. How does he explain the actions taken against two British subjects, Arbuthnot and Ambrister, found in the area?
4. What does this report reveal about Jackson as a military commander, instrument of United States policy, and, perhaps, representative of American public sentiment?

# John Quincy Adams

# Observations on Jackson and the Spanish Florida Situation (1818–19)

*When President Monroe made John Quincy Adams his secretary of state, Adams had long been engaged in diplomacy to good effect for his country: he had been part of the commission that negotiated the Treaty of Ghent that ended the War of 1812, and he had represented the United States in the Netherlands, Prussia, Russia, and Great Britain. Adams had also served in the Senate, the legislative branch with the duty to advise the president on treaties and ambassadors. His heritage, education, and experience molded his perceptions and policies to the point that he generally—the issue of slavery would later test him on this—put nation before section or state. He believed that the United States should have dominion over the North American continent and labored to that end. As secretary of state he negotiated the Convention of 1818 with the British, establishing, among other things, boundary and fishing rights as well as the Transcontinental Treaty of 1819 with Spain (also called the Adams-Onís Treaty). Adams was also a major influence in the creation of what has become known as the Monroe Doctrine. He was able to expand American property and power because of a growing American population, economy, and militarism. The last was seen in the actions of, and popular reactions to (especially in the South and West), General Jackson's campaign against the Seminoles.*

From Allan Nevins, ed., *The Diary of John Quincy Adams, 1794–1845* (1928; New York: Charles Scribner's Sons, 1951), pp. 196–201. [Editorial insertions appear in brackets—*Ed.*]

\*     \*     \*

*May.* 4. [1818]—The President sent me word this morning that he had returned from his short tour to Virginia. When I called at his house, I found there Mr. Calhoun and Mr. Crowninshield: Mr. Crawford came in shortly afterwards. The dispatches from General Jackson were just received, containing the account of his progress in the war against the Seminole Indians, and his having taken the Spanish fort of St. Mark's, in Florida, where they had taken refuge. They hung some of the Indian prisoners, as it appears, without due regard to humanity. A Scotchman by the name of Arbuthnot was found among them, and Jackson appears half inclined to take his life. Crawford some time ago proposed to send Jackson an order to give no quarter to any white man found with the Indians. I objected to it then, and this day avowed that I was not prepared for such a mode of warfare.

\*     \*     \*

*June 9.*—We spent the evening at the French Minister Hyde de Neuville's, a small musical party. Mr. Bagot [British minister Sir Charles Bagot] spoke to me of certain publications in the newspapers, mentioning the execution by sentences of court-martial, under the orders of General Jackson, of two Englishmen, named Arbuthnot and Ambrister, taken with the Seminole Indians in this war. These publications say that the evidence against them proved the greatest perfidy on the part of the British Government. Mr. Bagot was very much hurt by this charge of perfidy, for which he said there was not the slightest foundation.

*June* 18.—The President spoke of the taking of Pensacola by General Jackson, contrary to his orders, and, as it is now reported, by storm. This, and other events in this Indian war, makes many difficulties for the Administration.

*    *    *

*July* 10.—Had an interview at the office with Hyde de Neuville, the French Minister—all upon our affairs with Spain. He says that Spain will cede the Floridas to the United States, and let the lands go for the indemnities due to our citizens, and he urged that we should take the Sabine for the western boundary, which I told him was impossible. He urged this subject very strenuously for more than an hour. As to Onis's [Spanish minister Luís de Onís y Gonzales] note of invective against General Jackson, which I told him as a good friend to Onis he should advise him to take back, he said I need not answer it for a month or two, perhaps not at all, if in the meantime we could come to an arrangement of the other differences.

*July* 15.—Attended the Cabinet meeting at the President's, from noon till five o'clock. The subject of deliberation was General Jackson's late transactions in Florida, particularly the taking of Pensacola. The President and all the members of the Cabinet, except myself, are of opinion that Jackson acted not only without, but against, his instructions: that he has committed war upon Spain, which cannot be justified, and in which, if not disavowed by the Administration, they will be abandoned by the country. My opinion is that there was no real, though an apparent, violation of his instructions: that his proceedings were justified by the necessity of the case, and by the misconduct of the Spanish commanding officers in Florida. The question is embarrassing and complicated, not only as involving that of an actual war with Spain, but that of the Executive power to authorize hostilities without a declaration of war by Congress. There is no doubt that defensive acts of hostility may be authorized by the Executive; but Jackson was authorized to cross the Spanish line in pursuit of the Indian enemy . . . [.]

Calhoun, the Secretary at War, generally of sound, judicious, and comprehensive mind, seems in this case to be personally offended with the idea that Jackson has set at nought the instructions of the Department. The President supposes there might be cases which would have justified Jackson's measures, but that he has not made out his case.

*July* 16.—Second cabinet meeting at the President's, and the question of the course to be pursued with relation to General Jackson's proceedings in Florida recurred. As the opinion is unanimously against Jackson excepting mine, my range of argument now is only upon the degree to which his acts are to be disavowed. It was urged that the public dissatisfaction at the taking of Pensacola is so great that the Administration must immediately and publicly disclaim having given any authority for it, and publish all the instructions given to him to throw the blame entirely upon him.

*July* 17.—Cabinet meeting at the President's— the discussion continued upon the answer to be given to Onis, and the restoration of Florida to Spain. The weakness and palsy of my right hand make it impossible for me to report this discussion, in which I continue to oppose the unanimous opinions of the President, the Secretary of the Treasury Crawford, the Secretary of War Calhoun, and the Attorney-General Wirt. I have thought that the whole conduct of General Jackson was justifiable under his orders, although he certainly had none to take any Spanish fort. My principle is that everything he did was defensive; that as such it was neither war against Spain nor violation of the Constitution.

*July* 21.—A Cabinet meeting, at which the second draft of my letter to Mr. Onis was read and finally fixed. Mr. Wirt read what he called a second edition of his article for the *National Intelligencer*. I strenuously re-urged my objections, especially to a paragraph declaring that the President thought he had no constitutional power to have authorized General Jackson to take Pensacola . . . [.] I finally gave up the debate, acquiescing in the determination which had been taken. The Administration were placed in a dilemma from which it is impossible for them to escape censure by some, and factious crimination by many. If they avow and approve Jackson's conduct, they incur the double responsibility of having commenced a war against Spain, and of warring in violation of the Constitution without the authority of Congress. If they disavow him, they must give offence to all his friends, encounter the shock of his popularity, and have the appearance of truckling to Spain. For all this I should be prepared. But the mischief of this determination lies deeper: 1. It is weakness, and confession of weakness. 2. The disclaimer of power in the Executive is of dangerous example and of evil consequences. 3. There is injustice to the officer in disavowing him, when in principle he is strictly justifiable . . . [.]

Calhoun says he has heard that the court martial at first acquitted the two Englishmen, but that Jackson sent the case back to them. He says, also, that last winter there was a company formed in Tennessee, who sent Jackson's nephew to Pensacola and purchased Florida lands, and that Jackson himself is reported to be interested in the speculation. I hope not.

\*     \*     \*

*January* 23. [1819]—As I was going to the President's, General Jackson and his suite were going out. The President called him and Colonel Butler back, and introduced them to me. The General arrived this morning from his residence at Nashville, Tennessee, and had already called at my office. Among the rumors which have been circulated by the cabal now intriguing in Congress against Jack-

son, it has been very industriously whispered that Mr. Jefferson and Mr. Madison had declared themselves in very strong terms against him. I had mentioned this report a few days since to the President, who told me that he was convinced there was no foundation for it. This morning he showed me in confidence a letter he had just received from Mr. Jefferson. It not only expresses full satisfaction with the course pursued by the Administration, but mentions my letters of 12th March last to Onis, and of 28th November to Erving, in terms which it would not become me to repeat. He advises that they, with others of my letters to Onis, should be translated into French and communicated to every Government in Europe, as a thorough vindication of the conduct and policy of this Government.

\*     \*     \*

*February* 3.—General Jackson came to my house this morning, and I showed him the boundary line which has been offered to the Spanish Minister, and that which we proposed to offer upon Melish's map. He said there were many individuals who would take exception to our receding so far from the boundary of the Rio del Norte, which we claim, as the Sabine, and the enemies of the Administration would certainly make a handle of it to assail them: but the possession of the Floridas was of so great importance to the southern frontier of the United States, and so essential even to their safety, that the vast majority of the nation would be satisfied with the western boundary as we propose, if we obtain the Floridas. He showed me on the map the operations of the British force during the late war, and remarked that while the mouths of the Florida rivers should be accessible to a foreign naval force there would be no security for the United States.

He also entered into conversation upon the subject of discussion now pending in the House of Representatives on his proceedings in the late Seminole War, upon that which is preparing in the Senate under the auspices of Mr. Forsyth, of Georgia, and upon the general order given by Jackson in

1817, which was considered as setting at defiance the War Department. He imputed the whole to Mr. Crawford's resentments against him on account of his having at the last Presidential election supported Mr. Monroe against him; said there was not a single officer in the army known to have been at that time in favor of Monroe whom Crawford had not since insulted: that Mr. Monroe was of an open, fair, unsuspecting character, amiable in the highest degree, and would not believe human nature capable of the baseness which Crawford, while holding a confidential office under him, was practising against him.

I told Jackson that Mr. Crawford had never in any of the discussions on the Seminole War said a word which led me to suppose he had any hostile feeling against him. He replied that, however that might be, Crawford was now setting the whole delegation of Georgia against him, and by intentional insult and the grossest violation of all military principle had compelled him to issue the order of 1817. Crawford, he said, was a man restrained by no principle, and capable of any baseness . . . [.] Crawford was now canvassing for the next Presidential election, and actually wrote a letter to Clay proposing a coalition with him to overthrow Mr. Monroe's Administration.

That Crawford has written such a letter to Clay as Jackson has informed, is to the last degree improbable. He has too much discretion to have put himself so much in Clay's power. But that all his conduct is governed by his views to the Presidency, as the immediate successor to Mr. Monroe, and that his hopes depend upon a result unfavorable to the success, or at least to the popularity of the Administration, is perfectly clear. The important and critical interests of the country are those the management of which belongs to the Department of State. Those incidental to the Treasury are in a state which would give an able financier an opportunity to display his talents: but Crawford has no talents as a financier. He is just, and barely, equal to the current routine of the business of his office. His talent is intrigue. And as it is in the foreign affairs that the success or failure of the Administration

will be most conspicuous, and as their success would promote the reputation and influence, and their failure would lead to the disgrace, of the Secretary of State, Crawford's personal views centre in the ill success of the Administration in its foreign relations; and, perhaps unconscious of his own motives, he will always be impelled to throw obstacles in its way, and to bring upon the Department of State especially any feeling of public dissatisfaction that he can.

\*     \*     \*

*Feb.* 22.—Mr. Onis came at eleven, with Mr. Stoughton, one of the persons attached to his Legation. The two copies of the treaty made out at his house were ready: none of ours were entirely finished. We exchanged the original full powers on both sides, which I believe to be the correct course on the conclusion of treaties, though at Ghent, and on the conclusion of the Convention of 3d July, 1815, the originals were only exhibited and copies exchanged. I had one of the copies of the treaty, and Mr. Onis the other. I read the English side, which he collated, and he the Spanish side, which I collated. We then signed and sealed both copies on both sides—I first on the English and he first on the Spanish side . . . [.]

The acquisition of the Floridas has long been an object of earnest desire to this country. The acknowledgment of a definite line of boundary to the South Sea forms a great epoch in our history. The first proposal of it in this negotiation was my own, and I trust it is now secured beyond the reach of revocation. It was not even among our claims by the Treaty of Independence with Great Britain. It was not among our pretensions under the purchase of Louisiana—for that gave us only the range of the Mississippi and its waters. I first introduced it in the written proposal of 31st October last, after having discussed it verbally both with Onis and De Neuville. It is the only peculiar and appropriate right acquired by this treaty in the event of its ratification.

\*     \*     \*

## REVIEW QUESTIONS

1. Why did Jackson's actions create difficulties for Monroe's administration?
2. Did Adams approve or disapprove of Jackson's actions? Why?
3. Does it appear that Jackson's actions helped or hindered Adams in his negotiations with Spain?
4. Did Adams have to worry about domestic politics when implementing his foreign policy? Explain.

## JOHN QUINCY ADAMS

# Reflections on the Missouri Question (1820)

*The nation wrestled not only with matters of state but with matters within the states as well. The question of Missouri's admittance to the union had "excited feelings & raised difficulties, of an internal nature, which did not exist before." Actually the difficulties—those concerning the extension of slavery, the corresponding expansion of slaveholder power, and the respective rights of the people, states, and Congress—were not totally new, but while they had been subdued in the "Era of Good Feelings," they now burst forth in greater vigor and viciousness. The debate began in early 1819 when there were enough people in the territory around and including the town of St. Louis to constitute a new state. Considering how the nation had celebrated the admittance of each new state up to this time as a confirmation of America's power and prosperity, there should not have been a problem. One developed, however, when Representative James Tallmadge Jr. of New York proposed that Congress make a prohibition on the future importation of slaves into the area and introduce a system of gradual manumission as a condition of admission. Slaveowners in Missouri and elsewhere countered by arguing that Congress did not have the right to so restrict a state's power and an individual's right to control his property. John Quincy Adams, because of personal inclination as well as his professional responsibility to advise the president, observed and commented on the "Missouri question" as Congress and country debated the issue for over a year.*

From Allan Nevins, ed., *The Diary of John Quincy Adams, 1794–1845* (1928. New York: Charles Scribner's Sons, 1951), pp. 225–32. [Editorial insertions appear in square brackets—*Ed.*]

\*    \*    \*

*Jan. 24.*—I walked with R. M. Johnson to the Senate chamber and heard Mr. Pinkney close his Missouri speech. There was a great crowd of auditors. Many ladies, among whom several seated on the floor of the Senate. His eloquence was said to be less overpowering than it had been last Friday. His language is good, his fluency without interruption or hesitation, his manner impressive, but his argument weak, from the inherent weakness of his cause.

*Feb.* 11.—I went up to the Capitol and heard Mr. King in the Senate, upon what is called the Missouri question. He had been speaking perhaps an hour before I went in, and I heard him about an hour. His manner is dignified, grave, earnest, but not rapid or vehement. There was nothing new in his argument, but he unravelled with ingenious and subtle analysis many of the sophistical tissues of the slave-holders. He laid down the position of the natural liberty of man, and its incompatibility with slavery in any shape. He also questioned the Constitutional right of the President and Senate to make the Louisiana Treaty; but he did not dwell upon those points, nor draw the consequences from them which I should think important in speaking to that subject. He spoke, however, with great power, and the great slaveholders in the House gnawed their lips and clenched their fists as they heard him. . . . We attended an evening party at Mr. Calhoun's, and heard of nothing but the Missouri question and Mr. King's speeches. The slave-holders cannot hear of them without being seized with cramps. They call them seditious and inflammatory, when their greatest real defect is their timidity. Never since human sentiments and human conduct were influenced by human speech was there a theme for eloquence like the free side of this question now before Congress of this Union. By what fatality does it happen that all the most eloquent orators of the body are on its slav-ish side? There is a great mass of cool judgment and plain sense on the side of freedom and hu-manity, but the ardent spirits and passions are on the side of oppression. Oh, if but one man could arise with a genius capable of comprehending, a heart capable of supporting, and an utterance ca-pable of communicating those eternal truths that belong to this question, to lay bare in all its naked-ness that outrage upon the goodness of God, hu-man slavery, now is the time, and this is the occasion, upon which such a man would perform the duties of an angel upon earth!

*Feb.* 13.—Attended the divine service at the Capitol, and heard Mr. Edward Everett, the Professor of the Greek language at Harvard University, a young man of shining talents and of illustrious promise. His text was from I Cor. vii. 29: "Brethren, the time is short," and it was without comparison the most splendid composition as a sermon that I ever heard delivered. . . . Mr. Clay, with whom I walked, after the service, to call upon Chief-Justice Marshall, told me that although Everett had a fine fancy and a chaste style of composition, his manner was too theatrical, and he liked Mr. Holley's manner better.

Clay started, however, immediately to the Mis-souri question, yet in debate before both Houses of Congress, and, alluding to a strange scene at Rich-mond, Virginia, last Wednesday evening, said it was a shocking thing to think of, but he had not a doubt that within five years from this time the Union would be divided into three distinct con-federacies. I did not incline to discuss the subject with him. We found Judges Livingston and Story with the Chief Justice.

\*       \*       \*

*February* 23.—A. Livermore and W. Plumer, Junr, members of the House of Representatives from New Hampshire, called upon me, and, conversing on the Missouri slave question, which at this time agitates Congress and the Nation, asked my opin-ion of the propriety of agreeing to a compromise. The division in Congress and the nation is nearly equal on both sides. The argument on the free side is, the moral and political duty of preventing the extension of slavery in the immense country from the Mississippi River to the South Sea. The argu-ment on the slave side is, that Congress have no power by the Constitution to prohibit slavery in any State, and, the zealots say, not in any Territory. The proposed compromise is to admit Missouri, and hereafter Arkansas, as States, without any re-striction upon them regarding slavery, but to pro-hibit the future introduction of slaves in all Territories of the United States north of 36° 30' latitude. I told these gentlemen that my opinion was, the question could be settled no otherwise than by a compromise.

*Feb.* 24.—I had some conversation with Cal-houn on the slave question pending in Congress.

He said he did not think it would produce a dissolution of the Union, but, if it should, the South would be from necessity compelled to form an alliance, offensive and defensive, with Great Britain.

I said that would be returning to the colonial state.

He said, yes, pretty much, but it would be forced upon them. I asked him whether he thought, if by the effect of this alliance, offensive and defensive, the population of the North should be cut off from its natural outlet upon the ocean, it would fall back upon its rocks bound hand and foot, to starve, or whether it would not retain its powers of locomotion to move southward by land. Then, he said, they would find it necessary to make their communities all military. I pressed the conversation no further: but if the dissolution of the Union should result from the slave question, it is as obvious as anything that can be foreseen of futurity, that it must shortly afterwards be followed by the universal emancipation of the slaves. A more remote but perhaps not less certain consequence would be the extirpation of the African race on this continent, by the gradually bleaching process of intermixture, where the white portion is already so predominant, and by the destructive progress of emancipation, which, like all great religious and political reformations, is terrible in its means though happy and glorious in its end. Slavery is the great and foul stain upon the North American Union, and it is a contemplation worthy of the most exalted soul whether its total abolition is or is not practicable: if practicable, by what it may be effected, and if a choice of means be within the scope of the object, what means would accomplish it at the smallest cost of human suffering. A dissolution, at least temporary, of the Union, as now constituted, would be certainly necessary . . . [.] The Union might then be reorganized on the fundamental principle of emancipation. This object is vast in its compass, awful in its prospects, sublime and beautiful in its issue.

\*       \*       \*

*Washington, March 2, 1820.*—The compromise of the slave question was this day completed in Con-gress. The Senate have carried their whole point, barely consenting to the formality of separating the bill for the admission of the State of Maine into the Union from that for authorizing the people of the Territory of Missouri to form a State Government. The condition that slavery should be prohibited by their Constitution, which the House of Representatives had inserted, they have abandoned. Missouri and Arkansas will be slave States, but to the Missouri bill a section is annexed, prohibiting slavery in the remaining part of the Louisiana cession north of latitude 36° 30'. This compromise, as it is called, was finally carried this evening by a vote of ninety to eighty-seven in the House of Representatives, after successive days and almost nights of stormy debate.

*March* 3.—When I came this day to my office, I found there a note requesting me to call at one o'clock at the President's house. It was then one, and I immediately went over. He expected that the two bills, for the admission of Maine, and to enable Missouri to make a Constitution, would have been brought to him for his signature, and he had summoned all the members of the Administration to ask their opinions in writing, to be deposited in the Department of State, upon two questions: 1, Whether Congress had a Constitutional right to prohibit slavery in a Territory: and 2, Whether the eighth section of the Missouri bill (which interdicts slavery forever in the Territory north of thirty-six and a half latitude) was applicable only to the Territorial State, or could extend to it after it should become a State.

As to the first question, it was unanimously agreed that Congress have the power to prohibit slavery in the Territories . . . [.] I had no doubt of the right of Congress to interdict slavery in the Territories, and urged that the power contained in the term "dispose of" included the authority to do everything that could be done with it as mere property, and that the additional words, authorizing needful rules and regulations respecting it, must have reference to persons connected with it, or could have no meaning at all. As to the force of the term needful, I observed, it was relative, and must always be supposed to have reference to some end. Needful to what end? Needful in the Constitution of the United States to any of the ends for which that compact was formed. Those ends are declared in its preamble: to establish justice, for example. What can be more needful for the establishment of justice than the interdiction of slavery where it does not exist? . . [.]

After this meeting, I walked home with Calhoun, who said that the principles which I had avowed were just and noble: but that in the Southern country, whenever they were mentioned, they were always understood as applying only to white men. Domestic labor was confined to the blacks, and such was the prejudice, that if he, who was the most popular man in his district, were to keep a white servant in his house, his character and reputation would be irretrievably ruined.

I said that this confounding of the ideas of servitude and labor was one of the bad effects of slavery: but he thought it attended with many excellent consequences. It did not apply to all kinds of labor—not, for example, to farming. He himself had often held the plough: so had his father. Manufacturing and mechanical labor was not degrading. It was only manual labor—the proper work of slaves. No white person could descend to that. And it was the best guarantee to equality among the whites. It produced an unvarying level among them. It not only did not excite, but did not even admit of inequalities, by which one white man could domineer over another.

I told Calhoun I could not see things in the same light. It is, in truth, all perverted sentiment—mistaking labor for slavery and dominion for freedom. The discussion of this Missouri question has betrayed the secret of their souls. In the abstract they admit that slavery is an evil, they disclaim all participation in the introduction of it, and cast it all upon the shoulders of our old Grandam Britain. But when probed to the quick upon it, they show at the bottom of their souls pride and vainglory in their condition of masterdom. They fancy themselves more generous and noble-hearted than the plain freemen who labor for subsistence. They look down upon the simplicity of a Yankee's manners, because he has no habits of overbearing like theirs and cannot treat negroes like dogs. It is among the evils of slavery that it taints the very sources of moral principle. It establishes false estimates of virtue and vice: for what can be more false and heartless than this doctrine which makes the first and holiest rights of humanity to depend upon the color of the skin? . . [.]

I have favored this Missouri compromise, believing it to be all that could be effected under the present Constitution, and from extreme unwillingness to put the Union at hazard. But perhaps it would have been a wiser as well as a bolder course to have persisted in the restriction upon Missouri, till it should have terminated in a convention of the States to revise and amend the Constitution. This would have produced a new Union of thirteen or fourteen States unpolluted with slavery, with a great and glorious object to effect, namely, that of rallying to their standard the other States by the universal emancipation of their slaves. If the Union must be dissolved, slavery is precisely the question upon which it ought to break. For the present, however, this contest i[s] laid asleep.

\*    \*    \*

# REVIEW QUESTIONS

1. Why did the question of Missouri statehood provoke such a crisis? What were the moral and constitutional issues involved?
2. What appeared to have the most weight with the politicians? Does this issue appear to have affected the nature of the compromise?
3. What was Adams's position on the problem and the compromise?
4. Do these entries reveal Adams to be a believer in strict or loose construction of the Constitution? What do they reveal about Monroe?

# DAVID WALKER

# *Appeal to the Coloured Citizens of the World* (1829)

*The Missouri Compromise of 1820 paved the way for the admission of Missouri as a slave state in 1821, but by the end of the decade a growing number of reformers started to campaign against further compromises with slavery. David Walker was one of the most radical of those activists. Walker had been born out of slavery to a free black woman in North Carolina, but he saw and felt the effects of slavery and discrimination in his travels. He eventually settled in Boston where he had a small used-clothing shop and where he contributed to and distributed* Freedom's Journal, *a newspaper started by African Americans in New York City in 1827. Walker also lectured to Boston audiences promoting abolition and denouncing the colonization of free blacks to Africa. Ultimately he decided that he needed to reach larger audiences and, in particular, that he needed to reach the slaves of the South. He published the first edition of his* Appeal *in the fall of 1829 and then added material to a second and finally a third edition (excerpted here) that was published in June 1830, shortly before he died. Some sailors who bought his clothing goods and then traded them in the South smuggled the* Appeal *into southern ports (pages were sewn into their clothes). The* Appeal *energized antislavery activists, although most deplored its call to slaves to take extreme, even violent, measures. It enraged proslavery advocates and contributed to the passage of more repressive slave laws in many southern states.*

From *David Walker's Appeal . . . To the Coloured Citizens of the World*, edited with an introduction by Charles M. Wiltse (New York: Hill and Wang, 1965), pp. 7-8, 13–14, 16, 21–22, 26–28, 30–31. [Editorial insertions appear in brackets—*Ed.*]

## Article I.

### *Our Wretchedness in Consequence of Slavery.*

My beloved brethren:—The Indians of North and of South America—the Greeks—the Irish, subjected under the king of Great Britain—the Jews, that ancient people of the Lord—the inhabitants of the islands of the sea—in fine, all the inhabitants of the earth, (except however, the sons of Africa) are called *men*, and of course are, and ought to be free. But we, (coloured people) and our children are *brutes!!* and of course are, and *ought to be* SLAVES to the American people and their children forever! ! to dig their mines and work their farms; and thus go on enriching them, from one generation to another with our *blood* and our *tears! ! ! !*

I promised in a preceding page to demonstrate to the satisfaction of the most incredulous, that we, (coloured people of these United States of America) are the *most wretched, degraded* and *abject* set of beings that *ever lived* since the world began, and that the white Americans having reduced us to the wretched state of *slavery,* treat us in that condition *more cruel* (they being an enlightened and Christian people,) than any heathen nation did any people whom it had reduced to our condition. . . .

\*      \*      \*

Now I appeal to heaven and to earth, and particularly to the American people themselves, who cease not to declare that our condition is not *hard,* and that we are comparatively satisfied to rest in wretchedness and misery, under them and their children. Not, indeed, to show me a coloured President, a Governor, a Legislator, a Senator, a Mayor, or an Attorney at the Bar.—But to show me a man of colour, who holds the low office of a Constable, or one who sits in a Juror Box, even on a case of one of his wretched brethren, throughout this great Republic!! . . .

\*      \*      \*

The sufferings of the Helots among the Spartans, were somewhat severe, it is true, but to say that theirs, were as severe as ours among the Americans, I do most strenuously deny—for instance, can any man show me an article on a page of ancient history which specifies, that, the Spartans chained, and handcuffed the Helots, and dragged them from their wives and children, children from their parents, mothers from their suckling babes, wives from their husbands, driving them from one end of the country to the other? Notice the Spartans were heathens, who lived long before our Divine Master made his appearance in the flesh. Can  Christian Americans deny these barbarous cruelties? Have you not, Americans, having subjected us under you, added to these miseries, by insulting us in telling us to our face, because we are helpless, that we are not of the human family? I ask you, O! Americans, I ask you, in the name of the Lord, can you deny these charges? Some perhaps may deny, by saying, that they never thought or said that we were not men. But do not actions speak louder than words?—have they not made provisions for the Greeks, and Irish? Nations who have never done the least thing for them, while *we,* who have enriched their country with our blood and tears—have dug up gold and silver for them and

their children, from generation to generation, and are in more miseries than any other people under heaven, are not seen, but by comparatively, a handful of the American people? . . .

I have been for years troubling the pages of historians, to find out what our fathers have done to the *white Christians of America,* to merit such condign punishment as they have inflicted on them, and do continue to inflict on us their children. But I must aver, that my researches have hitherto been to no effect. I have therefore, come to the immoveable conclusion, that they (Americans) have, and do continue to punish us for nothing else, but for enriching them and their country. For I cannot conceive of anything else. Nor will I ever believe otherwise, until the Lord shall convince me.

The world knows, that slavery as it existed among the Romans, (which was the primary cause of their destruction) was, comparatively speaking, no more than a *cypher,* when compared with ours under the Americans. Indeed I should not have noticed the Roman slaves, had not the very learned and penetrating Mr. Jefferson said, "when a master was murdered, all his slaves in the same house, or within hearing, were condemned to death" [in *Notes on the State of Virginia* "Query XIV".]—Here let me ask Mr. Jefferson, (but he is gone to answer at the bar of God, for the deeds done in his body while living,) I therefore ask the whole American people, had I not rather die, or be put to death, than to be a slave to any tyrant, who takes not only my own, but my wife and children's lives by the inches? Yea, would I meet death with avidity far! far! ! in preference to such *servile submission* to the murderous hands of tyrants. . . .

\*      \*      \*

. . . Every body who has read history, knows, that as soon as a slave among the Romans obtained his freedom, he could rise to the greatest eminence in the State, and there was no law instituted to hinder a slave from buying his freedom. Have not the Americans instituted laws to hinder us from obtaining our freedom? Do any deny this charge? Read the laws of Virginia, North Carolina, &c. Further: have not the Americans instituted laws to prohibit a man of colour from obtaining and holding any office whatever, under the government of the United States of America? Now, Mr. Jefferson tells us, that our condition is not so hard, as the slaves were under the Romans! ! ! ! ! !

It is time for me to bring this article to a close. But before I close it, I must observe to my brethren that at the close of the first Revolution in this country, with Great Britain, there were but thirteen States in the Union, now there are twenty-four, most of which are slave-holding States, and the whites are dragging us around in chains and in handcuffs, to their new States and Territories to work their mines and farms, to enrich them and their children—and millions of them believing firmly that we being a little darker than they, were made by our Creator to be an inheritance to them and their children for ever—the same as a parcel of *brutes*.

Are we MEN! !—I ask you, O my brethren! are we MEN? Did our Creator make us to be slaves to dust and ashes like ourselves? Are they not dying worms as well as we? Have they not to make their appearance before the tribunal of Heaven, to answer for the deeds done in the body, as well as we? . . .

# Article II.

## *Our Wretchedness in Consequence of Ignorance.*

Ignorance and treachery one against the other—a grovelling servile and abject submission to the lash of tyrants, we see plainly, my brethren, are not the natural elements of the blacks, as the Americans try to make us believe; but these are misfortunes which God has suffered our fathers to be enveloped in for many ages, no doubt in consequence of their disobedience to their Maker, and which do, indeed, reign at this time among us, almost to the destruction of all other principles: for I must truly say, that ignorance, the mother of treachery and deceit, gnaws into our very vitals. Ignorance, as it now exists among us, produces a state of things, Oh my Lord! too horrible to present to the world. Any man who is curious to see the full force of ignorance developed among the coloured people of the United States of America, has only to go into the southern and western states of this confederacy, where, if he is not a tyrant, but has the feelings of a human being, who can feel for a fellow creature, he may see enough to make his very heart bleed! He may see there, a son take his mother, who bore almost the pains of death to give him birth, and by the command of a tyrant, strip her as naked as she came into the world, and apply the cow-hide to her, until she falls a victim to death in the road! He may see a husband take his dear wife, not unfrequently in a pregnant state, and perhaps far advanced, and beat her for an unmerciful wretch, until his infant falls a lifeless lump at her feet! Can the Americans escape God Almighty? If they do, can he be to us a God of Justice? God is just, and I know it—for he has convinced me to my satisfaction—I cannot doubt him. My observer may see fathers beating their sons, mothers their daughters, and children their parents, all to pacify the passions of unrelenting tyrants. He may also, see them telling news and lies, making mischief one upon another. These are some of the productions of ignorance, which he will see practised among my dear brethren, who are held in unjust slavery and wretchedness, by avaricious and unmerciful tyrants, to whom, and their hellish deeds, I would suffer my life to be taken before I would submit. And when my curious observer comes to take notice of those who are said to be free, (which assertion I deny) and who are making some frivolous pretentions to common sense, he will see that branch of ignorance among the slaves assuming a more cunning and deceitful course of procedure.—He may see some of my brethren in league with tyrants, selling their own brethren into *hell upon earth,* not dissimilar to the exhibitions in Africa, but in a more secret, servile and abject manner. . . . My observer may see some of those ignorant and treacherous creatures (coloured people) sneaking about in the large cities, endeavouring to find out all strange coloured people, where they work and where they reside, asking them questions, and trying to ascertain whether they are runaways or not, telling them, at the same time, that they always have been, are, and always will be, friends to their brethren; and, perhaps, that they themselves are absconders, and a thousand such treacherous lies to get the better information of the more ignorant! ! ! There have been and are at this day in Boston, New-York, Philadelphia, and Baltimore, coloured men, who are in league with tyrants, and who receive a great portion of their daily bread, of the moneys which they acquire from the blood and tears of their more miserable brethren, . . .

*    *    *

. . . Oh! coloured people of these United States, I ask you, in the name of that God who made us, have we, in consequence of oppression, nearly lost the spirit of man, and, in no very trifling degree, adopted that of brutes? Do you answer, no?—I ask you, then, what set of men can you point me to, in all the world, who are so abjectly employed by their oppressors, as we are by our *natural enemies?* How can, Oh! how can those enemies but say that we and our children are not of the HUMAN FAMILY, but were made by our Creator to be an inheritance to them and theirs for ever? How can the slaveholders but say that they can bribe the best coloured person in the country, to sell his brethren for a trifling sum of money, and take that atrocity to confirm them in their avaricious opinion, that we were made to be slaves to them and their children? How could Mr. Jefferson but say [in *Notes on Virginia,* "Query XIV"], "I advance it therefore as a suspicion only, that the blacks, whether originally a distinct race, or made distinct by time and circumstances, are *inferior* to the whites in the endowments both of body and mind?" . . ."Will not a lover of natural history, then, one who views the gradations in all the races of *animals* with the eye of philosophy, excuse an effort to keep those in the department of MAN as *distinct* as nature has formed them?"—I hope you will try to find out the meaning of this verse—its widest sense and all its bearings: whether you do or not, remember the whites do. This very verse, brethren, having emanated from Mr. Jefferson, a much greater philosopher the world never afforded, has in truth injured us more, and has been

as great a barrier to our emancipation as any thing that has ever been advanced against us. I hope you will not let it pass unnoticed. He goes on further, and says: "This *unfortunate* difference of colour, and *perhaps* of *faculty,* is a powerful obstacle to the emancipation of these people. Many of their advocates, while they wish to vindicate the liberty of human nature are anxious also to preserve its *dignity* and *beauty.* Some of these, embarrassed by the question, 'What further is to be done with them?' join themselves in opposition with those who are actuated by sordid avarice only." Now I ask you candidly, my suffering brethren in time, who are candidates for the eternal worlds, how could Mr. Jefferson but have given the world these remarks respecting us, when we are so submissive to them, and so much servile deceit prevail among ourselves—when we so *meanly* submit to their murderous lashes, to which neither the Indians nor any other people under Heaven would submit? No, they would die to a man, before they would suffer such things from men who are no better than themselves, and *perhaps not so good.* Yes, how can our friends but be embarrassed, as Mr. Jefferson says, by the question, "What further is to be done with these people?" For while they are working for our emancipation, we are, by our treachery, wickedness and deceit, working against ourselves and our children—helping ours, and the enemies of God, to keep us and our dear little children in their infernal chains of slavery! ! ! Indeed, our friends cannot but relapse and join themselves "with those who are actuated by *sordid avarice* only ! ! ! !" For my own part, I am glad Mr. Jefferson has advanced his positions for your sake; for you will either have to contradict or confirm him by your own actions, and not by what our friends have said or done for us; for those things are other men's labours, and do not satisfy the Americans, who are waiting for us to prove to them ourselves, that we are MEN, before they will be willing to admit the fact; for I pledge you my sacred word of honour, that Mr. Jefferson's remarks respecting us, have sunk deep into the hearts of millions of the whites, and never will be removed this side of eternity.—For how can they, when we are confirming him every day, by our *groveling submissions* and *treachery?* I aver, that when I look over these United States of America, and the world, and see the ignorant deceptions and consequent wretchedness of my brethren, I am brought oftimes solemnly to a stand, and in the midst of my reflections I exclaim to my God, "Lord didst thou make us to be slaves to our brethren, the whites?" But when I reflect that God is just, and that millions of my wretched brethren would meet death with glory—yea, more, would plunge into the very mouths of cannons and be torn into particles as minute as the atoms which compose the elements of the earth, in preference to a mean submission to the lash of tyrants, I am with streaming eyes, compelled to shrink back into nothingness before my Maker, and exclaim again, thy will be done, O Lord God Almighty.

Men of colour, who are also of sense, for you particularly is my APPEAL designed. Our more ignorant brethren are not able to penetrate its value. I call upon you therefore to cast your eyes upon the wretchedness of your brethren, and to do your utmost to enlighten them—*go to work and enlighten your brethren!* . . .

There is a great work for you to do, as trifling as some of you may think of it. You have to prove to the Americans and the world, that we are MEN, and not *brutes,* as we have been represented, and by millions treated. Remember, to let the aim of your labours among your brethren, and particularly the youths, be the dissemination of education and religion. It is lamentable, that many of our children go to school, from four until they are eight or ten, and sometimes fifteen years of age, and leave school knowing but a little more about the grammar of their language than a horse does about handling a musket—and not a few of them are really so ignorant, that they are unable to answer a person correctly, general questions in geography, and to hear them read, would only be to disgust a man who has a taste for reading; which, to do well, as trifling as it may appear to some, (to the ignorant in particular) is a great part of learning. Some few of them, may make out to scribble tolerably well, over a half sheet of paper, which I believe has hith-

erto been a powerful obstacle in our way, to keep us from acquiring knowledge. An ignorant father, who knows no more than what nature has taught him, together with what little he acquires by the senses of hearing and seeing, finding his son able to write a neat hand, sets it down for granted that he has as good learning as any body; the young, ignorant gump, hearing his father or mother, who perhaps may be ten times more ignorant, in point of literature, than himself, extolling his learning, struts about, in the full assurance, that his attainments in literature are sufficient to take him through the world, when, in fact, he has scarcely any learning at all! ! ! !

I promiscuously fell in conversation once, with an elderly coloured man on the topics of education, and of the great prevalency of ignorance among us: Said he, "I know that our people are very ignorant but my son has a good education: I spent a great deal of money on his education: he can write as well as any white man, and I assure you that no one can fool him," &c. Said I, what else can your son do, besides writing a good hand? Can he post a set of books in a mercantile manner? Can he write a neat piece of composition in prose or in verse? To these interrogations he answered in the negative. Said I, did your son learn, while he was at school, the width and depth of English Grammar? To which he also replied in the negative, telling me his son did not learn those things. Your son, said I, then, has hardly any learning at all—he is almost as ignorant, and more so, than many of those who never went to school one day in all their lives. My friend got a little put out, and so walking off, said that his son could write as well as any white man. Most of the coloured people, when they speak of the education of one among us who can write a neat hand, and who perhaps knows nothing but to scribble and puff pretty fair on a small scrap of paper, immaterial whether his words are grammatical, or spelt correctly, or not; if it only looks beautiful, they say he has as good an education as any white man—he can write as well as any white man, &c. The poor, ignorant creature, hearing this, he is ashamed, forever after, to let any person see him humbling himself to another for knowledge but going about trying to deceive those who are more ignorant than himself, he at last falls an ignorant victim to death in wretchedness. I pray that the Lord may undeceive my ignorant brethren, and permit them to throw away pretensions, and seek after the substance of learning. I would crawl on my hands and knees through mud and mire, to the feet of a learned man, where I would sit and humbly supplicate him to instil into me, that which neither devils nor tyrants could remove, only with my life—for coloured people to acquire learning in this country, makes tyrants quake and tremble on their sandy foundation.

\*      \*      \*

# REVIEW QUESTIONS

1. How did Walker use religious beliefs and language to appeal to both oppressed and oppressors?
2. How does he compare the present to the past? Was his use of history effective in making his argument?
3. Walker was not only angry with white Americans who maintained slavery but also with some black Americans. Why?
4. Walker disputes Thomas Jefferson's assumptions about African Americans but he also says, "I am glad Mr. Jefferson has advanced his positions for your sake." Why?
5. Why did Walker speak of learning while proclaiming for abolition and equality?

# FROM *McCulloch v. Maryland* (1819)

*Maryland's legislature passed an act that permitted the state to tax the operations of the Second Bank of the United States as it operated within its borders. An officer of the Baltimore branch, James McCulloch, then went to court to stop such taxation. When the Baltimore County Court decided against him, he appealed to the Court of Appeals of the State of Maryland, and when that court upheld the lower court, he appealed to the Supreme Court. John Marshall, the Chief Justice, delivered the unanimous ruling of the Court and provided an extensive justification. That the Court ruled for the bank was not surprising: by 1816, when the Second Bank was chartered, most Americans, Jeffersonian Republicans included, had come to accept that incorporation of the bank was constitutional. By 1819, however, the bank was coming under increasing attack as the people and states struggled with an economic depression. In the midst of this backlash, the question before the Court was that of the constitutionality of a state tax on a properly incorporated national institution. But Marshall did not focus on that alone; he went back to the whole issue of how to determine constitutionality. In effect, the decision itself was not as important—in terms of historical legal precedents—as how the decision was reached. McCulloch v. Maryland thus became much more than the case about the bank; it became a fundamental, nationalistic defense of a broad construction of the Constitution.*

From Gerald Gunther, ed., *John Marshall's Defense of* McCulloch v. Maryland (Stanford Calif.: Stanford University Press, 1969), pp. 23–51. [Editorial insertions appear in brackets—*Ed.*]

Mr. Chief Justice MARSHALL delivered the opinion of the Court.

\*      \*      \*

The first question made in the cause is, has Congress power to incorporate a bank?

It has been truly said, that this can scarcely be considered as an open question, entirely unprejudiced by the former proceedings of the nation respecting it. The principle now contested was introduced at a very early period of our history, has been recognized by many successive legislatures, and has been acted upon by the judicial department, in cases of peculiar delicacy, as a law of undoubted obligation.

\*      \*      \*

The power now contested was exercised by the first Congress elected under the present constitution. The bill for incorporating the bank of the United States did not steal upon an unsuspecting legislature, and pass unobserved. Its principle was completely understood, and was opposed with equal zeal and ability. After being resisted, first in the fair and open field of debate, and afterwards in the executive cabinet, with as much persevering talent as any measure has ever experienced, and being supported by arguments which convinced minds as pure and as intelligent as this country can boast, it became a law. The original act was permitted to expire; but a short experience of the embarrassments to which the refusal to revive it exposed the government, convinced those who were most prejudiced against the measure of its necessity, and induced the passage of the present law. It would require no ordinary share of intrepidity to assert that a measure adopted under these circumstances was a bold and plain usurpation, to which the constitution gave no countenance.

\*      \*      \*

In discussing this question, the counsel for the State of Maryland have deemed it of some importance, in the construction of the constitution, to consider that instrument not as emanating from the people, but as the act of sovereign and independent States. The powers of the general government, it has been said, are delegated by the States, who alone are truly sovereign; and must be exercised in subordination to the States, who alone possess supreme dominion.

It would be difficult to sustain this proposition. The Convention which framed the constitution was indeed elected by the State legislatures. But the instrument, when it came from their hands, was a mere proposal, without obligation, or pretensions to it. It was reported to the then existing Congress of the United States, with a request that it might "be submitted to a Convention of Delegates, chosen in each State by the people thereof, under the recommendation of its Legislature, for their assent and ratification." This mode of proceeding was adopted; and by the Convention, by Congress, and by the State Legislatures, the instrument was submitted to the people. They acted upon it . . . by assembling in Convention. . . .

From these Conventions the constitution derives its whole authority. The government proceeds directly from the people; . . . It required not the affirmance, and could not be negatived, by the State governments. The constitution, when thus adopted, was of complete obligation, and bound the State sovereignties.

\*      \*      \*

This government is acknowledged by all to be one of enumerated powers. The principle, that it can exercise only the powers granted to it, would seem too apparent to have required to be enforced by all those arguments which its enlightened friends . . . found it necessary to urge. That principle is now universally admitted. But the question respecting the extent of the powers actually granted, is perpetually arising, and will probably continue to arise, as long as our system shall exist.

In discussing these questions, the conflicting powers of the general and State governments must be brought into view, and the supremacy of their respective laws, when they are in opposition, must be settled.

If any one proposition could command the universal assent of mankind, we might expect it would be this—that the government of the Union, though limited in its powers, is supreme within its sphere of action. This would seem to result necessarily from its nature. It is the government of all; its powers are delegated by all; it represents all, and acts for all. . . . But this question is not left to mere reason: the people have, in express terms, decided it, by saying, "this constitution, and the laws of the United States, which shall be made in pursuance thereof," "shall be the supreme law of the land," and by requiring that the members of the State legislatures, and the officers of the executive and judicial departments of the States, shall take the oath of fidelity to it.

The government of the United States, then, though limited in its powers, is supreme; and its laws, when made in pursuance of the constitution, form the supreme law of the land, "any thing in the constitution or laws of any State to the contrary notwithstanding."

Among the enumerated powers, we do not find that of establishing a bank or creating a corporation. But there is no phrase in the instrument which, like the articles of confederation, excludes incidental or implied powers; and which requires that every thing granted shall be expressly and minutely described. . . . [A constitution's] nature, therefore, requires, that only its great outlines should be marked, its important objects designated, and the minor ingredients which compose those objects be deduced from the nature of the objects themselves. That this idea was entertained by the framers of the American constitution, is not only to be inferred from the nature of the instrument, but from the language. Why else were some of the limitations, found in the ninth section of the 1st article, introduced? It is also, in some degree, warranted by their having omitted to use any restrictive term which might prevent its receiving a fair and just interpretation. In considering this question, then, we must never forget, that it is *a constitution* we are expounding.

Although, among the enumerated powers of government, we do not find the word "bank" or

"incorporation," we find the great powers to lay and collect taxes; to borrow money; to regulate commerce; to declare and conduct a war; and to raise and support armies and navies. The sword and the purse, all the external relations, and no inconsiderable portion of the industry of the nation, are entrusted to its government. . . . [A] government, entrusted with such ample powers, on the due execution of which the happiness and prosperity of the nation so vitally depends, must also be entrusted with ample means for their execution. . . . Can we adopt that construction (unless the words imperiously require it), which would impute to the framers of that instrument . . . the intention of impeding their exercise by withholding a choice of means? If, indeed, such be the mandate of the constitution, we have only to obey; but that instrument does not profess to enumerate the means by which the powers it confers may be executed; nor does it prohibit the creation of a corporation, if the existence of such a being be essential to the beneficial exercise of those powers. It is, then, the subject of fair inquiry, how far such means may be employed.

\*     \*     \*

The government which has a right to do an act, and has imposed on it the duty of performing that act, must, according to the dictates of reason, be allowed to select the means; and those who contend that it may not select any appropriate means, that one particular mode of effecting the object is excepted, take upon themselves the burden of establishing that exception.

The creation of a corporation, it is said, appertains to sovereignty. This is admitted. But to what portion of sovereignty does it appertain? Does it belong to one more than to another? In America, the powers of sovereignty are divided between the government of the Union, and those of the States. They are each sovereign, with respect to the objects committed to it, and neither sovereign with respect to the objects committed to the other. . . . The power of creating a corporation, though appertaining to sovereignty, is not, like the power of making war, or levying taxes, or of regulating commerce, a great substantive and independent power, which cannot be implied as incidental to other powers, or used as a means of executing them. It is never the end for which other powers are exercised, but a means by which other objects are accomplished. . . . The power of creating a corporation is never used for its own sake, but for the purpose of effecting something else. No sufficient reason is, therefore, perceived, why it may not pass as incidental to those powers which are expressly given, if it be a direct mode of executing them.

But the constitution of the United States has not left the right of Congress to employ the necessary means, for the execution of the powers conferred on the government, to general reasoning. To its enumeration of powers is added that of making "all laws which shall be necessary and proper, for carrying into execution the foregoing powers, and all other powers vested by this constitution, in the government of the United States, or in any department thereof."

The counsel for the State of Maryland have urged various arguments, to prove that this clause, though in terms a grant of power, is not so in effect; but is really restrictive of the general right, which might otherwise be implied, of selecting means for executing the enumerated powers.

\*      \*      \*

But the argument on which most reliance is placed, is drawn from the peculiar language of this clause. Congress is not empowered by it to make all laws, which may have relation to the powers conferred on the government, but such only as may be "*necessary and proper*" for carrying them into execution. The word "*necessary*," is considered as controlling the whole sentence, and as limiting the right to pass laws for the execution of the granted powers, to such as are indispensable, and without which the power would be nugatory. That it excludes the choice of means, and leaves to Congress, in each case, that only which is most direct and simple.

Is it true, that this is the sense in which the word "necessary" is always used? . . . We think it does not . . . we find that it frequently imports no more than that one thing is convenient, or useful, or essential to another. To employ the means necessary to an end, is generally understood as employing any means calculated to produce the end, and not as being confined to those single means, without which the end would be entirely unattainable. Such is the character of human language, that no word conveys to the mind, in all situations, one single definite idea; and nothing is more common than to use words in a figurative sense. . . . It is essential to just construction, that many words which import something excessive, should be understood in a more mitigated sense—in that sense which common usage justifies. The word "necessary" is of this description. . . . It admits of all degrees of comparison; and is often connected with other words, which increase or diminish the impression the mind receives of the urgency it imports. A thing may be necessary, very necessary, absolutely or indispensably necessary. To no mind would the same idea be conveyed, by these several phrases. . . . This word, then, like others, is used in various senses; and, in its construction, the subject, the context, the intention of the person using them, are all to be taken into view.

Let this be done in the case under consideration. The subject is the execution of those great powers on which the welfare of a nation essentially depends. It must have been the intention of those who gave these powers, to insure, as far as human prudence could insure, their beneficial execution. This could not be done by confining the choice of means to such narrow limits as not to leave it in the power of Congress to adopt any which might be appropriate, and which were conducive to the end. This provision is made in a constitution intended to endure for ages to come, and, consequently, to be adapted to the various *crises* of human affairs. To have prescribed the means by which government should, in all future time, execute its powers, would have been to change, entirely, the character of the instrument . . .

\*      \*      \*

The result of the most careful and attentive consideration bestowed upon this clause is, that if it does not enlarge, it cannot be construed to restrain the powers of Congress, or to impair the right of the legislature to exercise its best judgment in the selection of measures to carry into execution the constitutional powers of the government. . . .

We admit, as all must admit, that the powers of the government are limited, and that its limits are not to be transcended. But we think the sound construction of the constitution must allow to the national legislature that discretion, with respect to the means by which the powers it confers are to be carried into execution, which will enable that body to perform the high duties assigned to it, in the manner most beneficial to the people. Let the end be legitimate, let it be within the scope of the constitution, and all means which are appropriate, which are plainly adapted to that end, which are not prohibited, but consist with the letter and spirit of the constitution, are constitutional.

\*    \*    \*

If a corporation may be employed indiscriminately with other means to carry into execution the powers of the government, no particular reason can be assigned for excluding the use of a bank, if required for its fiscal operations. To use one, must be within the discretion of Congress, if it be an appropriate mode of executing the powers of government. That it is a convenient, a useful, and essential instrument in the prosecution of its fiscal operations, is not now a subject of controversy. . . .

But, were its necessity less apparent, none can deny its being an appropriate measure; and if it is, the degree of its necessity, as has been very justly observed, is to be discussed in another place. Should Congress, in the execution of its powers, adopt measures which are prohibited by the constitution; or should Congress, under the pretext of executing its powers, pass laws for the accomplishment of objects not entrusted to the government; it would become the painful duty of this tribunal, should a case requiring such a decision come before it, to say that such an act was not the law of the land. But where the law is not prohibited, and is really calculated to effect any of the objects entrusted to the government, to undertake here to

inquire into the degree of its necessity, would be to pass the line which circumscribes the judicial department, and to tread on legislative ground. This court disclaims all pretensions to such a power.

\*    \*    \*

After the most deliberate consideration, it is the unanimous and decided opinion of this Court, that the act to incorporate the Bank of the United States is a law made in pursuance of the constitution, and is a part of the supreme law of the land.

\*    \*    \*

It being the opinion of the Court, that the act incorporating the bank is constitutional; and that the power of establishing a branch in the State of Maryland might be properly exercised by the bank itself, we proceed to inquire—

. . . Whether the State of Maryland may, without violating the constitution, tax that branch?

That the power of taxation is one of vital importance; that it is retained by the States; that it is not abridged by the grant of a similar power to the government of the Union; that it is to be concurrently exercised by the two governments: are truths which have never been denied. But, such is the paramount character of the constitution, that its capacity to withdraw any subject from the action of even this power, is admitted. The States are expressly forbidden to lay any duties on imports or exports, except what may be absolutely necessary for executing their inspection laws. If the obligation of this prohibition must be conceded—if it may restrain a State from the exercise of its taxing power on imports and exports; the same paramount character would seem to restrain, as it certainly may restrain, a State from such other exercise of this power, as is in its nature incompatible with, and repugnant to, the constitutional laws of the Union. . . .

On this ground the counsel for the bank place its claim to be exempted from the power of a State to tax its operations. There is no express provision for the case, but the claim has been sustained on a principle which so entirely pervades the constitution, is so intermixed with the materials which compose it, so interwoven with its web, so blended with its texture, as to be incapable of being separated from it, without rending it into shreds.

This great principle is, that the constitution and the laws made in pursuance thereof are supreme; that they control the constitution and laws of the respective States, and cannot be controlled by them. From this, which may be almost termed an axiom, other propositions are deduced as corollaries, . . . These are, 1st. that a power to create implies a power to preserve. 2nd. That a power to destroy, if wielded by a different hand, is hostile to, and incompatible with these powers to create and to preserve. 3d. That where this repugnancy exists, that authority which is supreme must control, not yield to that over which it is supreme.

\*    \*    \*

That the power of taxing [the bank] by the States may be exercised so as to destroy it, is too obvious to be denied. But taxation is said to be an absolute power, which acknowledges no other limits than those expressly prescribed in the constitution, and like sovereign power of every other description, is trusted to the discretion of those who use it. But the very terms of this argument admit that the sovereignty of the State, in the article of taxation itself, is subordinate to, and may be controlled by the constitution of the United States. . . . It is of the very essence of supremacy to remove all obstacles to its action within its own sphere, and so to modify every power vested in subordinate governments, as to exempt its own operations from their own influence. This effect need not be stated in terms. It is so involved in the declaration of supremacy, so necessarily implied in it, that the expression of it could not make it more certain. We must, therefore, keep it in view while construing the constitution.

The argument on the part of the State of Maryland, is, not that the States may directly resist a law of Congress, but that they may exercise their acknowledged powers upon it, and that the constitution leaves them this right in the confidence that they will not abuse it.

\*    \*    \*

The sovereignty of a State extends to every thing which exists by its own authority, or is introduced by its permission; but does it extend to those means which are employed by Congress to carry into execution powers conferred on that body by the people of the United States? We think it demonstrable that it does not. Those powers are not given by the people of a single State. They are given by the people of the United States, to a government whose laws, made in pursuance of the constitution, are declared to be supreme. Consequently, the people of a single State cannot confer a sovereignty which will extend over them.

\*    \*    \*

If we apply the principle for which the State of Maryland contends, to the constitution generally, we shall find it capable of changing totally the character of that instrument. We shall find it capable of arresting all the measures of the government, and of prostrating it at the foot of the States. The American people have declared their constitution, and the laws made in pursuance thereof, to be supreme; but this principle would transfer the supremacy, in fact, to the States.

If the States may tax one instrument, employed by the government in the execution of its powers, they may tax any and every other instrument. They may tax the mail; they may tax the mint; they may tax patent rights; they may tax the papers of the custom-house; they may tax judicial process; they may tax all the means employed by the government, to an excess which would defeat all the ends of government. This was not intended by the American people. They did not design to make their government dependent on the States.

\*    \*    \*

It has also been insisted, that, as the power of taxation in the general and State governments is acknowledged to be concurrent, every argument which would sustain the right of the general government to tax banks chartered by the States, will equally sustain the right of the States to tax banks chartered by the general government.

But the two cases are not on the same reason. The people of all the States have created the general government, and have conferred upon it the general power of taxation. The people of all the States, and the States themselves, are represented in Congress, and, by their representatives, exercise this power. When they tax the chartered institutions of the States, they tax their constituents; and these taxes must be uniform. But, when a State taxes the operations of the government of the United States, it acts upon institutions created, not by their own constituents, but by people over whom they claim no control. It acts upon the measures of a government created by others as well as themselves, for the benefit of others in common with themselves. The difference is that which always exists, and always must exist, between the action of the whole on a part, and the action of a part on the whole—between the laws of a government declared to be supreme, and those of a government which, when in opposition to those laws, is not supreme.

\*     \*     \*

The Court has bestowed on this subject its most deliberate consideration. The result is a conviction that the States have no power, by taxation or otherwise, to retard, impede, burden, or in any manner control, the operations of the constitutional laws enacted by Congress to carry into execution the powers vested in the general government. This is, we think, the unavoidable consequence of that supremacy which the constitution has declared.

We are unanimously of opinion, that the law passed by the legislature of Maryland, imposing a tax on the Bank of the United States, is unconstitutional and void.

\*     \*     \*

## REVIEW QUESTIONS

1. What was Maryland's argument against the Second Bank of the United States?
2. What historical and legal precedents did Marshall, speaking for his court, use to refute that argument?
3. How did Marshall interpret the Constitution so as to bind the states to the general government?
4. Why did Marshall believe that most of the Constitution's framers intended that its provisions be loosely rather than strictly construed?

## JAMES MONROE

### FROM THE Monroe Doctrine (1823)

*The Monroe administration had to deal with increasingly complex foreign and domestic relations. In foreign affairs, however, it was particularly successful due to the diplomatic abilities of both president and secretary of state. Both Monroe and Adams were intent on securing the expanded borders of the United States and preserving the trade connections that were essential to economic growth. To accomplish these aims, they had to counter a number of challenges: the insurrections in colonial Spanish America that ended in newly independent Latin American countries desiring recognition from the United States; the possibility of European intervention in Latin America so as to gain or regain economic and territorial control; and the European, specifically*

*Russian and British, claims to territory in North America. Adams opposed recognition of the new Latin American nations because he feared such an act could lead to direct involvement in their conflicts. He wished them well, but he did not want the United States to fight their battles. Monroe, however, wanted to extend recognition to show support for such independence and democratic movements and, more important, to forge beneficial economic ties. The two worked through their differences to produce a set of principles that eventually had a great impact on the definition and implementation of American foreign policy. Monroe presented the principles in his annual message to Congress in December 1823, which explains why they came to be known as the* Monroe Doctrine, *but they were primarily the creation of Adams.*

From James D. Richardson, comp., *A Compilation of the Messages and Papers of the Presidents, 1789–1902*, vol. II (Washington, DC, Bureau of National Literature and Art, 1904), pp. 207–20.

## Seventh Annual Message

WASHINGTON, *December 2, 1823*
*Fellow-Citizens of the Senate and*
*House of Representatives:*

Many important subjects will claim your attention during the present session, of which I shall endeavor to give, in aid of your deliberations, a just idea in this communication. I undertake this duty with diffidence, from the vast extent of the interests on which I have to treat and of their great importance to every portion of our Union. I enter on it with zeal from a thorough conviction that there never was a period since the establishment of our Revolution when, regarding the condition of the civilized world and its bearing on us, there was greater necessity for devotion in the public servants to their respective duties, or for virtue, patriotism, and union in our constituents.

Meeting in you a new Congress, I deem it proper to present this view of public affairs in greater detail than might otherwise be necessary. I do it, however, with peculiar satisfaction, from a knowledge that in this respect I shall comply more fully with the sound principles of our Government. The people being with us exclusively the sovereign, it is indispensable that full information be laid before them on all important subjects, to enable them to exercise that high power with complete effect. If kept in the dark, they must be incompetent to it. . . . Their interests in all vital questions are the same, and the bond, by sentiment as well as by interest, will be proportionably strengthened as they are better informed of the real state of public affairs, especially in difficult conjunctures. It is by such knowledge that local prejudices and jealousies are surmounted, and that a national policy, extending its fostering care and protection to all the great interests of our Union, is formed and steadily adhered to.

A precise knowledge of our relations with foreign powers as respects our negotiations and transactions with each is thought to be particularly necessary. Equally necessary is it that we should form a just estimate of our resources, revenue, and progress in every kind of improvement connected with the national prosperity and public defense. It is by rendering justice to other nations that we may expect it from them. It is by our ability to resent injuries and redress wrongs that we may avoid them.

The commissioners under the fifth article of the treaty of Ghent, having disagreed in their opinions respecting that portion of the boundary between the Territories of the United States and of Great Britain the establishment of which had been submitted to them, have made their respective reports in compliance with that article, that the same might be referred to the decision of a friendly power. It being manifest, however, that it would be difficult, if not impossible, for any power to perform that office without great delay and much inconvenience to itself, a proposal has been made by this Government, and acceded to by that of Great Britain, to endeavor to establish that boundary by amicable negotiation. It appearing from long experience that no satisfactory arrangement could be formed of the commercial intercourse between the United States and the British colonies in this hemisphere by legislative acts while each party pursued its own course without agreement or concert with the other, a proposal has been made to the British Government to regulate this commerce by treaty, as it has been to arrange in like manner the just claim of the citizens of the United States inhabiting the States and Territories bordering on the lakes and rivers which empty into the St. Lawrence to the navigation of that river to the ocean. For these and other objects of high importance to the interests of both parties a negotiation has been opened with the British Government which it is hoped will have a satisfactory result.

\*       \*       \*

At the proposal of the Russian Imperial Government, made through the minister of the Emperor residing here, a full power and instructions have been transmitted to the minister of the United States at St. Petersburg to arrange by amicable negotiation the respective rights and interests of the two nations on the northwest coast of this continent. A similar proposal had been made by His Imperial Majesty to the Government of Great Britain, which has likewise been acceded to. The Government of the United States has been desirous by this friendly proceeding of manifesting the great value which they have invariably attached to the friendship of the Emperor and their solicitude to cultivate the best understanding with his Government. In the discussions to which this interest has given rise and in the arrangements by which they may terminate the occasion has been judged proper for asserting, as a principle in which the rights and interests of the United States are involved, that the American continents, by the free and independent condition which they have assumed and maintain, are henceforth not to be considered as subjects for future colonization by any European powers.

\*       \*       \*

In compliance with a resolution of the House of Representatives adopted at their last session, instructions have been given to all the ministers of the United States accredited to the powers of Europe and America to propose the proscription of the African slave trade by classing it under the denomination, and inflicting on its perpetrators the punishment, of piracy. Should this proposal be acceded to, it is not doubted that this odious and criminal practice will be promptly and entirely suppressed. It is earnestly hoped that it will be acceded to, from the firm belief that it is the most effectual expedient that can be adopted for the purpose.

At the commencement of the recent war between France and Spain it was declared by the French Government that it would grant no commissions to privateers, and that neither the commerce of Spain herself nor of neutral nations should be molested by the naval force of France, except in the breach of a lawful blockade. This declaration, which appears to have been faithfully carried into effect, concurring with principles proclaimed and cherished by the United States from the first establishment of their independence, suggested the hope that the time had arrived when the proposal for adopting it as a permanent and invariable rule in all future maritime wars might meet the favorable consideration of the great European powers. Instructions have accordingly been given to our ministers with France, Russia, and Great Britain to make those proposals to their respective Governments, and when the friends of humanity reflect on the essential amelioration to the condition of the human race which would result from the abolition of private war on the sea and on the great facility by which it might be accomplished, requiring only the consent of a few sovereigns, an earnest hope is indulged that these overtures will meet with an attention animated by the spirit in which they were made, and that they will ultimately be successful.

\*       \*       \*

The state of the Army in its organization and discipline has been gradually improving for several years, and has now attained a high degree of perfection. The military disbursements have been regularly made and the accounts regularly and promptly rendered for settlement. The supplies of various descriptions have been of good quality, and regularly issued at all of the posts. A system of economy and accountability has been introduced into every branch of the service which admits of little additional improvement. This desirable state has been attained by the act reorganizing the staff of the Army, passed on the 14th of April, 1818.

\*    \*    \*

I transmit a return of the militia of the several States according to the last reports which have been made by the proper officers in each to the Department of War. By reference to this return it will be seen that it is not complete, although great exertions have been made to make it so. As the defense and even the liberties of the country must depend in times of imminent danger on the militia, it is of the highest importance that it be well organized, armed, and disciplined throughout the Union. . . .

\*    \*    \*

The usual orders have been given to all our public ships to seize American vessels engaged in the slave trade and bring them in for adjudication, and I have the gratification to state that not one so employed has been discovered, and there is good reason to believe that our flag is now seldom, if at all, disgraced by that traffic.

It is a source of great satisfaction that we are always enabled to recur to the conduct of our Navy with pride and commendation. As a means of national defense it enjoys the public confidence, and is steadily assuming additional importance. It is submitted whether a more efficient and equally economical organization of it might not in several respects be effected. It is supposed that higher grades than now exist by law would be useful. They would afford well-merited rewards to those who have long and faithfully served their country, pre-sent the best incentives to good conduct, and the best means of insuring a proper discipline; destroy the inequality in that respect between military and naval services, and relieve our officers from many inconveniences and mortifications which occur when our vessels meet

those of other nations, ours being the only service in which such grades do not exist.

\*    \*    \*

Having communicated my views to Congress at the commencement of the last session respecting the encouragement which ought to be given to our manufactures and the principle on which it should be founded, I have only to add that those views remain unchanged, and that the present state of those countries with which we have the most immediate political relations and greatest commercial intercourse tends to confirm them. Under this impression I recommend a review of the tariff for the purpose of affording such additional protection to those articles which we are prepared to manufacture, or which are more immediately connected with the defense and independence of the country.

\*    \*    \*

The sum which was appropriated at the last session for the repairs of the Cumberland road has been applied with good effect to that object. . . .

Many patriotic and enlightened citizens who have made the subject an object of particular investigation have suggested an improvement of still greater importance. They are of opinion that the waters of the Chesapeake and Ohio may be connected together by one continued canal, and at an expense far short of the value and importance of the object to be obtained. If this could be accomplished it is impossible to calculate the beneficial consequences which would result from it. A great portion of the produce of the very fertile country through which it would pass would find a market through that channel. Troops might be moved with great facility in war, with cannon and every kind of munition, and in either direction. Connecting the Atlantic with the Western country in a line passing through the seat of the National Government, it would contribute essentially to strengthen the bond of union itself. Believing as I do that Congress possess the right to appropriate money for such a national object (the jurisdiction remaining to the States through which the canal would pass), I submit it to your consideration whether it may not be advisable to authorize by an adequate appropriation the employment of a suitable number of the officers of the Corps of Engineers to examine the unexplored ground during the next season and to report their opinion thereon. It will likewise be proper to extend their examination to the several routes through which the waters of the Ohio may be connected by canals with those of Lake Erie.

As the Cumberland road will require annual repairs, and Congress have not thought it expedient to recommend to the States an amendment to the Constitution for the purpose of vesting in the United States a power to adopt and execute a system of internal improvement, it is also submitted to your consideration whether it may not be expedient to authorize the Executive to enter into an arrangement with the several States through which the road passes to establish tolls, each within its limits, for the purpose of defraying the expense of future repairs and of providing also by suitable penalties for its protection against future injuries.

*     *     *

It was stated at the commencement of the last session that a great effort was then making in Spain and Portugal to improve the condition of the people of those countries, and that it appeared to be conducted with extraordinary moderation. It need scarcely be remarked that the result has been so far very different from what was then anticipated. Of events in that quarter of the globe, with which we have so much intercourse and from which we derive our origin, we have always been anxious and interested spectators. The citizens of the United States cherish sentiments the most friendly in favor of the liberty and happiness of their fellow-men on that side of the Atlantic. In the wars of the European powers in matters relating to themselves we have never taken any part, nor does it comport with our policy so to do. It is only when our rights are invaded or seriously menaced that we resent injuries or make preparation for our defense. With the movements in this hemisphere we are of necessity more immediately connected, and by causes which must be obvious to all enlightened and impartial observers. The political system of the allied powers is essentially different in this respect from

that of America. This difference proceeds from that which exists in their respective Governments; and to the defense of our own, which has been achieved by the loss of so much blood and treasure, and matured by the wisdom of their most enlightened citizens, and under which we have enjoyed unexampled felicity, this whole nation is devoted. We owe it, therefore, to candor and to the amicable relations existing between the United States and those powers to declare that we should consider any attempt on their part to extend their system to any portion of this hemisphere as dangerous to our peace and safety. With the existing colonies or dependencies of any European power we have not interfered and shall not interfere. But with the Governments who have declared their independence and maintained it, and whose independence we have, on great consideration and on just principles, acknowledged, we could not view any interposition for the purpose of oppressing them, or controlling in any other manner their destiny, by any European power in any other light than as the manifestation of an unfriendly disposition toward the United States. In the war between those new Governments and Spain we declared our neutrality at the time of their recognition, and to this we have adhered, and shall continue to adhere, provided no change shall occur which, in the judgment of the competent authorities of this Government, shall make a corresponding change on the part of the United States indispensable to their security.

The late events in Spain and Portugal shew that Europe is still unsettled. Of this important fact no stronger proof can be adduced than that the allied powers should have thought it proper, on any principle satisfactory to themselves, to have interposed by force in the internal concerns of Spain. To what extent such interposition may be carried, on the same principle, is a question in which all independent powers whose governments differ from theirs are interested, even those most remote, and surely none more so than the United States. Our policy in regard to Europe, which was adopted at an early stage of the wars which have so long agitated that quarter of the globe, nevertheless remains the same, which is, not to interfere in the internal concerns of any of its powers; to consider the government *de facto* as the legitimate government for us; to cultivate friendly relations with it, and to preserve those relations by a frank, firm, and manly policy, meeting in all instances the just claims of every power, submitting to injuries from none. But in regard to those continents circumstances are eminently and conspicuously different. It is impossible that the allied powers should extend their political system to any portion of either continent without endangering our peace and happiness; nor can anyone believe that our southern brethren, if left to themselves, would adopt it of their own accord. It is equally impossible, therefore, that we should behold such interposition in any form with indifference. If we look to the comparative strength and resources of Spain and those new Governments, and their distance from each other, it must be obvious that she can never subdue them. It is still the true policy of the United States to leave the parties to themselves, in the hope that other powers will pursue the same course.

If we compare the present condition of our Union with its actual state at the close of our Revolution, the history of the world furnishes no example of a progress in improvement in all the important circumstances which constitute the happiness of a nation which bears any resemblance to it. At the first epoch our population did not exceed 3,000,000. By the last census it amounted to about 10,000,000, and, what is more extraordinary, it is almost altogether native, for the immigration from other countries has been inconsiderable. At the first epoch half the territory within our acknowledged limits was uninhabited and a wilderness. Since then new territory has been acquired of vast extent, comprising within it many rivers, particularly the Mississippi, the navigation of which to the ocean was of the highest importance to the original States. Over this territory our population has expanded in every direction, and new States have been established almost equal in number to those which formed the first bond of our Union. This expansion of our population and accession of new States to our Union have had the happiest effect on all its highest interests. That it has eminently augmented our resources and added to our strength and respectability as a power is admitted by all. But it is not in these important circumstances only that this happy effect is felt. It is manifest that by enlarging the basis of our system and increasing the number of States the system itself has been greatly strengthened in both its branches. Consolidation and disunion have thereby been rendered equally impracticable. Each Government, confiding in its own strength, has less to apprehend from the other, and in consequence each, enjoying a greater freedom of action, is rendered more efficient for all the purposes for which it was instituted. It is unnecessary to treat here of the vast improvement made in the system itself by the adoption of this Constitution and of its happy effect in elevating the character and in protecting the rights of the nation as well as of individuals. To what, then, do we owe these blessings? It is known to all that we derive them from the excellence of our institutions. Ought we not, then, to adopt every measure which may be necessary to perpetuate them?

# REVIEW QUESTIONS

1. How is Monroe's message both a plea and a program for national integrity?
2. What foreign policy principles does he present that succeeding generations have lumped together as the Monroe Doctrine?
3. How does he justify these principles? How does he propose to enforce them?
4. What are some of the other foreign and domestic issues that he deemed important?

## HENRY CLAY

# On the Election, the Court, and Improvements (1823)

*President Monroe may have been elected without opposition in 1820, but a number of individuals immediately began planning and politicking for the presidential election of 1824. One of those was Congressman Henry Clay from Kentucky. Clay was speaker of the house in 1823, but he wanted to move into the executive branch. He thought that he had a solid shot at the presidency when the competition consisted of John Quincy Adams, Secretary of the Treasury William Crawford, and Secretary of War John C. Calhoun. Then General Andrew Jackson entered the fray and changed the dynamics of the contest. Even before Jackson officially entered the race, Clay realized that his interpretation of the Constitution and national power, especially in his advocacy of certain programs, might alienate some voters.*

"On the Election, the Court, and Improvements," *The Papers of Henry Clay, Volume 3* edited by James F. Hopkins. Copyright © 1963 by The University Press of Kentucky. Reprinted by permission of The University Press of Kentucky. [Editorial insertions appear in square brackets]

## To Francis T. Brooke

Lexington 28h. August 1823.

I received, my dear Sir, your very obliging letter of the 14h instant, and I pray you to believe that I do not place less value on your friendship because you have nothing to communicate "more favorable to my prospects." On the subject to which you allude I assure you most sincerely, I look with great calmness, and with a most perfect determination to acquiesce chearfully in whatever choice the Nation may make. It would be a poor compliment to our institutions to say that their solidity, or the public happiness, materially depended upon any selection that shall take place. I really think however that Virginia cannot justify herself to the Union for the apathy which you say prevails there on the question. Judging as I have done, at this distance, from the Enquirer [Richmond newspaper] and other Virginia prints I had supposed that great interest was felt and generally taken in its decision; and that there was even danger of her overstep-

ing the line of cautious circumspection which her leading politicians were understood to have marked out for her.

This indifference, you say, arises from the absence of any pledge that the great interests of the people of Virginia will be taken care of by any of the competitors for the Chief Magistracy. If indeed no such pledge is to be found in the principles, integrity & character, as heretofore developed, of either of the Candidates, it is, I should think, quite too late in the day now for any pledge to be given or received. But, my dear Sir, what interests have Virginia and the South separate from the Union? You have mentioned a single subject only, that of the encroachments of the Federal Judiciary on State rights; and, as connected with this, the "broad doctrine now inculcated that Congress has the right to extend[,] not to regulate only[,] the jurisdiction of the Federal Courts." On that subject I am entirely at a loss to conceive any peculiar interest in the State of Virginia and the Southern States. All are equally concerned in the preservation of the State Sovereignties. All would be equally affected by Fœderal usurpation. But I must confess that it is the first time that I ever heard asserted such a doctrine as you say is now inculcated. The limit of the Federal Judiciary is to be found in the Constitution, and Congress can vest in it no power which is not there found. If such a doctrine as you state is really attempted to be inculcated you will find Kentucky now, as in the epoch of 1799, in spite of all your unkindness towards her, ready to co operate with you in opposing it. And no man in the Union will be more prompt than I shall be to second the opposition. I cannot suppose you to refer to the power which is claimed for the General Government to give effect to its laws through its own judiciary. For without that power; without Federal means to effectuate the constitutional resolves of the Federal will, there is an end to the General Government; there is inevitable if not instantaneous anarchy.

But, my dear Sir, on this subject of the Federal Judiciary and State rights I mean to say a few words to you, in the spirit of Virginia Independence, and in the frankness of sincere friendship. Has not Virginia exposed herself to the imputation of selfishness by the course of her conduct, or of that of many of her politicians? When, in the case of Cohens and Virginia, her authority was alone concerned, she made the most strenuous efforts against the exercise of power by the Supreme Court. But when the thunders of that Court were directed against poor Kentucky, in vain did she invoke Virginian aid.[1] The Supreme Court it was imagined would decide on the side of supposed interests of Virginia. It has so decided; and, in effect, cripples the Sovereign power of the State of Kentucky noore [*sic*] than any other measure ever affected the Independence of any state in this Union, and not a Virginia voice is heard against the decision. The Supreme Court is viewed with complacency, and as a very different sort of tribunal, from that Supreme Court which decided Cohens's

case. Again. Of all the irregular bodies none can be more so than a Congressional Caucus at Washington. None have a more consolodating tendency. Indeed it is espoused upon the principle of preventing the exercise of State or Federal rights through the medium of the H. of R. Yet the Virginia politicians (at least if we are to judge from the papers) warmly advocate the constitution of such a Caucus. Will it not be said that they are influenced by the consideration, not of preserving unimpaired State rights, but of giving to the State power of *Virginia* the utmost effect of which it is susceptible? Or that of securing the election of the alleged favorite of Virginia who, without the instrumentality of such an assemblage, is in danger of losing the election? [William H. Crawford] It is in vain to speak of the inconveniencies of a warmly contested election. They are incident to our system; and are happily provided for by it. And the transitions from a Congressional Caucus, to a Prætorian Cohort or Hereditary Monarchy, to escape from those vexations, are not so great as we might at first imagine.

I am aware that on two subjects I have the misfortune to differ with many of my Virginia friends—Internal Improvements and Home Manufactures. My opinion has been formed after much deliberation, and my best judgment yet tells me that I am right. I have not time nor would it be fitting as regards your comfort now to discuss the policy or the power of fostering those interests. I believe Virginia & the Southern States as much interested, directly or indirectly, as any other parts of the Union, in their encouragement. When this Government was first adopted, we had no interior. Our population was inclosed between the Sea and the Mountains which run parallel to it. Since then the West part of your State, the Western parts of N. York & Pennsa. & all the Western States have been settled. The Wars of Europe & the emigrants to the West consumed all the surplus produced on both sides of the Mountains. Those Wars have terminated; and emigration has ceased. We find ourselves annually in the possession of an immense surplus. There is no market for it abroad; there is none at home. If there were a foreign market, before we, in the interior, could reach it, the intervening population would have supplied it. There can be no Foreign market adequate

---

[1] Clay was probably referring to *Green v. Biddle* (1823), in which the Supreme Court declared unconstitutional Kentucky statutes on the disposition of land titles claimed by Kentucky settlers versus Virginia landowners (who had claimed the land before Kentucky separated from Virginia).

to the consumption of the vast & growing surplus of the produce of our Agriculture. We must then have a Home market. Some of us must cultivate; some fabricate. And we must have reasonable protection against the machinations of Foreign powers. On the Sea board you want a navy, fortifications, protection, foreign commerce. In the Interior we want Internal Improvements, Home Manufactures. You have what you want, and object to our getting what we want. Should not the interests of both parties be provided for?

It has appeared to me, in the administration of the General Government, to be a just principle, to enquire what great interests belong to each section of our Country, and to promote those interests as far as practicable consistently with the Constitution, having always an eye to the welfare of the whole. Assuming this principle, does any one doubt that if N. York, N. Jersey, Pennsa. Delaware Maryland & the Western States constituted an Independent Nation, it would immediately protect the two important interests in question? And is it not to be feared that, if protection is not to be found to vital interests, from the existing system, in great parts of the Confederacy, those parts will ultimately seek to establish a system that will afford the requisite protection? I would not, in the application of the principle indicated, give to the peculiar interests of great sections *all* the protection which they would probably receive if those sections constituted separate & independent States. I would however extend some protection & measure it by balancing the countervailing interests, if there be such, in other quarters of the Union.

I concur entirely with you in thinking that the North & East, but particularly New England, have laid in a great measure, the other parts of the Union under contribution. And of all the ill advised measures; of all the wasteful expenditures of public money, the Revolutionary pension list preeminently takes the lead. Never was there more public money spent with less practical benefit. But who proposed it? Your own Monroe [after Monroe pointed out that needy veterans of the Revolutionary war were not eligible for federal pensions, Congress enacted the pension law of 18 March 1818.]. I thought of it then as I think of it now; but opposition would have been silly & vain.

You will oppose my election I suppose in Virginia. I have no right to complain. Silence & Submission are my duty. You will oppose me because I think that the interests of all parts of the Union should be taken care of; in other words, that the interests of the Interior, on the two subjects mentioned, as well as those of the Maritime coast ought to be provided for. You will give your suffrages to Mr. Crawford or to Mr. Adams; and if Mr. Crawford or Mr. Adams be elected I venture to predict that we shall find either in his inaugural speech, or in his first message or speech (perhaps the latter mode of communication may be revived) to Congress, a recommendation of efficient encouragement to Domestic Manufactures & Internal improvements.

I am afraid that you will think me in a very bad humor. Far from it. I repeat, that I never enjoyed more perfect composure. My health, it is true, is extremely bad; and I am now confined at home by the endeavor to re establish it. But it neither affects my tranquillity nor gives me the spleen. In regard to the election, as to which I will make no professions of apathy or indifference, which I do not feel, my friends continue to be very confident; and my own opinion is that my prospects are not surpassed by those of either of the other gentlemen. Still I am not unaware that all things are uncertain. And I therefore continue resolved to preserve my philosophy, my principles & my conscience, be the event what it may.

\*     \*     \*

# REVIEW QUESTIONS

1. What part did Clay think state or regional interests should play in the presidential election?
2. Why did he criticize Virginia's interpretations and actions in regard to the powers of the federal judiciary?
3. Why did he criticize attempts to reinstitute a congressional caucus for the nomination of presidential candidates?
4. Why did he want the national government to take an active role in promoting internal improvements? How, according to Clay, would such action affect national and state interests?

# 11   THE JACKSONIAN ERA

*Tennessee militia soldiers, inspired by his toughness, had nicknamed Andrew Jackson "Old Hickory" during the War of 1812. Since that time, less inspired than aggravated, his political opponents called him quite a number of other names. Jackson probably deserved all of the monikers, good and bad, for he was a complex man whose personal and professional decisions produced conflicting reactions during his lifetime and thereafter. Although negative evaluations mounted in the late twentieth century, Jackson was a hero to most of his contemporaries. He seemed to embody the image many Americans had, or wanted to have, of themselves. They embraced the image of the frontiersman, someone they saw as self-reliant, someone whose character was based in action not intellect: someone who used might to make right and who knew instinctively what right was. These Americans applauded him as a self-made man: he was an example to their sons that in America any boy, through self-determination, direction, and diligence, could indeed become powerful. Jackson's opponents, however, pointed out that his conduct also demonstrated how action without full reflection could have negative repercussions. To them, his decisions showed why there had to be checks on the delegation and execution of power.*

*Jackson, over time, came to epitomize the myth and reality of a new era in American democracy. The Jacksonian Age was a time when many Americans started to define democracy more inclusively and equality more broadly than the Founders had. They celebrated greater participation by white men, no matter what their economic and social rank, in the political life of the nation. Yet in doing so, showing the complexity and contradictory nature of this age, they also expounded more fully on the ethnic and gendered limits to American democracy, equality, and opportunity. Some Americans did protest those restrictions, using the language of revolutionary America and building on the broader interpretations of Jacksonian America. During this period there was growing debate about the abolition of slavery and Native American rights and property.*

*Another issue of increasing concern was that of the allocation and exercise of power between national and state governments. Old compromises were fraying and new ones increasingly difficult to forge. In this new era of the common man there was no question of sovereignty remaining with the people, but there were many heated debates over which government—state or national—best protected the common man's rights and interests. When national and state legislation came into conflict, which one did citizens ultimately want to have precedence? Did they want the one that confirmed rule by the majority to hold sway, or did they want those that protected minorities (state contingents) to have the power to check a possible tyranny by the majority? Some believed that the primacy of the national government had already been spelled out in the Constitution and confirmed by Supreme Court decisions; others believed that the state governments, which were more closely tied to the people, better represented citizens' interests, and they increasingly challenged the former.*

*Jackson initially straddled the debate, but when put to the test during the nullification controversy, he came down firmly for the supremacy of the national government. Yet as a believer and practitioner in self-reliance, he also seemed to believe that the nation should not do what the state could do, nor should the state do what the individual could do. This showed in his constitutional scruples about national power in terms of internal improvements. As did Madison and Monroe before him, Jackson opposed federal support for local projects. Even so, Jackson was not a states-rights proponent; he supported issues only if they fit within his concept of national interests.*

*As a general and then as president, Jackson's duty was to execute national policy. In pursuing that end—ensuring the security and developing the strength of the country—Jackson assumed and exercised ever greater power, which sometimes got him into trouble. When he was a general, politicians accused him of exceeding his orders and delegating authority, and during his presidency, political opponents accused him of exceeding his constitutional authority. Operating within a rather expansive interpretation of executive limits, Jackson strengthened the power of the presidency through his use of appointments and the veto. While willing to work with the legislative branch, he refused to be ruled by it, just as he refused to allow the Supreme Court or the state governments to have the last say in national affairs. He believed that he knew what was best for the country and acted on that belief. His popularity with the voters suggests that they agreed with him.*

## SAMUEL ENNALS AND PHILIP BELL

# An Address to the Citizens
# of New-York (1831)

*In 1832 William Lloyd Garrison published* Thoughts on African Colonization. *The subtitle was* An Impartial Exhibition of the Doctrines, Principles and Purposes of the American Colonization Society, Together with the Resolutions, Addresses and Remonstrances of the Free People of Color. *Garrison began his book by saying that when he started his abolitionist work he knew that he would be persecuted for attacking slavery and that he also knew that it would be the same for opposing colonization. Even so, he refused to remain silent. The main reason that he was against the American Colonization Society (and related state societies) was because it refused to oppose the system of slavery even as it advocated freeing African Americans and then sending the freedmen to Liberia in Africa. He also decried how the society represented slaves and freedmen "as aliens and foreigners, wanderers from Africa—destitute of that* amor patriae, *which is the bond of union—seditious—without alliances—irresponsible—unambitious—cherishing no attachment to the soil—feeling no interest in our national prosperity . . . content to remain in ignorance and degradation—&c. &c. &c. (pt. II, p. 4). He proclaimed that all of that was a libel and one to be refuted not only by his words but also by those of African Americans. He included the objections voiced in twenty communities from Baltimore to Boston.*

---

From William Lloyd Garrison, ed., *Thoughts on African Colonization. Part II. Sentiments of the People of Color* (1832; New York: Arno Press, 1968), pp. 13–17. [Editorial insertions appear in brackets—Ed.]

## A Voice from New-York

New-York, January, 1831.

At a public meeting of the colored citizens of New-York, held at Boyer Lodge Room, on Tuesday evening, the 25th ult. Mr Samuel Ennals was called to the chair, and Mr Philip Bell appointed secretary. The chairman stated that the object of the meeting was to take into consideration the proceedings of an association, under the title of the 'New-York Colonization Society.' An address to the 'Citizens of New-York' relative to that Society, was read from the Commercial Advertiser of the 8th ult.; whereupon the following resolutions were unanimously adopted.

Whereas a number of gentlemen in this city, of mistaken views with respect to the wishes and welfare of the people of this state, on the subject of African colonization, and in pursuance of such mistaken views are using every exertion to form 'African Colonization Societies;' and whereas a public document, purporting to be an address to the people of the 'city of New-York' on this subject, contains opinions and assertions regarding the people of color as unfounded as they are unjust and derogatory to them—Therefore

Resolved, That this meeting do most solemnly protest against the said address, as containing sentiments with respect to the people of color, unjust, illiberal and unfounded; tending to excite the prejudice of the community.

Resolved, That in our opinion the sentiments put forth in the resolution at the formation of the

'Colonization Society of the city of New-York,' are such as to impress this community with the belief that the colored population are a growing evil, immoral, and destitute of religious principles.

Resolved, That we view the resolution calling on the worshippers of Christ to assist in the unholy crusade against the colored population of this country, as totally at variance with true Christian principles.

Resolved, That we claim *this country, the place of our birth, and not Africa,* as our mother country, and all attempts to send us to Africa we consider as gratuitous and uncalled for.

Resolved, That a committee of three persons be appointed to draft an address to the people of New-York, and to be published, together with these resolutions, and the same be signed by the Chairman and Secretary.

SAMUEL ENNALS, Chairman.
PHILIP BELL, Secretary.

## An Address to the Citizens of New-York.

In protesting against the sentiments and declarations to our prejudice with which the above noticed 'address' and 'resolutions' abound, we are well aware of the power and influence we have attempted to resist. The gentlemen named as officers of the 'Colonization Society' are men of high standing, their dictum is law in morals with our community; but we who feel the effect of their proscription, indulge the hope of an impartial hearing.

We believe many of those gentlemen are our friends, and we hope they all mean well; we care not how many Colonization Societies they form to send slaves from the south to a place where they may enjoy freedom; and if they can 'drain the ocean with a bucket,' may send '*with their own consent*,' the increasing free colored population: but we solemnly protest against that Christian philanthropy which in acknowledging our wrongs commits a greater by vilifying us. The conscientious man would not kill the animal, but cried 'mad dog,' and the rabble despatched him. These

gentlemen acknowledge the anomaly of those political ethics which make a distinction between man and man, when their foundation is, 'that all men are born equal,' and possess in common 'unalienable rights;' and to justify the withholding of these 'rights' would proclaim to foreigners that we are 'a distinct and inferior race,' without religion or morals, and implying that our condition cannot be improved here because there exists an unconquerable prejudice in the whites towards us. We absolutely deny these positions, and we call upon the learned author of the 'address' for the indications of distinction between us and other men. There are different *colors* among all species of animated creation. A difference of color is not a difference of species. Our structure and organization are the same, and not distinct from other men; and in what respects are we inferior? Our political condition we admit renders us less respectable, but does it prove us an inferior part of the human family? Inferior indeed we are as to the means which we possess of becoming wealthy and learned men; and it would argue well for the cause of justice, humanity and true religion, if the reverend gentlemen whose names are found at the bottom of President Duer's [William A. Duer, president of Columbia College] address, instead of showing their benevolence by laboring to move us some four thousand miles off, were to engage actively in the furtherance of plans for the improvement of our moral and political condition in the country of our birth. It is too late now to brand with inferiority any one of the races of mankind. We ask for proof. Time was when it was thought impossible to civilize the red man. Yet our own country presents a practical refutation of the vain assertion in the flourishing condition of the Cherokees, among whom intelligence and refinement are seen in somewhat fairer proportions than are exhibited by some of their white neighbors. In the language of a writer of expanded views and truly noble sentiments, 'the blacks must be regarded as the real authors of most of the arts and sciences which give the whites at present the advantage over them. While Greece and Rome were yet barbarous, we find the light of learning and improvement emanating from this, by supposition, degraded and accursed continent of Africa, out of the midst of this very woolly-haired, flat-nosed, thick lipped, and coal black race, which some persons are tempted to station at a pretty low intermediate point between men and monkeys' [Alexander H. Everett, 'America, or a General Survey,' pp. 212, 225]. It is needless to dwell on this topic; and we say with the same writer, the blacks had a long and glorious day: and after what they have been and done, it argues not so much a mistaken theory, as sheer ignorance of the most notorious historical facts, to pretend that they are naturally inferior to the whites.

We earnestly desire that this address may not be misunderstood. We have no objection in the abstract to the Colonization Society; but we do protest against the means which that Society uses to effect its purposes. It is evident, to any impartial observer, that the natural tendency of all their speeches, reports, sermons, &c. is to widen the breach between us and the whites, and give to prejudice a tenfold vigor. It has produced a mistaken sentiment toward us. Africa is considered the home of those who have never seen its shores. The poor ignorant slave, who, in all probability, has never heard the name of Christ, by the colonization process is suddenly transformed into a 'missionary,' to instruct in the principles of Christianity and the arts of civilized life. The Friends have been the last to aid the system pursued by the Society's advocates. And we say (for we feel it) that in proportion as they become colonizationists, they become less active and less friendly to our welfare as citizens of the United States.

There does exist in the United States a prejudice against us; but is it unconquerable? Is it not in the power of these gentlemen to subdue it? If their object is to benefit us, why not better our condition here? What keeps us down but the want of wealth? Why do we not accumulate wealth? Simply because we are not encouraged. If we wish to give our boys a classical education, they are refused admission into your colleges. If we consume our means in giving them a mercantile education, you will not employ them as clerks; if they are taught navigation, you will not employ them as captains.

If we make them mechanics, you will not encourage them, nor will white mechanics work in the same shop with them. And with all these disabilities, like a mill-stone about us, because we cannot point to our statesmen, bankers and lawyers, we are called an inferior race. Look at the glaring injustice towards us. (A foreigner, before he knows one of our streets from another, mounts a cart under the license of another man, or is a public porter, a lamp-lighter, a watchman, &c)

These gentlemen know but little of a large portion of the colored population of this city. Their opinions are formed from the unfortunate portion of our people whose characters are scrutinized by them as judges of courts. Their patrician principles prevent an intercourse with men in the middle walks of life, among whom a large portion of our people may be classed. We ask them to visit the dwellings of the respectable part of our people, and we are satisfied that they will discover more civilization and refinement than will be found among the same number of white families of an equal standing.

Finally, we hope that those who have so eloquently pleaded the cause of the Indian, will at least endeavor to preserve consistency in their conduct. They put no faith in Georgia, although she declares that the Indians shall not be removed but 'with their own consent.' Can they blame us if we attach the same credit to the declaration that they mean to colonize us 'only with our consent?' They cannot indeed use force; that is out of the question. But they harp so much on 'inferiority,' 'prejudice,' 'distinction,' and what not, that there will no alternative be left us but to fall in with their plans. We are content to abide where we are. We do not believe that things will always continue the same. The time must come when the declaration of independence will be felt in the heart as well as uttered from the mouth, and when the rights of all shall be properly acknowledged and appreciated. God hasten that time. This is our home, and this our country. Beneath its sod lie the bones of our fathers: for it some of them fought, bled, and died. Here we were born, and here we will die.

## REVIEW QUESTIONS

1. Why did some African American inhabitants of New York City meet on January 25, 1831? What does such a meeting reveal about the African-American community in the city?

2. Were the meeting's participants totally against colonization?
3. What did they protest?
4. What did they call on reformers to do?
5. Why did the address include references to Native Americans?

# South Carolina's Ordinance of Nullification (1832)

*In the ongoing tug of war between states and nation, the conflict over the 1828 tariff led to what has been called the nullification controversy. South Carolina was suffering from an agricultural depression when Congress passed what the state's citizens called the Tariff of Abominations. They believed that the tariff protected northern manufacturing at their expense. John C. Calhoun of South Carolina, who had been John Quincy Adams's vice president and then became Andrew Jackson's in 1829, wrote but published anonymously the* South Carolina Exposition and Protest. *Calhoun theorized that the states could nullify national legislation they deemed unconstitutional and outlined a procedure for such an action. South Carolina did not immediately do this, for with the election of Jackson and Calhoun, it decided to wait for a new tariff policy to be drawn up by the incoming administration. Then, in January 1830, Senator Samuel A. Foot of Connecticut proposed a resolution to restrict the sale of public land in the West. After Thomas Hart Benton of Missouri denounced it as an attack on the West, Robert Y. Hayne of South Carolina joined the fight. He hoped that southern advocacy of a policy of cheap lands in the West would result in western support for the lower tariffs sought by the South.*

*This sectional debate over land policy expanded quickly into one on national power. Opponents and supporters in both national and state governments, executive and legislative branches, rallied their forces. President Jackson split from Vice President Calhoun over the issue; the result was a new cabinet purged of Calhoun adherents and, in the next election, a new vice president, Martin Van Buren. Calhoun then moved into the Senate to promote and defend nullification there, as Hayne moved back to South Carolina to assume his gubernatorial duties. As governor, it was Hayne's responsibility to execute the will of the citizens of South Carolina as expressed not only by their representatives in the normal legislature but as presented in an ordinance passed on 24 November by a special convention. Despite some congressional concessions—the lowering of duties in 1830 and then the passage of the Tariff of 1832, which reduced rates even further—South Carolina nullifiers were determined to turn their political theory into reality.*

From *Statutes at Large of South Carolina*, vol. I (Columbia, SC: A. S. Johnston, 1836), pp. 329ff. [Editorial insertions that appear in square brackets are from the 1836 edition—*Ed.*]

*An Ordinance to Nullify certain acts of the Congress of the United States, purporting to be laws laying duties and imposts on the importation of foreign commodities.*

*Whereas* the Congress of the United States, by various acts, purporting to be acts laying duties and imposts on foreign imports, but in reality intended for the protection of domestic manufactures, and the giving of bounties to classes and individuals engaged in particular employments, at the expense and to the injury and oppression of other classes and individuals, and by wholly exempting from taxation certain foreign commodities, such as are not produced or manufactured in the United States, to afford a pretext for imposing higher and excessive duties on articles similar to those intended to be protected, hath exceeded its just powers under the Constitution, which confers on it no authority to afford such protection, and hath violated the true meaning and intent of the Constitution, which provides for equality in imposing the burthens of taxation upon the several States and portions of the Confederacy: *And whereas* the said Congress, exceeding its just power to impose taxes and collect revenue for the purpose of effecting and accomplishing the specific objects and purposes which the Constitution of the United States authorizes it to effect and accomplish, hath raised and collected unnecessary revenue for objects unauthorized by the Constitution:—

*We, therefore, the people of the State of South Carolina in Convention assembled, do declare and ordain,* . . . That the several acts and parts of acts of the Congress of the United States, purporting to be laws for the imposing of duties and imposts on the importation of foreign commodities, . . . and, more especially, . . . [the tariff acts of 1828 and 1832] . . . , are unauthorized by the Constitution of the United States, and violate the true meaning and intent thereof, and are null, void, and no law, nor binding upon this State, its officers or citizens; and all promises, contracts, and obligations, made or entered into, or to be made or entered into, with purpose to secure the duties imposed by the said acts, and all judicial proceedings which shall be hereafter had in affirmance thereof, are and shall be held utterly null and void.

*And it is further Ordained,* That it shall not be lawful for any of the constituted authorities, whether of this State or of the United States, to enforce the payment of duties imposed by the said acts within the limits of this State; but it shall be the duty of the Legislature to adopt such measures and pass such acts as may be necessary to give full effect to this Ordinance, and to prevent the enforcement and arrest the operation of the said acts and parts of acts of the Congress of the United States within the limits of this State, from and after the 1st day of February next, . . .

*And it is further Ordained,* That in no case of law or equity, decided in the courts of this State, wherein shall be drawn in question the authority of this ordinance, or the validity of such act or acts of the Legislature as may be passed for the purpose of giving effect thereto, or the validity of the aforesaid acts of Congress, imposing duties, shall any appeal be taken or allowed to the Supreme Court of the United States, nor shall any copy of the record be printed or allowed for that purpose; and if any such appeal shall be attempted to be taken, the courts of this State shall proceed to execute and enforce their judgments, according to the laws and usages of the State, without reference to such attempted appeal, and the person or persons attempting to take such appeal may be dealt with as for a contempt of the court.

*And it is further Ordained,* That all persons now holding any office of honor, profit, or trust, civil or military, under this State, (members of the Legislature excepted), shall, within such time, and in such manner as the Legislature shall prescribe, take an oath well and truly to obey, execute, and enforce, this Ordinance, and such act or acts of the Legislature as may be passed in pursuance thereof, according to the true intent and meaning of the same; and on the neglect or omission of any such person or persons so to do, his or their office or offices shall be forthwith vacated, . . . and no person hereafter elected to any office of honor, profit, or trust, civil or military, (members of the Legislature excepted), shall, until the Legislature shall otherwise provide and direct, enter on the execution of his office, . . . until he shall, in like manner, have taken a similar oath; and no juror shall be empannelled in any of the courts of this State, in any cause in which shall be in question this Ordinance, or any act of the Legislature passed in pursuance thereof, unless he shall first, in addition to the usual oath, have taken an oath that he will well and truly obey, execute, and enforce this Ordinance, and such act or acts of the Legislature as may be passed to carry the same into operation. . . .

And we, the People of South Carolina, to the end that it may be fully understood by the Government of the United States, and the people of the co-States, that we are determined to maintain this, our Ordinance and Declaration, at every hazard, *Do further Declare* that we will not submit to the application of force, on the part of the Federal Government, to reduce this State to obedience; but that we will consider the passage, by Congress, of any act . . . to coerce the State, shut up her ports, destroy or harass her commerce, or to enforce the acts hereby declared to be null and void, otherwise than through the civil tribunals of the country, as inconsistent with the longer continuance of South Carolina in the Union: and that the people of this State will thenceforth hold themselves absolved from all further obligation to maintain or preserve their political connexion with the people of the other States, and will forthwith proceed to organize a separate Government, and do all other acts and things which sovereign and independent States may of right to do.

## REVIEW QUESTIONS

1. What justification was given for the act?
2. How was the state to implement nullification?
3. Which was given precedence: obedience to the state or to the nation?
4. Did this ordinance leave an opening for compromise? If so, how?

## ANDREW JACKSON

# FROM The President's Nullification Proclamation (1832)

*President Jackson was not about to let South Carolina impose its interpretation of the Constitution on the national government or to empower its sister states by example. The old duelist fired back at the state, first with a moderate charge in his annual message on December 4, 1832, and then with a full explosive charge in a proclamation on 10 December.*

From James D. Richardson, comp., *A Compilation of the Messages and Papers of the Presidents, 1789–1902*, vol. II (Bureau of National Literature and Art, 1904), pp. 640–56. [Editorial insertions appear in square brackets—*Ed.*]

\*   \*   \*

To preserve this bond of our political existence from destruction, to maintain inviolate this state of national honor and prosperity, and to justify the confidence my fellow-citizens have reposed in me, I, Andrew Jackson, President of the United States, have thought proper to issue this my proclamation, stating my views of the Constitution and laws applicable to the measures adopted by the convention of South Carolina and to the reasons they have put forth to sustain them, declaring the course which duty will require me to pursue, and, appealing to the understanding and patriotism of the people, warn them of the consequences that must inevitably result from an observance of the dictates of the convention.

*　　*　　*

The ordinance is founded, not on the indefeasible right of resisting acts which are plainly unconstitutional and too oppressive to be endured, but on the strange position that any one State may not only declare an act of Congress void, but prohibit its execution; that they may do this consistently with the Constitution; that the true construction of that instrument permits a State to retain its place in the Union and yet be bound by no other of its laws than those it may choose to consider as constitutional. It is true, they add, that to justify this abrogation of a law it must be palpably contrary to the Constitution: but it is evident that to give the right of resisting laws of that description, coupled with the uncontrolled right to decide what laws deserve that character, is to give the power of resisting all laws; for as by the theory there is no appeal, the reasons alleged by the State, good or bad, must prevail. If it should be said that public opinion is a sufficient check against the abuse of this power, it may be asked why it is not deemed a sufficient guard against the passage of an unconstitutional act by Congress? There is, however, a restraint in this last case which makes the assumed power of a State more indefensible, and which does not exist in the other. There are two appeals from an unconstitutional act passed by Congress—one to the judiciary, the other to the people and the States. There is no appeal from the State decision in theory, and the practical illustration shows that the courts are closed against an application to review it, both judges and jurors being sworn to decide in its favor. But reasoning on this subject is superfluous when our social compact, in express terms, declares that the laws of the United States, its Constitution, and treaties made under it are the supreme law of the land, and, for greater caution, adds "that the

judges in every State shall be bound thereby, anything in the constitution or laws of any State to the contrary notwithstanding." . . .

*　　*　　*

. . . [T]he defects of the Confederation need not be detailed. Under its operation we could scarcely be called a nation. We had neither prosperity at home nor consideration abroad. This state of things could not be endured, and our present happy Constitution was formed, but formed in vain if this fatal doctrine prevails. It was formed for important objects that are announced in the preamble, made in the name and by the authority of the people of the United States, whose delegates framed and whose conventions approved it. The most important among these objects—that which is placed first in rank, on which all the others rest—is "*to form a more perfect union.*" Now, is it possible that even if there were no express provision giving supremacy to the Constitution and laws of the United States over those of the States, can it be conceived that an instrument made for the purpose of "*forming a more perfect union*" than that of the Confederation could be so constructed by the assembled wisdom of our country as to substitute for that Confederation a form of government dependent for its existence on the local interest, the party spirit, of a State, or of a prevailing faction in a State? Every man of plain, unsophisticated understanding who hears the question will give such an answer as will preserve the Union. Metaphysical subtlety, in pursuit of an impracticable theory, could alone have devised one that is calculated to destroy it.

I consider, then, the power to annul a law of the United States, assumed by one State, *incompatible with the existence of the Union, contradicted expressly by the letter of the Constitution, unauthorized by its spirit, inconsistent with every principle on which it was founded, and destructive of the great object for which it was formed.*

After this general view of the leading principle, we must examine the particular application of it which is made in the ordinance.

The preamble rests its justification on these grounds: It assumes as a fact that the obnoxious laws, although they purport to be laws for raising revenue, were in reality intended for the protection of manufactures, which purpose it asserts to be unconstitutional; that the operation of these laws is unequal; that the amount raised by them is greater than is required by the wants of the Government; and, finally, that the proceeds are to be applied to objects unauthorized by the Constitution. These are the only causes alleged to justify an open opposition to the laws of the country and a threat of seceding from the Union if any attempt should be made to enforce them. The first virtually acknowledges that the law in question was passed under a power expressly given by the Constitution to lay and collect imposts; but its constitutionality is drawn in question from the *motives* of those who passed it. However apparent this purpose may be in the present case, nothing can be more dangerous than to admit the position that an unconstitutional purpose entertained by the members who assent to a law enacted under a constitutional power shall make that law void. For how is that purpose to be ascertained? Who is to make the scrutiny? How often may bad purposes be falsely imputed, in how many cases are they concealed by false professions, in how many is no declaration of motive made? . . .

The next objection is that the laws in question operate unequally. This objection may be made with truth to every law that has been or can be passed. The wisdom of man never yet contrived a system of taxation that would operate with perfect equality. If the unequal operation of a law makes it unconstitutional, and if all laws of that description may be abrogated by any State for that cause, then, indeed, is the Federal Constitution unworthy of the slightest effort for its preservation. . . .

The two remaining objections made by the ordinance to these laws are that the sums intended to be raised by them are greater than are required and that the proceeds will be unconstitutionally employed.

The Constitution has given, expressly, to Congress the right of raising revenue and of determining the sum the public exigencies will require. The States have no control over the exercise of this right other than that which results from the power of changing the representatives who abuse it, and thus procure redress. Congress may undoubtedly abuse this discretionary power; but the same may be said of others with which they are vested. Yet the discretion must exist somewhere. The Constitution has given it to the representatives of all the people, checked by the representatives of the States and by the Executive power. The South Carolina construction gives it to the legislature or the convention of a single State, where neither the people of the different States, nor the States in their separate capacity, nor the Chief Magistrate elected by the people have any representation. . . .

The ordinance, with the same knowledge of the future that characterizes a former objection, tells you that the proceeds of the tax will be unconstitutionally applied. If this could be ascertained with certainty, the objection would with more propriety be reserved for the law so applying the proceeds, but surely can not be urged against the laws levying the duty.

*       *       *

The Constitution declares that the judicial powers of the United States extend to cases arising under the laws of the United States, and that such laws, the Constitution, and treaties shall be paramount to the State constitutions and laws. The judiciary act prescribes the mode by which the case may be brought before a court of the United States by appeal when a State tribunal shall decide against this provision of the Constitution. The ordinance declares there shall be no appeal—makes the State law paramount to the Constitution and laws of the United States, forces judges and jurors to swear that they will disregard their provisions, and even makes it penal in a suitor to attempt relief by appeal. It further declares that it shall not be lawful for the authorities of the United States or of that State to enforce the payment of duties imposed by the revenue laws within its limits.

Here is a law of the United States, not even pretended to be unconstitutional, repealed by the authority of a small majority of the voters of a single State. Here is a provision of the Constitution which is solemnly abrogated by the same authority.

On such expositions and reasonings the ordinance grounds not only an assertion of the right to annul the laws of which it complains, but to enforce it by a threat of seceding from the Union if any attempt is made to execute them.

This right to secede is deduced from the nature of the Constitution, which, they say, is a compact between sovereign States who have preserved their whole sovereignty and therefore are subject to no superior; that because they made the compact they can break it when in their opinion it has been departed from by the other States. Fallacious as this course of reasoning is, it enlists State pride and finds advocates in the honest prejudices of those who have not studied the nature of our Government sufficiently to see the radical error on which it rests.

The people of the United States formed the Constitution, acting through the State legislatures in making the compact, to meet and discuss its provisions, and acting in separate conventions when they ratified those provisions; but the terms used in its construction show it to be a Government in which the people of all the States, collectively, are represented. We are *one people* in the choice of President and Vice-President. Here the States have no other agency than to direct the mode in which the votes shall be given. The candidates having the majority of all the votes are chosen. The electors of a majority of States may have given their votes for one candidate, and yet another may be chosen. The people, then, and not the States, are represented in the executive branch.

In the House of Representatives there is this difference, that the people of one State do not, as in the case of President and Vice-President, all vote for the same officers. The people of all the States do not vote for all the members, each State electing only its own representatives. But this creates no material distinction. When chosen, they are all representatives of the United States, not representatives of the particular State from which they come. They are paid by the United States, not by the State; nor are they accountable to it for any act done in the performance of their legislative functions; and however they may in practice, as it is

their duty to do, consult and prefer the interests of their particular constituents when they come in conflict with any other partial or local interest, yet it is their first and highest duty, as representatives of the United States, to promote the general good.

The Constitution of the United States, then, forms a *government*, not a league; and whether it be formed by compact between the States or in any other manner, its character is the same. It is a Government in which all the people are represented, which operates directly on the people individually, not upon the States; they retained all the power they did not grant. But each State, having expressly parted with so many powers as to constitute, jointly with the other States, a single nation, can not, from that period, possess any right to secede, because such secession does not break a league, but destroys the unity of a nation; and any injury to that unity is not only a breach which would result from the contravention of a compact, but it is an offense against the whole Union. To say that any State may at pleasure secede from the Union is to say that the United States are not a nation, because it would be a solecism to contend that any part of a nation might dissolve its connection with the other parts, to their injury or ruin, without committing any offense. Secession, like any other revolutionary act, may be morally justified by the extremity of oppression; but to call it a constitutional right is confounding the meaning of terms, and can only be done through gross error or to deceive those who are willing to assert a right, but would pause before they made a revolution or incur the penalties consequent on a failure.

Because the Union was formed by a compact, it is said the parties to that compact may, when they feel themselves aggrieved, depart from it; but it is precisely because it is a compact that they can not. A compact is an agreement or binding obligation. It may by its terms have a sanction or penalty for its breach, or it may not. If it contains no sanction, it may be broken with no other consequence than moral guilt; if it have a sanction, then the breach incurs the designated or implied penalty. A league between independent nations generally has no sanction other than a moral one; or if it should contain a penalty, as there is no common superior it can not be enforced. A government, on the contrary, always has a sanction, express or implied; and in our case it is both necessarily implied and expressly given. An attempt, by force of arms, to destroy a government is an offense, by whatever means the constitutional compact may have been formed; and such government has the right by the law of self-defense to pass acts for punishing the offender, unless that right is modified, restrained, or resumed by the constitutional act. In our system, although it is modified in the case of treason, yet authority is expressly given to pass all laws necessary to carry its powers into effect, and under this grant provision has been made for punishing acts which obstruct the due administration of the laws.

*    *    *

The States severally have not retained their entire sovereignty. It has been shown that in becoming parts of a nation, not members of a league, they surrendered many of their essential parts of sovereignty. The right to make treaties, declare war, levy taxes, exercise exclusive judicial and legislative powers, were all of them functions of sovereign power. The States, then, for all these important purposes were no longer sovereign. The allegiance of their citizens was transferred, in the first instance, to the Government of the United States; they became American citizens and owed obedience to the Constitution of the United States and to laws made in conformity with the powers it vested in Congress. This last position has not been and can not be denied. How, then, can that State be said to be sovereign and independent whose citizens owe obedience to laws not made by it and whose magistrates are sworn to disregard those laws when they come in conflict with those passed by another? What shows conclusively that the States can not be said to have reserved an undivided sovereignty is that they expressly ceded the right to punish treason—not treason against their separate power, but treason against the United States. Treason is an offense against *sovereignty*,

and sovereignty must reside with the power to punish it. . . .

*    *    *

These are the alternatives that are presented by the convention—a repeal of all the acts for raising revenue, leaving the Government without the means of support, or an acquiescence in the dissolution of our Union by the secession of one of its members. When the first was proposed, it was known that it could not be listened to for a moment. It was known, if force was applied to oppose the execution of the laws, that it must be repelled by force; that Congress could not, without involving itself in disgrace and the country in ruin, accede to the proposition; and yet if this is not done in a given day, or if any attempt is made to execute the laws, the State is by the ordinance declared to be out of the Union. The majority of a convention assembled for the purpose have dictated these terms, or rather this rejection of all terms, in the name of the people of South Carolina. It is true that the governor of the State speaks of the submission of their grievances to a convention of all the States, which, he says, they "sincerely and anxiously seek and desire." Yet this obvious and constitutional mode of obtaining the sense of the other States on the construction of the federal compact, and amending it if necessary, has never been attempted by those who have urged the State on to this destructive measure. . . . If the legislature of South Carolina "anxiously desire" a general convention to consider their complaints, why have they not made application for it in the way the Constitution points out? The assertion that they "earnestly seek" it is completely negatived by the omission.

This, then, is the position in which we stand: A small majority of the citizens of one State in the Union have elected delegates to a State convention; that convention has ordained that all the revenue laws of the United States must be repealed, or that they are no longer a member of the Union. The governor of that State has recommended to the legislature the raising of an army to carry the secession into effect, and that he may be empowered to give clearances to vessels in the name of the

State. No act of violent opposition to the laws has yet been committed, but such a state of things is hourly apprehended. And it is the intent of this instrument to *proclaim*, not only that the duty imposed on me by the Constitution "to take care that the laws be faithfully executed" shall be performed to the extent of the powers already vested in me by law, or of such others as the wisdom of Congress shall devise and intrust to me for that purpose, but to warn the citizens of South Carolina who have been deluded into an opposition to the laws of the danger they will incur by obedience to the illegal and disorganizing ordinance of the convention; to exhort those who have refused to support it to persevere in their determination to uphold the Constitution and laws of their country; and to point out to all the perilous situation into which the good people of that State have been led, and that the course they are urged to pursue is one of ruin and disgrace to the very State whose rights they affect to support.

*     *     *

I have urged you [South Carolinians] to look back to the means that were used to hurry you on to the position you have now assumed and forward to the consequences it will produce. Something more is necessary. Contemplate the condition of that country of which you still form an important part. Consider its Government, uniting in one bond of common interest and general protection so many different States, giving to all their inhabitants the proud title of *American citizen*, protecting their commerce, securing their literature and their arts, facilitating their intercommunication, defending their frontiers, and making their name respected in the remotest parts of the earth. . . . If your leaders could succeed in establishing a separation, what would be your situation? Are you united at home? Are you free from the apprehension of civil discord, with all its fearful consequences? Do our neighboring republics, every day suffering some new revolution or contending with some new insurrection, do they excite your envy? But the dictates of a high duty oblige me solemnly to announce that you can not succeed. The laws of

the United States must be executed. I have no discretionary power on the subject; my duty is emphatically pronounced in the Constitution. Those who told you that you might peaceably prevent their execution deceived you; they could not have been deceived themselves. They know that a forcible opposition could alone prevent the execution of the laws, and they know that such opposition must be repelled. Their object is disunion. But be not deceived by names. Disunion by armed force is *treason*. Are you really ready to incur its guilt? If you are, on the heads of the instigators of the act be the dreadful consequences; on their heads be the dishonor, but on yours may fall the punishment. . . .

Fellow-citizens of the United States, the threat of unhallowed disunion, the names of those once respected by whom it is uttered, the array of military force to support it, denote the approach of a crisis in our affairs on which the continuance of our unexampled prosperity, our political existence, and perhaps that of all free governments may depend. . . . Having the fullest confidence in the justness of the legal and constitutional opinion of my duties which has been expressed, I rely with equal confidence on your undivided support in my determination to execute the laws, to preserve the Union by all constitutional means, to arrest, if possible, by moderate and firm measures the necessity of a recourse to force; and if it be the will of Heaven that the recurrence of its primeval curse on man for the shedding of a brother's blood should fall upon our land, that it be not called down by any offensive act on the part of the United States.

Fellow-citizens, the momentous case is before you. On your undivided support of your Government depends the decision of the great question it involves—whether your sacred Union will be preserved and the blessing it secures to us as one people shall be perpetuated. No one can doubt that the unanimity with which that decision will be expressed will be such as to inspire new confidence in republican institutions, and that the prudence, the wisdom, and the courage which it will bring to their defense will transmit them unimpaired and invigorated to our children.

May the Great Ruler of Nations grant that the signal blessings with which He has favored ours may not, by the madness of party or personal ambition, be disregarded and lost; and may His wise providence bring those who have produced this crisis to see the folly before they feel the misery of civil strife, and inspire a returning veneration for that Union which, if we may dare to penetrate His designs, He has chosen as the only means of attaining the high destinies to which we may reasonably aspire.

\*    \*    \*

## Review Questions

1. Did Jackson persuasively refute each of the points presented by the South Carolina nullificationists?
2. Why did Jackson believe that the interpretation of the Constitution as a state compact was incorrect? How did his perspective affect his view of secession?
3. Which branch of the national government did he indicate was the ultimate expression of the people's will? How does that help explain why he wielded the powers of his office as he did?

# ALEXIS DE TOCQUEVILLE

## FROM A Letter to Countess de Tocqueville (1831)

*General Jackson combated the Native Americans; President Jackson removed them. In doing so, he acted on his own desires and those of probably most—though not all—U.S. citizens. As the new Americans filled up the states east of the Mississippi River, they butted up against independent Indians holding prime land. Presidents Monroe and Adams dealt with the mounting crisis by turning to an idea first proposed in the Jefferson administration: that of removal. By 1830 Congress responded to the public's sentiments, the War Department's proposals, and the president's prodding by passing the Indian Removal Act. While the act seemed to reiterate the voluntary nature of removal by stating that certain allocated western lands were for "such tribes or nations of Indians as may choose to exchange the lands where they now reside, and remove there," it actually empowered the executive branch to follow a more coercive policy. The Indian Removal Act facilitated the transfer of almost all of the remaining eastern Native American tribes. Although the Cherokees were among the last uprooted by the government and forced to make the journey west, their fight, first by legal means and then, for some, by arms, meant that most of the nation's attention was on them. This continued as they made the terrible trip across the South to reach their new lands across the Mississippi. Their mental and physical anguish marked their path, along what became known as the Trail of Tears. They were not the only Indians to endure such travail. The Choctaws, Chickasaws, and Creeks blazed the way before them between 1830 and 1832. Their agonies did not go unremarked—indeed, as word got back to the Cherokees, that nation probably became all the more determined to resist—but they gained more sympathy from a foreign observer than from most Euro-Americans. Alexis de Tocqueville, a well-born Frenchman, traveled through the*

*United States to observe and record the attitudes and actions of the new nation and its people in the early 1830s. As his 25 December 1831 letter to his mother shows, he was both fascinated and repelled by what he saw.*

December 25, 1831,
on the Mississippi

Finally, finally, my dear mama, the signal is given; and here we are descending the Mississippi with all the swiftness that steam and current together can give to a vessel. We were beginning to despair of ever getting out of the wilderness in which we were confined. . . . Finally, one fine day, a little smoke was seen on the Mississippi, on the limits of the horizon; the cloud drew near little by little, and there emerged from it, neither a giant nor a dwarf as in fairy tales, but a huge steamboat, coming from New Orleans, and which, after parading before us for a quarter of an hour, as if to leave us in uncertainty as to whether it would stop or continue on its route, after spouting like a whale, finally headed toward us, broke through the ice with its huge framework and was tied to the bank. The entire population of our universe made its way to the riverside, which, as you know, then formed one of the furthest frontiers of our empire. The whole city of Memphis was in a flutter; no bells were rung because there are no bells, but people cried out hurrah! and the newcomers alighted on the bank in the manner of Christopher Columbus. We were not yet saved, however; the boat's destination was to go up the Mississippi to Louisville, and our purpose was to go to New Orleans. We happily had about fifteen companions in adversity who desired no more than we did to make their winter quarters in Memphis. So we made a general *push* on the captain. . . . I am nevertheless of the conviction that he would not have turned in his tracks, without a fortunate event, to which we owe our not becoming citizens of Memphis. As we were thus debating on the bank, an infernal music resounded in the forest; it was a noise composed of

drums, the neighing of horses, the barking of dogs. Finally a great troop of Indians, elderly people, women, children, baggage, all conducted by a European and heading toward the capital of our triangle. These Indians were the Chactas (or Choctaws), after the Indian pronunciation; . . . Be that as it may, you undoubtedly wish to know why these Indians had arrived there, and how they could be of use to us; patience, I beg you, now that I have time and paper, I want nothing to hurry me. You will thus know that the Americans of the United States, rational and unprejudiced people, moreover, great philanthropists, supposed, like the Spanish, that God had given them the new world and its inhabitants as complete property.

They have discovered, moreover, that, as it was proved (listen to this well) that a square mile could support ten times more civilized men than savage men, reason indicated that wherever civilized men could settle, it was necessary that the savages cede the place. You see what a fine thing logic is. Consequently, when the Indians begin to find themselves a little too near their brothers the whites, the President of the United States sends them a messenger, who represents to them that in their interest, properly understood, it would be good to draw back ever so little toward the West. The lands they have inhabited for centuries belong to them, undoubtedly: no one refuses them this incontestable right; but these lands, after all, are uncultivated wilderness, woods, swamps, truly poor property. On the other side of the Mississippi, by contrast, are magnificent regions, where the game has never been troubled by the noise of the pioneer's axe, where the Europeans will *never* reach. They are separated from it by more than a hundred leagues. Add to that gifts of inestimable price, ready to reward their compliance; casks of brandy, glass necklaces, pendant earrings and mirrors; all supported by the insinuation that if they refuse, people will perhaps see themselves as constrained to force them to move. What to do? The poor Indians take their old parents in their arms; the women load their children on their shoulders; the nation finally puts itself on the march, carrying with it its greatest riches. It abandons forever the soil on which, perhaps for a thousand years, its fathers have lived, in order to go settle in a wilderness where the whites will not leave them ten years in peace. Do you observe the results of a high civilization? The Spanish, truly brutal, loose their dogs on the Indians as on ferocious beasts; they kill, burn, massacre, pillage the new world as one would a city taken by assault, without pity as without discrimination. But one cannot destroy everything; fury has a limit. The rest of the Indian population ultimately becomes mixed with its conquerors, takes on their mores, their religion; it reigns today in several provinces over those who formerly conquered it. The Americans of the United States, more humane, more moderate, more respectful of law and legality, never bloodthirsty, are profoundly more destructive, and it is impossible to doubt that within a hundred years there will remain in North America, not a single nation, not even a single man belonging to the most remarkable of the Indian races. . . .

But I no longer know at all where I am in my story. It had to do, I think, with the Choctaws. The Choctaws formed a powerful nation that inhabited the frontier of the state of Alabama and that of Georgia. After long negotiations, they finally managed, this year, to persuade them to leave their country and to emigrate to the right bank of the Mississippi. Six to seven thousand Indians have already crossed the great river; those who arrived in Memphis came there with the aim of following their compatriots. The agent of the American government who accompanied them and was charged with paying for their passage, knowing that a steamboat had just arrived, hurried down to the bank. The price he offered for transporting the Indians sixty leagues down river managed to settle

the shaken mind of the captain; the signal to depart was given. The prow was turned toward the south and we cheerfully climbed the ladder down which descended the poor passengers who, instead of going to Louisville, saw themselves forced to await the thaw in Memphis. So goes the world.

But we had not yet left; there was still the matter of embarking our exiled tribe, its horses and its dogs. Here began a scene which was something truly lamentable. The Indians came forward toward the shore with a despondent air; they first made the horses go, several of which, little accustomed to the forms of civilized life, took fright and threw themselves into the Mississippi, from which they could be pulled out only with difficulty. Then came the men, who, following their usual custom, carried nothing except their weapons; then the women, carrying their children attached to their backs or wrapped up in the blankets that covered them; they were, moreover, overburdened with loads that contained all their riches. Finally the old people were led on. There was among them a woman of a hundred and ten years of age. I have never seen a more frightening figure. She was naked, with the exception of a blanket that allowed one to see, in a thousand places, the most emaciated body that one can imagine. She was escorted by two or three generations of grandchildren. To leave her country at that age to go seek her fate in a strange land, what misery! There was, amidst the old people, a young girl who had broken her arm a week before; for want of care, the arm was frostbitten below the fracture. She nonetheless had to follow the common march. When all had gone by, the dogs advanced toward the bank; but they refused to enter the boat and took to making frightful howls. Their masters had to lead them by force.

There was, in the whole of this spectacle, an air of ruin and destruction, something that savored of a farewell that was final and with no return; no one could witness this without being sick at heart; the Indians were calm, but somber and taciturn. There was one of them who knew English and of whom I asked why the Choctaws were leaving their country—"To be free," he answered—I could never draw anything else out of him. We will deposit them tomorrow in the solitudes of Arkansas. It has to be confessed that this is a singular accident, that made us come to Memphis to witness the expulsion, one might say the dissolution, of one of the most celebrated and most ancient American nations.

\*　　\*　　\*

## REVIEW QUESTIONS

1. What is the tone of Tocqueville's letter?
2. Did he accept the American justification for removal?
3. How did the Americans compare with the Spanish?
4. If, as that one man said, the Choctaws were moving so as "to be free," why were they so desolate?

# JOHN ROSS

# FROM The Chief's Annual Message (1831)

*Back East, both Jackson and Georgia wanted the Cherokees to move for a number of reasons: they desired Cherokee land, which encompassed not only rich soil for crops but deposits of gold as well; they deemed the Indians to be a threat to state and national security; and they believed the old "civilization" or assimilation program to have failed. In terms of the Cherokee Nation, the old program had not really failed, though it had not worked quite as the earlier administrations had planned. The Cherokee Nation had become what most white Americans recognized as a civilized tribe, but it had adopted and adapted facets of European-American civilization to suit its needs instead of simply assimilating into that engrossing culture. One of the concepts that the Cherokees adopted was that of constitutional government. In 1827 they wrote their own constitution, which established a chief executive, a bicameral legislature, and a judiciary. John Ross, a man grown wealthy through his trade and agricultural enterprises and who had been active in Cherokee public affairs since 1816, became their first chief elected under this constitution. In this capacity he tried to get federal intervention on the behalf of his nation against the state of Georgia. That state believed that it did, or should have, title to the Indian lands under the Compact of 1802. Upon that stand, Georgia passed legislation that ignored Cherokee tribal rights as part of a strategy to drive the Cherokees off their lands and, if possible, out of the state. Ross appealed first to the president and then to the Supreme Court in* Cherokee Nation v. Georgia.

From Gary E. Moulton, ed., *The Papers of Chief John Ross*, vol. I (Norman: University of Oklahoma Press, 1985), pp. 224–30. © by the University of Oklahoma Press, Norman. [Editorial insertions that appear in square brackets are from Moulton—*Ed.*]

Friends and Fellow Citizens

Chattoga, Cher. Nation,
Oct. 24, 1831

\*      \*      \*

It will be recollected that the President of the United States [Andrew Jackson], at an early day after his induction into office, made us a declaratory and positive assurance that *so far as we had rights we should be protected in them*, and that "*an interference to the extent of affording protection to the Cherokees, and the occupancy of their soil, is what is demanded of the justice of the U.S. and will not be withheld;*" and that "*the intruders would be removed.*" After the promulgation of this assurance, detachments of the Federal troops were ordered within our territorial limits. This movement was hailed with joy and approbation on our part, under the sanguine hope that the *protection* which had so recently been promised us by Pres't Jackson was now to be afforded. But to our astonishment and disappointment the troops were soon found employed under the orders of their superiors, in preventing our citizens from working gold mines, belonging to this nation, and thereby treating them as trespassers upon their own soil. And on being requested by the Governor of Georgia [George R. Gilmer], with the assurance that "whatever measures may be adopted by the State of Georgia in relation to the Cherokees, the strongest desire will be felt to make them accord with the *policy* which has been *adopted by the present administration* of the General Government," the President ordered these troops to be withdrawn from our territory! Thus the military of the United States figured and decamped before our eyes without affording that protection which we had a right to expect, and which had so recently been pledged, leaving undisturbed the numerous intruders who have settled down upon our lands on the frontiers of Georgia and other adjacent states. Immediately after this, Georgia, under her own authority, levied a military force, which is known by the appelation of the "Georgia Guard," and stationed it in this nation, at the encampment which had been established and vacated by the United States troops.

The numerous subsisting treaties between the United States and this nation were negotiated, entered into, and constitutionally ratified on the part of the States by the competent authorities thereof; and they compose a part of "*the supreme law of the land,*" and "*the judges in every state shall be bound thereby, any thing in the constitution or laws of any state to the contrary notwithstanding.*" In reference to this clause of the Federal Constitution I may well borrow an expression of one of the most eminent Judges of Georgia, "can language be plainer or can words be stronger." Such was the language of an Honorable Judge in delivering an opinion from the bench in that state some years ago, in favor of some individuals who claimed title to land reserved to them by the treaty of 1819, between the United States and this nation, & against the title claimed under a grant from Georgia by certain citizens thereof.

The Judicial power extends to all cases in law & equity, arising under the constitution, the laws of the U. States, and treaties made, or which shall be made under their authority; and no state can enter into any treaty, alliance or confederation, or pass any law impairing the obligation of contracts; and Congress alone possesses the power to regulate commerce with foreign nations, among the several states and with the Indian tribes. Here then, in the face of all these constitutional provisions, all the treaties made with the Cherokee Nation and the laws enacted by Congress in the spirit of those treaties for our protection, the present administration of the General Government, has tolerated Ga. in the recklessness of her own glory and reputation, to march across the line of her constitutional boundary to pass laws repugnant to those treaties and laws of the United States for the express object of perplexing and distressing our citizens by intolerable oppression, that we may be forced to surrender our lands for her benefit. Georgia has surveyed our country into districts—she has placed numerous intruders upon our soil, and in time of *profound peace* has levied *troops*, and still continues to keep them in service. Those troops without civil precepts have arrested our citizens at the point of the bayonet, marched them over the country with chains around their necks, and without trials have imprisoned them in a jail at their military station! Missionaries of the cross, who under the approbation of the authorities of the General Government were sent hither by the benevolence of religious associations, to instruct the Cherokees in the precepts of the Gospel and the arts of civilization, and who have met a welcome reception in this nation, and were successfully prosecuting the objects of their laudable and peaceful mission, have also been cruelly torn from their families and ministerial charge and similarly treated! Two of these worthy and inoffensive men [Samuel Worcester and Elizur Butler], who had been delivered over to the civil authority of Georgia, under the charge merely of *residing* in this Nation, and refusing to comply with a law of that state which goes to infringe upon the rights and liberties guaranteed to every free and loyal citizen under the constitution of the United States, have been sentenced by Judge [Augustin S.] Clayton to the penitentiary of Georgia, there to endure hard labor for the term of four years.

Being fully convinced that President [George] Washington and his successors well understood the constitutional powers of the General Government, and the rights of the individual states, as well as those belonging to the Indian Nations, and that the treaties made under their respective administrations with the Cherokee Nation were intended to be faithfully & honestly regarded on the part of the United States; and that the judicial power would extend to all cases of litigation that might arise under those treaties; it was determined on the expediency of employing legal Counsel to defend the rights of the Nation before the Courts of the United States. Finding, however, that the Courts of Georgia were disposed to prevent as far as possible any case from going up to the Supreme Court of the United States, our counsel advised the propriety of trying the original jurisdiction of the Court by applying, in the character of a *foreign state* for an injunction to restrain Georgia, her officers, citizens &c. from enforcing her laws within our territorial limits. Copies of the Bill for an injunction, and notice of the intended motion were accord-ingly served upon the Governor and Attorney General of that state. On the 5th of March last the motion was made by John Sergeant Esqr, who also delivered an able speech in favor of the application. William Wirt, Esqr, concluded with equal ability and force of argument on the same side. No counsel appeared on the part of Georgia but some of her representatives in Congress and other friends attended the Court and anxiously awaited the decision. The Court denied the injunction on the ground that the Cherokee Nation was not a *foreign state in the sense of the Constitution*. A majority, however, decided that "the Cherokees are a distinct political society, separate from others, capable of managing its own affairs and governing itself,["] and that the acts of the United States Government plainly recognized the Cherokee Nation as a *state* and the courts are bound by these acts. The Honorable Judges [Smith] Thompson and [Joseph] Story dissented from the majority—in a part of their opinion, and gave a very able and luminous opinion in favor of the jurisdiction of the Court and awarding the injunction. There can be no doubt that a majority of the Judges of the Supreme Court holds the law of Georgia extending jurisdiction within our limits to be unconstitutional, and whenever a case between proper parties can be brought before them, they will so decide . . .

*       *       *

By innumerable acts of injustice and oppression, the rights, liberties and lives our Citizens, have been threatened and jeopardized; and after placing our citizens almost in a state of duresse, the President has been induced by the urgent solicitations of Governor Gilmore [Gilmer], to send into the Nation special agents for the purpose of urging our Citizens to enroll their names for emigration west of the Mississippi river. These Agents are now in the Nation, and a part of them have been seen conversing with a few individuals at their houses, but with no success. By fair and honorable means there can be no danger as it regards the sentiments and disposition of our people on this subject. It is said their fears and credulity are to be operated upon—how far this may be true time will soon develope—at all events, by the admission of Governor Gilmer, the people are no longer *afraid of their chiefs,* nor under the influence of *white men,* and that they will *now* think and act for themselves by emigration. When this project fails it is not known to what cause the failure will be imputed, as our opponents seem determined not to believe the truth, that the opposition of the Cherokees is owing purely to a correct sense of their rights, and to their love of country.

Much has been said from time to time to make a false impression on the public mind in regard to our present controversy and difficulties with Georgia. There can be no subject easier understood than the true relationship between this Nation and the United States; nor the justness of any cause more obvious than ours when fairly investigated. The expediency of removing of our Nation west of the Mississippi has also been urged upon the incompatibility of permitting an independent Government to grow up within the limits of the United States. A correct understanding of our Treaties with the United States will show the absurdity of this argument and remove all fears of the possibility of any evil ever arising to any one of the States from our present location. A weak defenceless community as we are, forming an alliance with, and placed in the heart of so powerful a Nation as the United States, and having surrendered a portion of our sovereignty, as a security for our protection, and our intercourse being confined exclusively with our protector, must necessarily produce that identity of interest and bond of friendship so natural to the ties of such an alliance. Something has also been said on the score of the public defence. It is true our population at present is small, but it is increasing as rapidly as could be expected. And have not the Cherokees at all times been ready to meet the common foe of the United States? Did they not sufficiently prove to the world their disposition on this subject during the last war? Did they not meet and fight the enemy as be-

came warriors? Let the gallant commander, who now administers the affairs of the United States Government answer. Situated, therefore, as we are under the fostering care and protection of a magnanimous Government, there is every reason to cherish the hope that, under the auspices of a kind and generous administration, time would soon put to shame and lull to silence all the sophistry and unnatural clamour so boisterously paraded against our peaceful continuance upon the land of our fathers. By suitable encouragement and proper culture the arts and sciences would soon flourish in every section of our Nation, & the happy period be hastened when an incorporation into the great family of the American Republic would be greeted by every patriot, & posterity hail the event with grateful rejoicings. May such ever be the views and the prospects to guide us in our efforts to secure for our posterity the inestimable advantages and enjoyments, rights, and liberties, guarantied by treaties in our present location. On the other hand, by a removal West of the Mississippi, under the policy of the present administration of the General Government, to a barren and inhospitable region, we can flatter ourselves with no other prospect than the degradation, dispersion and ultimate extinction of our race.

\*   \*   \*

# REVIEW QUESTIONS

1. Did Ross charge Georgia with violations of the Cherokee constitution or the U.S. Constitution? What evidence did he present?
2. Of what did he accuse the U.S. government?
3. What measures did the Cherokee Nation take to protect and promote its interests?
4. Was Ross optimistic or pessimistic about his nation's chances for redress and the retention of their property? Explain.

# FROM *Worcester v. Georgia* (1832)

*In* Cherokee Nation v. Georgia, *the Supreme Court refused to rule on the issue being disputed, that of the enforcement of state law within Cherokee territory, because, as Ross mentioned in his 1831 annual message, the Court did not deem the Cherokee Nation to be a foreign nation that could, as stated in the Constitution, bring a case before it. Chief Justice John Marshall referred to the Cherokee nation as a "domestic dependent nation." Yet even as that case closed, another opened. Georgia had required that whites living in Cherokee territory get a license to reside there and take an oath of allegiance to the state. In July the Georgia Guard arrested eleven missionaries who had refused to do so. Eventually nine of the missionaries either took the oath or left the state, but Samuel Worcester and Elizur Butler, who continued to refuse, were sentenced to four years of hard labor by a state court. They appealed their cases up to the Supreme Court, which in March 1832 ruled on Worcester's case and then extended its decision to Butler's.*

From Theda Perdue and Michael D. Green, eds., *The Cherokee Removal: A Brief History with Documents* (Boston: Bedford Books, 1995), pp. 70–75. [Editorial insertions appear in square brackets—*Ed.*]

March 1832

Mr. Chief Justice Marshall delivered the opinion of the Court.

This cause, in every point of view in which it can be placed, is of the deepest interest.

The defendant is a state, a member of the Union, which has exercised the powers of government over a people who deny its jurisdiction, and are under the protection of the United States.

The plaintiff is a citizen of the state of Vermont, condemned to hard labour for four years in the penitentiary of Georgia; under colour of an act which he alleges to be repugnant to the Constitution, laws, and treaties of the United States. . . .

The indictment charges the plaintiff in error, and others, being white persons, with the offence of "residing within the limits of the Cherokee nation without a license," and "without having taken the oath to support and defend the constitution and laws of the state of Georgia."

The defendant in the state Court appeared in proper person, and filed the following plea:

"And the said Samuel A. Worcester, in his own proper person, comes and says, that this Court ought not to take further cognisance of the action and prosecution aforesaid, because, he says, that, on the 15th day of July, in the year 1831, he was, and still is, a resident in the Cherokee nation; and that the said supposed crime or crimes, and each of them, were committed, if committed at all, at the town of New Echota, in the said Cherokee nation, out of the jurisdiction of this Court, and not in the county Gwinnett, or elsewhere, within the jurisdiction of this Court: and this defendant saith, that he is a citizen of the state of Vermont, one of the United States of America, and that he entered the aforesaid Cherokee nation in the capacity of a duly authorized missionary of the American Board of Commissioners for Foreign Missions, under the authority of the President of the United States, and has not since been required by him to leave it: that he was, at the time of his arrest, engaged in preaching the gospel to the Cherokee Indians, and in translating the sacred Scriptures into their language, with the permission and approval of the said Cherokee nation, and in accordance with the humane policy of the government of the United States for the civilization and improvement of the

Indians; and that his residence there, for this purpose, is the residence charged in the aforesaid indictment: and this defendant further saith, that this prosecution the state of Georgia ought not to have or maintain, because, he saith, that several treaties have, from time to time, been entered into between the United States and the Cherokee nation of Indians. . . . all which treaties have been duly ratified by the Senate of the United States of America; and, by which treaties, the United States of America acknowledge the said Cherokee nation to be a sovereign nation, authorized to govern themselves, and all persons who have settled within their territory, free from any right of legislative interference by the several states composing the United States of America, in reference to acts done within their own territory; and, by which treaties, the whole of the territory now occupied by the Cherokee nation, on the east of the Mississippi, has been solemnly guarantied to them; all of which treaties are existing treaties at this day, and in full force. . . ."

This plea was overruled by the [state] Court. And the prisoner being arraigned, plead not guilty. The jury found a verdict against him, and the Court sentenced him to hard labour, . . .

The indictment and plea in this case draw in question, we think, the validity of the treaties made by the United States with Cherokee Indians; if not so, their construction is certainly drawn in question; and the decision has been, if not against their validity, "against the right, privilege, or exemption, specially set up and claimed under them." They also draw into question the validity of a statute of the state of Georgia, "on the ground of its being repugnant to the Constitution, treaties, and laws of the United States, and the decision is in favour of its validity. . . ."

It has been said at the bar, that the acts of the legislature of Georgia seize on the whole Cherokee country, parcel it out among the neighbouring counties of the state, extend her code over the whole country, abolish its institutions and its laws, and annihilate its political existence.

If this be the general effect of the system, let us inquire into the effect of the particular statute and section on which the indictment is founded.

It enacts that "all white persons residing within the limits of the Cherokee nation on the 1st day of March next, or at any time thereafter, without a license or permit from his excellency the governor, or from such agent as his excellency the governor shall authorize to grant such permit or license, and who shall not have taken the oath hereinafter required, shall be guilty of a high misdemeanor, and, upon conviction thereof, shall be punished by confinement to the penitentiary, at hard labour, for a term not less than four years."

The eleventh section authorizes "the governor, should he deem it necessary for the protection of the mines, or the enforcement of the laws in force within the Cherokee nation, to raise and organize a guard," &c.

The thirteenth section enacts, "that the said guard or any member of them, shall be, and they are hereby authorized and empowered to arrest any person legally charged with or detected in a violation of the laws of this state, and to convey, as soon as practicable, the person so arrested, before a justice of the peace, judge of the Superior, or justice of inferior Court of this state, to be dealt with according to law."

The extra-territorial power of every legislature being limited in its action to its own citizens or subjects, the very passage of this act is an assertion of jurisdiction over the Cherokee nation, and of the rights and powers consequent on jurisdiction.

The first step, then, in the inquiry, which the Constitution and laws impose on this Court, is an examination of the rightfulness of this claim.

America, separated from Europe by a wide ocean, was inhabited by a distinct people, divided into separate nations, independent of each other and of the rest of the world, having institutions of their own, and governing themselves by their own laws. It is difficult to comprehend the proposition, that the inhabitants of either quarter of the globe could have rightful original claims of dominion over the inhabitants of the other, or over the lands they occupied; or that the discovery of either by the other should give the discoverer rights in the country discovered, which annulled the pre-existing right of its ancient possessors. . . .

The Indian nations had always been considered as distinct, independent political communities, retaining their original natural rights, as the undisputed possessors of the soil, from time immemorial, with the single exception of that imposed by irresistible power, which excluded them from intercourse with any other European potentate than the first discoverer of the coast of the particular region claimed; and this was a restriction which those European potentates imposed on themselves, as well as on the Indians. The very term "nation," so generally applied to them, means "a people distinct from others." The Constitution, by declaring treaties already made, as well as those to be made, to be the supreme law of the land, has adopted and sanctioned the previous treaties with the Indian nations, and consequently admits their rank among those powers who are capable of making treaties. The words "treaty" and "nation" are words of our own language, selected in our diplomatic and legislative proceedings, by ourselves, having each a definite and well understood meaning. We have applied them to Indians, as we have applied them to the other nations of the earth. They are applied to all in the same sense.

Georgia, herself, has furnished conclusive evidence that her former opinions on this subject concurred with those entertained by her sister states, and by the government of the United States. Various acts of her legislature have been cited in the argument, including the contract of cession made in the year 1802, all tending to prove her acquiescence in the universal conviction that the Indian nations possessed a full right to the lands they occupied, until that right should be extinguished by the United States, with their consent: that their territory was separated from that of any state within whose chartered limits they might reside, by a boundary line, established by treaties: that, within their boundary, they possessed rights with which no state could interfere; and that the whole power of regulating the intercourse with them was vested in the United States. A review of these acts, on the part of Georgia, would occupy too much time, and is the less necessary, because they have been accurately detailed in the argument at the bar.

Her new series of laws, manifesting her abandonment of these opinions, appears to have commenced in December, 1828.

In opposition to this original right, possessed by the undisputed occupants of every country; to this recognition of that right, which is evidenced by our history, in every change through which we have passed; is placed the charters granted by the monarch of a distant and distinct region, parcelling out a territory in possession of others whom he could not remove and did not attempt to remove, and the cession made of his claims by the treaty of peace.

The actual state of things at the time, and all history since, explain these charters; and the King of Great Britain, at the treaty of peace, could cede only what belonged to his crown. These newly asserted titles can derive no aid from the articles so often repeated in Indian treaties; extending to them, first, the protection of Great Britain, and afterwards that of the United States. These articles are associated with others, recognising their title to self-government. The very fact of repeated treaties with them recognises it; and the settled doctrine of the law of nations is, that a weaker power does not surrender its independence—its right to self-government, by associating with a stronger, and taking its protection. A weak state, in order to provide for its safety, may place itself under the protection of one more powerful, without stripping itself of the right of government, and ceasing to be a state. Examples of this kind are not wanting in Europe. "Tributary and feudatory states," says Vattel, "do not thereby cease to be sovereign and independent states, so long as self-government and sovereign and independent authority are left in the administration of the state." At the present day, more than one state may be considered as holding its right of self-government under the guarantee and protection of one or more allies.

The Cherokee nation, then, is a distinct community, occupying its own territory, with boundaries accurately described, in which the laws of Georgia can have no force, and which the citizens of Georgia have no right to enter, but with the assent of the Cherokees themselves, or in conformity with treaties, and with the acts of Congress. The whole intercourse between the United States and this nation, is, by our Constitution and laws, vested in the government of the United States.

The act of the state of Georgia, under which the plaintiff in error was prosecuted, is consequently void, and the judgment a nullity. Can this Court revise and reverse it?

If the objection to the system of legislation, lately adopted by the legislature of Georgia, in relation to the Cherokee nation, was confined to its extra-territorial operation, the objection, though complete, so far as respected mere right, would give this Court no power over the subject. But it goes much further. If the review which has been taken be correct, and we think it is, the acts of Georgia are repugnant to the Constitution, laws, and treaties of the United States.

They interfere forcibly with the relations established between the United States and the Cherokee nation, the regulation of which, according to the settled principles of our Constitution, are committed exclusively to the government of the Union.

They are in direct hostility with treaties, repeated in a succession of years, which mark out the boundary that separates the Cherokee country from Georgia; guaranty to them all the land within their boundary; solemnly pledge the faith of the United States to restrain their citizens from trespassing on it; and recognise the pre-existing power of the nation to govern itself.

They are in equal hostility with the acts of Congress for regulating this intercourse, and giving effect to the treaties.

The forcible seizure and abduction of the plaintiff in error, who was residing in the nation with its permission, and by authority of the President of the United States, is also a violation of the acts which authorize the chief magistrate to exercise this authority. . . .

It is the opinion of this Court that the judgment of the Superior Court for the county of Gwinnett, in the state of Georgia, condemning Samuel A. Worcester to hard labour in the penitentiary of the state of Georgia, for four years, was pronounced by that Court under colour of a law which is void, as being repugnant to the Constitution, treaties, and laws of the United States, and ought, therefore, to be reversed and annulled.

## REVIEW QUESTIONS

1. What was Worcester's defense?
2. Did the Court believe that Georgia could rightfully claim jurisdiction over the Cherokee Nation on the basis of historical discovery and settlement? Why or why not?
3. Did the Court accept Georgia's contention that Indians had ceded their sovereignty in the charters or treaties they had made? Why or why not?
4. How did Marshall show that there were degrees of sovereignty—that this case was not predicated on a simple matter of having sovereignty or not having it?

# INTERPRETING VISUAL SOURCES: PICTURING DEVELOPMENT VERSUS NATURE

*A picture of nature may not merely record an expanse of scenery; it may also represent an intellectual image. In such a case the artists depict not only what is seen by the eye but what is felt or believed by the heart and mind. Interpreting such a source as artwork, therefore, requires not only a visual examination of the picture and a knowledge of the method by which it was created but also an understanding of the context in which it was created and that it represents. That representation of context—of a particular place, person, idea, or sentiment—is of prime importance for a student of history. A picture for an artist may be a matter of "what is," but for an historian it is a matter of "what was."*

*Drawings and paintings are material remains that present another form of historical documentation. Historians tend to concentrate on deciphering the written evidence of the past, but they find that attention to other kinds of evidence deepens their understanding of that past. Writings themselves can be interpreted as material artifacts: one need only take the time to look at the paper, ink, and even formation of the letters. When examined in their original forms, written sources physically manifest the past in the way they look, feel, and smell. Some people like to examine physical remnants because such things help them picture the worlds that the words describe. Material artifacts, which include clothing and jewelry, pottery and porcelain, glass and silver, needlework and furniture, as well as architecture and art, are especially helpful when one tries to visualize cultures that existed before photographic records.*

*Just as Americans today like to take pictures of their new cars and houses on their digital cameras and then download those images onto their computers and zip them out to friends and family, Americans in the early nineteenth century enjoyed using and recording their personal and technological advances. One of the new mechanical processes, as well as its product, was an early form of photography called the daguerreotype; but drawings, engravings, and paintings were more common and easier to reproduce for public consumption. Americans celebrated national development by hanging images of their changing country in public buildings as well as in private homes and by publishing them in books, newspapers, and magazines. It is interesting that at the same time as they worshipfully depicted their technical feats, they also increasingly revered the depiction of nature in artwork.*

*As many Americans embraced the expansion of the nation's territory and celebrated the transformation of wilderness into farms, artisan shops into factories, and dirt roads into canals and railroads, others worried about how such development would affect the natural world and, in turn, the human psyche. Using oils, watercolors, and pen and ink, artists depicted Americans' enthusiasm for change and mastery of their world as well as the ramifications of their attempts to remodel their environment. Their pictures provided a visual counterpoint to the images composed by the writers of the time.*

LOCKPORT—ERIE CANAL
Bettmann/Corbis

## Lockport—Erie Canal

This town, so suddenly sprung into existence, is about thirty miles from Lake Erie, and exhibits one of those wonders of enterprise which astonish calculation. The waters of Lake Erie, which have come thus far without much descent, are here let down sixty feet by five double locks and thence pursue a perfectly level course, sixty-five miles, to Rochester. The remarkable thing at Lockport, however, is a deep cut from here to the Torenanta Creek, seven miles in length, and partly through solid rock, at an average depth of twenty feet. The canal boat glides through this flinty bed, with jagged precipices on each side; and the whole route has very much the effect of passing through an immense cavern.

\*    \*    \*

RAILROAD TO UTICA
From N. P. Willis, *American Scenery: with 121 Steelplate Engravings from Drawings by W. H. Bartlett* (Barre, Mass: Imprint Society, 1971), pp. 135–36.

## View of the Railroad to Utica (taken at Little Falls)

Before the completion of the Railroad, when travellers to the West were contented with the philosophic pace of the canal-boat, one might take up a novel at Little Falls, and come fairly to the sequel by the time the steersman cried out "Bridge!" at Utica. There were fifteen miles between them in those days; but now (to a man of indistinct ideas of geography, at least, and a traveller on the Railroad) they are as nearly run together as two drops on the window-pane. The intermediate distance is, by all the usual measurements of wear and time, annihilated.

All this is very pleasant to people in a hurry; and as most people in our busy country come under that category, it is a very pleasant thing for the white man altogether. There is a class of inhabitants [the Oneida] of the long valley of the Mohawk, however, of whose sufferings, by the advance of the white man's enterprise, this is not the first, though it may be the least, and last.

## Passenger Pigeon

The Passenger Pigeon, or, as it is usually named in America, the Wild Pigeon, moves with extreme rapidity, . . . Like the Domestic Pigeon, it often flies, during the love season, in a circling manner, . . .

PASSENGER PIGEON, *ECTOPISTES MIGRATORIUS*
Bettmann/Corbis

Their great power of flight enables them to survey and pass over an astonishing extent of country in a very short time. This is proved by facts well known in America. Thus, Pigeons have been killed in the neighbourhood of New York, with their crops full of rice, which they must have collected in the fields of Georgia and Carolina, these districts being the nearest in which they could possibly have procured a supply of that kind of food. . . .

The multitudes of Wild Pigeons in our woods are astonishing. . . . [Audubon relates a trip that he made in 1813 to Louisville, Kentucky. Over the course of his journey pigeons filled the air. When he reached Louisville the pigeons were still flying overhead and continued to do so for three days.] The banks of the Ohio were crowded with men and boys, incessantly shooting at the pilgrims, which there flew lower as they passed the river. Multitudes were thus destroyed. For a week or more, the population fed on no other flesh than that of Pigeons, and talked of nothing but Pigeons. . . .

Persons unacquainted with these birds might naturally conclude that such dreadful havock would soon put an end to the species. But I have satisfied myself, by long observation, that nothing but the gradual diminution of our forests can accomplish their decrease, as they not unfrequently quadruple their numbers yearly, and always at least double it. . . . In the month of March 1830, they were so abundant in the markets of New York, that piles of them met the eye in every direction. [By the early twentieth century, there were no more passenger pigeons to be found in the wild. The breeding of surviving captive birds was not successful. The last known passenger pi-geon died at the Cincinnati Zoological Garden in 1914.]

AMERICAN BISON, *BISON BISON*
From John James Audubon, *Missouri River Journals* (New York: Library of America, 1999), plate 64 and pp. 564, 585, 588–89.

## American Bison

*May 3* [1843; traveling the Missouri River]. . . . After leaving [Fort Leavenworth] we fairly entered the Indian country on the west side of the river, for the State of Missouri, by the purchase of the Platte River country, continues for about 250 miles further on the east side, where now we see the only settlements. We saw a good number of Indians in the woods and on the banks, gazing at us as we passed; these are, however, partly civilized, and are miserable enough. . . .

*May 18, Thursday.* Our good captain called us all up at a quarter before four this fair morning, to tell us that four barges had arrived from Fort Pierre, . . . They had ten thousand Buffalo robes on the four boats; the men live entirely on Buffalo meat and pemmican. They told us that about a hundred miles above us the Buffalo were by thousands, that the prairies were covered with dead calves, and the shores [where too steep to be climbed easily by the animals] lined with dead of all sorts; that Antelopes were there also, and a great number of Wolves, etc.; . . .

*May 21, Sunday.* . . . We have seen this day about fifty Buffaloes; two which we saw had taken to the river, with intent to swim across it, but on the approach of our thundering, noisy vessel, turned about and after struggling for a few minutes, did make out to reach the top of the bank, after which they travelled at a moderate gait for some hundreds of yards; then, perhaps smelling or seeing the steamboat, they went off at a good though not very fast gallop, on the prairie by our side, and were soon somewhat ahead of us; . . .

*May 22, Monday.* . . . We began seeing Buffaloes again in small gangs, but this afternoon and evening we have seen a goodly number, probably more than a hundred. We also saw fifteen or twenty Antelopes. I saw ten at once, and it was beautiful to see them running from the top of a high hill down to its base, . . . The whole of the prairies as well as the hills have been so trampled by [Buffaloes] that I should have considered it quite unsafe for a man to travel on horseback. The ground was literally covered with their tracks, and also with bunches of hair, while the bushes and the trunks of the trees, between which they had passed, were hanging with the latter substance. . . .

[Although these animals have been called buffalo in American histories, their proper name is bison. By the mid-nineteenth century hundreds of thousands of bison were killed annually on the Great Plains. There may have been only a few hundred left by the 1890s. A few concerned individuals founded the American Bison Society in 1905 and made Theodore Roosevelt the society's honorary president. Roosevelt, in turn, persuaded Congress to establish some wildlife preserves. By 1930 there were more than three thousand bison. Today they number in the hundreds of thousands with some protected on public lands and others bred privately.]

# Progress

The artist Thomas Cole (1801–1848) created powerful landscapes that presented a vision of unspoiled American wilderness that in turn suggested an unsullied spiritual state. He also wrote about the need for what he called the liberal arts (today defined as the fine arts) "to soften our manners" and "mend our hearts." In his "Essay on American Scenery" (American Monthly Magazine, January 1836), he wrote:

> In this age, when a meagre utilitarianism seems ready to absorb every feeling and sentiment, and what is sometimes called improvement in its march makes us fear that the bright and tender flowers of the imagination shall all be crushed beneath its iron tramp, it would be well to cultivate the oasis [meaning not just nature but "taste" or refinement] that yet remains to us, and thus preserve the germs of a future and a purer system. . . . The spirit of our society is to contrive but not to enjoy—toiling to produce more toil— accumulating in order to aggrandize. The pleasures of the imagination, among which the love of scenery holds a conspicuous place, will alone temper the harshness of such a state; and, like the atmosphere that softens the most rugged forms of the landscape, cast a veil of tender beauty over the asperities of life.[1]

Cole's paintings and words inspired Asher B. Durand (1796–1886), and the two founded what became known as the Hudson River School of landscape art (for early members generally focused on that area). Cole may have been somewhat conflicted over the encroachment of civilization in both his country and scenes, but Durand and other artists in the school tended to paint Manifest Destiny in a good light. While they certainly extolled the beauty of nature with every brushstroke, the small human figures and elements betokening human industry that often appeared in their works indicated their belief that civilization could coexist with nature in America. Yet coexistence would be on man's terms. In the 1853 painting Progress, Durand essentially showed his own form of dominion over nature as well as documented human penetration of the wilderness and claims on the land.

Durand echoed Cole in touting nature's "influence on the mind and heart." He believed that nature's appearance, "apart from its wondrous structure and functions that minister to our well-being, is fraught with lessons of high and holy meaning, only surpassed by the light of Revelation." Such sentiments showed that Durand was a colleague not just of painters such as Cole, but of writers such as Ralph Waldo Emerson. He also showed a distinct pride in America's natural as well as productive bounty in an 1855 article in the Crayon, an art journal:

> Go not abroad then in search of material for the exercise of your pencil, while the virgin charms of our native land have claims on your deepest affections. . . . I desire not to limit the universality of the Art, or require that the artist shall sacrifice aught to patriotism; but, . . . why should not the American landscape painter, in accordance with the principle of self-government, boldly originate a high and independent style, based on his native resources?[2]

---

[1]Thomas Cole, *The Collected Essays and Prose Sketches*, edited by Marshall Tymn (St. Paul, Minn: John Colet Press, 1980), pp. 3, 6.

[2]John W. McCoubrey, *American Art, 1700–1960: Sources and Documents* (Englewood Cliffs, N.J.: Prentice-Hall, 1965), pp. 111–13.

*PROGRESS* (1853)
The Warner Collection, Gulf States Paper Corporation, Tuscaloosa, Alabama.

# REVIEW QUESTIONS

1. What do the first two scenes and their captions reveal about the state of transportation technology? What do they reveal about how transportation technology both met the demands of and made its own mark on the American landscape?

2. Do they indicate or imply that progress had a price? Was this presented as good or bad?

3. How are the human and natural elements juxtaposed in the first two scenes as compared to those in Durand's *Progress*?

4. What do the Audubon pictures and captions reveal about the human interest in and impact on America's native animals? How does Audubon's focus on and painting of specific animals compare to Durand's wider view of nature?

5. Consider how Americans might have interpreted Durand's *Progress* in the 1850s, in the early 1900s, and then in 2000. What might such a comparison reveal about the nature of progress in America?

# 12   THE OLD SOUTH

Southerners wrote about their world, extolling their culture and defending their peculiar institution, but many other people—Northerners and foreign visitors—journeyed to the South to see it for themselves. To them such a trip was a combination of exotic adventure and reformist crusade, for southern lands and ways fascinated, confused, and, sometimes, repelled them. The South embodied such powerful dichotomies under its strong sun and shielding shade trees—beauty versus ugliness, good against evil—that the stories about it, fictional and factual, could not help but reflect that.

The tales were many and varied as the witnesses to southern society and slavery each experienced different aspects of the culture. Slaves, and many free blacks, looked at the South from the bottom up: from the bottom of the cotton and tobacco rows, the receiving end of the whip, and the rough floors of their quarters. Slaveowners saw it from quite a different perspective as they surveyed their fields from horseback or carriage, labored over the financial equation of provisions versus profits, and tried to establish or maintain comfortable, if not always genteel, lifestyles. Their non-slaveowner neighbors wrestled with desire and distress: many desired to own their own laborers and thereupon build their estates, but some were distressed at the cost—both financial and moral. Visiting diarists and reporters often brought with them preconceived notions by which to interpret this southern scene, while the readers of their publications added their own interpretations.

Observers' accounts were published overseas as well as in the United States, indicating that southern society and the growing conflict between North and South captivated and concerned foreign as well as domestic audiences. Slavery was an international issue. As the British and Foreign Anti-slavery Society noted in 1839, slavery existed in "British India, in the colonies of several of the nations of Europe, in the United States of America, in Texas, and in the Empire of Brazil." Antislavery organizations attempted to end it in all of these places. Such interna-

*tional agitation and cooperation did serve to contain, though not eradicate, the transatlantic slave trade in the early nineteenth century, but such activism faced greater resistance within nations. Although England abolished slavery in the British Isles by the late eighteenth century and outlawed its slave trade in 1807, some in England did not want the issue to interfere with other strategic and economic interests. Across the ocean, in accordance with a constitutional provision, Congress abolished the external slave trade in America in 1808, but smuggling, often via Cuban traders, continued. Furthermore, when foreign reformers condemned the institution as it existed within the States, slavery proponents and even some abolitionists decried outside intervention in the country's internal affairs.*

*Antislavery sentiment had appeared with the introduction of slavery in the colonial era, but the creation of a formal organization against the institution did not occur until the Revolution. As Americans debated and fought for liberty and freedom, some saw the inherent contradiction of slavery. That perception, especially when added to certain religious beliefs, led to antislavery activism. Quakers founded the Pennsylvania Society for Promoting the Abolition of Slavery in 1775. The society was essentially inactive during the war years, but in 1785 and especially 1787, when constitutional debate led to hopes of reform, the society vigorously pushed for abolition. It did not get what it wanted in the new Constitution, but at that time, even in the South, many agreed that slavery's days were numbered; the fact that manumission was on the rise seemed to give proof of that. Due to no sense of urgency, abolitionism languished. But when planters moved out into the rich lands of the Old Southwest, and after the cotton gin made the processing of that crop easier, slavery grew—and that growth spurred the development of a new abolitionist movement.*

*Advocates on both sides of this great struggle presented their basic premises in the 1830s and then rehashed them again and again throughout the 1840s and 1850s, until they threw away the words to pick up arms. Slavery may not have been the only cause of the Civil War, but as a physical presence and ideological issue it helped dig the grave of the early union. Attacked and defended culturally, socially, politically, and religiously, the South's peculiar institution became America's particular problem.*

*Many nations of the Atlantic world and beyond contended with the issue of slavery in the nineteenth century. As part of their internal reforms and international relations, these countries sometimes struggled to define and implement notions of citizenship and universal human rights. Yet although slavery was an international problem, it was a distinctly American tragedy. In the United States, it contributed to a particularly bloody civil war and illuminated discrepancies between ideology and practice in the republic that was supposed to stand as an enlightened example to the rest of the world.*

# FREDERICK DOUGLASS

## FROM *Narrative of the Life of Frederick Douglass* (1845)

*Frederick Douglass (1818–1895) wrote and spoke about the institution of slavery and southern culture based on his own youthful experiences as a slave in Maryland as well as on the stories of others. He could vividly describe how people lived within its constraints because he had suffered its blows. He constantly strove to make his audiences understand the inhumanity of the institution and the humanity of its victims so that the first would be abolished and the second accepted in American society. Douglass escaped from bondage, or as he liked to put it, stole himself from his master, when he was twenty years old. His accomplishment was due, at least in part, to the fact that, unlike most slaves, he had learned to read and had access to the wider world through his work in Baltimore. That education in both bondage and books served as the foundation for his success as an abolitionist, publisher, politician, and ultimately the United States' consul general to Haiti.*

From Michael Meyer, ed., *Frederick Douglass: The Narrative and Selected Writings* (New York: The Modern Library, 1984), pp. 24–30. [Editorial insertions appear in brackets —*Ed.*]

. . . [Colonel Edward Lloyd's] plantation is about twelve miles north of Easton, in Talbot county, and is situated on the border of Miles River. The principal products raised upon it were tobacco, corn, and wheat. These were raised in great abundance; . . .

Colonel Lloyd kept from three to four hundred slaves on his home plantation, and owned a large number more on the neighboring farms belonging to him. . . . The overseers of these, and all the rest of the farms, numbering over twenty, received advice and direction from the managers of the home plantation. This was the great business place. It was the seat of government for the whole twenty farms. All disputes among the overseers were settled here. If a slave was convicted of any high misdemeanor, became unmanageable, or evinced a determination to run away, he was brought immediately here, severely whipped, put on board the sloop, carried to Baltimore, and sold to Austin Woolfolk, or some other slave-trader, as a warning to the slaves remaining.

Here, too, the slaves of all the other farms received their monthly allowance of food, and their yearly clothing. The men and women slaves received, as their monthly allowance of food, eight pounds of pork, or its equivalent in fish, and one bushel of corn meal. Their yearly clothing consisted of two coarse linen shirts, one pair of linen trousers, like the shirts, one jacket, one pair of trousers for winter, made of coarse negro cloth, one pair of stockings, and one pair of shoes; the whole of which could not have cost more than seven dollars. The allowance of the slave children was given to their mothers, or the old women having the care of them. The children unable to work in the field had neither shoes, stockings, jackets, nor trousers, given to them; their clothing consisted of two coarse linen shirts per year. When these failed them, they went naked until the next allowance-day. Children from seven to ten years old, of both sexes, almost naked, might be seen at all seasons of the year.

There were no beds given the slaves, unless one coarse blanket be considered such, and none but the men and women had these. This, however, is not considered a very great privation. They find less difficulty from the want of beds, than from the want of time to sleep; for when their day's work in the field is done, the most of them having their washing, mending, and cooking to do, and having few or none of the ordinary facilities for doing either of these, very many of their sleeping hours are consumed in preparing for the field the coming day; and when this is done, old and young, male and female, married and single, drop down side by side, on one common bed,—the cold, damp floor,—each covering himself or herself with their miserable blankets; and here they sleep till they are summoned to the field by the driver's horn. At the sound of this, all must rise, and be off to the field. There must be no halting; every one must be at his or her post; and woe betides them who hear not this morning summons to the field; for if they are not awakened by the sense of hearing, they are by the sense of feeling: no age nor sex finds any favor. Mr. Severe, the overseer, used to stand by the door of the quarter, armed with a large hickory stick and heavy cowskin, ready to whip any one who was so unfortunate as not to hear, or, from any other cause, was prevented from being ready to start for the field at the sound of the horn.

Mr. Severe was rightly named: he was a cruel man. I have seen him whip a woman, causing the blood to run half an hour at the time; and this, too, in the midst of her crying children, pleading for their mother's release. He seemed to take pleasure in manifesting his fiendish barbarity. Added to his cruelty, he was a profane swearer. . . . The field was the place to witness his cruelty and profanity. His presence made it both the field of blood and of blasphemy. From the rising till the going down of the sun, he was cursing, raving, cutting, and slashing among the slaves of the field, in the most frightful manner. His career was short. He died very soon after I went to Colonel Lloyd's; and he died as he lived, uttering, with his dying groans, bitter curses and horrid oaths. His death was regarded by the slaves as the result of a merciful providence.

Mr. Severe's place was filled by a Mr. Hopkins. He was a very different man. He was less cruel, less profane, and made less noise, than Mr. Severe. His course was characterized by no extraordinary demonstrations of cruelty. He whipped, but seemed to take no pleasure in it. He was called by the slaves a good overseer.

The home plantation of Colonel Lloyd wore the appearance of a country village. All the mechanical operations for all the farms were performed here. The shoemaking and mending, the blacksmithing, cartwrighting, coopering, weaving, and grain-grinding, were all performed by the slaves on the home plantation. The whole place wore a business-like aspect very unlike the neighboring farms. The number of houses, too, conspired to give it advantage over the neighboring farms. It was called by the slaves the *Great House Farm*. Few privileges were esteemed higher, by the slaves of the out-farms, than that of being selected to do errands at the Great House Farm. . . . He was called the smartest and most trusty fellow, who had this honor conferred upon him the most frequently. The competitors for this office sought as diligently to please their overseers, as the office-seekers in the political parties seek to please and deceive the people. The same traits of character might be seen in Colonel Lloyd's slaves, as are seen in the slaves of the political parties.

The slaves selected to go to the Great House Farm, for the monthly allowance for themselves and their fellow-slaves, were peculiarly enthusiastic. While on their way, they would make the dense old woods, for miles around, reverberate with their wild songs, revealing at once the highest joy and the deepest sadness. They would compose and sing as they went along, consulting neither time nor tune. . . . They would sometimes sing the most pathetic sentiment in the most rapturous tone, and the most rapturous sentiment in the most pathetic tone. . . . I have sometimes thought that the mere hearing of those songs would do more to impress some minds with the horrible character of slavery, than the reading of whole volumes of philosophy on the subject could do.

I did not, when a slave, understand the deep meaning of those rude and apparently incoherent songs. I was myself within the circle; so that I neither saw nor heard as those without might see and hear. They told a tale of woe which was then altogether beyond my feeble comprehension; they were tones loud, long, and deep; they breathed the prayer and complaint of souls boiling over with the bitterest anguish. Every tone was a testimony against slavery, and a prayer to God for deliverance from chains. The hearing of those wild notes always depressed my spirit, and filled me with ineffable sadness. I have frequently found myself in tears while hearing them. . . . To those songs I trace my first glimmering conception of the dehumanizing character of slavery. I can never get rid of that conception. Those songs still follow me, to deepen my hatred of slavery, and quicken my sympathies for my brethren in bonds. . . .

I have often been utterly astonished, since I came to the north, to find persons who could speak of the singing, among slaves, as evidence of their contentment and happiness. It is impossible to conceive of a greater mistake. Slaves sing most when they are most unhappy. The songs of the slave represent the sorrows of his heart; and he is relieved by them, only as an aching heart is relieved by its tears. At least, such is my experience. I have often sung to drown my sorrow, but seldom to express my happiness. Crying for joy, and singing for joy, were alike uncommon to me while in the jaws of slavery. The singing of a man cast away upon a desolate island might be as appropriately considered as evidence of contentment and happiness, as the singing of a slave; the songs of the one and of the other are prompted by the same emotion.

## REVIEW QUESTIONS

1. Does Douglass describe Lloyd's plantation and its outlying farms as a microcosm of the larger southern society? Explain.
2. Are material rewards, or the lack thereof, part of Douglass's definition of slavery?
3. How does Douglass refute the prevailing southern—and, indeed, northern—perception of slave songs? Why was that important?
4. What is the difference between a bad overseer and a good one?

## GEORGE SKIPWITH

# Letters from "Your Servant" (1847)

*John Hartwell Cocke (1780–1866), the master of many plantations and hundreds of slaves in Fluvanna County, Virginia, sent dozens of his slaves to Alabama in 1840 as a financial investment and reform experiment. Cocke was an agricultural and social reformer; for instance, he railed against tobacco cultivation for what it did to the soil, Virginia's economy, and people's health. He also campaigned against intemperance and ignorance. Cocke also worried about how to end slavery and deal with those freed from it. His solution was the colonization of African Americans to Africa, tying emancipation to deportation, as a way to defuse racial issues in America and introduce civilization and Christianity to Africa. As the colonization movement withered under criticism from both blacks and whites, Cocke developed his own program for manumission. He educated some slaves in reading, writing, and religion and then offered freedom in conjunction with passage to Liberia to those who worked off their cost and proved to be good, temperate Christians. Peyton Skipwith and his family sailed to Liberia in 1833 as a result. Others, including Peyton's brother George (b. 1810), were then given a chance to do the same at a cotton plantation, "Hopewell," in Alabama. They could try to earn their freedom by the sale of the cotton (profits after subtracting cost of maintenance would be applied to this) and showing moral, religious progress. As neither profit nor progress proved big or fast enough, by late 1846 Skipwith the slave driver found himself increasingly squeezed between his master's demands and demoralized, restless slaves. Skipwith had to exercise power over his fellow slaves or lose his privileges; yet he also had to be careful in applying discipline so as not to undermine his prestige and authority within his community. Ultimately George Skipwith could not balance those challenges or remain temperate, and so he lost power and remained a slave until the emancipation that came with the Civil War.*

---

From Randall M. Miller, ed., *"Dear Master": Letters of a Slave Family. Part II: Letters from Alabama, 1847–1865* (Ithaca, N.Y., and London: Cornell University Press, 1978), pp. 154–58. [Editorial insertions appear in square brackets—Ed.]

June the 17 1847

Sir

I would hav written to you a few days suner but i was wating to see if you found any fault in my letter or not   I hav nothing perticulerly to say more than how we have spent our time sence i wrote to you. I mentioned in my letter that i could not write untel mas John returned but i signed no reason. I will now sign my reason   I wanted mas John [John Hartwell Cocke's cousin, John Cocke, acted as steward] to see my letters so that you may knoe that what I write is so. I hav ploued my cotten over the second time putting four furrows in a roe with the sweeps and we will finish in three days from to day   the hoes will also finish the last of this week or the first of next the third time in the cotten. then you may consider your cotten crop out of the danger of grass, tho we have had grass and a plenty of it and so has every boddy in green County for grass hav never growed so before. the Lice hav ingured the cotten cropes in our naberhood very much. they hav been very plentyful with us but hav not done us no great damage. mas John told me to chop it out in large bunches and that was all that saved it. it is now growing and ses it is the best cotten he has seen. I hav also ploued my corn the third

time and hav laid it by and i dont see any thing to pervent us from makine an elogent crop of corn for it [is] much such a crop as we made the first year that we come into the country and it is praised by every boddy that speakes about it. there was about thirty acers of sandy land corn that was too thick, and mas John told me to thin it out and give it the second working over with the hoes and i hav don so and it is improveing every day. we expect rane every day and if we can get it in eight or ten days I shall not dought it for a moment. I Thought at one time that our oats would not be worth cutting but they mend very fast and I think that we will make a pretty good crope. I think that our last years crope will last us untel the new crope comes. our potatoes looks better this year than any we hav had since we hav been into this country   our muls stands well after hard driven and i can shoe them all with second sholders except too. I hav ten regelar worke muls but I hav been oblige to worke the three mares and the horse utill, but i can spell them in a few days. we hav six young coalts   amonge them are four horse coalts two of them which will be three years old this coming spring   they are boath very likely coalts. the other too, one is about ten days old and the other about a year old. we also hav two filies among them    one is two years old and the other is one year old, and the one at one year old is the finest colt I ever saw. I hav sixty hogs for this years killing. our fouls hav failed this year  we have hatched hundreds of turkeys and chickins but the Rats destroied them all so that we have not raised none. we are all well and hav had no sickness since i wrote except Spencer [Spencer Kellor, plantation blacksmith] he is got a risen hand, and i am in hopes that this letter will fine them all as well there as they are here. Lee and Archa are done ther Job at home (haveing Quitt cotton Prep) and are hierd out. Remember me to the family boath black and white a[nd] Beleave me your servant

George Skipwith

hopewell  July the 8 1847

Sir

on the forth day of July I reseved your letter dated may the 25. I wrote to yo the 15 of June the second time giveing you a true statement of the crops, horses, hogs, and chickeins but I am sorry that I shall have to write yo princerble about other matters. I hav a good crop on hand for you, boath of cotten and corn. this you knoe could not be don without hard worke. I have worked the people but not out of reason, and I have whiped none without a caus  the persons whome I have correct I will tell you thir name and thir faults.

Suky [Ann Suky Faulcon was liberated by Cocke in 1851] who I put to plant som corn and after she had been there long anuf to hav been done I went there and she had hardly began it    I gave her som four or five licks over her clothes    I gave isham [Isham Gault, field worker] too licks over his clothes for covering up cotton with the plow.

I put frank [Frank Randall, often made trouble and Cocke ordered him sold or hired out in 1853] isham, violly, Dinah Jinny [Jinny Randall, Frank's wife, also sold or hired out in 1853], evealine and Charlotte to Sweeping cotten going twice in a roe, and at a Reasonable days worke they aught to hav plowed seven accers a peice, and they had been at it a half of a day, and they had not done more than one accer and a half and I gave them ten licks a

peace upon thir skins   I gave Julyann eight or ten licks for misplacing her hoe. that was all the whiping I hav done from the time that I pitched the crop untell we comenced cutting oats. I put Shadrack [Shadrack Cocke became driver after George's downfall], Robert [Robert Lewis, Charlotte's husband], Armstead, and frank to cutting, they comemince on friday, but they did not more than urn the salt in thir bread, but the next morning i went out there and staid untill a late breackfast, and i saw that the lick that they had then, they were about to do a pretty good days worke. I then leave them and went to the hoe hands, marking the last roe they cut while I was there. when I come to them at twelve o clocke, they had cut me nineteen roes, and it would not take them more than ten minits to cut one roe    as Shedrack was the ruler among them, I spoke these words to him. you do not intend to cut these oats untill I whip every one of you. Shedrack did not say any thing to me, but Robert spoke these words saying that he knoed when he worked. I told him to shut his lips and if he spoke a nother worde I would whip him right of[f] but he spoke again the second time saying that he was not afraid of being whiped by no man. I then gave him a cut with the whip. he then flong down his cradle, and made a oath and said that he had as live die as to live and he said that he did not intend to stay here. he then tried to take the whip out of my hand, but I caught him fast by the collar and holed him. I then told the other boys to stripe him and they don so   I then whiped untell I thought that he was pretty could but I was desieved for as soon as I leave him and went to the hoe hands, he come of to the house to our preacher [the Reverend Isaac Taylor, Methodist minister hired by Cocke to preach to slaves] and his family becaus he knoed that they would protect him in his Rascality for he had herd that they had said that they were worked to death, and that they were lowed no more chance for lieving than if they were dogs or hogs. tho the preacher did not say any thing to me about whiping Robert neither to mas John but went down to the shop and holed about an hours chat with the negros  I do not knoe what his chat was to them but [he] ask Dr Weeb [Dr.

Willis T. Webb, Greensboro physician] what was good for a negro that was whipt albut to death, and he had much to say about it   Dr Weeb saw that his chat was calculated to incurage the people to rebel aganst me, and he went and told mas John about what he had herd and mas John took him and come up here to see if he was punised in the way that he had herd, but as soon as the Dr put his hand apon him, he told mas John that there was nothing the matter with him. mas John then ordered him to his worke and told him that he did not have what his crime was deserving him, and at som lasure time he intend to give him a good willering and then he would knoe how to behave him self. he rode over the land and saw what they had done and instead of finding fault of me he said I ought to have given the other three the same

we did not plant any ceaders last winter becaus we had a great deal of fencing to do that was oblige to be done for we have Joined fences with mr Smith [neighbor Isaac Smith] for he would not keep a good fence and his stork was often in our crops. mas John said that he would not be plaged with him no longer, to make my fence the whole line out and he gave me a half a mile of fence and was to hawl them at every lasure chance and the nearist rails was a mile and a half and from that to a mile and three quarters

I have not room to write you as I would wish. I will inform you in my next letter what fenceing I have done. then you can Judge whither I had any time or not. I have a nuf yet to write you to fill up another Sheat. permit me to say a few words to you in James [George's son at Hopewell] letter. we have our family worship every morning. Beleave me to be your servant

George Skipwith

## REVIEW QUESTIONS

1. What tasks did Skipwith oversee on the plantation?
2. What do the letters reveal about Skipwith's knowledge of farming? What kind of things supported or undermined plant or livestock production?
3. How did Skipwith manage the slaves under his supervision?
4. In analyzing the tone and content of the letters, what can you discern about Skipwith's relationship with his immediate supervisor, "mas John," and his master, John Hartwell Cocke?

# LYDIA MARIA CHILD

# FROM Propositions Defining Slavery and Emancipation (1833)

*Lydia Maria Child (1802–1880) was already a well-known writer when she took up the abolitionist cause. She had published novels and works on domestic management and child care and had founded a children's magazine. Promoting reform within the household was not enough for her, however; she wanted to help put the country's house in order by sweeping out slavery. In this desire and in her endeavors, she was at the forefront of the abolitionist movement that burst on the national scene in the 1830s. Child was ostracized by some people and organizations because of her activism, and her outspoken advocacy adversely affected the sales of both her books and her magazine, but she remained a leader in the antislavery movement and then, after the Civil War, in endeavors to help the freed slaves and promote equality. In her book* An Appeal in Favor of that Class of Americans called Africans, *first published in 1833, she strove to make clear just what slavery was and what could and should be done about it.*

---

From *An Appeal in Favor of That Class of Americans Called Africans* (1836; New York: Arno Press and The New York Times, 1968), pp. 41–42, 76–77, 82–83, 95–100. [Editorial insertions appear in square brackets—*Ed.*]

\*    \*    \*

In order to show the true aspect of slavery among us, I will state distinct propositions, each supported by the evidence of actually existing laws.

1. *Slavery is hereditary and perpetual, to the last moment of the slave's earthly existence, and to all his descendants, to the latest posterity.*

2. *The labor of the slave is compulsory and uncompensated; while the kind of labor, the amount of toil, and the time allowed for rest, are dictated solely by the master. No bargain is made, no wages given. A pure despotism governs the human brute; and even his covering and provender, both as to quantity and quality, depend entirely on the master's discretion.*

3. *The slave being considered a personal chattel, may be sold, or pledged, or leased, at the will of his master. He may be exchanged for marketable commodities, or taken in execution for the debts, or taxes, either of a living, or a deceased master. Sold at auction, "either individually, or in lots to suit the purchaser," he may remain with his family, or be separated from them for ever.*

4. *Slaves can make no contracts, and have no legal right to any property, real or personal. Their own honest earnings, and the legacies of friends belong, in point of law, to their masters.*

5. *Neither a slave, nor free colored person, can be a witness against any white or free man, in a court of justice, however atrocious may have been the crimes they have seen him commit: but they may give testimony against a fellow-slave, or free colored man, even in cases affecting life.*

6. *The slave may be punished at his master's discretion—without trial—without any means of legal redress,—whether his offence be real, or imaginary: and the master can transfer the same despotic power to any person, or persons, he may choose to appoint.*

7. *The slave is not allowed to resist any free man under any circumstances: his only safety consists in the fact that his owner may bring suit, and recover, the price of his body, in case his life is taken, or his limbs rendered unfit for labor.*

8. *Slaves cannot redeem themselves, or obtain a change of masters, though cruel treatment may have rendered such a change necessary for their personal safety.*

9. *The slave is entirely unprotected in his domestic relations.*

10. *The laws greatly obstruct the manumission of slaves, even where the master is willing to enfranchise them.*

11. *The operation of the laws tends to deprive slaves of religious instruction and consolation.*

12. *The whole power of the laws is exerted to keep slaves in a state of the lowest ignorance.*

13. *There is in this country a monstrous inequality of law and right. What is a trifling fault in the white man, is considered highly criminal in the slave; the same offences which cost a white man a few dollars only, are punished in the negro with death.*

14. *The laws operate most oppressively upon free people of color.*

\*    \*    \*

. . . [A] very brief glance will show that slavery is inconsistent with *economy*, whether domestic or political.

The slave is bought, sometimes at a very high price; in free labor there is no such investment of capital. When the slave is ill, a physician must be paid by the owner; the free laborer defrays his own expenses. The children of the slave must be supported by his master; the free man maintains his own. The slave is to be taken care of in his old age, which his previous habits render peculiarly helpless; the free laborer is hired when he is wanted, and then returns to his home. The slave does not care how slowly or carelessly he works; it is the free man's interest to do his business well and quickly. The slave is indifferent how many tools he spoils; the free man has a motive to be careful. The slave's clothing is indeed very cheap, but it is of no consequence to him how fast it is destroyed—his master *must* keep him covered, and that is all he is likely to do; the hired laborer pays more for his garments, but makes them last three times as long. The free man will be honest for reputation's sake; but reputation will make the slave none the richer, nor invest him with any of the privileges of a human being—while his poverty and sense of wrong both urge him to steal from his master. A salary must be paid to an overseer to compel the slave to work; the free man is impelled by the desire of increasing the comforts of himself and family. Two hired laborers will perform as much work as three slaves; by some it is supposed to be a more correct estimate that slaves perform only *half* as much labor as the same number of free laborers. Finally, *where* slaves are employed, manual industry is a degradation to white people, and indolence becomes the prevailing characteristic.

Slave-owners have indeed frequently shown great adroitness in defending this bad system; but, with few exceptions, they base their arguments upon the necessity of continuing slavery because it is already begun. Many of them have openly acknowledged that it was highly injurious to the prosperity of the State.

\*    \*    \*

The inhabitants of free States are often told that they cannot argue fairly upon the subject of slavery because they know nothing about its actual operation; and any expression of their opinions and feelings with regard to the system, is attributed to ignorant enthusiasm, fanatical benevolence, or a wicked intention to do mischief.

But Mr. Clay, Mr. Brodnax, and Mr. Faulkner [from whom she had just quoted passages noting defects in the system] belong to slaveholding States; and the two former, if I mistake not, are slave-owners. *They* surely are qualified to judge of the system; and I might fill ten pages with other quotations from southern writers and speakers, who acknowledge that slavery is a great evil. . . . This system is so closely entwined with the apparent interests and convenience of individuals, that it will never want for able defenders, so long as it exists. But I believe I do not misrepresent the truth, when I say the prevailing opinion at the South is, that it would have been much better for those States, and for the country in general, if slavery had never been introduced.

\*    \*    \*

But to return to the subject of emancipation. Nearly every one of the States north of Mason and Dixon's line once held slaves. These slaves were manumitted without bloodshed, and there was no trouble in making free colored laborers obey the laws.

I am aware that this desirable change must be attended with much more difficulty in the Southern States, simply because the evil has been suffered until it is fearfully overgrown; but it must not be forgotten that while they are using their ingenuity and strength to sustain it for the present, the mischief is increasing more and more rapidly. If this be not a good time to apply a remedy, when will be a better? They must annihilate slavery, or slavery will annihilate them.

It seems to be forgotten that emancipation from tyranny is not an emancipation from law; the negro, after he is made free, is restrained from the commission of crimes by the same laws which restrain other citizens: if he steals, he will be imprisoned: if he commits murder, he will be hung.

It will, perhaps, be said that the free people of color in the slave portions of *this* country are peculiarly ignorant, idle, and vicious? It may be so: for our laws and our influence are peculiarly calculated to make them bad members of society. But we trust the civil power to keep in order the great mass of ignorant and vicious foreigners continually pouring into the country; and if the laws are strong enough for this, may they not be trusted to restrain the free blacks?

In those countries where the slaves codes are mild, where emancipation is rendered easy, and inducements are offered to industry, insurrections are not feared, and free people of color form a valuable portion of the community. If we persist in acting in opposition to the established laws of nature and reason, how can we expect favorable results? But it is pronounced *unsafe* to change our policy. Every progressive improvement in the world has been resisted by despotism, on the ground that changes were dangerous. The Emperor of Austria thinks there is need of keeping his subjects ignorant, that good order may be preserved. But what he calls good order, is sacrificing the happiness of many to the advancement of a few; and no doubt knowledge *is* unfavorable to the continuation of such a state of things. It is precisely so with the slaveholder; he insists that the welfare of millions must be subordinate to his private interest, or else all good order is destroyed.

\*      \*      \*

But if slaves were allowed to redeem themselves progressively, by purchasing one day of the week after another, as they can in the Spanish colonies, habits of industry would be gradually formed, and enterprise would be stimulated, by their successful efforts to acquire a little property. And if they afterward worked better as free laborers than they now do as slaves, it would surely benefit their masters as well as themselves.

\*      \*      \*

It is commonly urged against emancipation that white men cannot possibly labor under the sultry climate of our most southerly States. This is a good reason for not sending the slaves out of the country, but it is no argument against making them free. No doubt we do need their labor; but we ought to pay for it. Why should their presence be any more disagreeable as hired laborers, than as slaves? In Boston, we continually meet colored people in the streets, and employ them in various ways, without being endangered or even incommoded. There is no moral impossibility in a perfectly kind and just relation between the two races.

If white men think otherwise, let *them* remove from climates which nature has made too hot for their constitutions. Wealth or pleasure often induces men to change their abode; an emigration for the sake of humanity would be an agreeable novelty. . . .

But the slaveholders try to stop all the efforts of benevolence, by vociferous complaints about infringing upon their *property*; and justice is so subordinate to self-interest, that the unrighteous claim is silently allowed, and even openly supported, by those who ought to blush for themselves, as Christians and as republicans. Let men *simplify* their arguments—let them confine themselves to one single question, "What right can a man have to compel his neighbor to toil without reward, and leave the same hopeless inheritance to his children, in order that *he* may live in luxury and indolence?" Let the doctrines of *expediency* return to the Father of Lies, who invented them, and gave them power to turn every way for evil. The Christian knows no appeal from the decisions of God, plainly uttered in his conscience.

\*      \*      \*

. . . Personal freedom is the birthright of every human being. God himself made it the first great law of creation; and no human enactment can render it null and void. . . .

. . . Have the negroes no right to ask compensation for their years and years of unrewarded toil? It is true that they have food and clothing, of such kind, and in such quantities, as their masters think proper. But it is evident that this is not the worth of their labor; for the proprietors can give from one hundred to five and six hundred dollars for a slave, beside the expense of supporting those who are too old or too young to labor. They could not *afford* to do this, if the slave did not earn more than he receives in food and clothing. If the laws allowed the slave to redeem himself progressively, the owner would receive his money back again; and the negro's years of uncompensated toil would be more than lawful interest.

\*    \*    \*

1. How does Child define slavery? Is hers a complete definition?
2. Does she make emancipation sound like a rational as opposed to an emotional proposition?
3. What argument does she make to convince her readers that emancipation would not lead to social disorder?
4. How does she propose to make emancipation economically viable?

# WILLIAM LLOYD GARRISON

## FROM *Declaration of Sentiments of the American Anti-Slavery Society* (1833)

*In 1833, the same year that Lydia Maria Child published her appeal, a group of abolitionists gathered together to found the American Anti-Slavery Society. A number of the representatives had been involved in the creation of the New England Anti-Slavery Society in 1832 and the New York society that followed, but they believed that there should be a national organization. Prominent among them was William Lloyd Garrison (1805–1879). Garrison gave his first public address against slavery in 1829 and soon after, in 1831, began publishing the Boston* Liberator. *Over the next three decades he vigorously fought slavery with words even as he opposed violence to free the slaves. Besides his public speeches and* Liberator *editorials, Garrison helped draft the New England society's constitution as well as the* Declaration of Sentiments of the American Anti-Slavery Society. *He also served as president of the latter society from 1843 to 1865.*

From *Selections from the Writings and Speeches of William Lloyd Garrison* (R. F. Wallcut, 1852; New York: Negro Universities Press, 1968), pp. 66–71.

The Convention assembled in the city of Philadelphia, to organize a National Anti-Slavery Society, promptly seize the opportunity to promulgate the following Declaration of Sentiments, as cherished by them in relation to the enslavement of one-sixth portion of the American people.

More than fifty-seven years have elapsed, since a band of patriots convened in this place, to devise measures for the deliverance of this country from a foreign yoke. The corner-stone upon which they founded the Temple of Freedom was broadly this—'that all men are created equal; that they are endowed by their Creator with certain inalienable rights; that among these are life, LIBERTY, and the pursuit of happiness.' . . .

We have met together for the achievement of an enterprise, without which that of our fathers is incomplete; and which, for its magnitude, solemnity, and probable results upon the destiny of the world, as far transcends theirs as moral truth does physical force.

*    *    *

Their principles led them to wage war against their oppressors, and to spill human blood like water, in order to be free. Ours forbid the doing of evil that good may come, and lead us to reject, and to entreat the oppressed to reject, the use of all carnal weapons for deliverance from bondage; relying solely upon those which are spiritual, and mighty through God to the pulling down of strong holds.

Their measures were physical resistance—the marshalling in arms—the hostile array—the mortal encounter. Ours shall be such only as the opposition of moral purity to moral corruption—the destruction of error by the potency of truth—the overthrow of prejudice by the power of love—and the abolition of slavery by the spirit of repentance.

Their grievances, great as they were, were trifling in comparison with the wrongs and sufferings of those for whom we plead. Our fathers were never slaves—never bought and sold like cattle—never shut out from the light of knowledge and religion—never subjected to the lash of brutal taskmasters.

But those, for whose emancipation we are striving—constituting at the present time at least one-sixth part of our countrymen—are recognized by law, and treated by their fellow-beings, as marketable commodities, as goods and chattels, as brute beasts; . . . For the crime of having a dark complexion, they suffer the pangs of hunger, the infliction of stripes, the ignominy of brutal servitude. They are kept in heathenish darkness by laws expressly enacted to make their instruction a criminal offence.

These are the prominent circumstances in the condition of more than two millions of our people, the proof of which may be found in thousands of indisputable facts, and in the laws of the slaveholding States.

Hence we maintain—that, in view of the civil and religious privileges of this nation, the guilt of its oppression is unequalled by any other on the face of the earth; and, therefore, that it is bound to repent instantly, to undo the heavy burdens, and to let the oppressed go free.

We further maintain—that no man has a right to enslave or imbrute his brother—to hold or acknowledge him, for one moment, as a piece of merchandize—to keep back his hire by fraud—or to brutalize his mind, by denying him the means of intellectual, social and moral improvement.

The right to enjoy liberty is inalienable. To invade it is to usurp the prerogative of Jehovah. Every man has a right to his own body—to the products of his own labor—to the protection of law—and to the common advantages of society. It is piracy to buy or steal a native African, and subject him to servitude. Surely, the sin is as great to enslave an American as an African.

Therefore we believe and affirm—that there is no difference, in principle, between the African slave trade and American slavery:

That every American citizen, who detains a human being in involuntary bondage as his property, is, according to Scripture, (Ex. xxi. 16,) a man-stealer:

That the slaves ought instantly to be set free, and brought under the protection of law:

That if they had lived from the time of Pharaoh down to the present period, and had been entailed through successive generations, their right to be free could never have been alienated, but their claims would have constantly risen in solemnity:

That all those laws which are now in force, admitting the right of slavery, are therefore, before God, utterly null and void; being an audacious usurpation of the Divine prerogative, a daring infringement on the law of nature, a base overthrow of the very foundations of the social compact, a complete extinction of all the relations, endearments and obligations of mankind, and a presumptuous transgression of all the holy commandments; and that therefore they ought instantly to be abrogated.

We further believe and affirm—that all persons of color, who possess the qualifications which are demanded of others, ought to be admitted forthwith to the enjoyment of the same privileges, and the exercise of the same prerogatives, as others; and that the paths of preferment, of wealth, and of intelligence, should be opened as widely to them as to persons of a white complexion.

We maintain that no compensation should be given to the planters emancipating their slaves:

Because it would be a surrender of the great fundamental principle, that man cannot hold property in man:

Because slavery is a crime, and therefore is not an article to be sold:

Because the holders of slaves are not the just proprietors of what they claim; freeing the slave is not depriving them of property, but restoring it to its rightful owner; it is not wronging the master, but righting the slave—restoring him to himself:

Because immediate and general emancipation would only destroy nominal, not real property; it would not amputate a limb or break a bone of the slaves, but by infusing motives into their breasts, would make them doubly valuable to the masters as free laborers; and

Because, if compensation is to be given at all, it should be given to the outraged and guiltless slaves, and not to those who have plundered and abused them.

We regard as delusive, cruel and dangerous, any scheme of expatriation which pretends to aid, either directly or indirectly, in the emancipation of the slaves, or to be a substitute for the immediate and total abolition of slavery.

We fully and unanimously recognise the sovereignty of each State, to legislate exclusively on the subject of the slavery which is tolerated within its limits; we concede that Congress, under the present national compact, has no right to interfere with any of the slave States, in relation to this momentous subject:

But we maintain that Congress has a right, and is solemnly bound, to suppress the domestic slave trade between the several States, and to abolish slavery in those portions of our territory which the Constitution has placed under its exclusive jurisdiction.

We also maintain that there are, at the present time, the highest obligations resting upon the people of the free States to remove slavery by moral and political action, as prescribed in the Constitution of the United States. They are now living under a pledge of their tremendous physical force, to fasten the galling fetters of tyranny upon the limbs of millions in the Southern States; they are liable to be called at any moment to suppress a general insurrection of the slaves; they authorize the slave owner to vote for three-fifths of his slaves as property, and thus enable him to perpetuate his oppression; they support a standing army at the South for its protection; and they seize the slave, who has escaped into their territories, and send him back to be tortured by an enraged master or a brutal driver. This relation to slavery is criminal, and full of danger: IT MUST BE BROKEN UP.

\*    \*    \*

We shall organize Anti-Slavery Societies, if possible, in every city, town and village in our land.

We shall send forth agents to lift up the voice of remonstrance, of warning, of entreaty, and of rebuke.

We shall circulate, unsparingly and extensively, antislavery tracts and periodicals.

We shall enlist the pulpit and the press in the cause of the suffering and the dumb.

We shall aim at a purification of the churches from all participation in the guilt of slavery.

We shall encourage the labor of freemen rather than that of slaves, by giving a preference to their productions: and

We shall spare no exertions nor means to bring the whole nation to speedy repentance.

Our trust for victory is solely in God. We may be personally defeated, but our principles never. Truth, Justice, Reason, Humanity, must and will gloriously triumph. . . .

\*      \*      \*

*Done at Philadelphia, December 6th, A.D. 1833*

## REVIEW QUESTIONS

1. Did the abolitionists at the convention believe that their work continued the Revolution? Did they think it of more value than the Revolution? Explain.

2. How do their sentiments illustrate both the romanticism and reform impulses of the time?

3. Given that other nations still had slavery, why did the abolitionists believe that the guilt for such oppression lay more heavily on the United States? And why did they accuse the national and free-state governments of aiding and abetting the southern states in the continuation of slavery?

4. What kind of emancipation program did they propose? Was it similar to the one suggested by Lydia Maria Child?

# H. MANLY, PUBLISHER

# FROM *The South Vindicated from the Treason and Fanaticism of the Northern Abolitionists* (1836)

*Slaveowners and other white Southerners did not tamely endure attacks on an institution they now believed to be essential to both their economy and society. Whereas many—though certainly not all—Southerners of the late eighteenth century had accepted and even promoted the gradual end of slavery, their descendants had a change of heart as they pursued their fortunes. Some were initially rather apologetic about their continued use of slaves, explaining that necessity was a strict taskmaster, but as the attacks mounted and widened to include criticism of southern culture, Christianity, and honor, Southerners rallied to the defense of their peculiar institution and, by extension, their way of life. They also counterattacked by pointing out the ties between the regional economies and the problems in northern society.*

From *The South Vindicated from the Treason and Fanaticism of the Northern Abolitionists* (1836; New York: Negro Universities Press, 1969), pp. 66–69, 71–72, 81–84, 93–94, 98, 109–14, 180–81, 288–90. [Editorial insertions appear in square brackets—*Ed.*]

## Condition of Slaves in the United States

The extent of slavery in the different slave-holding states of this union, may be seen by the following table, digested from the census of 1830.

| | Whites. | Free col'd. | Slaves. | Total col'd. | Total. |
|---|---|---|---|---|---|
| Maryland, | 291,093 | 52,912 | 102,873 | 155,820 | 446,913 |
| Virginia | 694,270 | 47,348 | 469,757 | 517,105 | 1,211,375 |
| North Carolina, | 472,843 | 19,543 | 245,601 | 265,444 | 737,987 |
| South Carolina, | 275,863 | 7,921 | 315,401 | 323,322 | 518,185 |
| Georgia, | 296,806 | 2,486 | 217,531 | 220,017 | 516,823 |
| Alabama, { North, | 81,173 | 422 | 44,130 | 44,552 | 125,725 |
| { South, | 109,233 | 1,150 | 73,419 | 74,569 | 183,802 |
| Mississippi, | 114,795 | 569 | 25,091 | 25,660 | 140,455 |
| Kentucky, | 517,787 | 4,917 | 165,213 | 170,130 | 687,917 |
| Louisiana, | 89,291 | 16,710 | 109,588 | 126,298 | 215,589 |
| Tennessee, | 535,748 | 4,555 | 141,603 | 146,158 | 681,906 |
| Missouri, | 114,795 | 569 | 25,091 | 25,660 | 140,455 |
| District of Columbia, | 27,647 | 6,093 | 6,058 | 12,151 | 39,868 |
| —— Missouri, | | | | | |
| —— Arkansaw, | 25,671 | 141 | 4,576 | 4,717 | 30,388 |
| —— Florida, | 18,375 | 844 | 15,501 | 16,345 | 34,720 |

The states in which slavery prevails, have been distinguished for their affluence. Notwithstanding the policy of the national government has borne heavily upon the South, notwithstanding the occasional depression of her staples, and the proverbially unfortunate pecuniary habits of her citizens, that portion of the union may still be regarded as peculiarly favoured. The slave-labour of the South has thus far practically disproved the theories of the North; and demonstrated that the institution of slavery, whatever objections may be alleged against it, is not calculated to diminish the national wealth, or retard the national prosperity. It will be seen hereafter, that the South pays nearly one-third of the revenue of the government; and of the one hundred millions of dollars annual exports sent from the country, *nine-tenths are raised by the South.* Of the productiveness of slave-labour, who can, after a knowledge of these facts, affect a doubt? The North, as well as the South, is enriched by that labour; and should any disastrous occurrences disturb the institutions of the South, not only the whites and negroes of the slave-holding states would sink into poverty and suffering, but the decayed manufactures, shrunken commerce, and ruined prosperity of the North, would show how near and vital is the connexion of the different sections of our common country.

Every country must have its labourers, men who are willing to be directed by the mind and capital of others, and to undergo, in consideration of support, the physical toil requisite for the attainment of the goods of life. In the North, this labour is done by the poor; in the South, by the negro. In both, the labourer is forced to endure the privations of his condition in life. In the North, not only is his toil severe, but poverty and anxiety attend him in his humble path in life. His family must be sustained; his wife attended in sickness; his children supported in youth. His means are often inadequate to his wants. He is bowed down by the consciousness of inequality, and haunted by the fear of the prison. Incertitude and anxiety are with him each hour of his life; and when sickness or age steals upon him, it often finds him without resources or hope. Thus is he dogged through life by poverty, fear, humiliation and oppression (for the title of freeman does not protect the poor from oppression) and dies with the unhappy consciousness that for his children is reserved the same lot of wretchedness. The labourer of the South knows none of these evils. He is scarcely acquainted with the meaning of the word care. He never suffers from inordinate labour—he never sickens from unwholesome food. No fear of want disturbs his slumbers. Hunger and cold are strangers to him; and in sickness or age he knows that he has a protector and a friend able and willing to shield him from suffering. His pleasures are such as his nature enjoys, and are unrestricted. He enjoys all the privileges which his simple heart craves, and which are wholesome for him. Thus protected from all the other has to fear, and secured in the enjoyment of all he desires—he is as happy as circumstances can render him.

We are aware that certain pseudo philanthropists affect great concern for the benighted state of the negro, and condemn the enactments which, in some of the states, discourage his education. We may be permitted to remark, that, but for the intrusive and intriguing interference of prag-matical fanatics, such precautionary enactments would never have been necessary. When such foes are abroad, industrious in scattering the seeds of insurrection, it becomes necessary to close every avenue by which they may operate upon the slaves. It becomes necessary to check or turn aside the stream, which instead of flowing health-fully upon the negro, is polluted and poisoned by the abolitionists, and rendered the source of discontent and excitement. Education, thus per-verted, would become equally dangerous to the master and the slave: and while fanaticism continue, its war upon the South, the measures of necessary precaution and defence must be continued.

The situation of the slave is, in every particular, incompatible with the cultivation of his mind. It would not only unfit him for his station in life, and prepare him for insurrection, but would be found wholly impracticable in the performance of the duties of a labourer. . . .

\*　　\*　　\*

The slaves of the South are protected from abuse or wrong by liberal laws, justly adminis-tered. Improper punishment, under-feeding or over-working, are prevented by enactments, which, should any master incur their penalties, effectually vindicate the cause of justice. The laws protect the slave as fully as the white man: they go further, and, as the slave is supposed to be completely dependent upon his master, they require that he should be supplied with the nec-essaries and comforts of his station, and treated with unvarying kindness. In some of the states it has, indeed, been necessary to pass rigid po-lice laws to protect the country from insurrec-tions; but these laws remain a dead letter, until the interference of insidious and evil men ex-cites and stirs up the slaves, and renders caution and severity indispensable for the safety of the master. When abolitionists make the application of these laws necessary, it is they, and they alone, who are the authors of the restraint placed upon the slaves.

\*　　\*　　\*

It should be distinctly understood, that while the South acknowledges no accountability to any power under heaven for her course or sentiments on the subject of slavery, she freely avows her con-viction of her right to hold the negroes in bondage, and her persuasion that the domestic slavery of that section of our country, is not a moral or po-litical evil. These sentiments are the result of a full and general investigation of the subject: and were the people of the North equally well acquainted with it, they would probably subscribe to the opin-ions of the South. The original importation of the African is regarded by us as a moral wrong, be-cause associated with acts of violence and cruelty, which nothing can justify. But of the justice, nec-essity, and advantages of the institution, as now entailed upon the South, we cannot, after an exam-ination of the subject, feel a doubt. To the negro himself, we consider it no calamity. He is happier here than on the shores of his own degraded, sav-age, and most unhappy country—or rather the country of his fathers. He is happier, also, as a slave, than he could be as a freeman. . . .

The abolitionists deny the right of the people of the South, under any circumstances, to hold their fellow men in bondage. Upon what grounds is this position assumed? . . . It is their duty to prove that an institution, which has existed almost from the creation of the world to the present time, which has been encouraged by the best men of the most enlightened ages, and which has met the sanction of the Highest—has become, since these moral luminaries arose upon the world, guilty and calamitous. It will be found difficult to obtain a di-rect and rational answer to so plain a demand. They deal wholly in rhetorical flourishes; and if they reply at all, will tell us that the negro slave should not be a slave, because "he was created free." The fact is exactly the reverse. He comes into the world a slave. . . . But they tell us—"it is the will of God that he should be free." It is somewhat strange, that the will of God, in this point, has never been expressed until it came from the oracular mouths of the abolitionists. Such manifestations of the di-vine will never took place among the Jews, where slavery was universal, nor among the nations to which the disciples of our Saviour preached—nations which were overrun with slaves. The will and desire of God is the welfare of the species. If negro slavery in the South be inconsistent with the happiness of the human family, the argument may apply: but if, as we confidently assert, its existence is not at war with the well-being of the greatest number of those interested, it is wholly justifiable. And if, to go one step further, the measures of abolition, projected by the fanatics, are calculated to result in consequences calamitous to the race, they are, notwithstanding their ostentatious and obtrusive piety, guilty, in the face of heaven and earth, of crimes of the darkest and deepest crimson.

The phrase which occurs in the Declaration of American Independence—"all men are created free and equal"—is perpetually upon the lips of the abolitionist, to sanction his violation of the rights of the South. The following extract from a speech, delivered at the late public meeting in Philadelphia, by Mr. J. R. Burden, formerly Speaker of the Senate, and an early, fervent, and fearless advocate of the rights of the slave-holder, admirably illustrates the perversion and desecration of that celebrated sentence of Jefferson.

"On the 4th of July, 1776, in the immediate neighbourhood of this place, the Declaration of Independence was made. From it the advocates of black emancipation take their text, 'All men are created free and equal,' &c. The construction they put upon it is unlimited. Let us examine the subject carefully. Did the framers of the Declaration, the representatives of the people, intend to declare that domestic slavery was incompatible with the freedom of the colonies? If they did not, their words are of no use in the defence of negro emancipation. If they did, *why were not all the slaves then emancipated?*

\* \* \*

"The people of the United States, in order to form a more perfect union and secure the blessings of liberty, established the constitution in 1787. Domestic slavery still existed. No constitution could have been formed, had emancipation been persisted in. No union could have been perfected, if theorists and dreamers had determined to deprive the slave-holding states of their property.

"The constitution was adopted; the union was established; the world looked on it with admiration; yet it did not prohibit domestic slavery. So far from it, one of its main features, that of representation, was based upon it. Further, it declared that the *traffic should not be prohibited* by Congress prior to the year 1808. Perhaps the framers of the constitution thought that, by that period, the increased population of the blacks, would supersede the necessity of importation.

"We hear, in our day, much prating about liberty and philanthropy. The signers of the Declaration of Independence, and the framers of the constitution, were quite as conversant with the rights of man, as the best of us; they had as much philanthropy; and, if you will have it, as much Christianity as we profess to have. They possessed the confidence of the people, and deserved it; they passed through the times that tried men's souls; and, without the fear, favour, or affection of power, but in the spirit of virtue, wisdom, and patriotism, perfected a union as imperishable as the globe we inhabit. Shall it be said that such men put a blot and a stain upon our country?—So much for the text of emancipation!"

\* \* \*

At the period of the advent of Christ, slavery prevailed throughout the world. In that portion of Asia, in which Christianity was first preached, it existed in its severest form, and to a very great extent. Had it been regarded as an evil, it could not have escaped the animadversion, not only of Christ, but of all the holy men who became, at his departure, the preachers of his faith. A subject so nearly connected with the happiness of the mass of mankind, could not have escaped, and did not escape, their attention: and, had it not possessed their approbation, must have been condemned. Instead of this, however, we find the institution sanctioned, slaveholders admitted into the bosom of the church, and slaves admonished to humility and obedience. . . .

\*    \*    \*

[The abolitionists'] application of the "golden rule," strips it of its golden attributes, and makes it sanction all that it was intended to condemn. They insist that the maxim, as interpreted by them, requires that the authority of the master over the slave should be immediately relinquished. We may add that, it requires further, that the authority of the father over his child, of the master over his apprentice, of the tutor over his pupil, should also be given up. It requires that the ruler should not control the private citizen; that the judge should not sentence the convict, nor the jailor confine the thief. Neither the child, servant, nor scholar—the citizen, convict, nor thief are dealt with according to their desires; nor as those, in whose power they are placed, would desire, if their relative position were reversed. That rule which would require that their wishes should be regarded as rights, and conceded accordingly, would abrogate all law, would place the innocent at the mercy of the guilty, involve right and wrong in indistinguishable confusion, and render society a chaotic and jarring mass of wretchedness and crime.

\*    \*    \*

It will be admitted, that one of the first and most essential requisites in the formation of republican character is intelligence. Without that, patriotism is blind and inefficient. Without it, a virtuous people may be readily deceived and betrayed, and lose their freedom before they dream that it is in peril. The slave-holder has, in this particular, the inestimable advantage of leisure. Relieved from the labour required for actual support, he is enabled to direct his attention to public affairs; to investigate political subjects, and exercise his privileges understandingly. This result has been fully attained at the south. In no population in the world is the same time devoted to political investigations; and nowhere are the rights of man so fully canvassed and understood by the mass of the citizens.

While we acknowledge that some of the noblest spirits which our race has boasted have been linked, through life, with poverty, and while we are proud to be enabled to boast that in no country are the poor more pure and virtuous than in our own, yet we must also admit that poverty has its temptations. Men who enter into politics, as do many in the north, for the purpose of making money, are but dangerous agents. . . . The institution of slavery, by forming the character of the citizen on a more elevated standard, by lifting him above the necessities and temptations of poverty, secures, to the councils of the country, men for whom, to repeat the words of Ferguson, "danger has no terror, interest no means to corrupt."

There is one result which has been accomplished by slavery, and which no other cause has hitherto completely effected—it has introduced a complete equality among the whites. Professor Dew thus describes the difference which prevails in the north and south in this particular. "The menial and low offices being all performed by the blacks, there is at once taken away the greatest cause of distinction and separation of the ranks of society. The man at the north will not shake hands familiarly with his servant, and converse and laugh, and dine with him, no matter how honest and respectable he may be. But go to the south, and you will find that no white man feels such inferiority of rank as to be unworthy of association with those around him. Colour alone is here the badge of distinction, the true mark of aristocracy, and all who are white are equal in spite of variety of occupation." . . .

\*    \*    \*

The abolitionists, as another auxiliary in the attainment of their ends, have succeeded in enlisting female societies in their support. They sew for the cause; collect money for it; and render it all the aid which extraordinary zeal, combined with activity and leisure, can yield. When the most profound intellects in our country regard this exciting and momentous subject with awe, we cannot, without regret, see ladies rushing boldly into it. They forget that it is a political subject of the most important character: and, easily led away by the religious appeals of the abolitionists and the gentle and generous, but in this case misguided, promptings of their own nature, they unreflectingly lend their aid to designs, the tendency and consequence of which they are incapable of understanding. Politics is not the sphere in which the sex is either useful or honored; and their interference with subjects of this character, if sufficiently important to have *any* influence, must have an evil one. It is peculiarly to be regretted, that the false eloquence of the abolition preachers could ever have attained such influence over them, as to render them forgetful of the situation of their fair and gentle sisters of the South. Have they studied the history of St. Domingo; and are they prepared to let loose upon the refined and innocent ladies of the South, the savage negro, incapable of restraint, and wild with ungovernable passions? Are they aware of the present apprehensions of the females of the slave-holding states; and are they willing to add another to the fears that now haunt their pillows? It is impossible that fanatacism can so far have perverted their sympathies, or steeled the holier charities of their nature. The *possibility* of insurrection and the negroes' saturnalia of blood and lust, should appal every female bosom, and deter them from a scheme of *benevolence* so dubious in its character, and so fearful in its consequences.

*      *      *

If the scheme of emancipation were entitled to our approbation and support, the manner in which it is urged, would be sufficient to excite just and general suspicion and alarm. A political cause that comes before the people, sustained on the one side by English influence, and on the other by an aspiring priesthood—may well be regarded, by republicans, with distrust and terror.

It is not difficult to divine the motives which induce Great Britain to encourage the incendiary efforts of the abolitionists. . . . Our ruined commerce and manufactures, would afford Great Britain a new and boundless source of affluence; while the destruction of a former foe and a present rival, would be regarded with feelings of malicious satisfaction. Many of her people also regard the example of republicanism in this country, as dangerous to the existing institutions of Europe, and would rejoice to see the fabric of our Union torn to pieces, and our land bleeding and groaning beneath the parricidal arms of her own infuriated children.

Such, we have every reason to believe, are the motives that have induced England to send her emissaries into this country, to aid the incendiary schemes of the emancipationists, to volunteer and contribute pecuniary support, in forwarding the same cause; and in short, to exercise every means in her power, to excite division and insurrection, and consummate the infamy of our people, and the downfall of our country. It is true, that she avows only motives of philanthropy. But why is that philanthropy directed hither? Why does it not turn to their brethren, the oppressed and starving people of Ireland, whose condition is so much worse than that of our slaves? Why does it overlook the perishing thousands, in the manufactories in England? Why is it not turned to the almost countless millions of slaves who groan beneath English tyranny in India? . . . It remains to be seen, whether British money will be allowed openly to circulate, in maintaining an opposition to our Union and our Constitution; and whether English emissaries will be permitted to go from state to state, preaching treason against those sacred rights, which were wrested from English tyranny, and established at the price of hundreds of thousands of American lives.

*      *      *

# REVIEW QUESTIONS

1. What does the author offer as proof that man had the right "to hold his fellow-man in bondage"?
2. Why does the author argue that the slave of the South was better off than the laborer of the North?
3. What are his arguments against educating slaves?
4. How effective is the argument that slavery had allowed Southerners—rather than Northerners—to embody more fully the virtues of the republic?
5. Is the author against the methods as well as the goal of abolitionism? Why?

# LYDIA MARIA CHILD

## FROM Prejudices against People of Color (1836)

*As slavery proponents shrewdly pointed out, many Americans, including some aboli-*
*tionists, were racist. Given that, they asked their opponents whether freedom for the*
*slaves was to mean equality. It was a tough question, for it required people to think*
*beyond abolition itself and to consider how they defined humanity. Child, Douglass,*
*and others in the antislavery movement acknowledged the truth of the charge and the*
*importance of the question. Child and others like her realized that they had a dual*
*mission: to eradicate the spirit as well as the form of slavery. Some, including Doug-*
*lass, hoped that abolition of the institution of slavery would erase the attitudes*
*that had maintained it, for they believed slavery had created the prejudice against*
*people of color. Others argued that differences between races—a perception that*
*leads to racism—created slavery, and thus the solution would not be as simple*
*as abolition. These issues of cause, effect, and cure entangled reformers for*
*decades.*

From *An Appeal in Favor of That Class of Americans Called Africans* (1836; New York: Arno Press and The New York Times, 1968), pp. 195–99, 206–07.

While we bestow our earnest disapprobation on the system of slavery, let us not flatter ourselves that we are in reality any better than our brethren of the South. Thanks to our soil and climate, and the early exertions of the excellent Society of Friends, the *form* of slavery does not exist among us; but the very *spirit* of the hateful and mischievous thing is here in all its strength. The manner in which we use what power we have, gives us ample reason to be grateful that the nature of our institutions does not intrust us with more. Our prejudice against colored people is even more inveterate than it is at the South. The planter is often attached to his negroes, and lavishes caresses and kind words upon them, as he would on a favorite hound: but our cold-hearted, ignoble prejudice admits of no exception—no intermission.

The Southerners have long continued habit, apparent interest and dreaded danger, to palliate the wrong they do; but we stand without excuse.

They tell us that Northern ships and Northern capital have been engaged in this wicked business; and the reproach is true. Several fortunes in this city have been made by the sale of negro blood. If these criminal transactions are still carried on, they are done in silence and secrecy, because public opinion has made them disgraceful. But if the free States wished to cherish the system of slavery for ever, they could not take a more direct course than they now do. Those who are kind and liberal on all other subjects, unite with the selfish and the proud in their unrelenting efforts to keep the colored population in the lowest state of degradation; and the influence they unconsciously exert over children early infuses into their innocent minds the same strong feelings of contempt.

The intelligent and well-informed have the least share of this prejudice; and when their minds can be brought to reflect upon it, I have generally observed that they soon cease to have any at all. But such a general apathy prevails and the subject is so seldom brought into view, that few are really aware how oppressively the influence of society is made to bear upon this injured class of the community. . . . In order that my readers may not be ignorant of the extent of this tyrannical prejudice, I will as briefly as possible state the evidence, and leave them to judge of it, as their hearts and consciences may dictate.

In the first place, an unjust law exists in this Commonwealth, by which marriages between persons of different color is pronounced illegal. . . . In the first place, the government ought not to be invested with power to control the affections, any more than the consciences of citizens. A man has at least as good a right to choose his wife, as he has to choose his religion. His taste may not suit his neighbors; but so long as his deportment is correct, they have no right to interfere with his concerns. In the second place, this law is a *useless* disgrace to Massachusetts. Under existing circumstances, none but those whose condition in life is too low to be much affected by public opinion, will form such alliances; and they, when they choose to do so, *will* make such marriages, in spite of the law. I know two or three instances where women of the laboring class have been united to reputable, industrious colored men. These husbands regularly bring home their wages, and are kind to their families. If by some of the odd chances, which not unfrequently occur in the world, their wives should become heirs to any property, the children may be wronged out of it, because the law pronounces them illegitimate. And while this injustice exists with regard to *honest*, industrious individuals, who are merely guilty of differing from us in a matter of taste, neither the legislation nor customs of slaveholding States exert their influence against *immoral* connexions.

\*   \*   \*

There is among the colored people an increasing desire for information, and laudable ambition to be respectable in manners and appearance. Are we not foolish as well as sinful, in trying to repress a tendency so salutary to themselves, and so beneficial to the community? Several individuals of this class are very desirous to have persons of their own color qualified to teach something more than mere reading and writing. But in the public schools, colored children are subject to many discouragements and difficulties; and into the private schools they cannot gain admission. . . .

In a town adjoining Boston, a well behaved colored boy was kept out of the public school more than a year, by vote of the trustees. His mother, having some information herself, knew the importance of knowledge, and was anxious to obtain it for her family. She wrote repeatedly and urgently; and the schoolmaster himself told me that the correctness of her spelling, and the neatness of her hand-writing, formed a curious contrast with the notes he received from many white parents. At last, this spirited woman appeared before the committee, and reminded them that her husband, having for many years paid taxes as a citizen, had a right to the privileges of a citizen; and if her claim were refused, or longer postponed, she declared her determination to seek justice from a higher source. The trustees were, of course, obliged to yield to the equality of the laws, with the best grace they could. The boy was admitted, and made good progress in his studies. Had his mother been too ignorant to know her rights, or too abject to demand them, the lad would have had a fair chance to get a living out of the State as the occupant of a workhouse, or penitentiary.

\*   \*   \*

Will any candid person tell me why respectable colored people should not be allowed to make use of public conveyances, open to all who are able and willing to pay for the privilege? Those who enter a vessel, or a stage-coach, cannot expect to select their companions. If they can afford to take a carriage or boat for themselves, then, and then only, they have a right to be exclusive. I was lately talking with a young gentleman on this subject, who professed to have no prejudice against colored people, except so far as they were ignorant and vulgar; but still he could not tolerate the idea of allowing them to enter stages and steam-boats. "Yet, you allow the same privilege to vulgar and ignorant white men, without a murmur," I replied; "Pray give a good republican reason why a respectable colored citizen should be less favored." For want of a better argument, he said—(pardon me, fastidious reader)—he implied that the presence of colored persons was less agreeable than Otto of Rose, or Eau de Cologne; and this distinction, he urged was made by God himself. I answered, "Whoever takes his chance in a public vehicle, is liable to meet with uncleanly white passengers, whose breath may be redolent with the fumes of American cigars, or American gin. Neither of these articles have a fragrance peculiarly agreeable to nerves of delicate organization. Allowing your argument double the weight it deserves, it is utter nonsense to pretend that the inconvenience in the case I have supposed is not infinitely greater. But what is more to the point, do you dine in a fashionable hotel, do you sail in a fashionable steam-boat, do you sup at a fashionable house, without having negro servants behind your chair. Would they be any more disagreeable, as *passengers* seated in the corner of a stage, or a steam-boat, than as *waiters* in such immediate attendance upon your person?"

Stage-drivers are very much perplexed when they attempt to vindicate the present tyrannical customs; and they usually give up the point, by saying they themselves have no prejudice against colored people—they are merely afraid of the public. But stage-drivers should remember that in a popular government, they, in common with every other citizen, form a part and portion of the dreaded public.

The gold was never coined for which I would barter my individual freedom of acting and thinking upon any subject, or knowingly interfere with the rights of the meanest human being. The only true courage is that which impels us to do right without regard to consequences. To fear a populace is as servile as to fear an emperor. . . .

*    *    *

The state of public feeling not only makes it difficult for the Africans to obtain information, but it prevents them from making profitable use of what knowledge they have. A colored man, however intelligent, is not allowed to pursue any business more lucrative than that of a barber, a shoe-black, or a waiter. These, and all other employments, are truly respectable, whenever the duties connected with them are faithfully performed; but it is unjust that a man should, on account of his complexion, be prevented from performing more elevated uses in society. Every citizen ought to have a fair chance to try his fortune in any line of business, which he thinks he has ability to transact. Why should not colored men be employed in the manufactories of various kinds? If their ignorance is an objection, let them be enlightened, as speedily as possible. If their moral character is not sufficiently pure, remove the pressure of public scorn, and thus supply them with motives for being respectable. All this can be done. It merely requires an earnest wish to overcome a prejudice, which has "grown with our growth and strengthened with our strength," but which is in fact opposed to the spirit of our religion, and contrary to the instinctive good feelings of our nature. When examined by the clear light of reason, it disappears. Prejudices of all kinds have their strongest holds in the minds of the vulgar and the ignorant. In a community so enlightened as our own, they must gradually melt away under the influence of public discussion. . . .

*    *    *

# REVIEW QUESTIONS

1. What did Child mean when she wrote of the spirit of slavery? Do you agree with her definition?
2. How did the spirit of slavery manifest itself in the North?
3. What kind of social system did Northerners appear to be implementing?
4. In arguing against racial bias, does Child reveal the existence of other biases? Explain.

# 13 RELIGION, ROMANTICISM, AND REFORM

An English visitor, Frances Trollope, scathingly wrote that "if the citizens of the United States were indeed the devoted patriots they call themselves, they would surely not thus encrust themselves in the hard, dry, stubborn persuasion, that they are the first and best of the human race, that nothing is to be learnt, but what they are able to teach, and that nothing is worth having, which they do not possess." She then criticized how such an attitude served as an antidote to— meaning it countered or prevented—improvement.

While it was true that Americans tended to crow like cocks on a dunghill, Trollope failed to recognize the concerns behind the cock-a-doodle-doos. There was bravado as well as bravery in American actions, qualms as well as convictions in their attitudes, but they were not about to reveal their doubts and weaknesses to an Englishwoman who represented what to many of them was still the enemy. Yes, Americans did generally believe that their nation and its citizens were the best in the world, an attitude distasteful to others who reserved that title for themselves, but many also thought that their society could and should be improved, and it was up to them—not a foreign observer—to determine what needed to be fixed and how it was to be done.

The 1830s through the 1850s were thus years of great cultural and political ferment. The energetic, egalitarian spirit that marked Jacksonian democracy spilled over into a variety of reform crusades. A new generation of American moralists and thinkers saw themselves as inhabiting a nation of providential destiny and infinite potential, and they expressed an exuberant faith in the perfectibility of both individuals and society as a whole. As the poet-philosopher Ralph Waldo Emerson proclaimed in 1841, "the doctrine of Reform had never such scope as the present hour." Indeed, at midcentury the United States was awash in organized efforts to redress every social evil and conquer every personal failing.

*Religious life during the decades before the Civil War took on a more optimistic and fervent tone as many Protestants adopted more inclusive visions of God's grace and rejected the predestinarian tenets of orthodox Calvinism. Ministers of the New Divinity theology, while accepting God's will, preached that people effected their own destiny by electing between good and evil. People of faith still believed in original sin, but more and more believers embraced the concept of a benevolent God who offered everyone the gift of salvation through the experience of spiritual conversion and a life of faith. Evangelical firebrands such as Charles G. Finney and the Methodist circuit rider Peter Cartwright were especially skilled at challenging orthodox theology and attracting throngs of believers to an emotional rather than reasoned piety. Finney's enthusiasm did not stop with conversion: he exhorted the converted to express their faith not only in church but through good works, including social reform.*

*In the midst of this so-called Second Great Awakening, new religious denominations appeared that embraced people without regard to social standing or educational achievement. Such egalitarianism affected the status quo in other areas of culture as well, as Americans set out to correct their society's faults. The most profound version of reform idealism during this period was the peculiar romanticism practiced by the Transcendentalists, an eclectic coterie of New England poets and philosophers. This fluid group of geniuses and cranks included clergymen such as Theodore Parker and Ralph Waldo Emerson, philosopher-writers such as Henry David Thoreau and Bronson Alcott, and such learned women as Elizabeth Peabody and Margaret Fuller.*

*The Transcendentalists exercised an influence on American thought that far exceeded their numbers. Full of burning enthusiasm and perfectionist illusions about the boundless possibilities of human nature and the American social experiment, they broke away from what Emerson called the cultural domination of "reverent and conservative minds" and the dry logic of Enlightenment rationalism. They celebrated the individual spirit over the collective state and intuitive over rational knowledge.*

*These visionaries—and the authors and artists of the Romantic movement they affected—gave free rein to their fertile imaginations so as to transcend the limits of reason and cultivate inner states of consciousness, for they believed that human existence encompassed more experiences than reason and logic could explain. Such philosophical idealism traced its roots to Plato and Kant and led the Transcendentalists to use the lamp of personal inspiration to illuminate changing states of consciousness and spirituality—and to wield the rod of personal revelation to beat on the status quo.*

*The Transcendentalists emphasized self-reliance but also supported many of the organized efforts to reform social ills. Of course, many of the reform organizations were created to promote self-reliance as well as social responsibility. Activists, many of whom were women, promoted the abolition of slavery, aid* to the physically handicapped and mentally ill, prison improvements, state-supported public schools, temperance legislation, and women's rights.

Although this spirit of social reform was centered in New England and often fueled by an evangelical Protestant moralism, it penetrated all regions of the country and displayed secular motives as well. Burdened as well as bolstered by a naive optimism about human nature and the sufficiency of individual moral regeneration, the antebellum reform movements exercised a powerful influence on the country's culture and helped reveal to the young nation how much remained to be done to ensure the realization of the American dream.

# CHARLES GRANDISON FINNEY

## FROM *Lectures on Revivals of Religion* (1835, with 1868 revisions)

*Charles Grandison Finney (1792–1875) was the most celebrated revivalist of the Second Great Awakening. Born in Connecticut, he was raised in various frontier towns in central New York, an area known as the "Burned-Over District" for the revivals that had swept through it. In 1821 Finney experienced a soul-wrenching conversion during which God told him "to plead his cause" to others, so he abandoned his legal career and became a celebrated converter of souls in upstate New York and New England. A man of imposing height, forceful appearance, and vibrant rhetoric, he mesmerized the thousands who flocked to hear him preach his appealing theology of conversion and redemption. Although initially ordained as a Presbyterian minister, Finney was not a Calvinist; indeed, he contributed to the breakdown of Calvinism in American religion. He insisted that sin was a voluntary act rather than a foreordained certainty, and therefore people could choose to be saved and elect to embrace a life of holiness. This focus on the individual—a religious belief shared by most middle-class churchgoers—shows how Finney was both a product and representative of the Jacksonian era. So too did his belief in progress. According to Finney, revivalism and reform went hand in hand, and he inspired many people to take up such causes as abolition and temperance.*

Reprinted by permission of the publisher from *Lectures on Revivals of Religion* by Charles Grandison Finney, edited by William G. McLoughlin, pp. 9–12, 293–305, Cambridge, Mass.: The Belknap Press of Harvard University Press, Copyright © 1960 by the President and Fellows of Harvard College. [Editorial insertions appear in square brackets, except when otherwise noted—*Ed.*]

\*    \*    \*

A "Revival of Religion" presupposes a declension. Almost all the religion in the world has been produced by revivals. God has found it necessary to take advantage of the excitability there is in mankind, to produce powerful excitements among them, before he can lead them to obey. Men are so [spiritually][1] sluggish, there are so many things to lead their minds off from religion, and to oppose the influence of the gospel, that it is necessary to raise an excitement among them, till the tide rises so high as to sweep away the opposing obstacles. They must be so excited that they will break over these counteracting influences, before they will obey God. [Not that excited feeling is religion, for it is not; but it is excited desire, appetite, and feeling that prevents religion. The will is, in a sense, enslaved by the carnal and worldly desires. Hence it is necessary to awaken men to a sense of guilt and danger, and thus produce an excitement of counter-feeling and desire which will break the power of carnal and worldly desire and leave the will free to obey God.][2]

\*    \*    \*

---

[1] From the revised 1868 edition.

[2] From the revised 1868 edition.

There is so little *principle* in the church, so little firmness and stability of purpose, that [unless the religious feelings are awakened and kept excited, counter worldly feelings and excitements will prevail, and men will not obey God].[3] They have so little knowledge, and their principles are so weak, that unless they are excited, they will go back from the path of duty, and do nothing to promote the glory of God. The state of the world is still such, and probably will be till the millennium is fully come, that religion must be mainly promoted by these excitements. How long and how often has the experiment been tried, to bring the church to act steadily for God, without these periodical excitements! Many good men have supposed, and still suppose, that the best way to promote religion, is to go along *uniformly*, and gather in the ungodly gradually, and without excitement. But however such reasoning may appear in the abstract, *facts* demonstrate its futility. If the church were far enough advanced in knowledge, and had stability of principle enough to *keep awake*, such a course would do; but the church is so little enlightened, and there are so many counteracting causes, that the church will not go steadily to work without a special excitement. . . .

. . . The great political, and other worldly excitements that agitate Christendom, are all unfriendly to religion, and divert the mind from the interests of the soul. Now these excitements can only be counteracted by *religious* excitements. And until there is religious principle in the world to put down irreligious excitements, it is in vain to try to promote religion, except by counteracting excitements. This is true in philosophy, and it is a historical fact.

It is altogether improbable that religion will ever make progress among *heathen* nations except through the influence of revivals. The attempt is now making to do it by education, and other cautious and gradual improvements. But so long as the laws of mind remain what they are, it cannot be done in this way. There must be excitement sufficient to wake up the dormant moral powers, and roll back the tide of degradation and sin. And precisely so far as our own land approximates to heathenism, it is impossible for God or man to promote religion in such a state of things but by powerful excitements. . . .

\*       \*       \*

III. I proceed to mention some things *which ought to be done*, to continue this great and glorious revival of religion, which has been in progress for the last ten years.

1. *There should be great and deep repentings on the part of ministers.* WE, my brethren, must humble *ourselves* before God. It will not do for us to suppose that it is enough to call on the *people* to repent. We must repent, we must take the lead in repentance, and then call on the churches to follow.

\*       \*       \*

4. *The church must take right ground in regard to politics.* Do not suppose, now, that I am going to preach a political sermon, or that I wish to have you join and get up a *Christian party* in politics. No, I do not believe in that. But the time has come that Christians must vote for honest men, and take consistent ground in politics, or the Lord will curse them. They must be honest men themselves, and instead of voting for a man because he belongs to their party, Bank or Anti-Bank, Jackson, or Anti-Jackson, they must find out whether he is honest and upright, and fit to be trusted. They must let the world see that the church will uphold no man in office, who is known to be a knave, or an adulterer, or a Sabbath-breaker, or a gambler. Such is the spread of intelligence and the facility of communication in our country, that every man can know for whom he gives his vote. And if he will give his vote only for honest men, the country will be obliged to have upright rulers. . . . As on the subject of slavery and temperance, so on this subject, the church must act right or the country will be ruined. God cannot sustain this free and blessed country, which

---

[3] From the revised 1868 edition.

we love and pray for, unless the church will take right ground. Politics are a part of religion in such a country as this, and Christians must do their duty to the country as a part of their duty to God. It seems sometimes as if the foundations of the nation were becoming rotten, and Christians seem to act as if they thought God did not see what they do in politics. But I tell you, he does see it, and he will bless or curse this nation, according to the course they take.

5. *The churches must take right ground on the subject of slavery.* And here the question arises, what is right ground? And FIRST I will state some things that should be avoided.

(1.) First of all, *a bad spirit* should be avoided. Nothing is more calculated to injure religion, and to injure the slaves themselves, than for Christians to get into an angry controversy on the subject. It is a subject upon which there needs to be no angry controversy among Christians. Slave-holding professors, like rum-selling professors, may endeavor to justify themselves, and may be angry with those who press their consciences, and call upon them to give up their sins. Those proud professors of religion who think a man to blame, or think it is a shame to have a black skin, may allow their prejudices so far to prevail, as to shut their ears, and be disposed to quarrel with those who urge the subject upon them. But I repeat it, the subject of slavery is a subject upon which Christians, praying men, *need not* and *must not* differ.

(2.) Another thing to be avoided is *an attempt to take neutral ground* on this subject. Christians can no more take neutral ground on this subject, since it has come up for discussion, than they can take neutral ground on the subject of the sanctification of the Sabbath. It is a great national sin. It is a sin of the church. The churches by their silence, and by permitting slave-holders to belong to their communion, have been consenting to it. All denominations have been more or less guilty, although the Quakers have of late years washed their hands of it. It is in vain for the churches to pretend it is merely a political sin. I repeat it, it is the sin of the church, to which all denominations have consented. They have virtually declared that it is lawful. . . .

\*     \*     \*

In the SECOND place, I will mention several things, that in my judgment the church are imperatively called upon to do, on this subject:

(1.) Christians of all denominations, should lay aside prejudice and *inform themselves* on this subject, without any delay. Vast multitudes of professors of religion have indulged prejudice to such a degree as to be unwilling to read and hear, and come to a right understanding of the subject. But Christians cannot pray in this state of mind. I defy any one to possess the spirit of prayer, while he is too prejudiced to examine this, or any other question of duty. . . .

(2.) Writings, containing temperate and judicious discussions on this subject, and such developments of facts as are before the public, should be quietly and extensively circulated, and should be carefully and prayerfully examined by the whole church. . . . [P]raying men should act judiciously, and that, as soon as sufficient information can be diffused through the community, the churches should meekly, but FIRMLY take decided ground on the subject, and express before the whole nation and the world, their abhorrence of this sin.

\*     \*     \*

I believe the time has come, and although I am no prophet, I believe it will be found to have come, that the revival in the United States will continue and prevail, no farther and faster than the church take right ground upon this subject. The church are God's witnesses. The fact is that slavery is, pre-eminently, the *sin of the church*. It is the very fact that ministers and professors of religion of different denominations hold slaves, which sanctifies the whole abomination, in the eyes of ungodly men. Who does not know that on the subject of temperance, every drunkard in the land, will skulk behind some rum-selling deacon, or wine-drinking minister? It is the most common objection and refuge of the intemperate, and of moderate drinkers, that it is practised by professors of religion. It is *this* that creates the imperious necessity for excluding traffickers in ardent spirit, and rum-drinkers from the communion. Let the churches of all denominations speak out on the subject of temperance, let them close their doors against all who have any thing to do with the death-dealing abomination, and the cause of temperance is triumphant. A few years would annihilate the traffic. Just so with slavery.

It is the church that mainly supports this sin. Her united testimony upon this subject would settle the question. Let Christians of all denominations meekly but firmly come forth, and pronounce their verdict, let them clear their communions, and wash their hands of this thing, let them give forth and write on the head and front of this great abomination, SIN! and in three years, a public sentiment would be formed that would carry all before it, and there would not be a shackled slave, nor a bristling, cruel slave-driver in this land.

\*     \*     \*

6. If the church wishes to promote revivals, *she must sanctify the Sabbath.* There is a vast deal of Sabbath-breaking in the land. Merchants break it, travellers break it, the government breaks it. . . .

7. The church must take right ground on the subject of Temperance, and Moral Reform, and all the subject of practical morality which come up for decision from time to time.

There are those in the churches who are standing aloof from the subject of Moral Reform, and

who are as much afraid to have any thing said in the pulpit against lewdness, as if a thousand devils had got up into the pulpit. On this subject, the church need not expect to be permitted to take neutral ground. In the providence of God, it is up for discussion. The evils have been exhibited, the call has been made for reform. . . .

\*     \*     \*

## REVIEW QUESTIONS

1. How does Finney justify his efforts to provoke an emotional state in his listeners?
2. What does Finney mean by "so little principle in the church"? Is he referring to a particular church?
3. Why did Finney promote political and social activism instead of calling for a withdrawal from such worldly concerns?
4. According to Finney, what role should the churches play in the abolition of slavery? In what sense did he charge that they had "consented" to the practice of slavery?
5. Did Finney perhaps underestimate the entrenchment of slavery and overestimate the power of converted Christians to effect change?

# HENRY DAVID THOREAU

## FROM *Walden* (1854)

*After graduating from Harvard and teaching school for several years, Henry David Thoreau (1817–1862) decided to focus his energies on his true passions—nature study and poetry. The rebellious son of a pencil-maker father and abolitionist mother, Thoreau exuded a spirit of uncompromising integrity, manly vigor, self-reliant simplicity, and tart individuality. The short and sinewy Thoreau joyfully mastered the woodland arts. He loved to muck about in swamps and fields, communing with mud turtles and loons as well as his inner self. Such introspection was fostered by the leading founder of trascendentalism, Ralph Waldo Emerson. On 4 July 1845, Thoreau moved into a small cabin he had built on land owned by Emerson bordering Walden Pond, about two miles from Concord. Armed with jackknife, spyglass, diary, and pencil, he found the woods and fields alive with fascinating sights, spiritual meaning, and elemental truths. During his twenty-six months at Walden Pond, Thoreau learned to simplify his material wants so as to "entertain the true problems of life." In* Walden *he offered readers a richly textured journal of his thoughts and activities while engaged in plain living and high thinking at Walden Pond. Although he returned to live in his family's household in 1847, Thoreau's heart remained in the woods.*

From *The Writings of Henry David Thoreau*, vol. 2 (Boston: Houghton Mifflin, 1906), pp. 8–10, 100–03, 108–09, 355–56.

*       *       *

The mass of men lead lives of quiet desperation. What is called resignation is confirmed desperation. From the desperate city you go into the desperate country, and have to console yourself with the bravery of minks and muskrats. A stereotyped but unconscious despair is concealed even under what are called the games and amusements of mankind. There is no play in them, for this comes after work. But it is a characteristic of wisdom not to do desperate things.

When we consider what, to use the words of the catechism, is the chief end of man, and what are the true necessaries and means of life, it appears as if men had deliberately chosen the common mode of living because they preferred it to any other. Yet they honestly think there is no choice left. But alert and healthy natures remember that the sun rose clear. It is never too late to give up our prejudices. No way of thinking or doing, however ancient, can be trusted without proof. What everybody echoes or in silence passes by as true to-day may turn out to be falsehood tomorrow, mere smoke of opinion, which some had trusted for a cloud that would sprinkle fertilizing rain on their fields. What old people say you cannot do, you try and find that you can. Old deeds for old people, and new deeds for new. . . . I have lived some thirty years on this planet, and I have yet to hear the first syllable of valuable or even earnest advice from my seniors. They have told me nothing, and probably cannot tell me anything to the purpose. Here is life, an experiment to a great extent untried by me; but it does not avail me that they have tried it. If I have any experience which I think valuable, I am sure to reflect that this my Mentors said nothing about.

*       *       *

I went to the woods because I wished to live deliberately, to front only the essential facts of life, and see if I could not learn what it had to teach, and not, when I came to die, discover that I had not lived. I did not wish to live what was not life, living is so dear; nor did I wish to practise resignation, unless it was quite necessary. I wanted to live deep and suck out all the marrow of life, to live so sturdily and Spartan-like as to put to rout all that was not life, to cut a broad swath and shave close, to drive life into a corner, and reduce it to its lowest terms, and, if it proved to be mean, why then to get the whole and genuine meanness of it, and publish its meanness to the world; or if it were sublime, to know it by experience, and be able to give a true account of it in my next excursion. For most men, it appears to me, are in a strange uncertainty about it, whether it is of the devil or of God, and have *somewhat hastily* concluded that it is the chief end of man here to "glorify God and enjoy him forever."

Still we live meanly, like ants; though the fable tells us that we were long ago changed into men; . . . Our life is frittered away by detail. An honest man has hardly need to count more than his ten fingers, or in extreme cases he may add his ten toes, and lump the rest. Simplicity, simplicity, simplicity! I say, let your affairs be as two or three, and not a hundred or a thousand; instead of a million count half a dozen, and keep your accounts on your thumb-nail. In the midst of this chopping sea of civilized life, such are the clouds and storms and quicksands and thousand-and-one items to be allowed for, that a man has to live, if he would not founder and go to the bottom and not make his port at all, by dead reckoning, and he must be a great calculator indeed who succeeds. Simplify, simplify. Instead of three meals a day, if it be necessary eat but one; instead of a hundred dishes, five; and reduce other things in proportion. . . . The nation itself, with all its so-called internal improvements, which, by the way are all external and superficial, is just such an unwieldy and overgrown establishment, cluttered with furniture and tripped up by its own traps, ruined by luxury and heedless expense, by want of calculation and a worthy aim, as the million households in the land; and the only cure for it, as for them, is in a rigid economy, a stern and more than Spartan simplicity of life and elevation of purpose. It lives too fast. Men think that it is essential that the *Nation* have commerce, and export ice, and talk through a telegraph, and ride thirty miles an hour, without a doubt, whether *they* do or not; but whether we should live like baboons or like men, is a little uncertain. If we do not get out sleepers, and forge rails, and devote days and nights to the work, but go to tinkering upon our *lives* to improve *them*, who will build railroads? And if railroads are not built, how shall we get to heaven in season? But if we stay at home and mind our business, who will want railroads? We do not ride on the railroad; it rides upon us. Did you ever think what those sleepers are that underlie the railroad? Each one is a man, an Irishman, or a Yankee man. The rails are laid on them, and they are covered with sand, and the cars run smoothly over them. They are sound sleepers, I assure you. And every few years a new lot is laid down and run over; so that, if some have the pleasure of riding on a rail, others have the misfortune to be ridden upon. . . .

Why should we live with such hurry and waste of life? We are determined to be starved before we are hungry. Men say that a stitch in time saves nine, and so they take a thousand stitches to-day to save nine to-morrow. . . .

*        *        *

Let us spend one day as deliberately as Nature, and not be thrown off the track by every nutshell and mosquito's wing that falls on the rails. Let us rise early and fast, or break fast, gently and without perturbation; let company come and let company go, let the bells ring and the children cry,— determined to make a day of it. Why should we knock under and go with the stream? Let us not be upset and overwhelmed in that terrible rapid and whirlpool called a dinner, situated in the meridian shallows. Weather this danger and you are safe, for the rest of the way is down hill. With unrelaxed nerves, with morning vigor, sail by it, looking another way, tied to the mast like Ulysses. If the engine whistles, let it whistle till it is hoarse for its pains. If the bell rings, why should we run? We will consider what kind of music they are like. Let us settle ourselves, and work and wedge our feet downward through the mud and slush of opinion, and prejudice, and tradition, and delusion, and appearance, that alluvion which covers the globe, through Paris and London, through New York and Boston and Concord, through Church and State, through poetry and philosophy and religion, till we come to a hard bottom and rocks in place, which we can call *reality*, . . . Be it life or death, we crave only reality. If we are really dying, let us hear the rattle in our throats and feel cold in the extremities; if we are alive, let us go about our business.

*        *        *

I left the woods for as good a reason as I went there. Perhaps it seemed to me that I had several more lives to live, and could not spare any more time for that one. It is remarkable how easily and insensibly we fall into a particular route, and make a beaten track for ourselves. I had not lived there a week before my feet wore a path from my door to the pond-side; and though it is five or six years since I trod it, it is still quite distinct. It is true, I fear that others may have fallen into it, and so helped to keep it open. The surface of the earth is soft and impressible by the feet of men; and so with the paths which the mind travels. How worn and dusty, then, must be the highways of the world, how deep the ruts of tradition and conformity! . . .

I learned this, at least, by my experiment; that if one advances confidently in the direction of his dreams, and endeavors to live the life which he has imagined, he will meet with a success unexpected in common hours. He will put some things behind, will pass an invisible boundary; new, universal, and more liberal laws will begin to establish themselves around and within him; or the old laws be expanded, and interpreted in his favor in a more liberal sense, and he will live with the license of a higher order of beings. In proportion as he simplifies his life, the laws of the universe will appear less complex, and solitude will not be solitude, nor

poverty poverty, nor weakness weakness. If you have built castles in the air, your work need not be lost; that is where they should be. Now put the foundations under them.

\*   \*   \*

## REVIEW QUESTIONS

1. Why did Thoreau believe that most people led lives of "quiet desperation"? Was his experiment in simple living a response to that belief?
2. What was the significance of his comparing the nation's "establishment" with the "households" of its citizens?
3. What does he think about the notion of improvement in antebellum American society?
4. What did Thoreau mean by his references to the "ruts of tradition" and "castles in the air"?

## HORACE MANN

# Moral and Religious Education (1848)

*While Finney lectured about the revival of religion in America, Americans debated whether and how religion should be taught in the developing systems of state-supported public schools. As the nation's society and economy became more complex, reformers called for changes in education so that the United States and its citizens could continue to prosper. Prosperity, however, was not enough. Many social and political leaders were also exploring new ways to provide external guidance and inculcate the values needed to manage a growing and increasingly diverse population. Horace Mann (1796–1859) was the most prominent advocate of state-supported common schools as the means to create not only a literate but also a virtuous people. In 1837 he resigned his position as a state legislator and gave up his law practice to become the secretary of the first board of education established by the state of Massachusetts. For the next eleven years, he championed universal free education so that the children of workers and immigrants as well as those from the middle and upper classes could benefit from and contribute to the land of opportunity. He presented his arguments in published reports to the Massachusetts Board of Education. The follow-*

*ing excerpt comes from his twelfth report, in which he answered critics who believed he was secularizing public schools and thus demoralizing pupils as he restricted the nature of religious education in those schools.*

From *Life and Works of Horace Mann*, vol. 4, *Annual Reports of the Secretary of the Board of Education of Massachusetts for the Years 1845–1848* (Boston: Lee and Shepard, 1891), pp. 283, 287–88, 292, 296–300, 302–03, 305–12.

## Moral Education.

Moral education is a primal necessity of social existence. The unrestrained passions of men are not only homicidal, but suicidal; and a community without a conscience would soon extinguish itself. . . .

\*      \*      \*

. . . Education has never yet been brought to bear with one-hundredth part of its potential force upon the natures of children, and, through them, upon the character of men and of the race. In all the attempts to reform mankind which have hitherto been made, whether by changing the frame of government, by aggravating or softening the severity of the penal code, or by substituting a government-created for a God-created religion,— in all these attempts, the infantile and youthful mind, its amenability to influences, and the enduring and self-operating character of the influences it receives, have been almost wholly unrecognized. Here, then, is a new agency, whose powers are but just beginning to be understood, and whose mighty energies hitherto have been but feebly invoked. . . .

\*      \*      \*

## Religious Education.

But it will be said that this grand result in practical morals is a consummation of blessedness that can never be attained without religion, and that no community will ever be religious without a religious education. Both these propositions I regard as eternal and immutable truths. Devoid of religious principles and religious affections, the race can never fall so low but that it may sink still lower; animated and sanctified by them, it can never rise so high but that it may ascend still higher. . . .

\*      \*      \*

I here place the argument in favor of a religious education for the young upon the most broad and general grounds, purposely leaving it to every individual to add for himself those auxiliary arguments which may result from his own peculiar views of religious truth. But such is the force of the conviction to which my own mind is brought by these general considerations, that I could not avoid regarding the man who should oppose the religious education of the young as an insane man. . . .

I can, then, confess myself second to no one in the depth and sincerity of my convictions and desires respecting the necessity and universality, both on abstract and on practical grounds, of a religious education for the young; and, if I had stronger words at command in which to embody these views, I would not fail to use them. But the question still remains, How shall so momentous an object be pursued? In the measures we adopt to give a religious education to others, shall we ourselves abide by the dictates of religion? or shall we do, as has almost universally been done ever since the unhallowed union between Church and State under Constantine,—shall we seek to educate the community religiously through the use of the most irreligious means?

On this subject I propose to speak with freedom and plainness, and more at length than I should feel required to do but for the peculiar circumstances in which I have been placed. It is matter of notoriety, that the views of the Board of Education,— and my own, perhaps, still more than those of the Board,— on the subject of religious instruction in our public schools, have been subjected to animadversion. Grave charges have been made against us, that our purpose was to exclude religion, and to exclude that, too, which is the common exponent of religion,—the Bible,—from the common schools of the State; or, at least, to derogate from its authority, and destroy its influence in them. . . .

It is known, too, that our noble system of free schools for the whole people is strenuously opposed by a few persons in our own State, and by no inconsiderable numbers in some of the other states of this Union; and that a rival system of "parochial" or "sectarian schools" is now urged upon the public by a numerous, a powerful, and a well-organized body of men. It has pleased the advocates of this rival system, in various public addresses, in reports, and through periodicals devoted to their cause, to denounce our system as irreligious and anti-Christian. They do not trouble themselves to describe what our system is, but adopt a more summary way to forestall public opinion against it by using general epithets of reproach, and signals of alarm.

. . . In making this final Report, therefore, I desire to vindicate my conduct from the charges that have been made against it; and, so far as the Board has been implicated in these charges, to leave my testimony on record for their exculpation. . . . I desire, also, to vindicate the system with which I have been so long and so intimately connected, not only from the aspersion, but from the suspicion, of being an irreligious or anti-Christian or an un-Christian system. I know full well, that it is unlike the systems which prevail in Great Britain, and in many of the Continental nations of Europe, where the Established Church controls the education of the young in order to keep itself established. But this is presumptive evidence in its favor, rather than against it.

All the schemes ever devised by governments to secure the prevalence and permanence of religion among the people, however variant in form they may have been, are substantially resolvable into two systems. One of these systems holds the regulation and control of the religious belief of the people to be one of the functions of government, like the command of the army or the navy, or the establishment of courts, or the collection of revenues. According to the other system, religious belief is a matter of individual and parental concern; and, while the government furnishes all practicable facilities for the independent formation of that belief, it exercises no authority to prescribe, or coercion to enforce it. The former is the system, which, with very few exceptions, has prevailed throughout Christendom for fifteen hundred years. Our own government is almost a solitary example among the nations of the earth, where freedom of opinion, and the inviolability of conscience, have been even theoretically recognized by the law.

The argument in behalf of a government-established religion, at the time when it was first used, was not without its plausibility; but the principle, once admitted, drew after it a train of the most appalling consequences. If religion is absolutely essential to the stability of the State as well as to the present and future happiness of the subject, why, it was naturally asked, should not the government enforce it? And, if government is to enforce religion, it follows, as a necessary consequence, that it must define it; for how can it enforce a duty, which, being undefined, is uncertain? And again: if government begins to define religion, it must define what it is not, as well as what it is; and, while it upholds whatever is included in the definition, it must suppress and abolish whatever is excluded from it. . . . If the non-conformist feels himself, by the aid of a higher power, to be secure against threats of future perdition, the civil magistrate has terrible resources at command in this life,—imprisonment, scourging, the rack, the fagot, death. Should it ever be said that these are excessive punishments for exercising freedom of thought, and for allowing the heart to pour forth those sentiments of adoration to God with which it believes God himself has inspired it, the answer is always ready, that nothing is so terrible as the heresy that draws after it the endless wrath of the Omnipotent. . . .

But, in all the persecutions and oppressions ever committed in the name of religion, one point has been unwarrantably assumed; namely, *that the faith of their authors was certainly and infallibly the true faith*. With the fewest exceptions, the advocates of all the myriad conflicting creeds that have ever been promulgated have held substantially the same language: "*Our* faith we know to be true." . . . The advocates of hundreds and thousands of hostile creeds have placed themselves upon the same ground. Each has claimed the same proof from reason and conscience, the same external revelation from God, and the same inward light of his Spirit. But if truth be *one*, and hence necessarily harmonious; if God be its author; and if the voice of God be not more dissonant than the tongues of Babel,—then, at least, all but one of the different forms of faith ever promulgated by human authority, so far as these forms conflict with each other, cannot have emanated from the Fountain of all truth. These faiths must have been more or less erroneous. The believers in them must have been more or less mistaken. Who, on an impartial survey of the whole, and a recollection of the confidence with which each one has been claimed to be infallibly true, shall dare to affirm that any one of them all is a perfect transcript of the perfect law as it exists in the Divine Mind, *and that that one is his*?

But here arises a practical distinction, which the world has lost sight of. It is this: after seeking all possible light from within, from without, and from above, each man's belief is his own standard of truth; *but it is not the standard for any other man*. The believer is bound to live by his belief under all circumstances, in the face of all perils, and at the cost of any sacrifice. But his standard of truth is the standard for himself alone; *never for his neighbor*. That neighbor must have his own standard, which to him must be supreme. And the fact that each man is bound to follow his own best light and guidance is an express negation of any other man's right, and of any government's right, of forcible interference. Here is the dividing-line. On one side lie personal freedom and the recognition of freedom in others; on the other side are intolerance, oppression, and all the wrongs and woes of persecution for conscience' sake. The hierarchs of the world have generally reversed this rule of duty.

They have been more rigid in demanding that others should live according to their faith than in living in accordance with it themselves.

Did the history of mankind show that there has been the most of virtue and piety in those nations where religion has been most rigorously enforced by law, the advocates of ecclesiastical domination would have a powerful argument in favor of their measures of coercion; but the united and universal voice of history, observation, and experience, gives the argument to the other side. . . .

Among the infinite errors and enormities resulting from systems of religion devised by man, and enforced by the terrors of human government, have been those dreadful re-actions which have abjured all religion, spurned its obligations, and voted the Deity into non-existence. This extreme is, if possible, more fatal than that by which it was produced. Between these extremes, philanthropic and godly men have sought to find a medium, which should avoid both the evils of ecclesiastical tyranny and the greater evils of atheism. And this medium has at length been supposed to be found. It is promulgated in the great principle, that government should do all that it can to facilitate the acquisition of religious truth, but shall leave the decision of the question, what religious truth is, to the arbitrament, without human appeal, of each man's reason and conscience; in other words, that government shall never, by the infliction of pains and penalties, or by the privation of rights or immunities, call such decision either into prejudgment or into review. The formula in which the constitution of Massachusetts expresses it is in these words: "All religious sects and denominations demeaning themselves peaceably and as good citizens shall be equally under the protection of law; and no subordination of one sect or denomination to another shall ever be established by law."

The great truth recognized and expressed in these few words of our constitution is one which it has cost centuries of struggle and of suffering, and the shedding of rivers of blood, to attain; and he who would relinquish or forfeit it, virtually impetrates upon his fellow-men other centuries of suffering and the shedding of other rivers of blood.

Nor are we as yet entirely removed from all danger of relapse. The universal interference of government in matters of religion, for so many centuries, has hardened the public mind to its usurpations. Men have become tolerant of intolerance; and, among many nations of Christendom, the common idea of religious freedom is satisfied by an exemption from fine and imprisonment for religious belief. They have not yet reached the conception of equal privileges and franchises for all. Doubtless the time will come when any interference, either by positive infliction or by legal disability, with another man's conscience in religious concernments, so long as he molests no one by the exercise of his faith, will be regarded as the crowning and supereminent act of guilt which one human being can perpetrate against another. But this time is far from having yet arrived, and nations otherwise equally enlightened are at very different distances from this moral goal. The oppressed, on succeeding to power, are prone to become oppressors in their turn, and to forget, as victors, the lessons, which, as victims, they had learned.

*    *    *

All know the energetic tendency of men's minds to continue in a course to which long habit has accustomed them. The same law is as true in regard to institutions administered by bodies of men as in regard to individual minds. . . . A statute may be enacted, and may even be executed by the courts, long before it is ratified and enforced by public opinion. . . . And such was the case in regard to the law of 1827, prohibiting sectarian instruction in our public schools. It was not easy for committees at once to withdraw or to exclude the books, nor for teachers to renounce the habits, by which this kind of instruction had been given. Hence, more than ten years subsequent to the passage of that law, at the time when I made my first educational and official circuits over the State, I found books in the schools as strictly and exclusively *doctrinal* as any on the shelves of a theological library. I heard teachers giving oral instruction as strictly and purely *doctrinal* as any ever heard from the

pulpit or from the professor's chair. And more than this: I have now in my possession printed directions, given by committee-men to teachers, enjoining upon them the use of a catechism in school, which is wholly devoted to an exposition of the doctrines of one of the denominations amongst us. . . .

In the first place, then, I believed these proceedings not only to be wholly unwarranted by law, but to be in plain contravention of law. . . . I believed then, as now, that religious instruction in our schools, to the extent which the constitution and laws of the State allowed and prescribed, was indispensable to their highest welfare, and essential to the vitality of moral education. Then as now, also, I believed that sectarian books and sectarian instruction, if their encroachments were not resisted, would prove the overthrow of the schools. . . .

No person, then, in the whole community, could have been more surprised or grieved than myself at finding my views in regard to the extent and the limitation of religious instruction in our public schools attributed to a hostility to religion itself, or a hostility to the Scriptures, which are the "lively oracles" of the Christian's faith. As the Board was implicated with me in these charges (they never having dissented from my views, and continuing to re-elect me annually to the office of Secretary), it is well known to its earlier members that I urged the propriety of their meeting these charges with a public and explicit denial of their truth. . . .

*    *    *

After years of endurance, after suffering under misconstructions of conduct, and the imputation of motives whose edge is sharper than a knife, it was at my suggestion, and by making use of materials which I had laboriously collected, that the Board made its Eighth Annual Report,—a document said to be the ablest argument in favor of the use of the Bible in schools anywhere to be found. This Report had my full concurrence. Since its appearance, I have always referred to it as explanatory of the views of the Board, and as setting forth the law of a wise commonwealth and the policy of a Christian people. . . .

But it may still be said, and it is said, that however sincere, or however religiously disposed, the advocates of our school-system may be, still the character of the system is not to be determined by the number nor by the sincerity of its defenders, but by its own inherent attributes; and that, if judged by these attributes, it is, in fact and in truth, an irreligious, an un-Christian, and an anti-Christian system. Having devoted the best part of my life to the promotion of this system, and believing it to be the only system which ought to prevail, or can permanently prevail, in any free country, I am not content to see it suffer, unrelieved, beneath the weight of imputations so grievous; nor is it right that any hostile system should be built up by so gross a misrepresentation of ours. That our public schools are not theological seminaries, is admitted. That they are debarred by law from inculcating the peculiar and distinctive doctrines of any one religious denomination amongst us, is claimed; and that they are also prohibited from ever teaching that what they do teach is the whole of religion, or all that is essential to religion or to salvation, is equally certain. But our

system earnestly inculcates all Christian morals; it founds its morals on the basis of religion; it welcomes the religion of the Bible; and, in receiving the Bible, it allows it to do what it is allowed to do in no other system,—*to speak for itself.* But here it stops, not because it claims to have compassed all truth, but because it disclaims to act as an umpire between hostile religious opinions.

*       *       *

## REVIEW QUESTIONS

1. Did Mann believe that education was the ultimate way to reform humanity? If so, why?
2. Did he deem religious education essential to the development of morality?
3. What problems did he see in the teaching of religion in the common schools?
4. How did he correct, or intend to correct, such problems?
5. Did he have a strong rebuttal to critics who accused him and the board of education of having created an irreligious and anti-Christian school system?

---

# MARGARET FULLER

## FROM *Woman in the Nineteenth Century* (1845)

*Rebellion and nonconformity were not found solely among American men. While some reformers, such as Catharine Beecher, sought increased educational opportunities for women so that they could better serve their families and society within the domestic sphere, others, echoing American revolutionary and egalitarian sentiments, disputed such segregation and limitation. Some of these reformers concentrated on the passage of legislation that would protect a woman's rights in various situations, as in property settlements and divorce proceedings. Other reformers preferred to focus on the struggle for suffrage so as to have a public voice and power. Among the most radical of these reformers was Margaret Fuller (1810–1850). Educated by a father who believed that girls and boys were intellectually equal, Fuller (who later became an associate of the Transcendentalists) advocated the simple but disturbing doctrine of equal rights for women. She promoted this cause, along with her other artistic, literary, and social ideas, while she was the editor of the transcendentalist journal* The Dial *in the early 1840s and then when she was a writer for the New York* Daily-Tribune. *The revolutionary sentiments in her book,* Woman in the Nineteenth Century, *shocked many Americans at the time, but she was not the first or the last woman of her generation to argue against inequities based on gender.*

---

From *Woman in the Nineteenth Century,* introduction by Bernard Rosenthal (New York: W. W. Norton, 1971), pp. 24–26, 28–30, 37–38, 93–96, 119–20.

*    *    *

It should be remarked that, as the principle of liberty is better understood, and more nobly interpreted, a broader protest is made in behalf of Woman. As men become aware that few men have had a fair chance, they are inclined to say that no women have had a fair chance. . . .

*    *    *

Though the national independence be blurred by the servility of individuals; though freedom and equality have been proclaimed only to leave room for a monstrous display of slave-dealing and slave-keeping; though the free American so often feels himself free, like the Roman, only to pamper his appetites and his indolence through the misery of his fellow-beings; still it is not in vain that the verbal statement has been made, "All men are born free and equal." There it stands, a golden certainty wherewith to encourage the good, to shame the bad. . . .

*    *    *

Of all its banners, none has been more steadily upheld, and under none have more valor and willingness for real sacrifices been shown, than that of the champions of the enslaved African. And this band it is, which, partly from a natural following out of principles, partly because many women have been prominent in that cause, makes, just now, the warmest appeal in behalf of Woman.

Though there has been a growing liberality on this subject, yet society at large is not so prepared for the demands of this party, but that its members are, and will be for some time, coldly regarded as the Jacobins of their day.

"Is it not enough," cries the irritated trader, "that you have done all you could to break up the national union, and thus destroy the prosperity of our country, but now you must be trying to break up family union, to take my wife away from the cradle and the kitchen-hearth to vote at polls, and preach from a pulpit? Of course, if she does such things, she cannot attend to those of her own sphere. She is happy enough as she is. She has more leisure than I have,—every means of improvement, every indulgence."

"Have you asked her whether she was satisfied with these *indulgences*?"

"No, but I know she is. She is too amiable to desire what would make me unhappy, and too judicious to wish to step beyond the sphere of her sex. I will never consent to have our peace disturbed by any such discussions."

" 'Consent—you?' it is not consent from you that is in question—it is assent from your wife."

"Am not I the head of my house?"

"You are not the head of your wife. God has given her a mind of her own."

"I am the head, and she the heart."

"God grant you play true to one another, then! I suppose I am to be grateful that you did not say she was only the hand. . . . But our doubt is whether the heart *does* consent with the head, or only obeys its decrees with a passiveness that precludes the exercise of its natural powers, or a repugnance that turns sweet qualities to bitter, or a doubt that lays waste the fair occasions of life. It is to ascertain the truth that we propose some liberating measures."

Thus vaguely are these questions proposed and discussed at present. But their being proposed at all implies much thought, and suggests more. Many women are considering within themselves what they need that they have not, and what they can have if they find they need it. Many men are considering whether women are capable of being and having more than they are and have, *and* whether, if so, it will be best to consent to improvement in their condition.

*        *        *

. . . We would have every arbitrary barrier thrown down. We would have every path laid open to Woman as freely as to Man. Were this done, and a slight temporary fermentation allowed to subside, we should see crystallizations more pure and of more various beauty. We believe the divine energy would pervade nature to a degree unknown in the history of former ages, and that no discordant collision, but a ravishing harmony of the spheres, would ensue.

Yet, then and only then will mankind be ripe for this, when inward and outward freedom for Woman as much as for Man shall be acknowledged as a *right*, not yielded as a concession. As the friend of the negro assumes that one man cannot by right hold another in bondage, so should the friend of Woman assume that Man cannot by right lay even well-meant restrictions on Woman. . . .

Were thought and feeling once so far elevated that Man should esteem himself the brother and friend, but nowise the lord and tutor, of Woman,— were he really bound with her in equal worship,— arrangements as to function and employment would be of no consequence. What Woman needs is not as a woman to act or rule, but as a nature to grow, as an intellect to discern, as a soul to live freely and unimpeded, to unfold such powers as were given her when we left our common home. If fewer talents were given her, yet if allowed the free and full employment of these, so that she may render back to the giver his own with usury, she will not complain; nay, I dare to say she will bless and rejoice in her earthly birth-place, her earthly lot. Let us consider what obstructions impede this good era, and what signs give reason to hope that it draws near.

*        *        *

Another sign of the times is furnished by the triumphs of Female Authorship. These have been great, and are constantly increasing. Women have taken possession of so many provinces for which men had pronounced them unfit, that, though these still declare there are some inaccessible to them, it is difficult to say just *where* they must stop.

*        *        *

The influence has been such, that the aim certainly is, now, in arranging school instruction for girls, to give them as fair a field as boys. As yet, indeed, these arrangements are made with little judgment or reflection. . . . Women are, often, at the head of these institutions; but they have, as yet, seldom been thinking women, capable of organizing a new whole for the wants of the time, and choosing persons to officiate in the departments. And when some portion of instruction of a good sort is got from the school, the far greater proportion which is infused from the general atmosphere of society contradicts its purport. Yet books and a little elementary instruction are not furnished in vain. Women are better aware how great and rich the universe is, not so easily blinded by narrowness or partial views of a home circle. "Her mother did so before her" is no longer a sufficient excuse. Indeed, it was never received as an excuse to mitigate the severity of censure, but was adduced as a reason, rather, why there should be no effort made for reformation.

Whether much or little has been done, or will be done,—whether women will add to the talent of narration the power of systematizing,— whether they will carve marble, as well as draw and paint,—is not important. But that it should be acknowledged that they have intellect which needs developing—that they should not be considered complete, if beings of affection and habit alone—is important.

Yet even this acknowledgment, rather conquered by Woman than proferred by Man, has been sullied by the usual selfishness. Too much is said of women being better educated, that they may become better companions and mothers *for men*. They should be fit for such companionship, and we have mentioned, with satisfaction, instances where it has been established. Earth knows no fairer, holier relation than that of a mother. It is one which, rightly understood, must both promote and require the highest attainments. But a being of infinite scope must not be treated with an exclusive view to any one relation. Give the soul free course, let the organization, both of body and mind, be freely developed, and the being will be fit for any and every relation to which it may be called. The intellect, no more than the sense of hearing, is to be cultivated merely that Woman may be a more valuable companion to Man, but because the Power who gave a power, by its mere existence signifies that it must be brought out toward perfection.

\*    \*    \*

It is therefore that I would have Woman lay aside all thought, such as she habitually cherishes, of being taught and led by men. I would have her, like the Indian girl, dedicate herself to the Sun, the Sun of Truth, and go nowhere if his beams did not make clear the path. I would have her free from compromise, from complaisance, from helplessness, because I would have her good enough and strong enough to love one and all beings, from the fulness, not the poverty of being.

\*    \*    \*

## REVIEW QUESTIONS

1. Why did Fuller believe that the phrase "All men are born free and equal" was not made in vain?
2. Why were some people afraid of giving women equal rights?
3. Did Fuller believe that society had made some progress in gender issues?
4. How did her advocacy of woman's rights fit within the transcendentalist school?

# WOMAN'S RIGHTS CONVENTION, SENECA FALLS

## FROM *Declaration of Sentiments and Resolutions* (1848)

*Margaret Fuller's voice was but one among many, thus when she left America for Europe in 1846 the call for woman's rights was far from extinguished. Elizabeth Cady Stanton (1815–1902) became active in woman's rights issues, as did many other women, by way of her involvement in the antislavery movement. After living in Boston in the mid-1840s and there enjoying the stimulating company of other reformers, the Stantons moved to Seneca Falls, New York, where husband Henry practiced law and Elizabeth continued her activism. Stanton wanted full legal equality as well as educational, political, and economic opportunities for women. In July 1848, Elizabeth Cady Stanton, Lucretia Mott, Jane Hunt, Mary McClintock, and Martha C. Wright organized a woman's rights convention that was held at the Wesleyan*

*Methodist Church in Seneca Falls. On the agenda was a* Declaration of Sentiments *and various resolutions calling for change. Stanton, who drafted the* Declaration of Sentiments *using an earlier revered American document as her model, also submitted a resolution calling for suffrage—the vote—for women. The fight for suffrage and equal rights would continue beyond her lifetime.*

From Elizabeth Cady Stanton, Susan B. Anthony, and Matilda Joslyn Gage, eds., *History of Woman Suffrage*, vol. I (1881; New York: Arno Press and The New York Times, 1969), pp. 70–72.

\*    \*    \*

We hold these truths to be self-evident: that all men and women are created equal; that they are endowed by their Creator with certain inalienable rights; that among these are life, liberty, and the pursuit of happiness; that to secure these rights governments are instituted, deriving their just powers from the consent of the governed. . . . But when a long train of abuses and usurpations, pursuing invariably the same object evinces a design to reduce them under absolute despotism, it is their duty to throw off such government, and to provide new guards for their future security. Such has been the patient sufferance of the women under this government, and such is now the necessity which constrains them to demand the equal station to which they are entitled.

The history of mankind is a history of repeated injuries and usurpations on the part of man toward woman, having in direct object the establishment of an absolute tyranny over her. To prove this, let facts be submitted to a candid world.

He has never permitted her to exercise her inalienable right to the elective franchise.

He has compelled her to submit to laws, in the formation of which she had no voice.

He has withheld from her rights which are given to the most ignorant and degraded men—both natives and foreigners.

Having deprived her of this first right of a citizen, the elective franchise, thereby leaving her without representation in the halls of legislation, he has oppressed her on all sides.

He has made her, if married, in the eye of the law, civilly dead.

He has taken from her all right in property, even to the wages she earns.

He has made her, morally, an irresponsible being, as she can commit many crimes with impunity, provided they be done in the presence of her husband. In the covenant of marriage, she is compelled to promise obedience to her husband, he becoming, to all intents and purposes, her master—the law giving him power to deprive her of her liberty, and to administer chastisement.

He has so framed the laws of divorce, as to what shall be the proper causes, and in case of separation, to whom the guardianship of the children shall be given, as to be wholly regardless of the happiness of women—the law, in all cases, going upon a false supposition of the supremacy of man, and giving all power into his hands.

After depriving her of all rights as a married woman, if single, and the owner of property, he has taxed her to support a government which recognizes her only when her property can be made profitable to it.

He has monopolized nearly all the profitable employments, and from those she is permitted to follow, she receives but a scanty remuneration. He closes against her all the avenues to wealth and distinction which he considers most honorable to himself. As a teacher of theology, medicine, or law, she is not known.

He has denied her the facilities for obtaining a thorough education, all colleges being closed against her.

He allows her in Church, as well as State, but a subordinate position, claiming Apostolic authority for her exclusion from the ministry, and, with some exceptions, from any public participation in the affairs of the Church.

He has created a false public sentiment by giving to the world a different code of morals for men and women, by which moral delinquencies which exclude women from society, are not only tolerated, but deemed of little account in man.

He has usurped the prerogative of Jehovah himself, claiming it as his right to assign for her a sphere of action, when that belongs to her conscience and to her God.

He has endeavored, in every way that he could, to destroy her confidence in her own powers, to lessen her self-respect, and to make her willing to lead a dependent and abject life.

Now, in view of this entire disfranchisement of one-half the people of this country, their social and religious degradation—in view of the unjust laws above mentioned, and because women do feel themselves aggrieved, oppressed, and fraudulently deprived of their most sacred rights, we insist that they have immediate admission to all the rights and privileges which belong to them as citizens of the United States.

In entering upon the great work before us, we anticipate no small amount of misconception, misrepresentation, and ridicule; but we shall use every instrumentality within our power to effect our object. We shall employ agents, circulate tracts, petition the State and National legislatures, and endeavor to enlist the pulpit and the press in our behalf. We hope this Convention will be followed by a series of Conventions embracing every part of the country.

The following resolutions . . . were adopted:

*    *    *

*Resolved,* That such laws as conflict, in any way, with the true and substantial happiness of woman, are contrary to the great precept of nature and of no validity, for this is "superior in obligation to any other."

*Resolved,* That all laws which prevent woman from occupying such a station in society as her conscience shall dictate, or which place her in a position inferior to that of man, are contrary to the great precept of nature, and therefore of no force or authority.

*Resolved,* That woman is man's equal—was intended to be so by the Creator, and the highest good of the race demands that she should be recognized as such.

*Resolved,* That the women of this country ought to be enlightened in regard to the laws under which they live, that they may no longer publish their degradation by declaring themselves satisfied with their present position, nor their ignorance, by asserting that they have all the rights they want.

*Resolved,* That inasmuch as man, while claiming for himself intellectual superiority, does accord to woman moral superiority, it is pre-eminently his duty to encourage her to speak and teach, as she has an opportunity, in all religious assemblies.

*Resolved,* That the same amount of virtue, delicacy, and refinement of behavior that is required of woman in the social state, should also be required of man, and the same transgressions should be visited with equal severity on both man and woman.

*Resolved,* That the objection of indelicacy and impropriety, which is so often brought against woman when she addresses a public audience, comes with a very ill-grace from those who encourage, by their attendance, her appearance on the stage, in the concert, or in feats of the circus.

*Resolved,* That woman has too long rested satisfied in the circumscribed limits which corrupt customs and a perverted application of the Scriptures have marked out for her, and that it is time she should move in the enlarged sphere which her great Creator has assigned her.

*Resolved,* That it is the duty of the women of this country to secure to themselves their sacred right to the elective franchise.

*Resolved,* That the equality of human rights results necessarily from the fact of the identity of the race in capabilities and responsibilities.

*Resolved, therefore,* That, being invested by the Creator with the same capabilities, and the same consciousness of responsibility for their exercise, it is demonstrably the right and duty of woman, equally with man, to promote every righteous cause by every righteous means; and especially in regard to the great subjects of morals and religion, it is self-evidently her right to participate with her brother in teaching them, both in private and in public, by writing and by speaking, by any instrumentalities proper to be used, and in any assemblies proper to be held; and this being a self-evident truth growing out of the divinely implanted principles of human nature, any custom or authority adverse to it, whether modern or wearing the hoary sanction of antiquity, is to be regarded as a self-evident falsehood, and at war with mankind.

\*       \*       \*

*Resolved,* That the speedy success of our cause depends upon the zealous and untiring efforts of both men and women, for the overthrow of the monopoly of the pulpit, and for the securing to woman an equal participation with men in the various trades, professions, and commerce.

## REVIEW QUESTIONS

1. In what ways, according to the delegates who accepted this *Declaration,* were women treated unequally?
2. Although the *Declaration* states that man made woman "morally, an irresponsible being," a resolution states that man "does accord to woman moral superiority." Was this a contradiction? Explain.
3. Why did men see women as intellectually inferior?
4. Why were the sentiments expressed in the *Declaration* and resolutions revolutionary?
5. Were they more revolutionary than those stated in the Declaration of Independence? Explain.

# SOJOURNER TRUTH

# FROM Address to the Woman's Rights Convention, Akron, Ohio (1851)

*Enslaved people, of course, had no rights, but among the free people of color, black women faced double discrimination based on race and gender. One black woman named Isabella (1797–1883), who was born a slave to a master of Dutch descent in the state of New York, served a number of masters before gaining her freedom in 1827. She then moved to New York City, worked as a house servant, and became involved in evangelical activities. In 1843 she experienced a mystical conversation with God in which she was told to "travel up and down the land" preaching the sins of slavery and the need for conversion. After changing her name to Sojourner Truth, she began crisscrossing the nation, exhorting audiences to be born again and take up the cause of abolitionism. Although unable to read or write, she was a woman of rare intelligence and uncommon courage. During the late 1840s she began promoting the woman's rights movement and in 1851 she attended the convention in Akron, Ohio. There she discovered that many participants objected to her presence for fear that her abolitionist sentiments would deflect attention from women's issues. Hisses greeted the tall, gaunt woman as she rose to speak: "Woman's rights and niggers!" "Go it, darkey!" "Don't let her speak!" By the time she finished, however, the audience gave her a standing ovation.*

From Frances D. Gage's reminiscences in Elizabeth Cady Stanton, Susan B. Anthony, and Matilda Joslyn Gage, eds., *History of Woman Suffrage*, vol. I (1881; New York: Arno Press and The New York Times, 1969), p. 116.

\*    \*    \*

"Wall, chilern, whar dar is so much racket dar must be somethin' out o' kilter. I tink dat 'twixt de niggers of de Souf and de womin at de Norf, all talkin' 'bout rights, de white men will be in a fix pretty soon. But what's all dis here talkin' 'bout?

"Dat man ober dar say dat womin needs to be helped into carriages, and lifted ober ditches, and to hab de best place everywhar. Nobody eber helps me into carriages, or ober mud-puddles, or gibs me any best place!" . . . "And a'n't I a woman? Look at me! Look at my arm! . . . I have ploughed, and planted, and gathered into barns, and no man could head me! And a'n't I a woman? I could work as much and eat as much as a man—when I could get it—and bear de lash as well! And a'n't I a woman? I have borne thirteen chilern, and seen 'em mos' all sold off to slavery, and when I cried out with my mother's grief, none but Jesus heard me! And a'n't I a woman?

"Den dey talks 'bout dis ting in de head; what dis dey call it?" ("Intellect," whispered some one near.) "Dat's it, honey. What's dat got to do wid womin's rights or nigger's rights? If my cup won't hold but a pint, and yourn holds a quart, wouldn't ye be mean not to let me have my little half-measure full?" And she pointed her significant finger, and sent a keen glance at the minister who had made the argument. The cheering was long and loud.

"Den dat little man in black dar, he say women can't have as much rights as men, 'cause Christ wan't a woman! Whar did your Christ come from?" Rolling thunder couldn't have stilled that crowd, as did those deep, wonderful tones, as she stood there with outstretched arms and eyes of fire. Raising her voice still louder, she repeated, "Whar did your Christ come from? From God and a woman! Man had nothin' to do wid Him." Oh, what a rebuke that was to that little man.

Turning again to another objector, she took up the defense of Mother Eve. I can not follow her through it all. It was pointed, and witty, and solemn; eliciting at almost every sentence deafening applause; and she ended by asserting: "If de fust woman God ever made was strong enough to turn de world upside down all alone, dese women togedder (and she glanced her eye over the platform) ought to be able to turn it back, and get it right side up again! And now dey is asking to do it, de men better let 'em." Long-continued cheering greeted this. " 'Bleeged to ye for hearin' on me, and now ole Sojourner han't got nothin' more to say."

\*    \*    \*

## REVIEW QUESTIONS

1. How did Sojourner Truth equate the treatment of slaves with the treatment of women?
2. Did she suggest that laboring women, working-class women, had been ignored by the movement for women's rights?
3. How did she justify rights for women?
4. What factors made her presentation so effective?

# 14 ∽ AN EMPIRE IN THE WEST

*Most Americans may no longer have believed in predestination in a religious
sense by the 1830s, but a great many did espouse national predestination. They
not only nodded in agreement when they read John Louis O'Sullivan's articles
advocating expansion but also packed up and headed out. O'Sullivan, the editor
of the* United States Magazine and Democratic Review, *coined a now familiar
term when in 1845 he wrote that "our manifest destiny is to overspread the continent allotted by Providence for the free development of our yearly multiplying
millions." Both the idea of manifest destiny and the reality of expansion showed
the nature of the American character and nation and profoundly influenced their
continuing development.*

 *Contradictions abounded in the ideas and actions supporting expansion. For
instance, some citizens promoted expansion as a way of incorporating other peoples into American culture, while others used it to push them out. There were also
regional variations to the arguments for and against expansion as northerners,
southerners, and westerners pursued their own agendas. Some contemporaries
noted these problems in their arguments against expansion. Opponents believed
that expansion—either in its means or ends—would hurt, not help, the nation.
The majority of Americans, however, supported such growth.*

 *United States citizens generally celebrated their self-proclaimed manifest des-
tiny; Native Americans, Mexicans, and Europeans who still had claims in the
Western Hemisphere did not. As Americans moved west they trampled tribal
lands, trespassed over territorial boundaries, and ignored international agree-
ments. Those confronting the Americans were seen as impediments to be surmounted, removed, or destroyed rather than as peoples or nations with legitimate
cultures and claims. Indians who had endured dispossession in the East, such as
the Cherokee, found themselves under attack again in the West by white pioneers
as well as those native to the areas in which they settled. Many of the peoples native to the West, such as the Apache, Comanche, Crow, and Sioux (referring to*

the Dakota/Lakota) sharpened their combat skills and made some concessions to ensure their own survival. American movement also created conflict with neighboring countries. The Mexicans, who upon their independence in 1821 had claimed the Spanish possessions in North America, and the British in Canada, who via the Hudson Bay Company had established posts in the Northwest, struggled to contain the expansion of the United States.

The British eventually decided to compromise with the Americans over the Oregon territory. In accordance with the Buchanan-Pakenham Treaty of 1846, Britain accepted the lands north of the 49th parallel while the United States took those south of it. The Mexicans, however, did not see possession of the Texas territory as something open to compromise. As they were not willing to concede their claim, they fought two wars in attempts to retain it.

Mexico had initially encouraged American immigration into Texas, but upset by the newcomers who would not learn their language, respect their religion, or adhere to their laws (such as the abolition of slavery), the Mexicans under General Antonio López de Santa Anna tried to drive the Americans out of Texas in 1836. Although the Texans took a beating initially, they rallied to defeat the Mexicans at San Jacinto that April. The Texans established the Lone Star Republic and asked for annexation to the United States.

The American people and their Congress debated the annexation of Texas for nine years. They argued over whether its contributions to the nation's economy and security outweighed such effects as the probable extension of slavery as well as the possibility of war with Mexico. Finally, however, President John Tyler convinced Congress to annex Texas via a joint resolution in 1845. His successor, James K. Polk, immediately stepped into a crisis as Mexico protested the annexation of a state it claimed as its own territory. The Mexicans drew a line in the sand at the Nueces River over which they told the Americans not to step. First the Texans and then the Americans did: to the Rio Grande and beyond in the war that started in May 1846.

Pioneering was a contributing factor in the movement to war; it was also a result of that war. Once the United States took possession of the lands it claimed via conquest, more and more Americans headed out to populate them. And while men may have won the West, women settled it. Neither the winning nor the settling was easy: both challenged the courage, convictions, and constitutions of white and black, American-born and immigrant pioneers. Whereas war tested the resolve of the nation, pioneering tested the resolve of individuals. Exploration and settlement was, as it had been for centuries, the great American adventure.

# CATHERINE HAUN

# A Pioneer Woman's Westward Journey (1849)

*Although pioneering was usually initiated by men, they were by no means the only ones engaged in that endeavor. Many single men—and married men acting as temporary bachelors—seduced by the thought of rich lands and lodes, traveled west; but settlement was often contingent on the possibility of making and maintaining families there. Thousands of women, therefore, trudged the Overland Trail after 1840 when the great westward migration took off. Most of these women were married, and while some were forced to make the move, many others insisted on accompanying their men, for they were determined to maintain family unity despite the great potential risks to their health and safety. Some of the single women married on the trip or soon thereafter, while numerous married women were widowed. Many of these female pioneers had to deal with the rigors of the journey while pregnant or while caring for young children. Taken away from civilization, they were determined to take civilization with them. While the journey was liberating for a few, most battled the constant challenges to their feminine and domestic identities. Catherine Haun, young, newly married, and of the middle class, was one of the women who met the challenges with considerable strength and grace.*

From "A Woman's Trip across the Plains in 1849," in Lillian Schlissel, ed., *Women's Diaries of the Westward Journey* (New York: Schocken Books, 1992), pp. 166–85. [Editorial insertions appear in brackets—*Ed.*]

Early in January of 1849 we first thought of emigrating to California. It was a period of National hard times and we being financially involved in our business interests near Clinton, Iowa, longed to go to the new El Dorado and "pick up" gold enough with which to return and pay off our debts.

\*     \*     \*

At that time the "gold fever" was contagious and few, old or young, escaped the malady. On the streets, in the fields, in the workshops and by the fireside, golden California was the chief topic of conversation. Who were going? How was best to "fix up" the "outfit"? What to take as food and clothing? Who would stay at home to care for the farm and womenfolks? Who would take wives and children along? Advice was handed out quite free of charge and often quite free of common sense. However, as two heads are better than one, all proffered ideas helped as a means to the end. The intended adventurers dilligently collected their belongings and after exchanging such articles as were not needed for others more suitable for the trip, begging, buying or borrowing what they could, with buoyant spirits started off.

Some half dozen families of our neighborhood joined us and probably about twenty-five persons constituted our little band.

\*     \*     \*

. . . It was more than three months before we were thoroughly equipped and on April 24th, 1849 we left our comparatively comfortable homes—and the uncomfortable creditors—for the uncertain and dangerous trip, beyond which loomed up, in our mind's eye, castles of shining gold.

There was still snow upon the ground and the roads were bad, but in our eagerness to be off we ventured forth. This was a mistake as had we delayed for a couple of weeks the weather would have been more settled, the roads better and much of the discouragement and hardship of the first days of travel might have been avoided.

\*     \*     \*

At the end of the month we reached Council Bluffs, having only travelled across the state of Iowa, a distance of about 350 miles every mile of which was beautifully green and well watered. . . .

As Council Bluffs was the last settlement on the route we made ready for the final plunge into the wilderness by looking over our wagons and disposing of whatever we could spare. . . .

\*     \*     \*

The canvas covered schooners were supposed to be, as nearly as possible, constructed upon the principle of the "wonderful one-horse shay." It was very essential that the animals be sturdy, whether oxen, mules or horses. Oxen were preferred as they were less liable to stampede or be stolen by Indians and for long hauls held out better and though slower they were steady and in the long run performed the journey in an equally brief time. Besides, in an emergency they could be used as beef. When possible the provisions and ammunition were protected from water and dust by heavy canvas or rubber sheets.

Good health, and above all, not too large a proportion of women and children was also taken into consideration. The morning starts had to be made early—always before six o'clock—and it would be hard to get children ready by that hour. Later on experience taught the mothers that in order not to delay the trains it was best to allow the smaller children to sleep in the wagons until after several hours of travel when they were taken up for the day.

Our caravan had a good many women and children and although we were probably longer on the journey owing to their presence—they exerted a good influence, as the men did not take such risks with Indians and thereby avoided conflict; were more alert about the care of the teams and seldom had accidents; more attention was paid to cleanliness and sanitation and, lastly but not of less importance, the meals were more regular and better cooked thus preventing much sickness and there was less waste of food.

\*     \*     \*

After a sufficient number of wagons and people were collected at this rendezvous we proceeded to draw up and agree upon a code of general regulations for train government and mutual protection— a necessary precaution when so many were to travel together. Each family was to be independent yet a part of the grand unit and every man was expected to do his individual share of general work and picket duty.

John Brophy was selected as Colonel. He was particularly eligible having served in the Black Hawk War and as much of his life had been spent along the frontier his experience with Indians was quite exceptional.

Each week seven Captains were appointed to serve on "Grand Duty." They were to protect the camps and animals at night. One served each night and in case of danger gave the alarm.

When going into camp the "leader wagon" was turned from the road to the right, the next wagon turned to the left, the others following close after and always alternating to right and left. In this way a large circle, or corral, was formed within which the tents were pitched and the oxen herded. The horses were picketed near by until bed time when they were tethered to the tongues of the wagons.

While the stock and wagons were being cared for, the tents erected and camp fires started by the side of the wagons outside the corral, the cooks busied themselves preparing the evening meal for the hungry, tired, impatient travelers.

When the camp ground was desirable enough to warrant it we did not travel on the Sabbath.

Although the men were generally busy mending wagons, harness, yokes, shoeing the animals etc., and the women washed clothes, boiled a big mess of beans, to be warmed over for several meals, or perhaps mended clothes or did other household straightening up, all felt somewhat rested on Monday morning, for the change of occupation had been refreshing.

\*     \*     \*

During the entire trip Indians were a source of anxiety, we being never sure of their friendship. Secret dread and alert watchfulness seemed always necessary for after we left the prairies they were more treacherous and numerous being in the language of the pioneer trapper: "They wus the most onsartainest vermints alive."

One night after we had retired, some sleeping in blankets upon the ground, some in tents, a few under the wagons and others in the wagons, Colonel Brophy gave the men a practice drill. It was impromptu and a surprise. He called: "Indians, Indians!" We were thrown into great confusion and excitement but he was gratified at the promptness and courage with which the men responded. Each immediately seized his gun and made ready for the attack. The women had been instructed to seek shelter in the wagons at such times of danger, but some screamed, others fainted, a few crawled under the wagons and those sleeping in wagons generally followed their husbands out and all of us were nearly paralized with fear. Fortunately, we never had occasion to put into actual use this maneuver, but the drill was quite reassuring and certainly we womenfolk would have acted braver had the alarm ever again been sounded. . . .

\*     \*     \*

Finally after a couple of weeks' travel the distant mountains of the west came into view.

This was the land of the buffalo. One day a herd came in our direction like a great black cloud, a threatening moving mountain, advancing towards us very swiftly and with wild snorts, noses almost to the ground and tails flying in midair. I haven't any idea how many there were but they seemed to be innumerable and made a deafening terrible noise As is their habit, when stampeding, they did not turn out of their course for anything.

Some of our wagons were within their line of advance and in consequence one was completely demolished and two were overturned. Several persons were hurt, one child's shoulder being dislocated, but fortunately no one was killed.

Two of these buffaloes were shot and the humps and tongues furnished us with fine fresh meat. They happened to be buffalo cows and, in consequence, the meat was particularly good flavor and tender. It is believed that the cow can run faster than the bull. The large bone of the hind leg, after being stripped of the flesh, was buried in coals of buffalo chips and in an hour the baked marrow was served. I have never tasted such a rich, delicious food!

\*     \*     \*

Buffalo chips, when dry, were very useful to us as fuel. On the barren plains when we were without wood we carried empty bags and each pedestrian "picked up chips" as he, or she, walked along. Indeed we could have hardly got along without thus useful animal, were always appropriating either his hump, tongue, marrowbone, tallow, skin or chips! . . .

\*     \*     \*

Trudging along within the sight of the Platte, whose waters were now almost useless to us on account of the Alkali, we one day found a post with a cross board pointing to a branch road which seemed better than the one we were on. . . . We decided to take it but before many miles suddenly found ourselves in a desolate, rough country that proved to be the edge of the "Bad Lands." I shudder yet at the thought of the ugliness and danger of the territory. . . .

\*     \*     \*

We saw nothing living but Indians, lizards and snakes. Trying, indeed, to feminine nerves. Surely Inferno can be no more horrible in formation. The pelting sun's rays reflected from the parched ground seemed a furnace heat by day and our campfires, as well as those of the Indians cast grotesque glares and terrifying shadows by night.

The demen needed only horns and cloven feet to complete the soul stirring picture!

To add to the horrors of the surroundings one man was bitten on the ankle by a venemous snake. Although every available remidy was tried upon the wound, his limb had to be amputated with the aid of a common handsaw. Fortunately, for him, he had a good, brave wife along who helped and cheered him into health and usefulness; for it was not long before he found much that he could do and was not considered a burden, although the woman had to do a man's work as they were alone. He was of a mechanical turn, and later on helped mend wagons, yokes and harness; and when the train was "on the move" sat in the wagon, gun by his side, and repaired boots and shoes. He was one of the most cheery members of the company and told good stories and sang at the campfire, putting to shame some of the able bodied who were given to complaining or selfishness. . . .

Finally after several days we got back onto the road and were entering the Black Hills Country. . . .

＊　　＊　　＊

We had not traveled many miles in the Black Hills—the beginning of the Rocky Mountains— before we realized that our loads would have to be lightened as the animals were not able to draw the heavily laden wagons over the slippery steep roads. We were obliged to sacrifice most of our merchandise that was intended for our stock in trade in California and left it by the wayside; burying the barrels of alcohol least the Indians should drink it and frenzied thereby might follow and attack us. . . .

＊　　＊　　＊

During the day we womenfolk visited from wagon to wagon or congenial friends spent an hour walking, ever westward, and talking over our home life back in "the states" telling of the loved ones left behind; voicing our hopes for the future in the far west and even whispering a little friendly gossip of emigrant life.

High teas were not popular but tatting, knitting, crocheting, exchanging recipes for cooking beans or dried apples or swapping food for the sake of variety kept us in practice of feminine occupations and diversions.

We did not keep late hours but when not too engrossed with fear of the red enemy or dread of impending danger we enjoyed the hour around the campfire. The menfolk lolling and smoking their pipes and guessing or maybe betting how many miles we had covered the day. We listened to readings, story telling, music and songs and the day often ended in laughter and merrymaking.

It was the fourth of July when we reached the beautiful Laramie River. Its sparkling, pure waters were full of myriads of fish that could be caught with scarcely an effort. It was necessary to build barges to cross the river and during the enforced delay our animals rested and we had one of our periodical "house cleanings." This general systematic re-adjustment always freshened up our wagon train very much, for after a few weeks of travel things got mixed up and untidy and often wagons had to be abandoned if too worn for repairs, and generally one or more animals had died or been stolen.

＊　　＊　　＊

Cholera was prevalent on the plains at this time; the train preceding as well as the one following ours had one or more deaths, but fortunately we had not a single case of the disease. Often several graves together stood as silent proof of smallpox or cholera epidemic. The Indians spread the disease among themselves by digging up the bodies of the victims for the clothing. The majority of the Indians were badly pock-marked. . . .

＊　　＊　　＊

It was with considerable apprehension that we started to traverse the treeless, alkali region of the Great Basin or Sink of the Humboldt. Our wagons were badly worn, the animals much the worse for wear, food and stock feed was getting low with no chance of replenishing the supply. During the month of transit we, like other trains, experienced the greatest privations of the whole trip. It was no unusual sight to see graves, carcasses of animals and abandoned wagons. In fact the latter furnished us with wood for the campfires as the sagebrush was scarce and unsatisfactory and buffalo chips were not as plentiful as on the plains east of the Rocky Mountains.

\*   \*   \*

Across this drear country I used to ride horseback several hours of the day which was a great relief from the continual jolting of even our spring wagon. I also walked a great deal and this lightened the wagon. One day I walked fourteen miles and was not very fatigued.

. . . The men seemed more tired and hungry than were the women. Our only death on the journey occurred in this desert. The Canadian woman, Mrs. Lamore, suddenly sickened [after childbirth] and died, leaving her two little girls and grief stricken husband. We halted a day to bury her and the infant that had lived but an hour, in this weird, lonely spot on God's footstool away apparently from everywhere and everybody.

\*   \*   \*

. . . we reached Sacramento on November 4, 1849, just six months and ten days after leaving Clinton, Iowa, we were all in pretty good condition

Although very tired of tent life many of us spent Thanksgiving and Christmas in our canvas houses. I do not remember ever having had happier holiday times. For Christmas dinner we had a grizzly bear steak for which we paid $2.50, one cabbage for $1.00 and—oh horrors—some *more* dried apples! And for a Christmas present the Sacramento river rose very high and flooded the whole town! . . . It was past the middle of January before we . . . reached Marysville—there were only a half dozen houses; all occupied at exorbitant prices. Some one was calling for the services of a lawyer to draw up a will and my husband offered to do it for which he charged $150.00.

This seemed a happy omen for success and he hung out his shingle, abandoning all thought of going to the mines. As we had lived in a tent and had been on the move for nine months, traveling 2400 miles we were glad to settle down and go housekeeping in a shed that was built in a day of lumber purchased with the first fee. . . .

\*   \*   \*

# REVIEW QUESTIONS

1. According to Haun's account, what did it take to be a successful pioneer?
2. What hazards did the pioneers face?
3. Did the journey have an effect on gender roles? Why or why not?
4. What does her story reveal about Haun herself?

# Interesting from Minnesota (1849)

*Pioneers like Catherine Haun were not the only Americans crossing the continent's plains, mountains, and rivers in the 1840s and 1850s. Native Americans were also on the move. Some moved within their own territories and on their own terms, but many northern Plains peoples, not just the Cherokee and other tribes to the South, were pushed West by population and treaty pressures from the East. A writer provided clues as to why there were such pressures in "Intelligence from Minnesota," which was published first in the* Minnesota Register *on 7 April 1849, and then excerpted in* The New York Herald *on 2 May: "The summer of 1850 will doubtless witness the extinction of the Indian title to that magnificent region west of the 'Great River,' which is now in possession of the Sioux. . . . for beauty of scenery, for excellence in the quality of the soil, for the salubrity of the climate, for the abundance of pure and wholesome water, and for every other desideratum to make an earthly paradise, [that region] cannot be excelled." It did not happen quite as quickly as the* Minnesota Register *reported, but the U.S. government and its citizens claimed paradise to settle it. As its original inhabitants moved, its newer residents recorded their passing in both words and paintings. Characterizations often depended upon whether relations were good or bad at a particular time and place and whether the writer (or painter) preferred to demonize or romanticize Native Americans. Also, as may be seen with "Interesting from Minnesota," which was first published in St. Paul's* Chronicle *(probably the* Minnesota Chronicle and Register*) on 29 September, the accounts were often transmitted across the country to pop up in other newspapers, in this case* The Weekly Herald *in New York City on 20 October, so that readers could be armchair pioneers.*

---

"Interesting from Minnesota," *The Weekly Herald* (New York City), Saturday, 20 October 1849, issue 42, p. 331. col. E. [Editorial insertions noted in square brackets—*Ed.*]

## Interesting from Minnesota

### CONFERENCE WITH THE INDIANS— EMIGRATION OF THE WINNEBAGOES— THE SIOUX VISITORS—THE NAVIGATION OF THE MISSISSIPPI.

[FROM THE ST. PAUL'S (MIN. CHRONICLE, SEPT. 29.)]

### Conference with the Indians.

The expedition, composed of two companies of dragoons, under Major Woods and Capt. Pope of the Engineer corps, which left Fort Snelling [Fort Snelling was built in the 1820s at the juncture of the Minnesota and Mississippi Rivers] in June last, has returned—the Major and his dragoons several days ago, and Captain Pope on Thursday of this week. They visited our settlements on Red river [The Red River of the North borders Minnesota and North Dakota and flows into Canada], and examined the country, with a view to millitary defenses in that quarter, as far north as the British line. Capt. Pope returned by water ascending Red river and making a portage from its head waters, by way of Otter Tail Lake, to Crow Wing River, and thence down that stream and the Mississippi to Fort

Snelling. Capt. Pope had as *voyageurs* from Pembina Louis Vasseur, Antoine De Jarlais, Pierre Barare, Baptista Clutier, Jose Morril, Jose Martin, Jose Montory, Francois De Marais, Jose Madeau, Arsenne Morisette, and one or two others—Chippewa half-breeds—all stout, burly looking fellows from the Red river country. They had a long "talk" with Gov. Ramsey [Alexander Ramsey was the first territorial governor between 1849 and 1853.], in the Representatives' Hall yesterday, during which they entered a complaint of aggressions upon their rights by persons on the other side of the line. They stated that certain obnoxious men on the British side had been appointed Chiefs over them; that they were restricted in their hunting privileges, &c., and that they came here to claim protection as American citizens. The Governor replied, in substance, that the United States was strong, and able to protect all her citizens. That they might rest assured she would do so on all occasions when required—and that he would represent their grievances to the authorities at Washington, and see that right and justice was done them. They left well pleased and satisfied.

## Emigration of the Winnebagoes.

About 100 Winnebagoes, men, women and children, arrived here in the last boat from Iowa; they are on their way to their own country, where they say they are going to remain. They report not more than 75 of the tribe left in Iowa. An old man along with this party, says he was encamped on the Iowa river last summer when a war party of Pottawatomies and Sacs and Foxes returned from an expedition into the Sioux country. He says these were the men that killed the eighteen Wachapoota Sioux; they brought four scalps in.

## A Sioux Visit.

On last Saturday our town was visited by almost the entire population composing the two lower bands of Sioux Indians (Wabashaw's and Red Wing's, on their way to the payment at Fort Snelling[)]. They came in their canoes, a fleet of some eighty or ninety vessels, laden, besides men, women and children, with dogs, cooking utensils, buffalo skins forming the covering of their "tepees," &c. They called a halt opposite the lower landing, and proceeded to moor their fleet along the shore of the sand bar opposite, at the foot of Raspberry Island. In quick time the squaws had the baggage unpacked, lodge poles cut and erected, their buflaloes thrown over them; and an Indian village, numbering five hundred inhabitants, greeted the eye!

The warriors betook themselves to their toilets, and presently made their appearance in our streets, stripped and painted for the "Begging Dance." This is a dance performed in front of the doors of the citizens, and the store houses of merchants and traders; the Indians expecting by way of compensation, a barrel of flour or pork, or anything in the way of provisions that the person victimized may choose to give. The dancing was kept up till dark, when the braves returned to their quarters on the Island, well paid by our liberal citizens for the few hours' amusement they had afforded them.

The night was clear, faintly lighted by the mellow rays of a new moon. From any position along the top of the high bluff fronting our town, a scene presented itself worthy the eye of a poet or a painter. We viewed it until lost in reverie; and wished that a Cole, a Durand or a Somtag [Thomas Cole, Asher Brown Durand and William Louis Sonntag, Sr. were all artists of the Hudson River School.] were present to catch the inspiration of the moment, and transfer the landscape and figures to living canvas. Far away in the distance stretched the lofty hills and precipitous bluffs that confine the Father of Waters [Mississippi] within his path, their tops and intervening vallies crowned with forests of oak, ash and maple just beginning to assume the rich hues of autumn. At four feet lay the mighty river itself, its waters moving placidly along, calm as a sleeping infant, and only disturbed at intervals, by an Indian canoe gliding gracefully from the shore, as swift and straight as one of their own unerring arrows. Across the main channel, upon the clean white sandy beach, rose the hundred tepees of the Dakotas, the smoke curling majestically from their tops, casting long grotesque, shades in the transparent waters at their base. Along the margin of the beach were moored in order, as regular as shipping at the wharf of a commercial city, the fleet of light canoes. Back of us stood St Paul, with its scores of white cottages and neatly finished business houses gleaming in the soft moonlight.

We lingered until no sound broke the grand solemnity of the scene, save the sport of Indian children, as they chased each other in gleesome frolic over the smooth camping ground; and the low, plaintive tones of the Dakota lover's flute, serenading his favorite dark-eyed maid, reposing as sweetly, as contentedly, and as proudly on her rude couch, as castled lady on her bed of down. It was indeed a scene we shall never forget.

Sabbath morning. All is bustle and activity in the camp. The scene is changed from one of comparatively still life to the greatest degree of animation. Pale faces line the bluff, watching the movements of the active groups on the island, who are evidently preparing to leave. In less time than it would take to narrate the circumstance, the lodges are down, packed and shipped, with the rest of the household goods. All embark, and the fleet is moving off in regular order up the river. Nothing remains to mark the spot of the deserted village save the rude poles of the tepees. Such is Indian life.

## REVIEW QUESTIONS

1. What was the tone of the article? Celebratory, critical, or pensive? Why might that be important to interpreting the information?
2. What do the descriptions of the various peoples reveal about those people and about the author of the piece?
3. Does the article imply that manifest destiny was at work? Explain.

# JAMES K. POLK

## FROM The President's War Message to Congress (11 May 1846)

*President John Tyler signed the congressional resolution offering Texas annexation and statehood on 1 March 1845. He then left his successor, James K. Polk, to deal with the repercussions: one of the first was Mexico's dissolution of diplomatic relations. Mexico, which still disputed Texas's independence to the point that Texans could talk about an ongoing quasi-war with that nation, was firmly set against the annexation. Polk, an ardent expansionist, proceeded to duel against Mexico with one hand and against Britain with the other. He was determined to secure Texas (the territory of which both he and the Texans defined rather broadly); plant the flag of the United States in the ranches, ports, and presidios of California; and take sole possession of the Oregon territory. He was able to accomplish the last through diplomatic negotiations and compromise over the northern border at the 49th parallel, but to achieve the other two goals he had to go to war.*

---

From James D. Richardson, comp., *A Compilation of the Messages and Papers of the Presidents*, vol. V (New York: Bureau of National Literature, 1897), pp. 2287–93. [Editorial insertions appear in square brackets—*Ed.*]

*To the Senate and House of Representatives:*

The existing state of the relations between the United States and Mexico renders it proper that I should bring the subject to the consideration of Congress. . . .

\*      \*      \*

The strong desire to establish peace with Mexico on liberal and honorable terms, and the readiness of this Government to regulate and adjust our boundary and other causes of difference with that power on such fair and equitable principles as would lead to permanent relations of the most friendly nature, induced me in September last to seek the reopening of diplomatic relations between the two countries. Every measure adopted on our part had for its object the furtherance of these desired results. In communicating to Congress a succinct statement of the injuries which we had suffered from Mexico and which have been accumulating during a period of more than twenty years, every expression that could tend to inflame the people of Mexico or defeat or delay a pacific result was carefully avoided. An envoy of the United States repaired to Mexico with full powers to adjust every existing difference. But though present on the Mexican soil by agreement between the two Governments, invested with full powers, and bearing evidence of the most friendly dispositions, his mission has been unavailing. The Mexican Government not only refused to receive him or listen to his propositions, but after a long-continued series of menaces have at last invaded our territory and shed the blood of our fellow-citizens on our own soil.

It now becomes my duty to state more in detail the origin, progress, and failure of that mission. In pursuance of the instructions given in September last, an inquiry was made on the 13th of October, 1845, in the most friendly terms, through our consul in Mexico, of the minister for foreign affairs, whether the Mexican Government "would receive an envoy from the United States intrusted with full powers to adjust all the questions in dispute between the two Governments," with the assurance that "should the answer be in the affirmative such an envoy would be immediately dispatched to Mexico." The Mexican minister on the 15th of October gave an affirmative answer to this inquiry, requesting at the same time that our naval force at Vera Cruz might be withdrawn, lest its continued presence might assume the appearance of menace and coercion pending the negotiations. This force was immediately withdrawn. On the 10th of November, 1845, Mr. John Slidell, of Louisiana, was commissioned by me as envoy extraordinary and minister plenipotentiary of the United States to Mexico, and was intrusted with full powers to adjust both the questions of the Texas boundary and of indemnification to our citizens. The redress of the wrongs of our citizens naturally and inseparably blended itself with the question of boundary. The settlement of the one question in any correct view of the subject involves that of the other. I could not for a moment entertain the idea that the claims of our much-injured and long-suffering citizens, many of which had existed for more than twenty years, should be postponed or separated from the settlement of the boundary question.

Mr. Slidell arrived at Vera Cruz on the 30th of November, and was courteously received by the authorities of that city. But the Government of General Herrera was then tottering to its fall. The revolutionary party had seized upon the Texas question to effect or hasten its overthrow. Its determination to restore friendly relations with the United States, and to receive our minister to negotiate for the settlement of this question, was violently assailed, and was made the great theme of denunciation against it. The Government of General Herrera, there is good reason to believe, was sincerely desirous to receive our minister; but it yielded to the storm raised by its enemies, and on the 21st of December refused to accredit Mr. Slidell upon the most frivolous pretexts. . . .

Five days after the date of Mr. Slidell's note [24 December] General Herrera yielded the Government to General Paredes without a struggle, and on the 30th of December resigned the Presidency. This revolution was accomplished solely by the army, the people having taken little part in the contest; and thus the supreme power in Mexico passed into the hands of a military leader.

Determined to leave no effort untried to effect an amicable adjustment with Mexico, I directed Mr. Slidell to present his credentials to the Government of General Paredes and ask to be officially received by him. . . .

Under these circumstances, Mr. Slidell, in obedience to my direction, addressed a note to the Mexican minister of foreign relations, under date of the 1st of March last, asking to be received by that Government in the diplomatic character to which he had been appointed. This minister in his reply, under date of the 12th of March, reiterated the arguments of his predecessor, and in terms that may be considered as giving just grounds of offense to the Government and people of the United States denied the application of Mr. Slidell. . . .

Thus the Government of Mexico, though solemnly pledged by official acts in October last to receive and accredit an American envoy, violated their plighted faith and refused the offer of a peaceful adjustment of our difficulties. . . .

In my message at the commencement of the present session I informed you that upon the earnest appeal both of the Congress and convention of Texas I had ordered an efficient military force to take a position "between the Nueces and the Del Norte." This had become necessary to meet a threatened invasion of Texas by the Mexican forces, for which extensive military preparations

had been made. The invasion was threatened solely because Texas had determined, in accordance with a solemn resolution of the Congress of the United States, to annex herself to our Union, and under these circumstances it was plainly our duty to extend our protection over her citizens and soil.

This force was concentrated at Corpus Christi, and remained there until after I had received such information from Mexico as rendered it probable, if not certain, that the Mexican Government would refuse to receive our envoy.

Meantime Texas, by the final action of our Congress, had become an integral part of our Union. The Congress of Texas, by its act of December 19, 1836, had declared the Rio del Norte to be the boundary of that Republic. Its jurisdiction had been extended and exercised beyond the Nueces. The country between that river and the Del Norte had been represented in the Congress and in the convention of Texas, had thus taken part in the act of annexation itself, and is now included within one of our Congressional districts. Our own Congress had, moreover, with great unanimity, by the act approved December 31, 1845, recognized the country beyond the Nueces as a part of our territory by including it within our own revenue system, and a revenue officer to reside within that district has been appointed by and with the advice and consent of the Senate. It became, therefore, of urgent necessity to provide for the defense of that portion of our country. Accordingly, on the 13th of January last instructions were issued to the general in command of these troops to occupy the left bank of the Del Norte. This river, which is the southwestern boundary of the State of Texas, is an exposed frontier. From this quarter invasion was threatened; upon it and in its immediate vicinity, in the judgment of high military experience, are the proper stations for the protecting forces of the Government. . . .

The movement of the troops to the Del Norte was made by the commanding general under positive instructions to abstain from all aggressive acts toward Mexico or Mexican citizens and to regard the relations between that Republic and the United States as peaceful unless she should declare war or commit acts of hostility indicative of a state of war.

He was specially directed to protect private property and respect personal rights.

The Army moved from Corpus Christi on the 11th of March, and on the 28th of that month arrived on the left bank of the Del Norte opposite to Matamoras, where it encamped on a commanding position, which has since been strengthened by the erection of fieldworks. A depot has also been established at Point Isabel, near the Brazos Santiago, 30 miles in rear of the encampment. The selection of his position was necessarily confided to the judgment of the general in command.

The Mexican forces at Matamoras assumed a belligerent attitude, and on the 12th of April General Ampudia, then in command, notified General Taylor to break up his camp within twenty-four hours and to retire beyond the Nueces River, and in the event of his failure to comply with these demands announced that arms, and arms alone, must decide the question. But no open act of hostility was committed until the 24th of April. On that day General Arista, who had succeeded to the command of the Mexican forces, communicated to General Taylor that "he considered hostilities commenced and should prosecute them." A party of dragoons of 63 men and officers were on the same day dispatched from the American camp up the Rio del Norte, on its left bank, to ascertain whether the Mexican troops had crossed or were preparing to cross the river, "became engaged with a large body of these troops, and after a short affair, in which some 16 were killed and wounded, appear to have been surrounded and compelled to surrender."

The grievous wrongs perpetrated by Mexico upon our citizens throughout a long period of years remain unredressed, and solemn treaties pledging her public faith for this redress have been disregarded. A government either unable or unwilling to enforce the execution of such treaties fails to perform one of its plainest duties.

Our commerce with Mexico has been almost annihilated. It was formerly highly beneficial to both nations, but our merchants have been deterred from prosecuting it by the system of outrage and extortion which the Mexican authorities have pursued against them, whilst their appeals through their own Government for indemnity have been made in vain. Our forbearance has gone to such an extreme as to be mistaken in its character. Had we acted with vigor in repelling the insults and redressing the injuries inflicted by Mexico at the commencement, we should doubtless have escaped all the difficulties in which we are now involved.

Instead of this, however, we have been exerting our best efforts to propitiate her good will. Upon the pretext that Texas, a nation as independent as herself, thought proper to unite its destinies with our own she has affected to believe that we have severed her rightful territory, and in official proclamations and manifestoes has repeatedly threatened to make war upon us for the purpose of reconquering Texas. In the meantime we have tried every effort at reconciliation. The cup of forbearance had been exhausted even before the recent information from the frontier of the Del Norte. But now, after reiterated menaces, Mexico has passed the boundary of the United States, has invaded our territory and shed American blood upon the American soil. She has proclaimed that hostilities have commenced, and that the two nations are now at war.

As war exists, and, notwithstanding all our efforts to avoid it, exists by the act of Mexico herself, we are called upon by every consideration of duty and patriotism to vindicate with decision the honor, the rights, and the interests of our country.

Anticipating the possibility of a crisis like that which has arrived, instructions were given in August last, "as a precautionary measure" against invasion or threatened invasion, authorizing General Taylor, if the emergency required, to accept volunteers, not from Texas only, but from the States of Louisiana, Alabama, Mississippi, Tennessee, and Kentucky, and corresponding letters were addressed to the respective governors of those States. . . .

In further vindication of our rights and defense of our territory, I invoke the prompt action of Congress to recognize the existence of the war, and to place at the disposition of the Executive the means of prosecuting the war with vigor, and thus hastening the restoration of peace. To this end I recommend that authority should be given to call into the public service a large body of volunteers to serve for not less than six or twelve months unless sooner discharged. A volunteer force is beyond question more efficient than any other description of citizen soldiers, and it is not to be doubted that a number far beyond that required would readily rush to the field upon the call of their country. I further recommend that a liberal provision be made for sustaining our entire military force and furnishing it with supplies and munitions of war.

The most energetic and prompt measures and the immediate appearance in arms of a large and overpowering force are recommended to Congress as the most certain and efficient means of bringing the existing collision with Mexico to a speedy and successful termination.

In making these recommendations I deem it proper to declare that it is my anxious desire not only to terminate hostilities speedily, but to bring all matters in dispute between this Government and Mexico to an early and amicable adjustment; and in this view I shall be prepared to renew negotiations whenever Mexico shall be ready to receive propositions or to make propositions of her own.

\*    \*    \*

## REVIEW QUESTIONS

1. Who provoked whom in the crisis between Mexico and the United States? Explain.
2. Did domestic issues play a role in the escalation of tensions between the two countries?
3. How did Polk try to resolve the issues causing conflict between the United States and Mexico?
4. Is there any indication in this message that the government's actions and attitudes may have hurt rather than helped its diplomatic efforts?
5. Was this call to arms in line with or a break from previously stated foreign policy aims (as in Washington's Farewell Address and the Monroe Doctrine for example)?

# HENRY CLAY

# Speech about the Mexican War (1847)

*After his unsuccessful run for the presidency in 1824, Henry Clay became John Quincy Adams's secretary of state. He then served in the U.S. Senate from 1831 to 1842 (and again from 1849 until his death in 1852). Clay also tried for the presidency again in 1832 and 1844. While out of office, the dynamic orator continued to address public issues, speaking in favor of those he believed fostered a positive national destiny and arguing against those he believed would have a negative impact. Worried that it would have the latter effect, Clay opposed annexation of Texas in 1844. The next year he criticized President Tyler's method of annexation as unconstitutional and moaned that it would "totally change the peaceful character of the Republic, converting us in the end into a warlike, conquering Nation."\* His fears were realized when war commenced after annexation and when expansion created further internal dissension. Initially, upon Texas's admission to the Union, Clay accepted the necessity of military action to defend the new state's borders. When, however, Polk and others started to wage a more ambitious campaign, Clay, the old "War Hawk" of*

*1812, began his own more offensive campaign against the war. There was also a personal dimension to Clay's opposition: he lost a son during the war, at Buena Vista in February 1847.*

---

*Clay, 219.

"Speech about the Mexican War," *The Papers of Henry Clay, Volume 10,* edited by Melba Porter Hay. Copyright © 1991 by The University Press of Kentucky. Reprinted by permission of The University Press of Kentucky.

## Lexington, KY.

November 13, 1847

The day is dark and gloomy, unsettled and uncertain, like the condition of our country, in regard to the unnatural war with Mexico. The public mind is agitated and anxious, and is filled with serious apprehensions as to its indefinite continuance, and especially as to the consequences which its termination may bring forth, menacing the harmony, if not the existence, of our Union.

ж        ж        ж

How did we unhappily get involved in this war? It was predicted as the consequence of the annexation of Texas to the United States. If we had not Texas, we should have no war. The people were told that if that event happened, war would ensue. They were told that the war between Texas and Mexico had not been terminated by a treaty of peace; that Mexico still claimed Texas as a revolted province: and that, if we received Texas in our Union, we took along with her, the war existing between her and Mexico. And the Minister of Mexico [Juan N. Almonte] formally announced to the Government at Washington, that his nation would consider the annexation of Texas to the United States as producing a state of war. But all this was denied by the partizans of annexation. They insisted we should have no war, and even imputed to those who foretold it, sinister motives for their groundless prediction.

But, notwithstanding a state of virtual war necessarily resulted from the fact of annexation of one of the belligerents to the United States, actual hostilities might have been probably averted by prudence, moderation and wise statesmanship. If General [Zachary] Taylor had been permitted to re-main, where his own good sense prompted him to believe he ought to remain, at the point of Corpus Christi; and, if a negotiation had been opened with Mexico, in a true spirit of amity and conciliation, war possibly might have been prevented. But, instead of this pacific and moderate course, whilst Mr. [John] Slidell was bending [*sic*, wending] his way to Mexico with his diplomatic credentials, General Taylor was ordered to transport his cannon, and to plant them, in a warlike attitude, opposite to Matamoras, on the east bank of the Rio Bravo [Rio Grande]; within the very disputed territory, the adjustment of which was to be the object of Mr. Slidell's mission. What else could have transpired but a conflict of arms?

Thus the war commenced, and the President [James K. Polk] after having produced it, appealed to Congress. A bill was proposed to raise 50,000 volunteers, and in order to commit all who should vote for it, a preamble was inserted falsely attributing the commencement of the war to the act of Mexico. I have no doubt of the patriotic motives of those who, after struggling to divest the bill of that flagrant error, found themselves constrained to vote for it. . . .

The exceptionable conduct of the Federal party, during that last British War [of 1812], has excited an influence in the prosecution of the present war, and prevented a just discrimination between the two wars. That was a war of National defence, required for the vindication of the National rights and honor, and demanded by the indignant voice of the People. President [James] Madison himself, I know, at first, reluctantly and with great doubt and hesitation, brought himself to the conviction that it ought to be declared. . . . It was a just war, and its great object, as announced at the time, was "Free Trade and Sailors Rights," against the intolerable and oppressive acts of British power on the ocean. The justice of the war, far from being denied or controverted, was admitted by the Federal party, which only questioned it on considerations of policy. Being deliberately and constitutionally declared, it was, I think, their duty to have given to it their hearty co-operation. But the mass of them did not. They continued to oppose and thwart it, to discourage loans and enlistments, to deny the power of the General Government to march the militia beyond our limits, and to hold a Hartford Convention, which, whatever were its real objects, bore the aspect of seeking a dissolution of the Union itself. They lost and justly lost the public confidence.—But has not an apprehension of a similar fate, in a state of case widely different, repressed a fearless expression of their real sentiments in some of our public men?

How totally variant is the present war! This is no war of defence, but one unnecessary and of offensive aggression. It is Mexico that is defending her fire-sides, her castles and her altars, not we. And how different also is the conduct of the Whig party of the present day from that of the major part of the Federal party during the war of 1812! Far from interposing any obstacles to the prosecution of the war, if the Whigs in office are reproachable at all, it is for having lent too ready a facility to it, without careful examination into the objects of the war. And, out of office, who have rushed to the prosecution of the war with more ardor and alacrity than the Whigs? . . .

But the havoc of war is in progress, and the no less deplorable havoc of an inhospitable and pestilential climate. Without indulging in an unneccessary retrospect and useless reproaches on the past, all hearts and heads should unite in the patriotic endeavor to bring it to a satisfactory close. Is there no way that this can be done? . . .

A declaration of war is the highest and most awful exercise of sovereignty. . . . Whenever called upon to determine upon the solemn question of peace or war, Congress must consider and deliberate and decide upon the motives, objects and causes of the war. And, if a war be commenced without any previous declaration of its objects, as in the case of the existing war with Mexico, Congress must necessarily possess the authority, at any time, to declare for what purposes it shall be further prosecuted. If we suppose Congress does not possess the controlling authority attributed to it; if it be contended that a war having been once commenced, the President of the United States may direct it to the accomplishment of any objects he pleases, without consulting and without any regard to the will of Congress, the Convention will have utterly failed in guarding the nation against the abuses and ambition of a single individual. Either Congress, or the President, must have the right of determining upon the objects for which a war shall be prosecuted. There is no other alternative. If the President possess it and may prosecute it for objects against the will of Congress, where is the difference between our free government and that of any other nation which may be governed by an absolute Czar, Emperor, or King?

Congress may omit, as it has omitted in the present war, to proclaim the objects for which it was commenced or has been since prosecuted, and in cases of such omission the President, being charged with the employment and direction of the national force is, necessarily, left to his own judgment to decide upon the objects, to the attainment of which that force shall be applied. But, whenever Congress shall think proper to declare, by some authentic act, for what purposes a war shall be commenced or continued it is the duty of the President to apply the national force to the attainment of those purposes. In the instance of the last war with Great Britain, the act of Congress by which it was declared was preceded by a message of President Madison enumerating the wrongs and injuries of which we complained against Great Britain. That message therefore, and without it the well known objects of the war, which was a war purely of defence, rendered it unnecessary that Congress should particularize, in the act, the specific objects for which it was proclaimed. The whole world knew that it was a war waged for Free Trade and Sailors' Rights.

It may be urged that the President and Senate possess the treaty making power, without any express limitation as to its exercise; that the natural and ordinary termination of a war is by a treaty of peace; and therefore, that the President and Senate must possess the power to decide what stipulations and conditions shall enter into such a treaty. But it is not more true that the President and Senate possess the treaty making power, without limitation, than that Congress possesses the war making power, without restriction. These two powers then ought to be so interpreted as to reconcile the one with the other; and, in expounding the constitution, we ought to keep constantly in view the nature and structure of our free government, and especially the great object of the Convention in taking the war-making power out of the hands of a single man and placing it in the safer custody of the representatives of the whole nation. The desirable reconciliation between the two powers is effected by attributing to Congress the right to declare what shall be the objects of war, and to the President the duty of endeavoring to obtain those objects by the direction of the national force and by diplomacy.

*   *   *

I conclude, therefore, Mr. President and Fellow-Citizens, with entire confidence, that Congress has the right either at the beginning or during the prosecution of any war, to decide the objects and purposes for which it was proclaimed, or for which it ought to be continued. And, I think, it is the duty of Congress, by some deliberate and authentic act, to declare for what objects the present war shall be longer prosecuted. . . . Let it resolve, simply, that the war shall, or shall not, be a war of conquest; and, if a war of conquest, what is to be conquered. Should a resolution pass, disclaiming the design of conquest, peace would follow, in less than sixty days, if the President would conform to his constitutional duty.

Here, fellow Citizens, I might pause, having indicated a mode by which the nation, through its accredited and legitimate representatives in Congress, can announce for what purposes and objects this war shall be longer prosecuted, and can thus let the whole people of the United States know for what end their blood is to be further shed and their treasure further expended, instead of the knowledge of it being locked up and concealed in the bosom of one man. . . . But I do not think it right to stop here. It is the privilege of the people, in their primitive assemblies, and of every private man, however humble, to express an opinion in regard to the purposes for which the war should be continued; and such an expression will receive just so much consideration and consequence as it is entitled to, and no more.

Shall this war be prosecuted for the purpose of conquering and annexing Mexico, in all its boundless extent, to the United States?

I will not attribute to the President of the United States any such design; but I confess that I have been shocked and alarmed by manifestations of it in various quarters[.] Of all the dangers and misfortunes which could befall this nation, I should regard that of its becoming a warlike and conquering power the most direful and fatal. History tells the mournful tale of conquering nations and conquerors. The three most celebrated conquerors, in the civilized world, were Alexander, Caesar and Napoleon. . . . Do you believe that the people of Macedon or Greece, of Rome, or France, were benefitted, individually or collectively, by the triumphs of their great Captains? Their sad lot was immense sacrifice of life, heavy and intolerable burdens, and the ultimate loss of liberty itself.

That the power of the United States is competent to the conquest of Mexico, is quite probable. But it could not be achieved without frightful carnage, dreadful sacrifices of human life, and the creation of an onerous national debt; nor could it be completely effected, in all probability, until after the lapse of many years. It would be necessary to occupy all its strongholds, to disarm its inhabitants, and to keep them in constant fear and subjection. To consummate the work, I presume that standing armies, not less than a hundred thousand men, would be necessary, to be kept perhaps always in the bosom of their country. These standing armies, revelling in a foreign land, and accustomed to trample upon the liberties of a foreign people, at some distant day, might be fit and ready instruments, under the lead of some daring and unprincipled chieftain, to return to their country and prostrate the public liberty.

Supposing the conquest to be once made, what is to be done with it? Is it to be governed, like Roman Provinces, by Proconsuls? Would it be compatible with the genius, character, and safety of our free institutions, to keep such a great country as Mexico, with a population of not less that nine millions, in a state of constant military subjection?

Shall it be annexed to the United States: Does any considerate man believe it possible that two such immense countries, with territories of nearly equal extent, with populations so incongruous, so different in race, in language, in religion and in laws, could be blended together in one harmonious mass, and happily governed by one common authority? Murmurs, discontent, insurrections, rebellion, would inevitably ensue, until the incompatible parts would be broken asunder, and possibly, in the frightful struggle, our present glorious Union itself would be dissevered or dissolved. We ought not to forget the warning voice of all history, which teaches the difficulty of combining and consolidating together, conquering and conquered nations. After the lapse of eight hundred years, during which the Moors held their conquest of Spain, the indomitable courage, perseverance and obstinacy of the Spanish race finally triumphed, and expelled the African invaders from the Peninsula. . . . And what has been the fact with poor, gallant, generous and oppressed Ireland? Centuries have passed away, since the overbearing Saxon overrun and subjugated the Emerald Isle. Rivers of Irish blood have flowed, during the long and arduous contest. Insurrection and rebellion have been the order of the day; and yet, up to this time, Ireland remains alien in feeling, affection and sympathy, towards the power which has so long borne her down. Every Irishman hates, with a mortal hatred, his Saxon oppressor. Although there are great territorial differences between the condition of England and Ireland, as compared to that of the United States and Mexico, there are some points of striking resemblance between them. Both the Irish and the Mexicans are probably of the same Celtic race. Both the English and the Americans are of the same Saxon origin. The Catholic religion predominates in both the former, the Protestant among both the latter. Religion has been the fruitful cause of dissatisfaction and discontent between the Irish and the English nations[.] Is there not reason to apprehend that it would become so between the people of the United States and those of Mexico, if they were united together? Why should we seek to interfere with them, in their mode of worship of a common Saviour? We believe that they are wrong, especially in the exclusive character of their faith, and that we are right. They think that they are right and we wrong. What other rule can there be than to leave the followers of each religion to their own solemn convictions of conscientious duty towards God? Who, but the great Arbiter of the Universe, can judge in such a question? . . .

But I suppose it to be impossible that those who favor, if there be any who favor the annexation of Mexico to the United States, can think that it ought to be perpetually governed by military sway. Certainly no votary of human liberty could deem it right that a violation should be perpetrated of the great principles of our own revolution, according to which, laws ought not to be enacted and taxes ought not to be levied, without representation on the part of those who are to obey the one, and pay the other. Then, Mexico is to participate in our councils and equally share in our legislation and government. But, suppose she would not voluntarily choose representatives to the national Congress, is our soldiery to follow the electors to the ballot-box, and by force to compel them, at the point of the bayonet, to deposit their ballots? And how are the nine millions of Mexican people to be represented in the Congress of the United States of America and the Congress of the United States of the Republic of Mexico combined? Is every Mexican, without regard to color or caste, per capitum, to exercise the elective franchise? How is the quota of representation between the two Republics, to be fixed? Where is their Seat of Common Government to be established? And who can foresee or foretell, if Mexico, voluntarily or by force, were to share in the common government what would be the consequences to her or to us? . . . Those, whom God and Geography have pronounced should live asunder, could never be permanently and harmoniously united together.

Do we want for our own happiness or greatness the addition of Mexico to the the existing Union of our States? If our population was too dense for our territory, and there was a difficulty in obtaining honorably the means of subsistence, there might be some excuse for an attempt to enlarge our dominions. But we have no such apology. We have already, in our glorious country, a vast and almost boundless territory. . . . Ought we not to be profoundly thankful to the Giver of all good things for such a vast and bountiful land? Is it not the height of ingratitude to Him to seek, by war and conquest, indulging in a spirit of rapacity, to acquire other lands, the homes and habitations of a large portion of his common children? If we pursue the object of such a conquest, besides mortgaging the revenue and resources of this country for ages to come, in the form of an onerous national debt, we should have greatly to augment that debt, by an assumption of the sixty or seventy millions of the national debt of Mexico. For I take it that nothing is more certain than that, if we obtain, voluntarily or by conquest, a foreign nation we acquire it with all the incumbrances attached to it. . . .

Of all the possessions which appertain to man, in his collective or individual condition, none should be preserved and cherished, with more sedulous and unremitting care, than that of an unsullied character. It is impossible to estimate it too highly, in society, when attached to an individual, nor can it be exaggerated or too greatly magnified in a nation. Those who lose or are indifferent to it become just objects of scorn and contempt. . . . I am afraid that we do not now stand well in the opinion of other parts of christendom. Repudiation has brought upon us much reproach. All the nations, I apprehend, look upon us, in the prosecution of the present war, as being actuated by a spirit of rapacity, and an inordinate desire for territorial aggrandizement. Let us not forfeit altogether their good opinions. Let us command their applause by a noble exercise of forbearance and justice. In the elevated station which we hold, we can safely afford to practice the Godlike virtues of moderation and magnanimity. The long series of glorious triumphs, achieved by our gallant commanders and their brave armies, unattended by a single reverse, justify us, without the least danger of tarnishing the national honor, in disinterestedly holding out the olive branch of peace. . . .

*     *     *

But, it will be repeated, are we to have no indemnity for the expenses of this war? Mexico is utterly unable to make us any pecuniary indemnity, if the justice of the war on our part entitled us to demand it. Her country has been laid waste, her cities burned or occupied by our troops, her means so exhausted that she is unable to pay even her own armies. And every day's prosecution of the war, whilst it would augment the amount of our indemnity, would lessen the ability of Mexico to pay it.—We have seen, however, that there is another form in which we are to demand indemnity. It is to be territorial indemnity! I hope, for reasons already stated that that fire-brand will not be brought into our country.

Among the resolutions, which it is my intention to present for your consideration, at the conclusion of this address, one proposes, in your behalf and mine, to disavow, in the most positive manner, any desire, on our part, to acquire any foreign territory whatever, for the purpose of introducing slavery into it. I do not know that any citizen of the United States entertains such a wish. But such a motive has been often imputed to the slave States, and I therefore think it necessary to notice it on this occasion. My opinions on the subject of slavery are well known. . . . I have ever regarded slavery as a great evil, a wrong, for the present, I fear, an irremediable wrong to its unfortunate victims. I should rejoice if not a single slave breathed the air or was within the limits of our country. But here they are, to be dealt with as well as we can, with a due consideration of all circumstances affecting the security, safety and happiness of both races. Every State has the supreme, uncontrolled and exclusive power to decide for itself whether slavery shall cease or continue within its limits, without any exterior intervention from any quarter. . . . In the State of Kentucky, near fifty years ago, I thought the proportion of slaves, in comparison with the whites, was so inconsiderable that we might safely adopt a system of gradual emancipation that would ultimately eradicate this evil in our State. That system was totally different from the immediate abolition of slavery for which the party of the Abolitionists of the present day contend. Whether they have intended it or not, it is my calm and deliberate belief, that they have done incalculable mischief even to the very cause which they have espoused, to say nothing of the discord which has been produced between different parts of the Union. According to the system, we attempted, near the close of the last century, all slaves in being were to remain such, but, all who might be born subsequent to a specified day, were to become free at the age of twenty-eight, and, during their service, were to be taught to read, write, and cypher. Thus, instead of being thrown upon the community, ignorant and unprepared, as would be the case by immediate emancipation, they would have entered upon the possession of their freedom, capable, in some degree, of enjoying it.—After a hard struggle, the system was defeated, and I regret it extremely, as, if it had been then adopted, our State would be now nearly rid of that reproach.

Since the epoch, a scheme of unmixed benevolence has sprung up, which, if it had existed at that time, would have obviated one of the greatest objections which was made to gradual emancipation, which was the continuance of the emancipated slaves to abide among us. That scheme is the American Colonization Society. About twenty-eight years ago, a few individuals, myself among them, met together in the city of Washington, and laid the foundations of that society. It has gone on, amidst extraordinary difficulties and trials, sustaining itself almost entirely, by spontaneous and voluntary contributions, from individual benevolence, without scarcely any aid from Government. The Colonies, planted under its auspices, are now well established communities, with churches, schools and other institutions appertaining to the civilized state. . . .

\* \* \*

It may be argued, that, in admitting the injustice of slavery, I admit the necessity of an instantaneous reparation of that injustice. Unfortunately, however, it is not always safe, practicable or possible, in the great movements of States and public affairs of nations, to remedy or repair the infliction of previous injustice. In the inception of it, we may oppose and denounce it, by our most strenuous exertions, but, after its consummation, there is often no other alternative left us but to deplore its perpetration, and to acquiesce as the only alternative, in its existence, as a less evil that the frightful consequences which might ensue from the vain endeavor to repair it. Slavery is one of those unfortunate instances. . . . The case of the annexation of Texas to the United States is a recent and obvious one where, if it were wrong, it cannot now be repaired. Texas is now an integral part of our Union, with its own voluntary consent. Many of us opposed the annexation with honest zeal and most earnest exertions. But who would now think of perpetrating the folly of casting Texas out of the confederacy and throwing her back upon her own independence, or into the arms of Mexico? Who would now seek to divorce her from this Union? The Creeks and the Cherokee Indians were, by the most exceptionable means, driven from their country, and transported beyond the Mississippi river. Their lands have been fairly purchased and occupied by inhabitants of Georgia, Alabama, Mississippi and Tennessee. Who would now conceive of the flagrant injustice of expelling those inhabitants and restoring the Indian country to the Cherokees and the Creeks, under color of repairing original injustice? During the war of our revolution, millions of paper money were issued by our ancestors, as the only currency with which they could achieve our liberties and independence.—Thousands and hundreds of thousands of families were stripped of their homes and their all and brought to ruin, by giving credit and confidence to that spurious currency. Stern necessity has prevented the reparation of that great national injustice.

\*      \*      \*

I have embodied, Mr. President and fellow-citizens, the sentiments and opinions which I have endeavored to explain and enforce in a series of resolutions which I beg now to submit to your consideration and judgment. They are the following:

\*      \*      \*

4. *Resolved*, as the further opinion of this meeting, that it is the right and duty of Congress to declare, by some authentic act, for what purposes and objects the existing war ought to be further prosecuted; that it is the duty of the President, in his official conduct, to conform to such a declaration of Congress; and that, if, after such declaration, the President should decline or refuse to endeavor, by all the means, civil, diplomatic, and military, in his power, to execute the announced will of Congress, and, in defiance of its authority, should continue to prosecute the war for purposes and objects other than those declared by that body, it would become the right and duty of Congress to adopt the most efficacious measures to arrest the further progress of the war, taking care to make ample provision for the honor, the safety and security of our armies in Mexico, in every contingency. And, if Mexico should decline or refuse to conclude a treaty with us, stipulating for the purposes and objects so declared by Congress, it would be the duty of the Government to prosecute the war with the utmost vigor, until they were attained by a treaty of peace.

5. *Resolved*, That we view with serious alarm, and are utterly opposed to any purpose of annexing Mexico to the United States, in any mode, and especially by conquest; that we believe the two nations could not be happily governed by one common authority, owing to their great difference of race, law, language and religion, and the vast extent of their respective territories, and large amount of their re-

spective populations; that such a union, against the consent of the exasperated Mexican people, could only be effected and preserved by large standing armies, and the constant application of military force—in other words, by despotic sway exercised over the Mexican people, in the first instance, but which, there would be just cause to apprehend, might, in process of time, be extended over the people of the United States. That we deprecate, therefore, such a union, as wholly incompatible with the genius of our Government, and with the character of free and liberal institutions; and we anxiously hope that each nation may be left in the undisturbed possession of its own laws, language, cherished religion and territory, to pursue its own happiness, according to what it may deem best for itself.

6. *Resolved*, That, considering the series of splendid and brilliant victories achieved by our brave armies and their gallant commanders, during the war with Mexico, unattended by a single reverse, The United States, without any danger of their honor suffering the slightest tarnish, can practice the virtues of moderation and magnanimity towards their discomfited foe. We have no desire for the dismemberment of the United States of the Republic of Mexico, but wish only a just and proper fixation of the limits of Texas.

7. *Resolved*, That we do, positively and emphatically, disclaim and disavow any wish or desire, on our part, to acquire any foreign territory whatever, for the purpose of propagating slavery, or of introducing slaves from the United States, into such foreign territory.

8. *Resolved*, That we invite our fellow citizens of the United States, who are anxious for the restoration of the blessings of peace, or, if the existing war shall continue to be prosecuted, are desirous that its purpose and objects shall be defined and known; who are anxious to avert present and future perils and dangers, with which it may be fraught; and who are also anxious to produce contentment and satisfaction at home, and to elevate the national character abroad, to assemble together in their respective communities, and to express their views, feelings, and opinions.

# REVIEW QUESTIONS

1. How does Clay differentiate between the War of 1812 and the Mexican War?
2. How does he compare and contrast the Federalists during the former war and the Whigs during the latter one? Why does he do so?
3. What were his concerns about the war-making powers of the executive and legislative branches? What did he want the government to do?
4. Why did Clay believe the possible conquest and annexation of Mexico to be undesirable?
5. What does his argument reveal about him and his society?

# 15 ∽ THE GATHERING STORM

*During the 1850s sectional interests and identities battered national ones. There was a contentiousness that threatened to tear the country apart; thus many American politicians, reflecting the concerns of their constituents, proposed compromises to divert, if not stop, the conflicts. Unfortunately for the nation, however, compromise did not work as it had in the past: it now acted as a catalyst to crisis. Compromise worked when the parties involved were each willing to relinquish some demands to gain others and when there was an underlying agreement on what issues were most important. Such a consensus had existed earlier when the majority of all the states' citizens held that maintaining the union took precedence over regional interests, but when that consensus crumbled there was but a weak foundation for a common, long-lasting solution.*

*The crisis had been building for some time. A few contemporaries traced its origins to the constitutional compromises, while others thought the first true signs of danger appeared in the nullification controversy of the 1830s. Certainly, many acknowledged that tempers had long been rising as people argued over individuals' and states' rights—issues raised by the institution of slavery. Americans contested a person's right to property versus an individual's right to himself—or herself. They debated whether the federal government could limit people's choices in the territories—as in the expansion of slavery—in ways it could not in the states. The Missouri Compromise had been an early effort to cap this volcano of public sentiment, the gag rule in Congress another, but as these measures were rescinded and new ones failed, Americans grappled with the possibility that there would be an eruption that could destroy the union.*

*Secession was not a new concept created in the 1850s, but receptivity to the idea had grown over the previous decades. In December 1844, for example, James Henry Hammond, a South Carolina planter and politician, wrote in his diary about his state's resolutions that denounced the repeal of the gag rule "as a flagrant outrage infringing on the Fed[eral] Compact." The resolutions declared that Congressional legislation restricting slavery would amount to a dissolution of the Union. Hammond believed the resolutions more openly threatened separation than any ever passed—harking back to the nullification controversy—before. He continued, "Nothing in my opinion but Dis-union now or very shortly can [save us]. Those who are for delaying this event for the sake of peace are taking the surest steps to render war inevitable." Almost six years later, in May 1850, he criticized Clay's compromise as presupposing "a desire on both sides to be at peace, when such is not the fact and, if it were, no compromise would be necessary." He thought the compromise would weaken the South while only temporarily suspending abolition agitation. He wanted the South to unite in its resistance to limits on its rights and be ready for action. It took the South ten years.*

*Over that decade politicians tried various measures to stop the geopolitical fissures from splitting the nation apart. The first was the Compromise of 1850. Questions about the establishment of states and the expansion of slavery in the country's vast territories rocked the nation. While a few old masters, such as John C. Calhoun, and their acolytes, one being Jefferson Davis of Mississippi, argued that the only way to halt the widening schism was through an acknowledgment of southern rights, others, such as Henry Clay and Daniel Webster, sought to mend the rift through concessions to both sides. When Clay's package deal was defeated, a rising young leader in the Democratic Party, Stephen A. Douglas of Illinois, took on the task of getting the resolutions passed. He broke down Clay's program into five measures so that the lack of consensus on the sum of these issues would not prevent majorities from voting for each of them. Douglas's strategy worked: Congress admitted California as a free state, set the Texas state boundary and established the New Mexico territory, set up the Utah territory (as in New Mexico) with the issue of slavery left to the territorial legislature, passed a new Fugitive Slave Act, and abolished the slave trade in the District of Columbia.*

*Most Americans accepted the compromise with relief if not joy. That relief was short lived, for the question of slavery in the territories—and by extension, in the states—came up again when Douglas sought to organize the Nebraska territory and build a transcontinental railroad through it. To get Southerners to vote for his bill, Douglas accommodated them on the slavery issue. He made "popular sovereignty," which enabled the people of the territories and new states to decide for themselves whether to include slavery, a part of his bill, and then supported the repeal of the Missouri Compromise's exclusion of slavery north of 36° 30'. He also agreed to organize two territories: Kansas and Nebraska. Douglas got what he wanted, but at great personal and national expense. He ruined his chances for the presidency and further undermined the Union.*

*The threats facing the Union became clearer as Kansas became a combat zone. Settlers and their supporters battled one another over the inclusion or exclusion of slavery in their territory. As Kansans bled, other Americans continued to exchange verbal punches over the nation's great problem. They fought it out within and between the political parties. They argued over it within the judiciary. And they kept electing different presidents in their search for strong executive guidance. One thing followed another so rapidly that the Union could not recover its equilibrium between blows. It reeled and staggered into war.*

## RALPH WALDO EMERSON

# The Fugitive Slave Law (1854)

*Many activists who had pushed for a variety of reforms in the 1830s and 1840s started to concentrate more on the slavery issue by the 1850s. Horace Mann, that champion of public schools, declared in 1848 that "before a man can be educated, he must be a free man." To work to that end, he took a seat in Congress. Ralph Waldo Emerson preferred intellectual to political activism, but the passage of the Fugitive Slave Law as part of the Compromise of 1850 and Douglas's Kansas-Nebraska Act in 1854 roused him to take a public stand. He urged his listeners and readers to examine their beliefs—which he trusted were against slavery and for liberty—and then act to ensure that political compromises did not undermine them.*

From *The Selected Writings of Ralph Waldo Emerson*, edited by Brooks Atkinson (1940; New York: The Modern Library, Random House, 1950), pp. 861–76.

I do not often speak to public questions—they are odious and hurtful, and it seems like meddling or leaving your work. . . . And then I see what havoc it makes with any good mind, a dissipated philanthropy. The one thing not to be forgiven to intellectual persons is, not to know their own task, or to take their ideas from others. . . .

My own habitual view is to the well-being of students or scholars. And it is only when the public event affects them, that it very seriously touches me. And what I have to say is to them. For every man speaks mainly to a class whom he works with and more or less fully represents. . . . And yet, when I say the class of scholars or students—that is a class which comprises in some sort all mankind, comprises every man in the best hours of his life; and in these days not only virtually but actually. For who are the readers and thinkers of 1854? Owing to the silent revolution which the newspaper has wrought, this class has come in this country to take in all classes. Look into the morning trains which, from every suburb, carry the business men into the city to their shops, counting-rooms, workyards and warehouses. With them enters the car— the newsboy, that humble priest of politics, finance, philosophy, and religion. He unfolds his magical sheets—twopence a head his bread of knowledge costs—and instantly the entire rectangular assembly, fresh from their breakfast, are bending as one man to their second breakfast. There is, no doubt, chaff enough in what he brings; but there is fact, thought, and wisdom in the crude mass, from all regions of the world.

I have lived all my life without suffering any known inconvenience from American Slavery. I never saw it; I never heard the whip; I never felt the check on my free speech and action, until, the other day, when Mr. Webster, by his personal influence, brought the Fugitive Slave Law on the country. I say Mr. Webster, for though the Bill was not his, it is yet notorious that he was the life and soul of it, that he gave it all he had: it cost him his life, and under the shadow of his great name inferior men sheltered themselves, threw their ballots for it and made the law. I say inferior men. There were all sorts of what are called brilliant men, accomplished men, men of high station, a President of the United States, Senators, men of eloquent speech, but men without self-respect, without character, and it was strange to see that office, age, fame, talent, even a repute for honesty, all count for nothing. They had no opinions, they had no memory for what they had been saying like the Lord's Prayer all their lifetime: they were only looking to what their great Captain did: if he jumped, they jumped, if he stood on his head, they did. In ordinary, the supposed sense of their district and State is their guide, and that holds them to the part of liberty and justice. But it is always a little difficult to decipher what this public sense is; and when a great man comes who knots up into himself the opinions and wishes of the people, it is so much easier to follow him as an exponent of this. He too is responsible; they will not be. It will always suffice to say—"I followed him."

\*　　\*　　\*

In what I have to say of Mr. Webster I do not confound him with vulgar politicians before or since. There is always base ambition enough, men who calculate on the immense ignorance of the masses; . . . There are those too who have power and inspiration only to do ill. Their talent or their faculty deserts them when they undertake anything right. Mr. Webster had a natural ascendancy of aspect and carriage which distinguished him over all his contemporaries. His countenance, his figure, and his manners were all in so grand a style, that he was, without effort, as superior to his most eminent rivals as they were to the humblest; . . .

\*　　\*　　\*

The history of this country has given a disastrous importance to the defects of this great man's mind. Whether evil influences and the corruption of politics, or whether original infirmity, it was the misfortune of his country that with this large understanding he had not what is better than intellect, and the source of its health. It is a law of our nature that great thoughts come from the heart. If his moral sensibility had been proportioned to the force of his understanding, what limits could have been set to his genius and beneficent power? But he wanted that deep source of inspiration. . . .

Four years ago to-night, on one of those high critical moments in history when great issues are determined, when the powers of right and wrong are mustered for conflict, and it lies with one man to give a casting vote—Mr. Webster, most unexpectedly, threw his whole weight on the side of Slavery, and caused by his personal and official authority the passage of the Fugitive Slave Bill.

It is remarked of the Americans that they value dexterity too much, and honor too little; that they think they praise a man more by saying that he is "smart" than by saying that he is right. Whether the defect be national or not, it is the defect and calamity of Mr. Webster; and it is so far true of his countrymen, namely, that the appeal is sure to be made to his physical and mental ability when his character is assailed. . . .

\*　　\*　　\*

But the question which History will ask is broader. In the final hour, when he was forced by the peremptory necessity of the closing armies to take a side—did he take the part of great principles, the side of humanity and justice, or the side of abuse and oppression and chaos?

Mr. Webster decided for Slavery, and that, when the aspect of the institution was no longer doubtful, no longer feeble and apologetic and proposing soon to end itself, but when it was strong, aggressive, and threatening an illimitable increase. He listened to State reasons and hopes, and left, with much complacency we are told, the testament of his speech to the astonished State of Massachusetts, *vera pro gratis*; a ghastly result of all those years of experience in affairs, this, that there was nothing better for the foremost American man to tell his countrymen than that Slavery was now at that strength that they must beat down their conscience and become kidnappers for it.

\*　　\*　　\*

Here was the question, Are you for man and for the good of man; or are you for the hurt and harm of man? It was the question whether man shall be treated as leather? Whether the negro shall be, as the Indians were in Spanish America, a piece of money? Whether this system, which is a kind of mill or factory for converting men into monkeys, shall be upheld and enlarged? And Mr. Webster and the country went for the application to these poor men of quadruped law.

People were expecting a totally different course from Mr. Webster. If any man had in that hour possessed the weight with the country which he had acquired, he could have brought the whole country to its senses. But not a moment's pause was allowed. Angry parties went from bad to worse, and the decision of Webster was accompanied with everything offensive to freedom and good morals. . . . He told the people at Boston "they must conquer their prejudices"; that "agitation of the subject of Slavery must be suppressed." . . .

I said I had never in my life up to this time suffered from the Slave Institution. Slavery in Virginia or Carolina was like Slavery in Africa or the Feejees, for me. There was an old fugitive law, but it had become, or was fast becoming, a dead letter, and, by the genius and laws of Massachusetts, inoperative. The new Bill made it operative, required me to hunt slaves, and it found citizens in Massachusetts willing to act as judges and captors. Moreover, it discloses the secret of the new times, that Slavery was no longer mendicant, but was become aggressive and dangerous.

The way in which the country was dragged to consent to this, and the disastrous defection (on the miserable cry of Union) of the men of letters, of the colleges, of educated men, nay, of some preachers of religion—was the darkest passage in the history. It showed that our prosperity had hurt us, and that we could not be shocked by crime. It showed that the old religion and the sense of the right had faded and gone out; that while we reckoned ourselves a highly cultivated nation, our bellies had run away with our brains, and the principles of culture and progress did not exist.

For I suppose that liberty is an accurate index, in men and nations, of general progress. The theory of personal liberty must always appeal to the most refined communities and to the men of the rarest perception and of delicate moral sense. For there are rights which rest on the finest sense of justice, and, with every degree of civility, it will be more truly felt and defined. A barbarous

tribe of good stock will, by means of their best heads, secure substantial liberty. But where there is any weakness in a race, and it becomes in a degree matter of concession and protection from their stronger neighbors, the incompatibility and offensiveness of the wrong will of course be most evident to the most cultivated. For it is—is it not?—the essence of courtesy, of politeness, of religion, of love, to prefer another, to postpone oneself, to protect another from oneself. That is the distinction of the gentleman, to defend the weak and redress the injured, as it is of the savage and the brutal to usurp and use others.

In Massachusetts, as we all know, there has always existed a predominant conservative spirit. We have more money and value of every kind than other people, and wish to keep them. The plea on which freedom was resisted was Union. I went to certain serious men, who had a little more reason than the rest, and inquired why they took this part? They answered that they had no confidence in their strength to resist the Democratic party; . . . and they stood stiffly on conservatism, and as near to monarchy as they could, only to moderate the velocity with which the car was running down the precipice. In short, their theory was despair; the Whig wisdom was only reprieve, a waiting to be last devoured. They side with Carolina, or with Arkansas, only to make a show of Whig strength, wherewith to resist a little longer this general ruin.

I have a respect for conservatism. I know how deeply founded it is in our nature, and how idle are all attempts to shake ourselves free from it. We are all conservatives, half Whig, half Democrat, in our essences: and might as well try to jump out of our skins as to escape from our Whiggery. There are two forces in Nature, by whose antagonism we exist; the power of Fate, Fortune, the laws of the world, the order of things, or however else we choose to phrase it, the material necessities, on the one hand—and Will or Duty or Freedom on the other.

May and Must, and the sense of right and duty, on the one hand, and the material necessities on the other: May and Must. In vulgar politics the Whig goes for what has been, for the old necessities—the Musts. The reformer goes for the Better, for the ideal good, for the Mays. But each of these parties must of necessity take in, in some measure, the principles of the other. Each wishes to cover the whole ground; to hold fast *and* to advance. Only, one lays the emphasis on keeping, and the other on advancing. I too think the *musts* are a safe company to follow, and even agreeable. But if we are Whigs, let us be Whigs of nature and science, and so for all the necessities. Let us know that, over and above all the *musts* of poverty and appetite, is the instinct of man to rise, and the instinct to love and help his brother.

\*　　\*　　\*

The events of this month are teaching one thing plain and clear, the worthlessness of good tools to bad workmen; that official papers are of no use; resolutions of public meetings, platforms of conventions, no, nor laws, nor constitutions, any more. These are all declaratory of the will of the moment, and are passed with more levity and on grounds far less honorable than ordinary business transactions of the street.

You relied on the constitution. It has not the word *slave* in it; and very good argument has shown that it would not warrant the crimes that are done under it; that, with provisions so vague for an object not named, and which could not be availed of to claim a barrel of sugar or a barrel of corn, the robbing of a man and of all his posterity is effected. You relied on the Supreme Court. The law was right, excellent law for the lambs. But what if unhappily the judges were chosen from the wolves, and give to all the law a wolfish interpretation? You relied on the Missouri Compromise. That is ridden over. You relied on State sovereignty in the Free States to protect their citizens. They are driven with contempt out of the courts and out of the territory of the Slave States—if they are so happy as to get out with their lives—and now you relied on these dismal guaranties infamously made in 1850; and, before the body of Webster is yet crumbled, it is found that they have crumbled. This eternal monument of his fame and of the Union is rotten in four years. They are no guaranty

to the free states. They are a guaranty to the slave states that, as they have hitherto met with no repulse, they shall meet with none.

I fear there is no reliance to be put on any kind or form of covenant, no, not on sacred forms, none on churches, none on bibles. For one would have said that a Christian would not keep slaves: but the Christians keep slaves. Of course they will not dare to read the Bible? Won't they? They quote the Bible, quote Paul, quote Christ, to justify slavery. If slavery is good, then is lying, theft, arson, homicide, each and all good, and to be maintained by Union societies.

These things show that no forms, neither constitutions, nor laws, nor covenants, nor churches, nor bibles, are of any use in themselves. The Devil nestles comfortably into them all. There is no help but in the head and heart and hamstrings of a man. Covenants are of no use without honest men to keep them; laws of none but with loyal citizens to obey them. . . . To make good the cause of Freedom, you must draw off from all foolish trust in others. You must be citadels and warriors yourselves, declarations of Independence, the charter, the battle and the victory. . . . And no man has a right to hope that the laws of New York will defend him from the contamination of slaves another day until he has made up his mind that he will not owe his protection to the laws of New York, but to his own sense and spirit. Then he protects New York. He only who is able to stand alone is qualified for society. And that I understand to be the end for which a soul exists in this world—to be himself the counterbalance of all falsehood and all wrong. . . .

\*　　\*　　\*

Whenever a man has come to this mind, that there is no Church for him but his believing prayer; no Constitution but his dealing well and justly with his neighbor; no liberty but his invincible will to do right—then certain aids and allies will promptly appear: for the constitution of the Universe is on his side. It is of no use to vote down gravitation of morals. What is useful will last, whilst that which is hurtful to the world will sink beneath all the opposing forces which it must exasperate. . . . A man who commits a crime defeats the end of his existence. He was created for benefit, and he exists for harm; and as well-doing makes power and wisdom, ill-doing takes them away. A man who steals another man's labor steals away his own faculties; his integrity, his humanity is flowing away from him. The habit of oppression cuts out the moral eyes, and, though the intellect goes on simulating the moral as before, its sanity is gradually destroyed. . . .

I suppose in general this is allowed, that if you have a nice question of right and wrong, you would not go with it to Louis Napoleon, or to a political hack, or to a slave-driver. The habit of mind of traders in power would not be esteemed favorable to delicate moral perception. American slavery affords no exception to this rule. No excess of good nature or of tenderness in individuals has been able to give a new character to the system, to tear down the whipping-house. . . .

Slavery is disheartening; but Nature is not so helpless but it can rid itself at last of every wrong. But the spasms of Nature are centuries and ages, and will tax the faith of short-lived men. Slowly, slowly the Avenger comes, but comes surely. The proverbs of the nations affirm these delays, but affirm the arrival. They say, "God may consent, but not forever. . . ."

These delays, you see them now in the temper of the times. The national spirit in this country is so drowsy, preoccupied with interest, deaf to principle. . . .

To faint hearts the times offer no invitation, and torpor exists here throughout the active classes on the subject of domestic slavery and its appalling aggressions. Yes, that is the stern edict of Providence, that liberty shall be no hasty fruit, but that event on event, population on population, age on age, shall cast itself into the opposite scale, and not until liberty has slowly accumulated weight enough to countervail and preponderate against all this, can the sufficient recoil come. All the great cities, all the refined circles, all the statesmen, Guizot, Palmerston, Webster, Calhoun, are sure to be found befriending liberty with their words, and crushing it with their votes. Liberty

is never cheap. It is made difficult, because freedom is the accomplishment and perfectness of man. . . .

Whilst the inconsistency of slavery with the principles on which the world is built guarantees its downfall, I own that the patience it requires is almost too sublime for mortals, and seems to demand of us more than mere hoping. And when one sees how fast the rot spreads—it is growing serious—I think we demand of superior men that they be superior in this—that the mind and the virtue shall give their verdict in their day, and accelerate so far the progress of civilization. Possession is sure to throw its stupid strength for existing power, and appetite and ambition will go for that. Let the aid of virtue, intelligence and education be cast where they rightfully belong. They are organically ours. Let them be loyal to their own. I wish to see the instructed class here know their own flag, and not fire on their comrades. We should not forgive the clergy for taking on every issue the immoral side; nor the Bench, if it put itself on the side of the culprit; nor the Government, if it sustain the mob against the law.

It is a potent support and ally to a brave man standing single, or with a few, for the right, and out-voted and ostracized, to know that better men in other parts of the country appreciate the service and will rightly report him to his own and the next age. Without this assurance, he will sooner sink. He may well say, 'If my countrymen do not care to be defended, I too will decline the controversy, from which I only reap invectives and hatred.' Yet the lovers of liberty may with reason tax the coldness and indifferentism of scholars and literary men. They are lovers of liberty in Greece and Rome and in the English Commonwealth, but they are lukewarm lovers of the liberty of America in 1854. The universities are not, as in Hobbes's time, "the core of rebellion," no, but the seat of inertness. They have forgotten their allegiance to the Muse, and grown worldly and political. . . .

But I put it to every noble and generous spirit, to every poetic, every heroic, every religious heart, that not so is our learning, our education, our poetry, our worship to be declared. Liberty is aggressive, Liberty is the Crusade of all brave and conscientious men, the Epic Poetry, the new religion, the chivalry of all gentlemen. This is the oppressed Lady whom true knights on their oath and honor must rescue and save.

Now at last we are disenchanted and shall have no more false hopes. I respect the Anti-Slavery Society. It is the Cassandra that has foretold all that has befallen, fact for fact, years ago: foretold all, and no man laid it to heart. It seemed, as the Turks say, "Fate makes that a man should not believe his own eyes." But the Fugitive Law did much to unglue the eyes of men, and now the Nebraska Bill leaves us staring. The Anti-Slavery Society will add many members this year. The Whig Party will join it; the Democrats will join it. The population of the free states will join it. I doubt not, at last, the slave states will join it. But be that sooner or later, and whoever comes or stays away, I hope we have reached the end of our unbelief, have come to a belief that there is a divine Providence in the world, which will not save us but through our own cooperation.

## REVIEW QUESTIONS

1. Daniel Webster was a renowned statesman who had worked to protect and strengthen the Union throughout his career. Emerson acknowledged that but condemned what Webster did in 1850. Why?

2. In censuring Webster and his adherents, Emerson provided a critique of leaders and followers and even, in reference to himself, those who had been somewhat disengaged in the growing crisis. What faults did Emerson see in both politicians and citizens?

3. What did Emerson want people to do? What did he want them to be?

4. How did sentiments such as Emerson's add to the crisis?

# THE DEMOCRATIC PARTY

## The Democratic Platform (1856)

*While the Whig Party shattered under sectional pressures, the Democratic Party struggled to hold on to its partisans throughout the country. It tried to appeal to all its people both in its nominees for the executive offices and in the planks of its platform. The delegates at the Democratic convention in Cincinnati ultimately decided not to endorse the incumbent president, Franklin Pierce, or Stephen Douglas for president because the issues of the last few years, especially the Kansas-Nebraska situation, undermined their chances in a national election. After seventeen ballots, the Democrats chose James Buchanan of Pennsylvania for their presidential nominee; although a Northerner, he was seen as willing to appease southern slaveowners. They nominated John Breckinridge of Kentucky for vice president. In their platform, the Democrats praised compromise and advocated limited federal government in domestic affairs and such traditional American concerns as freedom of the seas and free trade in foreign policy.*

From Thomas V. Cooper and Hector T. Fenton, *American Politics from the Beginning to Date* (Chicago: Charles R. Brodix, 1882), pp. 36–39.

*Resolved*, That the American democracy place their trust in the intelligence, the patriotism, and discriminating justice of the American people.

*Resolved*, That we regard this as a distinctive feature of our political creed, which we are proud to maintain before the world as a great moral element in a form of government springing from and upheld by the popular will; and we contrast it with the creed and practice of federalism, under whatever name or form, which seeks to palsy the will of the constituents, and which conceives no imposture too monstrous for the popular credulity.

*Resolved, therefore,* That entertaining these views, the Democratic party of this Union, through their delegates, assembled in general convention, coming together in a spirit of concord, of devotion to the doctrines and faith of a free representative government, and appealing to their fellow citizens for the rectitude of their intentions, renew and reassert, before the American people, the declaration of principles avowed by them, when, on former occasions, in general convention, they have presented their candidates for the popular suffrage.

1. That the Federal government is one of limited power, derived solely from the constitution, and the grants of power made therein ought to be strictly construed by all the departments and agents of the government, and that it is inexpedient and dangerous to exercise doubtful constitutional powers.

2. That the constitution does not confer upon the general government the power to commence and carry on a general system of internal improvements.

3. That the constitution does not confer authority upon the Federal government, directly or indirectly, to assume the debts of the several states, contracted for local and internal improvements or other state purposes; nor would such assumption be just or expedient.

4. That justice and sound policy forbid the Federal government to foster one branch of industry to the detriment of another, or to cherish the interests of one portion of our common country; that every citizen and every section of the country

has a right to demand and insist upon an equality of rights and privileges, and a complete and ample protection of persons and property from domestic violence and foreign aggression.

5. That it is the duty of every branch of the government to enforce and practice the most rigid economy in conducting our public affairs, and that no more revenue ought to be raised than is required to defray the necessary expenses of the government and gradual but certain extinction of the public debt.

6. That the proceeds of the public lands ought to be sacredly applied to the national objects specified in the constitution, and that we are opposed to any law for the distribution of such proceeds among the states, as alike inexpedient in policy and repugnant to the constitution.

7. That Congress has no power to charter a national bank; that we believe such an institution one of deadly hostility to the best interests of this country, dangerous to our republican institutions and the liberties of the people, and calculated to place the business of the country within the control of a concentrated money power and above the laws and will of the people. . . .

\*     \*     \*

9. That we are decidedly opposed to taking from the President the qualified veto power, by which he is enabled, under restrictions and responsibilities amply sufficient to guard the public interests, to suspend the passage of a bill whose merits can not secure the approval of two-thirds of the Senate and House of Representatives, until the judgment of the people can be obtained thereon, and which has saved the American people from the corrupt and tyrannical dominion of the Bank of the United States and from a corrupting system of general internal improvements.

10. That the liberal principles embodied by Jefferson in the Declaration of Independence, and sanctioned in the Constitution, which makes ours the land of liberty and the asylum of the oppressed of every nation, have ever been cardinal principles in the democratic faith; and every attempt to abridge the privilege of becoming citizens and

owners of soil among us, ought to be resisted with the same spirit which swept the alien and sedition laws from our statute books.

*And whereas,* Since the foregoing declaration was uniformly adopted by our predecessors in national conventions, an adverse political and religious test has been secretly organized by a party claiming to be exclusively Americans, and it is proper that the American democracy should clearly define its relations thereto; and declare its determined opposition to all secret political societies, by whatever name they may be called—

*Resolved,* That the foundation of this union of states having been laid in, and its prosperity, expansion, and pre-eminent example in free government built upon, entire freedom of matters of religious concernment, and no respect of persons in regard to rank or place of birth, no party can justly be deemed national, constitutional, or in accordance with American principles, which bases its exclusive organization upon religious opinions and accidental birth-place. And hence a political crusade in the nineteenth century, and in the United States of America, against Catholics and foreign-born, is neither justified by the past history or future prospects of the country, nor in unison with the spirit of toleration and enlightened freedom which peculiarly distinguishes the American system of popular government.

*Resolved,* That we reiterate with renewed energy of purpose the well-considered declarations of former conventions upon the sectional issue of domestic slavery, and concerning the reserved rights of the states—

1. That Congress has no power under the constitution to interfere with or control the domestic institutions of the several states, and that all such states are the sole and proper judges of everything appertaining to their own affairs not prohibited by the constitution; that all efforts of the Abolitionists or others, made to induce Congress to interfere with questions of slavery, or to take incipient steps in relation thereto, are calculated to lead to the most alarming and dangerous consequences, and that all such efforts have an inevitable tendency to diminish the happiness of the people and endanger the stability and permanency of the Union, and ought not to be countenanced by any friend of our political institutions.

2. That the foregoing proposition covers and was intended to embrace the whole subject of slavery agitation in Congress, and therefore the Democratic party of the Union, standing on this national platform, will abide by and adhere to a faithful execution of the acts known as the compromise measures, settled by the Congress of 1850—"the act for reclaiming fugitives from service or labor" included; which act, being designed to carry out an express provision of the constitution, can not, with fidelity thereto, be repealed, or so changed as to destroy or impair its efficiency.

3. That the Democratic party will resist all attempts at renewing in Congress, or out of it, the agitation of the slavery question, under whatever shape or color the attempt may be made.

4. That the Democratic party will faithfully abide by and uphold the principles laid down in the Kentucky and Virginia resolutions of 1792 and 1798, and in the report of Mr. Madison to the Virginia legislature in 1799; that it adopts these principles as constituting one of the main foundations of its political creed, and is resolved to carry them out in their obvious meaning and import.

And that we may more distinctly meet the issue on which a sectional party, subsisting exclusively on slavery agitation, now relies to test the fidelity of the people, north and south, to the constitution and the Union—

1. *Resolved,* That claiming fellowship with and desiring the co-operation of all who regard the preservation of the Union under the constitution as the paramount issue, and repudiating all sectional parties and platforms concerning domestic slavery which seek to embroil the states and incite to treason and armed resistance to law in the territories, and whose avowed purpose, if consummated, must end in civil war and disunion, the American democracy recognize and adopt the principles contained in the organic laws establishing the territories of Nebraska and Kansas, as embodying the only sound and safe solution of the slavery question, upon which the great national

idea of the people of this whole country can repose in its determined conservation of the Union, and non-interference of Congress with slavery in the territories or in the District of Columbia.

2. That this was the basis of the compromise of 1850, confirmed by both the Democratic and Whig parties in national conventions, ratified by the people in the election of 1852, and rightly applied to the organization of the territories in 1854.

3. That by the uniform application of the Democratic principle to the organization of territories and the admission of new states, with or without domestic slavery, as they may elect, the equal rights of all the states will be preserved intact, the original compacts of the constitution maintained inviolate, and the perpetuity and expansion of the Union insured to its utmost capacity of embracing, in peace and harmony, every future American state that may be constituted or annexed with a republican form of government.

*Resolved*, That we recognize the right of the people of all the territories, including Kansas and Nebraska, acting through the legally and fairly expressed will of the majority of the actual residents, and whenever the number of their inhabitants justifies it, to form a constitution, with or without domestic slavery, and be admitted into the Union upon terms of perfect equality with the other states.

*Resolved, finally*, That in view of the condition of the popular institutions in the old world (and the dangerous tendencies of sectional agitation, combined with the attempt to enforce civil and religious disabilities against the rights of acquiring and enjoying citizenship in our own land), a high and sacred duty is devolved, with increased responsibility, upon the Democratic party of this country, as the party of the Union, to uphold and maintain the rights of every state, and thereby the union of the states, and to sustain and advance among us constitutional liberty, by continuing to resist all monopolies and exclusive legislation for the benefit of the few at the expense of the many, and by a vigilant and constant adherence to those principles and compromises of the constitution which are broad enough and strong enough to embrace and uphold the Union as it was, the

Union as it is, and the Union as it shall be, in the full expression of the energies and capacity of this great and progressive people.

1. *Resolved*, That there are questions connected with the foreign policy of this country which are inferior to no domestic questions whatever. The time has come for the people of the United States to declare themselves in favor of free seas and progressive free trade throughout the world, and, by solemn manifestations, to place their moral influence at the side of their successful example.

2. *Resolved*, That our geographical and political position with reference to the other states of this continent, no less than the interest of our commerce and the development of our growing power, requires that we should hold sacred the principles involved in the Monroe doctrine. . . .

3. *Resolved*, That the great highway which nature, as well as the assent of states most immediately interested in its maintenance, has marked out for free communication between the Atlantic and Pacific oceans, constitutes one of the most important achievements realized by the spirit of modern times . . . ; and that result would be secured by a timely and efficient exertion of the control which we have the right to claim over it; and no power on earth should be suffered to impede or clog its progress by any interference with relations that may suit our policy to establish between our government and the governments of the states within whose dominions it lies; . . .

4. *Resolved*, That in view of so commanding an interest, the people of the United States cannot but sympathize with the efforts which are being made by the people of Central America to regenerate that portion of the continent which covers the passage across the inter-oceanic isthmus.

5. *Resolved*, That the Democratic party will expect of the next administration that every proper effort be made to insure our ascendency in the Gulf of Mexico, and to maintain permanent protection to the great outlets through which are emptied into its waters the products raised out of the soil and the commodities created by the industry of the people of our western valleys and of the Union at large.

6. *Resolved*, That the administration of Franklin Pierce has been true to Democratic principles, and, therefore, true to the great interests of the country; in the face of violent opposition, he has maintained the laws at home and vindicated the rights of American citizens abroad, and, therefore, we proclaim our unqualified admiration of his measures and policy.

## REVIEW QUESTIONS

1. What did the Democrats indicate was the greatest threat to the American nation?
2. Did they address the slavery problem as a civil rights or states rights issue?
3. Why did they praise the legislative compromises of the early 1850s?
4. How did the Democratic Party promote itself at the expense of the Republican Party?

## THE REPUBLICAN PARTY

# The Republican Platform (1856)

*The new Republican Party, accused of being a sectional rather than a national organization by the Democrats, held its convention in Philadelphia. The party's emphasis on the containment of slavery, as well as the composition of its membership, did give some validity to the charge. Many of its members had been Whigs, and their influence was seen in the economic planks that advocated internal improvements financed by the federal government. Abolitionists and Free Soilers, coming from the Whig and Democratic parties, also influenced the creation of the party's platform and the nomination of candidates. The Republicans elected John Fremont of California, formerly a Free Soil Democrat, as their presidential candidate and William Dayton of New Jersey, a former Whig, as his running mate.*

From Thomas V. Cooper and Hector T. Fenton, *American Politics from the Beginning to Date* (Chicago: Charles R. Brodix, 1882), pp. 39–40.

This convention of delegates, assembled in pursuance of a call addressed to the people of the United States, without regard to past political differences or divisions, who are opposed to the repeal of the Missouri Compromise, to the policy of the present administration, to the extension of slavery into free territory; in favor of admitting Kansas as a free state, of restoring the action of the Federal government to the principles of Washington and Jefferson; and who purpose to unite in presenting candidates for the offices of President and Vice-President, do resolve as follows:

*Resolved*, That the maintenance of the principles promulgated in the Declaration of Independence, and embodied in the federal constitution, is essential to the preservation of our Republican institutions, and that the federal constitution, the rights of the states, and the union of the states, shall be preserved.

*Resolved*, That with our republican fathers we hold it to be a self-evident truth that all men are endowed with the inalienable rights to life, liberty, and the pursuit of happiness, and that the primary object and ulterior design of our Federal government were, to secure these rights to all persons within its exclusive jurisdiction; that as our republican fathers, when they had abolished slavery in all our national territory, ordained that no person should be deprived of life, liberty, or property, without due process of law, it becomes our duty to maintain this provision of the constitution against all attempts to violate it for the purpose of establishing slavery in any territory of the United States, by positive legislation, prohibiting its existence or extension therein. That we deny the authority of Congress, of a territorial legislature, of any individual or association of individuals, to give legal existence to slavery in any territory of the United States, while the present constitution shall be maintained.

*Resolved*, That the constitution confers upon Congress sovereign power over the territories of the United States for their government, and that in the exercise of this power it is both the right and the imperative duty of Congress to prohibit in the territories those twin relics of barbarism—polygamy and slavery.

*Resolved*, That while the constitution of the United States was ordained and established, in order to form a more perfect union, establish justice, insure domestic tranquillity, provide for the common defense, promote the general welfare, and secure the blessings of liberty, and contains ample provisions for the protection of the life, liberty, and property of every citizen, the dearest constitutional rights of the people of Kansas have been fraudulently and violently taken from them; their territory has been invaded by an armed force; spurious and pretended legislative, judicial, and executive officers have been set over them, by whose usurped authority, sustained by the military power of the government, tyrannical and unconstitutional laws have been enacted and enforced; the rights of the people to keep and bear arms have been infringed; test oaths of an extraordinary and entangling nature have been imposed, as a condition of exercising the right of suffrage and holding office; the right of an accused person to a speedy and public trial by an impartial jury has been denied; the right of the people to be secure in their persons, houses, papers, and effects against

unreasonable searches and seizures, has been violated; they have been deprived of life, liberty, and property without due process of law; that the freedom of speech and of the press has been abridged; the right to choose their representatives has been made of no effect; murders, robberies, and arsons have been instigated or encouraged, and the offenders have been allowed to go unpunished; that all these things have been done with the knowledge, sanction, and procurement of the present national administration; and that for this high crime against the constitution, the Union, and humanity, we arraign the administration, the President, his advisers, agents, supporters, apologists, and accessories, either before or after the facts, before the country and before the world; and that it is our fixed purpose to bring the actual perpetrators of these atrocious outrages, and their accomplices, to a sure and condign punishment hereafter.

*Resolved*, That Kansas should be immediately admitted as a state of the Union with her present free constitution, as at once the most effectual way of securing to her citizens the enjoyment of the rights and privileges to which they are entitled, and of ending the civil strife now raging in her territory.

*Resolved*, That the highwayman's plea that "might makes right," embodied in the Ostend circular, was in every respect unworthy of American diplomacy, and would bring shame and dishonor upon any government or people that gave it their sanction.

*Resolved*, That a railroad to the Pacific ocean, by the most central and practicable route, is imperatively demanded by the interests of the whole country, and that the Federal government ought to render immediate and efficient aid in its construction, and, as an auxiliary thereto, the immediate construction of an emigrant route on the line of the railroad.

*Resolved*, That appropriations of Congress for the improvement of rivers and harbors of a national character, required for the accommodation and security of our existing commerce, are authorized by the constitution, and justified by the obligation of government to protect the lives and property of its citizens.

*Resolved*, That we invite the affiliation and co-operation of the men of all parties, however differing from us in other respects, in support of the principles herein declared; and believing that the spirit of our institutions, as well as the constitution of our country, guarantees liberty of conscience and equality of rights among citizens, we oppose all proscriptive legislation affecting their security.

## REVIEW QUESTIONS

1. What did Republicans advocate in their platform? What did they condemn?
2. Did they answer the Democrats' charge that their endeavors would destroy the Union?
3. Was the Republican platform primarily an idealistic or pragmatic document?
4. How did it reflect the influence of the Declaration of Independence?
5. Was the focus on the Declaration as opposed to the Constitution significant? Explain.

# FROM *Dred Scott v. Sandford* (1857)

*James Buchanan, the Democratic candidate, won the presidency in 1856, but the joy of that success was soon buried under mounting troubles. As Buchanan tried to use his executive powers and political alliances to soothe the savage beasts of special and sectional interests, the Supreme Court stepped into the fray. It did so through the case of* Dred Scott v. Sandford. *Scott, an African American, had brought suit in the state circuit court of St. Louis County, Missouri, in 1846 claiming that earlier residence in Illinois and the free territory of Wisconsin had made him free. The verdict and judgment were in his favor, but the state's supreme court later reversed them. In the meantime Scott sued his former master, John F. A. Sandford, for assault against himself, his wife, and his two daughters. When the case came up in 1854, Sandford defended himself by arguing that Scott and his wife and daughters were his slaves and that "at the times mentioned in the plaintiff's declaration, the defendant, claiming to be owner as aforesaid, laid his hands upon said plaintiff, Harriet, Eliza, and Lizzie, and imprisoned them, doing in this respect, however, no more than what he might lawfully do, if they were of right his slaves at such times." The jury found for Sandford. Scott then filed a bill of exceptions against some of the proceedings of the court. That bill led to the Supreme Court case that was first argued in 1855 and then re-argued at the 1856 December term. Chief Justice Roger B. Taney delivered the court's opinion in March 1857. In rendering its decision against Scott, the court also passed judgment on the constitutionality of the Missouri Compromise and challenged the concept of popular sovereignty.*

From *Report of the Decision of the Supreme Court . . . in the Case of Dred Scott versus John F. A. Sandford* (1857; New York: Da Capo Press, 1970), pp. 9–14, 16, 32–34, 36–38, 53–58. [Editorial insertions appear in square brackets—*Ed.*]

*    *    *

The question is simply this: Can a negro, whose ancestors were imported into this country, and sold as slaves, become a member of the political community formed and brought into existence by the Constitution of the United States, and as such become entitled to all the rights, and privileges, and immunities, guarantied by that instrument to the citizen? One of which rights is the privilege of suing in a court of the United States in the cases specified in the Constitution.

It will be observed, that the plea applies to that class of persons only whose ancestors were negroes of the African race, and imported into this country, and sold and held as slaves. The only matter in issue before the court, therefore, is, whether the descendants of such slaves, when they shall be emancipated, or who are born of parents who had become free before their birth, are citizens of a State, in the sense in which the word citizen is used in the Constitution of the United States. . . .

The situation of this population was altogether unlike that of the Indian race. The latter, it is true, formed no part of the colonial communities, and never amalgamated with them in social connections or in government. But although they were uncivilized, they were yet a free and independent people, associated together in nations or tribes, and governed by their own laws. Many of these political communities were situated in territories to which the white race claimed the ultimate right of dominion. But that claim was acknowledged to be subject to the right of the Indians to occupy it as long as they thought proper, and neither the English nor colonial Governments claimed or exercised any dominion over the tribe or nation by whom it was occupied, nor claimed the right to the possession of the territory, until the tribe or nation consented to cede it. These Indian Governments were regarded and treated as foreign Governments, . . . Treaties have been negotiated with them, and their alliance sought for in war; and the people who compose these Indian political communities have always been treated as foreigners not living under our Government. It is true that the course of events has brought the Indian tribes within the limits of the United States under subjection to the white race; and it has been found necessary, for their sake as well as our own, to regard them as in a state of pupilage, and to legislate to a certain extent over them and the territory they occupy. But they may, without doubt, like the subjects of any other foreign Government, be naturalized by the authority of Congress, and become citizens of a State, and of the United States; and if an individual should leave his nation or tribe, and take up his abode among the white population, he would be entitled to all the rights and privileges which would belong to an emigrant from any other foreign people.

We proceed to examine the case as presented by the pleadings.

The words "people of the United States" and "citizens" are synonymous terms, and mean the same thing. They both describe the political body who, according to our republican institutions, form the sovereignty, and who hold the power and conduct the Government through their representatives. They are what we familiarly call the "sovereign people," and every citizen is one of this people, and a constituent member of this sovereignty. The question before us is, whether the class of persons described in the plea in abatement compose a portion of this people, and are constituent members of this sovereignty? We think they are not, and that they are not included, and were not intended to be included, under the word "citizens" in the Constitution, and can therefore claim none of the rights and privileges which that instrument provides for and secures to citizens of the United States. On the contrary, they were at that time considered as a subordinate and inferior class of beings, who had been subjugated by the dominant race, and, whether emancipated or not, yet remained subject to their authority, and had no rights or privileges but such as those who held the power and the Government might choose to grant them.

It is not the province of the court to decide upon the justice or injustice, the policy or impolicy, of these laws. The decision of that question belonged to the political or law-making power; to those who formed the sovereignty and framed the Constitution. The duty of the court is, to interpret the instrument they have framed, . . .

In discussing this question, we must not confound the rights of citizenship which a State may confer within its own limits, and the rights of citizenship as a member of the Union. It does not by any means follow, because he has all the rights and privileges of a citizen of a State, that he must be a citizen of the United States. He may have all of the rights and privileges of the citizen of a State, and yet not be entitled to the rights and privileges of a citizen in any other State. For, previous to the adoption of the Constitution of the United States, every State had the undoubted right to confer on whomsoever it pleased the character of citizen, and to endow him with all its rights. But this character of course was confined to the boundaries of the State, and gave him no rights or privileges in other States beyond those secured to him by the laws of nations and the comity of States. Nor have the several States surrendered the power of conferring these rights and privileges by adopting the Constitution of the United States. Each State may still confer them upon an alien, or any one it thinks proper, or upon any class or description of persons; yet he would not be a citizen in the sense in which that word is used in the Constitution of the United States, nor entitled to sue as such in one of its courts, nor to the privileges and immunities of a citizen in the other States. The rights which he would acquire would be restricted to the State which gave them. The Constitution has conferred on Congress the right to establish an uniform rule of naturalization, and this right is evidently exclusive, and has always been held by this court to be so. Consequently, no State, since the adoption of the Constitution, can by naturalizing an alien invest him with the rights and privileges secured to a citizen of a State under the Federal Government, . . .

\*  \*  \*

The question then arises, whether the provisions of the Constitution, in relation to the personal rights and privileges to which the citizen of a State should be entitled, embraced the negro African race, at that time in this country, or who might afterwards be imported, who had then or should afterwards be made free in any State; and to put it in the power of a single State to make him a citizen of the United States, and endue him with the full rights of citizenship in every other State without their consent? Does the Constitution of the United States act upon him whenever he shall be made free under the laws of a State, and raised there to the rank of a citizen, and immediately clothe him with all the privileges of a citizen in every other State, and in its own courts?

The court think the affirmative of these propositions cannot be maintained. And if it cannot, the plaintiff in error could not be a citizen of the State of Missouri, within the meaning of the Constitution of the United States, and, consequently, was not entitled to sue in its courts.

It is true, every person, and every class and description of persons, who were at the time of the adoption of the Constitution recognised as citizens in the several States, became also citizens of this new political body; but none other; it was formed by them, and for them and their posterity, but for no one else. . . .

\*  \*  \*

In the opinion of the court, the legislation and histories of the times, and the language used in the Declaration of Independence, show, that neither the class of persons who had been imported as slaves, nor their descendants, whether they had become free or not, were then acknowledged as a part of the people, nor intended to be included in the general words used in that memorable instrument.

It is difficult at this day to realize the state of public opinion in relation to that unfortunate race, which prevailed in the civilized and enlightened portions of the world at the time of the Declaration of Independence, and when the Constitution of the United States was framed and adopted. But the public history of every European nation displays it in a manner too plain to be mistaken.

They had for more than a century before been regarded as beings of an inferior order, and altogether

unfit to associate with the white race, either in social or political relations; and so far inferior, that
they had no rights which the white man
was bound to respect; and that the negro might
justly and lawfully be reduced to slavery for his
benefit. . . .

*       *       *

The opinion thus entertained and acted upon in
England was naturally impressed upon the colonies they founded on this side of the Atlantic.
And, accordingly, a negro of the African race
was regarded by them as an article of property,
and held, and bought and sold as such, in every one
of the thirteen colonies which united in
the Declaration of Independence, and afterwards
formed the Constitution of the United States.
The slaves were more or less numerous in the different colonies, as slave labor was found more or less
profitable. But no one seems to have doubted the
correctness of the prevailing opinion of the time.

*       *       *

[The Declaration of Independence] proceeds to
say: "We hold these truths to be self-evident: that
all men are created equal; that they are endowed by
their Creator with certain unalienable rights; that
among them is life, liberty, and the pursuit of happiness; that to secure these rights, Governments are
instituted, deriving their just powers from the consent of the governed."

The general words above quoted would seem to
embrace the whole human family, and if they were
used in a similar instrument at this day would be
so understood. But it is too clear for dispute, that
the enslaved African race were not intended to be
included, and formed no part of the people who
framed and adopted this declaration; for if the language, as understood in that day, would embrace
them, the conduct of the distinguished men who
framed the Declaration of Independence would
have been utterly and flagrantly inconsistent with
the principles they asserted; and instead of the
sympathy of mankind, to which they so confidently appealed, they would have deserved and received universal rebuke and reprobation.

Yet the men who framed this declaration were
great men—high in literary acquirements—high in
their sense of honor, and incapable of asserting
principles inconsistent with those on which they
were acting. They perfectly understood the meaning of the language they used, and how it would be
understood by others; and they knew that it would
not in any part of the civilized world be supposed
to embrace the negro race, which, by common
consent, had been excluded from civilized Governments and the family of nations, and doomed to
slavery. They spoke and acted according to the then
established doctrines and principles, and in the ordinary language of the day, and no one misunderstood them. . . .

This state of public opinion had undergone
no change when the Constitution was adopted,
as is equally evident from its provisions and
language.

*       *       *

No one, we presume, supposes that any change in
public opinion or feeling, in relation to this unfortunate race, in the civilized nations of Europe or in
this country, should induce the court to give to the
words of the Constitution a more liberal construction in their favor than they were intended to bear
when the instrument was framed and adopted.
Such an argument would be altogether inadmissible in any tribunal called on to interpret it. If any
of its provisions are deemed unjust, there is a mode
prescribed in the instrument itself by which it may
be amended; but while it remains unaltered, it
must be construed now as it was understood at the
time of its adoption. . . . Any other rule of construction would abrogate the judicial character of
this court, and make it the mere reflex of the popular opinion or passion of the day. This court was
not created by the Constitution for such purposes.
Higher and graver trusts have been confided to it,
and it must not falter in the path of duty.

What the construction was at that time, we
think can hardly admit of doubt. We have the language of the Declaration of Independence and of
the Articles of Confederation, in addition to the
plain words of the Constitution itself; we have

the legislation of the different States, before, about the time, and since, the Constitution was adopted; we have the legislation of Congress, from the time of its adoption to a recent period; and we have the constant and uniform action of the Executive Department, all concurring together, and leading to the same result. And if anything in relation to the construction of the Constitution can be regarded as settled, it is that which we now give to the word "citizen" and the word "people."

And upon a full and careful consideration of the subject, the court is of opinion, that, upon the facts stated in the plea in abatement, Dred Scott was not a citizen of Missouri within the meaning of the Constitution of the United States, and not entitled as such to sue in its courts; and, consequently, that the Circuit Court had no jurisdiction of the case, and that the judgment on the plea in abatement is erroneous.

. . . [T]he question as to the jurisdiction of the Circuit Court is presented on the face of the bill of exception itself, taken by the plaintiff at the trial; for he admits that he and his wife were born slaves, but endeavors to make out his title to freedom and citizenship by showing that they were taken by their owner to certain places, hereinafter mentioned, where slavery could not by law exist, and that they thereby became free, and upon their return to Missouri became citizens of that State.

Now, if the removal of which he speaks did not give them their freedom, then by his own admission he is still a slave; and whatever opinions may be entertained in favor of the citizenship of a free person of the African race, no one supposes that a slave is a citizen of the State or of the United States. If, therefore, the acts done by his owner did not make them free persons, he is still a slave, and certainly incapable of suing in the character of a citizen.

The principle of law is too well settled to be disputed, that a court can give no judgment for either party, where it has no jurisdiction; and if, upon the showing of Scott himself, it appeared that he was still a slave, the case ought to have been dismissed, and the judgment against him and in favor of the defendant for costs, is, like that on the plea

in abatement, erroneous, and the suit ought to have been dismissed by the Circuit Court for want of jurisdiction in that court.

\*     \*     \*

. . . [I]n this case it *does appear* that the plaintiff was born a slave; and if the facts upon which he relies have not made him free, then it appears affirmatively on the record that he is not a citizen, and consequently his suit against Sandford was not a suit between citizens of different States, and the court had no authority to pass any judgment between the parties. The suit ought, in this view of it, to have been dismissed by the Circuit Court, and its judgment in favor of Sandford is erroneous, and must be reversed.

\*     \*     \*

We proceed, therefore, to inquire whether the facts relied on by the plaintiff entitled him to his freedom.

The case, as he himself states it, on the record brought here by his writ of error, is this:

The plaintiff was a negro slave, belonging to Dr. Emerson, who was a surgeon in the army of the United States. In the year 1834, he took the plaintiff from the State of Missouri to the military post at Rock Island, in the State of Illinois, and held him there as a slave until the month of April or May, 1836. At the time last mentioned, said Dr. Emerson removed the plaintiff from said military post at Rock Island to the military post at Fort Snelling, situate on the west bank of the Mississippi river, in the Territory known as Upper Louisiana, acquired by the United States of France, and situate north of the latitude of thirty-six degrees thirty minutes north, and north of the State of Missouri. Said Dr. Emerson held the plaintiff in slavery at said Fort Snelling, from said last-mentioned date until the year 1838.

In the year 1835, Harriet, who is named in the second count of the plaintiff's declaration, was the negro slave of Major Taliaferro, who belonged to the army of the United States. In that year, 1835, said Major Taliaferro took said Harriet to said Fort Snelling, a military post, situated as hereinbefore stated, and kept her there as a slave until the year 1836, and then sold and delivered her as a slave, at said Fort Snelling, unto the said Dr. Emerson hereinbefore named. Said Dr. Emerson held said Harriet in slavery at said Fort Snelling until the year 1838.

In the year 1836, the plaintiff and Harriet intermarried, at Fort Snelling, with the consent of Dr. Emerson, who then claimed to be their master and owner. Eliza and Lizzie, named in the third count of the plaintiff's declaration, are the fruit of that marriage. . . .

In the year 1838, said Dr. Emerson removed the plaintiff and said Harriet, and their said daughter Eliza, from said Fort Snelling to the State of Missouri, where they have ever since resided.

Before the commencement of this suit, said Dr. Emerson sold and conveyed the plaintiff, and Harriet, Eliza, and Lizzie, to the defendant, as slaves, and the defendant has ever since claimed to hold them, and each of them, as slaves.

In considering this part of the controversy, two questions arise: 1. Was he, together with his family, free in Missouri by reason of the stay in the territory of the United States hereinbefore mentioned? And 2. If they were not, is Scott himself free by reason of his removal to Rock Island, in the State of Illinois, as stated in the above admissions?

We proceed to examine the first question.

The act of Congress, upon which the plaintiff relies, declares that slavery and involuntary servitude, except as a punishment for crime, shall be forever prohibited in all that part of the territory ceded by France, under the name of Louisiana, which lies north of thirty-six degrees thirty minutes north latitude, and not included within the limits of Missouri. And the difficulty which meets us at the threshold of this part of the inquiry is, whether Congress was authorized to pass this law under any of the powers granted to it by the Constitution; for if the authority is not given by that instrument, it is the duty of this court to declare it void and inoperative, and incapable of conferring freedom upon any one who is held as a slave under the laws of any one of the States.

The counsel for the plaintiff has laid much stress upon that article in the Constitution which confers on Congress the power "to dispose of and make all needful rules and regulations respecting the territory or other property belonging to the United States;" but, in the judgment of the court, that provision has no bearing on the present controversy, and the power there given, whatever it may be, is confined, and was intended to be confined, to the territory which at that time belonged to, or was claimed by, the United States, and was within their boundaries as settled by the treaty with Great Britain, and can have no influence upon a territory afterwards acquired from a foreign Government. It was a special provision for a known and particular territory, and to meet a present emergency, and nothing more.

\*    \*    \*

. . . The power to expand the territory of the United States by the admission of new States is plainly given [to Congress]; and in the construction of this power by all the departments of the Government, it has been held to authorize the acquisition of territory, not fit for admission at the time, but to be admitted as soon as its population and situation would entitle it to admission. It is acquired to become a State, and not to be held as a colony and governed by Congress with absolute authority; . . . All we mean to say on this point is, that, as there is no express regulation in the Constitution defining the power which the General Government may exercise over the person or property of a citizen in a Territory thus acquired, the court must necessarily look to the provisions and principles of the Constitution, and its distribution of powers, for the rules and principles by which its decision must be governed.

Taking this rule to guide us, it may be safely assumed that citizens of the United States who migrate to a Territory belonging to the people of the United States, cannot be ruled as mere colonists, dependent upon the will of the General Government, and to be governed by any laws it may think proper to impose. The principle upon which our Governments rest, and upon which alone they continue to exist, is the union of States, sovereign and independent within their own limits in their internal and domestic concerns, and bound together as one people by a General Government, possessing certain enumerated and restricted powers, . . . A power, therefore, in the General Government to obtain and hold colonies and dependent territories, over which they might legislate without restriction, would be inconsistent with its own existence in its present form. Whatever it acquires, it acquires for the benefit of the people of the several States who created it. It is their trustee acting for them, and charged with the duty of promoting the interests of the whole people of the Union in the exercise of the powers specifically granted.

\*    \*    \*

. . . The power to acquire necessarily carries with it the power to preserve and apply to the purposes for which it was acquired. The form of government to be established necessarily rested in the discretion of Congress. . . . [T]he choice of the mode must depend upon the exercise of a discretionary power by Congress, acting within the scope of its constitutional authority, and not infringing upon the rights of person or rights of property of the citizen who might go there to reside, or for any other lawful purpose. It was acquired by the exercise of this discretion, and it must be held and governed in like manner, until it is fitted to be a State.

But the power of Congress over the person or property of a citizen can never be a mere discretionary power under our Constitution and form of Government. The powers of the Government and the rights and privileges of the citizen are regulated and plainly defined by the Constitution itself. And when the Territory becomes a part of the United States, the Federal Government enters into possession in the character impressed upon it by those who created it. It enters upon it with its powers over the citizen strictly defined, and limited by the Constitution, from which it derives its own existence, and by virtue of which alone it continues to exist and act as a Government and sovereignty. It has no power of any kind beyond it; and it cannot, when it enters a Territory of the United States, put off its character, and assume discretionary or despotic powers which the Constitution has denied to it. It cannot create for itself a new character sep-

arated from the citizens of the United States, and the duties it owes them under the provisions of the Constitution. The Territory being a part of the United States, the Government and the citizen both enter it under the authority of the Constitution, with their respective rights defined and marked out; and the Federal Government can exercise no power over his person or property, beyond what that instrument confers, nor lawfully deny any right which it has reserved.

A reference to a few of the provisions of the Constitution will illustrate this proposition.

For example, no one, we presume, will contend that Congress can make any law in a Territory respecting the establishment of religion, or the free exercise thereof, or abridging the freedom of speech or of the press, or the right of the people of the Territory peaceably to assemble, and to petition the Government for the redress of grievances.

\*    \*    \*

These powers, and others, in relation to rights of person, which it is not necessary here to enumerate, are, in express and positive terms, denied to the General Government; and the rights of private property have been guarded with equal care. Thus the rights of property are united with the rights of person, and placed on the same ground by the fifth amendment to the Constitution, which provides that no person shall be deprived of life, liberty, and property, without due process of law. And an act of Congress which deprives a citizen of the United States of his liberty or property, merely because he came himself or brought his property into a particular Territory of the United States, and who had committed no offence against the laws, could hardly be dignified with the name of due process of law.

\*    \*    \*

It seems, however, to be supposed, that there is a difference between property in a slave and other property, and that different rules may be applied to it in expounding the Constitution of the United States. . . .

\*    \*    \*

Now, as we have already said in an earlier part of this opinion, upon a different point, the right of property in a slave is distinctly and expressly affirmed in the Constitution. The right to traffic in it, like an ordinary article of merchandise and property, was guarantied to the citizens of the United States, in every State that might desire it, for twenty years. And the Government in express terms is pledged to protect it in all future time, if the slave escapes from his owner. This is done in plain words—too plain to be misunderstood. And no word can be found in the Constitution which gives Congress a greater power over slave property, or which entitles property of that kind to less protection than property of any other description. The only power conferred is the power coupled with the duty of guarding and protecting the owner in his rights.

Upon these considerations, it is the opinion of the court that the act of Congress which prohibited a citizen from holding and owning property of this kind in the territory of the United States north of the line therein mentioned, is not warranted by the Constitution, and is therefore void; and that neither Dred Scott himself, nor any of his family, were made free by being carried into this territory; even if they had been carried there by the owner, with the intention of becoming a permanent resident.

\* \* \*

## REVIEW QUESTIONS

1. Why does Chief Justice Taney note that African Americans did not hold the same status before the court as Native Americans?
2. Why does he make a distinction between state and national citizenship?
3. Was he completely accurate in his presentation of historical precedents to support the Court's contention that African Americans could not be citizens? Did historical precedents alone inform the decision of the Court?
4. What argument does he present to show that the Missouri Compromise was unconstitutional?
5. How does Chief Justice Taney's interpretation of the Constitution compare to Marshall's in earlier cases (see Chapters 8 and 10)?

# ABRAHAM LINCOLN AND STEPHEN DOUGLAS

## FROM The Lincoln-Douglas Debates (1858)

*Abraham Lincoln was practicing rather than making law at the beginning of the decade, but as acts he considered dangerous were passed, he left the courtroom for convention floors and speakers' platforms. Lincoln had served before in the Illinois legislature and for one term in Congress as a Whig. He was still a Whig in 1854 when he again entered the public arena to oppose the Kansas-Nebraska Act. In 1856, however, Lincoln left the weakened Whigs to help found the Republican Party of Illinois and, by extension, the national Republican Party. In June 1858 the Republican Party endorsed him for the Senate seat then held by Stephen Douglas. Once Lincoln had the Republican nomination he began following Douglas through the state of Illinois in order to hear and refute his opponent's charges more effectively. It was also a way to pressure Douglas into agreeing to public debates. Lincoln and Douglas debated seven times—21 and 27 August, 15 and 18 September, and 7, 13, and 15 October— at seven different places—Ottawa, Freeport, Jonesboro, Charleston, Galesburg, Quincy, and Alton—in Illinois. All except the Jonesboro debate drew audiences of over ten thousand people. The debates were set up so that one candidate would lead off, the other would answer, and then the first would have a short rejoinder. Lincoln and Douglas took turns on the lead position. In all of these debates they covered much of the same material, but the emphasis of each man's argument shifted a bit each time as he answered issues raised in the previous debate as well as any intervening speeches.*

From Abraham Lincoln, *Speeches and Writings, 1832–1858* (New York: The Library of America, 1989), pp. 774–81, 785–86, 788–95, 797–98, 800–08, 810–12, 814–15, 818–19. Reprinted by permission of the Abraham Lincoln Association.

## Seventh Lincoln-Douglas Debate, Alton, Illinois

*Seventh, and last joint debate. October 15, 1858. Douglas as reported in the* Chicago Times. *Lincoln as reported in the* Press & Tribune.

### Senator Douglas' Speech

\*   \*   \*

LADIES AND GENTLEMEN: It is now nearly four months since the canvass between Mr. Lincoln and myself commenced. On the 16th of June the Republican Convention assembled at Springfield and nominated Mr. Lincoln as their candidate for the U.S. Senate, and he, on that occasion, delivered a speech in which he laid down what he understood to be the Republican creed and the platform on which he proposed to stand during the contest. The principal points in that speech of Mr. Lincoln's were: First, that this government could not endure permanently divided into free and slave States, as our fathers made it; that they must all become free or all become slave; all become one thing or all become the other, otherwise this Union could not continue to exist. . . . His second proposition was a crusade against the Supreme court of the United States because of the Dred Scott decision; urging as an especial reason for his opposition to that decision that it deprived the negroes of the rights and benefits of that clause in the Constitution of the United States which guarantees to the citizens of each State, all the rights, privileges, and immunities of the citizens of the several States. On the 10th of July I returned home, and delivered a speech to the people of Chicago, in which I announced it to be my purpose to appeal to the people of Illinois to sustain the course I had pursued in Congress. In that speech I joined issue with Mr. Lincoln on the points which he had presented. Thus there was an issue clear and distinct made up between us on these two propositions laid down in the speech of Mr. Lincoln at Springfield, and controverted by me in my reply to him at Chicago. On the next day, the 11th of July, Mr. Lincoln replied to me at Chicago, explaining at some length, and re-affirming the positions which he had taken in his Springfield speech. In that Chicago speech he even went further than he had before, and uttered sentiments in regard to the negro being on an equality with the white man. ("That's so.") He adopted in support of this position the argument which Lovejoy and Codding, and other Abolition lecturers had made familiar in the northern and central portions of the State, to wit: that the Declaration of Independence having declared all men free and equal, by Divine law, also that negro equality was an inalienable right, of which they could not be deprived. . . .

The issue thus being made up between Mr. Lincoln and myself on three points, we went before the people of the State. . . . I took up Mr. Lincoln's three propositions in my several speeches, analyzed them, and pointed out what I believed to be the radical errors contained in them. First, in regard to his doctrine that this government was in violation of the law of God which says, that a house divided against itself cannot stand, I repudiated it as a slander upon the immortal framers of our constitution. I then said, have often repeated, and now again assert, that in my opinion this government can endure forever, ("Good.") divided into free and slave States as our fathers made it,—each State having the right to prohibit, abolish or sustain slavery just as it pleases. ("Good," "right," and cheers.) This government was made upon the great basis of the sovereignty of the States, the right of each State to regulate its own domestic institutions to suit itself, and that right was conferred with understanding and expectation that inasmuch as each locality had separate interests, each locality must have different and distinct local and domestic institutions, corresponding to its wants and interests. Our fathers knew when they made the government, that the laws and institutions which were well adapted to the green mountains of Vermont, were unsuited to the rice plantations of South Carolina. . . . They knew that in a Republic as broad as this, having such a variety of soil, climate and interest, there must necessarily be a corresponding variety of local laws—the policy and institutions of each State adapted to its condition and wants. For this reason this Union was established on the right of each State to do as it pleased on the question of slavery, and every other question; and the various States were not allowed to complain of, much less interfere, with the policy of their neighbors. ("That's good doctrine," "that's the doctrine," and cheers.)

\*   \*   \*

. . . Why can he not say whether he is willing to allow the people of each State to have slavery or not as they please, and to come into the Union when they have the requisite population as a slave or a free State as they decide? I have no trouble in answering the question. I have said everywhere, and now repeat it to you, that if the people of Kansas want a slave State they have a right, under the constitution of the United States, to form such a State, and I will let them come into the Union with slavery or without, as they determine. ("That's right," "good," "hurrah for Douglas all the time," and cheers.) If the people of any other territory desire slavery let them have it. If they do not want it let them prohibit it. It is their business not mine. ("That's the doctrine.") It is none of your business in Missouri whether Kansas shall adopt slavery or reject it. It is the business of her people and none of yours. The people of Kansas has as much right to decide that question for themselves as you have in Missouri to decide it for yourselves, or we in Illinois to decide it for ourselves. ("That's what we believe," "We stand by that," and cheers.)

\*   \*   \*

My friends, there never was a time when it was as important for the Democratic party, for all national men, to rally and stand together as it is today. We find all sectional men giving up past differences and continuing the one question of slavery, and when we find sectional men thus uniting, we should unite to resist them and their treasonable designs. Such was the case in 1850, when Clay left the quiet and peace of his home, and again entered upon public life to quell agitation and restore peace to a distracted Union. Then we Democrats, with Cass at our head, welcomed Henry Clay, whom the whole nation regarded as having been preserved by God for the times. He became our leader in that great fight, and we rallied around him the same as the Whigs rallied around old Hickory in 1832, to put down nullification. (Cheers.) Thus you see that whilst Whigs and Democrats fought fearlessly in old times about banks, the tariff, distribution, the specie circular, and the sub-treasury, all united as a band of brothers when the peace, harmony, or integrity of the Union was imperiled. (Tremendous applause.) It was so in 1850, when abolitionism had even so far divided this country, North and South, as to endanger the peace of the Union; Whigs and Democrats united in establishing the compromise measures of that year, and restoring tranquillity and good feeling. These measures passed on the joint action of the two parties. They rested on the great principle that the people of each State and each territory should be left perfectly free to form and regulate their domestic institutions to suit themselves. You Whigs and we Democrats justified them in that principle. In 1854, when it became necessary to organize the territories of Kansas and Nebraska, I brought forward the bill on the same principle. In the Kansas-Nebraska bill you find it declared to be the true intent and meaning of the act not to legislate slavery into any State or territory, nor to exclude it therefrom, but to leave the people thereof perfectly free to form and regulate their domestic institutions in their own way. ("That's so," and cheers.) I stand on that same platform in 1858 that I did in 1850, 1854, and 1856. . . .

\*     \*     \*

. . . The whole South are rallying to the support of the doctrine that if the people of a Territory want slavery they have a right to have it, and if they do not want it that no power on earth can force it upon them. I hold that there is no principle on earth more sacred to all the friends of freedom than that which says that no institution, no law, no constitution, should be forced on an unwilling people contrary to their wishes; and I assert that the Kansas and Nebraska bill contains that principle. . . . I say to you that there is but one hope, one safety for this country, and that is to stand immovably by that principle which declares the right of each State and each territory to decide these questions for themselves. ("Hear him, hear him.") This government was founded on that principle, and must be administered in the same sense in which it was founded.

But the Abolition party really think that under the Declaration of Independence the negro is equal to the white man, and that negro equality is an inalienable right conferred by the Almighty, and hence, that all human laws in violation of it are null and void. With such men it is no use for me to argue. I hold that the signers of the Declaration of Independence had no reference to negroes at all

when they declared all men to be created equal. They did not mean negro, nor the savage Indians, nor the Fejee Islanders, nor any other barbarous race. They were speaking of white men. . . . But it does not follow, by any means, that merely because the negro is not a citizen, and merely because he is not our equal, that, therefore, he should be a slave. On the contrary, it does follow, that we ought to extend to the negro race, and to all other dependent races all the rights, all the privileges, and all the immunities which they can exercise consistently with the safety of society. Humanity requires that we should give them all these privileges; christianity commands that we should extend those privileges to them. The question then arises what are those privileges, and what is the nature and extent of them. My answer is that that is a question which each State must answer for itself. We in Illinois have decided it for ourselves. We tried slavery, kept it up for twelve years, and finding that it was not profitable we abolished it for that reason, and became a free State. We adopted in its stead the policy that a negro in this State shall not be a slave and shall not be a citizen. We have a right to adopt that policy. For my part I think it is a wise and sound policy for us. You in Missouri must judge for yourselves whether it is a wise policy for you. If you choose to follow our example, very good; if you reject it, still well, it is your business, not ours. . . . If the people of all the States will act on that great principle, and each State mind its own business, attend to its own affairs, take care of its own negroes and not meddle with its neighbors, then there will be peace between the North and the South, the East and the West, throughout the whole Union. (Cheers.) Why can we not thus have peace? Why should we thus allow a sectional party to agitate this country, to array the North against the South, and convert us into enemies instead of friends, merely that a few ambitious men may ride into power on a sectional hobby? . . .

## Mr. Lincoln's Reply

On being introduced to the audience, after the cheering had subsided Mr. Lincoln said:

LADIES AND GENTLEMEN: . . .

\*    \*    \*

. . . I have heard the Judge state two or three times what he has stated to day—that in a speech which I made at Springfield, Illinois, I had in a very especial manner, complained that the Supreme Court in the Dred Scott case had decided that a negro could never be a citizen of the United States. I have omitted by some accident heretofore to analyze this statement, and it is required of me to notice it now. In point of fact it is *untrue*. I never have complained *especially* of the Dred Scott decision because it held that a negro could not be a citizen, and the Judge is always wrong when he says I ever did so complain of it. I have the speech here, and I will thank him or any of his friends to show where I said that a negro should be a citizen, and complained especially of the Dred Scott decision because it declared he could not be one. I have done no such thing, . . . I spoke of the Dred Scott decision . . . endeavoring to prove that the Dred Scott decision was a portion of a system or scheme to make slavery national in this country. I pointed out what things had been decided by the court. I mentioned as a fact that they had decided that a negro could not be a citizen—that they had done so, as I supposed, to deprive the negro, under all circumstances, of the remotest possibility of ever becoming a citizen and claiming the rights of a citizen of the United States under a certain clause of the Constitution. I stated that, without making any complaint of it at all. I then went on and stated the other points decided in the case, . . .

Out of this, Judge Douglas builds up his beautiful fabrication—of my purpose to introduce a perfect, social, and political equality between the white and black races. His assertion that I made an "especial objection" (that is his exact language) to the decision on this account, is untrue in point of fact.

\*    \*    \*

You have heard him frequently allude to my controversy with him in regard to the Declaration of Independence. I confess that I have had a struggle with Judge Douglas on that matter, and I will try briefly to place myself right in regard to it on this occasion. I said— . . .

It may be argued that there are certain conditions that make necessities and impose them upon us, and to the extent that a necessity is imposed upon a man he must submit to it. I think that was the condition in which we found ourselves when we established this government. We had slaves among us, we could not get our Constitution unless we permitted them to remain in slavery, we could not secure the good we did secure if we grasped for more; and having by necessity submitted to that much, it does not destroy the principle that is the charter of our liberties. Let that charter remain as our standard.

Now I have upon all occasions declared as strongly as Judge Douglas against the disposition to interfere with the existing institution of slavery. You hear me read it from the same speech from which he takes garbled extracts for the purpose of proving upon me a disposition to interfere with the institution of slavery, and establish a perfect social and political equality between negroes and white people.

Allow me while upon this subject briefly to present one other extract from a speech of mine, more than a year ago, at Springfield, in discussing this very same question, soon after Judge Douglas took his ground that negroes were not included in the Declaration of Independence:

I think the authors of that notable instrument intended to include *all* men, but they did not mean to declare all men equal *in all respects*. They did not mean to say all men were equal in color, size, intellect, moral development or social capacity. They defined with tolerable distinctness in what they did consider all men created equal—equal in certain inalienable rights, among which are life, liberty and the pursuit of happiness. This they said, and this they meant. They did not mean to assert the obvious untruth, that all were then actually enjoying that equality, nor yet, that they were about to confer it immediately upon them. In fact they had no power to confer such a boon. They meant simply to declare the *right* so that the *enforcement* of it might follow as fast as circumstances should permit.

They meant to set up a standard maxim for free society which should be familiar to all: constantly looked to, constantly labored for, and even though never perfectly attained, constantly approximated and thereby constantly spreading and deepening its influence and augmenting the happiness and value of life to all people, of all colors, everywhere.

There again are the sentiments I have expressed in regard to the Declaration of Independence upon a former occasion—sentiments which have been put in print and read wherever anybody cared to know what so humble an individual as myself chose to say in regard to it.

*    *    *

The principle upon which I have insisted in this canvass, is in relation to laying the foundations of new societies. I have never sought to apply these principles to the old States for the purpose of abolishing slavery in those States. It is nothing but a miserable perversion of what I *have* said, to assume that I have declared Missouri, or any other slave State shall emancipate her slaves. I have proposed no such thing. . . .

*    *    *

. . . I have said, and I repeat, my wish is that the further spread of it may be arrested, and that it may be placed where the public mind shall rest in the belief that it is in the course of ultimate extinction. (Great applause.) . . . I entertain the opinion upon evidence sufficient to my mind, that the fathers of this Government placed that institution where the public mind *did* rest in the belief that it was in the course of ultimate extinction. Let me ask why they made provision that the source of slavery—the African slave trade—should be cut off at the end of twenty years? Why did they make provision that in all the new territory we owned at that time slavery should be forever inhibited? Why stop its spread in one direction and cut off its source in another, if they did not look to its being placed in the course of ultimate extinction?

Again; the institution of slavery is only mentioned in the Constitution of the United States two or three times, and in neither of these cases does the word "slavery" or "negro race" occur; but covert

language is used each time, and for a purpose full of significance. . . .

*    *    *

. . . I understand the contemporaneous history of those times to be that covert language was used with a purpose, and that purpose was that in our Constitution, which it was hoped and is still hoped will endure forever—when it should be read by intelligent and patriotic men, after the institution of slavery had passed from among us—there should be nothing on the face of the great charter of liberty suggesting that such a thing as negro slavery had ever existed among us. (Enthusiastic applause.) This is part of the evidence that the fathers of the Government expected and intended the institution of slavery to come to an end. . . .

. . . I have not only made the declaration that I do not *mean* to produce a conflict between the States, but I have tried to show by fair reasoning, and I think I have shown to the minds of fair men, that I propose nothing but what has a most peaceful tendency. The quotation that I happened to make in that Springfield speech, that "a house divided against itself cannot stand," and which has proved so offensive to the Judge, was part and parcel of the same thing. He tries to show that variety in the domestic institutions of the different States is necessary and indispensable. I do not dispute it. I have no controversy with Judge Douglas about that. . . . I understand, I hope, quite as well as Judge Douglas or anybody else, that the variety in the soil and climate and face of the country, and consequent variety in the industrial pursuits and productions of a country, require systems of law conforming to this variety in the natural features of the country. I understand quite as well as Judge Douglas, that if we here raise a barrel of flour more than we want, and the Louisianians raise a barrel of sugar more than they want, it is of mutual advantage to exchange. That produces commerce, brings us together, and makes us better friends. We like one another the more for it. And I understand as well as Judge Douglas, or anybody else, that these mutual accommodations are the cements which bind together the different parts of this Union—that instead of being a thing to "divide the house"—figuratively expressing the Union,—they tend to sustain it; they are the props of the house tending always to hold it up.

But when I have admitted all this, I ask if there is any parallel between these things and this institution of slavery? I do not see that there is any parallel at all between them. . . . You may say and Judge Douglas has intimated the same thing, that all this difficulty in regard to the institution of slavery is the mere agitation of office seekers and ambitious Northern politicians. He thinks we want to get "his place," I suppose. (Cheers and laughter.) . . .

But is it true that all the difficulty and agitation we have in regard to this institution of slavery springs from office seeking—from the mere ambition of politicians? Is that the truth? How many times have we had danger from this question? Go back to the day of the Missouri Compromise. Go back to the Nullification question, at the bottom of which lay this same slavery question. Go back to the time of the Annexation of Texas. Go back to the troubles that led to the Compromise of 1850. You will find that every time, with the single exception of the Nullification question, they sprung from an endeavor to spread this institution. There never was a party in the history of this country, and there probably never will be of sufficient strength to disturb the general peace of the country. Parties themselves may be divided and quarrel on minor questions, yet it extends not beyond the parties themselves. But does *not* this question make a disturbance outside of political circles? Does it not enter into the churches and rend them asunder? . . . Is it not this same mighty, deep seated power that somehow operates on the minds of men, exciting and stirring them up in every avenue of society—in politics, in religion, in literature, in morals, in all the manifold relations of life? (Applause.) Is this the work of politicians? Is that irresistible power which for fifty years has shaken the government and agitated the people to be stilled and subdued by pretending that it is an exceedingly simple thing, and we ought not to talk about it? (Great cheers and laughter.) . . .

The Judge alludes very often in the course of his remarks to the exclusive right which the States have to decide the whole thing for themselves. I agree with him very readily that the different States have that right. . . . Our controversy with him is in regard to the new Territories. We agree that when the States come in as States they have the right and the power to do as they please. We have no power as citizens of the free States or in our federal capacity as members of the Federal Union through the general government, to disturb slavery in the States where it exists. We profess constantly that we have no more inclination than belief in the power of the Government to disturb it; yet we are driven constantly to defend ourselves from the assumption that we are warring upon the rights of the *States*. What I insist upon is, that the new Territories shall be kept free from it while in the Territorial condition. Judge Douglas assumes that we have no interest in them—that we have no right whatever to interfere. I think we have some interest. I think that as white men we have. Do we not wish for an outlet for our surplus population, if I may so express myself? Do we not feel an interest in getting to that outlet with such institutions as we would like to have prevail there? . . .

Now irrespective of the moral aspect of this question as to whether there is a right or wrong in enslaving a negro, I am still in favor of our new Territories being in such a condition that white men may find a home—may find some spot where they can better their condition—where they can settle upon new soil and better their condition in life. (Great and continued cheering.) I am in favor of this not merely, (I must say it here as I have elsewhere,) for our own people who are born amongst us, but as an outlet for *free white people everywhere*, the world over—in which Hans and Baptiste and Patrick, and all other men from all the world, may find new homes and better their conditions in life. (Loud and long continued applause.)

. . . The real issue in this controversy—the one pressing upon every mind—is the sentiment on the part of one class that looks upon the institution of slavery *as a wrong*, and of another class that *does not* look upon it as a wrong. The sentiment that contemplates the institution of slavery in this country as a wrong is the sentiment of the Republican party. It is the sentiment around which all their actions—all their arguments circle—from which all their propositions radiate. They look upon it as being a moral, social and political wrong; and while they contemplate it as such, they nevertheless have due regard for its actual existence among us, and the difficulties of getting rid of it in any satisfactory way and to all the constitutional obligations thrown about it. Yet having a due regard for these, they desire a policy in regard to it that looks to its not creating any more danger. They insist that it should as far as may be, *be treated* as a wrong, and one of the methods of treating it as a wrong is to *make provision that it shall grow no larger.* (Loud applause.) . . .

On this subject of treating it as a wrong, and limiting its spread, let me say a word. Has any thing ever threatened the existence of this Union save and except this very institution of Slavery? What is it that we hold most dear amongst us? Our own liberty and prosperity. What has ever threatened our liberty and prosperity save and except this institution of Slavery? . . .

That is the real issue. . . . It is the eternal struggle between these two principles—right and wrong—throughout the world. They are the two principles that have stood face to face from the beginning of time; and will ever continue to struggle. . . .

Whenever the issue can be distinctly made, and all extraneous matter thrown out so that men can fairly see the real difference between the parties, this controversy will soon be settled, and it will be done peaceably too. There will be no war, no violence. It will be placed again where the wisest and best men of the world, placed it. Brooks of South Carolina once declared that when this Constitution was framed, its framers did not look to the institution existing until this day. When he said this, I think he stated a fact that is fully borne out by the history of the times. But he also said they were better and wiser men than the men of these days; yet the men of these days had experience which they had not, and by the invention of the cotton gin it became a necessity in this country that slavery should be perpetual. I now say that willingly or unwillingly, purposely or without purpose, Judge Douglas has been the most prominent instrument in changing the position of the institution of slavery which the fathers of the government expected to come to an end ere this—*and putting it upon Brooks' cotton gin basis,* (Great applause,)—placing it where he openly confesses he has no desire there shall ever be an end of it. (Renewed applause.)

\*    \*    \*

## Mr. Douglas' Reply

\*    \*    \*

. . . Mr. Lincoln told you that the slavery question was the only thing that ever disturbed the peace and harmony of the Union. Did not nullification once raise its head and disturb the peace of this Union in 1832? Was that the slavery question, Mr. Lincoln? Did not disunion raise its monster head during the last war with Great Britain? Was that the slavery question, Mr. Lincoln? The peace of this country has been disturbed three times, once during the war with Great Britain, once on the tariff question, and once on the slavery question. ("Three cheers for Douglas.") His argument, therefore, that slavery is the only question that has ever created dissension in the Union falls to the ground. It is true that agitators are enabled now to use this slavery question for the purpose of sectional strife. ("That's so.") He admits that in regard to all things else, the principle that I advocate, making each State and territory free to decide for itself ought to prevail. . . . I say that all these laws are local and domestic, and that local and domestic concerns should be left to each State and each territory to manage for itself. If agitators would acquiesce in that principle, there never would be any danger to the peace and harmony of this Union. ("That's so," and cheers.)

Mr. Lincoln tries to avoid the main issue by attacking the truth of my proposition, that our fathers made this government divided into free and slave States, recognizing the right of each to decide all its local questions for itself. Did they not thus make it? . . . He says that he looks forward to a time when slavery shall be abolished everywhere. I look forward to a time when each State shall be allowed to do as it pleases. . . . Hence, I say, let us maintain this government on the principles that our fathers made it, recognizing the right of each State to keep slavery as long as its people determine, or to abolish it when they please. (Cheers.) But Mr. Lincoln says that when our fathers made this government they did not look forward to the state of things now existing; and therefore he thinks the doctrine was wrong; and he quotes Brooks, of South Carolina, to prove that our fathers then thought that probably slavery would be abolished, by each State acting for itself before this time. Suppose they did; suppose they did not foresee what has occurred,— does that change the principles of our government? They did not probably foresee the telegraph that transmits intelligence by lightning, nor did they foresee the railroads that now form the bonds of union between the different States, or the thousand mechanical inventions that have elevated mankind. But do these things change the principles of the government? Our fathers, I say, made this government on the principle of the right of each State to do as it pleases in its own domestic affairs, subject to the constitution, and allowed the people of each to apply to every new change of circumstance such remedy as they may see fit to improve their condition. This right they have for all time to come. (Cheers.)

\*    \*    \*

## REVIEW QUESTIONS

1. How did Douglas refute Lincoln's contention that the nation could not remain divided?
2. How did Douglas describe popular sovereignty to the audience?
3. What specific charges did he level against the Republican Party (and, by extension, against Lincoln)?
4. How did Lincoln answer those charges?
5. What do you think of Lincoln's interpretation of the Constitution and the Founders' intentions in terms of slavery? Why did he make the argument that he did?
6. Lincoln stated that slavery is the root of all dissension and disunion; Douglas rejected that interpretation. With whom do you agree? Why?

## HINTON ROWAN HELPER

## FROM *The Impending Crisis of the South* (1857)

*Hinton Rowan Helper (1829–1909) was born in Rowan County, North Carolina. It was a region of small farmers, many of whom were of German descent, and one with a substantial Quaker element. Thus, due to economic, ethnic, and religious blocks, slavery had not rooted deeply there. That may partly explain Helper's later anti-slavery stand. Another reason he may have argued against it was his upbringing, along with the fact that as a poor boy he could not succeed in the South because of the way slavery skewed its economy and society. He left the South in his search for fame and fortune, first moving to New York, then journeying west during an attack of gold fever. When that fever soon abated in failure, Helper returned to the East and wrote* The Land of Gold *(1855) to debunk the image of California as the promised land. He then wrote scathing critiques of the South that focused on the incompatibility of slavery and economic progress. Citing statistic after statistic he presented a strong, even if exaggerated, case that continued investment in land and slaves prevented the South from having a strong, diversified, and balanced economy. Helper also argued that slavery chained down white non-slaveholders. Abolitionists embraced his arguments as Southerners raged against this betrayal by one of their own. Yet Helper had never been a true southern agrarian: he was essentially a capitalist deriding a precapitalist economy, and as such he argued against the institution of slavery, not for the people in slavery. Helper was also a vehement racist, though he toned that down in this book—perhaps in consideration of the audience he wanted to attract. In later years Helper endeavored to exclude blacks from America, not give them equality within it.*

From Hinton Rowan Helper, *The Impending Crisis of the South: How to Meet It*, introduction by George M. Fredrickson (1857; Cambridge: The Belknap Press of Harvard University Press, 1968), pp. 21–26, 28, 42–45, 120–21.

## The Free and the Slave States

It is a fact well known to every intelligent Southerner that we are compelled to go to the North for almost every article of utility and adornment, from matches, shoepegs and paintings up to cotton-mills, steamships and statuary; that we have no foreign trade, no princely merchants, nor respectable artists; that, in comparison with the free states, we contribute nothing to the literature, polite arts and inventions of the age; that, for want of profitable employment at home, large numbers of our native population find themselves necessitated to emigrate to the West, whilst the free states retain not only the larger proportion of those born within their own limits, but induce, annually, hundreds of thousands of foreigners to settle and remain amongst them; that almost everything produced at the North meets with ready sale, while, at the same time, there is no demand, even among our own citizens, for the productions of Southern industry; that, owing to the absence of a proper system of business amongst us, the North becomes, in one way or another, the proprietor and dispenser of all our floating wealth, and that we are dependent on

Northern capitalists for the means necessary to build our railroads, canals and other public improvements; that if we want to visit a foreign country, even though it may lie directly South of us, we find no convenient way of getting there except by taking passage through a Northern port; and that nearly all the profits arising from the exchange of commodities, from insurance and shipping offices, and from the thousand and one industrial pursuits of the country, accrue to the North, and are there invested in the erection of those magnificent cities and stupendous works of art which dazzle the eyes of the South, and attest the superiority of free institutions!

The North is the Mecca of our merchants, and to it they must and do make two pilgrimages per annum—one in the spring and one in the fall. All our commercial, mechanical, manufactural, and literary supplies come from there. We want Bibles, brooms, buckets and books, and we go to the North; . . . we want toys, primers, school books, fashionable apparel, machinery, medicines, tombstones, and a thousand other things, and we go to the North for them all. Instead of keeping our money in circulation at home, by patronizing our own mechanics, manufacturers, and laborers, we send it all away to the North, and there it remains; it never falls into our hands again.

In one way or another we are more or less subservient to the North every day of our lives. In infancy we are swaddled in Northern muslin; in childhood we are humored with Northern gewgaws; in youth we are instructed out of Northern books; at the age of maturity we sow our "wild oats" on Northern soil; in middle-life we exhaust our wealth, energies and talents in the dishonorable vocation of entailing our dependence on our children and on our children's children, and, to the neglect of our own interests and the interests of those around us, in giving aid and succor to every department of Northern power; in the decline of life we remedy our eye-sight with Northern spectacles, and support our infirmities with Northern canes; in old age we are drugged with Northern physic; and, finally, when we die, our inanimate bodies, shrouded in Northern cambric, are stretched upon the bier, borne to the grave in a Northern carriage, entombed with a Northern spade, and memorized with a Northern slab!

*       *       *

And now to the point. In our opinion, . . . the causes which have impeded the progress and prosperity of the South, which have dwindled our commerce, and other similar pursuits, into the most contemptible insignificance; sunk a large majority of our people in galling poverty and ignorance, rendered a small minority conceited and tyrannical, and driven the rest away from their homes; entailed upon us a humiliating dependence on the Free States; disgraced us in the recesses of our own souls, and brought us under reproach in the eyes of all civilized and enlightened nations—may all be traced to one common source, and there find solution in the most hateful and horrible word, that was ever incorporated into the vocabulary of human economy—*Slavery!*

Reared amidst the institution of slavery, believing it to be wrong both in principle and in practice, and having seen and felt its evil influences upon individuals, communities and states, we deem it a duty, no less than a privilege, to enter our protest against it, and to use our most strenuous efforts to overturn and abolish it! Then we are an abolitionist? Yes! not merely a freesoiler, but an abolitionist, in the fullest sense of the term. We are not only in favor of keeping slavery out of the territories, but, carrying our opposition to the institution a step further, we here unhesitatingly declare ourself in favor of its immediate and unconditional abolition, in every state in this confederacy, where it now exists! Patriotism makes us a freesoiler; state pride makes us an emancipationist; a profound sense of duty to the South makes us an abolitionist; a reasonable degree of fellow feeling for the negro, makes us a colonizationist. . . .

*       *       *

. . . Nothing short of the complete abolition of slavery can save the South from falling into the vortex of utter ruin. Too long have we yielded a submissive obedience to the tyrannical domination of an inflated oligarchy; too long have we tolerated their arrogance and self-conceit; too long have we tolerated their arrogance and self-conceit; too long have we submitted to their unjust and savage exactions. Let us now wrest from them the sceptre of power, establish liberty and equal rights throughout the land, and henceforth and forever guard our legislative halls from the pollutions and usurpations of proslavery demagogues.

*       *       *

. . . Notwithstanding the fact that the white non-slaveholders of the South, are in the majority, as five to one, they have never yet had any part or lot in framing the laws under which they live. There is no legislation except for the benefit of slavery, and slaveholders. As a general rule, poor white persons are regarded with less esteem and attention than negroes, and though the condition of the latter is wretched beyond description, vast numbers of the former are infinitely worse off. A cunningly devised mockery of freedom is guarantied to them, and that is all. To all intents and purposes they are disfranchised, and outlawed, and the only privilege extended to them, is a shallow and circumscribed participation in the political movements that usher slaveholders into office.

\*     \*     \*

The lords of the lash are not only absolute masters of the blacks, who are bought and sold, and driven about like so many cattle, but they are also the oracles and arbiters of all non-slaveholding whites, whose freedom is merely nominal, and whose unparalleled illiteracy and degradation is purposely and fiendishly perpetuated. How little the "poor white trash," the great majority of the Southern people, know of the real condition of the country is, indeed, sadly astonishing. The truth is, they know nothing of public measures, and little of private affairs, except what their imperious masters, the slave-drivers, condescend to tell, and that is but precious little, and even that little, always garbled and one-sided, is never told except in public harangues; for the haughty cavaliers of shackles and handcuffs will not degrade themselves by holding private converse with those who have neither dimes nor hereditary rights in human flesh.

Whenever it pleases, and to the extent it pleases, a slaveholder to become communicative, poor whites may hear with fear and trembling, but not speak. . . . If they dare to think for themselves, their thoughts must be forever concealed. The expression of any sentiment at all conflicting with the gospel of slavery, dooms them at once in the community in which they live, and then, whether willing or unwilling, they are obliged to become heroes, martyrs, or exiles. . . . Non-slaveholders are not only kept in ignorance of what is transpiring at the North, but they are continually misinformed of what is going on even in the South. Never were the poorer classes of a people, and those classes so largely in the majority, and all inhabiting the same country, so basely duped, so adroitly swindled, or so damnably outraged.

It is expected that the stupid and sequacious masses, the white victims of slavery, will believe, and, as a general thing, they do believe, whatever the slaveholders tell them; and thus it is that they are cajoled into the notion that they are the freest, happiest and most intelligent people in the world, and are taught to look with prejudice and disapprobation upon every new principle or progressive movement. Thus it is that the South, woefully inert and inventionless, has lagged behind the North, and is now weltering in the cesspool of ignorance and degradation.

\*     \*     \*

Non-slaveholders of the South! farmers, mechanics and workingmen, we take this occasion to assure you that the slaveholders, the arrogant demagogues whom you have elected to offices of honor and profit, have hoodwinked you, trifled with you, and used you as mere tools for the consummation of their wicked designs. They have purposely kept you in ignorance, and have, by moulding your passions and prejudices to suit themselves, induced you to act in direct opposition to your dearest rights and interests. By a sytem of the grossest subterfuge and misrepresentation, and in order to avert, for a season, the vengeance that will most assuredly overtake them ere long, they have taught you to hate the abolitionists, who are your best and only true friends. Now, as one of your own number, we appeal to you to join us in our patriotic endeavors to rescue the generous soil of the South from the usurped and desolating control of these political vampires. Once and forever, at least so far as this country is concerned, the infernal question of slavery must be disposed of; a speedy and perfect abolishment of the whole institution is the true policy of the South— and this is the policy which we propose to pursue. Will you aid us, will you assist us, will you be freemen, or will you be slaves? These are questions of vital importance; weigh them well in your minds; come to a prudent and firm decision, and hold yourselves in readiness to act in accordance therewith. You must either be for us or against us— anti-slavery or pro-slavery; it is impossible for you to occupy a neutral ground; it is as certain as fate itself, that if you do not voluntarly oppose the usurpations and outrages of the slavocrats, they will force you into involuntary compliance with their infamous measures. Consider well the aggressive, fraudulent and despotic power which they have exercised in the affairs of Kanzas; and remember that, if, by adhering to erroneous principles of neutrality or non-resistance, you allow them to force the curse of slavery on that vast and fertile field, the broad area of all the surrounding States and Territories—the whole nation, in fact—will soon fall a prey to their diabolical intrigues and machinations. Thus, if you are not vigilant, will they take advantage of your neutrality, and make you and others the victims of their inhuman despotism. Do not reserve the strength of your arms until you shall have been rendered powerless to strike; . . .

\*    \*    \*

## REVIEW QUESTIONS

1. Did Helper essentially argue that slavery had enslaved the South? How so?
2. Was he worried about the morality of slavery? Explain.
3. Why did Helper's attack enrage, and perhaps frighten, Southerners more than Lincoln's did?

# FROM South Carolina's Ordinance of Secession and Declaration of Independence (1860)

*Southerners reeled from two shocks in 1859 and 1860. The first was John Brown's raid on the federal arsenal at Harpers Ferry, Virginia, so as to arm slaves to fight for their freedom. The second was Lincoln's election to the presidency. Many southern leaders then decided that the only way they could defend their peculiar institution, particular way of life, and political sentiments was to secede. They had to move quickly to mobilize support, for not every person, or every state, in the South was ready for such action when Lincoln won the presidential election in November 1860. "Secessionitis" was particularly strong in South Carolina, and that state consequently took the lead in disunion. On 20 December a special state convention unanimously passed an Ordinance of Secession; a few days later it justified its actions in its own Declaration of Independence (what has also been called a Declaration of the Causes of Secession). Copies were sent to the other southern states, which, already predisposed to "secessionitis," soon passed their own ordinances.*

From Howard W. Preston, ed., *Documents Illustrative of American History, 1606–1863* (New York: G. P. Putnam's Sons, 1886), pp. 305–12.

## Ordinance of Secession

An ordinance to dissolve the Union between the State of South Carolina and other States united with her under the compact entitled "The Constitution of the United States of America."

We, the People of the State of South Carolina, in Convention assembled, do declare and ordain, and it is hereby declared and ordained, that the Ordinance adopted by us in Convention, on the Twenty-third of May, in the year of our Lord one thousand seven hundred and eighty-eight, whereby the Constitution of the United States was ratified, and also all other Acts and parts of Acts of the General Assembly of the State ratifying amendments of the said Constitution, are hereby repealed, and the Union now subsisting between South Carolina and other States, under the name of the United States of America, is hereby dissolved.

## South Carolina Declaration of Independence

The State of South Carolina, having determined to resume her separate and equal place among nations, deems it due to herself, to the remaining United States of America, and to the nations of the world, that she should declare the causes which have led to this act.

In the year 1765, that portion of the British empire embracing Great Britain, undertook to make laws for the government of that portion composed of the thirteen American colonies. A struggle for the right of self-government ensued, which resulted, on the 4th of July, 1776, in a declaration by the colonies, "that they are, and of right ought to be, free and independent states, . . ."

They further solemnly declared, that whenever any "form of government becomes destructive of the ends for which it was established, it is the right of that people to alter or abolish it, and to institute a new government." . . .

In pursuance of this declaration of independence, each of the thirteen states proceeded to exercise its separate sovereignty; adopted for itself a constitution, and appointed officers for the administration of government in all its departments—legislative, executive, and judicial. For purpose of defense, they united their arms and their counsels; and, in 1778, they united in a league, known as the articles of confederation, whereby they agreed to intrust the administration of their external relations to a common agent, known as the Congress of the United States, expressly declaring in the first article, "that each state retains its sovereignty, freedom, and independence, and every power, jurisdiction, and right which is not, by this confederation,

expressly delegated to the United States in Congress assembled."

Under this consideration the war of the Revolution was carried on, and on the 3d of September, 1783, the contest ended, and a definite treaty was signed by Great Britain, in which she acknowledged the independence of the colonies in the following terms:

Article I. His Britannic Majesty acknowledges the said United States, viz.: New Hampshire, Massachusetts Bay, Rhode Island and Providence Plantation, Connecticut, New York, New Jersey, Pennsylvania, Delaware, Maryland, Virginia, North Carolina, South Carolina, and Georgia, to be free, sovereign, and independent states; that he treats them as such; and for himself, his heirs, and successors, relinquishes all claim to the government, proprietary and territorial rights of the same, and every part thereof.

Thus was established the two great principles asserted by the colonies, namely, the right of a state to govern itself, and the right of a people to abolish a government when it becomes destructive of the ends for which it was instituted. And concurrent with the establishment of these principles was the fact, that each colony became and was recognized by the mother country as a free, sovereign, and independent state.

In 1787, deputies were appointed by the states to revise the articles of confederation, and on September 17th, 1787, the deputies recommended for the adoption of the states the articles of union known as the constitution of the United States.

The parties to whom the constitution was submitted were the several sovereign states; they were to agree or disagree, and when nine of them agreed, the compact was to take effect among those concurring; and the general government, as the common agent, was then to be invested with their authority.

\*    \*    \*

By this constitution, certain duties were charged on the several states, and the exercise of certain of their powers not delegated to the United States by the constitution, nor prohibited by it to the states, are reserved to the states respectively, or to the people. On the 23d of May, 1788, South Carolina, by a convention of people, passed an ordinance assenting to this constitution, and afterwards altering her own constitution to conform herself to the obligation she had undertaken.

Thus was established, by compact between the states, a government with defined objects and powers, limited to the express words of the grant, and to so much more only as was necessary to execute the power granted. The limitations left the whole remaining mass of power subject to the clause reserving it to the state or to the people, and rendered unnecessary any specification of reserved powers.

We hold that the government thus established is subject to the two great principles asserted in the declaration of independence, and we hold further that the mode of its formation subjects it to a third fundamental principle, namely—the law of compact. We maintain that in every compact between two or more parties, the obligation is mutual—that the failure of one of the contracting parties to perform a material part of the agreement entirely released the obligation of the other, and that, where no arbiter is appointed, each party is remitted to his own judgment to determine the fact of failure with all its consequences.

In the present case that fact is established with certainty. We assert that fifteen of the states have deliberately refused for years past to fulfil their constitutional obligation, and we refer to their own statutes for the proof.

The constitution of the United States, in its fourth article, provides as follows:

"No person held to service or labor in one state, under the laws thereof, escaping into another, shall, in consequence of any law or regulation therein, be discharged from any service or labor, but shall be delivered up, on claim of party to whom such service or labor may be due."

This stipulation was so material to the compact that without it that compact would not have been made. . . .

The same article of the constitution stipulates also for the sedition by the several states of fugitives from justice from the other states.

The general government, as the common agent, passed laws to carry into effect these stipulations of the states. For many years these laws were executed. But an increasing hostility on the part of the northern states to the institution of slavery has led to a disregard of their obligations, and the laws of the general government have ceased to effect the objects of the constitution. The states of Maine, New Hampshire, Vermont, Massachusetts, Connecticut, Rhode Island, New York, Pennsylvania, Illinois, Indiana, Ohio, Michigan, Wisconsin, and Iowa have enacted laws which either nullify the acts of Congress, or render useless any attempt to execute them. In many of these states the fugitive is discharged from the service of labor claimed, and in none of them has the state government complied with the stipulation made in the constitution. . . . In the state of New York even the right of transit for a slave has been denied by her tribunals, and the states of Ohio and Iowa have refused to surrender to justice fugitives charged with murder and inciting servile insurrection in the state of Virginia. Thus the constitutional compact has been deliberately broken and disregarded by the non-slaveholding states, and the consequence follows that South Carolina is released from its obligation.

The ends for which this constitution was framed are declared by itself to be "to form a more perfect union, establish justice, insure domestic tranquillity, provide for the common defence, protect the general welfare, and secure the blessings of liberty to ourselves and posterity."

These ends it endeavored to accomplish by a federal government, in which each state was recognized as an equal, and had separate control over its own institutions. The right of property in slaves was recognized by giving to free persons distinct political rights; by giving them the right to represent, and burdening them with direct taxes for three-fifths of their slaves; by authorizing the importation of slaves for twenty years, and by stipulating for the rendition of fugitives from labor.

We affirm that these ends for which this government was instituted have been defeated, and the government itself has been made destructive of them by the action of the non-slaveholding state.

These states have assumed the right of deciding upon the propriety of our domestic institutions, and have denied the rights of property established in fifteen of the states and recognized by the constitution; they have denounced as sinful the institution of slavery; they have permitted the open establishment among them of societies whose avowed object is to disturb the peace and claim the property of the citizens of other states. They have encouraged and assisted thousands of our slaves to leave their homes, and those who remain have been incited by emissaries, books, and pictures to servile insurrection.

For twenty-five years this agitation has been steadily increasing, until it has now secured to its aid the power of the common government. Observing the forms of the constitution, a sectional party has found within that article establishing the executive department the means of subverting the constitution itself. A geographical line has been drawn across the Union, and all the states north of that line have united in the election of a man to the high office of President of the United States, whose opinions and purposes are hostile to slavery. He is to be entrusted with the administration of the common government, because he has declared that that "government cannot endure permanently half slave, half free," and that the public mind must rest in the belief that slavery is in the course of ultimate extinction.

This sectional combination for the subversion of the constitution has been aided in some of the states by elevating to citizenship persons who, by the supreme law of the land, are incapable of becoming citizens, and their votes have been used to inaugurate a new policy hostile to the south, and destructive of its peace and safety.

On the 4th of March next, this party will take possession of the government. It has announced that the south shall be excluded from the common territory; that the judicial tribunals shall be made sectional, and that a war must be waged against slavery until it shall cease throughout the United States.

The guarantees of the constitution will then no longer exist; the equal rights of the states will be lost. The slaveholding states will no longer have the power of self-government or self-protection, and the federal government will have become their enemies.

Sectional interest and animosity will deepen the irritation, and all hope of remedy is rendered vain by the fact that public opinion at the north has invested a great political error with the sanctions of a more erroneous religious belief.

We, therefore, the people of South Carolina, by our delegates in convention assembled, appealing to the Supreme Judge of the world for the rectitude of our intentions, have solemnly declared that the union heretofore existing between this state and the other states of North America is dissolved, and that the state of South Carolina has resumed her position among the nations of the world as a free, sovereign, and independent state, with full power to levy war, conclude peace, contract alliances, establish commerce, and to do all other acts and things which independent states may, of right, do.

And, for the support of this declaration, with a firm reliance on the protection of Divine Providence, we mutually pledge to each other, our lives, our fortunes, and our sacred honor.

## REVIEW QUESTIONS

1. Did South Carolina believe that secession was a legal or constitutional act?
2. What were the three great rights or principles upon which South Carolina was basing its actions?
3. What specific charges did it levy against the northern states? Were they, not the southern states, to blame for the disintegration of the union?
4. Did South Carolina essentially argue that secession was the last step in disunion, not the first?

# JEFFERSON DAVIS

## Speech upon Leaving the Senate
## (January 1861)

*Jefferson Davis (1808–1889) graduated from West Point and served in the Black Hawk and Mexican wars. At various times he had also been a congressman and senator from Mississippi before becoming secretary of war in 1853. Davis had thus given many years of service to the United States as well as to his state by the late 1850s. By the time he returned to the Senate in 1857, however, his priorities were definitely the interests of his state and the South. He still wanted to maintain the Union, but he wanted that union to sustain states' rights and powers as the South defined them. When it did not, he and his state decided to leave the Union. Mississippi seceded on 9 January 1861. Davis followed and confirmed that action on 21 January by leaving the Senate. Shortly thereafter, on 9 February, the Confederate Congress elected him provisional president of the Confederacy. He was formally elected that November.*

From *Jefferson Davis, Constitutionalist: His Letters, Papers and Speeches,* vol. 5, edited by Dunbar Rowland (1923; reprint, New York: AMS Press, 1973), pp. 40–45. [Editorial insertions appear in brackets—*Ed.*]

I rise, Mr. President [of the Senate], for the purpose of announcing to the Senate that I have satisfactory evidence that the State of Mississippi, by a solemn ordinance of her people in convention assembled, has declared her separation from the United States. Under these circumstances, of course my functions are terminated here. It has seemed to me proper, however, that I should appear in the Senate to announce that fact to my associates, and I will say but very little more. . . .

It is known to Senators who have served with me here, that I have for many years advocated, as an essential attribute of State sovereignty, the right of a State to secede from the Union. Therefore, if I had not believed there was justifiable cause; if I had thought that Mississippi was acting without sufficient provocation, or without an existing necessity, I should still, under my theory of the Government, because of my allegiance to the State of which I am a citizen, have been bound by her action. I, however, may be permitted to say that I do think she has justifiable cause, and I approve of her act. I conferred with her people

before that act was taken, counseled them then that if the state of things which they apprehended should exist when the convention met, they should take the action which they have now adopted.

I hope none who hear me will confound this expression of mine with the advocacy of the right of a State to remain in the Union, and to disregard its constitutional obligations by the nullification of the law. Such is not my theory. Nullification and secession, so often confounded, are indeed antagonistic principles. Nullification is a remedy which it is sought to apply within the Union, and against the agent [the federal government] of the States. It is only to be justified when the agent has violated his constitutional obligation, and a State, assuming to judge for itself, denies the right of the agent thus to act, and appeals to the other States of the Union for a decision; but when the States themselves, and when the people of the States, have so acted as to convince us that they will not regard our constitutional rights, then, and then for the first time, arises the doctrine of secession in its practical application.

A great man who now reposes with his fathers, and who has been often arraigned for a want of fealty to the Union, advocated the doctrine of nullification, because it preserved the Union. It was because of his deep-seated attachment to the Union, his determination to find some remedy for existing ills short of a severance of the ties which bound South Carolina to the other States, that Mr. Calhoun advocated the doctrine of nullification, which he proclaimed to be peaceful, to be within the limits of State power, not to disturb the Union, but only to be a means of bringing the agent before the tribunal of the States for their judgment.

Secession belongs to a different class of remedies. It is to be justified upon the basis that the States are sovereign. There was a time when none denied it. I hope the time may come again, when a better comprehension of the theory of our Government, and the inalienable rights of the people of the States, will prevent any one from denying that each State is a sovereign, and thus may reclaim the grants which it has made to any agent whomsoever.

I therefore say I concur in the action of the people of Mississippi, believing it to be necessary and proper, and should have been bound by their action if my belief had been otherwise; and this brings me to the important point which I wish on this last occasion to present to the Senate. It is by this confounding of nullification and secession that the name of a great man, whose ashes now mingle with his mother earth, has been invoked to justify coercion against a seceded State. The phrase "to execute the laws," was an expression which General Jackson applied to the case of a State refusing to obey the laws while yet a member of the Union. That is not the case which is now presented. The laws are to be executed over the United States, and upon the people of the United States. They have no relation to any foreign country. It is a perversion of terms, at least it is a great misapprehension of the case, which cites that expression for application to a State which has withdrawn from the Union. You may make war on a foreign State. If it be the purpose of gentlemen, they may make war against a State which has withdrawn from the Union; but there are no laws of the United States to be executed within the limits of a seceded State. A State

finding herself in the condition in which Mississippi has judged she is, in which her safety requires that she should provide for the maintenance of her rights out of the Union, surrenders all the benefits, (and they are known to be many,) deprives herself of the advantages, (they are known to be great,) severs all the ties of affection, (and they are close and enduring,) which have bound her to the Union; and thus divesting herself of every benefit, taking upon herself every burden, she claims to be exempt from any power to execute the laws of the United States within her limits.

I well remember an occasion when Massachusetts was arraigned before the bar of the Senate, and when then the doctrine of coercion was rife and to be applied against her because of the rescue of a fugitive slave in Boston. My opinion then was the same that it is now. Not in a spirit of egotism, but to show that I am not influenced in my opinion because the case is my own, I refer to that time and that occasion as containing the opinion which I then entertained, and on which my present conduct is based. I then said, if Massachusetts, following her through a stated line of conduct, chooses to take the last step which separates her from the Union, it is her right to go, and I will neither vote one dollar nor one man to coerce her back; but will say to her, God speed, in memory of the kind associations which once existed between her and the other States.

It has been a conviction of pressing necessity, it has been a belief that we are to be deprived in the Union of the rights which our fathers bequeathed to us, which has brought Mississippi into her present decision. She has heard proclaimed the theory that all men are created free and equal, and this made the basis of an attack upon her social institutions; and the sacred Declaration of Independence has been invoked to maintain the position of the equality of the races. That Declaration of Independence is to be construed by the circumstances and purposes for which it was made. The communities were declaring their independence; the people of those communities were asserting that no man was born—to use the language of Mr. Jefferson— booted and spurred to ride over the rest of mankind; that men were created equal—meaning the men of the political community; that there was no divine right to rule; that no man inherited the right to govern; that there were no classes by which power and place descended to families, but that all stations were equally within the grasp of each member of the body-politic. These were the great principles they announced; these were the purposes for which they made their declaration; these were the ends to which their enunciation was directed. They have no reference to the slave; else, how happened it that among the items of arraignment made against George III was that he endeavored to do just what the North has been endeavoring of late to do—to stir up insurrection among our slaves! Had the Declaration announced that the negroes were free and equal, how was the Prince to be arraigned for stirring up insurrection among them? And how was this to be enumerated among the high crimes which caused the colonies to sever their connection with the mother country? When our Constitution was formed, the same idea was rendered more palpable, for there we find provision made for that very class of persons as property; they were not put upon the footing of equality with white men—not even upon that of paupers and convicts; but, so far as representation was concerned, were discriminated against as a lower caste, only to be represented in the numerical proportion of three fifths.

Then, Senators, we recur to the compact which binds us together; we recur to the principles upon which our Government was founded; and when you deny them, and when you deny to us the right to withdraw from a Government which thus perverted threatens to be destructive of our rights, we but tread in the path of our fathers when we proclaim our independence, and take the hazard. This is done not in hostility to others, not to injure any section of the country, not even for our own pecuniary benefit; but from the high and solemn motive of defending and protecting the rights we inherited, and which it is our sacred duty to transmit unshorn to our children.

I find in myself, perhaps, a type of the general feeling of my constituents towards yours. I am sure I feel no hostility to you, Senators from the North. I am sure there is not one of you, whatever sharp discussion there may have been between us, to whom I cannot now say, in the presence of my God,

I wish you well; and such, I am sure, is the feeling of the people whom I represent towards those whom you represent. I therefore feel that I but express their desire when I say I hope, and they hope, for peaceful relations with you, though we must part. They may be mutually beneficial to us in the future, as they have been in the past, if you so will it. The reverse may bring disaster on every portion of the country; and if you will have it thus, we will invoke the God of our fathers, who delivered them from the power of the lion, to protect us from the ravages of the bear; and thus, putting our trust in God, and in our own firm hearts and strong arms, we will vindicate the right as best we may.

In the course of my service here, associated at different times with a great variety of Senators, I see now around me some with whom I have served long; there have been points of collision; but whatever of offense there has been to me, I leave here; I carry with me no hostile remembrance. Whatever offense I have given which has not been redressed, or for which satisfaction has not been demanded, I have, Senators, in this hour of our parting, to offer you my apology for any pain which, in heat of discussion, I have inflicted. I go hence unencumbered of the remembrance of any injury received, and having discharged the duty of making the only reparation in my power for any injury offered.

Mr. President, and Senators, having made the announcement which the occasion seemed to me to require, it only remains for me to bid you a final adieu.

## REVIEW QUESTIONS

1. How and why did Davis define nullification as a remedy for the preservation of the Union?
2. How did Davis differentiate secession from nullification?
3. Why was that distinction so important to Davis's argument for the independence of Mississippi and, by extension, the other states that seceded?
4. Davis argued that secession was due to both the North's and the South's interpretations and applications of the Declaration of Independence and the Constitution. Explain his argument.

# 16  &bull;  THE WAR OF THE UNION

*Rebellion—Civil War—War between the States—War of Northern Aggression: the words referred to the same event, but as seen from different perspectives. These titles at first simply gave a name to the climax of the nation's crisis, but later they came to define and be defined by the terrible toll of four years of bloody conflict. Although often talked about as a war between North and South and a war between brothers, this cataclysm engulfed all of America's regions and peoples as it devastated farms and families, strained resources, killed millions, and even scorched the nation's connections with other countries.*

*The war began with declarations and proclamations as adversaries justified their stands and drew lines in the sand. Then they called in their friends to stand with them as they dared their opponents to step over those lines. The southern states challenged the federal government with their declarations of secession and by arming and drilling their swelling militias. The new president of the United States, Abraham Lincoln, first responded with requests for dialogue and calm deliberation, but when South Carolina, taking the initiative again, fired on Fort Sumter in Charleston harbor on 12 April 1861, Lincoln fired back. On the 15th he issued a call for military volunteers from the loyal states, and then on the 19th, "with a view . . . to the protection of the public peace, and the lives and property of quiet and orderly citizens pursuing their lawful occupations," he proclaimed a blockade against the southern ports. Lincoln hoped that the use of such a naval blanket would suffocate the flames of rebellion; instead, it fanned them.*

*More southern states seceded and joined the compact that had been formalized between their sister states in March. The government of the Confederate States of America raised armies for defense and appointed ministers to pursue its interests abroad. The Confederacy wanted foreign powers to recognize its independence, for that acknowledgment would undermine the Union's contention that the war was an internal insurrection—a civil war—not a war between states or nations. Recognition was also a prerequisite to indispensable trade connections and perhaps military alliances. The United States government, by employing the diplomatic connections it had established over the years, wielding its economic might, and threatening war against those who intervened, countered the Confederacy abroad by warning other nations away from recognition and intervention. Foreign nations deliberated on the enticements of the South and demands of the North, and then made their decisions based on their own best interests, not America's. The fact that some nations, especially Britain, contemplated recognition instead of dismissing the southern suit was another powerful lesson on vulnerability for the United States.*

*While United States and Confederate ministers skirmished abroad, their governments and citizens focused on the vital, vicious battles being waged on American soil. Initially, many men (and a few women in disguise) flocked to enlist in their state regiments. They were eager to fight in what they were sure would be a short but glorious war. As the war lengthened and its toll—human casualties, property destruction, social disruption—mounted, however, Americans everywhere began to question the causes and costs. The war, a time of extermination, began a period of self-examination.*

*Southerners said that they fought so that they, using the words of 1776, would not be slaves. They, even less so than the Founders, failed to see the irony in that. Charles T. O'Ferrall, a cavalry officer in the Army of Northern Virginia who later became a congressman for and then governor of the state of Virginia, reflected back on Southerners' justifications when he published his memoirs in 1904. O'Ferrall wrote, "In spite of charters, compacts, and constitutions, a people who conscientiously believe they have been oppressed and wronged and can secure no redress have the inborn right to throw off the yoke that galls and strike for their liberties." While he declared, years after the war, that there was "no longer a spirit of revolt or rebellion" in his "bosom," he also said that he was proud to have been a rebel who stood "upon the eternal principles of the Declaration of Independence." If George Washington and his compatriots gloried in the term rebel, then O'Ferrall thought, so should the followers of Jefferson Davis and Robert E. Lee.*

*Northerners also declared that they fought for the ideas and fruits of the Revolution. As Lincoln intoned on 19 November 1863 at Gettysburg:*

> *Four score and seven years ago our fathers brought forth on this continent, a new nation, conceived in Liberty, and dedicated to the proposition that all men are created equal.*
>
> *Now we are engaged in a great civil war, testing whether that nation, or any nation so conceived and so dedicated, can long endure. . . .*
>
> *. . . It is for us the living, . . . to be dedicated here to the unfinished work which they who fought here have thus far so nobly advanced. . . . that this nation, under God, shall have a new birth of freedom—and that government of the people, by the people, for the people, shall not perish from the earth.*

# FREDERICK DOUGLASS

## FROM The Reasons for Our Troubles (1862)

*Was slavery truly the cause, or just the catalyst, of the cataclysm? That question, in turn, begs another: If the crisis was about slavery, was the war about it? Because neither side initially recruited and rallied its troops specifically for or against slavery, such questions engaged contemporaries of the war as well as later historians. Frederick Douglass was appalled by the avoidance of the issue, for he believed that "the mission of the war was the liberation of the slave as well as the salvation of the Union." He argued that the two parts of the mission were inseparable, contradicting others who not only separated them but made the former subordinate to the latter. Douglass refused to let the war distract Americans from the abolition of slavery and the emancipation of the slaves. He traveled through the northern states on extensive lecture tours in 1861 and the winter of 1862, urging his audiences to send petitions and delegations to Washington, D.C., so as to convince the administration to establish a policy in support of freedom. He presented his case to a Philadelphia audience at National Hall on 14 January 1862 and then published his speech in his journal,* Douglass' Monthly, *the following month.*

From *The Life and Writings of Frederick Douglass*, vol. III, edited by Philip S. Foner (New York: International Publishers, 1952), pp. 198–208.

\*     \*     \*

To what cause may we trace our present sad and deplorable condition? A man of flighty brain and flippant tongue will tell you that the cause of all our national troubles lies solely in the election of Abraham Lincoln to the President of the Republic. To the superficial this is final. Before Lincoln there was peace; after Lincoln there was rebellion. It stands to reason that Lincoln and rebellion are related as cause and effect. Such is their argument; such is their explanation. I hardly need waste your time in showing the folly and falsehood of either. Beyond all question, the facts show that this rebellion was planned and prepared long before the name of Abraham Lincoln was mentioned in connection with the office he now holds, and that though the catastrophe might have been postponed, it could not have been prevented, nor long delayed. The worst of our condition is not to be sought in our disaster on flood or field.—It is to be found rather in the character which contact with slavery has developed in every part of the country, so that at last there seems to be no truth, no candor left within us. We have faithfully copied all the cunning of the serpent without any of the harmlessness of the dove, or the boldness of the lion.

In dealing with the causes of our present troubles we find in quarters, high and low, the most painful evidences of dishonesty. It would seem, in the language of Isaiah, that the whole head is sick, and the whole heart is faint, that there is no soundness in it.—After-coming generations will remark with astonishment this feature in this dark chapter in our national history. They will find in no public document emanating from the loyal Government, anything like a frank and full statement of the real causes which have plunged us in the whirlpool of civil war. On the other hand, they will find the most studied and absurd attempts at concealment. Jefferson Davis is reticent. He seems ashamed to tell the world just what he is fighting for. Abraham Lincoln seems equally so, and is ashamed to tell the world what he is fighting against.

If we turn from the heads of the Government to the heads of the several Departments, we are equally befogged. The attempt is made to conceal the real facts of the case.—Our astute Secretary of State is careful to enjoin it upon our foreign ministers to remain dumb in respect to the real causes of the rebellion. They are to say nothing of the moral differences existing between the two sections of the country. There must be no calling things by their right names—no going straight to any point which can be reached by a crooked path. When slaves are referred to, they must be called persons held to service or labor. When in the hands of the Federal Governments, they are called contrabands— a name that will apply better to a pistol, than to a person. The preservation of slavery is called the preservation of the rights of the South under the Constitution. This concealment is one of the most contemptible features of the crisis. Every cause for the rebellion but the right one is pointed out and dwelt upon. Some make it geographical; others make it ethnographical.

\*      \*      \*

But even this cause does not hold true.—There is no geographical reason for national division. Every stream is bridged, and every mountain is tunnelled. All our rivers and mountains point to union, not division—to oneness, not to warfare. There is no earthly reason why the corn fields of Pennsylvania should quarrel with the cotton fields of South Carolina. The physical and climatic differences bind them together, instead of putting them asunder.

A very large class of persons charge all our national calamities upon the busy tongues and pens of the Abolitionists. Thus we accord to a handful of men and women, everywhere despised, a power superior to all other classes in the country. . . .

Others still explain the whole matter, by telling us that it is the work of defeated and disappointed politicians at the South. I shall waste no time upon either. The cause of this rebellion is deeper down than either Southern politicians or Northern Abolitionists. . . . The Southern politicians and the Northern Abolitionists are the fruits, not the trees. They indicate, but are not original causes. The trouble is deeper down, and is fundamental; there is nothing strange about it. The conflict is in every way natural.—"How can two walk together except they be agreed?" . . . It is something of a feat to ride two horses going the same way, and at the same pace, but a still greater feat when going in opposite directions.

Just here lies a true explanation of our troubles. . . . We have attempted to maintain our Union in utter defiance of the moral chemistry of the universe. We have endeavored to join together things which in their nature stand eternally asunder. We have sought to bind the chains of slavery on the limbs of the black man, without thinking that at last we should find the other end of that hateful chain about our own necks.

A glance at the history of the settlement of the two sections of this country will show that the causes which produced the present rebellion, reach back to the dawn of civilization on this continent. In the same year that the Mayflower landed her liberty-seeking passengers on the bleak New England shore, a Dutch galliot landed a company of African slaves on the banks of the James river, Virginia. The Mayflower planted liberty at the North, and the Dutch galliot slavery at the South.—There is the fire, and there is the gunpowder. Contact has produced the explosion. What has followed might have been easily predicted. Great men saw it from the beginning, but no great men were found great enough to prevent it.

The statesmanship of the last half century has been mainly taxed to perpetuate the American Union. A system of compromise and concessions has been adopted. A double-dealing policy—a facing-both-ways statesmanship, naturally sprung up, and became fashionable—so that political success was often made to depend upon political cheating. One section or the other must be deceived. Before railroads and electric wires were spread over the country, this trickery and fraud had a chance of success. The lighting made deception more difficult, and the Union by compromise impossible. Our Union is killed by lightning.

In order to have union, either in the family, in the church, or in the State, there must be unity of idea and sentiment in all essential interests. Find a man's treasure, and you have found his heart. Now, in the North, freedom is the grand and all-comprehensive condition of comfort, prosperity and happiness. All our ideas and sentiments grow out of this free element. Free speech, free soil, free men, free schools, free inquiry, free suffrage, equality before the law, are the natural outgrowths of freedom. Freedom is the centre of our Northern social system. It warms into life every other interest, and makes it beautiful in our eyes. Liberty is our treasure, and our hearts dwell with it, and receives its actuating motives from it.

What freedom is to the North as a generator of sentiment and ideas, *that* slavery is to the South. It is the treasure to which the Southern heart is fastened. It fashions all their ideas, and moulds all their sentiments.—Politics, education, literature, morals and religion in the South, all bear the bloody image and superscription of slavery. Here, then, are two direct, point-blank and irreconcilable antagonisms under the same form of government. The marvel is not that civil war has come, but that it did not come sooner. But the evil is now upon us, and the question as to the causes which produced it, is of less consequence than the question as to how it ought to be, and can be thrown off. How shall the civil war be ended?

It can be ended for a time in one of two ways. One by recognizing the complete independence of the Southern Confederacy, and indemnifying the traitors and rebels for all the expense to which they have been put, in carrying out this tremendous slaveholding rebellion; and the second is by receiving the slaveholding States back into the Union with such guarantees for slavery as they may de-mand for the better security and preservation of slavery. In either of these two ways it may be put down for a time; but God forbid that any such methods of obtaining peace shall be adopted; for neither the one nor the other could bring any permanent peace.

I take it that these United States are to remain united. National honor requires national unity. To abandon that idea would be a disgraceful, scandalous and cowardly surrender of the majority to a rebellious minority—the capitulation of twenty million loyal men to six million rebels—and would draw after it a train of disasters such as would heap curses on the very graves of the present generation. As to giving the slave States new guarantees for the safety of slavery, that I take to be entirely out of the question. The South does not want them, and the North could not give them if the South could accept them. To concede anything to these slave-holding traitors and rebels in arms, after all their atrocious crimes against justice, humanity, and every sentiment of loyalty, would be tantamount to the nation's defeat, and would substitute in the future the bayonet for the ballot, and cannon balls for Congress, revolution and anarchy for government, and the pronunciamentoes of rebel chiefs for regulating enacted laws.

*There is therefore no escape. The only road to national honor, and permanent peace to us, is to meet, fight, dislodge, drive back, conquer and subdue the rebels. . . .*

We have bought Florida, waged war with friendly Seminoles, purchased Louisiana, annexed Texas, fought Mexico, trampled on the right of petition, abridged the freedom of debate, paid ten million to Texas upon a fraudulent claim, mobbed the Abolitionists, repealed the Missouri Compromise, winked at the accursed slave trade, helped to extend slavery, given slave-holders a larger share of all the offices and honors than we claimed for ourselves, paid their postage, supported the Government, persecuted free Negroes, refused to recognize Haiti and Liberia, stained our souls by repeated compromises, borne with Southern bluster, allowed our ships to be robbed of their hardy sailors, defeated a central road to the Pacific, and have descended to the meanness and degradation of Negro dogs, and hunted down the panting slave escaping from his tyrant master—all to make the South love us; and yet how stand our relations?

At this hour there is everywhere at the South, nursed and cherished, the most deadly hate towards every man and woman of Northern birth. We, here at the North, do not begin to understand the strength and bitter intensity of this slaveholding malice. Mingled with it is a supercilious sense of superiority—a scornful contempt—the strutting pride of the turkey, with the cunning and poison of the rattlesnake. I say again, we must meet them, defeat them, and conquer them. Do I hear you say that this is more easily said than done? I admit it. . . .

*     *     *

But how shall the rebellion be put down? I will tell you; but before I do so, you must allow me to say that the plan thus far pursued does not correspond with my humble notion of fitness. Thus far, it must be confessed, we have struck wide of the mark, and very feebly withal. The temper of our steel has proved much better than the temper of our minds. While I do not charge, as some have done, that the Government at Washington is conducting the war upon peace principles, it is very plain that the war is not being conducted on war principles.

We are fighting the rebels with only one hand, when we ought to be fighting them with both. We are recruiting our troops in the towns and villages of the North, when we ought to be recruiting them on the plantations of the South. We are striking the guilty rebels with our soft, white hand, when we should be striking with the iron hand of the black man, which we keep chained behind us. We have been catching slaves, instead of arming them. We have thus far repelled our natural friends to win the worthless and faithless friendship of our unnatural enemies. We have been endeavoring to heal over the rotten cancer of slavery, instead of cutting out its death-dealing roots and fibres. We pay more attention to the advice of the half-rebel State of Kentucky, than to any suggestion coming from the loyal North. We have shouldered all the burdens of slavery, and given the slaveholders and traitors all its benefits; and robbed our cause of half its dignity in the eyes of an onlooking world.

I say here and now, that if this nation is destroyed—if the Government, shall, after all, be broken to pieces, and degraded in the eyes of the world—if the Union shall be shattered into fragments, it will neither be for the want of men, nor of money, nor even physical courage, for we have all these in abundance; but it will be solely owing to the want of moral courage and wise statesmanship in dealing with slavery, the *cause* and motive of the rebellion.

*     *     *

I have been often asked since this war began, why I am not at the South battling for freedom. My answer is with the Government. The Washington Government wants men for its army, but thus far, it has not had the boldness to recognize the manhood of the race to which I belong. It only sees in the slave an article of commerce—a contraband. I do not wish to say aught against our Government, for good or bad; it is all we have to save us from anarchy and ruin; but I owe it to my race, in view of the cruel aspersions cast upon it, to affirm that, in denying them the privileges to fight for their country, they have been most deeply and grievously wronged. Neither in the Revolution, nor in the last war did any such narrow and contemptible policy obtain. It shows the deep degeneracy of our times—the height from which we have fallen—that, while Washington, in 1776, and Jackson, in 1814, could fight side by side with Negroes, now, not even the best of our generals are willing so to fight. Is McClellan better than Washington? Is Halleck better than Jackson?

*     *     *

Thus far we have shown no lack of force. A call for men is answered by half a million. A call for money brings down a hundred million. A call for prayers brings a nation to its altars. But still the rebellion rages.—Washington is menaced. The Potomac is blockaded. Jeff Davis is still proud and defiant, and the rebels are looking forward hopefully to a recognition of their independence, the breaking of the blockade, and their final severance from the North.

Now, what is the remedy for all this? The answer is ready. Have done at once and forever with the wild and guilty phantasy that any one man can have a right of property in the body and soul of another man. Have done with the now exploded idea that the old Union, which has hobbled along through seventy years upon the crutches of compromise, is either desirable or possible, now, or in the future. Accept the incontestible truth of the "irrepressible conflict." It was spoken when temptations to compromise were less strong than now. Banish from your political dreams the last lingering adumbration that this great American nation can ever rest firmly and securely upon a mixed basis, part of iron, part of clay, part free, and part slave. . . .

To let this occasion pass unimproved, for getting rid of slavery, would be a sin against unborn generations. The cup of slave-holding iniquity is full and running over; now let it be disposed of and finished forever. Reason, common sense, justice, and humanity alike concur with this necessary step for the national safety. But it is contended that the nation at large has no right to interfere with slavery in the States  that the Constitution gives no power to abolish slavery. This pretext is flung at us at every corner, by the same men who, a few months ago, told us we had no Constitutional right to coerce a seceded State—no right to collect revenue in the harbors of such States—no right to subjugate such States—and it is part and parcel of the same nonsense.

In the first place, slavery has no Constitutional existence in the country. There is not a provision of that instrument which would be contravened by its abolition. But if every line and syllable of the Constitution contained an explicit prohibition of the abolition of slavery, the right of the nation to abolish it would still remain in full force. In virtue of a principle underlying all government—that of national self-preservation—the nation can no more be bound to disregard this, than a man can be bound to commit suicide. This law of self

preservation is the great end and object of all Governments and Constitutions. The means can never be superior to the end. But will our Government ever arrive at this conclusion? That will depend upon two very opposite elements.

First, it will depend upon the sum of Northern virtue.

Secondly, upon the extent of Southern villainy.

Now, I have much confidence in Northern virtue, but much more in Southern villainy.— Events are greater than either party to the conflict. We are fighting not only a wicked and determined foe, but a maddened and desperate foe. We are not fighting serviles, but our masters—men who have ruled over us for fifty years. If hard pushed, we may expect them to break through all the restraints of civilized warfare.

I am still hopeful that the Government will take direct and powerful abolition measures. That hope is founded on the fact that the Government has already traveled further in that direction than it promised. . . . No President, no Cabinet, no army can withstand the mighty current of events, or the surging billows of the popular will. The first flash of rebel gunpowder, ten months ago, pouring shot and shell upon the starving handful of men at Sumter, instantly changed the whole policy of the nation. Until then, the ever hopeful North, of all parties, was still dreaming of compromise. The heavens were black, the thunder rattled, the air was heavy, and vivid lightning flashed all around; but our sages were telling us there would be no rain. But all at once, down came the storm of hail and fire.

\*    \*    \*

Nothing stands to-day where it stood yesterday. Humanity sweeps onward. To-night with saints and angels, surrounded with the glorious army of martyrs and confessors, of whom our guilty world was not worthy, the brave spirit of old John Brown serenely looks down from his eternal rest, beholding his guilty murderers in torments of their own kindling, and the faith for which he nobly died steadily becoming the saving faith of the nation. . . .

We have seen great changes—everybody has changed—the North has changed—Republicans have changed—and even the Garrisonians, of whom it has been said that repentance is not among their virtues, even they have changed; and from being the stern advocates of a dissolution of the Union, they have become the uncompromising advocates of the perpetuity of the Union. I believed ten years ago that liberty was safer in the Union than out of the Union; but my Garrisonian friends could not then so see it, and of consequence dealt me some heavy blows. My crime was in being ten years in advance of them. But whether the Government shall directly abolish slavery or not, the war is essentially an abolition war. When the storm clouds of this rebellion shall be lifted from the land, the slave power, broken and humbled, will be revealed. Slavery will be a conquered power in the land. I am, therefore, for the war, for the Government, for the Union, for the Constitution in any and every event.

*Douglass' Monthly*, February, 1862

## REVIEW QUESTIONS

1. Douglass lists numerous causes of the war—as presented by his contemporaries. What are they?
2. Does Douglass trace the nation's calamity to its politics or its character? Why does he make that distinction?
3. What were some of the alternatives for ending the war? Does he advocate the more peaceful solutions? Why or why not?
4. How does he propose to strengthen the Union's military fitness? Would this also strengthen the nation's moral fiber?
5. Does he present a case for seeing the war as a fight for northern instead of southern independence?

## JAMES B. GRIFFIN

# Letters from a Confederate Officer (1862)

*James B. Griffin (1825–1881) was not one of the towering figures of the Confederacy, nor was he simply a soldier in the ranks: he was a southern gentleman, like many others, who went to war to defend his rights and to liberate the South from the North's attempts to subjugate her. He did not specifically state that he fought to preserve slavery, but among the rights he fought for was the right to continue his way of life. Griffin, as one of the wealthiest men in the Edgefield District of South Carolina, belonged to his society's elite class. He was, however, not rich enough or powerful enough to be part of its aristocracy. He did hold leadership positions in his community and state, the most prestigious being brigadier general in the South Carolina militia, but he generally preferred to focus on planting rather than politics. Griffin owned sixty-one slaves and fifteen hundred acres of land in 1860 and used both primarily in cotton production. When war threatened his world in 1861, he was primed to act. That spring Wade Hampton III of South Carolina created a special regiment, a legion that combined the three arms—infantry, cavalry, and artillery—of the mili-*

*tary. Hampton appointed Griffin to the post of major of the cavalry. When the legion's second in command was killed at Manassas (the cavalry missed the engagement as they had been left behind to continue their training), Griffin was promoted to lieutenant colonel. While fulfilling his duties on the Virginia front (attended by two slaves, Ned and Abram), he wrote regularly to his wife, Eliza, nicknamed Leila. Griffin remained with the legion until June of 1862, when, after it was reorganized and the field officer ranks were opened up to elections, he lost his position to another officer and resigned.*

From Judith N. McArthur and Orville Vernon Burton, eds., *"A Gentleman and an Officer": A Military and Social History of James B. Griffin's Civil War* (New York: Oxford University Press, 1996), pp. 132–37, 141–48, 159–65. Reprinted with permission. [Editorial insertions that appear in square brackets are from McArthur and Burton—*Ed.*]

Head Qrs. Legion Camp Wigfall
Sunday night January 5th 1862

My Darling Wife

. . . Camp life is so monotonous, so much of a sameness, that it is really trying to one's patience at times. This frequently accounts for the fact that Soldiers grow extremely eager for a fight. They want something to relieve the dull monotony of the camp life. This is the case, at this time with our troops. I believe they would, almost to a man, be delighted if the Enemy would come along. . . . Col Hampton had another regiment sent to him to day, he now has under his command, besides the Legion, three Regiments and a field battery. He will now be able to give the Yanks a warm reception, wherever they may choose to try to cross the Occoquan. It looked a little squally day before yesterday evening. There was a succession of fires apparently signal fires, from away up the lines near Alexandria, down the Potomac. I dont know what was the meaning of them—It may have been their signal for an advance, but if so they were deterred by a sleet which fell that night. . . . It is now exceedingly cold, but I dont suffer from the cold. A good many of our men have been skating for the last day or two. One poor fellow from the Ga Regiment, was drowned yesterday. Two men were skating when the ice broke and they both went down. This Georgian jumped in and saved them— And afterwards went back to show how he saved them, when the ice broke with him, he went down and drowned before they could get him out. I wrote

to you in my last that Maj'r Butler was sick. I am happy to inform you that he is convalescent—I saw him to day—I hope soon to see him again in the saddle. We have a good many Commissioned Officers now sick—On that account we are in bad condition for a fight—So far as the men are concerned we are in very good fighting condition. I am satisfied that the condition of our army would not be improved, by going into winter quarters, without an engagement. I feel the army would be a good deal demoralized, by such an event. I dont know what to think, whether they will attack us or not. I am fully confident if they do come that we will *lick* them. And if we give them a thorough licking, in their present shattered condition, I think they will begin to think about giving it up. I wish they would quit their foolishness[.] For I tell you, I would much prefer being at home with my Wife and Children—I am delighted to hear that the citizens of old South Carolina, and old Edgefield especially, have come up to the mark—without being drafted. It would have been an everlasting disgrace to have drafted the men when the Enemy were on our own soil. . . .

\*    \*    \*

Head Qrs Legion
Camp Near Occoquan Jany 10th
1862

My Darling Leila

. . . Oh, My Darling what a comfort to me it is, to know that you and the dear Children although separated from me, are well, and appear to be getting along so well. I am also delighted to hear that the Negroes are behaving so well—Do say to them that I hear with pleasure of their good behaviour, and hope they will continue to behave well—tell them they shall not loose anything by keeping it up. I hope also from what you and Willie both write, that our new overseer may do well. Tell him, I have entire confidence in him although a Stranger, from what I have heard of him, and he must do his best. Do ask him if he has a good stand of wheat and oats, and how they look. Has he fed away all the pea vines yet, and how does he get along with his business generally. Tell him to be economical with the corn, I think there is no doubt but he will have plenty, but still it is safest to be economical. Do tell him to see himself to measuring the corn when they go to the mill, and see that no more is sent than is necessary, and that it all comes back. Dont forget sometimes to have the wheat sunned. My Darling I do think you are getting to be a *first rate* manager. And whilst I hope that the time is not near at hand for you, Still, I believe you would make a right managing Widdow. But excuse me—My Darling that is too serious a subject to joke about just now. I am pleased to hear that you have your garden in such fine order. I hope to enjoy some of your nice vegetables this year. Dont forget the Watermelon patch when the proper time arrives. Tell your man Peter, that he knows my plan for planting, and he must pursue it just as if I were there to attend to it. Tell him to make some hills next month, dig the holes deep and put the manure low down, that is the secret of success. If you have an early Spring he might plant a few hills as early as the 10th of March and then keep on planting all the time after that, every week or two. By the way you have never written me how much cotton you and Peter made last year. . . . I really am at a loss to conjecture what is the programme of the Enemy. It was said when the weather was so fine that they were waiting for *hard* weather. Now we have had that and they still tarry. I am thoroughly satisfied, that McClelland [*sic*] doesnt want to come at all. It has been said by some that he has feigned sickness to give him an

excuse for not advancing. It seems that Public opinion would force him to move, as they are already speaking of one who is to supercede him. My opinion is that his reputation now hangs upon a rather slender thread. If he advances, and gets whipped, his reputation is gone—and if he does not advance, it appears as if they will call in another. I hear that he has pledged to advance by the 15th of this month. And I dont believe now he can do so if he wishes. The rains have made the roads so soft, that I dont believe Artillery can be carried over them. But as the Frenchman said, "we shall see what we shall see". My Darling I am really afraid that my letters are not very interesting to you but you must bear in mind that I have nothing else to write about. Tell Willie I am obliged to him for his letter, tell him he doesnt improve as much in writing as I would wish, but to keep trying, he will learn after awhile. Tell him to write to me every week. Give my love to all the Children and kiss them for me. Also remember me to all my friends and relatives. Abram and Ned beg to be remembered to all. Good night, My Love—

Your Jimmie

You asked me if I would like to have a pair of pants. Why, certainly I would be proud to wear them—spun[,] wove and made by your own direction.

JBG

Head Qrs of the Legion
Jany 30th 1862

My Dear Leila

. . . My Darling this is another gloomy day, been raining all day. Yesterday was a very pretty day, it seems as if we cant have more than one pretty day, and then pay for it by having three or four rainy ones. The sun hasnt shone, I dont think more than three or four days this whole month. I have been closely engaged to day, My Darling, examining the Commissary's quarterly report. It was an exceedingly tedious job. And consequently I feel rather tired. I should have written you last night, but for the fact that I didnt sleep much the night before, and was quite sleepy. I said, I didnt sleep much, night before last—It was quite an eventful night. Let me give you an account of it. In the first place a lot of young men from the "Washington Light Infantry" (Citizens of Charleston) took it into their heads to give a concert. They accordingly went to the village of Occoquan, distant from the camp about two miles, and about four from the camp of the Enemy. Just think of that, the idea of having an entertainment of that kind almost within gun shot of the Enemy's lines. But then we had the river Occoquan between us. I knew nothing of the affair until the arrangement was all completed. In the morning before the night of the concert—they asked through their Capt, permission to have it. I consented on condition that they would preserve good order, conduct themselves properly, and not report anything about it in the newspapers. They invited our Field and Staff and said it was gotten up for our express benefit. So that we all concluded to go. Col Hampton being in Richmond. I left the camp in charge of Capt Gary and went down. When I arrived, I found the audience already in attendance. The room was a very nice one, small, and pretty well filled. The crowd consisted mostly of Officers and about a dozen Ladies. I assure you I was surprised to see, in this country, such a collection of the "Fair Sex." True they were not so pretty but they were so dignified and Lady like. The Boys had erected a stage in one end of the house, and had one corner canvassed off for the performers to retire in. This canvass consisted of a very large and handsome quilt, which I suppose they had borrowed for the occasion, and a couple of Soldiers blankets. The curtain which was used to expose the Stage was made of the fly of a tent. They didnt have gas light, but good old *tallow candles*, with a wick about the size of your little finger. So you may imagine that the light wasnt very brilliant. The Performers were all blacked, and sung various songs, and performed beautifully on several instruments. They had the piano, two violins, a tamborine and one fellow played the banjo and another beat the bones. The music was really exquisite, and the whole affair passed off very pleasantly indeed. They closed about eleven oclock and we set out for camp—We had ridden about a mile when my ear caught the sound of a rifle, in the direction of Colchester. The very place we are guarding and

where we always keep a picket. In a few seconds I heard another, and then another, and then a volley. I was riding my fine mare "Belle Tucker". I gave her the spur and she soon carried me to the ferry where our Picket was stationed. I was accompanied by Adjt Barker. I found after seeing the Picket that the firing was over the river, in an old house just across the ferry. It had by this time all ceased. But I could distinctly hear the moaning and groaning of some one who was undoubtedly wounded. I immediately suspected the cause. We have for a long time had eight or ten Texians over the river who have been acting as scouts for us. They have harrassed the Enemy a great deal and they the Enemy have made many fruitless attempts to catch them. It turned out as I suspected[.] The Texians were all in this old house (there were eight of them in all[)], and had all gone to bed, leaving no watch at all. The Enemy were doubtless piloted to the house, and the first thing the Texians knew, the Enemy were trying to break the door down. The house was a two story one with several rooms in it—they separated some in each room, and the firing commenced. The night was exceedingly dark—and the Texians couldnt tell how many they were fighting. Certainly a pretty large crowd. The firing lasted only a few minutes, and the Cowardly rascals ran off—leaving two of their men dead and one badly wounded (died that night) in the yard. One of the Texians was wounded but not seriously. I ordered more men down to the river, and awaited to see what would turn up—It wasnt long before I heard a whistle across the river—I answered, and the Texians asked for a boat—I sent over and had them brought over and the wounded man attended to— He is now doing very well. Those Texians are number one men, and their conduct on that occasion was as gallant and brave as any thing that has occurred in this war. Just think of their cool courage, to be suddenly surprised by an Enemy, from whom they had no reason to expect any quarter— Surrounded in the night by these rascals, in an old house, which was but a shell—and see them separating themselves each man with his rifle in hand slipping to a window and firing at their opponents— who were also pouring the bullets into the old

House. Just think, I say of this conduct and compare it to the dastardly cowardice of the Enemy who had at last found the very men whom of all others they wanted to find—they had them completely surrounded and one would suppose just where they would like to have them. They also from the sign, next day, had a large force—And notwithstanding all this as soon as their men began to fall they actually ran off—The Texians say they carried off several wounded, they could distinctly hear them complaining and groaning as they went off. But they left one wounded man on the ground who hallooed and begged them to come back after him. I suppose he was the one I heard crying after I got down. The Texians came out after the Enemy were gone, and found this wounded man and two dead ones—They carried the wounded man in the house—built up a fire for him, gave him some water—took the arms of the three men, and then brought their own wounded man down to the river—When I sent for them as I have already told you. The next morning they went over and decently buried them. I didnt get back to camp that night until near three O Clock—and that is the reason I was so sleepy last night. Dont you think it was quite an adventerous night? . . .

*   *   *

Head Quarters of the Legion
Camp near Occoquan Feby 2nd
1862

My Dearest Wife

. . . This is the *rainiest—snowiest—muddiest* and with all, the most disagreeable country I ever met up with. This has been a clear sunny day—and now, (ten O Clock at night) it is raining—Night before last it snowed—Yesterday it thawed, and it seems that every thing combines to keep the earth saturated with water. The roads, being traveled over every day by wagons, of course continue to grow worse. I havent travelled over them but from accounts, and from what I see around here, I know they are awful. I have been trying for the last two weeks—to have some new batteries built—but owing to the dreadful weather, get along very slowly.

We never have two days in succession in which we can work. I never was so heartily tired of mud and water in my life. Col Hampton has not yet returned from Richmond—He has been gone a week—I am expecting him every day.

My Darling, you have no idea how proud I felt, yesterday while reading one of your very dear letters to find that you felt that you had reason (as you thought) to be proud of your Husband. It done me a *power* of good. For while I dont expect much from the cold Charity of the world—And indeed ask for little, It is really charming and enspiriting to feel that you are appreciated by one who loves you and one who is prompted by no deceitful motives, to bestow praise on you. But My Darling, let me say, while I thank you for the compliment, I have so far done nothing to merit it—Except perhaps, in showing a willingness to do, whenever an opportunity may offer. I have so far, never had the fortune (whether good or bad) to be engaged with the Enemy—I hope however, if it shall ever be my fortune to be engaged with them, that my conduct will be such, that if I do not merit your praise, will not cause you to feel ashamed—I, like every man, of course would not like the idea of being even wounded in battle—But I would dislike very much to go out of this Campaign without going through at least one battle—More especially as most of the officers of the Legion have had that good fortune. I assure you that the dangers of a battle, are not near so great as one, who is unacquainted, would suppose. I do not expect any fighting of consequence, in this army before Spring—But I think it will come then pretty heavy, if there is no change.

I honestly believe that the battle itself is about the least of dangers, to which the Soldier is exposed. Sickness is much more dangerous, caused from necessary exposure. The health of our Command is very good, at this time considering the quantity of bad weather we have had. My own health continues very good—I wouldnt have believed that I could have gone through what I have. But it doesnt hurt me at all. I have entire command of the Legion, during the Col's absence and flatter myself that we get along very well. I cant tell whether the men like me or not—they are very respectful to me, but that they are obliged to be— Military authority is the most powerful known to man. But doesnt do harm unless abused—I think the officers generally like me and most of the men two [*sic*] but some of them I reckon do not—An Officer, as a general rule, who does his duty is apt to make some Enemies.

\*      \*      \*

Head Qrs of the Legion
February 19th 1862

My Dear Leila

Well, my Darling, I have at last received my trunk, it came to day—Just four weeks from the time you started it. My Darling you just tried yourself to see how many nice things you could send. I opened the trunk to day (it came about twelve O Clock) and had a regular party. Invited the whole mess and Capt Gary, Lieut Tompkins and Ball from Laurens, a member of Gary's company. I cut one of the cakes, which was beautiful and very nice, and opened the apple cordial. All agreed in pronouncing it *splendid*. You were very highly complimented, while the cake & cordial was rapidly consumed. Every thing came perfectly safe and sound, notwithstanding the length of time it had been coming. The sausages were somewhat moulded, but I dont think are at all damaged, at least I hope not, for I am really *longing* for some. We also sampled the nice brandy peaches, I told the party that they were put up by your own fair hands, and four years ago at that. They were really very nice. Col Hampton is laid up in his tent with the mumps. (I tell him he is the largest case of mumps, I ever saw) So that he could not participate in the feast. I, sent him, however, a share of the good things. My darling every thing you sent is really a treat, but I believe I appreciate more than any thing else, the nice butter. I can eat it with a relish, and have the satisfaction of knowing it is *clean* and nice. We had such a nice lunch and enjoyed it so much, that we didnt have dinner until five O Clock, and it being a dark evening we had to

have a candle lit. I suppose you will think that we are quite aristocratic. And so we are. Our usual meal hours are as follows, Breakfast from nine to ten (Dark rainy mornings from ten to eleven.[)] Dinner from three to four, *tea* from eight to nine. Dont you think that is rather aristocratic. We sampled, at dinner, your catsup—it is splendid. Every thing is nice *very nice*, ham[,] biscuit and all. For all of which my Darling will please accept the sincere thanks of her husband, and also of the whole mess. I am also obliged to you for the clothing you sent. I didnt need any thing except the towels and handkerchiefs, I have lost some that I had. The shirts you sent are very pretty, I will wear them after the cold weather is gone. I wear nothing now but the calicoe. . . . My Darling the Mail has just come and the papers bring the unwelcome news of the capture of Fort Donnelson [*sic*] by the Federals. Our reverses have been frequent of late— It seems that we fought gallantly at the Fort—but the full particulars I havent seen. Our defeat at Roanoke was really disgraceful. Well, I hope the day of triumph is not far distant. I have no other news to write—It has been raining all day as usual.

Do remember me kindly to your Father and family, also to all friends. Give my love to all the Children, and accept for yourself the warmest love of your devoted

Jimmie

Camp of the Legion
February 26th 1862

My Darling Leila

I am delighted, my Darling to learn by your last letter that Minnie has at last "Come through". And I am also pleased, and tender my congratulations that she has another Boy. Notwithstanding you all were anxious for her to have a daughter. I really think she should be proud that she has another Boy. This is the time, above all others, that *men* should be raised. And this too, is the time above all others when females deserve sympathy. I assure you, I feel, far more anxiety about my dear little daughters, than I do about my Boys. For while men can manage to work for themselves, and can fight the battles of their Country if necessary, Females are very dependent. True, they too can do a great deal, and, 'tis true that our Southern Ladies have done and are still acting a conspicuous part in this war[.] In many instances (to the shame of our Sex be it said) a much bolder and more *manly* part than many men. But still, when it comes to the physical test, of course, they are helpless. It is on this account, that I think the Parents should congratulate themselves on the birth of a son rather than a daughter. We cannot see, My Darling, into the future, but I trust & have confidence in our people to believe, that if the unprincipled North shall persist in her policy of Subjugating the South, that we, who are able to resist them, will continue to do so, until we grow old and worn out in the service, and that then, our Sons will take the arms from our hands, and spend their lives, if necessary, in battling for Liberty and independence. As for my part, If this trouble should not be settled satisfactorily to us sooner—I would be proud of the thought that our youngest Boy—Yes Darling little Jimmie, will after awhile be able and I trust willing to take his Father's place in the field, and fight until he dies, rather than, be a Slave, *Yea* worse than a Slave to Yankee Masters—Have you ever anticipated, My Darling, what would be our probable condition, if we should be conquered in this war? The picture is really too horrible to contemplate. In the first place, the tremendous war tax, which will have accumulated, on the northern Government, would be paid entirely and exclusively by the property belonging to the Southerners. And more than this we would be an humbled, down trodden and disgraced, people. Not entitled to the respect of any body, and have no respect for ourselves. In fact we would be the most wretched and abject people on the face of the Earth. Just be what our Northern Masters say we may be. Would you, My Darling, desire to live, if this was the case? would you be willing to leave your Children under such a government? No—I know you would sacrifice every comfort on earth, rather than submit to it. Excuse me, My Darling, I didnt intend to, run off in this strain. You might think, from my painting this hor-

rid picture to you, that I had some doubts as to whether we might not have to experience it. But No, I havent the most remote idea that we will. I think our people will arouse themselves, shake off the lethargy, which seems now to have possession of them, and will meet the issue like *men.* We must see that we have *all*—Yes our all—staked upon the result—And we are obliged to succeed and we will do it. Just at this time the Enemy appears to have advantage of us. But this is no more than we have, all along, had of him, until lately. He did not succombe and give up for it—and shall we, Who have so much more to fight for than he has, do so? I am completely surprised and mortified at the feeling manifested by our people at this time. But they will soon rally and come with redoubled energy. Our Soldiers too, or rather our Generals have got to learn to fight better. The idea, of a Genl surrendering with 12000 men under his command,[1] is a species of bravery and Generalship, which I do not understand. I wish Congress would pass a law breaking an officer of his commission who surrenders. . . . My Darling tell Spradley, not to commence planting corn early[.] My land will not admit of early planting, of either corn or cotton. I generally, commence planting corn from the 15th to the 20th of March, and cotton about the same time in april. I see that Congress is about passing a bill, to impose a heavy tax on cotton raised this year[.] If they pass it—I wish no land planted in cotton except the new ground, and the field next to the overseers house, all the ballance planted in corn. I will write you, however in time. My Darling, Now is the time to bring out all your courage— Do not become despondent—Dont matter what *alarmists* and Croakers may say—take advice from him whom you *know* will advise you for the best. Keep up your spirits and your courage, and the clouds will soon pass away, and sun shine will return—My sheet is full—and I will close by begging to be remembered to all—My love to My Children and my Darling Leila

from your Husband

---

[1] Brigadier General Simon B. Buckner surrendered the garrison at Fort Donelson.

## REVIEW QUESTIONS

1. What kind of tone does Griffin take with his wife? What does that reveal about him and about their relationship?
2. Is there any evidence in the letters that the war affected gender roles and relations?
3. What does Griffin reveal about camp life near the enemy line?
4. What opinions did he hold of the North and Northerners?
5. What did he think about southern attitudes and actions at that time? Why did he believe the South would ultimately prevail?

# ELISHA HUNT RHODES

## FROM The Diary of a Union Soldier (1862)

*Elisha Hunt Rhodes (1842–1917) was a boy when he enlisted as a private in the Second Rhode Island Volunteers; he was a man and the colonel in charge of the regiment when it was disbanded in July 1865. His story shows how the war and the Union Army offered opportunities for advancement to able—and lucky, for many an able man died—young men who could face, survive, and grow through adversity. Rhodes's pluck, intelligence, and sense of responsibility showed at an early age. When his father died, the sixteen-year-old boy left school and became a clerk for a mill supplier so he could support his mother and two brothers. Because his family needed him, he resisted enlisting in the first regiment raised by Rhode Island, but when the call went out to form the second one, he could not contain his desire to join the army. After obtaining his mother's consent, he marched off to war.*

From Robert Hunt Rhodes, ed., *All for the Union: The Civil War Diary and Letters of Elisha Hunt Rhodes* (1985; New York: Orion Books, 1991), pp. 60–61, 64–65, 73–79, 81–85, 92–93. [Editorial insertions appear in square brackets—*Ed.*]

\*   \*   \*

*March 21/62*—I am twenty years of age today. The past year has been an eventful one to me, and I thank God for all his mercies to me. I trust my life in the future may be spent in his service. When I look back to March 21/61 I am amazed at what has transpired. Then I was a peaceful clerk in Frederick Miller's office. Today I am a soldier anxious to move. I feel to thank God that he has kept me within his fold while so many have gone astray, and trust that he will give me Grace to continue to serve Him and my country faithfully. I have now been in service ten months and feel like a veteran. Sleeping on the ground is fun, and a bed of pine boughs better than one of feathers. We are still waiting for orders which must come very soon. Many of the men are broken down by the late march, but I am stronger than ever.

*     *     *

*Camp Brightwood, Tuesday morning, March 25/62, One o'clock*—We are to leave Camp at 7 A.M. to take steamer, destination unknown. So Goodbye old Camp Brightwood where we have had lots of fun and learned a soldier's duty. May God bless and prosper us.

*     *     *

*Newport News, Va., March 29/62*—We are now at Newport News where the Union Army can be found. The next place is Yorktown where the Rebels will be found.

*March 31/62*—Our tents have come, and we are in comfort again. Plenty of beef, pork, ham, bacon, etc. Yesterday I had a beefsteak and sweet potatoes. Very good living for a soldier. I called at General Keyes' Headquarters yesterday. I am well and contented as usual. Camp life agrees with me.

*     *     *

*Battlefield of Williamsburg, Va., May 7th 1862*—Sunday last we received news of the evacuation of Yorktown, and we were ordered to leave our camp at Young's Farm and join the main Army. We crossed the river at Lee's Mills and then followed the line of forts and rifle pits until midnight when we encamped in a deserted Rebel camp. Everything denoted the haste in which the Rebels left their works. It rained hard all night, and we lay in the mud and water but felt happy, for now it was our turn to chase and the Rebels to run. Early Monday morning we moved towards Williamsburg, and about noon we began to hear the roar of cannon and rattle of musketry. We pushed on through mud that caused teams to be mired and batteries to halt, but by taking advantage of the woods and fields where the ground was not so soft or cut up, our Division arrived under fire at 4 P.M. Here we were placed in the reserves and remained until nearly dark when our Brigade was pushed to the front and took position in the edge of a piece of

woods about six hundred yards in front of Fort Magruder. Until dark we could see the Rebel gunners load and fire the cannon from the fort, and we had to stand it, for we were ordered for some reason not to fire. All night the shells continued to burst over our heads, and in the mud and discomfort we prayed for daylight. Sometime after midnight we could hear the rumble of teams in the direction of Williamsburg, and just as day began to break Major Nelson Viall and myself crawled towards the fort. After approaching quite near and not seeing anyone we arose and walked up the glacis and looked into an embrasure. Behold, the fort was deserted. We hurried around to the rear and entered the gate. The ground was covered with dead men and horses. I found in one of the tents left standing some documents that gave the number of the garrison. While we were in the fort the 10th Mass. charged across the open space and entered the fort. They were surprised to find two Rhode Island soldiers already in possession. Both General Couch and Gen. Charles Devens who commands our Brigade made speeches to our Regiment and thanked the men for their coolness under fire. The field presented a horrible appearance, and in one small spot I counted sixty dead bodies. The Rebels threw away much of their baggage, and the road is filled with broken teams and gun carriages. Our Cavalry are now in pursuit, and many prisoners are being sent to the rear. Thank God for this victory and may we have many more and so end the war.

*May 8th 1862*—Monday night orders were received for a Light Brigade under command of General George Stoneman to be formed and follow the retreating Rebels. The 2nd R.I. Vols, Col. Frank Wheaton; the 98th Penn. Vols, Col. John F. Ballier; the 6th U.S. Cavalry; the 8th Illinois Cavalry, Col. Farnsworth Robertson's and Tidball's regular Batteries were detailed for this duty. Colonel Wheaton commands the two Infantry Regiments and Lt. Colonel Steere the 2nd R.I. We are now fifteen miles from Williamsburg on the road to Richmond, and we pick up prisoners every mile. The bugle has just sounded the advance and we must move.

*Camp near Pamunkey River, Va., May 11/62*—Friday our Cavalry came up with the Rebels and charged through the lines, and falling into an ambush, turned and came back. The Cavalry lost three killed and several wounded but brought back a number of prisoners. The Rebels opened with skill and we were ordered to move up. Our Artillery replied and the Rebel rear guard moved on. We followed to this place and are now waiting orders. Food is scarce, and all that we have to eat is the cattle killed by the way. No bread or salt in the Regiment and I am most starved. But it is all for the Union and we do not complain.

*May 12th 1862*—Left camp in the evening and marched to White House Landing on the Pamunkey River. Here we found three gun boats, and we feel more comfortable. In the evening we attended an outdoor jubilee meeting held by the Negroes. One of them preached a sermon. He tried to prove from the Bible that truth that every man must seek his own salvation. . . .

\*        \*        \*

*Malvern Hill July 1/62*—O the horrors of this day's work, but at last we have stopped the Rebel advance, and instead of following us they are fleeing to Richmond. The battle of today is beyond description. The enemy advanced through fields of grain and attacked our lines posted upon a long range of hills. Our gun boat threw shell over our heads and into the Rebel lines. All attempts to drive us from our position failed and at night the Rebels retired. Our Regiment supported the Batteries of our camps and did not suffer much, but saw the whole of the grand fight.

*Harrison's Landing, James River, July 3/62*—We left Malvern Hill last night and in the midst of a pouring rain marched to this place where we arrived early this morning. O how tired and sleepy I am. We have had no rest since June 24th, and we are nearly dead. The first thing I noticed in the river was the steamer *Canonicus* of Providence. It made me think of home. We stacked arms and the men laid down in the rain and went to sleep. Lieutenant-Colonel Viall threw a piece of canvas over a bush and putting some straw upon the

ground invited me to share it with him. We had just gone to sleep when a Rebel Battery opened and sent their shells over our heads. We turned out in a hurry and just in time, too, for a shot or shell struck in the straw that we had just left. This shot covered Colonel Viall's horse with mud. We were ordered to leave our knapsacks and go after this Rebel Battery. But our men could hardly move, and after going a short distance we halted and other troops went on in pursuit. Battery "E" 1st R.I. Artillery sent out some guns and I hear that one of the Rebel guns was captured. We returned to our knapsacks and the men are trying to sleep.

*July 4th 1862*—This morning all the troops were put to work upon the line of forts that have been laid out. As I was going to the spring I met General McClellan who said good morning pleasantly and told our party that as soon as the forts were finished we should have rest. He took a drink of water from a canteen and lighted a cigar from one of the men's pipes. At Malvern Hill he rode in front of our Regiment and was loudly cheered. I have been down to the river. I rode the Adjutant's horse and enjoyed the sight of the vessels. Gun boats and transports are anchored in the stream. Rest is what we want now, and I hope we shall get it. I could sleep for a week. The weather is very hot, but we have moved our camp to a wood where we get the shade. This is a queer 4th of July, but we have not forgotten that it is our national birthday, and a salute has been fired. We expect to have something to eat before long. Soldiering is not fun, but duty keeps us in the ranks. Well, the war must end some time, and the Union will be restored. I wonder what our next move will be. I hope it will be more successful than our last.

*Harrison's Landing, Va., July 9/62*—The weather is extremely hot, and as the men are at work on the forts they suffer much. The Army is full of sick men, but so far our Regiment seems to have escaped. The swamp in which we lived while in front of Richmond caused chills and fever. I have been very well, in fact not sick at all. Lt. Col. Nelson Viall of our Regiment is now in command of the 10th Mass. Vols., their field officers being all sick or wounded. Fred Arnold is in the hospital in Washington. Last night President Lincoln made a visit to the Army. As he passed along the lines salutes were fired, and the men turned out and cheered. We see General McClellan nearly every day, and he often speaks to the men. How I should like to see my home. In God's own time we shall meet on earth or in Heaven. I have been busy all day preparing muster and pay rolls. We hope to get some money some day.

* * *

*Harrison's Landing Sunday July 27/62*—We are having a fine day and commenced regular camp duties the same as at Camp Brightwood. After "Guard Mount" the Regiment was paraded in front of Colonel Wheaton's quarters and we had church service. The men were seated in the form of a hollow square, and the Chaplain preached from the centre. Some of the men are very much interested, while others are totally indifferent to what is going on. The band is now playing in front of the Colonel's tent, and crowds of soldiers are listening to the music. The Colonel has returned from his visit to Mrs. Wheaton at Fortress Monroe. The Sloop of War *Dacotah* has arrived. Lieut. Wm. Ames' brother is an officer on board of her. Some of the Rhode Island Artillery boys paid me a visit today.

*July 31/62*—I have been quite sick for a few days but am all right again now. Col Wheaton has recommended me for promotion to Second Lieutenant, for as the letter reads: "Good conduct in the different engagements on the Peninsular." I suppose my commission will come soon. Hurrah. Yesterday the Army was under arms as it was reported that the Rebel iron clad *Merrimac* was coming. Well let her come, and bring the Rebel Army with her. We can take care of them now. I have received a box. The cake was spoiled, but the other things were all right.

*Harrison's Landing, Va. Aug. 2nd 1862*—Today we moved our camp back into a pine grove. Shelter tents have been issued to the men. Each man has one piece about six feet long and four feet wide. Two men button these pieces together, and by throwing it over a ridge pole, supported at each end, a shelter is formed. It is open at each end and

serves to shield from the sun, but makes a regular shower bath when it rains. The men carry each a piece of tent in their knapsacks. We have a fine camp with regular company streets. Tonight we had a fine dress parade followed by Divine Service. We have a large open field near our camp which we use for parades and drills. It is rumored that we are to move. I hope it will be towards Richmond.

*Aug. 3/62*—Thursday morning about 1 o'clock a gun was heard followed by the bursting of a shell near our camp. This was repeated, and soon the gunboats joined in with the heavy shots and we had music. We found that a Rebel Light Battery had taken position on the south side of the James and opened upon our fleet of transports, some of the shells coming over to the camps. The gunboats drove the enemy away, and the next morning troops crossed the river and burned the houses that gave the enemy shelter. We are looking for recruits, but so far in vain. If men are not patriotic enough to volunteer to save the country I hope a draft will be ordered.

* * *

*Camp near Yorktown, Va., Aug. 24/62*—Sunday night again and I fear we are no nearer the end of the war than we were when we first landed at Fortress Monroe five months ago. But then we have learned some things, and now I hope we shall go ahead and capture Richmond. We have moved our camp from near the river to a hill where we get plenty of pure water from a spring. This is a great luxury, for in most of our camps we have been obliged to go long distances for water. This hill was occupied by General Fitz-John Porter's Corps during the late siege, and we occasionally find shot and shell lying about. Each company has a wide street, and we have a parade ground in front of the camp. It looks now as if our Corps (Keyes 4th) would remain on the Peninsular, as most of the other troops have been sent away. I was much surprised at the appearance of Yorktown. We entered town through a gate in a fort built upon a bluff. There are not more than twenty houses in the village and some of these must have been built before the Revolutionary War for they are of the gamble roof style and all tumbling down. Passing through the main street we saw the old forts built by the British Army when it was beseiged by Washington in 1781. Some of these forts were used by the Rebels. Still further on we saw the Rebel works built of bags of sand covered with earth. Some of them were on high bluffs with deep ravines in front. Some of the Rebel guns are still mounted, while others lay upon the ground dismounted by our fire. Passing through another gate we came to the open plain which separated Yorktown from our batteries. Here we halted for a short time, and I visited a large lot enclosed by a rail fence over the entrance to which were the words: "Union Cemetery." . . . We marched on to our old lines where we saw the Batteries for heavy guns and mortars. A darkey said that the shell from our guns "played a tune like a fiddle." We passed through the old camps and encamped near the river. I visited with Levi Carr in one of our bayonet earthworks. It is in the yard of a plantation. The owner told me that he moved away when the fight began, but he might have remained in safety for not one Rebel shot struck his house. He said that he owned hundreds of acres of land, but could only raise two and a half dollars in money, and that he got from our people. The people are very poor indeed. They are reaping their reward. . . .

*        *        *

*Sunday Aug. 31/62*—We arrived at Alexandria this morning after a pleasant sail from Yorktown. Here we learned that a battle had been fought at, or near, Manassas. We landed and marched in the direction of the old Bull Run ground where we understand our forces have met the enemy.

*Sept. 1st 1862*—Today we passed through Fairfax Court House and formed line of battle at Germantown with a battle going on two miles in our front. It rained in torrents, and I never in all my life ever heard such thunder or saw such lightning. It seemed as if Nature was trying to outdo man in the way of noise, for all the time the cannon roared and muskets rattled while the air was filled with flying missiles. But Nature won, and the battle ceased. We camped on the field for the night amid the dead and dying.

*Sept. 2nd 1862*—This morning we found the entire Army retreating and our Division was left to protect and cover the rear. As soon as our lines were formed our troops that had been fighting the day before passed through to the rear. As the Rebels came in sight we too moved off with the gallant 1st Rhode Island Cavalry with us. The Rebels shelled us lively, but we did not stop and reached Alexandria all right about midnight.

*Sept. 3/62*—Today we took a steamer at Alexandria and went up the Potomac past Washington, through the draw at Long Bridge and landed at Georgetown. From here we marched up the river and crossed Chain Bridge into Virginia again. It is hard to have reached the point we started from last March, and Richmond is still the Rebel Capital.

*Camp near Chain Bridge, Va., Sept. 5/62*—Last Wednesday after landing at Alexandria, Levi Carr and myself procured a quart of milk, and as we had only one cup and one spoon sat down to take turns in enjoying our feast. As we were eating Colonel Wheaton called: "Lieutenant Rhodes!" I went across the railroad track to where he was standing where he took me by the hand and congratulated me on my promotion. Well, I am proud, and I think I have a right to be, for thirteen months ago I enlisted as a private and I am now an officer. I am grateful to God for all his mercies to me.

*        *        *

*Near Williamsport, Md., Sept. 23/62*— . . . [On] the 17th, we saw the Battle of Antietam fought almost at our feet. We could see the long lines of battle, both Union and Rebel and hear the roar as it came from the field. The Rebel trains of waggons were moving all day towards the river. At dark we marched down the mountain and started for the battlefield where we arrived and went into camp. The next morning we were put in the front lines. I have never in all my soldier life seen such a sight. The dead and wounded covered the ground. In one spot a Rebel officer and twenty men lay near a wreck of a Battery. It is said Battery "A" 1st R.I. Artillery did this work. The Rebel sharpshooters and skirmishers were still at work and the bullets whizzed merrily. At noon the Rebels asked and received permission to bury their dead, and the firing ceased for awhile but commenced again in the afternoon. The 2nd R.I. was ordered forward and we charged up a hill and driving the enemy away took possession. Here we lay all night with the bullets flying over us most of the time.

The next morning the enemy shelled our Regiment, but it was their last shots, for as we moved forward they retired, and we entered Sharpsburg. The town is all battered to pieces and is not worth much. Here we remained until midnight of the 19th when we moved to Williamsport. It was reported that the Rebels were here in force. After forming our lines the entire Division moved on the town with flags flying. It was a grand sight to see our long lines extending through fields and woods, hills and dales, make this advance. Picket or skirmish firing was going on in front, but after marching some distance we halted. Several were killed in the Division and many wounded. Sunday morning we found that the enemy had recrossed the river. O, why did we not attack them and drive them into the river? I do not understand these things. But then I am only a boy.

\*     \*     \*

*Near Downsville, Md., Tuesday Sept. 30th 1862—* Still in Maryland with all sorts of rumors about our next move. The days are hot and the nights cold, and just now we are having beautiful weather with moonlight nights, which makes guard duty very pleasant. I suppose that we shall be looking for winter quarters soon.

We have a mess composed of the following officers: Capt. Samuel B. M. Read and Lieut. Benjamin B. Manchester of Co. "I," Lieut. Edward A. Russell commanding Co. "C" and Captain Stephen H. Brown and Lieut. Elisha H. Rhodes of Co. "D." We have attached to our mess three servants to carry our blankets, shelter tents and a few simple cooking utensils. When we halt the servants put up our shelter tents and find us straw if possible. They do our cooking and look after things generally. Near our present camp there lives an old lady who supplies

our mess with soft bread. On the march salt pork toasted on a stick with hard bread and coffee is our principal diet. . . . Sunday last a soldier of Co. "A" died and was buried with military honors. It was not an unusual scene for us, yet it is always solemn. First came the muffled drums playing the "Dead March" then the usual escort for a private. Eight privates, commanded by a corporal, with arms reversed. Then an ambulance with the body in a common board coffin covered with the Stars and Stripes. Co. "A" with side arms only followed while the Company officers brought up the rear. On arriving at the grave the Chaplain offered prayer and made some remarks. The coffin was then lowered into the grave, and three volleys were fired by the guard, and then the grave was filled up. The procession returned to camp with the drums playing a "Quick March." Everything went on as usual in camp as if nothing had happened, for death is so common that little sentiment is wasted. It is not like death at home. May God prepare us all for this event which must sooner or later come to all of us.

\*     \*     \*

*Oct. 8/62—* . . . The people in Maryland appear as a rule to be loyal to our government and have suffered much during the past few weeks. The nights are cold, and, as our shelter tents furnish poor protection, the men spend a good deal of the night about huge camp fires. But we do not complain, as it is all for the Union. The war will not end until the North wakes up. As it is now conducted it seems to me to be a grand farce. When certain politicians, Army contractors and traitors North are put out of the way, we shall succeed. General McClellan is popular with the Army, and we feel that he has not had a fair chance.[1]

\*     \*     \*

*Near Downsville, Oct. 10th 1862—*Mrs. Wheaton, the wife of our Colonel, is in camp. She is very kind

---

[1]Since I wrote the above as a boy, I have changed my mind in regard to Gen. McClellan. I now honestly believe that while he was a good organizer of Armies, yet he lacked the skill to plan campaigns or handle large bodies of troops. [E. Hunt Rhodes, 1885]

to the officers and men and is a great favorite with all. Gen. Charles Devens is now in command of our Division and Colonel Wheaton commands the Brigade. Lt. William Ames is sick in Washington. It is reported that he is to be made Major of the 12th R.I. Vols. Well, he will make a good one. The weather is very fine and we have had no rain for a long time. Orders have come for us to move and we are all ready, but know nothing of our destination. Virginia probably.

*Camp near Downsville, Md., Oct. 15th 1862*— For the past four days it has been cloudy and very cold and as the men have no overcoats they suffer some. We are, however, expecting new clothing very soon. We are very much ashamed that the Rebels were allowed to make their late raid into Pennsylvania. If this Army cannot protect the loyal states we had better *sell out* and go home. I ought not to complain, but I am mortified to think that we did not catch some of the Rebel raiders. We are all ready for a move. Let me describe the camp after marching orders are received. We see an orderly or staff officer dash into camp with his horse covered with foam, and he says: "Colonel Wheaton, your Regiment will move in fifteen minutes." The orders are sent around to the Captains, and down comes the shelter tents, blankets are packed up and haversacks filled with rations. Perhaps, and it usually happens, all the straw is burned, when another orderly rides leisurely into camp and says: "The order to move is countermanded." Then we go to work, set up our shelters and get ready to live again. Some of the men will be quite glad while the growlers who always find fault say: "It is always so,

and we never shall leave this camp." The same men will want to get back after marching a few miles. I am acting Adjutant for a few days.

\*    \*    \*

*Dec. 31/62*—Well, the year 1862 is drawing to a close. As I look back I am bewildered when I think of the hundreds of miles I have tramped, the thousands of dead and wounded that I have seen, and the many strange sights that I have witnessed. I can truly thank God for his preserving care over me and the many blessings I have received. One year ago tonight I was an enlisted man and stood cap in hand asking for a furlough. Tonight I am an officer and men ask the same favor of me. It seems to me right that officers should rise from the ranks, for only such can sympathize with the private soldiers. The year has not amounted to much as far as the War is concerned, but we hope for the best and feel sure that in the end the Union will be restored. Good bye, 1862.

## REVIEW QUESTIONS

1. What does Rhodes reveal about camp life?
2. How does his description compare to Griffin's?
3. Does he provide realistic or romantic portrayals of camp and combat?
4. In his evaluations of northern attitudes and actions, what does he criticize?
5. How did Rhodes change between March and December 1862? What accounts for that change?

# ROBERT E. LEE

# Appomattox, Virginia (1865)

*As 1865 dawned, the Confederacy set. General William T. Sherman, who had completed a Union strategy of splitting the South into isolated and vulnerable sections with his destructive March to the Sea from Atlanta to Savannah in December 1864, began mowing through the Carolinas in February. That month Vice President Alexander Stephens of the Confederacy met with President Lincoln aboard a Union ship about ending the war, but although the meeting was evidence of a faltering South, Stephens still refused to surrender unless the Union recognized southern independence. Once again the politicians could not solve the conflict, so the military had to end it. The contest revolved around the forces of General Ulysses S. Grant (1822–1885), the commanding general of the Union Army, and those of General Robert E. Lee (1807–1870), commander of the Army of Northern Virginia. Grant was an 1843 West Point graduate who had served with distinction in the Mexican War but had become a particularly undistinguished civilian until the Civil War resurrected him as a bold and successful military leader. Lee, an 1829 graduate of West Point, had been one of the ablest and most respected officers in the United States Army before the war. He had been offered command of the federal forces when the war began, but turned down the job and the country: he resigned his commission. Soon thereafter he took command of Virginia's army. The last days of the war commenced with Lee's abandonment of Petersburg and Richmond on 2 April. In the hope that he could get around Grant and move south to join General Joseph E. Johnston's troops in North Carolina, he started his troops westward toward Lynchburg. They never arrived, for the Union forces soon had them surrounded. On 9 April 1865 Lee surrendered to Grant at Appomatox Court House.*

From Clifford Dowdey, ed., *The Wartime Papers of R. E. Lee* (Boston: Little, Brown, 1961), pp. 934–39.

## *General Order, No. 9*

Headquarters, Army of Northern Virginia
April 10, 1865

After four years of arduous service, marked by unsurpassed courage and fortitude, the Army of Northern Virginia has been compelled to yield to overwhelming numbers and resources.

I need not tell the brave survivors of so many hard fought battles, who have remained steadfast to the last, that I have consented to the result from no distrust of them.

But feeling that valor and devotion could accomplish nothing that would compensate for the loss that must have attended the continuance of the contest, I determined to avoid the useless sacrifice of those whose past services have endeared them to their countrymen.

By the terms of the agreement officers and men can return to their homes and remain until exchanged. You will take with you the satisfaction that proceeds from the consciousness of duty faithfully performed, and I earnestly pray that a Merciful God will extend to you His blessing and protection.

With an increasing admiration of your constancy and devotion to your country, and a grateful remembrance of your kind and generous considerations for myself, I bid you all an affectionate farewell.

R. E. LEE
Genl

\*     \*     \*

# To Jefferson Davis

Near Appomattox Court House, Virginia
April 12, 1865

Mr. President:

It is with pain that I announce to Your Excellency the surrender of the Army of Northern Virginia. The operations which preceded this result will be reported in full. I will therefore only now state that upon arriving at Amelia Court House on the morning of the 4th with the advance of the army, on its retreat from the lines in front of Richmond and Petersburg, and not finding the supplies ordered to be placed there, nearly twenty-four hours were lost in endeavoring to collect in the country subsistence for men and horses. This delay was fatal, and could not be retrieved. The troops, wearied by continued fighting and marching for several days and nights, obtained neither rest nor refreshment; and on moving on the 5th on the Richmond and Danville Railroad, I found at Jetersville the enemy's cavalry, and learned the approach of his infantry and the general advance of his army towards Burkeville. This deprived us of the use of the railroad, and rendered it impracticable to procure from Danville the supplies ordered to meet us at points of our march. Nothing could be obtained from the adjacent country. Our route to the Roanoke was therefore changed, and the march directed upon Farmville, where supplies were ordered from Lynchburg. The change of route threw the troops on the roads pursued by the artillery and wagon trains west of the railroad, which

impeded our advance and embarrassed our movements. On the morning of the 6th Genl Longstreet's corps reached Rice's Station on the Lynchburg Railroad. It was followed by the commands of Genls R. H. Anderson, Ewell, and Gordon, with orders to close upon it as fast as the progress of the trains would permit or as they could be directed (diverted) on roads farther west. Genl Anderson, commanding Pickett's and B. R. Johnson's divisions, became disconnected with Mahone's division, forming the rear of Longstreet. The enemy's cavalry penetrated the line of march through the interval thus left and attacked the wagon train moving towards Farmville. This caused serious delay in the march of the center and rear of the column, and enabled the enemy to mass upon their flank. After successive attacks Anderson's and Ewell's corps were captured or driven from their position. The latter general, with both of his division commanders, Kershaw and Custis Lee, and his brigadiers, were taken prisoners. Gordon, who all the morning, aided by Genl W. H. F. Lee's cavalry, had checked the advance of the enemy on the road from Amelia Springs and protected the trains, became exposed to his combined assaults, which he bravely resisted and twice repulsed; but the cavalry having been withdrawn to another part of the line of march, and the enemy massing heavily on his front and both flanks, renewed the attack about 6 p.m., and drove him from the field in much confusion. The army continued its march during the night, and every effort was made to reorganize the divisions which had been shattered by the day's operations. But the men depressed by fatigue and hunger, many threw away their arms, while others followed the wagon trains and embarrassed their progress. On the morning of the 7th rations were issued to the troops as they passed Farmville, but the safety of the trains requiring their removal upon the approach of the enemy, all could not be supplied. The army reduced to two corps under Longstreet and Gordon, moved steadily on the road to Appomattox Court House. Thence its march was ordered by Campbell Court House through Pittsylvania towards Danville. The roads were wretched and the progress of the trains slow.

By great efforts the head of the column reached Appomattox Court House on the evening of the 8th, and the troops were halted for rest. The march was ordered to be resumed at one (1) a.m. on the 9th. Fitz Lee with the cavalry, supported by Gordon, was ordered to drive the enemy from his front, wheel to the left, and cover the passage of the trains, while Longstreet, who from Rice's Station had formed the rear guard, should close up and hold the position. Two battalions of artillery and the ammunition wagons were directed to accompany the army. The rest of the artillery and wagons to move towards Lynchburg. In the early part of the night the enemy attacked Walker's artillery train near Appomattox Station on the Lynchburg Railroad, and were repelled. Shortly afterwards their cavalry dashed towards the Court House till halted by our line. During the night there were indications of a large force massing on our left and front. Fitz Lee was directed to ascertain its strength, and to suspend his advance till daylight if necessary. About five (5) a.m. on the 9th, with Gordon on his left, he moved forward and opened the way. A heavy force of the enemy was discovered opposite Gordon's right, which, moving in the direction of Appomattox Court House, drove back the left of the cavalry and threatened to cut off Gordon from Longstreet. His cavalry at the same time threatening to envelop his left flank, Gordon withdrew across the Appomattox River, and the cavalry advanced on the Lynchburg road and became separated from the army. Learning the condition of affairs on the lines, where I had gone under the expectation of meeting Genl Grant to learn definitely the terms he proposed in a communication received from him on the 8th, in the event of the surrender of the army, I requested a suspension of hostilities until these terms could be arranged. In the interview which occurred with Genl Grant in compliance with my request, terms having been agreed on, I surrendered that portion of the Army of Northern Virginia which was on the field, with its arms, artillery, and wagon trains; the officers and men to be paroled, retaining their side arms and private effects. I deemed this course the best under all the circumstances by which we were surrounded. On the morning of the 9th, according to the reports of the ordnance officers, there were seven thousand eight hundred and ninety-two (7892) organized infantry with arms, with an average of seventy-five (75) rounds of ammunition per man. The artillery, though reduced to sixty-three (63) pieces, with ninety-three (93) rounds of ammunition, was sufficient. These comprised all the supplies of ordnance that could be relied on in the State of Virginia. I have no accurate report of the cavalry, but believe it did not exceed two thousand and one hundred (2100) effective men. The enemy was more than five times our numbers. If we could have forced our way one day longer it would have been at a great sacrifice of life; at its end, I did not see how a surrender could have been avoided. We had no subsistence for man or horse, and it could not be gathered in the country. The supplies ordered to Pamplin's Station from Lynchburg could not reach us, and the men deprived of food and sleep for many days, were worn out and exhausted.

With great respect, yr obdt svt

R. E. Lee

Genl

# To Jefferson Davis

Richmond, Virginia
April 20, 1865

Mr. President:

The apprehensions I expressed during the winter, of the moral condition of the Army of Northern Virginia, have been realized. The operations which occurred while the troops were in the entrenchments in front of Richmond and Petersburg were not marked by the boldness and decision which formerly characterized them. Except in particular instances, they were feeble; and a want of confidence seemed to possess officers and men. This condition, I think, was produced by the state of feeling in the country, and the communications received by the men from their homes, urging their return and the abandonment of the field. The movement of the enemy on the 30th March to Dinwiddie Court House was consequently not as strongly met as similar ones had been. Advantages were gained by him which discouraged the troops, so that on the morning of the 2d April, when our lines between the Appomattox and Hatcher's Run were assaulted, the resistance was not effectual: several points were penetrated and large captures made. At the commencement of the withdrawal of the army from the lines on the night of the 2d, it began to disintegrate, and straggling from the ranks increased up to the surrender on the 9th. On that day, as previously reported, there were only seven thousand eight hundred and ninety-two (7892) effective infantry. During the night, when the surrender became known, more than ten thousand men came in, as reported to me by the Chief Commissary of the Army. During the succeeding days stragglers continued to give themselves up, so that on the 12th April, according to the rolls of those paroled, twenty-six thousand and eighteen (26,018) officers and men had surrendered. Men who had left the ranks on the march, and crossed James River, returned and gave themselves up, and many have since come to Richmond and surrendered. I have given these details that Your Excellency might know the state of feeling which existed in the army, and judge of that in the country. From what I have seen and learned, I believe an army

cannot be organized or supported in Virginia, and as far as I know the condition of affairs, the country east of the Mississippi is morally and physically unable to maintain the contest unaided with any hope of ultimate success. A partisan war may be continued, and hostilities protracted, causing individual suffering and the devastation of the country, but I see no prospect by that means of achieving a separate independence. It is for Your Excellency to decide, should you agree with me in opinion, what is proper to be done. To save useless effusion of blood, I would recommend measures be taken for suspension of hostilities and the restoration of peace.

I am with great respect, yr obdt svt
R. E. LEE
Genl

## REVIEW QUESTIONS

1. Was defeat the result of one particular factor or a concourse of circumstances?
2. Did Lee blame his soldiers for the defeat?
3. What were some of the terms of the surrender?
4. Why did Lee recommend a cessation of all hostilities and acceptance of reunion?

# FRANK MOORE

# FROM *Women of the War* (1866)

*Frank Moore (1828–1904) compiled and edited numerous works from the 1850s through 1880s. He gathered songs, speeches, and other materials related to the American Revolution and the Civil War. In 1866 he published* Women of the War: Their Heroism and Self-Sacrifice. *He was not the only person to write about women's contributions to the war, for quite a number of other people published accounts of and by women participants. In doing so, they provided evidence of women's growing participation in public affairs and of society's gratitude and yet uneasiness about the possible effect on gender roles and social norms. As Moore notes in his introduction of the book: "The histories of wars are records of the achievements of men, for the most part. . . . It has been different in our Conflict for the Union. . . . Everywhere there were humble and unknown laborers. But there were others, fine and adventurous spirits, whom the glowing fire of patriotism urged to more noticeable efforts. . . . Like the soldiers of the armies, they were from every rank in life, and they exhibited a like persistence, endurance, and faith."*

*Although many of his subjects were reluctant to be interviewed, their families and admirers obviously believed that their actions were a credit to the nation and to womanhood and thus worthy of publication and emulation. Reinforcing the latter point, that of what actions other women should imitate in similar situations, Moore focuses primarily on "ladies" rather than those "born in less-favored circles," though he does recount the story of Bridget Divers, the "Irish Biddy," who acted as chaplain, nurse, and sometimes surgeon. He provides only one short chapter on "Women as Soldiers," which notes the affecting death of one rash young woman, for he prefers dwelling on those who served in the hospitals and Sanitary and Christian Commissions and who organized other soldiers' aid societies. Most of his chapters provided a sketch, based on conversation and correspondence, of a woman whose deeds honored her country and whose country in turn should honor her.*

---

*Moore introduction, pp. iii–v.

From *Women of the War: Their Heroism and Self-Sacrifice* (Hartford, Conn.: S. S. Scranton & Co., 1866), pp. 148–57, 159–63, 168–69.

## Mrs. Mary W. Lee.

This name will recall to the minds of ten thousands of our brave soldiers who fought in the army of the Potomac the face and the figure of a cheerful, active, efficient, yet tender-hearted woman, herself the mother of a soldier boy, who for month after month, and year after year, while the war continued, moved about the hospitals of the army a blessing, a comfort, and a hope to thousands of weary sufferers.

\*       \*       \*

. . . In this great battle[1] Mrs. Lee was one of the first on the field; and her labors, commencing among the first wounded, continued, without weariness or abatement, till the last poor, mutilated hero of the "crutch brigade" was moved from the general hospital late in December.

Although it was her first experience in a great battle, Mrs. Lee prepared for the awful scenes that were to follow with the coolness and judgment of a veteran. She had two large buckets filled with water, one for washing wounds, the other for quenching thirst. As the action grew hot, the first tub grew of a deeper and deeper crimson, till it seemed almost as red as blood itself; and the other was again and again replenished, as the men came in with faces black with powder, and clothes stiff with gore. The hunger, too, in many cases, was clamorous. Many of the men had eaten nothing for more than twenty-four hours. Mrs. Lee found a sutler,[2] who, with enterprise that would have been becoming in anything less purely selfish, had urged his wagon well to the front, and was selling at exorbitant rates to the exhausted men. She took money from her private purse, and again and again bought his

---

[1]The Battle of Antietam.

[2]Peddler or vendor registered with and regulated by the army.

bread and soft crackers at his army rates. At last such repeated proofs of generosity touched the heart of the army Shylock, and he was determined not to be outdone so entirely by a woman. About the third or fourth time she pulled out her purse he exclaimed, "Great God, I can't stand this any longer. Give that woman the bread!" The ice was now broken, and from giving to her, he began to give away, himself, till his last cracker had gone down the throat of a half-famished hero, and he drove away with his wagon lighter and his heart softer for having met a noble-hearted woman.

*        *        *

Immediately after the battle there was that confusion and delay in the supply trains inevitable in the best-conducted army at the time of a great action. At one of the field hospitals where Mrs. Lee was doing the best she could for the crowd of sufferers, there was found nothing in the way of commissary supplies but a barrel of flour, a barrel of apples, and a keg of lard. To a practical housekeeper, as she is, this combination seemed to point to apple dumplings as the dish in which they could all be employed to the best advantage; and the good-natured astonishment of the poor fellows, who looked for nothing but black coffee and hard-tack, was merged in admiration for the accomplished cook who could there, almost on the battle-field, serve them with hot dumplings.

While the battle was still raging, and orderlies were galloping past where Mrs. Lee was at work, she asked one of them if Sumner's corps were yet engaged. "Yes," was the reply; "they have just been double-quicked into the fight." For a few moments her heart sank within her, and she grew sick, for her son was in that corps, and all her acquaintances in the army. Her anguish found relief in prayer; after which she grew so calm and cheerful that a wounded boy, who lay there on the grass beside her, said, "Madam, I suppose you haven't any one in the battle, or you couldn't be so calm."

The night after the battle she went to Sedgwick's division hospital, and while preparing some food for the sufferers, was greatly annoyed by some worthless camp-followers, who would not carry food to the wounded, and when she left to carry it, they stole everything she had cooked. She went up stairs, where most of the wounded were, and asked if any one was there who had sufficient authority to detail her a guard. A pleasant voice from one of the cots, where an officer lay bleeding, said, "I believe I have. Just take the first man you can find, and put a gun in his hand." It was General John Sedgwick; and she had no more annoyance from camp thieves.

*        *        *

Not long after the battle, all the field and regimental hospitals were merged into one general hospital at Smoketown; and here Mrs. Lee was aided by a noble and efficient corps of army workers—Miss Maria Hall, Mrs. Barlow, Mrs. Husband, Mrs. Harris, and others, most of whom labored through the war, and enjoyed the utmost confidence of the surgeons and all who observed the superior character and spirit of their work.

During the fall many touching instances of noble youths dying of their wounds, and making the last sacrifice for their country, occurred among those daily visited by Mrs. Lee. Among others was the case of Henry Cole, of the nineteenth Massachusetts. He had been wounded in the leg, and strong hopes were entertained that he might recover. His mother came on from Massachusetts to nurse him. He was her only child. As she bent over his cot, and saw him gradually becoming weaker and more pallid, tears fell fast on the coverlet, and she would exclaim, "O, if money could restore you, I'd gladly give all I have in this world."

He was a Christian, and a well-educated young gentleman; everything that a mother's heart, in its pride and its unfathomable love could hope for in a son. "O Henry, my son," she would say, amid her tears, "when you are gone, my light is gone out. I've nothing to live for."

"Mother," he would answer, "I am only going a little while before you; we shall meet again." Then, just before he died, repeating these farewells, he added, "Tell all the boys good by for me, and tell them never to give up our noble cause."

This hospital was blessed with the attendance and service of a superior surgeon-general in Dr. Vanderkieft, and a most excellent and praiseworthy chaplain in Rev. Mr. Sloan. Hardly a soldier in the Smoketown Hospital but loved him as a brother. Many a face tortured with pain grew smooth when his cheerful countenance entered the tent.

When the hospital was fully established, the tents were divided between Mrs. Husband, Miss Hall, and Mrs. Lee; and their labors, thus systematic and persistent, continued till some time in December, when the wounded at Fredericksburg demanded attention.

*    *    *

The religious exercises at this hospital were often deeply interesting. Mr. Sloan was as much respected for piety as he was beloved for his kindness. Miss Hall commonly led the singing; and many a touching, fervent, and whole-souled prayer for the Union and the army was offered by men who would hobble in on crutches. The more they suffered in the cause, the more they loved it.

While thus occupied at Antietam, Mrs. Lee heard with alarm of the great explosion of powder at Harper's Ferry, by which so many of the seventy-second Pennsylvania were killed or wounded. Her son was in that regiment. She hurried up there, and labored some time among those sufferers, compounding for their burns a salve that was found very grateful and healing. Her boy was fortunately not injured in the explosion.

From Antietam the hospital workers next went to Falmouth, on the Rappahannock, where the army was encamped, after Burnside's unfortunate attack at Fredericksburg. Upon leaving Antietam, Dr. Vanderkieft expressed his opinion of the character and worth of Mrs. Lee, and her labors there, in the following terms:—

"It is with great pleasure that I bear witness to the invaluable services of Mrs. Lee in this hospital. She knew no rest while there were any who needed her assistance. Her unwearied activity was a subject of universal comment, among officers and men, and her untiring efforts in behalf of patriots have won the love and esteem of all to whom she has

ministered. I commend Mrs. Lee to the highest position that a noble and Christian woman can fill."

Chaplain Sloan, also, in a letter from Antietam, in which he speaks of the workers there, says of Mrs. Lee: "None of the newspaper notices tell half the story of her good works. Many a poor boy, that suffered here, will long remember her kindness. She labored harder, and did more to alleviate the pains and sufferings of the wounded at Antietam than any three others."

This describes her labors at the Falmouth hospitals, and all the others with which she was connected during the three years of her army life. She was regular, persistent, thorough, and obedient to the surgeons in all she did, and all she gave to the soldiers. Her wards were always found in perfect order, and well supplied. For a great part of the time she was placed in charge of the light diet and special diet department, where her duties were laborious, and often vexatious.

The rickety old stove upon which she prepared her food for the sick was often in a wretched condition. When set up in a tent it generally smoked, and fuel was not always abundant, or of a good quality. Notwithstanding all these discouragements, her temper was always cheerful, her health perfect, and her duty performed with thoroughness and punctuality.

After a temporary absence from Falmouth, with her sick son, in March, she returned, and was on duty among the wounded at Chancellorsville.

She was at the Lacey House Hospital, and had a full view of the storming of Mayre's Heights, by Sedgwick's corps, on the 2d of May.

When that fierce engagement was at its height, the men that had been wounded in the skirmishes of the days previous all dragged themselves to the galleries and terraces of the house, Mrs. Lee helping them, and watched the conflict with eager forgetfulness of their own sufferings. When at length Sedgwick, and the brave sixth corps, after two repulses, made the final and triumphant charge, sweeping over the battlements from which Burnside had been so terribly repulsed in December, everybody that had a well arm raised it, with ringing cheers, over his head, and shouted, till their brave companions on the other side heard and answered back their triumph. Mrs. Lee stood by her little cooking tent, wiping dishes, and joined in the general delight by waving her towel, as a flag, and shouting with the rest. She did more than this. She fell upon her knees, and thanked God that those formidable lines, from which the Union forces had been so often repulsed with frightful carnage, were at last carried, and the national flag waved in triumph over them.

But the eight thousand wounded that came pouring across the Rappahannock soon engrossed the attention of every one who could do anything for their relief, and Mrs. Lee, with the other ladies, labored all day, and a considerable part of each night, striving to mitigate some of the accumulated suffering and pain.

\*       \*       \*

Mrs. Lee was at Gettysburg as soon as the cannon smoke had cleared away from the blood-stained hill-side, and labored in the second corps hospital, and also at Letterman General Hospital, for three months following the great battle.

\*       \*       \*

One of her most valued reminiscences of Gettysburg is a letter of thanks, drawn up and numerously signed by the boys in whose ward she had acted as nurse. They say,—

MRS. LEE.

Dear Madam: We now hasten to express to you our thanks for the numerous luxuries and kind services we have received from you, as from the hands of our own kind mothers, for which we shall ever feel grateful to you.

While endeavoring to meet the urgent calls of our wronged country, we had the misfortune to be wounded far from home, and, as we thought, from friends. Here we have found your kind hand to care for us, and alleviate our wants as much as possible. We shall ever feel grateful to you for such motherly care as can never be forgotten; and besides the thousand thanks bestowed on you, the God of our country will ever bless you with a special blessing—if not now, surely you will receive it hereafter.

This testimonial was signed by a large number in Ward B, sixth division, General Hospital, Gettysburg.

\*       \*       \*

There was, of course, a vast number of wounded, and the demand for hospital workers was never more urgent than during the months of May and June, 1864. Mrs. Lee made her way to Fredericksburg, and found that war-battered old town one vast hospital. The first and great clamor was for food. Transportation from Belle Plain was slow, on account of the fearful condition of the roads; and though the enemy was crippled and falling slowly back to Richmond, and Fredericksburg is only a days ride from Washington, thousands and thousands of our men suffered constantly from hunger. Upon Mrs. Lee's arrival, Dr. Bannister gave her the charge of the special diet of the second corps. The kitchen furniture with which she was supplied consisted of one small tin cup, and there was no source from which the proper utensils could be obtained. Mrs. Lee remembered, however, that the year before, Mrs. Harris, at the Lacey House, on the other side of the Rappahannock, had left a cooking stove, which might be there yet. Obtaining an ambulance, and going over on the pontoon, she found the old stove, dilapidated, indeed, and rusty; but she could make gruel and panada[3] on it. She found some old kettles, too, which she took over, and scoured up, so that in a few hours a kitchen had been extemporized. The boys broke up clapboards and pickets for fuel, and soon the buckets of gruel, tea, and coffee, and bowls of chicken soup, began to circulate among the famishing heroes. As long as she remained in Fredericksburg, and, in fact, all that summer, from daylight till long after the nine o'clock drum-taps, she did little but cook, cook, cook. Sometimes, just as the hospital had become composed for the night, and the old campaign stove had grown cool for the first time in eighteen hours, an immense

---

[3]Version of "pap" that was a mixture of boiled flour or bread and water or milk or both.

train of ambulances would come rolling in from the front, all loaded down with men, sick, wounded, dusty, and famishing. There was no other way but to rise, and work, perhaps, till long past midnight. It was fortunate that with such willingness of heart and such skill, nay, such genius, as she displayed for cooking under all the disadvantages of camp life, Mrs. Lee had also a robust constitution and excellent health; otherwise she must have broken down under the long-continued labors and sleeplessness of that last grand campaign against Richmond.

\*       \*       \*

Having thus sympathized in the sufferings and disasters of our soldiers, and in the agony that their death occasioned at so many firesides, it was fit that Mrs. Lee should be present at the happy consummation, and join in that grand pæan of victory, that, commencing at Richmond, in the first days of April, went swelling, in a glorious chorus, from the Atlantic to the Pacific shores.

In the hospital where Mrs. Lee then was, the exultations of the poor, languishing soldiers were full of almost frantic joy.

"Such a time!" she writes; "the people nearly went crazy. Hospital help, ladies, wounded and all, were beside themselves. Processions were formed, kettles improvised for drums; all kinds of noises were made to manifest our joy. Bells were rung, cannon fired, steam whistles blown; men cheered and shouted themselves hoarse. President Lincoln

visited the hospital while I was there. He went round to every man, and said he wanted to shake the hand of every man who had helped to gain so glorious a victory; and he had a kind word for all."

In the hospitals of Petersburg and Richmond Mrs. Lee continued for a month after Lee's surrender; for, though the war was ended, there remained a great multitude of the sick, and those wounded in the last engagements.

Then, when there were no more homeless and suffering patriots; no more wounds to be stanched; no more long trains of ambulances, with their groaning and bleeding freightage; no more caldrons of gruel and mutton soup to be cooked for great wards full of half-famished boys, Mrs. Lee went home, and slipped back into the happy routine of domestic usefulness.

\*       \*       \*

## REVIEW QUESTIONS

1. What did Mary Lee do?
2. Why was the way she performed her tasks noteworthy? Consider how Moore described Mrs. Lee and her actions.
3. How did Moore relate what he considered to be proper manly, not just womanly, behavior?
4. What does this excerpt reveal about the nature of support services in the war?

# INTERPRETING VISUAL SOURCES: PICTURING THE CIVIL WAR

## MATHEW BRADY AND ASSOCIATES

The Civil War was the first "modern" war in American history. People have de-scribed it as such because of who and what were involved in the conflict and how many people participated in or were affected by it. Americans of both sexes, all ethnic groups, and from the various regions either participated in or felt the im-pact of this "total war"—a term denoting warfare that extends beyond battle-fields and military forces to batter and even destroy civilian persons, property, and societies.

Technology contributed to the totality of this war. Modern military weapons were more powerful, more accurate, and more plentiful due to new manufacturing processes and the multiplying factories and factory workers producing them. These weapons were used not only on the battlefields but also against civilian communi-ties. Those "under the gun" certainly felt the impact of the technology, but even those away from the camps and battlefields of war could see and feel the impact through the product of another new mechanical and chemical marvel: the camera.

Photographers and combat artists, most associated with the Union forces, headed into camps and combat to record the war. Mathew B. Brady (1822–1896) was one of the most distinguished and, at least at the beginning of the conflict, perhaps most prolific of the group. In 1861 Brady not only set out to photograph the war himself, he assembled the material and human resources needed to cover more than one army or battlefield at a time. Over the following years, some of his associates, such as Alexander Gardner, Timothy H. O'Sullivan, and James F. Gib-son, left his employ and continued their work independently. Brady, on the other hand, became more dependent on assistants over time as his eyesight failed; even so, whether he was operating the cameras, supervising shoots, or putting on gallery shows, Brady provided the public with some remarkable images of the war.

Brady's work reflected his constant desire to perfect his craft and his strong drive to preserve the images of the people and events of his era for posterity. Soon after the photographic process invented by Louis Jacques Mandé

Daguerre became public knowledge in 1839, Brady set out to master it. He experimented with everything from preparing the photographic plates, modifying and maneuvering the camera boxes and lenses, seating a subject or finding the best place to record a scene, to mixing the chemicals and developing the plates with them. He soon became a very successful professional photographer and established studios in Washington, D.C., and New York City.

While many people commissioned him to take their pictures, Brady sought out America's leading figures in politics, the sciences, and the arts. Between 1845 and 1861 he managed to seat or stand many of these leaders before his cameras. In doing so Brady was already forging a connection between photography and the historical record, a link that grew during the war when Brady and other photographers headed out to record military scenes.

After receiving permission from President Lincoln to accompany the Union Army, Brady set up a black, hooded wagon that became known as the "What-is-it" wagon. He designed it to transport and shield his cameras and the exposed wet plates from which he and his people developed their photographs. Troops may have questioned what it was at first, but Brady, his assistants, his competitors, and their equipment soon became familiar sights.

The photographers set up their big cameras—and they were huge contraptions balanced on long legs and draped in dark cloth—in camps, where they could safely photograph soldiers at their everyday tasks and officers in meetings, but they also hazarded themselves and their equipment on battlefields. These cameramen did manage to produce a few action shots, but the fact that there were not many was due more to the limitations of the equipment than to any unwillingness on the part of the photographers to take them. Moving objects only produced blurs in photographs, and the lighting conditions had to be just right for anything to develop on the plates then in use. The photographers may not have taken many shots of the armies in action, but they made up for that in the numerous photographs they produced of the dead and destroyed at battles' end. Gardner, in particular, seemed especially interested in recording the human toll.

Brady was good at taking photographs, but he was even better at disseminating them. The master photographer showed and sold his work and that of his assistants at his galleries. In fact, his promotion of their work under his name may have been what drove some of them out of his employ (it also made proper attribution difficult for later historians). Most Americans then, however, were interested in the products, not the producers. Those who visited Brady's gallery shows, purchased copies of the photographs, or saw the woodcut illustrations based on his images in newspapers could examine the scenes and see the faces of war as they had never seen them before. Brady and his fellow photographers thus helped strip away some of the glory of war as they exposed both the humanity and inhumanity of camp and combat.

# Yorktown Fortifications (1862)

1862 PHOTOGRAPH OF ENTRENCHMENTS AND HEAVY ARTILLERY AT YORKTOWN, VA
Library of Congress

*The first year of the war, 1861, was actually rather quiet in terms of army operations. Both sides had to recruit soldiers, stockpile supplies, decide on strategies, and then move their troops into place. In 1862 fierce fighting in the West led to Union victories at Fort Henry, Fort Donnelson, and Shiloh. The morale and expectations raised by success in the West were, however, soon leveled by lost opportunities and defeat in the East. The Peninsular Campaign, for instance, which was supposed to have culminated with Union forces marching into Richmond, ended with the troops pulling out and heading north to defend against Confederate invasions there. General George B. McClellan actually built the Army of the Potomac into a very strong, disciplined force, which showed in the siege of Yorktown between 5 April and 4 May. He did not use it to advantage, however, in the following battles.*

*For much of the siege the weather hindered photographic operations, but whenever the rain lifted and the clouds blew away, Brady and his assistant operators were out in the camp and on the fortifications. Their photographs revealed the combination of old and new in this war: how McClellan built up massive fortifications (modified from older military engineering traditions) to house modern weaponry—their new, very heavy artillery pieces. As it turned out, the Confederates decided not to challenge those pieces—they abandoned their works instead. McClellan would have to leave the safe haven of his fortifications and pursue them, not something at which this cautious general excelled. When he had still not taken Richmond by July, Lincoln packed the general off to Washington.*

# Antietam/Sharpsburg (1862)

TROOPS DEPLOYED: UNION FORCES
Library of Congress

*Lincoln gave McClellan a chance to redeem himself against the Confederate forces, now under command of General Robert E. Lee, that invaded western Maryland in September. McClellan, with the advantage of having received critical intelligence about the disposition of Lee's troops, should have moved to the attack right away, but instead he waited (courageous about his own safety, he was perhaps overly careful of his soldiers) for sixteen hours before moving forward. McClellan thus lost the chance to strike a truly decisive if not fatal blow against the Confederate forces. The Union forces did win the battle of Antietam (called Sharpsburg by the Confederates) on 17 September, but victory came at a horrendous cost: over two thousand Union soldiers died and more than ten thousand others were pronounced wounded or missing, while Lee's dead, wounded, and missing combined to a total of over ten thousand. When McClellan failed to pursue that weakened Confederate army and prevent it from reaching safety (and the chance to fight again another day), the disgusted Lincoln removed him from command and commenced a search for a more aggressive general.*

*Two of Brady's operators, Gardner and Gibson, trekked after the Union forces to the village of Sharpsburg and from there out into the battlefields that had once been cornfields between the Antietam and Potomac rivers. There is some uncertainty as to whether the photographers arrived on the day of battle or the day after;*

not true
a stalemate

thus it was either on the 17th or 18th when they first set up their camera behind McClellan's headquarters. If it was on the 17th, as Gardner noted (with an eye to later public viewing, he may have taken dramatic license), then the photographers may have caught Sumner's Second Army Corps beginning to move against D. H. Hill's Confederate division. If the scene was shot on the 18th, then they actually recorded a reserve artillery unit that had moved up to replace the troops that had been active the day before.

On the day of the battle, the Confederates were pushed back to the Sunken Road, but they fought every step of the way. Once they were entrenched in the road, they repelled attack after attack by the federal forces until, finally, they had to leave it in the hands of their dead and dying. On the 19th, after the Union troops confirmed their possession of the field, Gardner and Gibson headed out to capture the carnage on their plates. Although a few European photographers had taken pictures of the victims of their mid-nineteenth-century wars, this was apparently the first time American photographers had been able or willing to set up their equipment before all the dead were buried. The resulting images of bloated, contorted corpses morbidly fascinated the American viewing public.

# Fredericksburg (1862–63)

AFTER THE BOMBARDMENT, DECEMBER 1862
National Archives

In December 1862 Union forces struck Confederate troops at Fredericksburg in northern Virginia. _General Ambrose E. Burnside was determined to cross the Rappahannock River and dislodge the southern forces that held the town on the river's west bank._ On 11 December, federal engineers struggled to construct a bridge as southern sharpshooters took aim to stop them. Burnside's solution to that threat was an artillery barrage that not only knocked out the snipers but destroyed a good bit of the town. Then General Joseph Hooker sent over two regiments to cover the bridge builders by fighting through the town. Nightfall brought a pause in the combat, but the next day, once pontoon bridges were in place, the federal army crossed the river. In the midst of vicious street fighting, Union soldiers sacked the town.

Brady, assisted by O'Sullivan, drove the "What-is-it" wagon across one of the bridges and quickly set up a camera to photograph the destroyed town. As it turned

_Failed attack_

*out, they only had that one day. On the 13th the two forces renewed the battle, and this time the southern troops won.*

*Brady returned to Fredericksburg in the spring of 1863 when once again Union and Confederate forces were facing off there. General Hooker, who had replaced Burnside, decided to leave a decoy force in place to deceive the Southerners and move the main part of his army to Chancellorsville to attack Lee's left flank. It was a good plan, but Lee managed to move his troops quickly enough to counter the threat. While the two primary forces clashed at Chancellorsville between 2–4 May, the remaining troops, with Brady driving his wagon in their wake, fought for Fredericksburg. The Union troops took the latter, but the Confederates won the former. Soldiers were wounded, as Brady showed, and killed at both.*

UNION WOUNDED, MAY 1863
Library of Congress

# Gettysburg (1863)

DEAD CONFEDERATE SOLDIER, DEVIL'S DEN, 6 JULY 1863
Library of Congress

DEAD CONFEDERATE SOLDIER, DEVIL'S DEN
Library of Congress

*Brady arrived at the Gettysburg, Pennsylvania, battlefield too late to record the hu-
man remains of that three-day engagement in July 1863. When he did arrive, he directed his assistants to photograph the landscape and landmarks of the area. The first
photographers to reach the battlefield and record the carnage were Brady's former associates, Gardner, O'Sullivan, and Gibson. Gardner, the leader of the group, apparently made it his mission to preserve the toll of war on his plates. This could have
been a statement about the destructiveness of war, but it was also a marketing ploy:
people paid to be horrified. Gardner and his crew took pictures of the dead on the 5th
and 6th of July. Their subjects were primarily Confederates, perhaps because the
Union Army buried its dead first, perhaps because northern audiences may have
found pictures of enemy dead more acceptable or palatable than such photographs of
their own soldiers.*

*The Gardner contingent did not merely record the fallen where they found them.
These cameramen, like others, moved their cameras around their subjects in attempts
to capture compelling photographic compositions. In a few instances they also moved
props—weapons and equipment—and even bodies so that they could create stronger
pictorial stories. Gardner and O'Sullivan did this when they found the body of a
young Confederate soldier amidst the boulders and stone walls of Devil's Den.*

DEAD CONFEDERATE SOLDIER IN NEW POSITION
Library of Congress

# Freedman's Camp (1865)

RICHMOND, VIRGINIA: FREEDMAN'S ENCAMPMENT
National Archives

*During the war many slaves fled to the Union Army. Called "contrabands," some served as laborers and servants while others eventually became soldiers. Once the war was over, many, though certainly not all, ex-slaves continued to move away from their former masters and homes. Some moved north or west, heading for the areas they had long heard described as free or full of opportunities. Many more freedmen, as they were known, gathered where there were federal military forces and government officials. The Bureau of Refugees, Freedmen, and Abandoned Lands attempted to care for their immediate needs and assist them in gaining the support and skills they required to help themselves. It could offer, however, only temporary solutions— as temporary as the tents in a Freedman's camp, such as this one within sight of Richmond, Virginia—to some of the very difficult problems of Reconstruction.*

## REVIEW QUESTIONS

1. In what ways do these photographs reveal aspects of modern warfare and total war?
2. What do they reveal about the people, including the photographers themselves, involved in or affected by armed conflict?
3. Do these photographs illuminate the reality of war? Do they romanticize war?
4. How could a photographic record of a scene affect someone's interpretation of a historical event?

# 17 ❧ RECONSTRUCTION: NORTH AND SOUTH

*The assassination of Abraham Lincoln in April 1865 brought Vice President Andrew Johnson into the White House. A Tennessee Democrat who served two terms as governor before being elected to the Senate in 1857, he was an ardent Unionist who blamed the slaveholding planter elite for secession and the Civil War. Johnson was the only southern senator who refused to embrace the Confederacy in 1861. Such credentials help explain why Lincoln invited him to be his running mate in 1864.*

*The Radical Republicans hoped that President Johnson would embrace their comprehensive effort to reconstruct the defeated South. Johnson shared their disdain for the former Confederate leaders and for the planter class, but he also cherished states' rights and feared any effort to expand federal authority. He also retained many of the racial prejudices of his native region. "White men alone must manage the South," Johnson told a journalist. Unlike the Radical Republicans, he balked at putting freed blacks in control of southern politics.*

*Like Lincoln, Andrew Johnson hoped that middle-class white southern Unionists, along with repentant ex-Confederates, would take control of restoring the South to the Union. He required that the new state constitutional conventions formally abolish slavery, renounce secession, and void all war debts that the state had incurred. The states then could hold elections and officially return to the Union. By April 1866 all of the southern states had fulfilled these requirements, albeit grudgingly, and had formed new governments. At the same time, they steadfastly refused to allow African Americans to vote. Johnson, however, was dismayed that the new political leaders were more often former Confederates than southern Unionists.*

*The Union victory in the Civil War and the official end of slavery created excited expectations among the freed slaves. Some adopted new names to express their new identity and to make a new beginning. Others discarded the clothes provided by their masters and took up new modes of dress. Many freed people left the plantations and migrated to neighboring towns and cities, where federal troops offered protection.*

*But freedom itself did not provide security or the resources necessary for meaningful lives. In March 1865 Congress created the Freedmen's Bureau, an agency administered by the War Department, to provide the former slaves with emergency supplies and to help them find employment, procure land, and pursue educational opportunities. By 1870 the Bureau was supervising more than four thousand schools.*

*Yet for all of its heroic efforts, the Freedmen's Bureau could help only a small percentage of former slaves. Few freed people were able to acquire land of their own. Most of them were forced to become wage laborers, or sharecroppers or tenant farmers contracting with white landowners to work their land in exchange for food, tools, clothing, and a place to live. This agrarian system, however necessary in the face of the social and economic realities confronting the region, soon placed the freed slaves in a dependent relationship reminiscent of slavery itself.*

*As the new "lily white" state governments coalesced in 1865 and 1866, most of them drafted "Black Codes" limiting the rights and freedoms of African Americans. These laws varied from state to state, but all of them restricted the independence of blacks and channeled them into the service of the white-dominated social and economic order.*

*Some whites decided that such restrictive laws did not sufficiently impress upon blacks their subordinate status. In an effort to promote white supremacy, they founded secret organizations such as the Ku Klux Klan. The Klan, organized by former Confederate soldiers, used violence and terror to intimidate blacks and to disrupt the efforts of Radical Republicans to "reconstruct" the South. During one campaign season in Louisiana, over two hundred African Americans were killed in one parish alone. Congress passed laws intended to suppress the Klan, but to little avail.*

*Reconstruction officially ended in 1877 with the withdrawal of the last federal troops from the South. African Americans in the region retained certain constitutional rights, but in practice white supremacy had been reestablished through force and terror. With the loss of federal protection, blacks found themselves not only at the mercy of the southern political elite but locked into a dependent economic relationship through the sharecrop system as well.*

THE NEW YORK TIMES

# FROM The Late Convention of Colored Men (1865)

*Freedom did not bring security to many former slaves after the Civil War. They were no longer slaves, but they had no property, no money, and little education. In each state, groups of former slaves met to share their concerns and to request assistance from the federal government. The following message was sent from a convention of freedmen in Alexandria, Virginia, in 1865.*

From "The Late Convention of Colored Men," *The New York Times*, August 13, 1865.

We, the undersigned members of a convention of colored citizens of the State of Virginia, would respectfully represent that, although we have been held as slaves, and denied all recognition as a constituent of your nationality for almost the entire period of the duration of your government, and that by your permission we have been denied either home or country, and deprived of the dearest rights of human nature; yet when you and our immediate oppressors met in deadly conflict upon the field of battle, the one to destroy and the other to save your government and nationality, we, with scarce an exception, in our inmost souls espoused your cause, and watched, and prayed, and waited, and labored for your success.

When the contest waxed long, and the result hung doubtfully, you appealed to us for help, and how well we answered is written in the rosters of the two hundred thousand colored troops now enrolled in your service; and as to our undying devotion to your cause, let the uniform acclamation of escaped prisoners, "Whenever we saw a black face we felt sure of a friend," answer.

Well, the war is over, the rebellion is "put down," and we are declared free! Four-fifths of our enemies are paroled or amnestied, and the other fifth are being pardoned, and the President has, in his efforts at the reconstruction of the civil government of the States, late in rebellion, left us entirely at the mercy of these subjugated but unconverted rebels, in everything save the privilege of bringing us, our wives and little ones, to the auction block. He has, so far as we can understand the tendency and bearing of his action in the case, remitted us for all our civil rights, to men, a majority of whom regard our devotions to your cause and flag as that which decided the contest against them! This we regard as destructive of all we hold dear, and in the name of God, of justice, of humanity, of good faith, of truth and righteousness, we do most solemnly and earnestly protest. Men and brethren, in the hour of your peril you called upon us, and despite all time-honored interpretation of constitutional obligations, we came at your call and you are saved—and now we beg, we pray, we entreat you not to desert us in this the hour of our peril!

We know these men—know them well—and we assure you that, with the majority of them, loyalty is only "lip deep," and that their professions of loyalty are used as a cover to the cherished design of getting restored to their former relation with the Federal Government, and then, by all sorts of "unfriendly legislation," to render the freedom you have given us more intolerable than the slavery they intended for us.

We warn you in time that our only safety is in keeping them under Governors of the military persuasion until you have so amended the Federal

Constitution that it will prohibit the States from making any distinction between citizens on account of race or color. In one word, the only salvation for us besides the power of the Government, is in the possession of the ballot. Give us this, and we will protect ourselves. No class of men relatively as numerous as we were ever oppressed when armed with the ballot. But, 'tis said we are ignorant. Admit it. Yet who denies we know a traitor from a loyal man, a gentleman from a rowdy, a friend from an enemy?

. . . All we ask is an equal chance with the white traitors varnished and japanned with the oath of amnesty. Can you deny us this and still keep faith with us? "But," say some, "the blacks will be overreached by the superior knowledge and cunning of the whites." Trust us for that. We will never be deceived a second time. "But," they continue, "the planters and landowners will have them in their power, and dictate the way their votes shall be cast." We did not know before that we were to be left to the tender mercies of these landed rebels for employment. Verily, we thought the Freedmen's Bureau was organized and clothed with power to protect us from this very thing, by compelling those for whom we labored to pay us, whether they liked our political opinions or not! . . .

We are "sheep in the midst of wolves," and nothing but the military arm of the Government prevents us and all the truly loyal white men from being driven from the land of our birth. Do not then, we beseech you, give to one of these "wayward sisters" the rights they abandoned and forfeited when they rebelled until you have secured our rights by the aforementioned amendment to the Constitution.

Let your action in our behalf be thus clear and emphatic, and our respected President, who, we feel confident, desires only to know your will, to act in harmony therewith, will give you his most earnest and cordial cooperation; and the Southern States, through your enlightened and just legislation, will speedily award us our rights. Thus not only will the arms of the rebellion be surrendered, but the ideas also.

## Review Questions

1. What services had former slaves performed that they believed entitled them to the protection of the federal government?
2. What did the petitioners mean when they said that the white southerner was "subjugated but unconverted"?
3. What two steps did the freed blacks claim would ensure that their own rights would be guaranteed?

# Black Codes of Mississippi (1865)

*The so-called Black Codes were enacted by the newly reconstituted southern state legislatures to address the legal status of the freed slaves after the Civil War. Some of the codes, such as Georgia's, were relatively lenient; others, such as those of Louisiana and Mississippi, sought to restore slavery in all but name. Most of the Black Codes were suspended by the federal military governors of the reconstructed states, and both the Civil Rights Act of 1866 and the Fourteenth Amendment were in part a response to these efforts to suppress the rights of blacks. The following sections from the Mississippi code deal with civil rights, apprenticeship, vagrancy, and penal crimes.*

From *Laws of the State of Mississippi*, 1865 (Jackson, Miss., 1866), pp. 82–90, 165.

# 1. Civil Rights of Freedmen in Mississippi

Sec. 1. *Be it enacted,* . . . That all freedmen, free negroes, and mulattoes may sue and be sued, implead and be impleaded, in all the courts of law and equity of this State, and may acquire personal property . . . by descent or purchase, and may dispose of the same in the same manner and to the same extent that white persons may: *Provided,* That the provisions of this section shall not be so construed as to allow any freedman, free negro, or mulatto to rent or lease any lands or tenements except in incorporated cities or towns, in which places the corporate authorities shall control the same. . . .

Sec. 3. . . . All freedmen, free negroes, or mulattoes who do now and have herebefore lived and cohabited together as husband and wife shall be taken and held in law as legally married, and the issue shall be taken and held as legitimate for all purposes: that it shall not be lawful for any freedman, free negro, or mulatto to intermarry with any white person; nor for any white person to intermarry with any freedman, free negro, or mulatto: and any person who shall so intermarry, shall be deemed guilty of felony, and on conviction thereof shall be confined in the State penitentiary for life; and those shall be deemed freedmen, free negroes, and mulattoes who are of pure negro blood, and those descended from a negro to the third generation, inclusive, though one ancestor in each generation may have been a white person.

Sec. 4. . . . In addition to cases in which freedmen, free negroes, and mulattoes are now by law competent witnesses, freedmen, free negroes, or mulattoes shall be competent in civil cases, when a party or parties to the suit, either plaintiff or plaintiffs, defendant or defendants, and a white person or white persons, is or are the opposing party or parties, plaintiff or plaintiffs, defendant or defendants. They shall also be competent witnesses in all criminal prosecutions where the crime charged is alleged to have been committed by a white person upon or against the person or property of a freedman, free negro, or mulatto: *Provided,* that in all cases said witnesses shall be examined in open court, on the stand; except, however, they may be examined before the grand jury, and shall in all cases be subject to the rules and tests of the common law as to competency and credibility. . . .

Sec. 6. . . . All contracts for labor made with freedmen, free negroes, and mulattoes for a longer period than one month shall be in writing, and in duplicate, attested and read to said freedman, free negro, or mulatto by a beat, city or county officer, or two disinterested white persons of the county in which the labor is to be performed, of which each party shall have one; and said contracts shall be taken and held as entire contracts, and if the laborer shall quit the service of the employer before the expiration of his term of service, without good cause, he shall forfeit his wages for that year up to the time of quitting.

Sec. 7. . . . Every civil officer shall, and every person may, arrest and carry back to his or her legal employer any freedman, free negro, or mulatto who shall have quit the service of his or her employer before the expiration of his or her term of service without good cause; and said officer and person shall be entitled to receive for arresting and carrying back every deserting employee aforesaid the sum of five dollars, and ten cents per mile from the place of arrest to the place of delivery; and the same shall be paid by the employer, and held as a set-off for so much against the wages of said deserting employee: *Provided,* that said arrested party, after being so returned, may appeal to the justice of the peace or member of the board of police of the county, who, on notice to the alleged employer, shall try summarily whether said appellant is legally employed by the alleged employer, and has good cause to quit said employer; either party shall have the right of appeal to the county court, pending which the alleged deserter shall be remanded to the alleged employer or otherwise disposed of, as shall be right and just; and the decision of the county court shall be final. . . .

Sec. 9. . . . If any person shall persuade or attempt to persuade, entice, or cause any freedman, free negro, or mulatto to desert from the legal employment of any person before the expiration of his or her term of service, or shall knowingly employ any such deserting freedman, free negro, or mulatto, or shall knowingly give or sell to any such deserting freedman, free negro, or mulatto, any food, raiment, or other thing, he or she shall be guilty of a misdemeanor, and, upon conviction, shall be fined not less than twenty-five dollars and not more than two hundred dollars and the costs; and if said fine and costs shall not be immediately paid, the court shall sentence said convict to not exceeding two months' imprisonment in the county jail, and he or she shall moreover be liable to the party injured in damages: *Provided*, if any person shall, or shall attempt to, persuade, entice, or cause any freedman, free negro, or mulatto to desert from any legal employment of any person, with the view to employ said freedman, free negro, or mulatto without the limits of this State, such person, on conviction, shall be fined not less than fifty dollars, and not more than five hundred dollars and costs; and if said fine and costs shall not be immediately paid, the court shall sentence said convict to not exceeding six months imprisonment in the county jail.

\* \* \*

## Mississippi Vagrant Law

Sec. 1. *Be it enacted, etc.,* . . . That all rogues and vagabonds, idle and dissipated persons, beggars, jugglers, or persons practicing unlawful games or plays, runaways, common drunkards, common night-walkers, pilferers, lewd, wanton, or lascivious persons, in speech or behavior, common railers and brawlers, persons who neglect their calling or employment, misspend what they earn, or do not provide for the support of themselves or their families, or dependents, and all other idle and disorderly persons, including all who neglect all lawful business, habitually misspend their time by frequenting houses of ill-fame, gaming-houses, or tippling shops, shall be deemed and considered vagrants, under the provisions of this act, and upon conviction thereof shall be fined not exceeding one

hundred dollars, with all accruing costs, and be imprisoned at the discretion of the court, not exceeding ten days.

Sec. 2. . . . All freedmen, free negroes and mulattoes in this State, over the age of eighteen years, found on the second Monday in January, 1866, or thereafter, with no lawful employment or business, or found unlawfully assembling themselves together, either in the day or night time, and all white persons so assembling themselves with freedmen, free negroes or mulattoes, or usually associating with freedmen, free negroes or mulattoes, on terms of equality, or living in adultery or fornication with a freed woman, free negro or mulatto, shall be deemed vagrants, and on conviction thereof shall be fined in a sum not exceeding, in the case of a freedman, free negro or mulatto, fifty dollars, and a white man two hundred dollars, and imprisoned at the discretion of the court, the free negro not exceeding ten days, and the white man not exceeding six months. . . .

Sec. 7. . . . If any freedman, free negro, or mulatto shall fail or refuse to pay any tax levied according to the provisions of the sixth section of this act, it shall be *prima facie* evidence of vagrancy, and it shall be the duty of the sheriff to arrest such freedman, free negro, or mulatto or such person refusing or neglecting to pay such tax, and proceed at once to hire for the shortest time such delinquent tax-payer to any one who will pay the said tax, with accruing costs, giving preference to the employer, if there be one.

\* \* \*

## 4. Penal Laws of Mississippi

Sec. 1. *Be it enacted,* . . . That no freedman, free negro or mulatto, not in the military service of the United States government, and not licensed so to do by the board of police of his or her county, shall keep or carry fire-arms of any kind, or any ammunition, dirk or bowie knife, and on conviction thereof in the county court shall be punished by fine, not exceeding ten dollars, and pay the costs of such proceedings, and all such arms or ammunition shall be forfeited to the informer; and it shall be the duty of every civil and military officer to arrest any freedman, free negro, or mulatto found with any such arms or ammunition, and cause him or her to be committed to trial in default of bail.

Sec. 2. . . . Any freedman, free negro, or mulatto committing riots, routs, affrays, trespasses, malicious mischief, cruel treatment to animals, seditious speeches, insulting gestures, language, or acts, or assaults on any person, disturbance of the peace, exercising the function of a minister of the Gospel without a license from some regularly organized church, vending spirituous or intoxicating liquors, or committing any other misdemeanor, the punishment of which is not specifically provided for by law, shall, upon conviction thereof in the county court, be fined not less than ten dollars, and not more than one hundred dollars, and may be imprisoned at the discretion of the court, not exceeding thirty days.

Sec. 3. . . . If any white person shall sell, lend, or give to any freedman, free negro, or mulatto any fire-arms, dirk or bowie knife, or ammunition, or any spirituous or intoxicating liquors, such person or persons so offending, upon conviction thereof

in the county court of his or her county, shall be fined not exceeding fifty dollars, and may be imprisoned, at the discretion of the court, not exceeding thirty days. . . .

. Sec. 5. . . . If any freedman, free negro, or mulatto, convicted of any of the misdemeanors provided against in this act, shall fail or refuse for the space of five days, after conviction, to pay the fine and costs imposed, such person shall be hired out by the sheriff or other officer, at public outcry, to any white person who will pay said fine and all costs, and take said convict for the shortest time.

## REVIEW QUESTIONS

1. Which crime carried the harshest penalty? Why?
2. Summarize the regulations related to employment of freed slaves. How did they represent a form of slavery?
3. The Black Codes were criticized for their vagueness. Cite an example of such vagueness, and note ways in which the codes could be interpreted or manipulated.

# JOURDON ANDERSON
# Letter to My Old Master (1865)

*The Civil War gave some four million slaves their freedom, but freedom wasn't quite so simple. Where would the former slaves live? How would they put food on the table? If those issues weren't challenging enough, freed slaves also had to contend with former owners who were not happy about what the war had done. Some ex-Confederates refused to acknowledge that defeat meant emancipation. They tried to force their slaves to stay under their control because they still needed help planting and harvesting their crops. Having become accustomed to the benefits of enslaved workers, most of them balked at paying their former slaves a living wage. Consider the example of Jourdon Anderson, who, like many slaves, had adopted the surname of his owner, Colonel P. H. Anderson of Big Spring, Tennessee. In 1864, as Union troops took control of Tennessee, Jourdon Anderson and his wife and children had seized their freedom and eventually relocated to Dayton, Ohio. Four months after the war ended, Colonel Anderson learned of Jourdon's whereabouts and sent him a letter urging him to return to work on the farm, promising to treat him well. Jourdon's tongue-in-cheek reply reveals both the complexities of emancipation and the resilience and courage that many freed slaves displayed.*

"Letter from a Freedman to His Old Master," *New York Daily Tribune*, August 22, 1865.

The following in a genuine document. It was dictated by the old servant, and contains his ideas and forms of expression. [Cincinnati Commercial.]

DAYTON, Ohio, August 7, 1865.

*To my Old Master, Col.* P. H. ANDERSON, *Big Spring, Tennessee.*

SIR: I got your letter and was glad to find that you had not forgotten Jourdon, and that you wanted me to come back and live with you again, promising to do better for me than anybody else can. I have often felt uneasy about you. I thought the Yankees would have hung you long before this for harboring Rebs, they found at your hourse. I suppose they never heard about your going to Col. Martin's to kill the Union soldier that was left by his company in their stable. Although you shot at me twice before I left you, I did not want to hear at your being hurt, and am glad you are still living. It would do me good to go back to the dear old home again and see Miss Mary and Miss Martin and Alion, Esther, Green and Leo. Give my love to them all, and tell them I hope we will meet in the better world, if not in this. I would have gone back to see you all when I was working in the Nashville Hospital, but one of the neighbors told me Henry intended to shoot me if he ever got a chance.

I want to know particularly what the good chance is you propose to give me. I am doing tolerably well here; I get $25 a month, with victuals and clothing; have a comfortable home for Mandy (the folks here call her Mrs. Anderson), and the children; Milly, Jane and Grandy, go to school and are learning well; the teacher says Grandy has a head for a preacher. They go to Sunday School, and Mandy and me attend church regularly. We are kindly treated; sometimes we overhear others saying, "Them colored people were slaves" down in Tennessee. The children feel hurt when they hear such remarks, but

I tell them it was no disgrace in Tennessee to belong to Col. Anderson. Many darkies would have been proud, as I used to was, to call you master. Now, if you will write and say what wages you will give me, I will be better able to decide whether it would be to my advantage to move back again.

As to my freedom, which you say I can have, there is nothing to be gained on that score, as I got my free-papers in 1861 from the Provost-Marshal-General of the Department at Nashville. Mandy says she would be afraid to go back without some proof that you are sincerely disposed to treat us justly and kindly—and we have concluded to test your sincerity by asking you to send us our wages for the time we served you. This will make us forget and forgive old sores, and rely on your justice and friendship in the future. I served you faithfully for thirty-two years, and Mandy twenty years, as $25 a month for me, and $2 a week for Mandy. Our earnings would amount to $11,680. Add to this the interest for the time our wages been kept back and deduct what you paid for our clothing and three doctor's visits to me, and pulling a tooth for Mandy, and the balance will show what we are in justice entitled to. Please send the money by Adams Express, in care of V. Winters, esq., Dayton, Ohio! If you fail to pay us for faithful labors in the past we can have little faith in your promises in the future. We trust the good Maker has opened your eyes to the wrongs which you and your fathers have done to me and my fathers, in making us toil for you for generations without recompense. Here I draw my wages every Saturday night, but in Tennessee there was never any pay day for the negroes any more than for the horses and cows. Surely there will be a day of reckoning for those who defraud the laborer of his hire.

In answering this letter please state if there would be any safety for my Milly and Jane, who are now grown up and both good looking girls. You know how it was with poor Matilda and Catherine.

I would rather stay here and starve and die if it come to that than have my girls brought to shame by the violence and wickedness of their young masters. You will also please state if there has been any schools opened for the colored children in your neighborhood, the great desire of my life now is to give my children an education, and have them form virtuous habits.

From your old servant,     JOURDON ANDERSON.

P. S.—Say howdy to George Carter, and thank him for taking the pistol from you when you were shooting at me.

## REVIEW QUESTIONS

1. What do you learn from this letter about the experience of enslaved African Americans in transitioning from being the property of others to being free?
2. Based on the information in the letter, how would you describe the conditions of being a slave in the former Confederacy?

# Organization and Principles of the Ku Klux Klan (1868)

*The Ku Klux Klan was the largest of several white supremacist societies that emerged in the post–Civil War era. Founded in Pulaski, Tennessee, in 1865, it grew rapidly among Confederate veterans across the South. Former Confederate general Nathan Bedford Forrest was the first grand wizard. The Klan used terror and violence to defy the efforts of Radical Republicans to reconstruct southern society. The following is an early statement of the Klan's principles.*

From *The Ku Klux Klan: Its Origin, Growth and Disbandment*, by W. L. Fleming, J. C. Lester, and D. L. Wilson (New York: Neale, 1905), pp. 154 ff.

## Creed

We, the Order of the . . . , reverentially acknowledge the majesty and supremacy of the Divine Being, and recognize the goodness and providence of the same. And we recognize our relation to the United States Government, the supremacy of the Constitution, the Constitutional Laws thereof, and the Union of States thereunder.

## Character and Objects of the Order

This is an institution of Chivalry, Humanity, Mercy, and Patriotism; embodying in its genius and its principles all that is chivalric in conduct, noble in sentiment, generous in manhood, and patriotic in purpose; its peculiar objects being

First: To protect the weak, the innocent, and the defenseless, from the indignities, wrongs, and outrages of the lawless, the violent, and the brutal; to relieve the injured and oppressed; to succor the suffering and unfortunate, and especially the widows and orphans of Confederate soldiers.

Second: To protect and defend the Constitution of the United States, and all laws passed in conformity thereto, and to protect the States and the people thereof from all invasion from any source whatever.

Third: To aid and assist in the execution of all constitutional laws, and to protect the people from unlawful seizure, and from trial except by their peers in conformity to the laws of the land.

*Their enemies* ↓

## Titles

*parku*

Sec. 1. The officers of this Order shall consist of a Grand Wizard of the Empire, and his ten Genii; a Grand Dragon of the Realm, and his eight Hydras; a Grand Titan of the Dominion, and his six Furies; a Grand Giant of the Province, and his four Goblins; a Grand Cyclops of the Den, and his two Night Hawks; a Grand Magi, a Grand Monk, a Grand Scribe, a Grand Exchequer, a Grand Turk, and a Grand Sentinel.

Sec. 2. The body politic of this Order shall be known and designated as "Ghouls."

## Territory and Its Divisions

*CSA = Empire "Empire*

Sec. 1. The territory embraced within the jurisdiction of this Order shall be coterminous with the States of Maryland, Virginia, North Carolina, South Carolina, Georgia, Florida, Alabama, Mississippi, Louisiana, Texas, Arkansas, Missouri, Kentucky, and Tennessee; all combined constituting the Empire.

Sec. 2. The Empire shall be divided into four departments, the first to be styled the Realm, and coterminous with the boundaries of the several States; the second to be styled the Dominion, and to be coterminous with such counties as the Grand Dragons of the several Realms may assign to the charge of the Grand Titan. The third to be styled the Province, and to be coterminous with the several counties; *Provided* the Grand Titan may, when he deems it necessary, assign two Grand Giants to one Province, prescribing, at the same time, the jurisdiction of each. The fourth department to be styled the Den, and shall embrace such part of a Province as the Grand Giant shall assign to the charge of a Grand Cyclops. . . .

*A*

## Interrogations to be asked

1st. Have you ever been rejected, upon application for membership in the . . . , or have you ever been expelled from the same?

2d. Are you now, or have you ever been, a member of the Radical Republican party, or either of the organizations known as the "Loyal League" and the "Grand Army of the Republic?"

3d. Are you opposed to the principles and policy of the Radical party, and to the Loyal League, and the Grand Army of the Republic, so far as you are informed of the character and purposes of those organizations?

4th. Did you belong to the Federal army during the late war, and fight against the South during the existence of the same?

5th. Are you opposed to negro equality, both social and political?

6th. Are you in favor of a white man's government in this country?

7th. Are you in favor of Constitutional liberty, and a Government of equitable laws instead of a Government of violence and oppression?

8th. Are you in favor of maintaining the Constitutional rights of the South?

9th. Are you in favor of the re-enfranchisement and emancipation of the white men of the South, and the restitution of the Southern people to all their rights, alike proprietary, civil, and political?

10th. Do you believe in the inalienable right of self-preservation of the people against the exercise of arbitrary and unlicensed power? . . .

## REVIEW QUESTIONS

1. How could the Klan express such reverence for the Constitution while castigating Union Army veterans?
2. Why would poor whites have been attracted to the Klan?
3. How would freed slaves have reacted to the Klan's principles?

# Lee Guidon

# Klan Terrorism in South Carolina (1872)

*During the early 1870s the Congress held hearings to investigate reports that the Ku Klux Klan was engaging in widespread intimidation and violence against blacks in the South. The following three documents relate to a series of racial incidents in York County, South Carolina, in 1871. Throughout the South, where Radical Reconstruction was being implemented, blacks were joining Union Leagues, Republican organizations that also had secret rituals. The first document is an article from the* Yorkville Enquirer *describing the rash of violence in the community. The second document is the courtroom testimony of an African American woman, Harriet Postle, whose family was assaulted by Klansmen. The third document is the testimony of Lawson B. Davis, a white Klansman accused of such terrorism.*

From U.S. Congress, *Report of the Joint Select Committee to Inquire into the Condition of Affairs in the Late Insurrectionary States* (Washington, D.C., 1872), 3:1540–41; 1951–52; 1943–44.

## Whipping and House-Burning.

The state of things which exists in many sections of our country is alarming. Scarcely a night passes but some outrage is perpetrated against the welfare of some community. Houses are burned, persons are whipped, and in some instances killed, by parties unknown, and for causes which no one can decipher. These things are not right; they are not prudent. They are grave crimes against God and the best interest of the country.

By common consent, the house-burning is charged upon the colored race, and the whipping and killing upon the so-called Ku-Klux. This is not certainly known to be the case, but the probability is that the supposition with regard to the perpetrators of these deeds is correct. One thing must be evident to every observing man: there is concert of action both in the house-burning and in the whipping and killing.

For some years there has been, and still is, we are informed by one who claims to know, an organization known as the Union League. Of this we know nothing, save what we have learned by observing its workings. From what we have been able to learn, we are convinced that the Union League is a secret political organization, and on this ground alone, if we knew nothing about its operations and results, we would condemn it. We take the broad ground that all secret political organizations are nothing but conspiracies against the established government of a country, and as such are ruinous to the peace and quiet and prosperity of the people.

Of the Ku-Klux we know even less than we do of the Union League. Sometimes we are disposed to believe that there is no such organization; at other times we think differently. Recent developments rather indicate that there is such an organization, and it is made of no mean material. This is mere conjecture on our part. We do not know one single individual who holds connection with the Ku-Klux. It is evident, however, that there is some sort of complicity of action in the whipping and killing that has recently been perpetrated in this country, and which is going on at present all over the State, and, in fact, all over the South.

We do not believe, from what we know of the political party which is opposed to the Union League and the political tenets of the dominant party in South Carolina, that the Ku-Klux is a political organization, in the strict sense of that term. Whatever may be its object, we are convinced that the Ku-Klux is doing much harm. To be honest and frank, we charge the Union League with the shameful state of things which now exists. It has placed its members in a predicament which is anything but enviable. The ostensible purpose for which the thing was organized was, we suppose, to protect the freedman; the real purpose, however, was, as is acknowledged by some of its members, to consolidate the votes of the freedman, that designing men might be elevated to positions of honor and profit. There is no doubt but the Union League has done the colored people a great injury. It has been the means of arraying them in hostility against the white man, and the result always has been that in every conflict between the white man and the colored man, the condition of the latter has been materially injured. We do not blame the colored people for joining the League; but we do blame those designing white men who enticed them into this snare of destruction.

However much we may reprobate the Union League, this does not cause us to love or approve of the Ku-Klux. Two wrongs never can make one right. Both the Union League and the Ku-Klux are founded upon dangerous principles, and are working the ruin of this county. We have no disposition to make prediction, especially while so unsettled a state of things continues as exists in this county at present; but we will venture to say that if this house-burning and whipping does not stop soon, it will culminate in a conflict which will be fatal to some party.

What is the duty of every good citizen, under existing circumstances? It is the duty, we believe, of the leading colored people to influence their race to abandon the League and to refrain from acts of violence. On the other hand, it is the duty of the white people, especially the old men, to advise the young men not to engage in whipping and murdering the colored people. So long as the present state of things exists, no one is safe. The minds of the white people are filled with anxiety lest their houses may be burned down at any time, and no doubt the minds of the colored people are filled with dread lest they be dragged from their beds and taken to the forest and whipped, or, perchance, shot. We have no party purposes to subserve by what we say. All we desire is to assist in restoring peace and quiet to our county. These outrages must stop now, or worse will come. If a few more houses are burned, the public mind will be so exasperated that, in all probability, something will be done that will be very injurious to the public good. It is the imperative duty of every good citizen to discourage house-burning and whipping. We must be permitted to say that it is our impression that, so long as the Union League exists, some kind of an opposing party will also exist. The sooner all such organizations cease to exist, the better it will be for all parties.

## Testimony of Harriet Postle.

Examination by Mr. CORBIN:

I live in the eastern part of York County, about four miles from Rock Hill, on Mr. James Smith's plantation; I am about thirty years old; my husband is a preacher; I have a family of six children; the oldest is about fourteen; the Ku-Klux visited me last spring; it was some time in March; I was asleep when they came; they made a great noise and waked me up, and called out for Postle; my husband heard them and jumped up, and I thought he was putting on his clothes, but when I got up I found he was gone; they kept on hallooing for Postle and knocking at the door; I was trying to get on my clothes, but I was so frightened I did not get on my clothes at all; it looked like they were going to knock the door down; then the rest of them began to come into the house, and my oldest child got out and ran under the bed; one of them saw him and said, "There he is; I see him;" and with that three of them pointed their pistols under the bed; I then cried out, "It is my child;" they told him to come out; when my child came out from under the bed, one of them said, "Put it on his neck;" and the child commenced hallooing and crying, and I begged them not to hurt my child; the man did not hurt it, but one of them ran the child back against the wall, and ground a piece of skin off as big as my hand; I then took a chair and sat it back upon a loose plank, and sat down upon it; one of the men stepped up; seeing the plank loose, he just jerked the chair and threw me over, while my babe was in my arms, and I fell with my babe to the floor, when one of them clapped his foot upon the child, and another had his foot on me; I begged him, for the Lord's sake, to save my child; I went and picked up my babe, and when I opened the door and looked I saw they had formed a line; they asked me if Postle was there; I said no; they told me to make up a light, but I was so frightened I could not do it well, and I asked my child to make it up for me; then they asked me where my husband was; I told them he was gone; they said, "He is here somewhere;" I told them he was gone for some meal; they said he was there somewhere, and they called me a damned liar; one of them said: "He is under the house;" then one of them comes to me and says: "I am going to have the truth tonight; you are a damned, lying bitch, and you are telling a lie;" and he had a line, and commenced putting it over my neck; said he: "You are telling a lie; I know it; he is here;" I told them again he was gone; when he had the rope round my head he said, "I want you to tell where your husband is;" and, said he, "The truth I've got to have;" I commenced hallooing, and says he: "We are men of peace, but you are telling me a damned lie, and you are not to tell me any lies to-night;" and the one who had his foot on my body mashed me badly, but not so badly as he might have done, for I was seven or eight months gone in travail; then I got outside of the house and sat down, with my back against the house, and I called the little ones to me, for they were all dreadfully frightened; they said my husband was there, and they would shoot into every crack; and they did shoot all over the place, and there are bullet-holes there and bullet-marks on the hearth yet; at this time there were some in the house and some outside, and says they to me: "We're going to have the truth out of you, you

damned, lying bitch; he is somewhere about here;" said I: "He is gone;" with that he clapped his hands on my neck, and with one hand put the line over my neck; and he says again: "We're going to have the truth out of you, you damned bitch;" and with that he beat my head against the side of the house till I had no sense hardly left; but I still had hold of my babe.

Mr. CORBIN:

*Question.* Did you recognize anybody?

*Answer.* Yes, sir; I did; I recognized the first man that came into the house; it was Dr. Avery, [pointing to the accused.] I recognized him by his performance, and when he was entangling the line round my neck; as I lifted my hand to keep the rope off my neck, I caught his lame hand; it was his left hand that I caught, his crippled hand; I felt it in my hand, and I said to myself right then, "I knows you;" and I knew Joe Castle and James Matthews—the old man's son; I didn't know any one else; I suppose there was about a dozen altogether there; Dr. Avery had on a red gown with a blue face, with red about his mouth, and he had two horns on his cap about a foot long; the line that he tried to put over my neck was a buggy-line, not quite so wide as three fingers, but wider than two; they said to me that they rode thirty-eight miles that night to see old Abe Broomfield and preacher Postle; they said that they had heard that preacher Postle had been preaching up fire and corruption; they afterward found my husband under the house, but I had gone to the big house with my children to take them out of the cold, and I did not see them pull him out from the house.

\*    \*    \*

# Testimony of Lawson B. Davis.

Witness for the prosecution:

I reside in York County, and have lived there two years. I was initiated as a member of the Ku-Klux Klan. I took the oath at my own house. Three persons were initiated at the same time. I attended one meeting and heard the constitution and by-laws. That was in last January. The contents of the oath, as near as I can remember, were that female friends, widows, and orphans were to be objects of our protection, and that we were to support the Constitution as it was bequeathed to us by our forefathers; and there was to be opposition to the thirteenth, fourteenth, and fifteenth amendments.[1] The fourteenth was particularly specified in the oath I took. The oath was repeated, and I repeated it after them. There was no written document present. The penalty for divulging its secrets was death.

The constitution and by-laws were here handed to the witness by Mr. Corbin.

The witness continued: That is the same oath that I took except the second section, which, as repeated to me, was "opposition to the thirteenth, fourteenth, and fifteenth amendments." The organization, when I joined it, was called the Invisible Empire of the South. After I joined I found it was the same as the Ku-Klux organization. When I found that I determined to leave them. The first meeting I attended there were eight or ten persons sworn in, and a proposition was brought forward to make a raid upon such and such persons. I inquired the reason, and they said they were prominently connected with the Union League. Their object was to discountenance people from joining the League. I heard this from the members. They said that those who belonged to the League were to be visited and warned; that they must discontinue their connection with the League. If they did not, on the second visit they were to leave the country, and if they didn't leave they were to be whipped; and if after this they did not leave, they were to be killed. I know this was how the purposes of the order were to be carried out. I have known of instances of raiding for guns.

---

[1] Amendments to the U.S. Constitution associated with the Civil War. The Thirteenth, ratified in 1865, abolished slavery; the Fourteenth (1866) provided people "equal protection under the law"; and the Fifteenth (1870) granted the right to vote to black males.

They made one raid upon Jerry Adams; Charley Byers told me they had whipped him; he was to be chief of the Klan; he said they had scared the boy very badly—they had fired several guns at him, but didn't mean to hit him. The only charge I ever heard against Jerry Adams was that he was a radical. He was a republican and a colored man. Charley Good, who was whipped very badly by the Klan, came to my house two or three days afterwards. He was a blacksmith, and a very good workman—the best in that part. Charley Good was whipped so badly that he could not follow his trade for several days. Two or three weeks after that he was killed.

Wesley Smith, and William Smith, and William White were among those who killed Charley Good. Smith said he was a member of Smarr's Klan, and some members of that Klan assisted in putting Charley Good's body out of the way. The two Smiths, I know, were members of the Klan. Charley Good was killed because he was a republican. He told me, in the presence of some other persons, that he knew who had whipped him. I told him it would be better for him to keep that to himself. Wesley Smith gave, as the reason for killing him, that Charley Good knew some of the party who had whipped him. I was ordered to assist in disposing of the body of Charley Good. I did not, till then, know that he was missing. They came and summoned me and Mr. Howard to go and secrete the body, which was lying near to where he was murdered.

Wesley Smith said that all who were members of the organization were required to assist, so that they might be connected with it, and that the matter might not get out. I told him that I did not want to go, but he said that all the members had to go. We were ordered to meet at the gate about a quarter of a mile from his house. I left about 9 o'clock and went up to Mr. Howard's, and Wesley Smith had given him the same instructions. He did not feel willing to go, and I said those were my feelings exactly. We waited until the hour had passed, and then when we left we met some ten or fifteen of the party. It was a dark night, and I only recognized Thomas L. Berry, Pinckney Caldwell, Wesley Smith, and Madison Smarr. He is said to be the chief of the Klan. Madison Smarr said I had escaped a scouring. He said the body was very heavy to carry. And Pinckney Caldwell told me that "Charley Good is now at the bottom of the river. The body would not sink, and I jumped in upon him," he said, "and fastened him there, as well as I could, with a stake."

Charley Good was at one time a member of a militia company, and, being told it was not to his interest, he left it and returned his gun. He was regarded as a man of republican principles, and was considered a person of some influence in that neighborhood. I never heard him charged with being a member of the Union League.

\*    \*    \*

## REVIEW QUESTIONS

1. Based on these testimonies, characterize the methods used by the Klan to intimidate blacks.
2. According to these excerpts, why did the KKK harass certain blacks?
3. How did blacks react to this kind of continuous treatment? What choices did they have?

## SOJOURNER TRUTH

# Address to the First Annual Meeting of the American Equal Rights Association (1867)

*In the aftermath of the Civil War, many Americans sought to help the almost four million former southern slaves, most of whom found themselves free but without jobs or homes or food—or civil rights. Most advocates for civil rights (voting privileges, social equality, equitable treatment, etc.) focused on black men and ignored the distinctive needs of black women. Sojourner Truth was one of the few advocates of equal rights for black women. Born a slave in 1797 in upstate New York and named Isabella Baumfree, she was sold several times to different owners before escaping with her infant daughter in 1826 (she later won custody of her son). As an adult she experienced an intense conversion to Christianity, renamed herself Sojourner Truth, and published her autobiography,* The Narrative of Sojourner Truth: A Northern Slave. *Thereafter she became the most celebrated female black abolitionist. During the Civil War, she helped recruit black men to serve in the Union Army. Afterward, she earnestly promoted equal rights for black women until her death in Michigan in 1883. In the following speech delivered two years after the end of the Civil War, Sojourner Truth explains why women deserved equal treatment.*

From Sojourner Truth, "Address to the First Annual Meeting of the American Equal Rights Association," in *History of Woman Suffrage*, eds. Elizabeth Cady Stanton, Susan B. Anthony, and Matilda Joslyn Gage (Source Books Press, 1970).

. . . My friends, I am rejoiced that you are glad, but I don't know how you will feel when I get through. I come from another field—the country of the slave. They have got their liberty—so much good luck to have slavery partly destroyed; not entirely. I want it root and branch destroyed. Then we will all be free indeed. I feel that if I have to answer for the deeds done in my body just as much as a man, I have a right to have just as much as a man. There is a great stir about colored men getting their rights, but not a word about the colored women; and if colored men get their rights, and not colored women theirs, you see the colored men will be masters over the women, and it will be just as bad as it was before. So I am for keeping the thing going while things are stirring; because if we wait till it is still, it will take a great while to get it going again. White women are a great deal smarter, and know more than colored women, while colored women do not know scarcely anything. They go out washing, which is about as high as a colored woman gets, and their men go about idle, strutting up and down; and when the women come home, they ask for their money and take it all, and then scold because there is no food. I want you to consider on that, chil'n. I call you chil'n; you are somebody's chil'n, and I am old enough to be mother of all that is here. I want women to have their rights. In the courts women have no right, no voice; nobody speaks for them. I wish woman to have her voice there among the pettifoggers. If it is not a fit place for women, it is unfit for men to be there.

I am above eighty years old; it is about time for me to be going. I have been forty years a slave and forty years free, and would be here forty years more to have equal rights for all. I suppose I am kept here because something remains for me to do; I suppose I am yet to help to break the chain. I have done a great deal of work; as much as a man, but did not get so much pay. I used to work in the field and bind grain, keeping up with the cradler; but men doing no more, got twice as much pay; so with the German women. They work in the field and do as much work, but do not get the pay. We do as much, we eat as much, we want as much. I suppose I am about the only colored woman that goes about to speak for the rights of the colored women. I want to keep the thing stirring, now that

the ice is cracked. What we want is a little money. You men know that you get as much again as women when you write, or for what you do. When we get our rights we shall not have to come to you for money, for then we shall have money enough in our own pockets; and may be you will ask us for money. But help us now until we get it. It is a good consolation to know that when we have got this battle once fought we shall not be coming to you any more. You have been having our rights so long, that you think, like a slave-holder, that you own us. I know that it is hard for one who has held the reins for so long to give up; it cuts like a knife. It will feel all the better when it closes up again. I have been in Washington about three years, seeing about these colored people. Now colored men have the right to vote. There ought to be equal rights now more than ever, since colored people have got their freedom. I am going to talk several times while I am here; so now I will do a little singing. I have not heard any singing since I came here.

Accordingly, suiting the action to the word, Sojourner sang, "We are going home." "There children," said she, "in heaven we shall rest from all our labors, first do all we have to do here. There I am determined to go, not to stop short of that beautiful place, and I do not mean to stop till I get there, and meet you there, too."

*    *    *

# REVIEW QUESTIONS

1. Truth claimed that "white women are a great deal smarter, and know more than colored women, while colored women do not know scarcely anything." What was her point? Did she mean to be taken literally?
2. How does Truth try to get black men to realize that they treat black women in ways comparable to the way that whites treated slaves?